# CSE 2111
## Modeling and Problem Solving with Spreadsheets and Databases

Third Custom Edition for The Ohio State University

D1262733

Taken from:

*Exploring Microsoft Office 2013*, Volume 1
by Mary Anne Poatsy, Keith Mulbery, Cynthia Krebs, Lynn Hogan,
Amy M. Rutledge, and Robert T. Grauer

*Exploring Microsoft Office 2013*, Volume 2
by Mary Anne Poatsy, Keith Mulbery, Eric Cameron, Jason Davidson,
Jerri Williams, Linda Lau, Rebecca Lawson,  Robert T. Grauer, and Sallie Dodson

*MIS Cases: Decision Making with Application Software*, Fourth Edition,
by M. Lisa Miller

Cover Image: Courtesy of Stockbyte/Getty Images.

Taken from:

*Exploring Microsoft Office 2013*, Volume 1,
by Mary Anne Poatsy, Keith Mulbery, Cynthia Krebs, Lynn Hogan, Amy M. Rutledge, and Robert T. Grauer
Copyright © 2014 by Pearson Education, Inc.
330 Hudson Street, New York, NY 10013

*Exploring Microsoft Office 2013*, Volume 2,
by Mary Anne Poatsy, Keith Mulbery, Eric Cameron, Jason Davidson, Jerri Williams, Linda Lau, Rebecca Lawson,
Robert T. Grauer, and Sallie Dodson
Copyright © 2014 by Pearson Education, Inc.
330 Hudson Street, New York, NY 10013

*MIS Cases: Decision Making with Application Software*, Fourth Edition,
by M. Lisa Miller
Copyright © 2009, 2007 by Pearson Education, Inc.
Published by Prentice Hall
Boston, Massachusetts 02116

This special edition published in cooperation with Pearson Learning Solutions.

Pearson Learning Solutions, 501 Boylston Street, Suite 900, Boston, MA 02116
A Pearson Education Company
www.pearsoned.com

Printed in the United States of America

9  16


000200010271962391

SR

ISBN 10: 1-323-13315-1
ISBN 13: 978-1-323-13315-6

# Brief Contents

**Excel**

| | | |
|---|---|---|
| CHAPTER 1 | Introduction to Excel | 1 |
| CHAPTER 2 | Formulas and Functions | 61 |
| CHAPTER 3 | Charts | 103 |
| CHAPTER 4 | Statistical Functions | 143 |
| CHAPTER 5 | Specialized Functions | 157 |
| CHAPTER 6 | Datasets and Tables | 169 |
| CHAPTER 7 | Multiple-Sheet Workbook Management | 231 |
| CHAPTER 8 | Imports, Web Queries, and XML | 267 |
| CHAPTER 9 | Templates, Styles, and Macros | 289 |
| CHAPTER 10 | Subtotals, Pivot Tables, and Pivot Charts | 327 |

**Access**

| | | |
|---|---|---|
| CHAPTER 11 | Action and Specialized Queries | 367 |

| | | |
|---|---|---|
| CHAPTER 12 | MIS Cases | 387 |
| INDEX | | 421 |

Chapters 1–3, 6 are taken from: *Exploring Microsoft Office 2013*, Volume 1, by Mary Anne Poatsy, Keith Mulbery, Cynthia Krebs, Lynn Hogan, Amy M. Rutledge, and Robert T. Grauer.

Chapters 4–5, 7–11 are taken from: *Exploring Microsoft Office 2013*, Volume 2, by Mary Anne Poatsy, Keith Mulbery, Eric Cameron, Jason Davidson, Jerri Williams, Linda Lau, Rebecca Lawson, Robert T. Grauer, and Sallie Dodson.

Chapter 12 is taken from: *MIS Cases: Decision Making with Application Software*, Fourth Edition, by M. Lisa Miller.

# Contents

## Microsoft Office Excel 2013

### ■ CHAPTER ONE  Introduction to Excel: What Is a Spreadsheet?  1

| | | | |
|---|---|---|---|
| OBJECTIVES | 1 | CLIPBOARD TASKS | 34 |
| CASE STUDY OK OFFICE SYSTEMS | 1 | Selecting, Moving, Copying, and Pasting Data | 34 |
| INTRODUCTION TO SPREADSHEETS | 2 | HANDS-ON EXERCISE 4: | |
| Exploring the Excel Window | 2 | Clipboard Tasks | 39 |
| Entering and Editing Cell Data | 5 | FORMATTING | 42 |
| HANDS-ON EXERCISE 1: | | Applying Alignment and Font Options | 42 |
| Introduction to Spreadsheets | 9 | Applying Number Formats | 44 |
| MATHEMATICS AND FORMULAS | 12 | HANDS-ON EXERCISE 5: | |
| Creating Formulas | 12 | Formatting | 47 |
| Using Auto Fill | 14 | PAGE SETUP AND PRINTING | 51 |
| Displaying Cell Formulas | 15 | Selecting Page Setup Options | 51 |
| HANDS-ON EXERCISE 2: | | Previewing and Printing a Worksheet | 55 |
| Mathematics and Formulas | 17 | HANDS-ON EXERCISE 6: | |
| WORKBOOK AND WORKSHEET MANAGEMENT | 22 | Page Setup and Printing | 56 |
| Managing Worksheets | 22 | | |
| Managing Columns and Rows | 25 | | |
| HANDS-ON EXERCISE 3: | | | |
| Workbook and Worksheet Management | 29 | | |

### ■ CHAPTER TWO  Formulas and Functions: Performing Quantitative Analysis  61

| | | | |
|---|---|---|---|
| OBJECTIVES | 61 | LOGICAL, LOOKUP, AND FINANCIAL FUNCTIONS | 85 |
| CASE STUDY TOWNSEND MORTGAGE COMPANY | 61 | Determining Results with the IF Function | 85 |
| FORMULA BASICS | 62 | Using Lookup Functions | 88 |
| Using Relative, Absolute, and Mixed Cell References | | Calculating Payments with the PMT Function | 91 |
| in Formulas | 62 | HANDS-ON EXERCISE 3: | |
| Correcting Circular References | 64 | Logical, Lookup, and Financial Functions | 92 |
| HANDS-ON EXERCISE 1: | | RANGE NAMES | 96 |
| Formula Basics | 66 | Creating and Maintaining Range Names | 96 |
| FUNCTION BASICS | 70 | Using Range Names in Formulas | 98 |
| Inserting a Function | 70 | HANDS-ON EXERCISE 4: | |
| Inserting Basic Math and Statistics Functions | 72 | Range Names | 99 |
| Using Date Functions | 77 | | |
| HANDS-ON EXERCISE 2: | | | |
| Function Basics | 80 | | |

### ■ CHAPTER THREE  Charts: Depicting Data Visually  103

| | | | |
|---|---|---|---|
| OBJECTIVES | 103 | HANDS-ON EXERCISE 1: | |
| CASE STUDY COMPUTER JOB OUTLOOK | 103 | Chart Creation Basics | 118 |
| CHART CREATION BASICS | 104 | CHART ELEMENTS | 123 |
| Selecting the Data Source | 104 | Adding Chart Elements | 123 |
| Choosing a Chart Type | 105 | Formatting Chart Elements | 126 |
| Moving, Sizing, and Printing a Chart | 115 | | |

**HANDS-ON EXERCISE 2:**
Chart Elements    131

**CHART DESIGN AND SPARKLINES**    135
Applying a Chart Style and Colors    135

Modifying the Data Source    136
Creating and Customizing Sparklines    137

**HANDS-ON EXERCISE 3:**
**Chart Design and Sparklines**    139

# ■ CHAPTER FOUR Statistical Functions: Analyzing Statistics    143

**OBJECTIVES**    143
**CASE STUDY: EDUCATION EVALUATION**    143
**MATH AND STATISTICAL FUNCTIONS**    144
Using Conditional Math and Statistical Functions    144
Calculating Relative Standing with Statistical Functions    147

**HANDS-ON EXERCISE 1:**
**Math and Statistical Functions**    152

# ■ CHAPTER FIVE Specialized Functions: Logical, Lookup, Databases, and Finances    157

**OBJECTIVES**    157
**CASE STUDY: TRANSPAYNE FILTRATION**    157
**LOGICAL AND LOOKUP FUNCTIONS**    158
Creating a Nested Logical Function    158
Using MATCH and INDEX Lookup Functions    162

**HANDS-ON EXERCISE 1:**
**Logical and Lookup Functions**    165

# ■ CHAPTER SIX Datasets and Tables: Managing Large Volumes of Data    169

**OBJECTIVES**    169
**CASE STUDY REID FURNITURE STORE**    169
**LARGE DATASETS**    170
Freezing Rows and Columns    171
Printing Large Datasets    171

**HANDS-ON EXERCISE 1:**
**Large Datasets**    175

**EXCEL TABLES**    179
Designing and Creating Tables    179
Applying a Table Style    183

**HANDS-ON EXERCISE 2:**
**Excel Tables**    185

**TABLE MANIPULATION**    190
Sorting Data    190
Filtering Data    192

**HANDS-ON EXERCISE 3:**
**Table Manipulation**    196

**TABLE AGGREGATION**    201
Using Structured References and a Total Row    201

**HANDS-ON EXERCISE 4:**
**Table Aggregation**    204

**CONDITIONAL FORMATTING**    208
Applying Conditional Formatting    208
Creating a New Rule    212

**HANDS-ON EXERCISE 5:**
**Conditional Formatting**    215

**CHAPTER OBJECTIVES REVIEW**    219
**KEY TERMS MATCHING**    220
**MULTIPLE CHOICE**    221
**PRACTICE EXERCISES**    222
**MID-LEVEL EXERCISES**    226
**BEYOND THE CLASSROOM**    228
**CAPSTONE EXERCISE**    230

# ■ CHAPTER SEVEN Multiple-Sheet Workbook Management: Ensuring Quality Control 231

| | | | | |
|---|---|---|---|---|
| OBJECTIVES | 231 | HANDS-ON EXERCISE 2: | | |
| CASE STUDY: CIRCLE CITY SPORTING GOODS | 231 | 3-D Formulas and Linked Workbooks | | 250 |
| MULTIPLE WORKSHEETS | 232 | FORMULA AUDITS AND DATA VALIDATION | | 254 |
| Working with Grouped Worksheets | 232 | Auditing Formulas | | 255 |
| Managing Windows and Workspaces | 235 | Setting Up a Watch Window | | 257 |
| Inserting Hyperlinks | 237 | Validating Data | | 258 |
| HANDS-ON EXERCISE 1: | | HANDS-ON EXERCISE 3: | | |
| Multiple Worksheets | 240 | Formula Audits and Data Validation | | 261 |
| 3-D FORMULAS AND LINKED WORKBOOKS | 245 | | | |
| Inserting a 3-D Formula | 245 | | | |
| Linking Workbooks | 247 | | | |

# ■ CHAPTER EIGHT Imports, Web Queries, and XML: Managing Data 267

| | | | |
|---|---|---|---|
| OBJECTIVES | 267 | TEXT MANIPULATION | 282 |
| CASE STUDY: STOCK ANALYSIS | 267 | Converting Text to Columns | 282 |
| EXTERNAL DATA | 268 | Manipulating Text with Functions | 283 |
| Importing Data from External Sources | 268 | Using Flash Fill | 285 |
| Creating a Web Query | 272 | HANDS-ON EXERCISE 2: | |
| Managing Connections | 274 | Text Manipulation | 286 |
| HANDS-ON EXERCISE 1: | | | |
| External Data | 276 | | |

# ■ CHAPTER NINE Templates, Styles, and Macros: Standardizing Workbooks 289

| | | | |
|---|---|---|---|
| OBJECTIVES | 289 | MACROS | 309 |
| CASE STUDY: STAFF ACCOUNTING SERVICES | 289 | Creating a Macro | 309 |
| TEMPLATES, THEMES, AND STYLES | 290 | Creating Macro Buttons | 312 |
| Selecting a Template | 290 | Setting Macro Security | 313 |
| Applying Themes and Backgrounds | 291 | HANDS-ON EXERCISE 3: | |
| Applying Cell Styles | 293 | Macros | 315 |
| HANDS-ON EXERCISE 1: | | VISUAL BASIC FOR APPLICATIONS | 319 |
| Templates, Themes, and Styles | 296 | Creating a Sub Procedure | 319 |
| CUSTOM TEMPLATES AND WORKBOOK PROTECTION | 299 | Creating a Custom Function | 321 |
| Creating and Using a Template | 299 | HANDS-ON EXERCISE 4: | |
| Protecting a Cell, a Worksheet, and a Workbook | 300 | Visual Basic for Applications | 323 |
| HANDS-ON EXERCISE 2: | | | |
| Custom Templates and Workbook Protection | 304 | | |

# ■ CHAPTER TEN Subtotals, PivotTables, and PivotCharts: Summarizing and Analyzing Data 327

| | | | |
|---|---|---|---|
| OBJECTIVES | 327 | PIVOTTABLE BASICS | 336 |
| CASE STUDY: IVORY HALLS PUBLISHING COMPANY | 327 | Creating a PivotTable | 336 |
| SUBTOTALS AND OUTLINES | 328 | Modifying a PivotTable | 339 |
| Subtotaling Data | 328 | HANDS-ON EXERCISE 2: | |
| Grouping and Ungrouping Data | 331 | PivotTable Basics | 344 |
| HANDS-ON EXERCISE 1: | | PIVOTTABLE OPTIONS | 349 |
| Subtotals and Outlines | 332 | Filtering and Slicing a PivotTable | 349 |
| | | Creating a Calculated Field | 352 |

HANDS-ON EXERCISE 3:
PivotTable Options                                                354
PIVOTTABLE DESIGN AND PIVOTCHARTS                                 359
Formatting a PivotTable                                           359

Using PowerPivot Functionality                                   360
Creating a PivotChart                                            362
HANDS-ON EXERCISE 4:
PivotTable Design and PivotCharts                                364

# Microsoft Office Access 2013

## ■ CHAPTER ELEVEN Action and Specialized Queries: Moving Beyond the Select Query    367

OBJECTIVES                                                       367
CASE STUDY: REPLACEMEMT CHINA, INC.                              367
ACTION QUERIES                                                   368
Determining When to Use an Action Query                          368
Updating Data with an Update Query                               370

Adding Records to a Table with an Append Query                   373
Creating a Table with a Make Table Query                         376
Deleting Records with a Delete Query                             377
HANDS-ON EXERCISE 1:
Action Queries                                                   380

## ■ CHAPTER TWELVE MIS Cases    387

CASE 1: PIEDMONT TRAILER MANUFACTURING COMPANY
CASE BACKGROUND                                                  387
CASE SCENARIO                                                    387
Design Specifications                                            389
Information Specifications                                       391
Implementation Concerns                                          391
Test Your Design                                                 392

CASE 2: FRANCISCO'S LAWN CARE
CASE BACKGROUND                                                  393
CASE SCENARIO                                                    393
Design Specifications                                            394
Information Specifications                                       395
Implementation Concerns                                          395
Test Your Design                                                 395

CASE 3: MAXI'S GROCERY MART
CASE BACKGROUND                                                  397
CASE SCENARIO                                                    397
Design Specifications                                            399
Information Specifications                                       399
Implementation Concerns                                          400
Test Your Design                                                 400

CASE 4: KELIN TECHNOLOGY SEMINARS
CASE BACKGROUND                                                  402
CASE SCENARIO                                                    402
Design Specifications                                            403
Information Specifications                                       405
Implementation Concerns                                          406
Test Your Design                                                 406

CASE 5: LAKE WEST UNIVERSITY
CASE BACKGROUND                                                  411
CASE SCENARIO                                                    411
Design Specifications                                            412
Information Specifications                                       413
Implementation Concerns                                          413
Test Your Design                                                 413

CASE 6: EDMUND GRANT PHARMACEUTICAL COMPANY
CASE BACKGROUND                                                  415
CASE SCENARIO                                                    415
Design Specifications                                            417
Information Specifications                                       418
Implementation Concerns                                          418
Test Your Design                                                 419

INDEX                                                            421

Chapters 1–3, 6 are taken from: *Exploring Microsoft Office 2013*, Volume 1, by Mary Anne Poatsy, Keith Mulbery, Cynthia Krebs, Lynn Hogan, Amy M. Rutledge, and Robert T. Grauer.

Chapters 4–5, 7–11 are taken from: *Exploring Microsoft Office 2013*, Volume 2, by Mary Anne Poatsy, Keith Mulbery, Eric Cameron, Jason Davidson, Jerri Williams, Linda Lau, Rebecca Lawson, Robert T. Grauer, and Sallie Dodson.

Chapter 12 is taken from: *MIS Cases: Decision Making with Application Software*, Fourth Edition, by M. Lisa Miller.

Excel

# Introduction to Excel

## CHAPTER 1

## What Is a Spreadsheet?

OBJECTIVES AFTER YOU READ THIS CHAPTER, YOU WILL BE ABLE TO:

1. Explore the Excel window p. 2
2. Enter and edit cell data p. 5
3. Create formulas p. 12
4. Use Auto Fill p. 14
5. Display cell formulas p. 15
6. Manage worksheets p. 22

7. Manage columns and rows p. 25
8. Select, move, copy, and paste data p. 34
9. Apply alignment and font options p. 42
10. Apply number formats p. 44
11. Select page setup options p. 51
12. Preview and print a worksheet p. 55

## CASE STUDY | OK Office Systems

You are an assistant manager at OK Office Systems (OKOS) in Oklahoma City. OKOS sells a wide range of computer systems, peripherals, and furniture for small- and medium-sized organizations in the metropolitan area. To compete against large, global, big-box office supply stores, OKOS provides competitive pricing by ordering directly from local manufacturers rather than dealing with distributors.

Alesha Bennett, the general manager, asked you to calculate the retail price, sale price, and profit analysis for selected items on sale this month. Using markup rates provided by Alesha, you need to calculate the retail price, the amount OKOS charges its customers for the products. For the sale, Alesha wants to give customers between a 10% and 30% discount on select items. You need to use those discount rates to calculate the sale prices. Finally, you will calculate the profit margin to determine the percentage of the final sale price over the cost.

After you create the initial pricing spreadsheet, you will be able to change values and see that the formulas update the results automatically. In addition, you will be able to insert data for additional sale items or delete an item based on the manager's decision.

Although your experience with Microsoft Office Excel 2013 may be limited, you are excited to apply your knowledge and skills to your newly assigned responsibility. In the Hands-On Exercises for this chapter, you will create and format the analytical spreadsheet to practice the skills you learn.

# Introduction to Spreadsheets

Organizing, calculating, and evaluating quantitative data are important skills needed today for personal and managerial decision making. You track expenses for your household budget, maintain a savings plan, and determine what amount you can afford for a house or car payment. Retail managers create and analyze their organizations' annual budgets, sales projections, and inventory records. Charitable organizations track the donations they receive, the distribution of those donations, and overhead expenditures.

You can use a spreadsheet to maintain data and perform calculations. A *spreadsheet* is an electronic file that contains a grid of columns and rows used to organize related data and to display results of calculations, enabling interpretation of quantitative data for decision making.

Performing calculations using a calculator and entering the results into a ledger can lead to inaccurate values. If an input value is incorrect or needs to be updated, you have to recalculate the results manually, which is time-consuming and can lead to inaccuracies. A spreadsheet makes data entry changes easy. If the formulas are correctly constructed, the results recalculate automatically and accurately, saving time and reducing room for error.

In this section, you will learn how to design spreadsheets. In addition, you will explore the Excel window and learn the name of each window element. Then, you will enter text, values, and dates in a spreadsheet.

## Exploring the Excel Window

In Excel, a *worksheet* is a single spreadsheet that typically contains descriptive labels, numeric values, formulas, functions, and graphical representations of data. A *workbook* is a collection of one or more related worksheets contained within a single file. By default, new workbooks contain one worksheet. Storing multiple worksheets within one workbook helps organize related data together in one file and enables you to perform calculations among the worksheets within the workbook. For example, you can create a budget workbook of 13 worksheets, one for each month to store your personal income and expenses and a final worksheet to calculate totals across the entire year.

Excel contains the standard interface of Microsoft Office applications:

- **Quick Access Toolbar:** Save, Undo, and Redo/Repeat commands
- **Title bar:** File name (such as Book1) and software name (such as Excel)
- **Control buttons:** Microsoft Excel Help, Full Screen Mode, Minimize, Restore Down, and Close
- **Ribbon:** Commands (such as Align Left) organized within groups (such as Alignment) on various tabs (such as Home)
- **Scroll bars:** Tools to scroll vertically and horizontally through a worksheet

### Identify Excel Window Elements

Figure 1.1 identifies elements specific to the Excel window, and Table 1.1 lists and describes the Excel window elements.

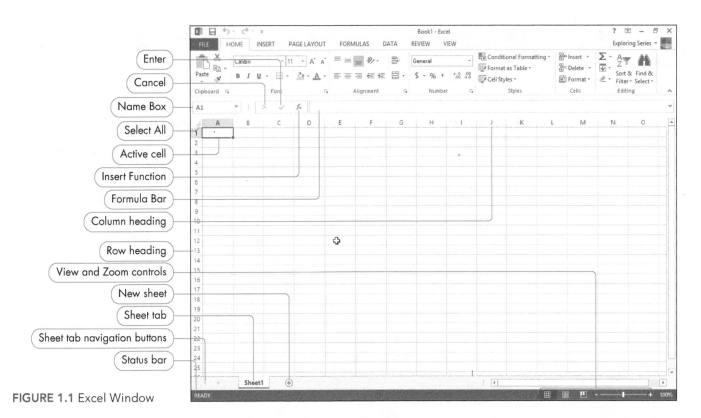

**FIGURE 1.1** Excel Window

## TABLE 1.1  Excel Elements

| Element | Description |
|---|---|
| Name Box | The **Name Box** is an identifier that displays the address of the current cell in the worksheet. Use the Name Box to go to a cell, assign a name to one or more cells, or select a function. |
| Cancel ✗ | When you enter or edit data, click Cancel to cancel the data entry or edit and revert back to the previous data in the cell, if any. The Cancel icon changes from gray to red when you position the mouse pointer over it. |
| Enter ✓ | When you enter or edit data, click Enter to accept data typed in the active cell and keep the current cell active. The Enter icon changes from gray to blue when you position the mouse pointer over it. |
| Insert Function 𝑓ₓ | Click to display the Insert Function dialog box to search for and select a function to insert into the active cell. The Insert Function icon changes from gray to green when you position the mouse pointer over it. |
| Formula Bar | The **Formula Bar** shows the contents of the active cell. You can enter or edit cell contents here or directly in the active cell. Drag the bottom border of the Formula Bar down to increase the height of the Formula Bar to display large amounts of data or a long formula contained in the active cell. |
| Select All ◺ | The triangle at the intersection of the row and column headings in the top-left corner of the worksheet. Click it to select everything contained in the active worksheet. |
| Column headings | The letters above the columns, such as A, B, C, and so on. |
| Row headings | The numbers to the left of the rows, such as 1, 2, 3, and so on. |
| Active cell | The active cell is the current cell, which is indicated by a dark green border. |
| Sheet tab | A **sheet tab** shows the name of a worksheet contained in the workbook. When you create a new Excel workbook, the default worksheet is named Sheet1. |
| New sheet ⊕ | Inserts a new worksheet to the right of the current worksheet. |
| Sheet tab navigation buttons | If your workbook contains several worksheets, Excel may not show all the sheet tabs at the same time. Use the buttons to display the first, previous, next, or last worksheet. |

TABLE 1.1  Excel Elements *(continued)*

| Element | Description |
|---------|-------------|
| Status bar | Displays information about a selected command or operation in progress. For example, it displays *Select destination and press ENTER or choose Paste* after you use the Copy command. |
| View controls | Click a view control to display the worksheet in Normal, Page Layout, or Page Break Preview. Normal view displays the worksheet without showing margins, headers, footers, and page breaks. Page Layout view shows the margins, header and footer area, and a ruler. Page Break Preview indicates where the worksheet will be divided into pages. |
| Zoom control | Drag the zoom control to increase the size of the worksheet onscreen to see more or less of the worksheet data. |

## Identify Columns, Rows, and Cells

A worksheet contains columns and rows, with each column and row assigned a heading. Columns are assigned alphabetical headings from columns A to Z, continuing from AA to AZ, and then from BA to BZ until XFD, which is the last of the possible 16,384 columns. Rows have numeric headings ranging from 1 to 1,048,576.

The intersection of a column and row is a *cell*; a total of more than 17 billion cells are available in a worksheet. Each cell has a unique *cell address*, identified by first its column letter and then its row number. For example, the cell at the intersection of column A and row 9 is cell A9. Cell references are useful when referencing data in formulas, or in navigation.

## Navigate In and Among Worksheets

The *active cell* is the current cell. Excel displays a dark green border around the active cell in the worksheet, and the cell address of the active cell appears in the Name Box. The contents of the active cell, or the formula used to calculate the results of the active cell, appear in the Formula Bar. You can change the active cell by using the mouse to click in a different cell. If you work in a large worksheet, use the vertical and horizontal scroll bars to display another area of the worksheet and click in the desired cell to make it the active cell.

To navigate to a new cell, click it or use the arrow keys on the keyboard. When you press Enter, the next cell down in the same column becomes the active cell. Table 1.2 lists the keyboard navigation methods. The Go To command is helpful for navigating to a cell that is not visible onscreen.

TABLE 1.2  Keystrokes and Actions

| Keystroke | Used to |
|-----------|---------|
| ↑ | Move up one cell in the same column. |
| ↓ | Move down one cell in the same column. |
| ← | Move left one cell in the same row. |
| → | Move right one cell in the same row. |
| Tab | Move right one cell in the same row. |
| Page Up | Move the active cell up one screen. |
| Page Down | Move the active cell down one screen. |
| Home | Move the active cell to column A of the current row. |
| Ctrl+Home | Make cell A1 the active cell. |
| Ctrl+End | Make the rightmost, lowermost active corner of the worksheet—the intersection of the last column and row that contains data—the active cell. Does not move to cell XFD1048576 unless that cell contains data. |
| F5 or Ctrl+G | Display the Go To dialog box to enter any cell address. |

To display the contents of another worksheet within the workbook, click the sheet tab at the bottom-left corner of the workbook window. The active sheet tab has a white background color. After you click a sheet tab, you can then navigate within that worksheet.

# Entering and Editing Cell Data

You should plan the structure before you start entering data into a worksheet. Using the OKOS case presented at the beginning of the chapter as an example, use the following steps to plan the worksheet design, enter and format data, and complete the workbook:

### Plan the Worksheet Design

1. **State the purpose of the worksheet.** The purpose of the OKOS worksheet is to store data about products on sale and to calculate important details, such as the retail price based on markup, the sales price based on a discount rate, and the profit margin.

2. **Decide what input values are needed.** Input values are the initial values, such as variables and assumptions. You may change these values to see what type of effects different values have on the end results. For the OKOS worksheet, the input values include the costs OKOS pays the manufacturers, the markup rates, and the proposed discount rates for the sale. In some worksheets, you can create an *input area*, a specific region in the worksheet to store and change the variables used in calculations. For example, if you applied the same Markup Rate and same Percent Off for all products, it would be easier to create an input area at the top of the worksheet to change the values in one location rather than in several locations.

3. **Decide what outputs are needed to achieve the purpose of the worksheet.** Outputs are the results you need to calculate. For the OKOS worksheet, the outputs include columns to calculate the retail price (i.e., the selling price to your customers), the sale price, and the profit margin. In some worksheets, you can create an *output area*, the region in the worksheet to contain formulas dependent on the values in the input area.

### Enter and Format the Data

4. **Enter the labels, values, and formulas in Excel.** Use the design plan (steps 2–3) as you enter labels, input values, and formulas to calculate the output. In the OKOS worksheet, descriptive labels (the product names) appear in the first column to indicate that the values on a specific row pertain to a specific product. Descriptive labels appear at the top of each column, such as Cost and Retail Price, to describe the values in the respective column. Change the input values to test that your formulas produce correct results. If necessary, correct any errors in the formulas to produce correct results. For the OKOS worksheet, change some of the original costs and markup rates to ensure the calculated retail price, selling price, and profit margin percentage results update correctly.

5. **Format the numerical values in the worksheet.** Align decimal points in columns of numbers and add number formats and styles. In the OKOS worksheet, use Accounting Number Format and the Percent Style to format the numerical data. Adjust the number of decimal places as needed.

6. **Format the descriptive titles and labels so that they stand out.** Add bold and color to headings so that they stand out and are attractive. Apply other formatting to headings and descriptive labels. In the OKOS worksheet, you will center the main title over all the columns, bold and center column labels over the columns, and apply other formatting to the headings. Figure 1.2 shows the completed OKOS worksheet.

**Complete the Workbook**

7. **Document the workbook as thoroughly as possible.** Include the current date, your name as the workbook author, assumptions, and purpose of the workbook. You can provide this documentation in a separate worksheet within the workbook. You can also add some documentation in the *Properties* section when you click the File tab.

8. **Save and share the completed workbook.** Preview and prepare printouts for distribution in meetings, send an electronic copy of the workbook to those who need it, or upload the workbook on a shared network drive or in the cloud.

Centered title
Formatted output range (calculated results)
Formatted column labels
Formatted input range (Cost, Markup Rate, and Percent Off)
Product data organized into rows

| | A | B | C | D | E | F | G | H |
|---|---|---|---|---|---|---|---|---|
| 1 | OK Office Systems Pricing Information | | | | | | | |
| 2 | | | | 9/1/2016 | | | | |
| 3 | | | | | | | | |
| 4 | Product | Cost | Markup Rate | Retail Price | Percent Off | Sale Price | Profit Amount | Profit Margin |
| 5 | Electronics | | | | | | | |
| 6 | Computer System | $475.50 | 50.0% | $ 713.25 | 15.0% | $ 606.26 | $ 130.76 | 21.6% |
| 7 | Color Laser Printer | $457.70 | 75.5% | $ 803.26 | 20.0% | $ 642.61 | $ 184.91 | 28.8% |
| 8 | 28" Monitor | $195.00 | 83.5% | $ 357.83 | 10.0% | $ 322.04 | $ 127.04 | 39.4% |
| 9 | Furniture | | | | | | | |
| 10 | Desk Chair | $ 75.00 | 100.0% | $ 150.00 | 25.0% | $ 112.50 | $ 37.50 | 33.3% |
| 11 | Solid Oak Computer Desk | $700.00 | 185.7% | $1,999.90 | 30.0% | $1,399.93 | $ 699.93 | 50.0% |
| 12 | Executive Desk Chair | $200.00 | 100.0% | $ 400.00 | 25.0% | $ 300.00 | $ 100.00 | 33.3% |
| 13 | | | | | | | | |

**FIGURE 1.2** Completed OKOS Worksheet

## Enter Text

*Text* is any combination of letters, numbers, symbols, and spaces not used in calculations. Excel treats phone numbers, such as 555-1234, and Social Security numbers, such as 123-45-6789, as text entries. You enter text for a worksheet title to describe the contents of the worksheet, as row and column labels to describe data, and as cell data. In Figure 1.2, the cells in column A, row 1, and row 4 contain text, such as *Product*. Text aligns at the left cell margin by default. To enter text in a cell, do the following:

STEP 1

1. Make sure the cell is active where you want to enter text.
2. Type the text.
3. Do one of the following to make another cell the active cell after entering data:

   - Press Enter on the keyboard.
   - Press an arrow key on the keyboard.
   - Press Tab on the keyboard.

   Do one of the following to keep the current cell the active cell after entering data:

   - Press Ctrl+Enter.
   - Click Enter (the check mark between the Name Box and the Formula Bar).

As soon as you begin typing a label into a cell, the **AutoComplete** feature searches for and automatically displays any other label in that column that matches the letters you typed. For example, *Computer System* is typed in cell A6 in Figure 1.2. When you start to type *Co* in cell A7, AutoComplete displays *Computer System* because a text entry previously typed starts with *Co*. Press Enter to accept the repeated label, or continue typing to enter a different label, such as *Color Laser Printer*.

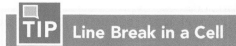

## TIP | Line Break in a Cell

If a long text label does not fit well in a cell, you can insert a line break to display the text label on multiple lines within the cell. To insert a line break while you are typing a label, press Alt+Enter where you want to start the next line of text within the cell.

## Enter Values

**STEP 2》** *Values* are numbers that represent a quantity or a measurable amount. Excel usually distinguishes between text and value data based on what you enter. The primary difference between text and value entries is that value entries can be the basis of calculations, whereas text cannot. In Figure 1.2, the data below the *Cost*, *Markup Rates*, and *Percent Off* labels are values. Values align at the right cell margin by default. After entering values, you can align decimal places and apply formatting by adding characters, such as $ or %.

## Enter Dates

**STEP 3》** You can enter dates and times in a variety of formats in cells, such as 9/1/2016; 9/1/16; September 1, 2016; or 1-Sep-16. You can also enter times, such as 1:30 PM or 13:30. You should enter a static date to document when you create or modify a workbook or to document the specific point in time when the data were accurate, such as on a balance sheet or income statement. Later, you will learn how to use formulas to enter dates that update to the current date. In Figure 1.2, cell A2 contains a date. Dates are values, so they align at the right cell margin. However, the date in Figure 1.2 has been centered by the user.

Excel displays dates differently from the way it stores dates. For example, the displayed date 9/1/2016 represents the first day in September in the year 2016. Excel stores dates as serial numbers starting at 1 with January 1, 1900, so 9/1/2016 is stored as 42614 so that you can create formulas, such as to calculate how many days exist between two dates.

## Enter Formulas

*Formulas* combine cell references, arithmetic operations, values, and/or functions used in a calculation. You must start the formula with an equal sign (=). In Figure 1.3, the data below the *Retail Price*, *Sale Price*, *Profit Amount*, and *Profit Margin* labels contain formulas. When a cell containing a formula is the active cell, the formula displays in the Formula Bar, and the result of the formula displays in the cell.

## Edit and Clear Cell Contents

You can edit a cell's contents by doing one of the following:

- Click the cell, click in the Formula Bar, make the changes, and then click Enter (the check mark between the Name Box and the Formula Bar) to keep the cell the active cell.
- Double-click the cell, make changes in the cell, and then press Enter.
- Click the cell, press F2, make changes in the cell, and then press Enter.

You can clear a cell's contents by doing one of the following:

- Click the cell and press Delete.
- Click the cell, click Clear in the Editing group on the HOME tab, and then select Clear Contents.

*Quick*
Concepts ✓

1. What are two major advantages of using an electronic spreadsheet instead of a paper-based ledger? *p. 2*

2. What visual indicators let you know which cell is the active cell? *p. 4*

3. What steps should you perform before entering data into a worksheet? *p. 5*

4. What are four major things you can enter into a cell? Give an example (different from those in the book) for each type. *pp. 6–7*

Hands-On Exercises

Watch the Video
for this Hands-
On Exercise!

MyITLab®
HOE1 Training

# 1 Introduction to Spreadsheets

As the assistant manager of OKOS, you need to create a worksheet that shows the cost (the amount OKOS pays its suppliers), the markup percentage (the amount by which the cost is increased), and the retail selling price. You also need to list the discount percentage (such as 25% off) for each product, the sale price, and the profit margin percentage.

**Skills covered:** Enter Text • Enter Values • Enter a Date and Clear Cell Contents

## STEP 1 ≫ ENTER TEXT

Now that you have planned the OKOS worksheet, you are ready to enter labels for the title, column labels, and row labels. You will type a title in cell A1, product labels in the first column, and row labels in the fourth row. Refer to Figure 1.3 as you complete Step 1.

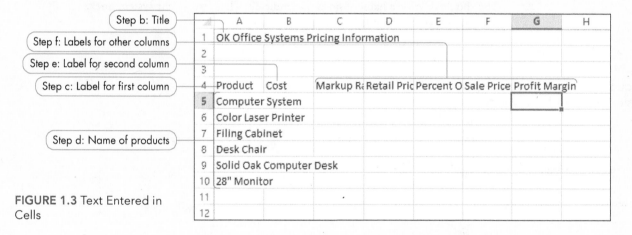

Step b: Title

Step f: Labels for other columns

Step e: Label for second column

Step c: Label for first column

Step d: Name of products

| | A | B | C | D | E | F | G | H |
|---|---|---|---|---|---|---|---|---|
| 1 | OK Office Systems Pricing Information | | | | | | | |
| 2 | | | | | | | | |
| 3 | | | | | | | | |
| 4 | Product | Cost | Markup Ra | Retail Pric | Percent O | Sale Price | Profit Margin | |
| 5 | Computer System | | | | | | | |
| 6 | Color Laser Printer | | | | | | | |
| 7 | Filing Cabinet | | | | | | | |
| 8 | Desk Chair | | | | | | | |
| 9 | Solid Oak Computer Desk | | | | | | | |
| 10 | 28" Monitor | | | | | | | |
| 11 | | | | | | | | |
| 12 | | | | | | | | |

**FIGURE 1.3** Text Entered in Cells

a. Start Excel and open a new blank workbook. Save the new workbook as **e01h1Markup_LastFirst**.

When you save files, use your last and first names. For example, as the Excel author, I would save my workbook as *e01h1Markup_MulberyKeith*.

b. Type **OK Office Systems Pricing Information** in **cell A1** and press **Enter**.

When you press Enter, the next cell down—cell A2 in this case—becomes the active cell. The text does not completely fit in cell A1, and some of the text appears in cells B1, C1, D1, and possibly E1. If you make cell B1, C1, D1, or E1 the active cell, the Formula Bar is empty, indicating that nothing is stored in those cells.

c. Click **cell A4**, type **Product**, and then press **Enter**.

d. Continue typing the rest of the text in **cells A5** through **A10** as shown in Figure 1.4. Text in column A appears to flow into column B.

When you start typing *Co* in cell A6, AutoComplete displays a ScreenTip suggesting a previous text entry starting with *Co—Computer System—*but keep typing to enter *Color Laser Printer* instead. You just entered the product labels to describe the data in each row.

e. Click **cell B4** to make it the active cell. Type **Cost** and press **Tab**.

Instead of pressing Enter to move down column B, you pressed Tab to make the cell to the right the active cell.

**f.** Type the following text in the respective cells, pressing **Tab** after typing each of the first four column labels and pressing **Enter** after the last column label:

- **Markup Rate** in **cell C4**
- **Retail Price** in **cell D4**
- **Percent Off** in **cell E4**
- **Sale Price** in **cell F4**
- **Profit Margin** in **cell G4**

The text looks cut off when you enter data in the cell to the right. Do not worry about this now. You will adjust column widths and formatting later in this chapter.

> **TROUBLESHOOTING:** If you notice a typographical error, click in the cell containing the error and retype the label. Or press F2 to edit the cell contents, move the insertion point using the arrow keys, press Backspace or Delete to delete the incorrect characters, type the correct characters, and then press Enter. If you type a label in an incorrect cell, click the cell and press Delete.

**g.** Save the changes you made to the workbook.

You should develop a habit of saving periodically. That way if your system unexpectedly shuts down, you will not lose everything you worked on.

## STEP 2 ≫ ENTER VALUES

Now that you have entered the descriptive labels, you need to enter the cost, markup rate, and percent off for each product. Refer to Figure 1.4 as you complete Step 2.

Steps e–f: Percent Off values

Steps c–d: Markup Rate values

Steps a–b: Cost values

| | A | B | C | D | E | F | G | H |
|---|---|---|---|---|---|---|---|---|
| 1 | OK Office Systems Pricing Information | | | | | | | |
| 2 | | | | | | | | |
| 3 | | | | | | | | |
| 4 | Product | Cost | Markup Ra | Retail Pric | Percent O | Sale Price | Profit Margin | |
| 5 | Computer | 400 | 0.5 | | 0.15 | | | |
| 6 | Color Lase | 457.7 | 0.75 | | 0.2 | | | |
| 7 | Filing Cab | 68.75 | 0.905 | | 0.1 | | | |
| 8 | Desk Chai | 75 | 1 | | 0.25 | | | |
| 9 | Solid Oak | 700 | 1.857 | | 0.3 | | | |
| 10 | 28" Monit | 195 | 0.835 | | 0.1 | | | |
| 11 | | | | | | | | |
| 12 | | | | | | | | |

**FIGURE 1.4** Values Entered in Cells

**a.** Click **cell B5**, type **400**, and then press **Enter**.

**b.** Type the remaining costs in **cells B6** through **B10** shown in Figure 1.4.

### TIP | Numeric Keypad

To improve your productivity, use the number keypad (if available) on the right side of your keyboard. It is much faster to type values and press Enter on the number keypad rather than using the numbers on the keyboard. Make sure Num Lock is active before using the number keypad to enter values.

**c.** Click **cell C5**, type **0.5**, and then press **Enter**.

You entered the markup rate as a decimal instead of a percentage. You will apply Percent Style later, but now you can concentrate on data entry. When you enter decimal values less than zero, you can type the period and value without typing the zero first, such as .5. Excel will automatically add the zero. You can also enter percentages as 50%, but the approach this textbook takes is to enter raw data without typing formatting such as % and to use number formatting options through Excel to display formatting symbols.

**d.** Type the remaining markup rates in **cells C6** through **C10** as shown in Figure 1.4.

**e.** Click **cell E5**, type **0.15**, and then press **Enter**.

You entered the Percent Off or markdown sale value as a decimal.

**f.** Type the remaining Percent Off values in **cells E6** through **E10** as shown in Figure 1.4 and save the workbook.

# STEP 3 ≫ ENTER A DATE AND CLEAR CELL CONTENTS

As you review the worksheet, you realize you need to provide a date to indicate when the sale starts. Refer to Figure 1.5 as you complete Step 3.

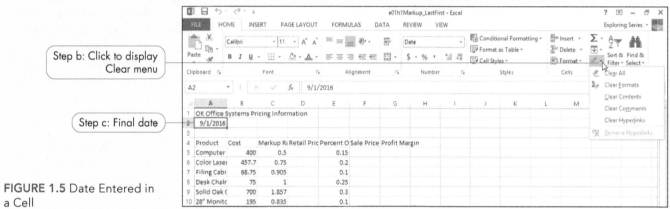

FIGURE 1.5 Date Entered in a Cell

**a.** Click **cell A2**, type **9/1**, and then press **Enter**.

The date aligns on the right cell margin by default. Excel displays *1-Sep* instead of *9/1*.

**b.** Click **cell A2**, click **Clear** in the Editing group on the HOME tab, and then select **Clear All**.

The Clear All command clears both cell contents and formatting in the selected cell(s).

**c.** Type **9/1/2016** in **cell A2** and press **Enter**.

> **TROUBLESHOOTING:** If you did not use Clear All and typed 9/1/2016 in cell A2, Excel would have retained the previous date format and displayed 1-Sep again.

**d.** Save the workbook. Keep the workbook open if you plan to continue with the next Hands-On Exercise. If not, close the workbook and exit Excel.

# Mathematics and Formulas

Formulas transform static numbers into meaningful results that can update as values change. For example, a payroll manager can build formulas to calculate the gross pay, deductions, and net pay for an organization's employees, or a doctoral student can create formulas to perform various statistical calculations to interpret his or her research data.

You can use formulas to help you analyze how results will change as the input data change. You can change the value of your assumptions or inputs and explore the results quickly and accurately. For example, if the interest rate changes from 4% to 5%, how would that affect your monthly payment? Analyzing different input values in Excel is easy after you build formulas. Simply change an input value and observe the change in the formula results.

In this section, you will learn how to use mathematical operations in Excel formulas. You will refresh your memory of mathematical order of precedence and how to construct formulas using cell addresses so that when the value of an input cell changes, the result of the formula changes without you having to modify the formula.

## Creating Formulas

Start a formula by typing the equal sign (=), followed by the arithmetic expression. Do not include a space before or after the arithmetic operator. Figure 1.6 shows a worksheet containing data and results of formulas. The figure also displays the actual formulas used to generate the calculated results. For example, cell B6 contains the formula =B2+B3. Excel uses the value stored in cell B2 (10) and adds it to the value stored in cell B3 (2). The result—12—appears in cell B6 instead of the actual formula. The Formula Bar displays the formula entered into the active cell.

| | A | B | C | D | E | F |
|---|---|---|---|---|---|---|
| 1 | Description | Values | | Description | Results | Formulas in Column E |
| 2 | First input value | 10 | | Sum of 10 and 2 | 12 | =B2+B3 |
| 3 | Second input value | 2 | | Difference between 10 and 2 | 8 | =B2-B3 |
| 4 | | | | Product of 10 and 2 | 20 | =B2*B3 |
| 5 | | | | Results of dividing 10 by 2 | 5 | =B2/B3 |
| 6 | | | | Results of 10 to the 2nd power | 100 | =B2^B3 |

**FIGURE 1.6** Formula Results

> **TROUBLESHOOTING:** If you type B2+B3 without the equal sign, Excel does not recognize that you entered a formula and stores the data as text.

### Use Cell References in Formulas

STEP 1 »
STEP 2 »
STEP 3 »

You should use cell references instead of values in formulas where possible. You may include values in an input area—such as dates, salary, or costs—that you will need to reference in formulas. Referencing these cells in your formulas, instead of typing the value of the cell to which you are referring, keeps your formulas accurate if the values change.

When you create a formula, you can type the cell references in uppercase, such as =B2+B3, or lowercase, such as =b2+b3. Excel changes cell references to uppercase.

In Figure 1.6, cell B2 contains 10, and cell B3 contains 2. Cell E2 contains =B2+B3 but shows the result, 12. If you change the value of cell B3 to 5, cell E2 displays the new result, which is 15. However, if you had typed actual values in the formula, =10+2, you would have to edit the formula each time an input value changes. This would be problematic, as you might forget to edit the formula or you might have a typographical error if you edit the formula. Always design worksheets in such a way as to be able to change input values without having to modify your formulas if an input value changes later.

## Apply the Order of Precedence

The **order of precedence** (also called order of operations) is a rule that controls the sequence in which arithmetic operations are performed, which affects the results of the calculation. Excel performs mathematical calculations left to right in this order: **P**ercent, **E**xponentiation, **M**ultiplication or **D**ivision, and finally **A**ddition or **S**ubtraction. Some people remember the order of precedence with the phrase *Please Excuse My Dear Aunt Sally*.

Table 1.3 lists the complete order of precedence. This chapter focuses on orders 4, 5, and 6.

**TABLE 1.3  Order of Precedence**

| Order | Description | Symbols |
|---|---|---|
| 1 | Reference Operators | colon (:), space, and comma (,) |
| 2 | Negation | - |
| 3 | Percent | % |
| 4 | Exponentiation | ^ |
| 5 | Multiplication and Division | * and / (respectively) |
| 6 | Addition and Subtraction | + and – (respectively) |
| 7 | Concatenation | ampersand symbol (&) to connect two text strings |
| 8 | Comparison | Equal sign (=), greater than (>), and less than (<) |

Figure 1.7 shows formulas, the sequence in which calculations occur, calculations, the description, and the results of each order of precedence. The highlighted results are the final formula results. This figure illustrates the importance of symbols and use of parentheses.

| | A | B | C | D | E | F |
|---|---|---|---|---|---|---|
| 1 | Input | | Formula | Sequence | Description | Result |
| 2 | 2 | | =A2+A3*A4+A5 | 1 | 3 (cell A3) * 4 (cell A4) | 12 |
| 3 | 3 | | | 2 | 2 (cell A2) + 12 (order 1) | 14 |
| 4 | 4 | | | 3 | 14 (order 2) + 5 (cell A5) | 19 |
| 5 | 5 | | | | | |
| 6 | | | =(A2+A3)*(A4+A5) | 1 | 2 (cell A2) + 3 (cell A3) | 5 |
| 7 | | | | 2 | 4 (cell A4) + 5 (cell A5) | 9 |
| 8 | | | | 3 | 5 (order 1) * 9 (order 2) | 45 |
| 9 | | | | | | |
| 10 | | | =A2/A3+A4*A5 | 1 | 2 (cell A2) / 3 (cell A3) | 0.666667 |
| 11 | | | | 2 | 4 (cell A4) * 5 (cell A5) | 20 |
| 12 | | | | 3 | 0.666667 (order 1) + 20 (order 2) | 20.66667 |
| 13 | | | | | | |
| 14 | | | =A2/(A3+A4)*A5 | 1 | 3 (cell A3) + 4 (cell A4) | 7 |
| 15 | | | | 2 | 2 (cell A2) / 7 (order 1) | 0.285714 |
| 16 | | | | 3 | 0.285714 (order 2) * 5 (cell A5) | 1.428571 |
| 17 | | | | | | |
| 18 | | | =A2^2+A3*A4% | 1 | 4 (cell A4) is converted to percentage | 0.04 |
| 19 | | | | 2 | 2 (cell A2) to the power of 2 | 4 |
| 20 | | | | 3 | 3 (cell A3) * 0.04 (order 1) | 0.12 |
| 21 | | | | 4 | 4 (order 2) + 0.12 (order 3) | 4.12 |

**FIGURE 1.7** Formula Results Based on Order of Precedence

## Use Semi-Selection to Create a Formula

To decrease typing time and ensure accuracy, you can use *semi-selection*, a process of selecting a cell or range of cells for entering cell references as you create formulas. Semi-selection is often called *pointing* because you use the mouse pointer to select cells as you build the formula. To use the semi-selection technique to create a formula, do the following:

1. Click the cell where you want to create the formula.
2. Type an equal sign (=) to start a formula.
3. Click the cell or drag to select the cell range that contains the value(s) to use in the formula. A moving marquee appears around the cell or range you select, and Excel displays the cell or range reference in the formula.
4. Type a mathematical operator.
5. Continue clicking cells, selecting ranges, and typing operators to finish the formula. Use the scroll bars if the cell is in a remote location in the worksheet, or click a worksheet tab to see a cell in another worksheet.
6. Press Enter to complete the formula.

# Using Auto Fill

*Auto Fill* enables you to copy the contents of a cell or a range of cells by dragging the *fill handle* (a small green square appearing in the bottom-right corner of the active cell) over an adjacent cell or range of cells. To use Auto Fill, do the following:

1. Click the cell with the content you want to copy to make it the active cell.
2. Point to the fill handle in the bottom-right corner of the cell until the mouse pointer changes to the fill pointer (a thin black plus sign).
3. Drag the fill handle to repeat the content in other cells.

## Copy Formulas with Auto Fill

**STEP 4 »** After you enter a formula in a cell, you can duplicate the formula without retyping it by using the fill handle to copy the formula in the active cell down a column or across a row, depending on how the data are organized. Excel adapts each copied formula based on the type of cell references in the original formula.

## Complete Sequences with Auto Fill

You can also use Auto Fill to complete a sequence. For example, if you enter January in a cell, you can use Auto Fill to enter the rest of the months in adjacent cells. Other sequences you can complete are quarters (Qtr 1, etc.), weekdays, and weekday abbreviations, by typing the first item and using Auto Fill to complete the other entries. For numeric sequences, however, you must specify the first two values in sequence. For example, if you want to fill in 5, 10, 15, and so on, you must enter 5 and 10 in two adjacent cells, select the two cells, and then use Auto Fill so that Excel knows to increment by 5. Figure 1.8 shows the results of filling in months, abbreviated months, quarters, weekdays, abbreviated weekdays, and increments of 5.

| | A | B | C | D | E | F | G | H | I |
|---|---|---|---|---|---|---|---|---|---|
| 1 | January | Jan | Qtr 1 | Monday | Mon | 5 | | | |
| 2 | February | Feb | Qtr 2 | Tuesday | Tue | 10 | | | |
| 3 | March | Mar | Qtr 3 | Wednesday | Wed | 15 | | | |
| 4 | April | Apr | Qtr 4 | Thursday | Thu | 20 | | | |
| 5 | May | May | | Friday | Fri | 25 | | | |
| 6 | June | Jun | | Saturday | Sat | 30 | | | |
| 7 | July | Jul | | Sunday | Sun | 35 | | | |
| 8 | August | Aug | | | | | | | |
| 9 | September | Sep | | | | ○ Copy Cells | | | |
| 10 | October | Oct | | | | ◉ Fill Series | | | |
| 11 | November | Nov | | | | ○ Fill Formatting Only | | | |
| 12 | December | Dec | | | | ○ Fill Without Formatting | | | |
| 13 | | | | | | ○ Flash Fill | | | |
| 14 | | | | | | | | | |
| 15 | | | | | | | | | |

Incremented values filled in

Click to see Auto Fill Options

**FIGURE 1.8** Auto Fill Examples

Immediately after you use Auto Fill, Excel displays the Auto Fill Options button in the bottom-right corner of the filled data (see Figure 1.8). Click Auto Fill Options to display five fill options: Copy Cells, Fill Series, Fill Formatting Only, Fill Without Formatting, or Flash Fill.

> **TIP  Double-Clicking the Fill Handle**
>
> You can double-click the fill handle to quickly copy a formula down a column. Excel will copy the formula in the active cell for each row of data to calculate in your worksheet.

# Displaying Cell Formulas

Excel shows the result of the formula in the cell (see the top half of Figure 1.9); however, you might want to display the formulas instead of the calculated results in the cells (see the bottom half of Figure 1.9). To display cell formulas, do one of the following:

**STEP 5 >>**

- Press Ctrl and the grave accent ( ` ) key, sometimes referred to as the tilde key, in the top-left corner of the keyboard, below the Esc key.
- Click Show Formulas in the Formula Auditing group on the FORMULAS tab.

To hide the formulas and display the formula results again, repeat the preceding process.

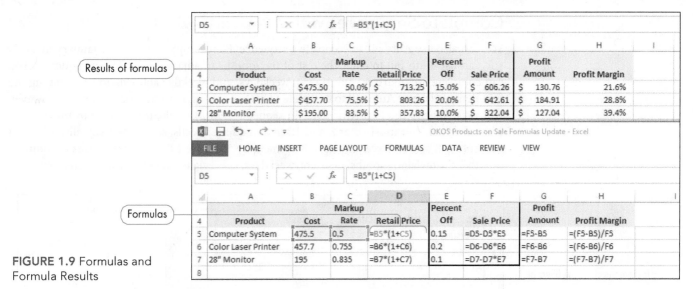

**Results of formulas**

| | A | B | C | D | E | F | G | H | I |
|---|---|---|---|---|---|---|---|---|---|
| | | | Markup | | Percent | | Profit | | |
| 4 | Product | Cost | Rate | Retail Price | Off | Sale Price | Amount | Profit Margin | |
| 5 | Computer System | $475.50 | 50.0% | $ 713.25 | 15.0% | $ 606.26 | $ 130.76 | 21.6% | |
| 6 | Color Laser Printer | $457.70 | 75.5% | $ 803.26 | 20.0% | $ 642.61 | $ 184.91 | 28.8% | |
| 7 | 28" Monitor | $195.00 | 83.5% | $ 357.83 | 10.0% | $ 322.04 | $ 127.04 | 39.4% | |

D5 · fx =B5*(1+C5)

OKOS Products on Sale Formulas Update - Excel

FILE    HOME    INSERT    PAGE LAYOUT    FORMULAS    DATA    REVIEW    VIEW

D5 · fx =B5*(1+C5)

**Formulas**

| | A | B | C | D | E | F | G | H | I |
|---|---|---|---|---|---|---|---|---|---|
| | | | Markup | | Percent | | Profit | | |
| 4 | Product | Cost | Rate | Retail Price | Off | Sale Price | Amount | Profit Margin | |
| 5 | Computer System | 475.5 | 0.5 | =B5*(1+C5) | 0.15 | =D5-D5*E5 | =F5-B5 | =(F5-B5)/F5 | |
| 6 | Color Laser Printer | 457.7 | 0.755 | =B6*(1+C6) | 0.2 | =D6-D6*E6 | =F6-B6 | =(F6-B6)/F6 | |
| 7 | 28" Monitor | 195 | 0.835 | =B7*(1+C7) | 0.1 | =D7-D7*E7 | =F7-B7 | =(F7-B7)/F7 | |
| 8 | | | | | | | | | |

**FIGURE 1.9** Formulas and Formula Results

*Quick Concepts* ✓

1. What is the order of precedence? Provide and explain two examples that use four different operators, one with parentheses and one without. **p. 13**

2. What is the purpose of Auto Fill? Provide an example of data you can complete using Auto Fill. **p. 14**

3. Why would it be useful to display formulas instead of formula results in a worksheet? **p. 15**

# Hands-On Exercises

## 2 Mathematics and Formulas

In Hands-On Exercise 1, you created the basic worksheet for OKOS by entering text, values, and a date for items on sale. Now you need to insert formulas to calculate the missing results—specifically, the retail (before sale) value, sale price, and profit margin. You will use cell addresses in your formulas, so when you change a referenced value, the formula results will update automatically.

**Skills covered:** Use Cell References in a Formula and Apply the Order of Precedence • Use the Semi-Selection Method to Enter a Formula • Use Cell References in a Formula and Apply the Order of Precedence • Copy Formulas with Auto Fill • Change Values and Display Cell Formulas

### STEP 1 >> USE CELL REFERENCES IN A FORMULA AND APPLY THE ORDER OF PRECEDENCE

The first formula you need to create will calculate the retail price. The retail price is the price you originally charge. It is based on a percentage of the original cost so that you earn a profit. Refer to Figure 1.10 as you complete Step 1.

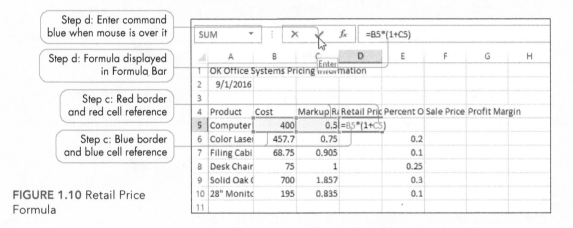

Step d: Enter command blue when mouse is over it

Step d: Formula displayed in Formula Bar

Step c: Red border and red cell reference

Step c: Blue border and blue cell reference

**FIGURE 1.10** Retail Price Formula

a. Open *e01h1Markup_LastFirst* if you closed it at the end of Hands-On Exercise 1 and save it as **e01h2Markup_LastFirst**, changing *h1* to *h2*.

> **TROUBLESHOOTING:** If you make any major mistakes in this exercise, you can close the file, open *e01h1Markup_LastFirst* again, and then start this exercise over.

b. Click **cell D5**, the cell where you will enter the formula to calculate the retail selling price of the first item.

c. Type **=B5*(1+C5)** and view the formula and the colored cells and borders on the screen.

   As you type or edit a formula, each cell address in the formula displays in a specific color, and while you type or edit the formula, the cells referenced in the formula have a temporarily colored border. For example, in the formula =B5*(1+C5), B5 appears in blue, and C5 appears in red. Cell B5 has a temporarily blue border and cell C5 has a temporarily red border to help you identify cells as you construct your formulas (see Figure 1.10).

An alternative formula also calculates the correct retail price: =B5*C5+B5 or =B5+B5*C5. In this formula, 400 (cell B5) is multiplied by 0.5 (cell C5); that result (200) represents the dollar value of the markup. Excel adds the value 200 to the original cost of 400 to obtain 600, the retail price. You were instructed to enter =B5*(1+C5) to demonstrate the order of precedence.

**d.** Click **Enter** (the check mark ☑ between the Name Box and the Formula Bar) and view the formula in the Formula Bar to check it for accuracy.

The result of the formula, 600, appears in cell D5, and the formula displays in the Formula Bar. This formula first adds 1 (the decimal equivalent of 100%) to 0.5 (the value stored in cell C5). Excel multiplies that sum of 1.5 by 400 (the value stored in cell B5). The theory behind this formula is that the retail price is 150% of the original cost.

> **TROUBLESHOOTING:** If the result is not correct, click the cell and look at the formula in the Formula Bar. Click in the Formula Bar, edit the formula to match the formula shown in Step c, and then click Enter (the check mark between the Name Box and the Formula Bar). Make sure you start the formula with an equal sign.

**e.** Save the workbook with the new formula.

## STEP 2 ≫ USE THE SEMI-SELECTION METHOD TO ENTER A FORMULA

Now that you have calculated the retail price, you need to calculate a sale price. This week, the computer is on sale for 15% off the retail price. Refer to Figure 1.11 as you complete Step 2.

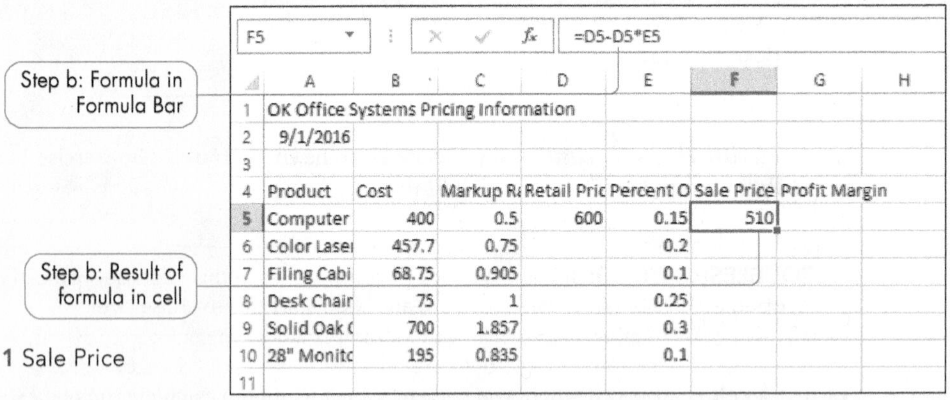

| F5 | | | ✕ | ✓ | $f_x$ | =D5-D5*E5 | | |
|---|---|---|---|---|---|---|---|---|
| | A | B | C | D | E | F | G | H |
| 1 | OK Office Systems Pricing Information | | | | | | | |
| 2 | 9/1/2016 | | | | | | | |
| 3 | | | | | | | | |
| 4 | Product | Cost | Markup R: | Retail Pric | Percent O | Sale Price | Profit Margin | |
| 5 | Computer | 400 | 0.5 | 600 | 0.15 | 510 | | |
| 6 | Color Lase | 457.7 | 0.75 | | 0.2 | | | |
| 7 | Filing Cabi | 68.75 | 0.905 | | 0.1 | | | |
| 8 | Desk Chair | 75 | 1 | | 0.25 | | | |
| 9 | Solid Oak ( | 700 | 1.857 | | 0.3 | | | |
| 10 | 28" Monitc | 195 | 0.835 | | 0.1 | | | |
| 11 | | | | | | | | |

Step b: Formula in Formula Bar

Step b: Result of formula in cell

**FIGURE 1.11** Sale Price Formula

**a.** Click **cell F5**, the cell where you will enter the formula to calculate the sale price.

**b.** Type **=**, click **cell D5**, type **-**, click **cell D5**, type **\***, and then click **cell E5**. Notice the color-coding in the cell addresses. Press **Ctrl+Enter** to keep the current cell the active cell.

You used the semi-selection method to enter a formula. The result is 510. Looking at the formula, you might think D5–D5 equals zero; remember that because of the order of precedence rules, multiplication is calculated before subtraction. The product of 600 (cell D5) and 0.15 (cell E5) equals 90, which is then subtracted from 600 (cell D5), so the sale price is 510. If it helps to understand the formula better, add parentheses: =D5-(D5*E5).

**c.** Save the workbook with the new formula.

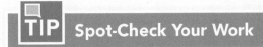

## TIP | Spot-Check Your Work

You should check the result for logic. Use a calculator to spot-check the accuracy of formulas. If you mark down merchandise by 15% of its regular price, you are charging 85% of the regular price. You can spot-check your formula to ensure that 85% of 600 is 510 by multiplying 600 by 0.85.

## STEP 3 ≫ USE CELL REFERENCES IN A FORMULA AND APPLY THE ORDER OF PRECEDENCE

After calculating the sale price, you want to know the profit margin OKOS will earn. OKOS paid $400 for the computer and will sell it for $510. The profit of $110 is then divided by the $400 cost, which gives OKOS a profit margin of 21.57%. Refer to Figure 1.12 as you complete Step 3.

Step b: Formula in Formula Bar

Step b: Result of formula in cell

| G5 | | | fx | =(F5-B5)/F5 | | | |
|---|---|---|---|---|---|---|---|
| | A | B | C | D | E | F | G | H |
| 1 | OK Office Systems Pricing Information | | | | | | | |
| 2 | 9/1/2016 | | | | | | | |
| 3 | | | | | | | | |
| 4 | Product | Cost | Markup Ra | Retail Pric | Percent O | Sale Price | Profit Margin | |
| 5 | Computer | 400 | 0.5 | 600 | 0.15 | 510 | 0.215686 | |
| 6 | Color Lase | 457.7 | 0.75 | | 0.2 | | | |
| 7 | Filing Cabi | 68.75 | 0.905 | | 0.1 | | | |
| 8 | Desk Chair | 75 | 1 | | 0.25 | | | |
| 9 | Solid Oak ( | 700 | 1.857 | | 0.3 | | | |
| 10 | 28" Monito | 195 | 0.835 | | 0.1 | | | |
| 11 | | | | | | | | |

**FIGURE 1.12** Profit Margin Formula

a. Click **cell G5**, the cell where you will enter the formula to calculate the profit margin.

The profit margin is the profit (difference in sales price and cost) percentage of the sale price.

b. Type **=(F5-B5)/F5** and notice the color-coding in the cell addresses. Press **Ctrl+Enter**.

The formula must first calculate the profit, which is the difference between the sale price (510) and the original cost (400). The difference (110) is then divided by the sale price (510) to determine the profit margin of 0.215686, or 21.6%.

> **TROUBLESHOOTING:** If you type a backslash (\) instead of a forward slash (/), Excel will display an error message box. Make sure you type / as the division operator.

c. Look at the Formula Bar and save the workbook with the new formula.

## STEP 4 ≫ COPY FORMULAS WITH AUTO FILL

After double-checking the accuracy of your calculations for the first product, you are ready to copy the formulas down the columns to calculate the retail price, sale price, and profit margin for the other products. Refer to Figure 1.13 as you complete Step 4.

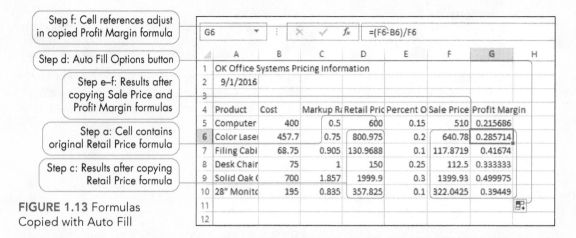

Step f: Cell references adjust in copied Profit Margin formula

Step d: Auto Fill Options button

Step e–f: Results after copying Sale Price and Profit Margin formulas

Step a: Cell contains original Retail Price formula

Step c: Results after copying Retail Price formula

**FIGURE 1.13** Formulas Copied with Auto Fill

a. Click **cell D5**, the cell containing the formula to calculate the retail price for the first item.

b. Position the mouse pointer on the **cell D5 fill handle**. When the pointer changes from a white plus sign to a thin black plus sign, double-click the **fill handle**.

Excel's Auto Fill feature copies the retail price formula for the remaining products in your worksheet. Excel detects when to stop copying the formula when it encounters a blank row, such as in row 11.

c. Click **cell D6**, the cell containing the first copied retail price formula, and look at the Formula Bar.

The formula in cell D5 is =B5*(1+C5). The copied formula in cell D6 is =B6*(1+C6). Excel adjusts the cell addresses in the formula as it copies the formula down a column so that the results are based on each row's data rather than using the original formula's cell addresses for other products.

> **TROUBLESHOOTING:** The result in cell D7 may show more decimal places than shown in Figure 1.13. This may be due to different screen resolutions. Do not worry about this slight difference.

d. Select the **range F5:G5**. Double-click the **fill handle** in the bottom-right corner of **cell G5**.

Auto Fill copies the selected formulas down their respective columns. Auto Fill Options are available down and to the right of the cell G10 fill handle, indicating you could select different fill options if you want.

> **TROUBLESHOOTING:** If Excel displays pound symbols, such as ####, instead of results, that means the column is not wide enough to show results. You will learn how to adjust column widths in the third section.

e. Click **cell F6**, the cell containing the first copied sale price formula, and view the Formula Bar.

The original formula was =D5-D5*E5. The copied formula in cell F6 is adjusted to =D6-D6*E6 so that it calculates the sales price based on the data in row 6.

f. Click **cell G6**, the cell containing the first copied profit margin formula, and look at the Formula Bar. Save the workbook.

The original formula was =(F5-B5)/F5, and the copied formula in cell G6 is =(F6-B6)/F6.

# STEP 5 >> CHANGE VALUES AND DISPLAY CELL FORMULAS

You want to see how the prices and profit margins are affected when you change some of the original cost values. For example, the supplier might notify you that the cost to you will increase. In addition, you want to see the formulas displayed in the cells temporarily. Refer to Figures 1.14 and 1.15 as you complete Step 5.

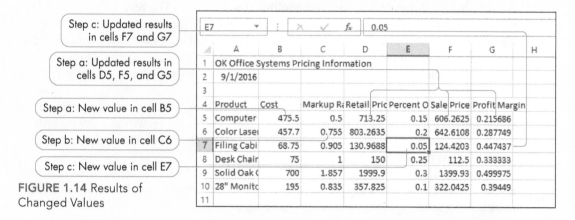

Step c: Updated results in cells F7 and G7

Step a: Updated results in cells D5, F5, and G5

Step a: New value in cell B5

Step b: New value in cell C6

Step c: New value in cell E7

**FIGURE 1.14** Results of Changed Values

a. Click **cell B5**, type **475.5**, and then press **Enter**.

The results of the retail price, sale price, and profit margin formulas change based on the new cost.

b. Click **cell C6**, type **0.755**, and then press **Enter**.

The results of the retail price, sale price, and profit margin formulas change based on the new markup rate.

c. Click **cell E7**, type **0.05**, and then press **Ctrl+Enter**.

The results of the sale price and profit margin formulas change based on the new markdown rate. Note that the retail price did not change, since that formula is not based on the markdown rate.

d. Press **Ctrl+`** (the grave accent mark).

The workbook now displays the formulas rather than the formula results (see Figure 1.15). This is helpful when you want to review several formulas at one time.

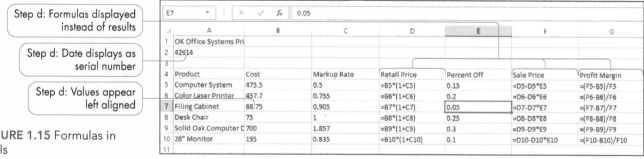

Step d: Formulas displayed instead of results

Step d: Date displays as serial number

Step d: Values appear left aligned

**FIGURE 1.15** Formulas in Cells

e. Press **Ctrl+`** (the grave accent mark).

The workbook now displays the formula results in the cells again.

f. Save the workbook. Keep the workbook open if you plan to continue with the next Hands-On Exercise. If not, close the workbook and exit Excel.

# Workbook and Worksheet Management

When you start a new blank workbook in Excel, the workbook contains one worksheet named Sheet1. However, you can add additional worksheets. The text, values, dates, and formulas you enter into the individual sheets are saved under one workbook file name. Having multiple worksheets in one workbook is helpful to keep related items together. For example, you might want one worksheet for each month to track your monthly income and expenses for one year. When tax time comes around, you have all your data stored in one workbook file.

Although you should plan the worksheet and workbook before you start entering data, you might need to add, delete, or rename worksheets. Furthermore, within a worksheet you may want to insert a new row to accommodate new data, delete a column that you no longer need, or adjust the size of columns and rows.

In this section, you will learn how to manage workbooks by renaming, inserting, and deleting worksheets. You will also learn how to make changes to worksheet columns and rows, such as inserting, deleting, and adjusting sizes.

## Managing Worksheets

Creating a multiple-worksheet workbook takes some planning and maintenance. Worksheet tab names should reflect the contents of the respective worksheets. In addition, you can insert, copy, move, and delete worksheets within the workbook. You can even apply background color to the worksheet tabs so that they stand out onscreen. Figure 1.16 shows a workbook in which the sheet tabs have been renamed, colors have been applied to worksheet tabs, and a worksheet tab has been right-clicked so that the shortcut menu appears.

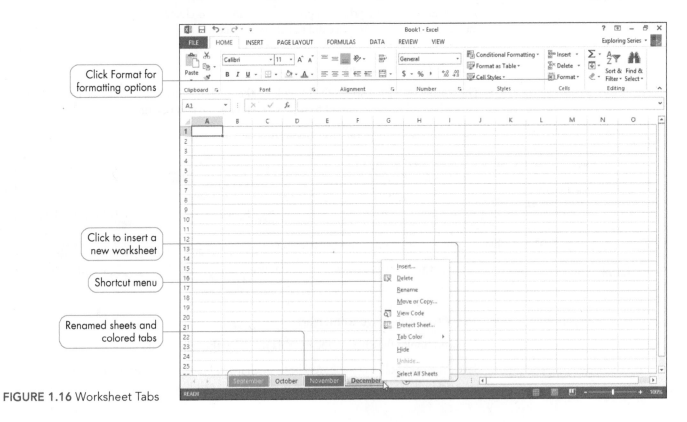

**FIGURE 1.16** Worksheet Tabs

## Rename a Worksheet

STEP 1 » The default worksheet name Sheet1 does not describe the contents of the worksheet. You should rename worksheet tabs to reflect the sheet contents. For example, if your budget workbook contains monthly worksheets, name the worksheets September, October, etc. Although you can have spaces in worksheet names, keep worksheet names relatively short. The longer the worksheet names, the fewer sheet tabs you will see at the bottom of the workbook window without scrolling.

To rename a worksheet, do one of the following:

- Double-click a sheet tab, type the new name, and then press Enter.

- Click the sheet tab for the sheet you want to rename, click Format in the Cells group on the HOME tab (refer to Figure 1.16), select Rename Sheet (see Figure 1.17), type the new sheet name, and then press Enter.

- Right-click the sheet tab, select Rename from the shortcut menu (see Figure 1.16), type the new sheet name, and then press Enter.

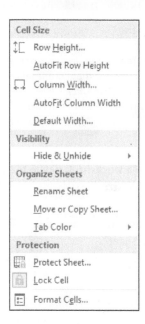

FIGURE 1.17 Format Menu

## Change Worksheet Tab Color

STEP 1 » The active worksheet tab is white with a green bottom border. When you use multiple worksheets, you might want to apply a different color to each worksheet tab to make the tab stand out or to emphasize the difference between sheets. For example, you might apply red to the September tab, green to the October tab, dark blue to the November tab, and purple to the December tab.

To change the color of a worksheet tab, do one of the following:

- Click the sheet tab for the sheet you want to rename, click Format in the Cells group on the HOME tab (refer to Figure 1.16), point to Tab Color (refer to Figure 1.17), and then click a color on the Tab Color palette.

- Right-click the sheet tab, point to Tab Color on the shortcut menu (refer to Figure 1.16), and then click a color on the Tab Color palette.

## Insert and Delete a Worksheet

Sometimes you need more than one worksheet in the workbook. For example, you might create a workbook that contains 12 worksheets—a worksheet for each month of the year. To insert a new worksheet, do one of the following:

- Click *New sheet* to the right of the last worksheet tab.
- Click the Insert arrow—either to the right or below Insert—in the Cells group on the HOME tab and select Insert Sheet.
- Right-click any sheet tab, select Insert from the shortcut menu (refer to Figure 1.16), click Worksheet in the Insert dialog box, and then click OK.
- Press Shift+F11.

---

**TIP  Ribbon Commands with Arrows**

Some commands, such as Insert in the Cells group, contain two parts: the main command and an arrow. The arrow may be below or to the right of the command, depending on the command, window size, or screen resolution. Instructions in the Exploring Series use the command name to instruct you to click the main command to perform the default action, such as *Click Insert in the Cells group* or *Click Delete in the Cells group*. Instructions include the word arrow when you need to select an additional option, such as *Click the Insert arrow in the Cells group* or *Click the Delete arrow in the Cells group*.

---

If you no longer need the data in a worksheet, delete the worksheet. Doing so will eliminate extra data in a file and reduce file size. To delete a worksheet in a workbook, do one of the following:

- Click the Delete arrow—either to the right or below Delete—in the Cells group on the HOME tab and select Delete Sheet.
- Right-click any sheet tab and select Delete from the shortcut menu (refer to Figure 1.16).

If the sheet you are trying to delete contains data, Excel will display a warning: *You can't undo deleting sheets, and you might be removing some data. If you don't need it, click Delete.* If you try to delete a blank worksheet, Excel will not display a warning; it will immediately delete the sheet.

## Move or Copy a Worksheet

After inserting and deleting worksheets, you can arrange the worksheet tabs in a different sequence, especially if the newly inserted worksheets do not fall within a logical sequence. To move a worksheet, do one of the following:

- Drag a worksheet tab to the desired location. As you drag a sheet tab, the pointer resembles a piece of paper. A down-pointing triangle appears between sheet tabs to indicate where the sheet will be placed when you release the mouse button.
- Click Format in the Cells group on the HOME tab (refer to Figure 1.16) and select *Move or Copy Sheet*, or right-click the sheet tab you want to move and select *Move or Copy* to display the *Move or Copy dialog box* (see Figure 1.18). You can move the worksheet within the current workbook, or you can move the worksheet to a different workbook. In the *Before sheet* list, select the worksheet you want to come after the moved worksheet and click OK. For example, you have just created a new worksheet named August and you want it to come before the September worksheet. You would select September in the *Before sheet* list.

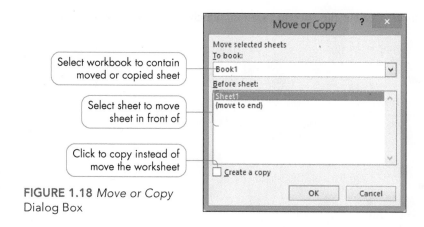

Select workbook to contain moved or copied sheet

Select sheet to move sheet in front of

Click to copy instead of move the worksheet

**FIGURE 1.18** *Move or Copy* Dialog Box

After creating a worksheet, you may want to copy it to use as a template or starting point for similar data. For example, if you create a worksheet for your September budget, you can copy the worksheet and then easily edit the data on the copied worksheet to enter data for your October budget. Copying the entire worksheet would save you a lot of valuable time in entering and formatting the new worksheet. The process for copying a worksheet is similar to moving a sheet. To copy a worksheet, press and hold Ctrl as you drag the worksheet tab. Alternatively, display the *Move or Copy* dialog box, select the *To book* and *Before sheet* options (refer to Figure 1.18), click the *Create a copy* check box, and then click OK.

# Managing Columns and Rows

As you enter and edit worksheet data, you can adjust the row and column structure. You can add rows and columns to add new data, or you can delete data you no longer need. Adjusting the height and width of rows and columns, respectively, can present the data better.

## Insert Cells, Columns, and Rows

**STEP 3 >>** After you construct a worksheet, you might need to insert cells, columns, or rows to accommodate new data. For example, you might need to insert a new column to perform calculations or a new row to list a new product. When you insert cells, rows, and columns, cell addresses in formulas adjust automatically.

To insert a new column or row, do one of the following:

- Click in the column or row for which you want to insert a new column to the left or a new row above, respectively. Click the Insert arrow in the Cells group on the HOME tab and select Insert Sheet Columns or Insert Sheet Rows.

- Right-click the column (letter) or row (number) heading for which you want to insert a new column to the left or a new row above, respectively, and select Insert from the shortcut menu.

Excel inserts new columns to the left of the current column and new rows above the active row. If the current column is column C and you insert a new column, the new column becomes column C, and the original column C data are now in column D. Likewise, if the current row is 5 and you insert a new row, the new row is row 5, and the original row 5 data are now in row 6.

Inserting a cell is helpful when you realize that you left out an entry in one column after you have entered columns of data. Instead of inserting a new row for all columns, you just want to move the existing content down in one column to enter the missing value. You can insert a single cell in a particular row or column. To insert a cell, click in the cell where you want the new cell, click the Insert arrow in the Cells group on the Home tab, and then select Insert Cells. Select an option from the Insert dialog box (see Figure 1.19) to position the new cell and click OK. Alternatively, click Insert in the Cells group. The default action of clicking Insert is to insert a cell at the current location, which moves existing data down in that column only.

FIGURE 1.19 Insert Dialog Box

## Delete Cells, Columns, and Rows

**STEP 4》** If you no longer need a cell, column, or row, you can delete it. In these situations, you are deleting the entire cell, column, or row, not just the contents of the cell to leave empty cells. As with inserting new cells, any affected formulas adjust the cell references automatically. To delete a column or row, do one of the following:

- Click the column or row heading for the column or row you want to delete. Click Delete in the Cells group on the HOME tab.
- Click in any cell within the column or row you want to delete. Click the Delete arrow in the Cells group on the HOME tab and select Delete Sheet Columns or Delete Sheet Rows, respectively.
- Right-click the column letter or row number for the column or row you want to delete and select Delete from the shortcut menu.

To delete a cell or cells, select the cell(s), click the Delete arrow in the Cells group, and then select Delete Cells to display the Delete dialog box (see Figure 1.20). Click the appropriate option to shift cells left or up and click OK. Alternatively, click Delete in the Cells group. The default action of clicking Delete is to delete the active cell, which moves existing data up in that column only.

FIGURE 1.20 Delete Dialog Box

## Adjust Column Width

**STEP 5》** After you enter data in a column, you often need to adjust the *column width*—the number of characters that can fit horizontally using the default font or the number of horizontal pixels—to show the contents of cells. For example, in the worksheet you created in Hands-On Exercises 1 and 2, the labels in column A displayed into column B when those adjacent cells were empty. However, after you typed values in column B, the labels in column A appeared cut off. You will need to widen column A to show the full name of all of your products.

**TIP** **Pound Signs Displayed**

Numbers appear as a series of pound signs (######) when the cell is too narrow to display the complete value, and text appears to be truncated.

To widen a column to accommodate the longest label or value in a column, do one of the following:

- Position the pointer on the vertical border between the current column heading and the next column heading. When the pointer displays as a two-headed arrow, double-click the border. For example, if column B is too narrow to display the content in that column, double-click the border between the column B and C headings.
- Click Format in the Cells group on the HOME tab (refer to Figure 1.16) and select AutoFit Column Width (refer to Figure 1.17).

To widen a column to an exact width, do one of the following:

- Drag the vertical border to the left to decrease the column width or to the right to increase the column width. As you drag the vertical border, Excel displays a ScreenTip specifying the width (see Figure 1.21) from 0 to 255 characters and in pixels.
- Click Format in the Cells group on the HOME tab (refer to Figure 1.16), select Column Width (refer to Figure 1.17), type a value in the Column width box in the Column Width dialog box, and then click OK.

ScreenTip displaying column width

Mouse pointer as you drag the border between column headings

Current column width

Column width when you release the mouse button

| | A | B | C | D | E | F | G | H |
|---|---|---|---|---|---|---|---|---|
| | | Width: 10.57 (79 pixels) | | | | | | |
| 1 | OK Office Systems Pricing Information | | | | | | | |
| 2 | 9/1/2016 | | | | | | | |
| 3 | | | | | | | | |
| 4 | Product | Cost | Markup R | Retail Pric | Percent O | Sale Price | Profit Margin | |
| 5 | Computer | 475.5 | 0.5 | 713.25 | 0.15 | 606.263 | 0.275 | |
| 6 | Color Lase | 457.7 | 0.755 | 803.264 | 0.2 | 642.611 | 0.404 | |
| 7 | Filing Cabi | 68.75 | 0.905 | 130.969 | 0.05 | 124.42 | 0.80975 | |
| 8 | Desk Chai | 75 | 1 | 150 | 0.25 | 112.5 | 0.5 | |
| 9 | Solid Oak | 700 | 1.857 | 1999.9 | 0.3 | 1399.93 | 0.9999 | |
| 10 | 28" Monit | 195 | 0.835 | 357.825 | 0.1 | 322.043 | 0.6515 | |

**FIGURE 1.21** Changing Column Width

## Adjust Row Height

When you increase the font size of cell contents, Excel automatically increases the *row height*—the vertical measurement of the row. However, if you insert a line break or wrap text to create multiple lines of text in a cell, Excel might not increase the row height. You can adjust the row height in a way similar to how you change column width by double-clicking the border between row numbers or by selecting Row Height or AutoFit Row Height from the Format menu (refer to Figure 1.17). In Excel, row height is a value between 0 and 409 based on point size (abbreviated as pt) and pixels. Whether you are measuring font sizes or row heights, one point size is equal to 1/72 of an inch. Your row height should be taller than your font size. For example, with an 11-pt font size, the default row height is 15.

**TIP   Multiple Column Widths and Row Heights**

You can set the size for more than one column or row at a time to make the selected columns or rows the same size. Drag across the column or row headings for the area you want to format, and then set the size using any method.

## Hide and Unhide Columns and Rows

**STEP 6** If your worksheet contains confidential information, you might need to hide some columns and/or rows before you print a copy for public distribution. However, the column or row is not deleted. If you hide column B, you will see columns A and C side by side. If you hide row 3, you will see rows 2 and 4 together. Figure 1.22 shows that column B and row 3 are hidden. Excel displays a double line between column headings (such as between A and C), indicating one or more columns are hidden, and a double line between row headings (such as between 2 and 4), indicating one or more rows are hidden.

Double vertical line indicates hidden column

Double horizontal line indicates hidden row

**FIGURE 1.22** Hidden Column and Row

To hide a column or row, do one of the following:

- Click in the column or row you want to hide, click Format in the Cells group on the HOME tab (refer to Figure 1.16), point to Hide & Unhide (refer to Figure 1.17), and then select Hide Columns or Hide Rows, depending on what you want to hide.
- Right-click the column or row heading(s) you want to hide and select Hide.

You can hide multiple columns and rows at the same time. To select adjacent columns (such as columns B through E) or adjacent rows (such as rows 2 through 4), drag across the adjacent column or row headings. To hide nonadjacent columns or rows, press and hold Ctrl while you click the desired column or row headings. After selecting multiple columns or rows, use any acceptable method to hide the selected columns or rows.

To unhide a column or row, select the columns or rows on both sides of the hidden column or row. For example, if column B is hidden, drag across column letters A and C. Then do one of the following:

- Click Format in the Cells group on the HOME tab (refer to Figure 1.16), point to Hide & Unhide (refer to Figure 1.17), and then select Unhide Columns or Unhide Rows, depending on what you want to display again.
- Right-click the column(s) or row(s) you want to hide and select Unhide.

### TIP Unhiding Column A, Row 1, and All Hidden Rows/Columns

Unhiding column A or row 1 is different because you cannot select the row or column on either side. To unhide column A or row 1, type A1 in the Name Box and press Enter. Click Format in the Cells group on the Home tab, point to Hide & Unhide, and then select Unhide Columns or Unhide Rows to display column A or row 1, respectively. If you want to unhide all columns and rows, click Select All and use the Hide & Unhide submenu.

*Quick* Concepts

1. What is the benefit of renaming a worksheet? *p. 23*

2. What are two ways to insert a new row in a worksheet? *p. 25*

3. How can you delete cell B5 without deleting the entire row or column? *p. 26*

4. When should you adjust column widths instead of using the default width? *p. 26*

# Hands-On Exercises

## 3 Workbook and Worksheet Management

After reviewing the OKOS worksheet, you decide to rename the worksheet, change the worksheet tab color, insert a worksheet, and delete an empty worksheet. In addition, you need to insert a column to calculate the amount of markup and delete a row containing data you no longer need. You also need to adjust column widths to display the labels in the columns.

**Skills covered:** Rename a Worksheet and Select a Tab Color • Insert, Move, and Delete a Worksheet • Insert a Column and Rows • Delete a Row • Adjust Column Width and Row Height • Hide and Unhide Columns

---

### STEP 1 ›› RENAME A WORKSHEET AND SELECT A TAB COLOR

You want to rename Sheet1 to describe the worksheet contents and add a color to the sheet tab. Refer to Figure 1.23 as you complete Step 1.

**FIGURE 1.23** Renamed
Worksheet with Tab Color

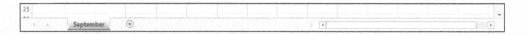

**a.** Open *e01h2Markup_LastFirst* if you closed it at the end of Hands-On Exercise 2 and save it as **e01h3Markup_LastFirst**, changing *h2* to *h3*.

**b.** Double-click the **Sheet1 sheet tab**, type **September**, and then press **Enter**.

You renamed Sheet1 September.

**c.** Right-click the **September sheet tab**, point to *Tab Color*, and then click **Red** in the *Standard Colors* section.

The worksheet tab color is red.

**d.** Save the workbook.

---

### STEP 2 ›› INSERT, MOVE, AND DELETE A WORKSHEET

Your supervisor asks you to add another worksheet to the workbook. She wants you to place it before the September worksheet so that she can add August data. After you do this, she calls you on the phone and tells you that she won't be adding the August data after all. Therefore, you will delete that worksheet. Refer to Figure 1.24 as you complete Step 2.

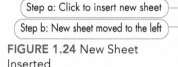

**FIGURE 1.24** New Sheet
Inserted

**a.** Click **New sheet**, the plus icon to the right of the September sheet tab.

Excel adds a new worksheet named either Sheet1 or Sheet2 to the right of the previously active sheet.

**b.** Drag the **Sheet tab** to the left of the September sheet tab.

**c.** Click the **Sheet tab**, click the **Delete arrow** in the Cells group on the HOME tab, and then select **Delete Sheet**.

You deleted the blank worksheet from the workbook.

> **TROUBLESHOOTING:** Delete in the Cells group, like some other commands in Excel, contains two parts: the main command icon and an arrow. Click the main command icon when instructed to click Delete to perform the default action. Click the arrow when instructed to click the Delete arrow for additional command options.

> **TROUBLESHOOTING:** Notice that Undo is unavailable on the Quick Access Toolbar. You cannot undo deleting a worksheet. It is deleted!

    **d.** Save the workbook.

## STEP 3 ≫ INSERT A COLUMN AND ROWS

You decide that you need a column to display the amount of profit. Because profit is a dollar amount, you want to keep the profit column close to another column of dollar amounts. Therefore, you will insert the profit column before the profit margin (percentage) column. You also want to insert new rows for product information and category names. Refer to Figure 1.25 as you complete Step 3.

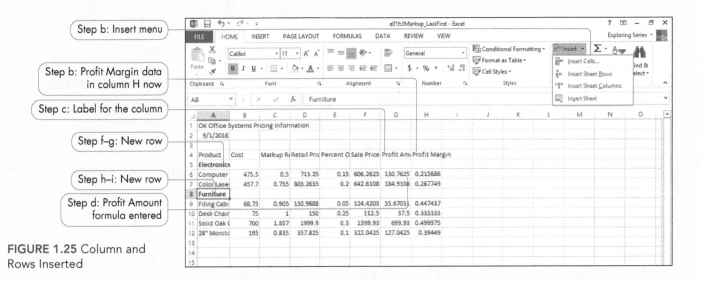

**FIGURE 1.25** Column and Rows Inserted

    **a.** Click **cell G5** (or any cell in column G), the column containing the Profit Margin.

        You want to insert a column between the Sale Price and Profit Margin columns so that you can calculate the profit amount in dollars.

    **b.** Click the **Insert arrow** in the Cells group and select **Insert Sheet Columns**.

        You inserted a new, blank column G. The data in the original column G are now in column H.

    **c.** Click **cell G4**, type **Profit Amount**, and then press **Enter**.

    **d.** Make sure the active cell is **cell G5**. Type **=F5-B5** and click **Enter** (the check mark between the Name Box and the Formula Bar). Double-click the **cell G5 fill handle** to copy the formula down the column.

        You calculated the profit amount by subtracting the original cost from the sale price. Although steps e and f below illustrate one way to insert a row, you can use other methods presented in this chapter.

    **e.** Right-click the **row 5 heading**, the row containing the Computer System data.

        Excel displays a shortcut menu consisting of commands you can perform.

**f.** Select **Insert** from the shortcut menu.

You inserted a new blank row 5, which is selected. The original rows of data move down a row each.

**g.** Click **cell A5**. Type **Electronics** and press **Ctrl+Enter**. Click **Bold** in the Font group on the HOME tab.

You typed and bolded the category name *Electronics* above the list of electronic products.

**h.** Right-click the **row 8 heading**, the row containing the Filing Cabinet data, and select **Insert** from the shortcut menu.

**i.** Click **cell A8**. Type **Furniture** and press **Ctrl+Enter**. Click **Bold** in the Font group on the HOME tab.

You typed and bolded the category name *Furniture* above the list of furniture products.

**j.** Save the workbook.

## STEP 4 ⟫ DELETE A ROW

You just realized that you do not have enough filing cabinets in stock to offer on sale, so you need to delete the Filing Cabinet row. Refer to Figure 1.26 as you complete Step 4.

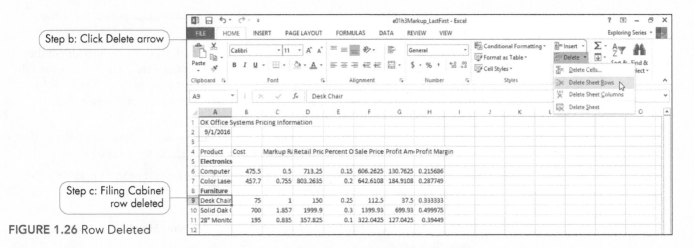

**FIGURE 1.26** Row Deleted

**a.** Click **cell A9** (or any cell on row 9), the row that contains the Filing Cabinet data.

**b.** Click the **Delete arrow** in the Cells group.

**c.** Select **Delete Sheet Rows** and save the workbook.

The Filing Cabinet row is deleted and the remaining rows move up one row.

---

**TROUBLESHOOTING:** If you accidentally delete the wrong row or accidentally select Delete Sheet Columns instead of Delete Sheet Rows, click Undo on the Quick Access Toolbar to restore the deleted row or column.

---

# STEP 5 ≫ ADJUST COLUMN WIDTH AND ROW HEIGHT

As you review your worksheet, you notice that the labels in column A appear cut off. You need to increase the width of that column to display the entire product names. In addition, you want to make row 1 taller. Refer to Figure 1.27 as you complete Step 5.

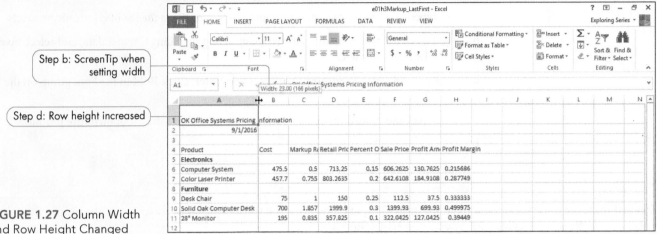

**FIGURE 1.27** Column Width and Row Height Changed

a. Position the pointer between the column A and B headings. When the pointer looks like a double-headed arrow, double-click the border.

   When you double-click the border between two columns, Excel adjusts the width of the column on the left side of the border to fit the contents of that column. Excel increased the width of column A based on the cell containing the longest content (the title in cell A1, which will eventually span over all columns). Therefore, you want to decrease the column to avoid so much empty space in column A.

b. Position the pointer between the column A and B headings again. Drag the border to the left until the ScreenTip displays **Width: 23.00 (166 pixels)**. Release the mouse button.

   You decreased the column width to 23 for column A. The longest product name is visible. You will not adjust the other column widths until after you apply formats to the column headings in Hands-On Exercise 5.

c. Click **cell A1**. Click **Format** in the Cells group and select **Row Height** to display the Row Height dialog box.

d. Type **30** in the **Row height box** and click **OK**. Save the workbook.

   You increased the height of the row that contains the worksheet title so that it is more prominent.

# STEP 6 ▶ HIDE AND UNHIDE COLUMNS

To focus on the dollar amounts, you decide to hide the markup rate, discount rate, and profit margin columns. Refer to Figure 1.28 as you complete Step 6.

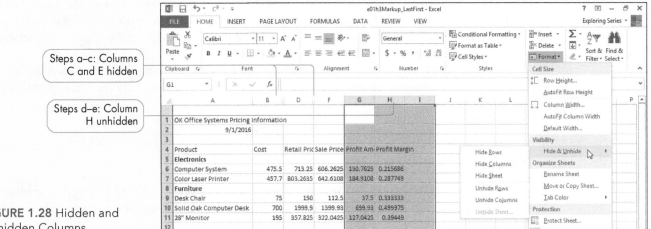

Steps a–c: Columns C and E hidden

Steps d–e: Column H unhidden

**FIGURE 1.28** Hidden and Unhidden Columns

**a.** Click the **column C heading**, the column containing the Markup Rate values.

**b.** Press and hold **Ctrl** as you click the **column E heading** and the **column H heading**. Release Ctrl after selecting the headings.

Holding down Ctrl enables you to select nonadjacent ranges. You want to hide the rate columns temporarily.

**c.** Click **Format** in the Cells group, point to *Hide & Unhide*, and then select **Hide Columns**.

Excel hides the selected columns. You see a gap in column heading letters, indicating columns are hidden (refer to Figure 1.28).

**d.** Drag to select the **column G and I headings**.

You want to unhide column H, so you must select the columns on both sides of the hidden column.

**e.** Click **Format** in the Cells group, point to *Hide & Unhide*, and then select **Unhide Columns**.

Column H, which contains the Profit Margin values, is no longer hidden. You will keep the other columns hidden and save the workbook as evidence that you know how to hide columns. You will unhide the remaining columns in the next Hands-On Exercise.

**f.** Save the workbook. Keep the workbook open if you plan to continue with the next Hands-On Exercise. If not, close the workbook and exit Excel.

# Clipboard Tasks

Although you plan worksheets before entering data, you might decide to move data to a different location in the same worksheet or even in a different worksheet. Instead of deleting the original data and then typing it in the new location, you can select and move data from one cell to another. In some instances, you might want to create a copy of data entered so that you can explore different values and compare the results of the original data set and the copied and edited data set.

In this section, you will learn how to select different ranges. Then you will learn how to move a range to another location, make a copy of a range, and use the Paste Special feature.

## Selecting, Moving, Copying, and Pasting Data

You may already know the basics of selecting, cutting, copying, and pasting data in other programs, such as Microsoft Word. These tasks are somewhat different when working in Excel.

### Select a Range

**STEP 1 >>**

A *range* refers to a group of adjacent or contiguous cells. A range may be as small as a single cell or as large as the entire worksheet. It may consist of a row or part of a row, a column or part of a column, or multiple rows or columns, but will always be a rectangular shape, as you must select the same number of cells in each row or column for the entire range. A range is specified by indicating the top-left and bottom-right cells in the selection. For example, in Figure 1.29, the date is a single-cell range in cell A2, the Color Laser Printer data are stored in the range A6:G6, the cost values are stored in the range B5:B10, and the sales prices and profit margins are stored in range F5:G10. A *nonadjacent range* contains multiple ranges, such as C5:C10 and E5:E10. At times, you need to select nonadjacent ranges so that you can apply the same formatting at the same time, such as formatting the nonadjacent range C5:C10 and E5:E10 with Percent Style.

| | A | B | C | D | E | F | G | H |
|---|---|---|---|---|---|---|---|---|
| 1 | OK Office Systems Pricing Information | | | | | | | |
| 2 | 9/1/2016 | | | | | | | |
| 3 | | | | | | | | |
| 4 | Product | Cost | Markup R | Retail Pric | Percent O | Sale Price | Profit Margin | |
| 5 | Computer System | 475.5 | 0.5 | 713.25 | 0.15 | 606.263 | 0.275 | |
| 6 | Color Laser Printer | 457.7 | 0.755 | 803.264 | 0.2 | 642.611 | 0.404 | |
| 7 | Filing Cabinet | 68.75 | 0.905 | 130.969 | 0.05 | 124.42 | 0.80975 | |
| 8 | Desk Chair | 75 | 1 | 150 | 0.25 | 112.5 | 0.5 | |
| 9 | Solid Oak Computer Desk | 700 | 1.857 | 1999.9 | 0.3 | 1399.93 | 0.9999 | |
| 10 | 28" Monitor | 195 | 0.835 | 357.825 | 0.1 | 322.043 | 0.6515 | |
| 11 | | | | | | | | |
| 12 | | | | | | | | |

Labels: Quick Analysis button, Single-cell range, Range of cells, Range in a row, Range in a column

**FIGURE 1.29** Sample Ranges

Table 1.4 lists methods you can use to select ranges, including nonadjacent ranges.

## TABLE 1.4 Selecting Ranges

| To Select: | Do This: |
|---|---|
| A range | Drag until you select the entire range. Alternatively, click the first cell in the range, press and hold Shift, and then click the last cell in the range. |
| An entire column | Click the column heading. |
| An entire row | Click the row heading. |
| Current range containing data | Click in the range of data and press Ctrl+A. |
| All cells in a worksheet | Click Select All or press Ctrl+A twice. |
| Nonadjacent range | Select the first range, press and hold Ctrl, and then select additional range(s). |

A green border appears around a selected range, and the Quick Analysis button displays in the bottom-right corner of the selected range. Any command you execute will affect the entire range. The range remains selected until you select another range or click in any cell in the worksheet.

 **TIP** Name Box

You can use the Name Box to select a range by clicking in the Name Box, typing a range address such as B15:D25, and then pressing Enter.

## Move a Range to Another Location

STEP 1 ›› You can move cell contents from one range to another. For example, you might need to move an input area from the right side of the worksheet to above the output range. When you move a range containing text and values, the text and values do not change. However, any formulas that refer to cells in that range will update to reflect the new cell addresses. To move a range, do the following:

1. Select the range.
2. Use the Cut command to copy the range to the Clipboard. Unlike cutting data in other Microsoft Office applications, the data you cut in Excel remain in their locations until you paste them elsewhere. After you click Cut, a moving dashed green border surrounds the selected range and the status bar displays *Select destination and press ENTER or choose Paste*.
3. Make sure the destination range—the range where you want to move the data—is the same size or greater than the size of the cut range. If any cells within the destination range contain data, Excel overwrites that data when you use the Paste command.
4. Click in the top-left corner of the destination range, and then use the Paste command to insert the data contained in the selected range and remove that data from the original range.

## Copy and Paste a Range

STEP 2 ›› You may need to copy cell contents from one range to another. For example, you might copy your January budget to another worksheet to use as a model for creating your February budget. When you copy a range, the original data remain in their original locations. Cell references in copied formulas adjust based on their relative locations to the original data. To copy a range, do the following:

1. Select the range.
2. Use the Copy command to copy the contents of the selected range to the Clipboard. After you click Copy, a moving dashed green border surrounds the selected range and the status bar displays *Select destination and press ENTER or choose Paste*.
3. Make sure the destination range—the range where you want to copy the data—is the same size or greater than the size of the copied range. If any cells within the destination range contain data, Excel overwrites that data when you use the Paste command.
4. Click in the top-left corner of the destination range where you want the duplicate data, and then use the Paste command. The original range still has the moving dashed green border, and the pasted copied range is selected with a solid green border. Figure 1.30 shows a selected range and a copy of the range.
5. Press Esc to turn off the moving dashed border around the originally selected range.

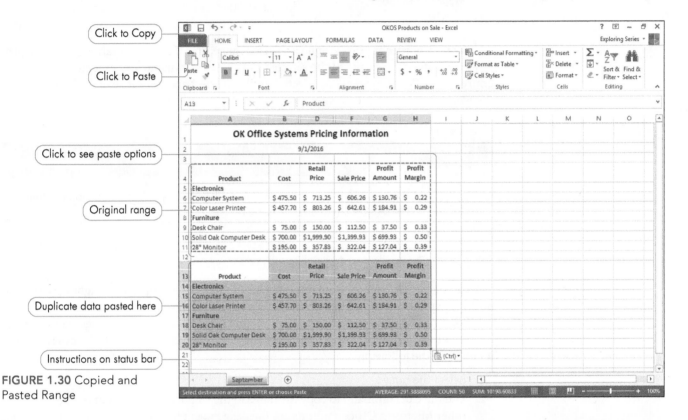

**FIGURE 1.30** Copied and Pasted Range

---

## TIP  Copy as Picture

Instead of clicking Copy, if you click the Copy arrow in the Clipboard group, you can select Copy (the default option) or Copy as Picture. When you select Copy as Picture, you copy an image of the selected data. You can then paste the image elsewhere in the workbook or in a Word document or PowerPoint presentation. However, when you copy the data as an image, you cannot edit individual cell data after you paste the image.

## Use Paste Options and Paste Special

STEP 3 ▶▶  Sometimes you might want to paste data in a different format than they are in the Clipboard. For example, you might want to copy a range containing formulas and cell references, and paste the range as values in another workbook that does not have the referenced cells. If you want to copy data from Excel and paste them into a Word document, you can paste the Excel data as a worksheet object, as unformatted text, or in another format. To paste data from the Clipboard into a different format, click the Paste arrow in the Clipboard group, and hover over a command to see a ScreenTip and a preview of how the pasted data will look. In Figure 1.31, the preview shows that a particular paste option will maintain formulas and number formatting; however, it will not maintain the text formatting, such as font color and centered text. After previewing different paste options, click the one you want in order to apply it.

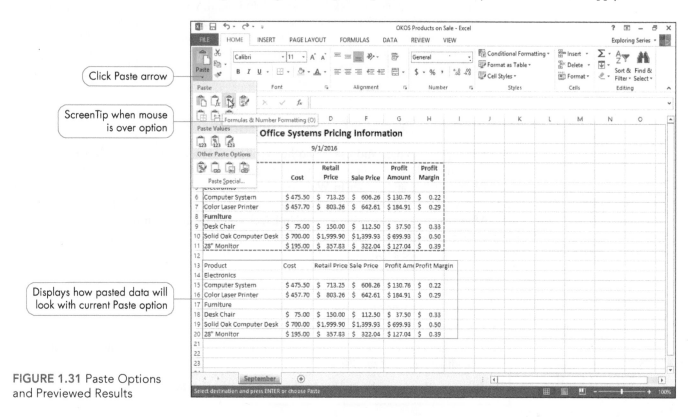

**FIGURE 1.31** Paste Options and Previewed Results

For more specific paste options, click the Paste arrow, and then select Paste Special to display the Paste Special dialog box (see Figure 1.32). This dialog box contains more options than the Paste menu. Click the desired option and click OK.

**FIGURE 1.32** Paste Special Dialog Box

## TIP  Paste Options Button

When you copy or paste data, Excel displays the *Paste Options button* in the bottom-right corner of the pasted data (refer to Figure 1.30). Click Paste Options to see different results for the pasted data.

After entering data into a worksheet, you might want to transpose the columns and rows so that the data in the first column appear as column labels across the first row, or the column labels in the first row appear in the first column. To transpose worksheet data, select and copy the original range, click the top-left corner of the destination range, click the Paste arrow, and then click Transpose.

## Copy Excel Data to Other Programs

You can copy Excel data and use it in other applications, such as in a Word document or in a PowerPoint slide show. For example, you might perform statistical analyses in Excel, copy the data into a research paper in Word or create a budget in Excel, and then copy the data into a PowerPoint slide show for a meeting.

After selecting and copying a range in Excel, you must decide how you want the data to appear in the destination application. Click the Paste arrow in the destination application, such as Word, to see a gallery of options or to select the Paste Special option.

*Quick*
Concepts

1. When you move or copy a worksheet, what are some of the decisions you must make? *pp. 35–36*

2. How can you select nonadjacent ranges, such as B5:B10 and F5:F10? Why would you select nonadjacent ranges? *pp. 34–35*

3. Why would you use the Paste Special options in Excel? *p. 36*

# Hands-On Exercises

Watch the Video for this Hands-On Exercise!

MyITLab®
HOE4 Training

## 4 Clipboard Tasks

You realize the 28" Monitor data is in the Furniture category instead of the Electronics category. You need to move the product to its appropriate location. In addition, your supervisor will ask you to enter data for a new product. Because it is almost identical to an existing product, you can copy the original data and edit the copied data to save time. You also want to experiment with the Paste Special option to see the results of using it in the OKOS workbook.

**Skills covered:** Select a Range and Move a Row to a New Location • Copy and Paste a Range • Use Paste Special

### STEP 1 ›› SELECT A RANGE AND MOVE A ROW TO A NEW LOCATION

You want to move the 28" Monitor product to be immediately after the Color Laser Printer product. Before moving the 28" Monitor row, you need to insert a blank row between the Color Laser Printer and Furniture rows. Refer to Figure 1.33 as you complete Step 1.

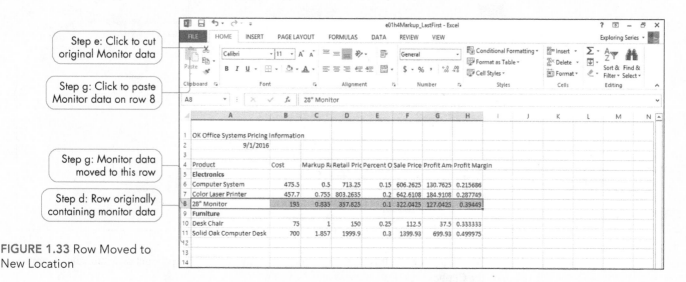

Step e: Click to cut original Monitor data

Step g: Click to paste Monitor data on row 8

Step g: Monitor data moved to this row

Step d: Row originally containing monitor data

**FIGURE 1.33** Row Moved to New Location

a. Open *e01h3Markup_LastFirst* if you closed it at the end of Hands-On Exercise 3 and save it as **e01h4Markup_LastFirst**, changing *h3* to *h4*.

b. Select the **column B, D, and F headings**. Unhide columns C and E as you learned in Hands-On Exercise 3.

   You kept those columns hidden when you saved the *e01h3Markup_LastFirst* workbook to preserve evidence that you know how to hide columns. Now you need the columns visible to continue.

c. Right-click the **row 8 heading** and select **Insert** from the menu.

   You need to insert a blank row so that you can move the *28" Computer Monitor* data to be between the *Color Laser Printer* and *Furniture* rows.

d. Select the **range A12:H12**.

   You selected the range of cells containing the 28" Monitor data.

e. Click **Cut** in the Clipboard group.

   A moving dashed green border outlines the selected range. The status bar displays the message *Select destination and press ENTER or choose Paste.*

**f.** Click **cell A8**, the new blank row you inserted in step c.

This is the first cell in the destination range.

**g.** Click **Paste** in the Clipboard group and save the workbook.

The 28" Monitor data are now located on row 8.

> **TROUBLESHOOTING:** If you cut and paste a row without inserting a new row first, Excel will overwrite the original row of data, which is why you inserted a new row in step c. If you forgot to do step c, click Undo until the 28" Monitor data is back in its original location and start with step c again.

## STEP 2 ≫ COPY AND PASTE A RANGE

Alesha told you that a new chair is on its way. She asked you to enter the data for the Executive Desk Chair. Because most of the data is the same as the Desk Chair data, you will copy the original Desk Chair data, edit the product name, and then change the cost to reflect the cost of the second chair. Refer to Figure 1.34 as you complete Step 2.

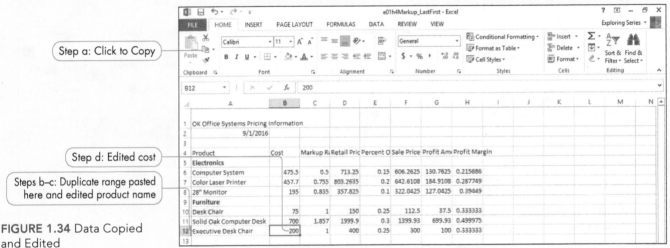

**FIGURE 1.34** Data Copied and Edited

**a.** Select the **range A10:H10**, the row containing the Desk Chair product data, and click **Copy** in the Clipboard group.

**b.** Click **cell A12**, the location for the duplicate data, and click **Paste** in the Clipboard group. Press **Esc**.

The pasted range is selected in row 12.

**c.** Click **cell A12**, press **F2** to activate Edit Mode, press **Home**, type **Executive**, press **Spacebar**, and then press **Enter**.

You edited the product name.

**d.** Change the value in **cell B12** to **200**. Save the workbook.

The formulas calculate the results based on the new cost of 200 for the Executive Desk Chair.

# STEP 3 ≫ USE PASTE SPECIAL

During your lunch break, you want to experiment with some of the Paste Special options. Particularly, you are interested in pasting Formulas and Value & Source Formatting. First, you will bold the title and apply a font color to help you test these Paste Special options. Refer to Figure 1.35 as you complete Step 3.

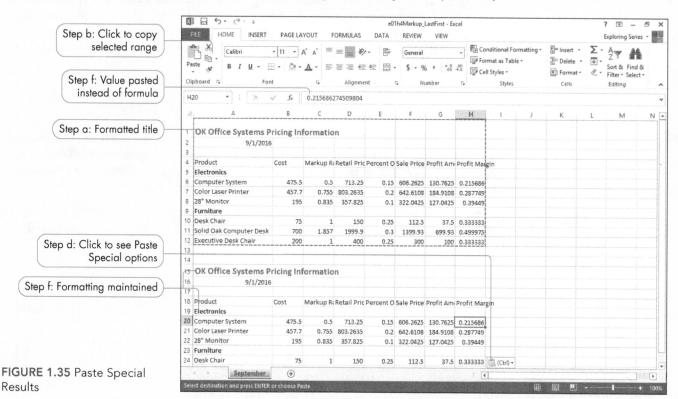

Step b: Click to copy selected range

Step f: Value pasted instead of formula

Step a: Formatted title

Step d: Click to see Paste Special options

Step f: Formatting maintained

**FIGURE 1.35** Paste Special Results

a. Click **cell A1**. Apply these font formats to the title: **14 pt**, **Bold**, and **Gold, Accent 4, Darker 50% font color** in the Font group on the HOME tab.

   You need to format text to see the effects of using different Paste Special options.

b. Select the **range A1:H12** and click **Copy** in the Clipboard group.

c. Click **cell A15**, the top-left corner of the destination range.

d. Click the **Paste arrow** in the Clipboard group and position the mouse pointer over *Formulas*.

   Without clicking the command, Excel shows you a preview of what that option would do. The pasted copy would not contain the font formatting you applied to the title or the bold on the two category names. In addition, the pasted date would appear as a serial number. The formulas would be maintained.

e. Position the mouse pointer over *Values & Source Formatting*.

   This option would preserve the formatting, but it would convert the formulas into the current value results.

f. Click **Values & Source Formatting**, click **cell H6** to see a formula, and then click **cell H20**. Press **Esc** to turn off the border.

   Cell H6 contains a formula, but in the pasted version, the equivalent cell H20 has converted the formula result into an actual value. If you were to change the original cost on row 20, the contents of cell H20 would not change. In a working environment, this is useful only if you want to capture the exact value in a point in time before making changes to the original data.

g. Save the workbook. Keep the workbook open if you plan to continue with the next Hands-On Exercise. If not, close the workbook and exit Excel.

# Formatting

After entering data and formulas, you should format the worksheet. A professionally formatted worksheet—through adding appropriate symbols, aligning decimals, and using fonts and colors to make data stand out—makes finding and analyzing data easy. You apply different formats to accentuate meaningful details or to draw attention to specific ranges in a worksheet.

In this section, you will learn to apply different alignment options, including horizontal and vertical alignment, text wrapping, and indent options. In addition, you will learn how to format different types of values.

## Applying Alignment and Font Options

*Alignment* refers to how data are positioned in cells. Text aligns at the left cell margin, and dates and values align at the right cell margin. You can change the alignment of cell contents to improve the appearance of data within the cells. The Alignment group (see Figure 1.36) on the Home tab contains several features to help you align and format data.

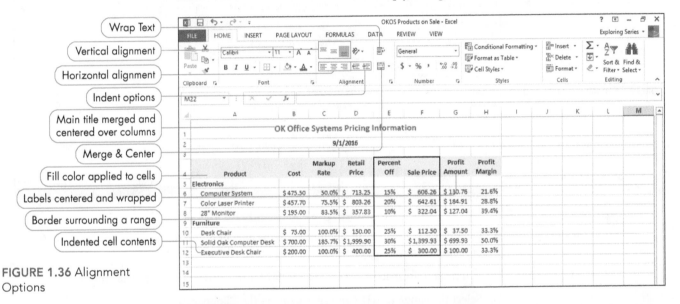

**FIGURE 1.36** Alignment Options

---

**TIP** **Alignment Options**

The Format Cells dialog box contains additional alignment options. To open the Format Cells dialog box, click the Dialog Box Launcher in the Alignment group on the Home tab. The Alignment tab in the dialog box contains the options for aligning data.

---

## Merge and Center Labels

You may want to place a title at the top of a worksheet and center it over the columns of data in the worksheet. You can center main titles over all columns in the worksheet, and you can center category titles over groups of related columns. To create a title, enter the text in the far left cell of the range. Select the range of cells across which you want to center the title and click Merge & Center in the Alignment group on the Home tab. Only data in the far left cell (or top right cell) are merged. Any other data in the merged cells are deleted. Excel merges the selected cells together into one cell, and the merged cell address is that of the original cell on the left. The data are centered between the left and right sides of the merged cell.

If you merge too many cells and want to split the merged cell back into its original multiple cells, click the merged cell and click Merge & Center. Unmerging places the data in the top-left cell.

For additional options, click the Merge & Center arrow. Table 1.5 lists the four merge options.

| TABLE 1.5 Merge Options | |
|---|---|
| **Option** | **Results** |
| Merge & Center | Merges selected cells and centers data into one cell. |
| Merge Across | Merges the selected cells but keeps text left aligned or values right aligned. |
| Merge Cells | Enables you to merge a range of cells on multiple rows as well as in multiple columns. |
| Unmerge Cells | Separates a merged cell into multiple cells again. |

## Change Horizontal and Vertical Cell Alignment

**STEP 2》**  *Horizontal alignment* specifies the position of data between the left and right cell margins, and *vertical alignment* specifies the position of data between the top and bottom cell margins. Bottom Align is the default vertical alignment (as indicated by the light green background), and Align Left is the default horizontal alignment for text. In Figure 1.36, the labels on row 4 have Center horizontal alignment and the title in row 1 has Middle Align vertical alignment.

If you increase row height, you might need to change the vertical alignment to position data better in conjunction with data in adjacent cells. To change alignments, click the desired alignment setting(s) in the Alignment group on the Home tab.

**TIP** Rotate Cell Data

People sometimes rotate headings in cells. You can rotate data in a cell by clicking Orientation in the Alignment group and selecting an option, such as Angle Clockwise.

## Wrap Text

**STEP 2》**  Sometimes you have to maintain specific column widths, but the data do not fit entirely. You can use *wrap text* to make data appear on multiple lines by adjusting the row height to fit the cell contents within the column width. When you click Wrap Text in the Alignment group, Excel wraps the text on two or more lines within the cell. This alignment option is helpful when the column headings are wider than the values contained in the column. In Figure 1.36, the *Markup Rate* and *Percent Off* labels on row 4 are examples of wrapped text.

## Increase and Decrease Indent

**STEP 3》**  To offset labels, you can indent text within a cell. **Indenting** helps others see the hierarchical structure of data. Accountants often indent the word *Totals* in financial statements so that it stands out from a list of items above the total row. To indent the contents of a cell, click Increase Indent in the Alignment group on the Home tab. The more you click Increase Indent, the more text is indented in the cell. To decrease the indent, click Decrease Indent in the Alignment group. In Figure 1.36, *Computer System* and *Desk Chair* are indented.

Values right align by default. You should align the decimal places in a column of values. If the column label is wide, the values below it appear too far on the right. To preserve the values aligning at the decimal places, use the Align Right horizontal alignment and click Increase Indent to shift the values over to the left a little for better placement.

### Apply Borders and Fill Color

**STEP 4 »**

You can apply a border or fill color to accentuate data in a worksheet. A **border** is a line that surrounds a cell or a range of cells. You can use borders to offset some data from the rest of the worksheet data. To apply a border, select the cell or range that you want to have a border, click the Borders arrow in the Font group, and then select the desired border type. In Figure 1.36, a border surrounds the range E4:F12. To remove a border, select No Border from the Borders menu.

To add some color to your worksheet to add emphasis to data or headers, you can apply a fill color. **Fill color** is a background color that displays behind the data. You should choose a fill color that contrasts with the font color. For example, if the font color is Black, you might want to choose Yellow fill color. If the font color is White, you might want to apply Blue or Dark Blue fill color. To apply a fill color, select the cell or range that you want to have a fill color, click the Fill Color arrow on the Home tab, and then select the color choice from the Fill Color palette. In Figure 1.36, the column labels in row 4 contain the Gold, Accent 4, Lighter 80% fill color. If you want to remove a fill color, select No Fill from the bottom of the palette.

For additional border and fill color options, click the Dialog Box Launcher in the Font group to display the Format Cells dialog box. Click the Border tab to select border options, including the border line style and color. Click the Fill tab to set the background color, fill effects, and patterns.

## Applying Number Formats

Values have no special formatting when you enter data. You should apply **number formats** based on the type of values in a cell, such as applying either the Accounting or Currency number format to monetary values. Changing the number format changes the way the number displays in a cell, but the format does not change the number's value. If, for example, you enter 123.456 into a cell and format the cell with the Currency number type, the value shows as $123.46 onscreen, but the actual value 123.456 is used for calculations. When you apply a number format, you can specify the number of decimal places to display onscreen.

### Apply a Number Format

**STEP 5 »**

The default number format is General, which displays values as you originally enter them. General does not align decimal points in a column or include symbols, such as dollar signs, percent signs, or commas. Table 1.6 lists and describes the primary number formats in Excel.

## TABLE 1.6 Number Formats

| Format Style | Display |
|---|---|
| General | A number as it was originally entered. Numbers are shown as integers (e.g., 12345), decimal fractions (e.g., 1234.5), or in scientific notation (e.g., 1.23E+10) if the number exceeds 11 digits. |
| Number | A number with or without the 1,000 separator (e.g., a comma) and with any number of decimal places. Negative numbers can be displayed with parentheses and/or red. |
| Currency | A number with the 1,000 separator and an optional dollar sign (which is placed immediately to the left of the number). Negative values are preceded by a minus sign or are displayed with parentheses or in red. Two decimal places display by default. |
| Accounting Number Format | A number with the 1,000 separator, an optional dollar sign (at the left border of the cell, vertically aligned within a column), negative values in parentheses, and zero values as hyphens. Two decimal places display by default. Changes alignment slightly within the cell. |
| Comma | A number with the 1,000 separator. Used in conjunction with Accounting Number Style to align commas and decimal places. |
| Date | The date in different ways, such as Long Date (March 14, 2016) or Short Date (3/14/16 or 14-Mar-16). |
| Time | The time in different formats, such as 10:50 PM or 22:50. |
| Percent Style | The value as it would be multiplied by 100 (for display purpose), with the percent sign. The default number of decimal places is zero if you click Percent Style in the Number group or two decimal places if you use the Format Cells dialog box. However, you should typically increase the number of decimal points to show greater accuracy. |
| Fraction | A number as a fraction; use when no exact decimal equivalent exists. A fraction is entered into a cell as a formula such as =1/3. If the cell is not formatted as a fraction, the formula results display. |
| Scientific | A number as a decimal fraction followed by a whole number exponent of 10; for example, the number 12345 would appear as 1.23E+04. The exponent, +04 in the example, is the number of places the decimal point is moved to the left (or right if the exponent is negative). Very small numbers have negative exponents. |
| Text | The data left aligned; is useful for numerical values that have leading zeros and should be treated as text, such as postal codes or phone numbers. Apply Text format before typing a leading zero so that the zero displays in the cell. |
| Special | A number with editing characters, such as hyphens in a Social Security number. |
| Custom | Predefined customized number formats or special symbols to create your own customized number format. |

The Number group on the Home tab contains commands for applying *Accounting Number Format*, *Percent Style*, and *Comma Style* numbering formats. You can click the Accounting Number Format arrow and select other denominations, such as English pounds or euros. For other number formats, click the Number Format arrow and select the numbering format you want to use. For more specific numbering formats than those provided, select More Number Formats from the Number Format menu or click the Number Dialog Box Launcher to open the Format Cells dialog box with the Number tab options readily available. Figure 1.37 shows different number formats applied to values.

|  | A | B |
|---|---|---|
| 1 | General | 1234.567 |
| 2 | Number | 1234.57 |
| 3 | Currency | $1,234.57 |
| 4 | Accounting | $            1,234.57 |
| 5 | Comma | 1,234.57 |
| 6 | Percent | 12% |
| 7 | Short Date | 3/1/2016 |
| 8 | Long Date | Tuesday, March 1, 2016 |

**FIGURE 1.37** Number Formats

## Increase and Decrease Decimal Places

 **STEP 5 >>** After applying a number format, you may need to adjust the number of decimal places that display. For example, if you have an entire column of monetary values formatted in Accounting Number Format, Excel displays two decimal places by default. If the entire column of values contains whole dollar values and no cents, displaying .00 down the column looks cluttered. You can decrease the number of decimal places to show whole numbers only.

To change the number of decimal places displayed, click Increase Decimal in the Number group on the Home tab to display more decimal places for greater precision or Decrease Decimal to display fewer or no decimal places.

*Quick*
Concepts

1. What is the importance of formatting a worksheet? *p. 42*

2. Describe five alignment and font formatting techniques used to format labels that are discussed in this section. *pp. 42–44*

3. What are the main differences between Accounting Number Format and Currency format? Which format has its own command on the Ribbon? *p. 45*

# Hands-On Exercises

Watch the Video
for this Hands-
On Exercise!

MyITLab®
HOE5 Training

# 5 Formatting

In the first four Hands-On Exercises, you entered data about products on sale, created formulas to calculate markup and profit, and inserted new rows and columns to accommodate the labels *Electronics* and *Furniture* to identify the specific products. You are ready to format the worksheet. Specifically, you need to center the title, align text, format values, and then apply other formatting to enhance the readability of the worksheet.

**Skills covered:** Merge and Center the Title • Align Text Horizontally and Vertically and Wrap Text • Increase Indent • Apply Borders and Fill Color • Apply Number Formats and Increase and Decrease Decimal Places

---

## STEP 1 ≫ MERGE AND CENTER THE TITLE

To make the title stand out, you want to center it over all the data columns. You will use the Merge & Center command to merge cells and center the title at the same time. Refer to Figure 1.38 as you complete Step 1.

Step e: Date merged, centered, and bold A2:H2

| | A | B | C | D | E | F | G | H | I |
|---|---|---|---|---|---|---|---|---|---|
| 1 | | | OK Office Systems Pricing Information | | | | | | |
| 2 | | | | 9/1/2016 | | | | | |
| 3 | | | | | | | | | |
| 4 | Product | Cost | Markup R | Retail Pric | Percent O | Sale Price | Profit Am | Profit Margin | |
| 5 | Electronics | | | | | | | | |
| 6 | Computer System | 475.5 | 0.5 | 713.25 | 0.15 | 606.2625 | 130.7625 | 0.215686 | |
| 7 | Color Laser Printer | 457.7 | 0.755 | 803.2635 | 0.2 | 642.6108 | 184.9108 | 0.287749 | |
| 8 | 28" Monitor | 195 | 0.835 | 357.825 | 0.1 | 322.0425 | 127.0425 | 0.39449 | |
| 9 | Furniture | | | | | | | | |
| 10 | Desk Chair | 75 | 1 | 150 | 0.25 | 112.5 | 37.5 | 0.333333 | |
| 11 | Solid Oak Computer Desk | 700 | 1.857 | 1999.9 | 0.3 | 1399.93 | 699.93 | 0.499975 | |
| 12 | Executive Desk Chair | 200 | 1 | 400 | 0.25 | 300 | 100 | 0.333333 | |
| 13 | | | | | | | | | |

**FIGURE 1.38** Title and Date Merged and Centered

a. Open *e01h4Markup_LastFirst* if you closed it at the end of Hands-On Exercise 4 and save it as **e01h5Markup_LastFirst**, changing *h4* to *h5*.

b. Select the **range A15:H26** and press **Delete**.

You maintained a copy of your Paste Special results in the *e01h4Markup_LastFirst* workbook, but you do not need it to continue.

c. Select the **range A1:H1**.

You want to center the title over all columns of data.

d. Click **Merge & Center** in the Alignment group.

Excel merges cells in the range A1:H1 into one cell and centers the title horizontally within the merged cell, which is cell A1.

> **TROUBLESHOOTING:** If you merge too many or not enough cells, you can unmerge the cells and start again. To unmerge cells, click in the merged cell. The Merge & Center command is shaded in green when the active cell is merged. Click Merge & Center to unmerge the cell. Then select the correct range to merge and use Merge & Center again.

**e.** Select the **range A2:H2**. Merge and center the date and bold it.

> **TROUBLESHOOTING:** If you try to merge and center data in the range A1:H2, Excel will keep the top-left data only and delete the date. To merge separate data on separate rows, you must merge and center data separately.

**f.** Save the workbook.

## STEP 2 ≫ ALIGN TEXT HORIZONTALLY AND VERTICALLY AND WRAP TEXT

You will wrap the text in the column headings to avoid columns that are too wide for the data, but which will display the entire text of the column labels. In addition, you will horizontally center column labels between the left and right cell margins. Refer to Figure 1.39 as you complete Step 2.

Step d: Title with Middle (vertical) Align

Steps b–c: Column labels wrapped, centered, and bold

| | A | B | C | D | E | F | G | H | I |
|---|---|---|---|---|---|---|---|---|---|
| 1 | OK Office Systems Pricing Information | | | | | | | | |
| 2 | 9/1/2016 | | | | | | | | |
| 3 | | | | | | | | | |
| 4 | Product | Cost | Markup Rate | Retail Price | Percent Off | Sale Price | Profit Amount | Profit Margin | |
| 5 | Electronics | | | | | | | | |
| 6 | Computer System | 475.5 | 0.5 | 713.25 | 0.15 | 606.2625 | 130.7625 | 0.215686 | |
| 7 | Color Laser Printer | 457.7 | 0.755 | 803.2635 | 0.2 | 642.6108 | 184.9108 | 0.287749 | |
| 8 | 28" Monitor | 195 | 0.835 | 357.825 | 0.1 | 322.0425 | 127.0425 | 0.39449 | |
| 9 | Furniture | | | | | | | | |
| 10 | Desk Chair | 75 | 1 | 150 | 0.25 | 112.5 | 37.5 | 0.333333 | |
| 11 | Solid Oak Computer Desk | 700 | 1.857 | 1999.9 | 0.3 | 1399.93 | 699.93 | 0.499975 | |
| 12 | Executive Desk Chair | 200 | 1 | 400 | 0.25 | 300 | 100 | 0.333333 | |
| 13 | | | | | | | | | |

**FIGURE 1.39** Formatted Column Labels

**a.** Select the **range A4:H4** to select the column labels.

**b.** Click **Wrap Text** in the Alignment group.

The multiple-word column headings are now visible on two lines within each cell.

**c.** Click **Center** in the Alignment group. Bold the selected column headings.

The column headings are centered horizontally between the left and right edges of each cell.

**d.** Click **cell A1**, which contains the title, click **Middle Align** in the Alignment group, and then save the workbook.

Middle Align vertically centers data between the top and bottom edges of the cell.

## STEP 3 ≫ INCREASE INDENT

As you review the first column, you notice that the category names, Electronics and Furniture, do not stand out. You decide to indent the labels within each category to better display which products are in each category. Refer to Figure 1.40 as you complete Step 3.

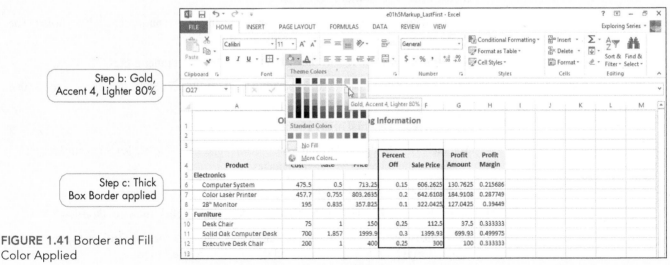

Step d: Column A width increased to 26.00

Step b: Electronics product labels indented twice

Step c: Furniture product labels indented twice

| Product | Cost | Markup Rate | Retail Price | Percent Off | Sale Price | Profit Amount | Profit Margin |
|---|---|---|---|---|---|---|---|
| Electronics | | | | | | | |
| Computer System | 475.5 | 0.5 | 713.25 | 0.15 | 606.2625 | 130.7625 | 0.215686 |
| Color Laser Printer | 457.7 | 0.755 | 803.2635 | 0.2 | 642.6108 | 184.9108 | 0.287749 |
| 28" Monitor | 195 | 0.835 | 357.825 | 0.1 | 322.0425 | 127.0425 | 0.39449 |
| Furniture | | | | | | | |
| Desk Chair | 75 | 1 | 150 | 0.25 | 112.5 | 37.5 | 0.333333 |
| Solid Oak Computer Desk | 700 | 1.857 | 1999.9 | 0.3 | 1399.93 | 699.93 | 0.499975 |
| Executive Desk Chair | 200 | 1 | 400 | 0.25 | 300 | 100 | 0.333333 |

**FIGURE 1.40** Indented Cell Contents

a. Select the **range A6:A8**, the cells containing electronic products labels.

b. Click **Increase Indent** in the Alignment group twice.

The three selected product names are indented below the *Electronics* heading.

c. Select the **range A10:A12**, the cells containing furniture products, and click **Increase Indent** twice.

The three selected product names are indented below the *Furniture* heading. Notice that the one product name appears cut off.

d. Increase the column A width to **26.00**. Save the workbook.

## STEP 4 ≫ APPLY BORDERS AND FILL COLOR

You want to apply a light gold fill color to highlight the column headings. In addition, you want to emphasize the percent off and sale prices. You will do this by applying a border around that range. Refer to Figure 1.41 as you complete Step 4.

Step b: Gold, Accent 4, Lighter 80%

Step c: Thick Box Border applied

**FIGURE 1.41** Border and Fill Color Applied

a. Select the **range A4:H4** and click the **Fill Color arrow** in the Font group.

b. Click **Gold, Accent 4, Lighter 80%** in the *Theme Colors* section. It is the second color down in the third column from the right.

You applied a fill color to the selected cells to draw attention to these cells.

c. Select the **range E4:F12**, click the **Border arrow** in the Font group, and then select **Thick Box Border**.

You applied a border around the selected cells.

d. Click in an empty cell below the columns of data to deselect the cells. Save the workbook.

## STEP 5 ≫ APPLY NUMBER FORMATS AND INCREASE AND DECREASE DECIMAL PLACES

You need to format the values to increase readability and look more professional. You will apply number formats and adjust the number of decimal points displayed. Refer to Figure 1.42 as you complete Step 5.

Step f: Percent Style, Align Right, Indent twice

Step e: Percent Style

Steps c–d: Percent Style with one decimal place

Step b: Accounting Number Format

**FIGURE 1.42** Number Formats and Decimal Places

| | A | B | C | D | E | F | G | H | I |
|---|---|---|---|---|---|---|---|---|---|
| 1 | | | OK Office Systems Pricing Information | | | | | | |
| 2 | | | | 9/1/2016 | | | | | |
| 3 | | | | | | | | | |
| 4 | Product | Cost | Markup Rate | Retail Price | Percent Off | Sale Price | Profit Amount | Profit Margin | |
| 5 | Electronics | | | | | | | | |
| 6 | Computer System | $475.50 | 50.0% | $ 713.25 | 15% | $ 606.26 | $ 130.76 | 21.6% | |
| 7 | Color Laser Printer | $457.70 | 75.5% | $ 803.26 | 20% | $ 642.61 | $ 184.91 | 28.8% | |
| 8 | 28" Monitor | $195.00 | 83.5% | $ 357.83 | 10% | $ 322.04 | $ 127.04 | 39.4% | |
| 9 | Furniture | | | | | | | | |
| 10 | Desk Chair | $ 75.00 | 100.0% | $ 150.00 | 25% | $ 112.50 | $ 37.50 | 33.3% | |
| 11 | Solid Oak Computer Desk | $700.00 | 185.7% | $1,999.90 | 30% | $1,399.93 | $ 699.93 | 50.0% | |
| 12 | Executive Desk Chair | $200.00 | 100.0% | $ 400.00 | 25% | $ 300.00 | $ 100.00 | 33.3% | |
| 13 | | | | | | | | | |

a. Select the **range B6:B12**. Press and hold **Ctrl** as you select the **ranges D6:D12** and **F6:G12**.

Because you want to format nonadjacent ranges with the same formats, you hold down Ctrl.

b. Click **Accounting Number Format** in the Number group. If some cells contain pound signs, increase the column widths as needed.

You formatted the selected nonadjacent ranges with the Accounting Number Format. The dollar signs align on the left cell margins and the decimals align.

c. Select the **range C6:C12** and click **Percent Style** in the Number group.

You formatted the values in the selected ranges with Percent Style, showing whole numbers only.

d. Click **Increase Decimal** in the Number group.

You increased the decimal to show one decimal place to avoid misleading your readers by displaying the values as whole percentages.

e. Apply **Percent Style** to the **range E6:E12**.

f. Select the **range H6:H12**, apply **Percent Style**, and then click **Increase Decimal**.

g. Select the **range E6:E12**, click **Align Right**, and then click **Increase Indent** twice. Select the **range H6:H12**, click **Align Right**, and then click **Increase Indent**.

With values, you want to keep the decimal points aligned, but you can then use Increase Indent to adjust the indent so that the values appear more centered below the column labels.

h. Save the workbook. Keep the workbook open if you plan to continue with the next Hands-On Exercise. If not, close the workbook and exit Excel.

# Page Setup and Printing

Although you might distribute workbooks electronically as e-mail attachments or you might upload workbooks to a corporate server, you should prepare the worksheets in the workbook for printing. You should prepare worksheets in case you need to print them or in case others who receive an electronic copy of your workbook need to print the worksheets. The Page Layout tab provides options for controlling the printed worksheet (see Figure 1.43).

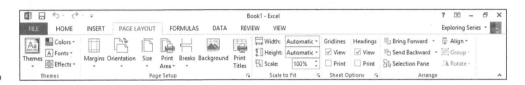

**FIGURE 1.43** Page Layout Tab

In this section, you will select options on the Page Layout tab. Specifically, you will use the Page Setup, Scale to Fit, and Sheet Options groups. After selecting page setup options, you are ready to print your worksheet.

## Selecting Page Setup Options

The Page Setup group on the Page Layout tab contains options to set the margins, select orientation, specify page size, select the print area, and apply other options. The *Scale to Fit* group contains options for adjusting the scaling of the spreadsheet on the printed page. When possible, use the commands in these groups to apply page settings. Table 1.7 lists and describes the commands in the Page Setup group.

**TABLE 1.7   Page Setup Commands**

| Command | Description |
|---|---|
| Margins | Displays a menu to select predefined margin settings. The default margins are 0.75" top and bottom and 0.7" left and right. You will often change these margin settings to balance the worksheet data better on the printed page. If you need different margins, select Custom Margins. |
| Orientation | Displays orientation options. The default page orientation is portrait, which is appropriate for worksheets that contain more rows than columns. Select landscape orientation when worksheets contain more columns than can fit in portrait orientation. For example, the OKOS worksheet might appear better balanced in landscape orientation because it has eight columns. |
| Size | Displays a list of standard paper sizes. The default size is 8 1/2" by 11". If you have a different paper size, such as legal paper, select it from the list. |
| Print Area | Displays a list to set or clear the print area. When you have very large worksheets, you might want to print only a portion of that worksheet. To do so, select the range you want to print, click Print Area in the Page Setup group, and then select Set Print Area. When you use the Print commands, only the range you specified will be printed. To clear the print area, click Print Area and select Clear Print Area. |
| Breaks | Displays a list to insert or remove page breaks. |
| Background | Enables you to select an image to appear as the background behind the worksheet data when viewed onscreen (backgrounds do not appear when the worksheet is printed). |
| Print Titles | Enables you to select column headings and row labels to repeat on multiple-page printouts. |

### Specify Page Options

**STEP 1》** To apply several page setup options at once or to access options not found on the Ribbon, click the Page Setup Dialog Box Launcher. The Page Setup dialog box organizes options into four tabs: Page, Margins, Header/Footer, and Sheet. All tabs contain Print and Print Preview buttons. Figure 1.44 shows the Page tab.

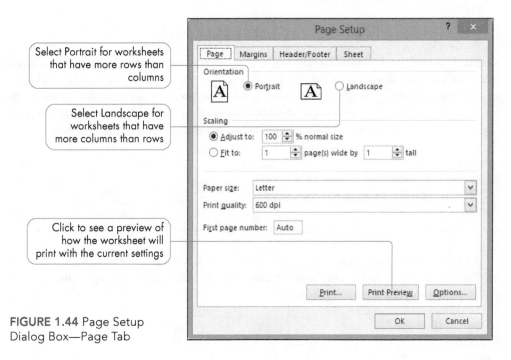

Select Portrait for worksheets that have more rows than columns

Select Landscape for worksheets that have more columns than rows

Click to see a preview of how the worksheet will print with the current settings

**FIGURE 1.44** Page Setup Dialog Box—Page Tab

The Page tab contains options to select the orientation and paper size. In addition, it contains scaling options that are similar to the options in the *Scale to Fit* group on the Page Layout tab. You use scaling options to increase or decrease the size of characters on a printed page, similar to using a zoom setting on a photocopy machine. You can also use the *Fit to* option to force the data to print on a specified number of pages.

## Set Margins Options

STEP 2 »

The Margins tab (see Figure 1.45) contains options for setting the specific margins. In addition, it contains options to center the worksheet data horizontally or vertically on the page. To balance worksheet data equally between the left and right margins, Excel users often center the page horizontally.

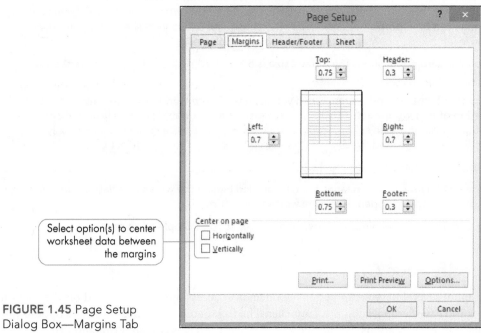

Select option(s) to center worksheet data between the margins

**FIGURE 1.45** Page Setup Dialog Box—Margins Tab

## Create Headers and Footers

STEP 3 » The Header/Footer tab (see Figure 1.46) lets you create a header and/or footer that appears at the top and/or bottom of every printed page. Click the arrows to choose from several preformatted entries, or alternatively, you can click Custom Header or Custom Footer, insert text and other objects, and then click the appropriate formatting button to customize your headers and footers. You can use headers and footers to provide additional information about the worksheet. You can include your name, the date the worksheet was prepared, and page numbers, for example.

You can create different headers or footers on different pages, such as one header with the file name on odd-numbered pages and a header containing the date on even-numbered pages. Click the *Different odd and even pages* check box in the Page Setup dialog box (see Figure 1.46).

You might want the first page to have a different header or footer from the rest of the printed pages, or you might not want a header or footer to show up on the first page but want the header or footer to display on the remaining pages. Click the *Different first page* check box in the Page Setup dialog box to specify a different first page header or footer (see Figure 1.46).

Click to see list of preformatted headers

Specify if you want a different header/footer on odd and even pages

Specify if you want the first page to have a different header/footer from the rest of the pages

**FIGURE 1.46** Page Setup Dialog Box—Header/Footer Tab

Instead of creating headers and footers using the Page Setup dialog box, you can click the Insert tab and click Header & Footer in the Text group. Excel displays the worksheet in Page Layout view with the insertion point in the center area of the header. You can click inside the left, center, or right section of a header or footer. When you do, Excel displays the Header & Footer Tools Design contextual tab (see Figure 1.47). You can enter text or insert data from the Header & Footer Elements group on the tab. Table 1.8 lists and describes the options in the Header & Footer Elements group. To get back to Normal view, click any cell in the worksheet and click Normal in the Workbook Views group on the View tab.

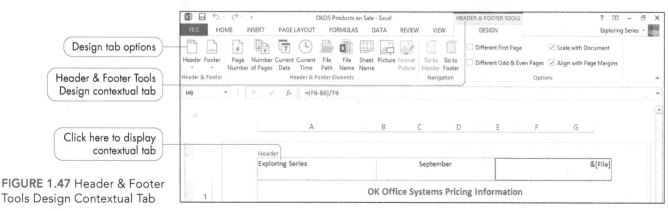

Design tab options

Header & Footer Tools Design contextual tab

Click here to display contextual tab

**FIGURE 1.47** Header & Footer Tools Design Contextual Tab

## TABLE 1.8 Header & Footer Elements Options

| Option Name | Result |
| --- | --- |
| Page Number | Inserts the code &[Page] to display the current page number. |
| Number of Pages | Inserts the code &[Pages] to display the total number of pages that will print. |
| Current Date | Inserts the code &[Date] to display the current date, such as 5/19/2016. The date updates to the current date when you open or print the worksheet. |
| Current Time | Inserts the code &[Time] to display the current time, such as 5:15 PM. The time updates to the current time when you open or print the worksheet. |
| File Path | Inserts the code &[Path]&[File] to display the path and file name, such as C:\Documents\e01h4Markup. This information changes if you save the workbook with a different name or in a different location. |
| File Name | Inserts the code &[File] to display the file name, such as e01h4Markup. This information changes if you save the workbook with a different name. |
| Sheet Name | Inserts the code &[Tab] to display the worksheet name, such as September. This information changes if you rename the worksheet. |
| Picture | Inserts the code &[Picture] to display and print an image as a background behind the data, not just the worksheet. |
| Format Picture | Enables you to adjust the brightness, contrast, and size of an image after you use the Picture option. |

**TIP   View Tab**

If you click the View tab and click Page Layout, Excel displays an area *Click to add header* at the top of the worksheet.

## Select Sheet Options

**STEP 5 »**   The Sheet tab (see Figure 1.48) contains options for setting the print area, print titles, print options, and page order. Some of these options are also located in the Sheet Options group on the Page Layout tab on the Ribbon. By default, Excel displays gridlines onscreen to show you each cell's margins, but the gridlines do not print unless you specifically select the Gridlines check box in the Page Setup dialog box or the Print Gridlines check box in the Sheet Options group on the Page Layout tab. In addition, Excel displays row (1, 2, 3, etc.) and column (A, B, C, etc.) headings onscreen. However, these headings do not print unless you click the *Row and column headings* check box in the Page Setup dialog box or click the Print Headings check box in the Sheet Options group on the Page Layout tab.

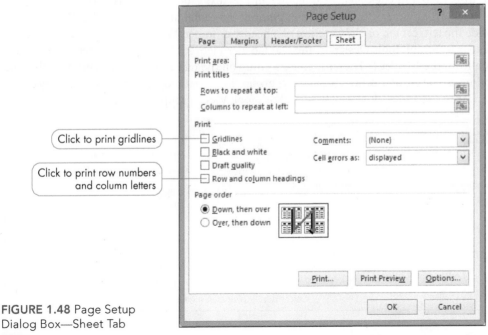

**FIGURE 1.48** Page Setup Dialog Box—Sheet Tab

## TIP | Printing Gridlines and Headings

For most worksheets, you do not need to print gridlines and row/column headings. However, when you want to display and print cell formulas instead of formula results, you might want to print the gridlines and row/column headings. Doing so will help you analyze your formulas. The gridlines help you see the cell boundaries, and the headings help you identify what data are in each cell. At times, you might want to display gridlines to separate data on a regular printout to increase readability.

# Previewing and Printing a Worksheet

**STEP 4**   Before printing a worksheet, you should click the File tab and select Print. The Microsoft Office Backstage view displays print options and displays the worksheet in print preview mode. This mode helps you see in advance if the data are balanced on the page or if data will print on multiple pages.

You can specify the number of copies to print and which printer to use to print the worksheet. The first option in the Settings area enables you to specify what to print. The default option is Print Active Sheets. You can choose other options, such as Print Entire Workbook or Print Selection. You can also specify which pages to print. If you are connected to a printer capable of duplex printing, you can print on only one side or print on both sides. You can also collate, change the orientation, specify the paper size, adjust the margins, and adjust the scaling.

The bottom of the Print window indicates how many pages will print. If you do not like how the worksheet will print, click the Page Layout tab so that you can adjust margins, scaling, column widths, and so on until the worksheet data appear the way you want them to print.

## TIP | Printing Multiple Worksheets

To print more than one worksheet at a time, select the sheets you want to print. To select adjacent sheets, click the first sheet tab, press and hold Shift, and then click the last sheet tab. To select nonadjacent sheets, press and hold Ctrl as you click each sheet tab. When you display the Print options in the Microsoft Office Backstage view, Print Active Sheets is one of the default settings. If you want to print all of the worksheets within the workbook, change the setting to Print Entire Workbook.

*Quick* Concepts

1. What helps determine whether you use portrait or landscape orientation for a worksheet? *p. 52*

2. Why would you select a *Center on page* option if you have already set the margins? *p. 52*

3. List at least five elements you can insert in a header or footer. *p. 54*

4. Why would you want to print gridlines and row and column headings? *p. 55*

# Hands-On Exercises

## 6 Page Setup and Printing

You are ready to complete the OKOS worksheet. Before printing the worksheet for your supervisor, you want to make sure the data will appear professional when printed. You will adjust some page setup options to put the finishing touches on the worksheet.

**Skills covered:** Set Page Orientation • Set Margin Options • Create a Header • View in Print Preview and Print • Adjust Scaling and Set Sheet Options

### STEP 1 ≫ SET PAGE ORIENTATION

Because the worksheet has several columns, you decide to print it in landscape orientation.

a. Open *e01h5Markup_LastFirst* if you closed it at the end of Hands-On Exercise 5 and save it as **e01h6Markup_LastFirst**, changing *h5* to *h6*.

b. Click the **PAGE LAYOUT tab**.

c. Click **Orientation** in the Page Setup group.

d. Select **Landscape** from the list. Save the workbook.

If you print the worksheet, the data will print in landscape orientation.

### STEP 2 ≫ SET MARGIN OPTIONS

You want to set a 1" top margin and center the data between the left and right margins.

a. Click **Margins** in the Page Setup group on the PAGE LAYOUT tab.

As you review the list of options, you notice the list does not contain an option to center the worksheet data horizontally.

b. Select **Custom Margins**.

The Page Setup dialog box opens with the Margins tab options displayed.

c. Click the **Top spin arrow** to display **1**.

You set a 1" top margin. For the OKOS worksheet, you do not need to change the left and right margins because you will center the worksheet data horizontally between the original margins.

d. Click the **Horizontally check box** in the *Center on page* section and click **OK**. Save the workbook.

The worksheet data are centered between the left and right margins.

**TIP  Page Setup Dialog Box**

You can click the Page Setup Dialog Box Launcher in the Page Setup group to quickly display the Page Setup dialog box. From there, you can click the Margins tab and set the desired margins.

# STEP 3 ›› CREATE A HEADER

To document the worksheet, you want to include your name, the current date, and the worksheet tab name in a header. Refer to Figure 1.49 as you complete Step 3.

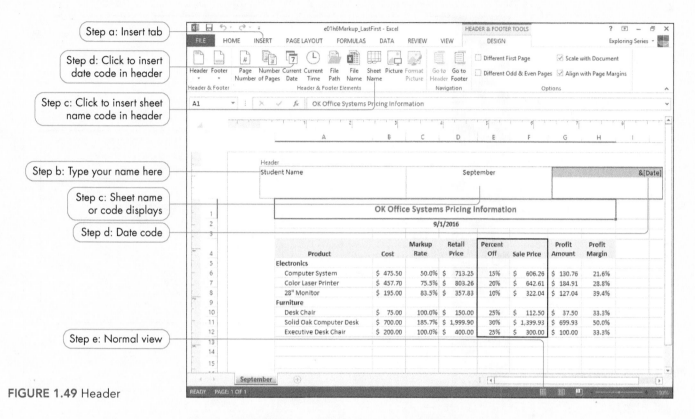

**FIGURE 1.49** Header

a. Click the **INSERT tab** and click **Header & Footer** in the Text group.

Excel displays the DESIGN tab and the worksheet displays in Page Layout view, which displays the header area, margin space, and ruler. The insertion point blinks inside the center section of the header.

b. Click in the left section of the header and type your name.

c. Click in the center section of the header and click **Sheet Name** in the Header & Footer Elements group on the DESIGN tab.

Excel inserts the code &[Tab]. This code displays the name of the worksheet. If you change the worksheet tab name, the header will reflect the new sheet name.

d. Click in the right section of the header and click **Current Date** in the Header & Footer Elements group on the DESIGN tab.

Excel inserts the code &[Date]. This code displays the current date based on the computer clock when you print the worksheet. If you want a specific date to appear regardless of the date you open or print the worksheet, you would have to type that date manually. When you click in a different header section, the codes, such as &[Tab], display the actual tab name instead of the code.

e. Click in any cell in the worksheet, click **Normal** on the status bar, and then save the workbook.

Normal view displays the worksheet, but does not display the header or margins.

## STEP 4 ≫ VIEW IN PRINT PREVIEW AND PRINT

Before printing the worksheet, you should preview it. Doing so helps you detect margin problems and other issues, such as a single row or column of data flowing onto a new page. Refer to Figure 1.50 as you complete Step 4.

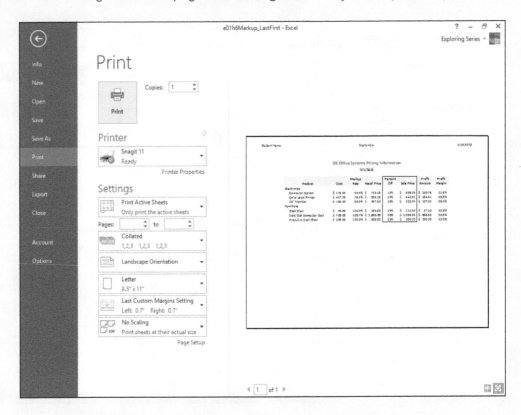

**FIGURE 1.50** Worksheet in Print Preview

a. Click the **FILE tab** and click **Print**.

   The Microsoft Office Backstage view displays print options and a preview of the worksheet.

b. Verify the Printer box displays the printer that you want to use to print your worksheet.

c. Click **Print** to print the worksheet and save the workbook.

   Check your printed worksheet to make sure the data are formatted correctly. After you click Print, the HOME tab displays. If you decide not to print at this time, click the **Back arrow** to display the Ribbon again.

## STEP 5 ≫ ADJUST SCALING AND SET SHEET OPTIONS

You want to print a copy of the worksheet formulas to check the logic of the formulas. You need to display the formulas, select options to print gridlines and headings, and then decrease the scaling so that the data print on one page. Refer to Figure 1.51 as you complete Step 5.

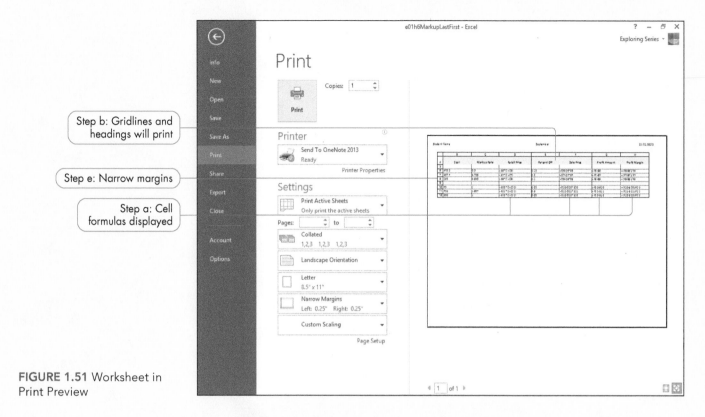

Step b: Gridlines and headings will print

Step e: Narrow margins

Step a: Cell formulas displayed

**FIGURE 1.51** Worksheet in Print Preview

a. Press **Ctrl+`** to display cell formulas.

b. Click the **PAGE LAYOUT tab**. Click the **Print Gridlines check box** in the Sheet Options group and click the **Print Headings check box** in the Sheet Options group.

Because you want to print cell formulas, it is helpful to display the gridlines and row and column headings on that printout.

c. Click the **FILE tab** and click **Print**.

The bottom of the Print Preview displays 1 of 2, indicating the worksheet no longer prints on one page.

d. Click **Next Page** (the right triangle at the bottom of the Microsoft Office Backstage view) to view the contents of the second page and click the **Back arrow** to display the Ribbon again.

e. Click **Margins** in the Page Setup group and select **Narrow**.

f. Select the **range B4:H12**, click **Print Area** in the Page Setup group, and then select **Set Print Area**.

g. Click the **Scale spin arrow** in the *Scale to Fit* group on the PAGE LAYOUT tab until it displays **90%**.

If you want to verify that the worksheet will print on one page, display it in print preview.

h. Save and close the workbook and submit based on your instructor's directions.

Check your printed worksheet to make sure the data are formatted correctly.

# Formulas and Functions

## CHAPTER 2

## Performing Quantitative Analysis

## OBJECTIVES AFTER YOU READ THIS CHAPTER, YOU WILL BE ABLE TO:

1. Use relative, absolute, and mixed cell references in formulas p. 62
2. Correct circular references p. 64
3. Insert a function p. 70
4. Insert basic math and statistics functions p. 72
5. Use date functions p. 77

6. Determine results with the IF function p. 85
7. Use lookup functions p. 88
8. Calculate payments with the PMT function p. 91
9. Create and maintain range names p. 96
10. Use range names in formulas p. 98

## CASE STUDY | Townsend Mortgage Company

You are an assistant to Erica Matheson, a mortgage broker at the Townsend Mortgage Company. Erica spends her days reviewing mortgage rates and trends, meeting with clients, and preparing paperwork. She relies on your expertise in using Excel to help analyze mortgage data.

Today, Erica provided you with sample mortgage data: loan number, house cost, down payment, mortgage rate, and the length of the loan in years. She asked you to perform some basic calculations so that she can check the output provided by her system to verify if it is calculating results correctly. She needs you to calculate the amount financed, the periodic interest rate, the total number of payment periods, the percent of the house cost that is financed, and the payoff year for each loan. In addition, you will calculate totals, averages, and other basic statistics.

Furthermore, you need to complete another worksheet that uses functions to look up interest rates from another table, calculate the monthly payments, and determine how much (if any) the borrower will have to pay for private mortgage insurance (PMI).

# Formula Basics

When you increase your understanding of formulas, you can build robust workbooks that perform a variety of calculations for quantitative analysis. Your ability to build sophisticated workbooks and to interpret the results increases your value to any organization. By now, you should be able to build simple formulas using cell references and mathematical operators and using the order of precedence to control the sequence of calculations in formulas.

In this section, you will create formulas in which cell addresses change or remain fixed when you copy them. Finally, you will learn how to identify and prevent circular references in formulas.

## Using Relative, Absolute, and Mixed Cell References in Formulas

When you copy a formula, Excel either adjusts or preserves the cell references in the copied formulas based on how the cell references appear in the original formula. Excel uses three different ways to reference a cell in a formula: relative, absolute, and mixed. When you create a formula that you will copy to other cells, ask yourself the following question:

> Do the cell references need to adjust for the copied formulas, or should the cell references always refer to the same cell location, regardless of where the copied formula is located?

### Use a Relative Cell Reference

**STEP 1 >>** A *relative cell reference* indicates a cell's relative location, such as five rows up and one column to the left, from the cell containing the formula. When you copy a formula containing a relative cell reference, the cell references in the copied formula change relative to the position of the copied formula. Regardless of where you copy the formula, the cell references in the copied formula maintain the same relative distance from the cell containing the copied formula, as the cell references the relative location to the original formula cell.

In Figure 2.1, the formulas in column F contain relative cell references. When you copy the original formula =D2-E2 from cell F2 down to cell F3, the copied formula changes to =D3-E3. Because you copy the formula *down* the column to cell F3, the column letters in the formula stay the same, but the row numbers change to reflect the row to which you copied the formula. Using relative cell addresses to calculate the amount financed ensures that each borrower's down payment is subtracted from his or her respective house cost.

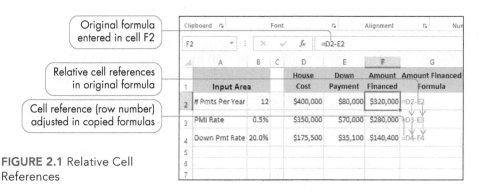

**FIGURE 2.1** Relative Cell References

### Use an Absolute Cell Reference

**STEP 2 >>** An *absolute cell reference* provides a permanent reference to a specific cell. When you copy a formula containing an absolute cell reference, the cell reference in the copied formula does not change, regardless of where you copy the formula. An absolute cell reference appears with a dollar sign before both the column letter and row number, such as $B$4.

In Figure 2.2, each down payment is calculated by multiplying the respective house cost by the down payment rate (20%). Cell E2 contains =D2*$B$4 ($400,000*20.0%) to calculate the first borrower's down payment ($80,000). When you copy the formula down to the next row, the copied formula in cell E3 is =D3*$B$4. The relative cell reference D2 changes to D3 (for the next house cost) and the absolute cell reference $B$4 remains the same to refer to the 20.0% down payment rate. This formula ensures that the cell reference to the house cost changes for each row but that the house cost is always multiplied by the rate in cell B4.

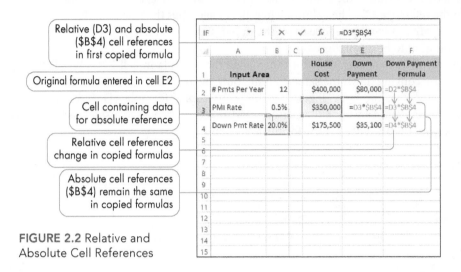

**FIGURE 2.2** Relative and Absolute Cell References

---

**TIP  Input Area and Absolute Cell References**

Figure 2.2 illustrates an input area, a range in a worksheet that contains values that you can change. You build formulas using absolute references to the cells in the input area. By using cell references from an input area, you can change the value in the input area and the formulas that refer to those cells will update automatically. If an input value changes (e.g., the down payment rate changes from 20% to 25%), enter the new input value in only one cell (e.g., B4), and Excel recalculates the amount of down payment for all the formulas.

---

Figure 2.3 shows what happens if the down payment formula used a relative reference to cell B4. If the original formula in cell E2 is =D2*B4, the copied formula becomes =D3*B5 in cell E3. The relative cell reference to B4 changes to B5 when you copy the formula down. Because cell B5 is empty, the $350,000 house cost in cell D3 is multiplied by 0, giving a $0 down payment, which is not a valid down payment amount.

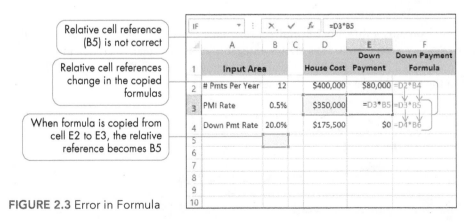

**FIGURE 2.3** Error in Formula

## Use a Mixed Cell Reference

STEP 3 A *mixed cell reference* combines an absolute cell reference with a relative cell reference. When you copy a formula containing a mixed cell reference, either the column letter or the row number that has the absolute reference remains fixed while the other part of the cell reference that is relative changes in the copied formula. $B4 and B$4 are examples of mixed cell references. In the reference $B4, the column B is absolute, and the row number is relative; when you copy the formula, the column letter, B, does not change, but the row number will change. In the reference B$4, the column letter, B, changes, but the row number, 4, does not change. To create a mixed reference, type the dollar sign to the left of the part of the cell reference you want to be absolute.

In the down payment formula, you can change the formula in cell E2 to be =D2*B$4. Because you are copying down the same column, only the row reference 4 must be absolute; the column letter stays the same. Figure 2.4 shows the copied formula =D3*B$4 in cell E3. In situations where you can use either absolute or mixed references, consider using mixed references to shorten the length of the formula.

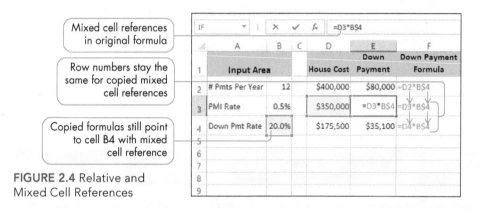

Mixed cell references in original formula

Row numbers stay the same for copied mixed cell references

Copied formulas still point to cell B4 with mixed cell reference

**FIGURE 2.4** Relative and Mixed Cell References

---

### TIP  The F4 Key

The F4 key toggles through relative, absolute, and mixed references. Click a cell reference within a formula on the Formula Bar and press F4 to change it. For example, click in B4 in the formula =D2*B4. Press F4 and the relative cell reference (B4) changes to an absolute cell reference ($B$4). Press F4 again and $B$4 becomes a mixed reference (B$4); press F4 again and it becomes another mixed reference ($B4). Press F4 a fourth time and the cell reference returns to the original relative reference (B4).

---

# Correcting Circular References

If a formula contains a direct or an indirect reference to the cell containing the formula, a *circular reference* exists. Figure 2.5 shows an example of a circular reference in a formula. The formula in cell E2 is =E2*$B$4. Because the formula is in cell E2, using the cell address E2 within the formula creates a circular reference.

Active cell

Formula contains reference to active cell

Error message

**FIGURE 2.5** Circular Reference

Circular references usually cause inaccurate results. Excel displays a warning message when you enter a formula containing a circular reference or when you open an Excel workbook that contains an existing circular reference. Click Help to display the *Find and fix a circular reference* Help topic or click OK to accept the circular reference. Until you resolve a circular reference, the status bar indicates the location of a circular reference, such as CIRCULAR REFERENCES: E2.

---

### TIP Green Triangles

Excel displays a green triangle in the top-left corner of a cell if it detects a potential error in a formula. Click the cell to see the Trace Error button (yellow diamond with exclamation mark). When you click Trace Error, Excel displays information about the potential error and how to correct it. In some cases, Excel may anticipate an inconsistent formula or the omission of adjacent cells in a formula. For example, if a column contains values for the year 2016, the error message indicates that you did not include the year itself. However, the year 2016 is merely a label and should not be included; therefore, you would ignore that error message.

---

*Quick* Concepts ✓

1. What happens when you copy a formula containing a relative cell reference one column to the right? *p. 62*

2. Why would you use an absolute reference in a formula? *p. 63*

3. What is a circular reference? Provide an example. *p. 64*

# Hands-On Exercises

Watch the Video
for this Hands-
On Exercise!

MyITLab®
HOE1 Training

## 1 Formula Basics

Erica prepared a workbook containing data for five mortgages financed with the Townsend Mortgage Company. The data include house cost, down payment, mortgage rate, number of years to pay off the mortgage, and the financing date for each mortgage.

**Skills covered:** Use a Relative Cell Reference in a Formula • Use an Absolute Cell Reference in a Formula • Use a Mixed Cell Reference in a Formula • Correct a Circular Reference

### STEP 1 ≫ USE A RELATIVE CELL REFERENCE IN A FORMULA

You need to calculate the amount financed by each borrower by creating a formula with relative cell references that calculates the difference between the house cost and the down payment. After verifying the results of the amount financed by the first borrower, you will copy the formula down the Amount Financed column to calculate the other borrowers' amounts financed. Refer to Figure 2.6 as you complete Step 1.

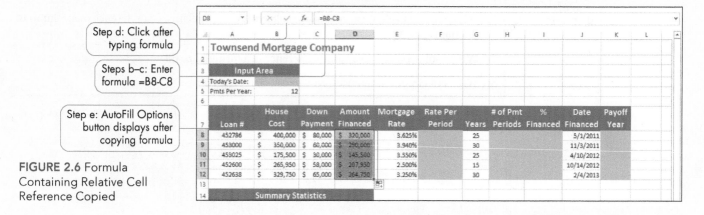

Step d: Click after typing formula

Steps b–c: Enter formula =B8-C8

Step e: AutoFill Options button displays after copying formula

**FIGURE 2.6** Formula Containing Relative Cell Reference Copied

a.   Open *e02h1Loans* and save it as **e02h1Loans_LastFirst**.

> **TROUBLESHOOTING:** If you make any major mistakes in this exercise, you can close the file, open *e02h1Loans* again, and then start this exercise over.

The workbook contains two worksheets: Details (for Hands-On Exercises 1 and 2) and Payment Info (for Hands-On Exercises 3 and 4). You will enter formulas in the shaded cells.

b.   Click **cell D8** in the Details sheet. Type = and click **cell B8**, the cell containing the first borrower's house cost.

c.   Type - and click **cell C8**, the cell containing the down payment by the first borrower.

d.   Click **Enter** (the check mark between the Name Box and Formula Bar) to complete the formula.

The first borrower financed (i.e., borrowed) $320,000, the difference between the cost ($400,000) and the down payment ($80,000).

e.   Double-click the **cell D8 fill handle**.

You copied the formula down the Amount Financed column for each mortgage row.

# TIP | Auto Fill Options

The Auto Fill Options button appears in the bottom-right corner of the copied formulas. If you click it, you can see that the default is Copy Cells. If you want to copy only formatting, click Fill Formatting Only. If you want to copy data only, click Fill Without Formatting.

f. Click **cell D9** and view the formula in the Formula Bar.

The formula in cell D8 is =B8-C8. The formula pasted in cell D9 is =B9-C9. Because the original formula contained relative cell references, when you copy the formula down to the next row, the row numbers for the cell references change. Each result represents the amount financed for that particular borrower.

g. Press ⬇ and look at the cell references in the Formula Bar to see how the references change for each formula you copied. Save the workbook with the new formula you created.

## STEP 2 ≫ USE AN ABSOLUTE CELL REFERENCE IN A FORMULA

Column E contains the annual percentage rate (APR) for each mortgage. Because the borrowers will make monthly payments, you need to calculate the monthly interest rate by dividing the APR by 12 (the number of payments in one year) for each borrower. Refer to Figure 2.7 as you complete Step 2.

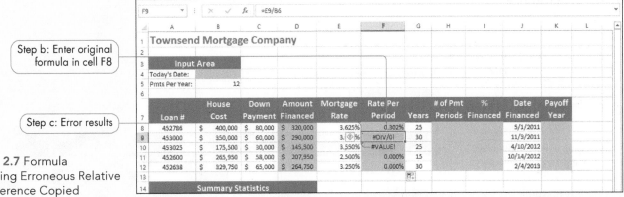

Step b: Enter original formula in cell F8

Step c: Error results

**FIGURE 2.7** Formula Containing Erroneous Relative Cell Reference Copied

a. Click **cell F8**.

You need to create a formula to calculate the monthly interest rate for the first borrower.

b. Type **=E8/B5** and click **Enter** (the checkmark between the Name Box and the Formula Bar).

Typically, you should avoid typing values directly in formulas. Although the number of months in one year is always 12, use a reference to cell B5, where the number of payments per year is placed in the input area, so that the company can change the payment period to bimonthly (24 payments per year) or quarterly (four payments per year) without adjusting the formula.

c. Double-click the **cell F8 fill handle**, click **cell F9**, and then view the results (see Figure 2.7).

An error icon displays to the left of cell F9, cell F9 displays #DIV/0!, and cell F10 displays #VALUE!. The original formula was =E8/B5. Because you copied the formula =E8/B5 down the column, the first copied formula is =E9/B6, and the second copied formula is =E10/B7. Although you want the mortgage rate cell reference (E8) to change (E9, E10, etc.) from row to row, you do not want the divisor (cell B5) to change. You need all formulas to divide by the value stored in cell B5, so you will edit the formula to make B5 an absolute reference.

You can position the mouse pointer over the error icon to see a tip indicating what is wrong, such as *The formula or function used is dividing by zero or empty cells.* You can click the icon to see a menu of options to learn more about the error and how to correct it.

d. Click **Undo** in the Quick Access Toolbar to undo the Auto Fill process. Click within or to the right of **B5** in the Formula Bar.

e. Press **F4** and click **Enter** (the checkmark between the Name Box and the Formula Bar).

Excel changes the cell reference from B5 to $B$5, making it an absolute cell reference.

f. Copy the formula down the Rate Per Period column. Click **cell F9** and view the formula in the Formula Bar. Save the workbook.

The formula in cell F9 is =E9/$B$5. The reference to E9 is relative and the reference to B5 is absolute.

## STEP 3 ≫ USE A MIXED CELL REFERENCE IN A FORMULA

The next formula you create will calculate the total number of payment periods for each loan. Refer to Figure 2.8 as you complete Step 3.

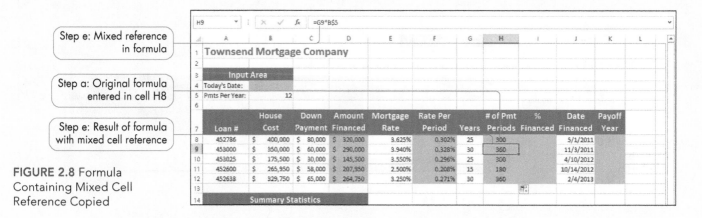

Step e: Mixed reference in formula

Step a: Original formula entered in cell H8

Step e: Result of formula with mixed cell reference

**FIGURE 2.8** Formula Containing Mixed Cell Reference Copied

a. Click **cell H8** and type **=G8*B5**.

You need to multiply the number of years (25) by the number of payment periods in one year (12) using cell references.

b. Press **F4** to make the B5 cell reference absolute and click **Enter** (the checkmark between the Name Box and Formula Bar).

You want B5 to be absolute so that the cell reference remains B5 when you copy the formula. The product of 25 years and 12 months is 300 months or payment periods.

c. Copy the formula down the # of Pmt Periods column.

The first copied formula is =G9*$B$5, and the result is 360. You want to see what happens if you change the absolute reference to a mixed reference and copy the formula again. Because you are copying down a column, the column letter B can be relative because it will not change either way, but the row number 5 must be absolute.

d. Click **Undo** on the Quick Access Toolbar to undo the copied formulas.

Cell H8 is the active cell.

e. Click within the **$B$5 cell reference** in the Formula Bar. Press **F4** to change the cell reference to a mixed cell reference: B$5. Press **Ctrl+Enter** and copy the formula down the # of Pmt Periods column. Click **cell H9**. Save the workbook.

The first copied formula is =G9*B$5 and the result is still 360. In this situation, using either an absolute reference or a mixed reference provides the same results.

## STEP 4 ≫ CORRECT A CIRCULAR REFERENCE

Erica wants to know what percentage of the house cost each borrower will finance. As you create the formula, you enter a circular reference. After studying the results, you correct the circular error and plan future formulas that avoid this problem. Refer to Figure 2.9 as you complete Step 4.

Step d: Corrected formula in cell I8

Step d: Results of copied formulas

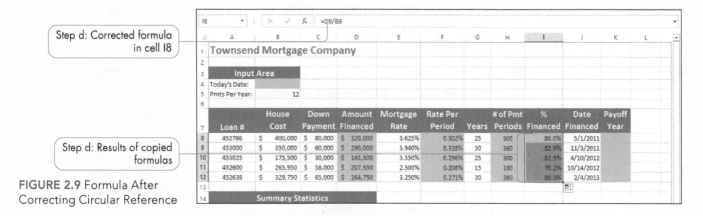

**FIGURE 2.9** Formula After Correcting Circular Reference

a. Click **cell I8**, type **=I8/B8**, and then press **Enter**.

The Circular Reference Warning message box displays.

> **TROUBLESHOOTING:** If the message box does not display, close the workbook and exit Excel. Start Excel, open the workbook again, and then repeat Step 4a. Sometimes the message box appears only once while Excel is running. If you had previously experimented with a circular reference during a work session, the message box might not display. However, exiting Excel and opening it again will enable the message box to display.

b. Read the description of the error and click **Help**.

The Excel Help window opens, displaying information about circular references.

c. Read the circular reference information, close the Excel Help window, and then click **OK** in the message box.

The left side of the status bar displays *CIRCULAR REFERENCES: I8*.

Because the formula is stored in cell I8, the formula cannot refer to the cell itself. You need to divide the value in the Amount Financed column by the value in the House Cost column.

d. Click **cell I8** and edit the formula to be **=D8/B8**. Copy the formula down the % Financed column.

The first borrower financed 80% of the cost of the house: $320,000 financed divided by $400,000 cost.

e. Save the workbook. Keep the workbook open if you plan to continue with the next Hands-On Exercise. If not, close the workbook and exit Excel.

# Function Basics

An Excel *function* is a predefined computation that simplifies creating a formula that performs a complex calculation. Excel contains more than 400 functions, which are organized into 14 categories. Table 2.1 lists and describes the primary function categories used in this chapter.

**TABLE 2.1  Function Categories and Descriptions**

| Category | Description |
| --- | --- |
| Date & Time | Provides methods for manipulating date and time values. |
| Financial | Performs financial calculations, such as payments, rates, present value, and future value. |
| Logical | Performs logical tests and returns the value of the tests.  Includes logical operators for combined tests, such as AND, OR, and NOT. |
| Lookup & Reference | Looks up values, creates links to cells, or provides references to cells in a worksheet. |
| Math & Trig | Performs standard math and trigonometry calculations. |
| Statistical | Performs common statistical calculations, such as averages and standard deviations. |

When using functions, you must adhere to correct *syntax*, the rules that dictate the structure and components required to perform the necessary calculations. Start a function with an equal sign, followed by the function name, and then its arguments in parentheses.

- The function name describes the purpose of the function. For example, the function name SUM indicates that the function sums, or adds, values.

- A function's *arguments* specify the inputs—such as cells, values, or arithmetic expressions—that are required to complete the operation. In some cases, a function requires multiple arguments separated by commas.

In this section, you will learn how to insert common functions using the keyboard and the Insert Function and Function Arguments dialog boxes.

## Inserting a Function

To insert a function by typing, first type an equal sign, and then begin typing the function name. *Formula AutoComplete* displays a list of functions and defined names that match letters as you type a formula. For example, if you type =SU, Formula AutoComplete displays a list of functions and names that start with *SU* (see Figure 2.10). You can double-click the function name from the list or continue typing the function name. You can even scroll through the list to see the ScreenTip describing the function.

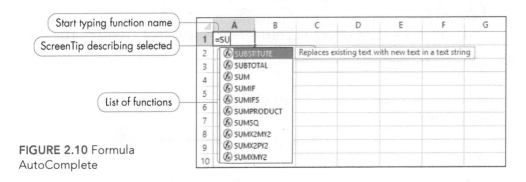

**FIGURE 2.10** Formula AutoComplete

After you type the function name and opening parenthesis, Excel displays the ***function ScreenTip***, a small pop-up description that displays the function's arguments. The argument you are currently entering is bold in the function ScreenTip (see Figure 2.11). Square brackets indicate optional arguments. For example, the SUM function requires the number1 argument, but the number2 argument is optional. Click the argument name in the function ScreenTip to select the actual argument in the formula you are creating if you want to make changes to the argument.

**FIGURE 2.11** Function ScreenTip

| | A | B | C | D | E | F | G |
|---|---|---|---|---|---|---|---|
| 1 | =SUM( | | | | | | |
| 2 | | SUM(**number1**, [number2], ...) | | | | | |
| 3 | | | | | | | |

You can also use the Insert Function dialog box to search for a function, select a function category, and select a function from the list (see Figure 2.12). The dialog box is helpful if you want to browse a list of functions, especially if you are not sure of the function you need and want to see descriptions.

To display the Insert Function dialog box, click Insert Function $f_x$ (located between the Name Box and the Formula Bar) or click Insert Function in the Function Library group on the Formulas tab. From within the dialog box, select a function category, such as Most Recently Used, and select a function to display the syntax and a brief description of that function. Click *Help on this function* to display details about the selected function.

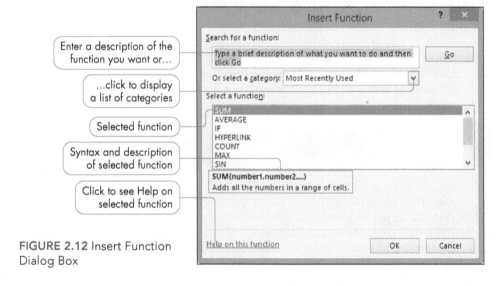

Enter a description of the function you want or...

...click to display a list of categories

Selected function

Syntax and description of selected function

Click to see Help on selected function

**FIGURE 2.12** Insert Function Dialog Box

When you find the function you want, click OK. The Function Arguments dialog box opens so that you can enter the arguments for that specific function (see Figure 2.13). The following list explains the arguments in the Function Arguments dialog box:

- Argument names in **bold** (such as Number1 in the SUM function) are required.

- Argument names that are not bold (such as Number2 in the SUM function) are optional. The function can operate without the optional argument, which is used when you need additional specifications to calculate a result.

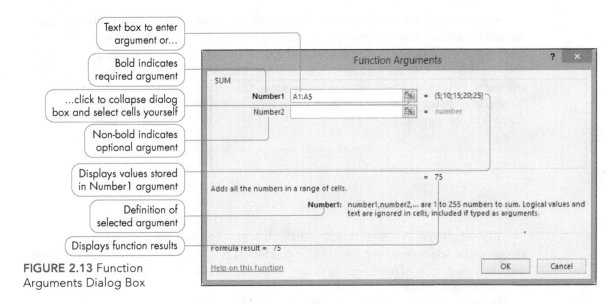

Text box to enter argument or...

Bold indicates required argument

...click to collapse dialog box and select cells yourself

Non-bold indicates optional argument

Displays values stored in Number1 argument

Definition of selected argument

Displays function results

**FIGURE 2.13** Function Arguments Dialog Box

Type the cell references in the argument boxes or click a collapse button to the right side of an argument box to collapse the dialog box and select the cell or range of cells in the worksheet to designate as that argument. If you click the collapse button to select a range, you need to click the expand button to expand the dialog box again. The value, or results, of a formula contained in the argument cell displays on the right side of the argument box (such as 5; 10; 15; 20; 25—the values stored in the range A1:A5 used for the Number1 argument). If the argument is not valid, Excel displays an error description on the right side of the argument box.

The bottom of the Function Arguments dialog box displays a description of the function and a description of the argument containing the insertion point. As you enter arguments, the bottom of the dialog box also displays the results of the function, such as 75.

**TIP   #Name?**

If you enter a function and #NAME? displays in the cell, you might have mistyped the function name. To avoid this problem, select the function name from the Formula AutoComplete list as you type the function name, or use the Insert Function dialog box. You can type a function name in lowercase letters. If you type the name correctly, Excel converts the name to all capital letters when you press Enter, indicating that you spelled the function name correctly.

# Inserting Basic Math and Statistics Functions

Excel includes commonly used math and statistical functions that you can use for a variety of calculations. For example, you can insert functions to calculate the total amount you spend on dining out in a month, the average amount you spend per month downloading music from iTunes®, your highest electric bill, and your lowest time to run a mile this week.

## Calculate a Total with the SUM Function

STEP 1 »   The **SUM function** totals values in two or more cells and displays the result in the cell containing the function. This function is more efficient to create when you need to add the values contained in three or more cells. For example, to add the contents of cells A2 through A14, you could enter =A2+A3+A4+A5+A6+A7+A8+A9+A10+A11+A12+A13+A14, which is time-consuming and increases the probability of entering an inaccurate cell reference, such as entering a cell reference twice or accidentally leaving out a cell reference. Instead, you should use the SUM function, =SUM(A2:A14).

=SUM(number 1, [number 2],...)

## TIP  Function Syntax

In this book, the function syntax lines are highlighted. Brackets [ ] indicate optional arguments; however, do not actually type the brackets when you enter the argument.

The SUM function contains one required argument (Number1) that represents a range of cells to add. The range, such as A2:A14, specifies the first and last cells containing values to SUM. Excel will sum all cells within that range. The Number2 optional argument is used when you want to sum values stored in nonadjacent cells or ranges, such as =SUM(A2:A14,F2:F14). The ellipsis in the function syntax indicates you can add as many additional ranges as desired, separated by commas.

## TIP  Avoiding Functions for Basic Formulas

Do not use a function for a basic mathematical expression. For example, although =SUM(B4/C4) produces the same result as =B4/C4, the SUM function is not needed to perform the basic arithmetic division. Furthermore, someone taking a quick look at that formula might assume it performs addition instead of division. Use the most appropriate, clear-cut formula, =B4/C4.

To insert the SUM function (for example, to sum the values in the range A2:A14), do one of the following:

- Type =SUM(A2:A14) and press Enter.
- Type =SUM(and drag to select the range A2:A14 with the mouse. Type the ending #) and press Enter.
- Click in cell A15, click Sum in the Editing group on the HOME tab, press Enter to select the suggested range or type (or drag to select) A2:A14, and then press Enter.
- Click in cell A15, click Sum in the Function Library group on the FORMULAS tab, press Enter to select the suggested range or type A2:A14, and then press Enter.

Figure 2.14 shows the result of using the SUM function in cell D2 to total scores (898).

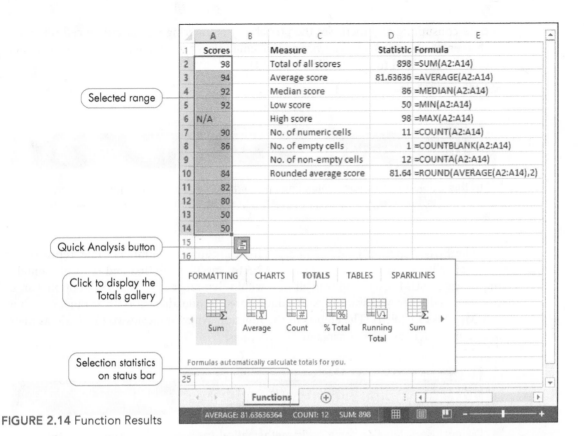

Selected range

Quick Analysis button

Click to display the Totals gallery

Selection statistics on status bar

| | A | B | C | D | E |
|---|---|---|---|---|---|
| 1 | Scores | | Measure | Statistic | Formula |
| 2 | 98 | | Total of all scores | 898 | =SUM(A2:A14) |
| 3 | 94 | | Average score | 81.63636 | =AVERAGE(A2:A14) |
| 4 | 92 | | Median score | 86 | =MEDIAN(A2:A14) |
| 5 | 92 | | Low score | 50 | =MIN(A2:A14) |
| 6 | N/A | | High score | 98 | =MAX(A2:A14) |
| 7 | 90 | | No. of numeric cells | 11 | =COUNT(A2:A14) |
| 8 | 86 | | No. of empty cells | 1 | =COUNTBLANK(A2:A14) |
| 9 | | | No. of non-empty cells | 12 | =COUNTA(A2:A14) |
| 10 | 84 | | Rounded average score | 81.64 | =ROUND(AVERAGE(A2:A14),2) |
| 11 | 82 | | | | |
| 12 | 80 | | | | |
| 13 | 50 | | | | |
| 14 | 50 | | | | |
| 15 | | | | | |
| 16 | | | | | |

FORMATTING    CHARTS    **TOTALS**    TABLES    SPARKLINES

Sum    Average    Count    % Total    Running Total    Sum

Formulas automatically calculate totals for you.

AVERAGE: 81.63636364    COUNT: 12    SUM: 898

**FIGURE 2.14** Function Results

---

**TIP** **Sum Arrow**

If you click Sum, Excel inserts the SUM function. However, if you click the Sum arrow in the Editing group on the Home tab or in the Function Library group on the Formulas tab, Excel displays a list of basic functions to select: Sum, Average, Count Numbers, Max, and Min. If you want to insert another function, select More Functions from the list.

## Find Central Tendency with AVERAGE and MEDIAN

STEP 2 >> People often describe data based on central tendency, which means that values tend to cluster around a central value. Excel provides two functions to calculate central tendency: AVERAGE and MEDIAN. The **AVERAGE function** calculates the arithmetic mean, or average, for the values in a range of cells. You can use this function to calculate the class average on a biology test or the average number of points scored per game by a basketball player. In Figure 2.14, =AVERAGE(A2:A14) in cell D3 returns 81.63636 as the average test score. The AVERAGE function ignores empty cells and cells containing N/A or text.

=AVERAGE(number 1,[number2],...)

STEP 3 >> The **MEDIAN function** finds the midpoint value, which is the value that one half of the data set is above or below. The median is particularly useful because extreme values often influence arithmetic mean calculated by the AVERAGE function. In Figure 2.14, the two extreme test scores of 50 distort the average. The rest of the test scores range from 80 to 98. Cell D4 contains =MEDIAN(A2:A14). The median for test scores is 86, which indicates that half the test scores are above 86 and half the test scores are below 86. This statistic is more reflective of the data set than the average is. The MEDIAN function ignores empty cells and cells containing N/A or text.

=MEDIAN(number 1,[number 2],...)

## Identify Low and High Values with MIN and MAX

STEP 4 >>

The *MIN function* analyzes an argument list to determine the lowest value, such as the lowest score on a test. Manually inspecting a range of values to identify the lowest value is inefficient, especially in large spreadsheets. If you change values in the range, the MIN function will identify the new lowest value and display it in the cell containing the MIN function. In Figure 2.14, =MIN(A2:A14) in cell D5 identifies that 50 is the lowest test score.

=MIN(number 1,[number 2],...)

The *MAX function* analyzes an argument list to determine the highest value, such as the highest score on a test. Like the MIN function, when the values in the range change, the MAX function will display the new highest value within the range of cells. In Figure 2.14, =MAX(A2:A14) in cell D6 identifies 98 as the highest test score.

=MAX(number 1,[number 2],...)

 **TIP  Nonadjacent Ranges**

You can use multiple ranges as arguments, such as finding the largest number within two nonadjacent (nonconsecutive) ranges. For example, you can find the highest test score where some scores are stored in cells A2:A14 and others are stored in cells K2:K14. Separate each range with a comma in the argument list, so that the formula is =MAX(A2:A14,K2:K14).

## Identify the Total Number with COUNT Functions

Excel provides three basic count functions—COUNT, COUNTBLANK and COUNTA—to count the cells in a range that meet a particular criterion. The *COUNT function* tallies the number of cells in a range that contain values you can use in calculations, such as numerical and date data, but excludes blank cells or text entries from the tally. In Figure 2.14, the selected range spans 13 cells; however, =COUNT(A2:A14) in cell D7 returns 11, the number of cells that contain numerical data. It does not count the cell containing the text *N/A* or the blank cell.

The *COUNTBLANK function* tallies the number of cells in a range that are blank. In Figure 2.14, =COUNTBLANK(A2:A14) in cell D8 identifies that one cell in the range A2:A14 is blank. The *COUNTA function* tallies the number of cells in a range that are not blank, that is, cells that contain data, whether a value, text, or a formula. In Figure 2.14, =COUNTA(A2:A14) in cell D9 returns 12, indicating the range A2:A14 contains 12 cells that contain some form of data. It does not count the blank cell.

=COUNT(number 1,[number 2],...)
=COUNTBLANK(number 1,[number 2],...)
=COUNTA(number 1,[number 2],...)

 **TIP  Status Bar Statistics: Average, Count, and Sum**

When you select a range of cells containing values, by default Excel displays the average, count, and sum of those values on the status bar (see Figure 2.14). You can customize the status bar to show other selection statistics, such as the minimum and maximum values for a selected range. To display or hide particular selection statistics, right-click the status bar and select the statistic.

## Perform Calculations with Quick Analysis Tools

Excel 2013 contains a new feature called *Quick Analysis*, which is a set of analytical tools you can use to apply formatting, create charts or tables, and insert basic functions. When you select a range of data, the Quick Analysis button displays in the bottom-right corner of the selected range. Click the Quick Analysis button to display the Quick Analysis gallery and select the analytical tool to meet your needs.

Figure 2.14 shows the TOTALS options so that you can sum, average, or count the values in the selected range. Select % Total to display the percentage of the grand total of two or more columns. Select Running Total to provide a cumulative total at the bottom of multiple columns.

## Use Other Math and Statistical Functions

In addition to the functions you have learned in this chapter, Excel provides more than 100 other math and statistical functions. Table 2.2 lists and describes some of these functions that you might find helpful in your business, education, and general statistics courses.

TABLE 2.2   Math and Statistical Functions

| Function Syntax | Description |
|---|---|
| =ABS(number) | Displays the absolute (i.e., positive) value of a number. |
| =FREQUENCY(data_array,bins_array) | Counts how often values appear in a given range. |
| =INT(number) | Rounds a value number down to the nearest whole number. |
| =MODE.SNGL(number1,[number2],…) | Displays the most frequently occurring value in a list. |
| =RANK.AVG(number,ref,[order]) | Identifies a value's rank within a list of values; returns an average rank for identical values. |
| =RANK.EQ(number,ref,[order]) | Identifies a value's rank within a list of values; the top rank is identified for all identical values. |
| =ROUND(number,num_digits) | Rounds a value to a specific number of digits. Rounds numbers of 5 and greater up and those less than 5 down. |

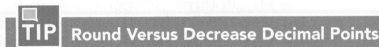

**TIP   Round Versus Decrease Decimal Points**

When you click Decrease Decimal in the Number group to display fewer or no digits after a decimal point, Excel still stores the original value's decimal places so that those digits can be used in calculations. The ROUND function changes the stored value to its rounded state.

## Nest Functions as Arguments

A *nested function* occurs when one function is embedded as an argument within another function. Each function has its own set of arguments that must be included. For example, cell D10 in Figure 2.14 contains =ROUND(AVERAGE(A2:A14),2). The ROUND function requires two arguments: number and num_digits.

The AVERAGE function is nested in the *number* argument of the ROUND function. AVERAGE(A2:A14) returns 81.63636. That value is then rounded to two decimal places, indicated by 2 in the *num_digits* argument. The result is 81.64. If you change the second argument from 2 to 0, such as =ROUND(AVERAGE(A2:A14),0), the result would be 82.

# Using Date Functions

Because Excel treats dates as serial numbers, you can perform calculations using dates. For example, assume today is January 1, 2016, and you graduate on May 6, 2016. To determine how many days until graduation, subtract today's date from the graduation date. Excel uses the serial numbers for these dates (42370 and 42494) to calculate the difference of 126 days.

## Insert the TODAY Function

The **TODAY function** displays the current date, such as 6/14/2016, in a cell. Excel updates the function results when you open or print the workbook. The TODAY() function does not require arguments, but you must include the parentheses. If you omit the parentheses, Excel displays #NAME? in the cell with a green triangle in the top-left corner of the cell. When you click the cell, an error icon appears that you can click for more information.

=TODAY()

## Insert the NOW Function

The **NOW function** uses the computer's clock to display the date and military time, such as 6/14/2016 15:30, that you last opened the workbook. (Military time expresses time on a 24-hour period where 1:00 is 1 a.m. and 13:00 is 1 p.m.) The date and time will change every time the workbook is opened. Like the TODAY function, the NOW function does not require arguments, but you must include the parentheses. Omitting the parentheses creates a #NAME? error.

=NOW()

> **TIP** **Update the Date and Time**
>
> Both the TODAY and NOW functions display the date/time the workbook was last opened or last calculated. These functions do not continuously update the date and time while the workbook is open. To update the date and time, press F9 or click the Formulas tab and click *Calculate now* in the Calculation group.

## Use Other Date & Time Functions

Excel contains a variety of other date functions. You can use these functions to calculate when employees are eligible for certain benefits, what the date is six months from now, or what day of the week a particular date falls on. Table 2.3 describes and Figure 2.15 shows examples of some date functions.

## TABLE 2.3  Date Functions

| Function Syntax | Description |
|---|---|
| =DATE(year,month,day) | Returns the serial number for a date. |
| =DAY(serial_number) | Displays the day (1–31) within a given month for a date or its serial number. |
| =EDATE(start_date,months) | Displays the serial number using the General format of a date a specified number of months in the future (using a positive value) or past (using a negative value). Displays the actual future or past date in Short Date format. |
| =EOMONTH(start_date,months) | Identifies the serial number of the last day of a month using General format or the exact last day of a month using Short Date format for a specified number of months from a date's serial number. |
| =MONTH(serial_number) | Returns the month (1–12) for a serial number, where 1 is January and 12 is December. |
| =WEEKDAY(serial_number, [return_type]) | Identifies the weekday (1–7) for a serial number, where 1 is Sunday and 7 is Saturday (the default with no second argument); can specify a second argument for different numbers assigned to weekdays (see Help). |
| =YEAR(serial_number) | Identifies the year for a serial number. |
| =YEARFRAC(start_date,end_date,[basis]) | Calculates the fraction of a year between two dates based on the number of whole days. |

FIGURE 2.15 Date Function Examples

| | A | B | C | D | E | F |
|---|---|---|---|---|---|---|
| 1 | Inputs: | 7 | 11 | 2016 | 10/17/2016 | |
| 2 | | | | | | |
| 3 | Description | | | Format | Result | Formula |
| 4 | Today's Date | | | Short Date | 10/17/2016 | =TODAY() |
| 5 | Today's Date | | | Other Date | October 17, 2016 | =TODAY() |
| 6 | Today's Date and Military Time | | | Date/Time | 10/17/2016 17:15 | =NOW() |
| 7 | Serial # of Date | | | General | 42562 | =DATE(D1,B1,C1) |
| 8 | Serial # of Date | | | Short Date | 7/11/2016 | =DATE(D1,B1,C1) |
| 9 | Day within the Month | | | General | 17 | =DAY(E4) or =DAY(TODAY()) |
| 10 | Serial # of Date 3 Months in Future | | | General | 42752 | =EDATE(E4,3) |
| 11 | Date 3 Months in Future | | | Short Date | 1/17/2017 | =EDATE(E4,3) |
| 12 | Date 3 Years in Future | | | Short Date | 10/17/2019 | =EDATE(E4,3*12) |
| 13 | Date 2 Months Ago | | | Short Date | 8/17/2016 | =EDATE(E4,-2) |
| 14 | Serial # of Date 6 Months in Future | | | General | 42746 | =EDATE(DATE(D1,B1,C1),6) |
| 15 | Serial # of Last Day in 6 Months | | | General | 42855 | =EOMONTH(E4,6) or =EOMONTH(TODAY()) |
| 16 | Last Day of 6 Months in Future | | | Short Date | 4/30/2017 | =EOMONTH(E4,6) or =EOMONTH(TODAY()) |
| 17 | Month Number (where 6=June) | | | General | 10 | =MONTH(E5) or =MONTH(TODAY()) |
| 18 | Week day (1=Sunday; 7=Saturday) | | | General | 2 | =WEEKDAY(E4) |
| 19 | Week day (1=Monday; 7=Sunday) | | | General | 1 | =WEEKDAY(E4,2) |
| 20 | Year for a Serial Date | | | General | 2016 | =YEAR(E4) or =YEAR(TODAY()) |
| 21 | Fraction of Year 7/11/2016-10/17/2016 | | | General | 0.266666667 | =YEARFRAC(DATE(D1,B1,C1),E1) |

You can nest a date function inside another date function, such as =DAY(TODAY()). This nested function TODAY() first identifies today's date, and from that date, the DAY function identifies the day of the month. In Figure 2.15, cell E21 contains =YEARFRAC(DATE(D1,B1,C1),E1). The DATE function is nested to combine values in three cells (D1, B1, and C1) to build a date (7/11/2016). Excel finds the number of days between that date and 10/17/2016, the date stored in cell E1. From there, the YEARFRAC function calculates the fraction of a year (26.667%) between those two dates. Had 7/11/2016 been stored as a date in a single cell, the formula would simplify to something like =YEARFRAC(D1,E1).

## TIP | Date Functions and Arithmetic Operations

You can combine date functions with arithmetic operations. For example, you sign a lease on June 14, 2016, for three years. The starting date is stored in cell E4. What date does your lease expire? Enter =EDATE(E4,3*12)-1 to calculate the expiration date. The first argument, E4, is the cell containing the start date, and the second argument, 3*12, equals three years containing 12 months each, or 36 months. (In an actual worksheet, you should store the value 36 in a cell instead of typing numbers in the argument.) That result is June 14, 2019, but the lease actually expires the day before. So you must then subtract 1 from the function result to calculate the June 13, 2019, date.

*Quick* Concepts ✓

1. What visual features help guide you through typing a function directly in a cell? **pp. 70–71**

2. What type of data do you enter in a Function Arguments dialog box, and what are four things the dialog box tells you? **pp. 71–72**

3. What is the difference between the AVERAGE and MEDIAN functions? **p. 74**

4. What is a nested function, and why would you create one? **p. 76**

5. Provide three examples of using date functions to determine something specific. **p. 78**

# Hands-On Exercises

Watch the Video
for this Hands-
On Exercise!

MyITLab®
HOE2 Training

## 2 Function Basics

The Townsend Mortgage Company's worksheet contains an area in which you must enter summary statistics. In addition, you need to include today's date and identify the year in which each mortgage will be paid off.

**Skills covered:** Use the SUM Function • Use the AVERAGE Function • Use the MEDIAN Function • Use the MIN, MAX, and COUNT Functions • Use the TODAY and YEAR Functions

### STEP 1 >> USE THE SUM FUNCTION

The first summary statistic you need to calculate is the total value of the houses bought by the borrowers. You will use the SUM function. Refer to Figure 2.16 as you complete Step 1.

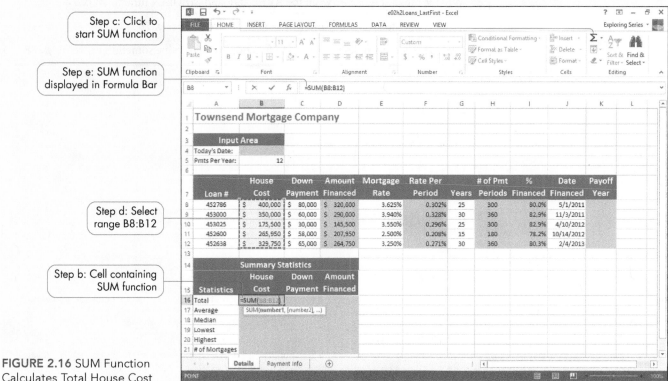

**FIGURE 2.16** SUM Function Calculates Total House Cost

a. Open *e02h1Loans_LastFirst* if you closed it at the end of Hands-On Exercise 1 and save it as **e02h2Loans_LastFirst**, changing *h1* to *h2*.

b. Make sure the Details worksheet is active and click **cell B16**, the cell where you will enter a formula for the total house cost.

c. Click **Sum** in the Editing group on the HOME tab.

> **TROUBLESHOOTING:** Click the main part of the Sum command. If you click the Sum arrow, select Sum.

Excel anticipates the range of cells containing values you want to sum based on where you enter the formula—in this case, A8:D15. This is not the correct range, so you must enter the correct range.

**d.** Select the **range B8:B12**, the cells containing house costs.

As you use the semi-selection process, Excel enters the range in the SUM function.

> **TROUBLESHOOTING:** If you entered the function without changing the arguments, repeat steps b–d or edit the arguments in the Formula Bar by deleting the default range, typing B8:B12 between the parentheses and pressing Enter.

**e.** Click **Enter** (the checkmark between the Name Box and Formula Bar) and save the workbook.

Cell B16 contains the function = SUM(B8:B12), and the result is $1,521,200.

## STEP 2 ≫ USE THE AVERAGE FUNCTION

Before copying the functions to calculate the total down payments and amounts financed, you want to calculate the average house cost bought by the borrowers in your list. Refer to Figure 2.17 as you complete Step 2.

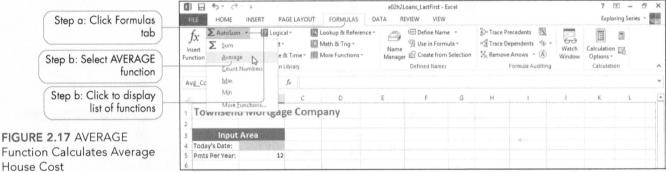

Step a: Click Formulas tab

Step b: Select AVERAGE function

Step b: Click to display list of functions

**FIGURE 2.17** AVERAGE Function Calculates Average House Cost

**a.** Click the **FORMULAS tab** and click **cell B17**, the cell where you will display the average cost of the houses.

**b.** Click the **Sum arrow** in the Function Library group and select **Average**.

Excel selects cell B15, which is the total cost of the houses. You need to change the range.

> **TROUBLESHOOTING:** Sum, like some other commands in Excel, contains two parts: the main command icon and an arrow. Click the main command icon when instructed to click Sum to perform the default action. Click the arrow when instructed to click the Sum arrow for additional options. If you accidentally clicked Sum instead of the arrow, press Esc to cancel the SUM function from being completed and try step b again.

**c.** Select the **range B8:B12**, the cells containing the house costs.

The function is =AVERAGE(B8:B12).

**d.** Press **Enter**, make **cell B18** the active cell, and save the workbook.

The average house cost is $304,240.

You realize that extreme house costs may distort the average. Therefore, you decide to identify the median house cost to compare it to the average house cost. Refer to Figure 2.18 as you complete Step 3.

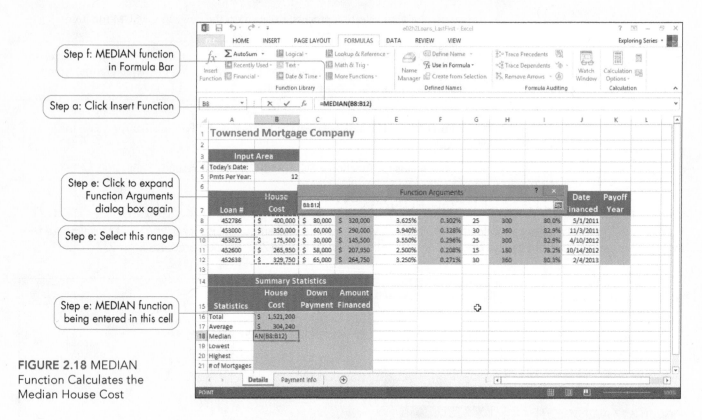

**FIGURE 2.18** MEDIAN Function Calculates the Median House Cost

a. Make sure **cell B18** is the active cell. Click **Insert Function** between the Name Box and the Formula Bar, or in the Function Library group on the FORMULAS tab.

The Insert Function dialog box opens. Use this dialog box to select the MEDIAN function since it is not available on the Ribbon.

b. Type **median** in the **Search for a function box** and click **Go**.

Excel displays a list of functions in the *Select a function* list. The MEDIAN function is selected at the top of the list; the bottom of the dialog box displays the syntax and the description.

c. Read the MEDIAN function's description and click **OK**.

The Function Arguments dialog box opens. It contains one required argument, Number1, representing a range of cells containing values. It has an optional argument, Number2, which you can use if you have nonadjacent ranges that contain values.

d. Click the **collapse button** to the right of the Number1 box.

You collapsed the Function Arguments dialog box so that you can select the range.

e. Select the **range B8:B12** and click the **expand button** in the Function Arguments dialog box.

The Function Arguments dialog box expands, displaying B8:B12 in the Number1 box.

f. Click **OK** to accept the function arguments and close the dialog box. Save the workbook.

Half of the houses purchased cost more than the median, $329,750, and half of the houses cost less than this value. Notice the difference between the median and the average: The average is lower because it is affected by the lowest-priced house, $175,500.

# STEP 4 ❯❯ USE THE MIN, MAX, AND COUNT FUNCTIONS

Erica wants to know the least and most expensive houses so that she can analyze typical customers of the Townsend Mortgage Company. You will use the MIN and MAX functions to obtain these statistics. In addition, you will use the COUNT function to tally the number of mortgages in the sample. Refer to Figure 2.19 as you complete Step 4.

Step f: Formulas copied to these columns

Step g: Value changed in cell B9

Step b: Cell contains MIN function

Step c: Cell contains MAX function

Step d: Cell contains COUNT function

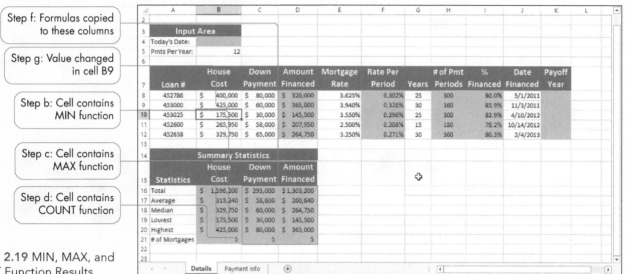

**FIGURE 2.19** MIN, MAX, and COUNT Function Results

**a.** Click **cell B19**, the cell to display the cost of the lowest-costing house.

**b.** Click the **Sum arrow** in the Function Library group, select **Min**, select the **range B8:B12**, and then press **Enter**.

The MIN function identifies that the lowest-costing house is $175,500.

**c.** Click **cell B20**, if necessary. Click the **Sum arrow** in the Function Library group, select **Max**, select the **range B8:B12**, and then press **Enter**.

The MAX function identifies that the highest-costing house is $400,000.

**d.** Click **cell B21**, if necessary. Type **=COUNT(B8:B12)** and press **Enter**.

As you type the letter *C*, Formula AutoComplete suggests functions starting with *C*. As you continue typing, the list of functions narrows. After you type the beginning parenthesis, Excel displays the function ScreenTip, indicating the arguments for the function. The range B8:B12 contains five cells.

**e.** Select the **range B16:B21**.

You want to select the range of original statistics to copy the cells all at one time to the next two columns.

**f.** Drag the fill handle to the right by two columns to copy the functions. Click **cell D21**.

Because you used relative cell references in the functions, the range changes from =COUNT(B8:B12) to =COUNT(D8:D12).

**g.** Change the value in **cell B9** to **425000**. Save the workbook.

The results of several formulas and functions change, including the total, average, and max house costs.

# STEP 5 ≫ USE THE TODAY AND YEAR FUNCTIONS

You have two date functions (TODAY and YEAR) to enter to complete the first worksheet. The TODAY function will display today's date, and you will use the YEAR function in a formula to calculate the payoff year for each mortgage. Refer to Figure 2.20 as you complete Step 5.

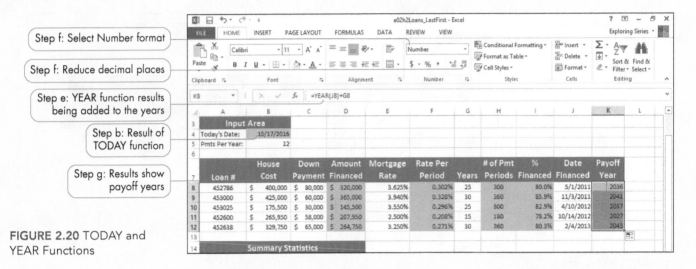

Step f: Select Number format

Step f: Reduce decimal places

Step e: YEAR function results being added to the years

Step b: Result of TODAY function

Step g: Results show payoff years

**FIGURE 2.20** TODAY and YEAR Functions

a.  Click **cell B4**, the cell to contain the current date.

b.  Click **Date & Time** in the Function Library group, select **TODAY** to display the Function Arguments dialog box, and then click **OK** to close the dialog box.

    The Function Arguments dialog box opens, although no arguments are necessary for this function. Excel inserts the current date in Short Date format, such as 1/2/2016, based on the computer system's date.

c.  Click **cell K8**, click **Date & Time** in the Function Library group, scroll through the list, and then select **YEAR**.

    The Function Arguments dialog box opens so that you can enter the argument, a serial number for a date.

d.  Click **cell J8** to enter it in the **Serial_number box**. Click **OK**.

    The function returns 2011, the year the first mortgage was taken out. However, you want the year the mortgage will be paid off. The YEAR function returns the year from a date. You need to add the years to the result of the function to calculate the year that the borrower will pay off the mortgage.

e.  Press **F2** to edit the formula stored in **cell K8**. With the insertion point on the right side of the closing parenthesis, type **+G8** and press **Ctrl+Enter**.

    Pressing Ctrl+Enter is the alternative to clicking Enter by the Formula Bar. It keeps the current cell as the active cell. The results show a date: 7/28/1905. You need to apply the Number format to display the year.

f.  Click the **HOME tab**, click the **Number Format arrow** in the Number group, and then select **Number**. Decrease the number of decimal places to show the value as a whole number.

    You applied the Number format instead of the Comma format because although the Comma format is correct for quantities, such as 2,036 units, it is not appropriate for the year 2036.

g.  Copy the formula down the Payoff Year column.

h.  Save the workbook. Keep the workbook open if you plan to continue with the next Hands-On Exercise. If not, close the workbook and exit Excel.

# Logical, Lookup, and Financial Functions

As you prepare complex spreadsheets using functions, you will frequently use three function categories: logical, lookup and reference, and finance. Logical functions test the logic of a situation and return a particular result. Lookup and reference functions are useful when you need to look up a value in a list to identify the applicable value. Financial functions are useful to anyone who plans to take out a loan or invest money.

In this section, you will learn how to use the logical, lookup, and financial functions.

## Determining Results with the IF Function

STEP 3 »  The most common logical function is the *IF function*, which returns one value when a condition is met or is true and returns another value when the condition is not met or is false. For example, a company gives a $500 bonus to employees who sold *over* $10,000 in merchandise this week, but no bonus to employees who did not sell over $10,000 in merchandise. Figure 2.21 shows a worksheet containing the sales data for three representatives and their bonuses, if any.

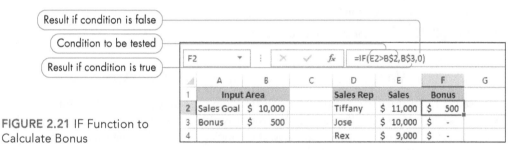

**FIGURE 2.21** IF Function to Calculate Bonus

The IF function has three arguments: (1) a condition that is tested to determine if it is either true or false, (2) the resulting value if the condition is true, and (3) the resulting value if the condition is false.

=IF(logical_test,value_if_true,value_if_false)

You might find it helpful to create two flowcharts to illustrate an IF function. First, construct a flowchart that uses words and numbers to illustrate the condition and results. For example, the left flowchart in Figure 2.22 illustrates the condition to see if sales are greater than $10,000, and the $500 bonus if the condition is true or $0 if the condition is false. Then, create a second flowchart similar to the one on the right side of Figure 2.22 that replaces the words and values with actual cell references. Creating these flowcharts can help you construct the IF function that is used in cell F2 in Figure 2.21.

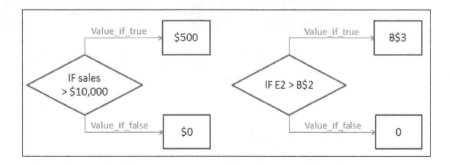

**FIGURE 2.22** Flowcharts Illustrating IF Function

## Design the Logical Test

The first argument for the IF function is the logical test. The **logical test** is a formula that contains either a value or an expression that evaluates to true or false. The logical expression is typically a binary expression, meaning that it requires a comparison between at least two variables, such as the values stored in cells E2 and B2. Table 2.4 lists and describes the logical operators to make the comparison in the logical test.

In Figure 2.21, cell F2 contains an IF function where the logical test is E2>B$2 to determine if Tiffany's sales in cell E2 are greater than the sales goal in cell B2. The reference to cell B2 can be mixed B$2 or absolute $B$2. Either way, copying the function down the column will compare each sales representative's sales with the $10,000 value in cell B2.

| TABLE 2.4 | Logical Operators |
|---|---|
| **Operator** | **Description** |
| = | Equal to |
| <> | Not equal to |
| < | Less than |
| > | Greater than |
| <= | Less than or equal to |
| >= | Greater than or equal to |

## Design the Value_If_True and Value_If_False Arguments

The second and third arguments of an IF function are value_if_true and value_if_false. When Excel evaluates the logical test, the result is either true or false. If the logical test is true, the value_if_true argument executes. If the logical test is false, the value_if_false argument executes. Only one of the last two arguments is executed; both arguments cannot be executed, because the logical test is either true or false but not both.

The value_if_true and value_if_false arguments can contain text, cell references, formulas, or constants (not recommended unless –1, 1, or 0). In Figure 2.21, cell F2 contains an IF function in which the value_if_true argument is B$3 and the value_if_false argument is 0. Because the logical test (E2>B$2) is true—that is, Tiffany's sales of $11,000 are greater than the $10,000 goal—the value_if_true argument is executed, and the result displays $500, the value that is stored in cell B3.

Jose's sales of $10,000 are not *greater than* $10,000, and Rex's sales of $9,000 are not *greater than* $10,000. Therefore, the value_if_false argument is executed and returns no bonus in cells F3 and F4.

**TIP**  **At Least Two Possible Right Answers**

Every IF function can have at least two right solutions to produce the same results. For example, if the logical test is E2<=B$2 for Figure 2.21, the value_if_true is 0, and the value_if_false is B$3.

## Create Other IF Functions

Figure 2.23 illustrates several IF functions, how they are evaluated, and their results. The input area contains values that are used in the logical tests and results. You can create this worksheet with the input area and IF functions to develop your understanding of how IF functions work.

| | A | B | C |
|---|---|---|---|
| 1 | **Input Values** | | |
| 2 | $1,000 | | |
| 3 | $2,000 | | |
| 4 | 10% | | |
| 5 | 5% | | |
| 6 | $250 | | |
| 7 | | | |
| 8 | **IF Function** | **Evaluation** | **Result** |
| 9 | =IF(A2=A3,A4,A5) | $1,000 is equal to $2,000: FALSE | 5% |
| 10 | =IF(A2<A3,A4,A5) | $1,000 is less than $2,000: TRUE | 10% |
| 11 | =IF(A2<>A3,"Not Equal","Equal") | $1,000 and $2,000 are not equal: TRUE | Not Equal |
| 12 | =IF(A2>A3,(A2*A4),(A2*A5)) | $1,000 is greater than $2,000: FALSE | $50 |
| 13 | =IF(A2>A3,A2*A4,MAX(A2*A5,A6)) | $1,000 is greater than $2,000: FALSE | $250 |
| 14 | =IF(A2*A4=A3*A5,A6,0) | $100 (A2*A4) is equal to $100 (A3*A5): TRUE | $250 |

**FIGURE 2.23** Sample IF Functions

- **Cell A9.** The logical test A2=A3 compares the values in cells A2 and A3 to see if they are equal. Because $1,000 is not equal to $2,000, the logical test is false. The value_if_false argument is executed, which displays 5%, the value stored in cell A5.

- **Cell A10.** The logical test A2<A3 determines if the value in cell A2 is less than the value in A3. Because $1,000 is less than $2,000, the logical test is true. The value_if_true argument is executed, which displays the value stored in cell A4, which is 10%.

- **Cell A11.** The logical test A2<>A3 determines if the values in cells A2 and A3 are not equal. Because $1,000 and $2,000 are not equal, the logical test is true. The value_if_true argument is executed, which displays the text *Not Equal*.

- **Cell A12.** The logical test A2>A3 is false. The value_if_false argument is executed, which multiplies the value in cell A2 ($1,000) by the value in cell A5 (5%) and displays $50. The parentheses in the value_if_true (A2*A4) and value_if_false (A2*A5) arguments are optional. They are not required but may help you read the function arguments better.

- **Cell A13.** The logical test A2>A3 is false. The value_if_false argument, which contains a nested MAX function, is executed. The MAX function, MAX(A2*A5,A6), multiplies the values in cells A2 ($1,000) and A5 (5%) and returns the higher of the product ($50) and the value stored in cell A6 ($250).

- **Cell A14.** The logical test A2*A4=A3*A5 is true. The contents of cell A2 ($1,000) are multiplied by the contents of cell A4 (10%) for a result of $100. That result is then compared to the result of A3*A5, which is also $100. Because the logical test is true, the function returns the value of cell A6 ($250).

### TIP  Using Text in Formulas

You can use text within a formula. For example, you can build a logical test comparing the contents of cell A1 to specific text, such as A1="Input Values". The IF function in cell A11 in Figure 2.23 uses "Not Equal" and "Equal" in the value_if_true and value_if_false arguments. When you use text in a formula or function, you must enclose the text in quotation marks. However, do not use quotation marks around formulas, cell references, or values.

### TIP  Nest Functions in IF Functions

You can nest functions in the logical test, value_if_true, and value_if_false arguments of the IF function. When you nest functions as arguments, make sure the nested function contains the required arguments for it to work and that you nest the function in the correct argument to calculate accurate results. For example, cell C13 in Figure 2.23 contains a nested MAX function in the value_if_false argument.

# Using Lookup Functions

You can use lookup and reference functions to look up values to perform calculations or display results. For example, when you order merchandise on a Web site, the Web server looks up the shipping costs based on weight and distance, or at the end of a semester, your professor uses your average, such as 88%, to look up the letter grade to assign, such as B+.

## Create the Lookup Table

A **lookup table** is a range containing a table of values or text that can be retrieved. The table should contain at least two rows and two columns, not including headings. Figure 2.24 illustrates a college directory with three "columns." The first column contains professors' names. You look up a professor's name in the first column to see his or her office (second "column") and phone extension (third "column").

| | | |
|---|---|---|
| Brazil, Estivan | GT 218b | 7243 |
| Fiedler, Zazilia | CS 417 | 7860 |
| Lam, Kaitlyn | SC 124a | 7031 |
| Rodriquez, Lisa | GT 304 | 7592 |
| Yeung, Bradon | CS 414 | 7314 |

**FIGURE 2.24** College Directory Lookup Table Analogy

It is important to plan the table so that it conforms to the way in which Excel can utilize the data in it. Excel cannot interpret the structure of Table 2.5. To look up a value in a range (such as the range 80–89), you must arrange data from the lowest to the highest value and include only the lowest value in the range (such as 80) instead of the complete range. If the values you look up are *exact* values, you can arrange the first column in any logical order. The lowest value for a category or in a series is the **breakpoint**. The first column contains the breakpoints—such as 60, 70, 80, and 90—or the lowest values to achieve a particular grade. The lookup table contains one or more additional columns of related data to retrieve. Table 2.6 shows how to construct the lookup table in Excel.

| TABLE 2.5 Grading Scale | |
|---|---|
| **Range** | **Grade** |
| 90–100 | A |
| 80–89 | B |
| 70–79 | C |
| 60–69 | D |
| Below 60 | F |

| TABLE 2.6 Grades Lookup Table | |
|---|---|
| **Range** | **Grade** |
| 0 | F |
| 60 | D |
| 70 | C |
| 80 | B |
| 90 | A |

## Understand the VLOOKUP Function Syntax

STEP 1 »

The **VLOOKUP function** accepts a value, looks the value up in a vertical lookup table, and returns a result. Use VLOOKUP to search for exact matches or for the nearest value that is less than or equal to the search value, such as assigning a B grade for an 87% class average. The VLOOKUP function has the following three required arguments and one optional argument: (1) lookup_value, (2) table_array, (3) col_index_number, and (4) range_lookup.

=VLOOKUP(lookup_value,table_array,col_index_number,[range_lookup])

Figure 2.25 shows a partial grade book that contains a vertical lookup table, as well as the final scores and letter grades. The function in cell F3 is =VLOOKUP(E3,$A$3:$B$7,2).

Value (final score) to look up

Table array range

Use second column within the table to return letter grade

| F3 | ▼ | : | × | ✓ | fx | =VLOOKUP(E3,$A$3:$B$7,2) |

| ⊿ | A | B | C | D | E | F | G |
|---|---|---|---|---|---|---|---|
| 1 | Grading Scale | | | Partial Gradebook | | | |
| 2 | Breakpoint | Grade | | Names | Final Score | Letter Grade | |
| 3 | 0 | F | | Abbott | 85 | B | |
| 4 | 60 | D | | Carter | 69 | D | |
| 5 | 70 | C | | Hon | 90 | A | |
| 6 | 80 | B | | Jackson | 74 | C | |
| 7 | 90 | A | | Miller | 80 | B | |
| 8 | | | | Nelsen | 78 | C | |

**FIGURE 2.25** VLOOKUP Function for Grade Book

The **lookup value** is the cell reference of the cell that contains the value to look up. The lookup value for the first student is cell E3, which contains 85. The **table array** is the range that contains the lookup table: $A$3:$B$7. The table array range must be absolute and cannot include column labels for the lookup table. The **column index number** is the column number in the lookup table that contains the return values. In this example, the column index number is 2.

---

### TIP  Using Values in Formulas

You know to avoid using values in formulas because the input values in a worksheet cell might change. However, the value 2 is used in the col_index_number argument of the VLOOKUP function. The 2 refers to a particular column within the lookup table and is an acceptable use of a number within a formula.

---

## Understand How Excel Processes the Lookup

Here is how the VLOOK function works:

1. The function identifies the value-stored cell used as the lookup value argument.
2. Excel searches the first column of the lookup table until it (a) finds an exact match (if possible) or (b) identifies the correct range if the lookup table contains breakpoints for range.
3. If Excel finds an exact match, it returns the value stored in the column designated by the column index number on that same row. If breakpoints are used and the lookup value is larger than the breakpoint, it looks to the next breakpoint to see if the lookup value is larger than that breakpoint also. When Excel detects that the lookup value is not greater than the next breakpoint, it stays on that row. It then uses the column index number to identify the column containing the value to return for the lookup value. Because Excel goes sequentially through the breakpoints, it is mandatory that the breakpoints are arranged from the lowest value to the highest value for ranges.

In Figure 2.25, the VLOOKUP function assigns letter grades based on final scores. Excel identifies the lookup value (85 in cell E3) and compares it to the values in the first column of the lookup table (range A3:B7). It tries to find an exact match of 85; however, the table contains breakpoints rather than every conceivable score. Because the lookup table is arranged from the lowest to the highest breakpoints, Excel detects that 85 is greater than the 80 breakpoint but is not greater than the 90 breakpoint. Therefore, it stays on the 80 row. Excel looks at the second column (column index number of 2) and returns the letter grade of B. The B grade is then stored in cell F3.

## Use the Range_Lookup Argument

Instead of looking up values in a range, you can look up a value for an exact match using the optional range_lookup argument in the VLOOKUP function. By default, the range_lookup is set implicitly to TRUE, which is appropriate to look up values in a range. Omitting the optional argument or typing TRUE in it enables the VLOOKUP function to find the closest match in the table to the lookup value.

To look up an exact match, enter FALSE in the range_lookup argument. For example, if you are looking up product numbers, you must find an exact match to display the price. The function would look like this: =VLOOKUP(D15,$A$1:$B$50,2,FALSE). The function returns a value for the first lookup value that matches the first column of the lookup table. If no exact match is found, the function returns #N/A.

## Nest Functions Inside the VLOOKUP Function

You can nest functions as arguments inside the VLOOKUP function. For example, Figure 2.26 illustrates shipping amounts that are based on weight and location (Boston or Chicago). In the VLOOKUP function in cell C3, the lookup_value argument looks up the weight of a package in cell A3. That weight (14 pounds) is looked up in the table_array argument, which is $E$3:$G$5. To determine which column of the lookup table to use, an IF function is nested as the column_index_number argument. The nested IF function compares the city stored in cell B3 to the text *Boston*. If cell B3 contains *Boston*, it returns 2 to use as the column_index_number to identify the shipping value for a package that is going to Boston. If cell B3 does not contain *Boston* (i.e., the only other city in this example is *Chicago*), the column_index_number is 3.

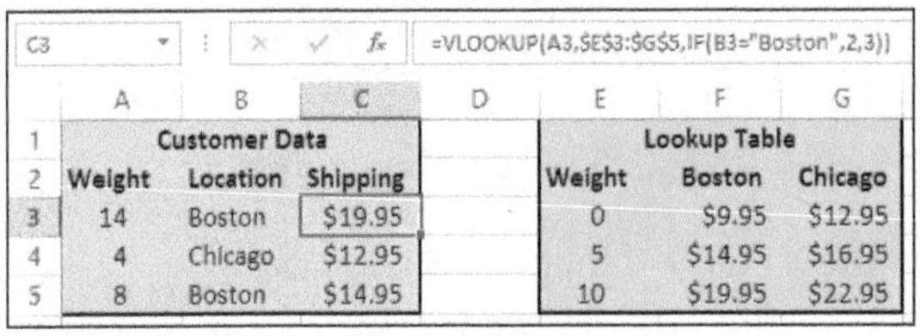
C3 =VLOOKUP(A3,$E$3:$G$5,IF(B3="Boston",2,3))

| | A | B | C | D | E | F | G |
|---|---|---|---|---|---|---|---|
| 1 | Customer Data | | | | Lookup Table | | |
| 2 | Weight | Location | Shipping | | Weight | Boston | Chicago |
| 3 | 14 | Boston | $19.95 | | 0 | $9.95 | $12.95 |
| 4 | 4 | Chicago | $12.95 | | 5 | $14.95 | $16.95 |
| 5 | 8 | Boston | $14.95 | | 10 | $19.95 | $22.95 |

**FIGURE 2.26** IF Function Nested in VLOOKUP Function

## Use the HLOOKUP Function

You can design a lookup table horizontally where the first row contains the values for the basis of the lookup or the breakpoints, and additional rows contain data to be retrieved. With a horizontal lookup table, use the ***HLOOKUP function***. Table 2.7 shows how the grading scale would look as a horizontal lookup table.

TABLE 2.7 Horizontal Lookup Table

| | | | | |
|---|---|---|---|---|
| 0 | 60 | 70 | 80 | 90 |
| F | D | C | B | A |

The syntax is almost the same as the syntax for the VLOOKUP function, except the third argument is row_index_number instead of col_index_number.

=HLOOKUP(lookup_value,table_array,row_index_number,[range_lookup])

# Calculating Payments with the PMT Function

STEP 2》 Excel contains several financial functions to help you perform calculations with monetary values. If you take out a loan to purchase a car, you need to know the monthly payment, which depends on the price of the car, the down payment, and the terms of the loan, in order to determine if you can afford the car. The decision is made easier by developing the worksheet in Figure 2.27 and by changing the various input values as indicated.

| B9 | ▼ | : | × | ✓ | fx | =PMT(B6,B8,-B3) |
| --- | --- | --- | --- | --- | --- | --- |

| ◢ | A | B | C | D |
| --- | --- | --- | --- | --- |
| 1 | Purchase Price | $25,999.00 | | |
| 2 | Down Payment | $ 5,000.00 | | |
| 3 | Amount to Finance | $20,999.00 | | |
| 4 | Payments per Year | 12 | | |
| 5 | Interest Rate (APR) | 3.500% | | |
| 6 | Periodic Rate (Monthly) | 0.292% | | |
| 7 | Term (Years) | 5 | | |
| 8 | No. of Payment Periods | 60 | | |
| 9 | Monthly Payment | $ 382.01 | | |
| 10 | | | | |

**FIGURE 2.27** Car Loan Worksheet

Creating a loan model helps you evaluate options. You realize that the purchase of a $25,999 car is prohibitive because the monthly payment is $382.01. Purchasing a less expensive car, coming up with a substantial down payment, taking out a longer-term loan, or finding a better interest rate can decrease your monthly payments.

The **PMT function** calculates payments for a loan with a fixed amount at a fixed periodic rate for a fixed time period. The PMT function uses three required arguments and up to two optional arguments: (1) rate, (2) nper, (3) pv, (4) fv, and (5) type.

=PMT(rate,nper,pv,[fv],[type])

The **rate** is the periodic interest rate, the interest rate per payment period. If the annual percentage rate (APR) is 12% and you make monthly payments, the periodic rate is 1% (12%/12 months). With the same APR and quarterly payments, the periodic rate is 3% (12%/4 quarters). Divide the APR by the number of payment periods in one year. However, instead of dividing the APR by 12 within the PMT function, calculate the periodic interest rate in cell B6 in Figure 2.27 and use that calculated rate in the PMT function.

The **nper** is the total number of payment periods. The term of a loan is usually stated in years; however, you make several payments per year. For monthly payments, you make 12 payments per year. To calculate the nper, multiply the number of years by the number of payments in one year. Instead of calculating the number of payment periods in the PMT function, calculate the number of payment periods in cell B8 and use that calculated value in the PMT function.

The **pv** is the present value of the loan. The result of the PMT function is a negative value because it represents your debt. However, you can display the result as a positive value by typing a minus sign in front of the present value cell reference in the PMT function.

*Quick* Concepts

1. Describe the three arguments for an IF function. **pp. 85–86**

2. How should you structure a vertical lookup table if you need to look up values in a range? **p. 88**

3. What are the first three arguments of a PMT function? Why would you have to divide by or multiply an argument by 12? **p. 91**

# Hands-On Exercises

**Watch the Video for this Hands-On Exercise!**

**MyITLab®**
HOE3 Training

## 3 Logical, Lookup, and Financial Functions

Erica wants you to complete another model that she might use for future mortgage data analysis. As you study the model, you realize you need to incorporate logical, lookup, and financial functions.

**Skills covered:** Use the VLOOKUP Function • Use the PMT Function • Use the IF Function

### STEP 1 » USE THE VLOOKUP FUNCTION

Rates vary based on the number of years to pay off the loan. Erica created a lookup table for three common mortgage years, and she entered the current APR. The lookup table will provide efficiency later when the rates change. You will use the VLOOKUP function to display the correct rate for each customer based on the number of years of the respective loans. Refer to Figure 2.28 as you complete Step 1.

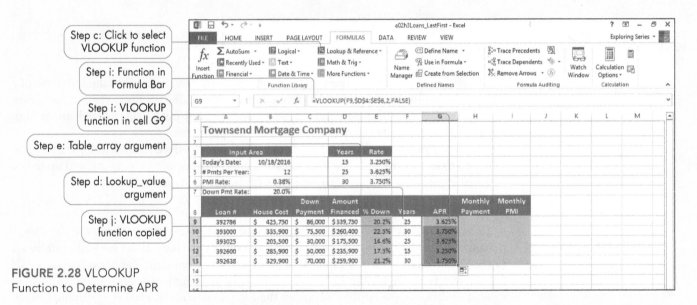

- Step c: Click to select VLOOKUP function
- Step i: Function in Formula Bar
- Step i: VLOOKUP function in cell G9
- Step e: Table_array argument
- Step d: Lookup_value argument
- Step j: VLOOKUP function copied

**FIGURE 2.28** VLOOKUP Function to Determine APR

a. Open *e02h2Loans_LastFirst* if you closed it at the end of Hands-On Exercise 2 and save it as **e02h3Loans_LastFirst**, changing *h2* to *h3*.

b. Click the **Payment Info worksheet tab** to display the worksheet containing the data to complete. Click **cell G9**, the cell that will store the APR for the first customer.

c. Click the **FORMULAS tab**, click **Lookup & Reference** in the Function Library group, and then select **VLOOKUP**.

   The Function Arguments dialog box opens.

d. Click **F9** to enter F9 in the **Lookup_value box**.

   Cell F9 contains the value you need to look up from the table: 25 years.

> **TROUBLESHOOTING:** If you cannot see the cell you need to use in an argument, click the Function Arguments dialog box title bar and drag the dialog box on the screen until you can see and click the cell you need for the argument. Alternatively, you can click the collapse button to the right of the argument box to collapse the dialog box so that you can select the range. After selecting the range, click the expand button to expand the dialog box.

e. Press **Tab** and select the **range D4:E6** in the **Table_array box**.

This is the range that contains that data for the lookup table. The Years values in the table are arranged from lowest to highest. Do **not** select the column labels for the range.

Anticipate what will happen if you copy the formula down the column. What do you need to do to ensure that the cell references always point to the exact location of the table? If your answer is to make the table array cell references absolute, then you answered correctly.

f. Press **F4** to make the range references absolute.

The Table_array box now contains $D$4:$E$6.

g. Press **Tab** and type **2** in the **Col_index_num box**.

The second column of the lookup table contains the APRs that you want to return and display in the cells containing the formulas.

h. Press **Tab** and type **False** in the **Range_lookup box**.

You want the formula to display an error if an incorrect number of years has been entered. To ensure an exact match to look up in the table, you enter *False* in the optional argument.

i. Click **OK**.

The VLOOKUP function looks up the first person's years (25), finds an exact match in the first column of the lookup table, and then returns the corresponding APR, which is 3.625%.

j. Copy the formula down the column and save the workbook.

Spot check the results to make sure the function returned the correct APR based on the number of years.

## STEP 2 » USE THE PMT FUNCTION

The worksheet now has all the necessary data for you to calculate the monthly payment for each loan: the APR, the number of years for the loan, the number of payment periods in one year, and the initial loan amount. You will use the PMT function to calculate the monthly payment, which includes paying back the principal amount with interest. This calculation does not include escrow amounts, such as property taxes or insurance. Refer to Figure 2.29 as you complete Step 2.

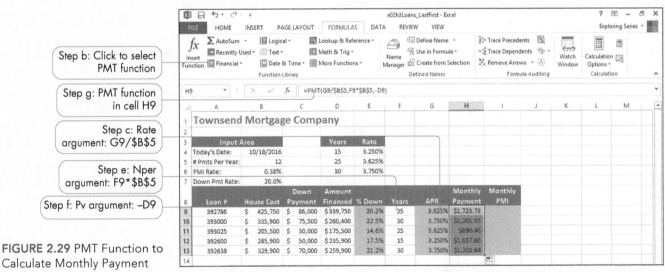

**FIGURE 2.29** PMT Function to Calculate Monthly Payment

a. Click **cell H9**, the cell that will store the payment for the first customer.

b. Click **Financial** in the Function Library group, scroll through the list, and then select **PMT**.

> **TROUBLESHOOTING:** Make sure you select PMT, not PPMT. The PPMT function calculates the principal portion of a particular monthly payment, not the total monthly payment itself.

The Function Arguments dialog box opens.

c. Type **G9/B5** in the **Rate box**.

Think about what will happen if you copy the formula. The argument will be G10/B6 for the next customer. Are those cell references correct? G10 does contain the APR for the next customer, but B6 does not contain the correct number of payments in one year. Therefore, you need to make B5 an absolute cell reference because the number of payments per year does not vary.

d. Press **F4** to make the reference to cell B5 absolute.

e. Press **Tab** and type **F9*$B$5** in the **Nper box**.

You calculate the nper by multiplying the number of years by the number of payments in one year. You must make B5 an absolute cell reference so that it does not change when you copy the formula down the column.

f. Press **Tab** and type **-D9** in the **Pv box**.

The bottom of the dialog box indicates that the monthly payment is 1723.73008 or $1,723.73.

> **TROUBLESHOOTING:** If the payment displays as a negative value, you probably forgot to type the minus sign in front of the D9 reference in the Pv box. Edit the function and type the minus sign in the correct place.

g. Click **OK**. Copy the formula down the column and save the workbook.

## STEP 3 ≫ USE THE IF FUNCTION

Lenders often want borrowers to have a 20% down payment. If borrowers do not put in 20% of the cost of the house as a down payment, they pay a private mortgage insurance (PMI) fee. PMI serves to protect lenders from absorbing loss if the borrower defaults on the loan, and it enables borrowers with less cash to secure a loan. The PMI fee is about 0.38% of the amount financed. Some borrowers have to pay PMI for a few months or years until the balance owed is less than 80% of the appraised value. The worksheet contains the necessary values input area. You need to use the IF function to determine which borrowers must pay PMI and how much they will pay. Refer to Figure 2.30 as you complete Step 3.

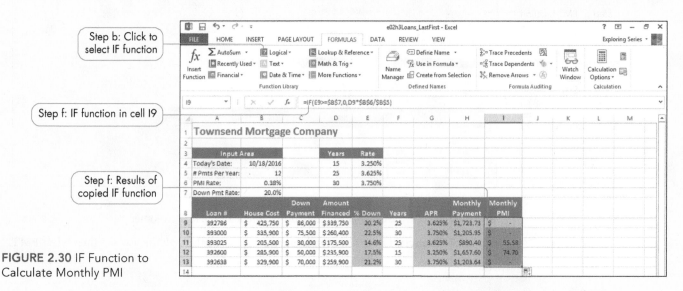

**FIGURE 2.30** IF Function to Calculate Monthly PMI

**a.** Click **cell I9**, the cell that will store the PMI, if any, for the first customer.

**b.** Click **Logical** in the Function Library group and select **IF**.

The Function Arguments dialog box opens. You need to enter the three arguments.

**c.** Type **E9>=$B$7** in the **Logical_test box**.

The logical test compares the down payment percentage to see if the customer's down payment is at least 20%, the threshold stored in B7, of the amount financed. The customer's percentage cell reference needs to be relative so that it will change when you copy it down the column; however, cell B7 must be absolute because it contains the threshold value.

**d.** Press **Tab** and type **0** in the **Value_if_true box**.

If the customer makes a down payment that is at least 20% of the purchase price, the customer does not pay PMI. The first customer paid 20% of the purchase price, so he or she does not have to pay PMI.

**e.** Press **Tab** and type **D9*$B$6/$B$5** in the **Value_if_false box**.

If the logical test is false, the customer must pay PMI, which is calculated by dividing the yearly PMI (0.38%) by 12 and multiplying the result by the amount financed.

**f.** Click **OK** and copy the formula down the column.

The third and fourth customers must pay PMI because their respective down payments were less than 20% of the purchase price.

---

**TROUBLESHOOTING:** If the results are not as you expected, check the logical operators. People often mistype < and > or forget to type = for >= situations. Correct any errors in the original formula and copy the formula again.

---

**g.** Save the workbook. Keep the workbook open if you plan to continue with the next Hands-On Exercise. If not, close the workbook and exit Excel.

# Range Names

To simplify entering ranges in formulas, you can use range names. A ***range name*** is a word or string of characters assigned to one or more cells. Think of range names in this way: Your college identifies you by your student ID; however, your professors call you by an easy-to-remember name, such as Micah or Vanessa. Similarly, instead of using cell addresses, you can use descriptive range names in formulas. Going back to the VLOOKUP example shown in Figure 2.25, you can assign the range name *Grades* to cells A3:B7 and modify the VLOOKUP function to be =VLOOKUP(E3,Grades,2), using the range name *Grades* in the formula. Another benefit of using range names is that they are absolute references, which helps ensure accuracy in your calculations.

In this section, you will work with range names. First, you will learn how to create and maintain range names. Then you will learn how to use a range name in a formula.

## Creating and Maintaining Range Names

Each range name within a workbook must be unique. For example, you cannot assign the name *COST* to ranges on several worksheets or on the same sheet. After you create a range name, you might need to change its name or range. If you no longer need a range name, you can delete it. You can also insert in the workbook a list of range names and their respective cell ranges for reference.

### Create a Range Name

STEP 1 ≫ A range name can contain up to 255 characters, but it must begin with a letter or an underscore. You can use a combination of upper- or lowercase letters, numbers, periods, and underscores throughout the range name. A range name cannot include spaces or special characters. You should create range names that describe the range of cells being named, but names cannot be identical to the cell contents. Keep the range names short to make them easier to use in formulas. Table 2.8 lists acceptable and unacceptable range names.

| TABLE 2.8 Range Names | |
|---|---|
| **Name** | **Description** |
| Grades | Acceptable range name |
| COL | Acceptable abbreviation for cost-of-living |
| Tax_Rate | Acceptable name with underscore |
| Commission Rate | Unacceptable name; cannot use spaces in names |
| Discount Rate % | Unacceptable name; cannot use special symbols and spaces |
| 2016_Rate | Unacceptable name; cannot start with a number |
| Rate_2016 | Acceptable name with underscore and numbers |

To create a range name, select the range you want to name and do one of the following:

- Click in the Name Box, type the range name, and then press Enter.
- Click the FORMULAS tab, click Define Name in the Defined Names group to open the New Name dialog box (see Figure 2.31), type the range name in the Name Box, and then click OK.
- Click the FORMULAS tab, click Name Manager in the Defined Names group to open the Name Manager dialog box, click New, type the range name in the Name Box, click OK, and then click Close.

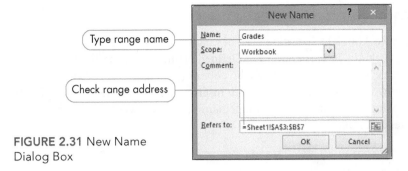

**FIGURE 2.31** New Name Dialog Box

You can create several range names at the same time if your worksheet includes ranges with values and descriptive labels. To do this, select the range of cells containing the labels that you want to become names and the cells that contain the values to name, click *Create from Selection* in the Defined Named group on the Formulas tab, and then select an option in the *Create Names from Selection* dialog box (see Figure 2.32).

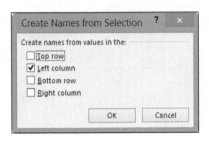

**FIGURE 2.32** Create Names from Selection Dialog Box

## Edit or Delete a Range Name

**STEP 2 »** Use the Name Manager dialog box to edit, delete, and create range names. To open the Name Manager dialog box shown in Figure 2.33, click Name Manager in the Defined Names group on the Formulas tab. To edit a range or range name, click the range name in the list and click Edit. In the Edit Name dialog box, make your edits and click OK.

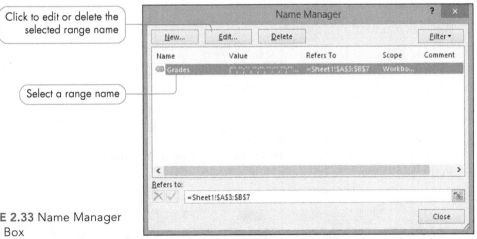

**FIGURE 2.33** Name Manager Dialog Box

To delete a range name, open the Name Manager dialog box, select the name you want to delete, click Delete, and then click OK in the confirmation message box.

If you change a range name, any formulas that use the range name reflect the new name. For example, if a formula contains =cost*rate and you change the name rate to tax_rate, Excel updates the formula to be =cost*tax_rate. If you delete a range name and a formula depends on that range name, Excel displays #NAME?—indicating an Invalid Name Error.

## Insert a Table of Range Names

STEP 4 » You can document a workbook by inserting a list of range names in a worksheet. To insert a list of range names, click *Use in Formula* in the Defined Names group on the Formulas tab and select Paste Names. The Paste Name dialog box opens (see Figure 2.34), listing all range names in the current workbook. Click Paste List to insert a list of range names in alphabetical order. The first column contains a list of range names, and the second column contains the worksheet names and range locations.

Click to select option to display Paste Name dialog box

Click to insert a list of range names

Names pasted starting in active cell

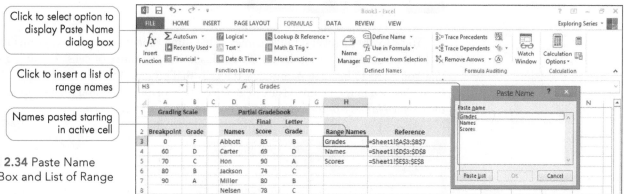

**FIGURE 2.34** Paste Name Dialog Box and List of Range Names

## Using Range Names in Formulas

STEP 3 » You can use range names in formulas instead of cell references. For example, if cell C15 contains a purchase amount, and cell C5 contains the sales tax rate, instead of typing =C15*C5, you can type the range names in the formula, such as =purchase*tax_rate. When you type a formula, Formula AutoComplete displays a list of range names, as well as functions, that start with the letters as you type (see Figure 2.35). Double-click the range name to insert it in the formula.

Indicates function

Part of range name being entered

Indicates range name

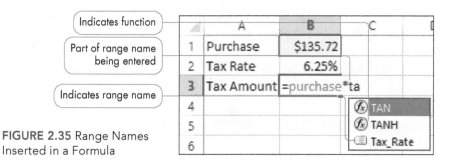

**FIGURE 2.35** Range Names Inserted in a Formula

Another benefit of using range names is that if you have to copy the formula, you do not have to make the cell reference absolute in the formula. Furthermore, if you share your workbook with others, range names in formulas help others understand what values are used in the calculations.

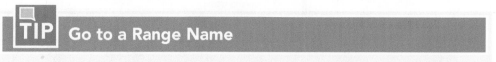

**TIP** **Go to a Range Name**

Use the Go To dialog box to go to the top-left cell in a range specified by a range name.

*Quick* Concepts

1. What is a range name? *p. 96*

2. List at least five guidelines and rules for naming a range. *p. 96*

3. What is the purpose of inserting a list of range names in a worksheet? What is contained in the list, and how is it arranged? *p. 98*

# Hands-On Exercises

## 4 Range Names

You decide to simplify the VLOOKUP function by using a range name for the APR rates lookup table instead of the actual cell references. After creating a range name, you will modify some range names Erica created and create a list of range names.

**Skills covered:** Create a Range Name • Edit and Delete Range Names • Use a Range Name in a Formula • Insert a List of Range Names

### STEP 1 ≫ CREATE A RANGE NAME

You want to assign a range name to the lookup table of years and APRs. Refer to Figure 2.36 as you complete Step 1.

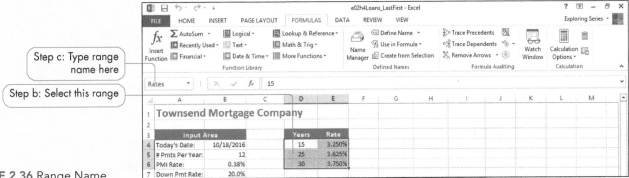

FIGURE 2.36 Range Name

a. Open *e02h3Loans_LastFirst* if you closed it at the end of Hands-On Exercise 3 and save it as **e02h4Loans_LastFirst**, changing *h3* to *h4*.

b. Make sure the **Payment Info worksheet tab** is active. Select **range D4:E6** (the lookup table).

c. Click in the **Name Box**, type **Rates**, and then press **Enter**. Save the workbook.

### STEP 2 ≫ EDIT AND DELETE RANGE NAMES

You noticed that Erica added some range names. You will use the Name Manager dialog box to view and make changes to the range names, such as reducing the length of two range names and deleting another range name. Refer to Figure 2.37 as you complete Step 2.

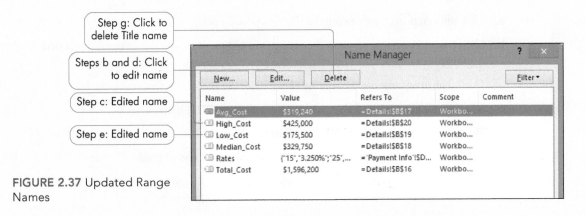

FIGURE 2.37 Updated Range Names

a. Click **Name Manager** in the Defined Names group on the FORMULAS tab.

The Name Manager dialog box opens.

b. Select **Highest_House…** and click **Edit** to open the Edit Name dialog box.

c. Type **High_Cost** in the **Name Box** and click **OK**.

d. Select **Lowest_House…** and click **Edit**.

e. Type **Low_Cost** in the **Name Box** and click **OK**.

f. Select **Title** in the Name Manager dialog box.

This range name applies to a cell containing text, which does not need a name as it cannot be used in calculations. You decide to delete the range name.

g. Click **Delete**, read the warning message box, and then click **OK** to confirm the deletion of the Title range name.

h. Click **Close** and save the workbook.

## STEP 3 ≫ USE A RANGE NAME IN A FORMULA

You will modify the VLOOKUP function by replacing the existing Table_array argument with the range name. This will help Erica interpret the VLOOKUP function. Refer to Figure 2.38 as you complete Step 3.

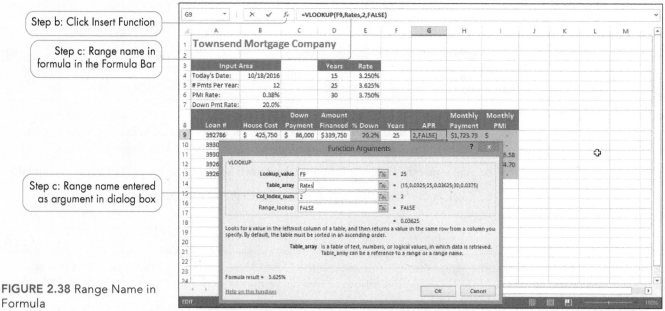

**FIGURE 2.38** Range Name in Formula

a. Click **cell G9**, the cell containing the VLOOKUP function.

b. Click **Insert Function** between the Name Box and the Formula Bar to open the Function Arguments dialog box.

The Table_array argument contains $D$4:$E$6, the absolute reference to the lookup table.

c. Select **$D$4:$E$6** in the **Table_array box**, type **Rates**, and then click **OK**.

The new function is =VLOOKUP(F9,Rates,2,FALSE).

d. Copy the updated formula down the column and save the workbook.

The results are the same as they were when you used the absolute cell references. However, the formulas are shorter and easier to read with the range names.

# STEP 4 ≫ INSERT A LIST OF RANGE NAMES

Before submitting the completed workbook to Erica, you want to create a documentation worksheet that lists all of the range names in the workbook. Refer to Figure 2.39 as you complete Step 4.

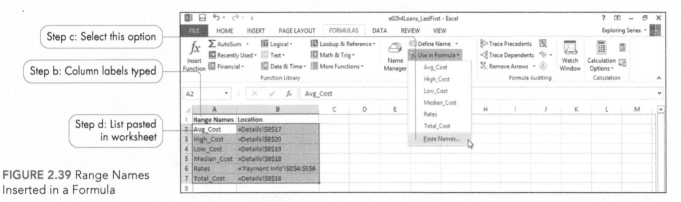

**FIGURE 2.39** Range Names Inserted in a Formula

**a.** Click **New sheet** to the right of the worksheet tabs and double-click the default sheet name, **Sheet1**. Type **Range Names** and press **Enter**.

You inserted and renamed the new worksheet to reflect the data you will add to it.

**b.** Type **Range Names** in **cell A1** and type **Location** in **cell B1**. Bold these headings.

These column headings will display above the list of range names.

**c.** Click **cell A2**, click **Use in Formula** in the Defined Names group on the FORMULAS tab, and then select **Paste Names**.

The Paste Name dialog box opens, displaying all of the range names in the workbook.

**d.** Click **Paste List**.

Excel pastes an alphabetical list of range names starting in cell A2. The second column displays the locations of the range names.

**e.** Increase the widths of columns A and B to fit the data.

**f.** Save and close the workbook, and submit based on your instructor's directions.

---

### TIP   List of Range Names

When you paste range names, the list will overwrite any existing data in a worksheet, so consider pasting the list in a separate worksheet. If you add, edit, or delete range names, the list does not update automatically. To keep the list current, you would need to paste the list again.

# Charts

## Depicting Data Visually

## CHAPTER 3

## OBJECTIVES | AFTER YOU READ THIS CHAPTER, YOU WILL BE ABLE TO:

1. Select the data source p. 104

2. Choose a chart type p. 105

3. Move, size, and print a chart p. 115

4. Add chart elements p. 123

5. Format chart elements p. 126

6. Apply a chart style and colors p. 135

7. Modify the data source p. 136

8. Create and customize sparklines p. 137

## CASE STUDY | Computer Job Outlook

You are an academic advisor for the School of Computing at a private university in Seattle, Washington. You will be visiting high schools in the state over the next few weeks to discuss the computing programs at the university and to inform students about the job outlook in the computing industry.

Your assistant, Doug Demers, researched growing computer-related jobs in the *Occupational Outlook Handbook* published by the Bureau of Labor Statistics on the U.S. Department of Labor's Web site. In particular, Doug listed seven jobs, the number of those jobs in 2010, the projected number of jobs by 2020, the growth in percentage increase and number of jobs, and the 2010 median pay. This data set shows an 18%–31% increase in computer-related jobs in that 10-year time period.

To prepare for your presentation to encourage students to enroll in your School of Computing, you want to create several charts that depict the job growth in the computer industry. You know that different charts provide different perspectives on the data. After you complete the charts, you will be able to use them in a variety of formats, such as presentations, fliers, brochures, and press releases.

# Chart Creation Basics

The expression "a picture is worth a thousand words" means that a visual can be a more effective way to communicate or interpret data than words or numbers. Storing, organizing, and performing calculations on quantitative data are important, but you must also be able to analyze the data. A *chart* is a visual representation of numerical data that compares data and helps reveal trends or patterns to help people make informed decisions. An effective chart depicts data in a clear, easy-to-interpret manner and contains enough data to be useful without overwhelming your audience.

A chart may include several chart elements. The *chart area* contains the entire chart and all of its elements, including the plot area, titles, legend, and labels. The *plot area* is the region containing the graphical representation of the values in the data series. Two axes form a border around the plot area.

The *X-axis* is a horizontal border that provides a frame of reference for measuring data horizontally. The *Y-axis* is a vertical border that provides a frame of reference for measuring data vertically. Excel refers to the axes as the category axis and value axis. The *category axis* displays descriptive group names or labels (such as college names, cities, or equal amounts of time) to identify data. Categories are usually defined by column or row labels (such as job titles or years) in the worksheet. The *value axis* displays incremental numbers to identify the worksheet values (such as number of jobs or revenue) used to create the chart. A *legend* is a key that identifies the color, gradient, picture, texture, or pattern assigned to each data series in a chart. For example, blue might represent values for 2010, and orange might represent values for 2020.

In this section, you will select the data source, choose the best chart type to represent numerical data, and designate the chart's location.

## Selecting the Data Source

Before creating a chart, organize the worksheet data so that the values in columns and rows are on the same value system (such as dollars or units), make sure labels are descriptive, and delete any blank rows or columns that exist in the primary data set. Look at the structure of the worksheet—the column labels, the row labels, the quantitative data, and the calculated values. Decide what you want to convey to your audience by answering these questions:

- Does the worksheet hold a single set of data, such as average snowfall at one ski resort, or multiple sets of data, such as average snowfall at several ski resorts?

- Do you want to depict data for one specific time period or over several time periods, such as several years or decades?

Identify the data range by selecting values and labels that you want to include in the chart. If the values and labels are not stored in adjacent cells, hold Ctrl while selecting the nonadjacent ranges. Do not select worksheet titles or subtitles; doing so would add unnecessary data to the chart.

Figure 3.1 shows a worksheet containing computer-related job titles, the number of jobs in 2010, the projected number of jobs by 2020, and other details. Row 3 contains labels merged and centered over individual column labels in row 5. Row 4 is blank and hidden. It is a good practice to insert a blank row between merged labels and individual column labels. Without the blank row, you would not be able to correctly sort data; the column headings would be sorted with the data.

Each cell containing a value is a *data point*. For example, the value 110,800 is a data point for the number of Database Administrators in 2010. A group of related data points that display in row(s) or column(s) in the worksheet create a *data series*. For example, the values 110,800 and 144,800 comprise the Database Administrators data series. Row and column labels (such as job titles, years, growth, etc.) are used to create *category labels* in charts.

| | A | B | C | D | E | F |
|---|---|---|---|---|---|---|
| 1 | | Computer-Related Jobs | | | | |
| 2 | | | | | | |
| 3 | | # of Jobs | | Job Growth | | Median Pay |
| 5 | | 2010 | 2020 Est. | % Growth | # of New Jobs | 2010 |
| 6 | Database Administrators | 110,800 | 144,800 | 31% | 34,000 | $ 73,490 |
| 7 | Info Security Analysts | 302,300 | 367,900 | 22% | 65,600 | $ 75,600 |
| 8 | CIS Managers | 307,900 | 363,700 | 18% | 55,800 | $ 115,780 |
| 9 | Network/System Admins | 347,200 | 443,800 | 28% | 96,600 | $ 69,160 |
| 10 | Programmers | 363,100 | 406,800 | 12% | 43,700 | $ 71,380 |
| 11 | Software App Developers | 520,800 | 664,500 | 28% | 143,700 | $ 90,530 |
| 12 | Systems Analysts | 544,400 | 664,800 | 22% | 120,400 | $ 77,740 |
| 14 | Source: Bureau of Labor Statistics, U.S. Department of Labor, *Occupational Outlook Handbook, 2012-13 Edition*, on the Internet at http://www.bls.gov/ | | | | | |

**FIGURE 3.1** Sample Data Set

 **TIP** **Avoid Using Data Aggregates and Individual Values**

Make sure that each data series uses the same scale. For example, do not include data aggregates (such as totals or averages) with individual values. The data source used to create the chart in Figure 3.2 mixes individual number of jobs by title with the total number of jobs, which distorts the scale from the comparison of the number of jobs for each job title.

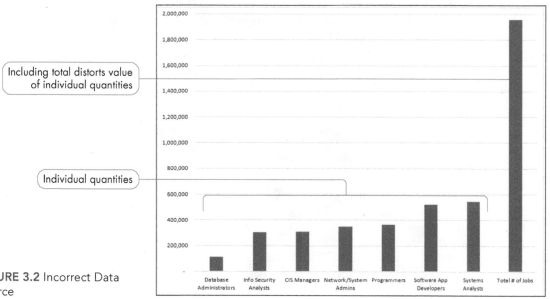

Including total distorts value of individual quantities

Individual quantities

**FIGURE 3.2** Incorrect Data Source

**TIP** **Charts Update When Data Change**

After you create a chart, you may need to change the worksheet data. When you change the worksheet data, Excel updates any charts that you created based on the data.

## Choosing a Chart Type

When you select a range of cells and position the mouse pointer over that selected range, Excel displays the Quick Analysis button in the bottom-right corner of the selected area. The Excel 2013 Quick Analysis tool enables you to use analytical tools, such as charts, to quickly examine data. You should select a chart type that appropriately represents the data and tells a story. You can create different charts from the same data set, but each chart tells a different story. For example, one chart might compare the number of computer-related jobs between 2010 and 2020, and another chart might indicate the percentage of new jobs by job title. The most commonly used chart types are column, bar, line, and pie (see Table 3.1). Each chart type is designed to provide a unique perspective to the selected data.

**TABLE 3.1  Common Chart Types**

| Chart | Chart Type | Description |
|---|---|---|
| | Column | Displays values in vertical columns where the height represents the value; the taller the column, the larger the value. Categories display along the horizontal (category) axis. |
| | Bar | Displays values in horizontal bars where the width represents the value; the wider the bar, the larger the value. Categories display along the vertical (category) axis. |
| | Line | Displays category data on the horizontal axis and value data on the vertical axis. Appropriate to show continuous data to depict trends over time, such as months, years, or decades. |
| | Pie | Shows proportion of individual data points to the sum of all those data points. |

To create a chart, do the following:

1. Select the data and click the Quick Analysis button.
2. Click CHARTS in the Quick Analysis gallery (see Figure 3.3).
3. Position the mouse over each recommended chart thumbnail to see the type of chart that would be created from the selected data.
4. Click the thumbnail of the chart you want to create.

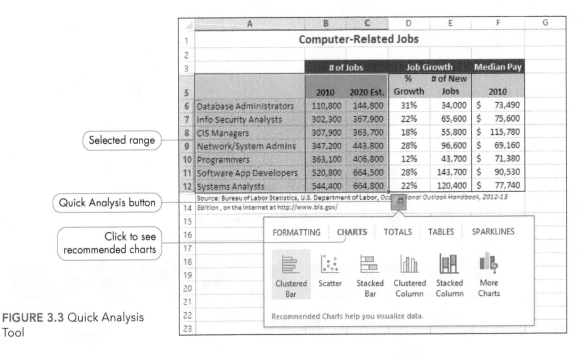

**FIGURE 3.3** Quick Analysis Tool

Another way to create a chart is to click the Insert tab and do one of the following:

- Click the chart type (such as Column) in the Charts group and click a chart subtype (such as Clustered Column) from the chart gallery (see Figure 3.4).
- Click Recommended Charts in the Charts group to open the Insert Chart dialog box (see Figure 3.5), click a thumbnail of the chart you want, and then click OK.

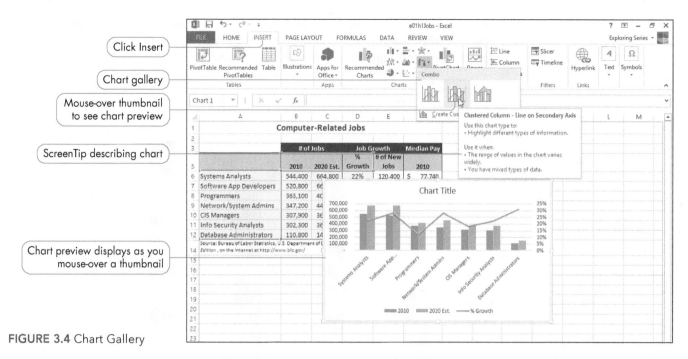

**Click Insert**

**Chart gallery**

**Mouse-over thumbnail to see chart preview**

**ScreenTip describing chart**

**Chart preview displays as you mouse-over a thumbnail**

**FIGURE 3.4** Chart Gallery

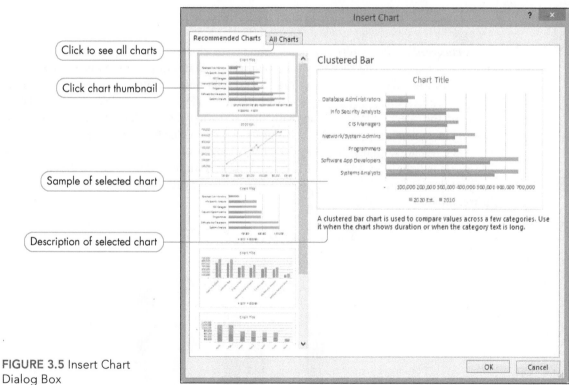

**Click to see all charts**

**Click chart thumbnail**

**Sample of selected chart**

**Description of selected chart**

**FIGURE 3.5** Insert Chart Dialog Box

## Create a Column Chart

STEP 1 ≫

A *column chart* displays data vertically in columns. Create a column chart to compare values across different categories, such as population among cities in a state or number of computer-related jobs between two years. Column charts are most effective when they are limited to seven or fewer categories. If more categories exist, the columns appear too close together, making it difficult to read the labels.

The column chart in Figure 3.6 compares the number of projected jobs by job title for 2020 using the data in Figure 3.1. The first four job titles stored in the first column (range A6:A9) form the category axis, and the increments of the number of jobs in 2020 (range C6:C9) form the value axis. The height of each column represents the value of individual data points: The larger the value, the taller the column. For example, the Info Security Analysts column is taller than the Database Administrators column, indicating that more jobs are projected for Info Security Analysts than Database Administrators.

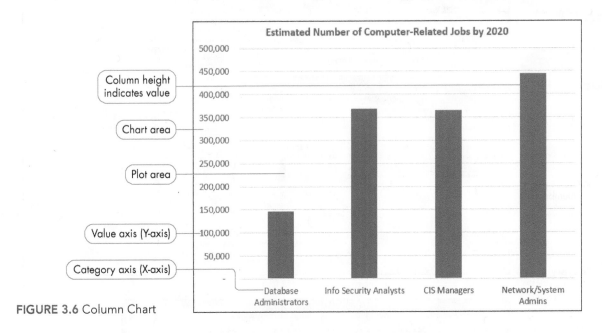

**FIGURE 3.6** Column Chart

A *clustered column chart* compares groups—or clusters—of columns set by side for easy comparison. The clustered column chart facilitates quick comparisons across data series, and it is effective for comparing several data points among categories. Figure 3.7 shows a clustered column chart created from the data in Figure 3.1. By default, the row labels appear on the category axis, and the yearly data series appear as columns with the value axis showing incremental numbers. Excel assigns a different color to each yearly data series and includes a legend so that you will know what color represents which data series. The 2010 data series is light blue, and the 2020 data series is dark blue. This chart makes it easy to compare the predicted job growth from 2010 to 2020 for each job title and then to compare the trends among job titles.

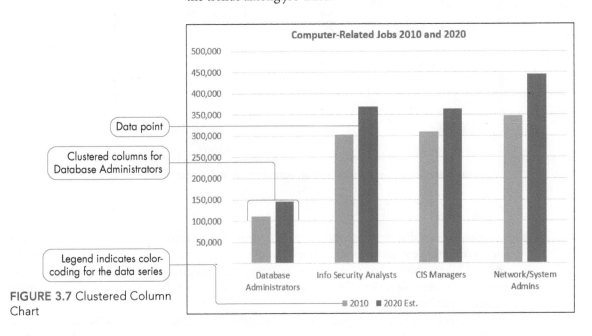

**FIGURE 3.7** Clustered Column Chart

Figure 3.8 shows a clustered column chart in which the categories and data series are reversed. The years appear on the category axis, and the job titles appear as color-coded data series and in the legend. This chart gives a different perspective from that in Figure 3.7 in that it compares the number of jobs within a given year, such as 2010.

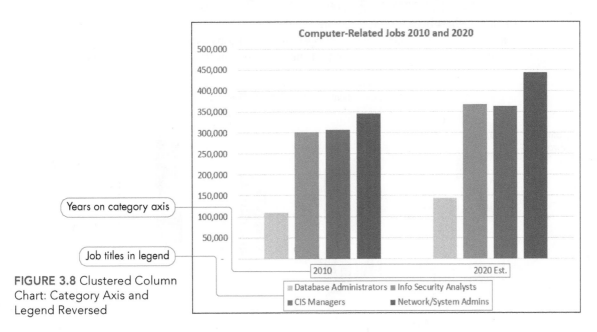

FIGURE 3.8 Clustered Column Chart: Category Axis and Legend Reversed

A *stacked column chart* shows the relationship of individual data points to the whole category. A stacked column chart displays only one column for each category. Each category within the stacked column is color-coded for one data series. Use the stacked column chart when you want to compare total values across categories, as well as to display the individual category values. Figure 3.9 shows a stacked column chart in which a single column represents each categorical year, and each column stacks color-coded data-point segments representing the different jobs. The stacked column chart enables you to compare the total number of computer-related jobs for each year. The height of each color-coded data point enables you to identify the relative contribution of each job to the total number of jobs for a particular year. A disadvantage of the stacked column chart is that the segments within each column do not start at the same point, making it more difficult to compare individual segment values across categories.

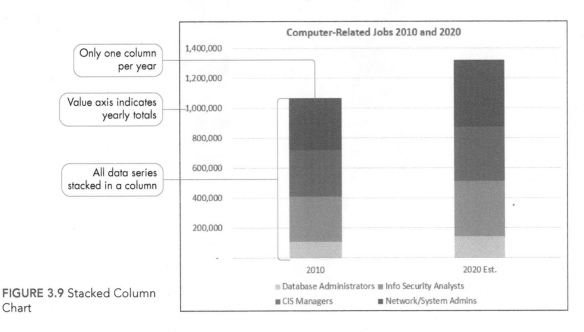

FIGURE 3.9 Stacked Column Chart

When you create a stacked column chart, make sure data are *additive*: each column represents a sum of the data for each segment. Figure 3.9 correctly uses years as the category axis and the jobs as data series. Within each year, Excel adds the number of jobs, and the columns display the total number of jobs. For example, the estimated total number of computer-related jobs in 2020 is about 1,300,000. Figure 3.10 shows an incorrectly constructed stacked column chart because the yearly number of jobs by job title is *not* additive. It is incorrect to state that about 800,000 Network/System Admin jobs exist. Be careful when constructing stacked column charts to ensure that they lead to logical interpretation of data.

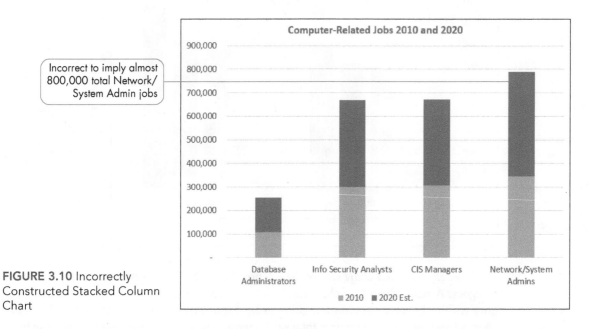

**FIGURE 3.10** Incorrectly Constructed Stacked Column Chart

A **100% stacked column chart** converts individual data points into percentages of the total value. Each data series is a different color of the stack, representing a percentage. The total of each column is 100%. This type of chart depicts contributions to the whole. For example, the chart in Figure 3.11 illustrates that Network/System Admins account for over 30% of the computer-related jobs represented by the four job categories.

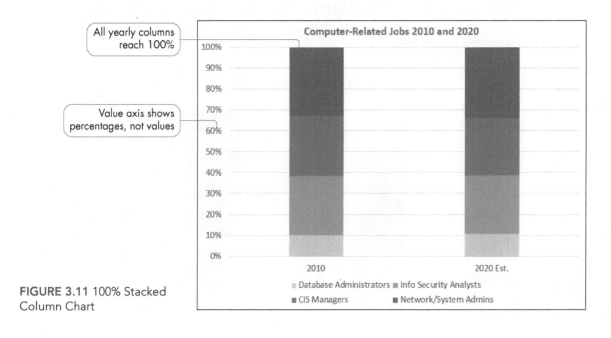

**FIGURE 3.11** 100% Stacked Column Chart

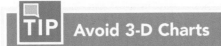
## Create a Bar Chart

**STEP 3**  A *bar chart* compares values across categories using horizontal bars. The horizontal axis displays values, and the vertical axis displays categories (see Figure 3.12). Bar charts and column charts tell a similar story: they both compare categories of data. A bar chart is preferable when category names are long, such as *Database Administrators*. A bar chart enables category names to appear in an easy-to-read format, whereas a column chart might display category names at an awkward angle or in a smaller font size. The overall decision between a column and a bar chart may come down to the fact that different data may look better with one chart type than the other.

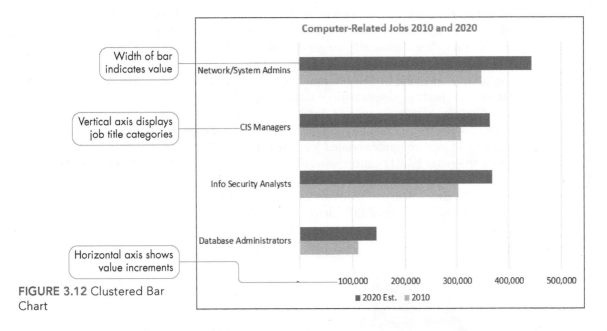

**FIGURE 3.12** Clustered Bar Chart

## Create a Line Chart

A *line chart* displays lines connecting data points to show trends over equal time periods. Excel displays each data series with a different line color. The category axis (X-axis) represents time, such as 10-year increments, whereas the value axis (Y-axis) represents the value, such as money or quantity. A line chart enables you to detect trends because the line continues to the next data point. To show each data point, choose the Line with Markers chart type. Figure 3.13 shows a line chart indicating the number of majors from 2005 to 2020 at five-year increments. The number of Arts majors remains relatively constant, but the number of Tech & Computing majors increases significantly over time, especially between the years 2010 and 2020.

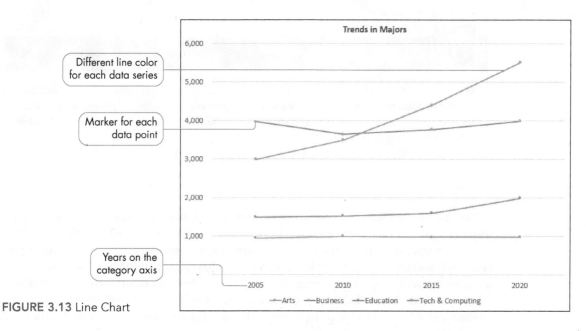

**FIGURE 3.13** Line Chart

## Create a Pie Chart

**STEP 4》** A *pie chart* shows each data point as a proportion to the whole data series. The pie chart displays as a circle, or "pie," where the entire pie represents the total value of the data series. Each slice represents a single data point. The larger the slice, the larger percentage that data point contributes to the whole. Use a pie chart when you want to convey percentage or market share. Unlike column, bar, and line charts that typically chart multiple data series, pie charts represent a single data series only.

The pie chart in Figure 3.14 divides the pie representing the estimated number of new jobs into seven slices, one for each job title. The size of each slice is proportional to the percentage of total computer-related jobs for that year. The chart depicts a single data series from the range E6:E12 on the worksheet in Figure 3.1. Excel creates a legend to indicate which color represents which pie slice. When you create a pie chart, limit it to about seven slices. Pie charts with too many slices appear too busy to interpret, or shades of the same color scheme become too difficult to distinguish.

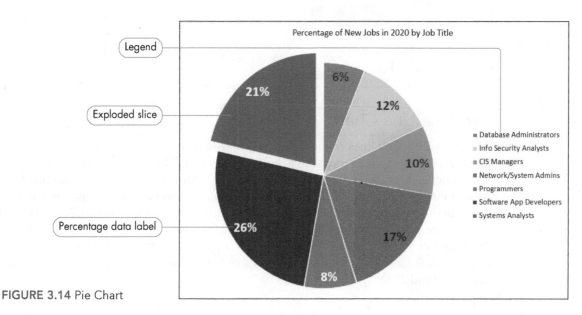

**FIGURE 3.14** Pie Chart

The projected number of new Systems Analyst jobs is 33,900, which accounts for 21% of the new jobs. You can focus a person's attention on a particular slice by separating one or more slices from the rest of the chart in an *exploded pie chart*, as shown in Figure 3.14.

## Change the Chart Type

After you create a chart, you may decide that the data would be better represented by a different type of chart. For example, you might decide a bar chart would display the labels better than a column chart. When you select a chart, Chart Tools displays on the Ribbon with the Design and Format tabs. To change the type of an existing chart, do the following:

1. Select the chart and click the DESIGN tab.
2. Click Change Chart Type in the Type group to open the Change Chart Type dialog box, which is similar to the Insert Chart dialog box.
3. Click the ALL CHARTS tab within the dialog box.
4. Click a chart type on the left side of the dialog box.
5. Click a chart subtype on the right side of the dialog box and click OK.

## Create Other Chart Types

Two other chart types that are used for specialized analysis are X Y (scatter) charts and stock charts.

An *X Y (scatter) chart* shows a relationship between two numerical variables using their X and Y coordinates. Excel plots one variable on the horizontal X-axis and the other variable on the vertical Y-axis. Scatter charts are often used to represent data in educational, scientific, and medical experiments. Figure 3.15 shows the relationship between the number of minutes students view a training video and their test scores.

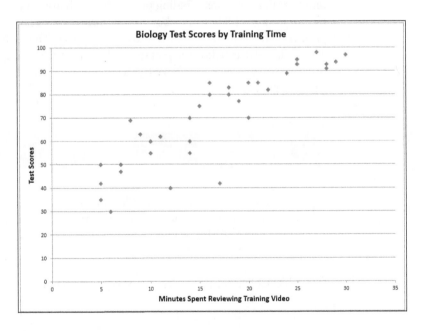

**FIGURE 3.15** X Y (Scatter) Chart

A *stock chart* shows fluctuations in stock changes. You can select one of four stock subtypes: High-Low-Close, Open-High-Low-Close, Volume-High-Low-Close, and Volume-Open-High-Low-Close. The High-Low-Close stock chart marks a stock's trading range on a given day with a vertical line from the lowest to the highest stock prices. Rectangles mark the opening and closing prices. Figure 3.16 shows three days of stock prices for a particular company.

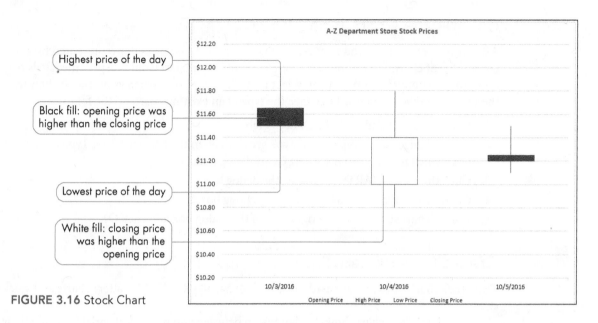

**FIGURE 3.16** Stock Chart

The rectangle represents the difference in the opening and closing prices. If the rectangle has a white fill, the closing price is higher than the opening price. If the rectangle has a black fill, the opening price is higher than the closing price. In Figure 3.16, on October 3, the opening price was $11.65, and the closing price was $11.50. A line below the rectangle indicates that the lowest trading price is lower than the opening and closing prices. The lowest price was $11.00 on October 3. A line above the rectangle indicates the highest trading price is higher than the opening and closing prices. The highest price was $12.00 on October 3. If no line exists below the rectangle, the lowest price equals either the opening or closing price, and if no line exists above the rectangle, the highest price equals either the opening or closing price.

### TIP Arrange Data for a Stock Chart

To create an Open-High-Low-Close stock chart, you must arrange data with Opening Price, High Price, Low Price, and Closing Price as column labels in that sequence. If you want to create other variations of stock charts, you must arrange data in a structured sequence required by Excel.

Table 3.2 lists and describes other types of charts you can create in Excel.

## TABLE 3.2 Other Chart Types

| Chart | Chart Type | Description |
|---|---|---|
| | **Area** | Similar to a line chart in that it shows trends over time; however, the area chart displays colors between the lines to help illustrate the magnitude of changes. |
| | **Surface** | Represents numeric data and numeric categories. Takes on some of the same characteristics as a topographic map of hills and valleys. |
| | **Doughnut** | A derivative of a pie chart showing relationship of parts to a whole, but the doughnut chart can display more than one data series. |
| | **Bubble** | A derivative of a scatter chart in which both the horizontal and vertical axes are value axes. The third value determines the size of the bubble, where the larger the value, the larger the bubble. Do not select the column labels, as they might distort the data. |
| | **Radar** | Uses each category as a spoke radiating from the center point to the outer edges of the chart. Each spoke represents each data series, and lines connect the data points between spokes, similar to a spider web. You can create a radar chart to compare aggregate values for several data series. |
| | **Combo** | Combines two chart types (such as column and line) to plot different data types (such as values and percentages). |

# Moving, Sizing, and Printing a Chart

Excel inserts the chart as an embedded object in the current worksheet, often to the right side of, but sometimes on top of and covering up, the data area. After you insert a chart, you usually need to move it to a different location, adjust its size, and prepare to print it.

## Move a Chart

To move the chart on the active worksheet, position the mouse pointer over the chart area. When you see the Chart Area ScreenTip and the mouse pointer includes the white arrowhead and a four-headed arrow, drag the chart to the desired location.

You can place the chart in a separate worksheet, called a *chart sheet*. A chart sheet contains a single chart only; you cannot enter data and formulas on a chart sheet. If you leave the chart in the same worksheet, you can print the data and chart on the same page. If you want to print or view a full-sized chart, move the chart to its own chart sheet. To move a chart to another sheet or a chart sheet, do the following:

1. Select the chart.
2. Click the DESIGN tab and click Move Chart in the Location group to open the Move Chart dialog box (see Figure 3.17).
3. Select one of these options to indicate where you want to move the chart:
   - Click *New sheet* to move the chart to its own sheet.
   - Click *Object in*, click the *Object in* arrow, and select the worksheet to which you want to move the chart. The default chart sheet is Chart1, but you can rename it in the Move Chart dialog box or similarly to the way you rename other sheet tabs. Click OK.

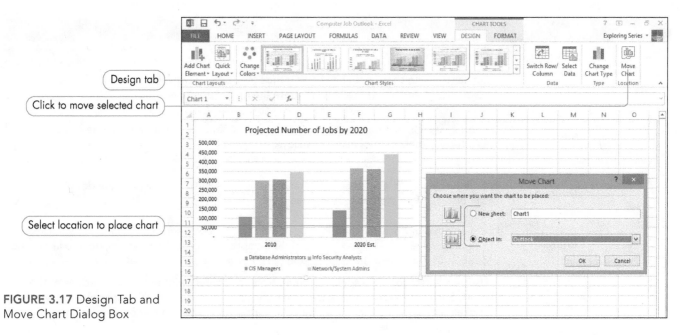

**FIGURE 3.17** Design Tab and Move Chart Dialog Box

## Size a Chart

If you keep a chart in a worksheet, you can size it to fit in a particular range or to ensure the chart elements are proportional. To change the chart size, do the following:

1. Select the chart.
2. Position the mouse pointer on the outer edge of the chart where you see eight small white-filled squares, called *sizing handles*.
3. When the mouse pointer changes to a two-headed arrow, drag the border to adjust the chart's height or width. Drag a corner sizing handle to increase or decrease the height and width of the chart at the same time. Press and hold down Shift as you drag a corner sizing handle to change the height and width proportionately.

You can also change the chart size by clicking the Format tab and changing the height and width values in the Size group (see Figure 3.18).

**FIGURE 3.18** Sizing a Chart

## Print a Chart

If you embedded a chart on the same sheet as the data source, you need to decide if you want to print the data only, the data *and* the chart, or the chart only. To print the data only, select the data, click the File tab, click Print, click the first arrow in the Settings section and select Print Selection, and then click Print. To print only the chart, select the chart, click the File tab, click Print, make sure the default setting is Print Selected Chart, and then click Print to print the chart as a full-page chart. If the data and chart are on the same worksheet, print the worksheet contents to print both, but do not select either the chart or the data before displaying the Print options. The preview shows you what will print. Make sure it displays what you want to print before clicking Print.

If you moved the chart to a chart sheet, the chart is the only item on that worksheet. When you display the print options, the default is Print Active Sheets, and the chart will print as a full-page chart.

*Quick*
Concepts

1. Why should you not include aggregates, such as totals or averages, along with individual data series in a chart? *p. 105*

2. What is the purpose of each of these chart types: (a) column, (b) bar, (c) line, and (d) pie? *p. 106*

3. How can you use the Quick Analysis button to create a chart? *p. 106*

4. After you create a chart, where is it located by default? What do you usually do to the chart immediately after creating it? *p. 115*

MyITLab®

HOE1 Training

# 1 Chart Creation Basics

Doug Demers, your assistant, gathered data about seven computer-related jobs from the *Occupational Outlook Handbook* online. He organized the data into a structured worksheet that contains the job titles, the number of jobs in 2010, the projected number of jobs by 2020, and other data. Now you are ready to transform the data into visually appealing charts.

**Skills covered:** Create a Clustered Column Chart • Create a Bar Chart • Change the Chart Position, Size, and Type • Create a Pie Chart

## STEP 1 ≫ CREATE A CLUSTERED COLUMN CHART

You want to compare the number of jobs in 2010 to the projected number of jobs in 2020 for all seven computer-related professions that Doug entered into the worksheet. You decide to create a clustered column chart to depict this data. After you create this chart, you will move it to its own chart sheet. Refer to Figure 3.19 as you complete Step 1.

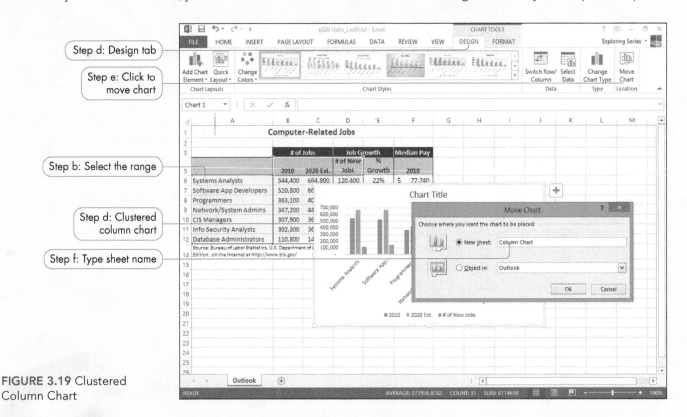

**FIGURE 3.19** Clustered Column Chart

a. Open *e03h1Jobs* and save it as **e03h1Jobs_LastFirst**.

> **TROUBLESHOOTING:** If you make any major mistakes in this exercise, you can close the file, open *e03h1Jobs* again, and then start this exercise over.

b. Select the **range A5:D12**.

You selected the job titles, the number of jobs in 2010, the projected number of jobs in 2020, and the number of new jobs.

c. Click the **Quick Analysis button** at the bottom-right corner of the selected range and click **CHARTS**.

The Quick Analysis gallery displays recommended charts based on the selected range.

d. Position the mouse pointer over *Clustered Column* to see a live preview of what the chart would look like and click **Clustered Column**.

Excel inserts a clustered column chart based on the selected data.

The DESIGN tab displays on the Ribbon.

e. Click **Move Chart** in the Location group to open the Move Chart dialog box.

f. Click **New sheet**, type **Column Chart**, and click **OK**. Save the workbook.

Excel moves the clustered column chart to a new sheet called Column Chart. Later, you will modify the chart.

## STEP 2 » CREATE A BAR CHART

You want to create a bar chart to depict the number of jobs in 2010 and the number of new jobs that will be created by 2020. Refer to Figure 3.20 as you complete Step 2.

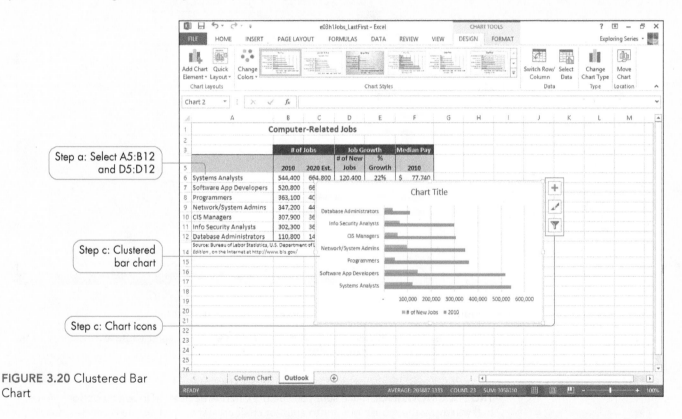

Step a: Select A5:B12 and D5:D12

Step c: Clustered bar chart

Step c: Chart icons

**FIGURE 3.20** Clustered Bar Chart

a. Click the **Outlook sheet tab**, select the **range A5:B12**, press and hold **Ctrl**, and then select the **range D5:D12**.

You selected the job title labels, the number of jobs in 2010, and the number of new jobs.

 **Parallel Ranges**

Nonadjacent ranges should be parallel so that the legend will correctly reflect the data series. This means that each range should contain the same number of related cells. For example, A5:A12, B5:B12, and D5:D12 are parallel ranges.

**b.** Click the **INSERT tab** and click **Insert Bar Chart** in the Charts group.

A gallery containing thumbnails of different bar charts displays.

**c.** Click **Clustered Bar** in the 2-D Bar group. Save the workbook.

Excel inserts the clustered bar chart in the worksheet. Three icons display to the right side of the selected chart: Chart Elements, Chart Styles, and Chart Filters.

## STEP 3 >> CHANGE THE CHART POSITION, SIZE, AND TYPE

Because the bar chart overlaps the data, you need to move it. You decide to position it below the job outlook data and adjust its size. Finally, you want to change the chart to a stacked bar chart to show the total jobs in 2020 based on the number of jobs in 2010 and the number of new jobs. Refer to Figure 3.21 as you complete Step 3.

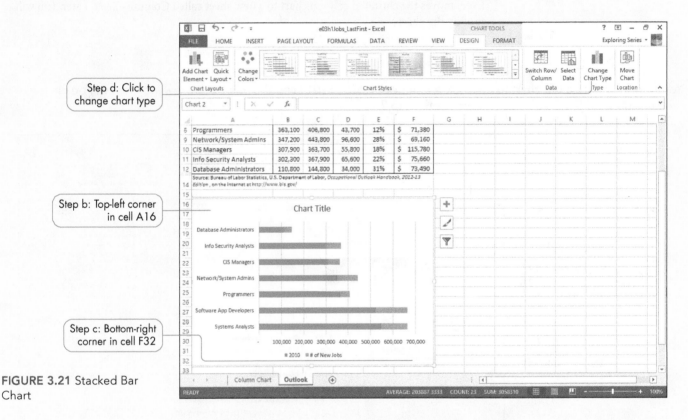

**FIGURE 3.21** Stacked Bar Chart

**a.** Position the mouse pointer over the empty area of the chart area.

The mouse pointer includes a four-headed arrow with the regular white arrowhead, and the Chart Area ScreenTip displays.

---

**TROUBLESHOOTING:** Make sure you see the Chart Area ScreenTip as you perform step b. If you move the mouse pointer to another chart element—such as the legend—you will move or size that element instead of moving the entire chart.

---

**b.** Drag the chart so that the top-left corner of the chart appears in **cell A16**.

You positioned the chart below the worksheet data.

**c.** Drag the bottom-right sizing handle through **cell F32**.

You changed both the height and the width at the same time.

**d.** Click **Change Chart Type** in the Type group, click **Stacked Bar** in the top center of the dialog box, and then click **OK**. Save the workbook.

Excel stacks the 2010 number of new jobs data series into one column per job title. This chart tells the story of where the projected number of jobs in 2020 come from: the number of existing jobs in 2010 (blue) and the number of new jobs (orange).

## STEP 4 ▶ CREATE A PIE CHART

You decide to create a pie chart that depicts the percentage of new jobs by job title created out of the total number of new jobs created, which is 559,800. After creating the pie chart, you will move it to its own sheet. Finally, you want to draw attention to the job that has the largest slice by exploding it. Refer to Figure 3.22 as you complete Step 4.

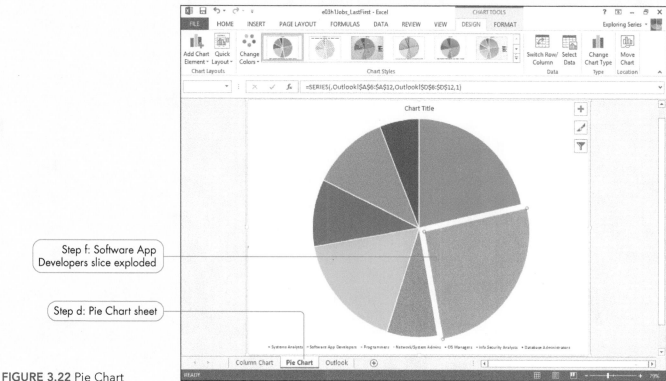

**FIGURE 3.22** Pie Chart

**a.** Select the **range A6:A12** and press and hold **Ctrl** as you select the **range D6:D12**.

> **TROUBLESHOOTING:** Do not select cells A5 and D5 this time because you are creating a pie chart. Doing so would add unnecessary data to the chart.

**b.** Click the **INSERT tab**, click **Insert Pie or Doughnut** in the Charts group, and then select **Pie** in the 2-D Pie group on the gallery.

The pie chart may overlap part of the worksheet data and the stacked bar chart.

**c.** Click **Move Chart** in the Location group on the DESIGN tab.

The Move Chart dialog box opens.

**d.** Click **New sheet**, type **Pie Chart**, and then click **OK**.

Excel creates a new sheet called Pie Chart. The pie chart is the only object on that sheet.

**e.** Click the **Software App Developers orange slice**, pause, and then click it again.

The first click selects all slices of the pie. The second click selects only the Software App Developers slice.

> **TROUBLESHOOTING:** If you double-click the pie chart, the Format Data Series task pane opens on the right side of the chart. Click its Close button and click the orange slice one time.

    **f.** Drag the **Software App Developers orange slice** away from the pie a little bit.

    **g.** Save the workbook. Keep the workbook open if you plan to continue with the next Hands-On Exercise. If not, close the workbook and exit Excel.

# Chart Elements

After you create a chart, you usually need to add components to describe the chart. Adding descriptive text for labels provides information for the reader to comprehend the chart. When you create a chart, one or more components may display by default. For example, when you created the charts in Hands-On Exercise 1, Excel displayed a placeholder for the chart title and displayed a legend so that you know which color represents which data series.

When you select a chart, Excel displays three icons to the right side the chart, the first of which is Chart Elements. In addition, the Design tab contains the Chart Layouts group so that you can add and customize chart elements.

In this section, you will learn how to add and format chart elements.

## Adding Chart Elements

A *chart element* is a component that completes or helps clarify the chart. Some chart elements, such as chart titles, should be included in every chart. Other elements are optional. Table 3.3 describes the chart elements, and Figure 3.23 illustrates several chart elements.

| TABLE 3.3 | Chart Elements |
|---|---|
| **Element** | **Description** |
| **Axes** | Category axis labels, such as job titles, and the value axis quantities in increments in column, bar, and line charts. Axes display by default. |
| **Axis titles** | Labels that describe the category and value axes. You can display axis titles, such as *In Millions of Dollars* or *Top 7 Computer Job Titles*, to clarify the axes. Axis titles are not displayed by default. |
| **Chart title** | Label that describes the entire chart. It should reflect the purpose of the chart. For example, *Houses Sold* is too generic, but *Houses Sold in Seattle in 2016* indicates the what (Houses), the where (Seattle), and the when (2016). The default is *Chart Title*. |
| **Data labels** | Descriptive labels that show exact value or name of a data point. Data labels are not displayed by default. |
| **Data table** | A grid that contains the data source values and labels. If you embed a chart on the same worksheet as the data source, you might not need to include a data table. Only add a data table with a chart that is on a chart sheet. |
| **Error bars** | Visuals that indicate the standard error amount, a percentage, or a standard deviation for a data point or marker. Error bars are not displayed by default. |
| **Gridlines** | Horizontal or vertical lines that span across the chart to help people identify the values plotted by the visual elements, such as a column. Excel displays horizontal gridlines for column, line, scatter, stock, surface, and bubble charts and vertical gridlines for bar charts. Gridlines may display by default, depending on the chart type. |
| **Legend** | A key that identifies the color, gradient, picture, texture, or pattern assigned to each data series. The legend is displayed by default for particular charts. |
| **Trendline** | A line that depicts trends or helps forecast future data, such as estimating future sales or number of births in a region. You can add a trendline to column, bar, line, stock, scatter, and bubble charts. Excel will analyze the current trends to display a line indicating future values based on the current trend. |

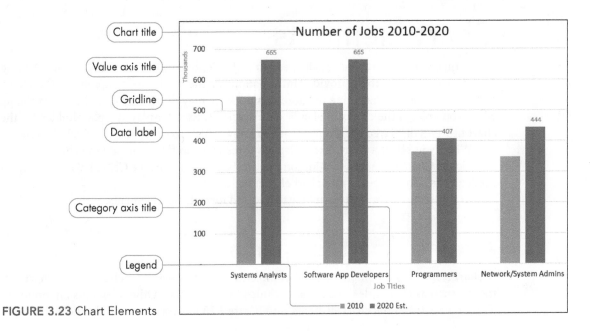
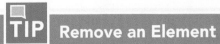

FIGURE 3.23 Chart Elements

Labels (top to bottom on left):
Chart title
Value axis title
Gridline
Data label
Category axis title
Legend

To add a chart element, do the following:

1. Click the Chart Elements button to the right side of the chart (see Figure 3.24).
2. Click an empty check box to display an element, or position the mouse pointer on an element and click the triangle to select more specific chart elements. For example, if you click the triangle to the right of Axis Titles, you select on which axis to include a title.
3. If you selected a title, type the text for the title, and then press Enter.
4. Click the Chart Elements button again to close the menu.

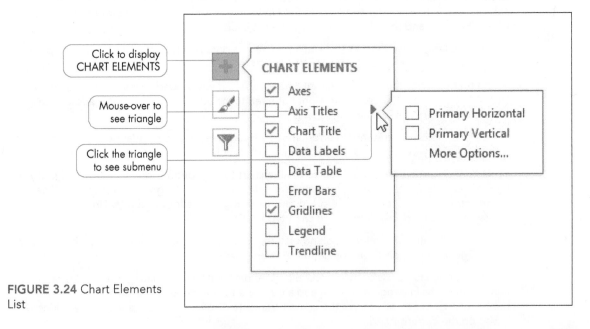

FIGURE 3.24 Chart Elements List

Labels:
Click to display CHART ELEMENTS
Mouse-over to see triangle
Click the triangle to see submenu

CHART ELEMENTS
☑ Axes
☐ Axis Titles ▸   ☐ Primary Horizontal
☑ Chart Title      ☐ Primary Vertical
☐ Data Labels      More Options...
☐ Data Table
☐ Error Bars
☑ Gridlines
☐ Legend
☐ Trendline

---

**TIP** Remove an Element

To remove an element, click Chart Elements and deselect a check box. Alternatively, click Add Chart Element in the Chart Layouts group on the Chart Tools Design tab, position the mouse pointer over the element name, and then select None.

To use the Design tab to add or remove a chart element, do the following:

1. Click the DESIGN tab.
2. Click Add Chart Element in the Chart Layouts group.
3. Point to an element and select from that element's submenu (see Figure 3.25).
4. If you selected a title, type the text for the title and press Enter.

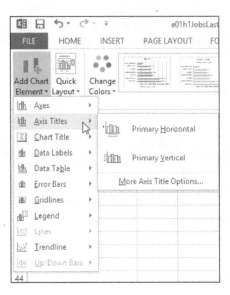

**FIGURE 3.25** Chart Elements Menu and Submenu

## Position the Chart Title

Excel includes the placeholder text *Chart Title* above the chart when you create a chart. You should replace that text with a descriptive title. To change the chart title text, click the Chart Title placeholder, type the text, and then press Enter. You can select the position of the title by doing the following:

1. Click the Chart Elements button to the right side of the chart.
2. Position the mouse pointer over Chart Title and click the triangle on the right side.
3. Select one of the options:
   - Above Chart: Centers the title above the plot area, decreasing the plot area size to make room for the chart title.
   - Centered Overlay: Centers the chart title horizontally without resizing the plot area; the title displays over the top of the plot area.
   - More Options: Opens the Format Chart Title task pane so that you can apply fill, border, and alignment settings.
4. Click the Chart Elements button to close the menu.

## Include and Position Axis Titles

**STEP 2 >>** Excel does not include axis titles by default; however, you can display titles. When you click Chart Elements and click the triangle on the right side of Axis Titles, you can select Primary Horizontal and Primary Vertical. The horizontal axis title displays below the category labels, and the rotated vertical axis title displays on the left side of the value axis. After including these titles, you can click the respective title, type the text for the title, and then press Enter.

## Include and Position Data Labels

**STEP 3 >>** Excel does not include data labels by default; however, you can display the exact values of the data points in the chart. When you click Chart Elements and click the triangle on the right side of Data Labels, you can select where the labels display.

By default, Excel adds data labels to all data series. If you want to display data labels for only one series, select the data labels for the other data series and press Delete. In Figure 3.23, data labels are included for the 2020 data series but not the 2010 data series.

## Position the Legend

When you create a multiple series chart, the legend displays, providing a key to the color-coded data series. You can position the legend to the right, top, bottom, or left of the plot area. Choose the position based on how the legend's placement affects the chart. Make sure that the columns, bars, or lines appear proportionate and well balanced after you position the legend. You may need to adjust the height and/or width of the entire chart to achieve a balanced appearance.

### TIP  Quick Layout

Use Quick Layout to apply predefined layouts to a chart. Specifically, you can apply a layout to add several chart elements at one time. Click Quick Layout in the Chart Layouts group on the Design tab (see Figure 3.26) and select a layout. Each layout contains predefined chart elements and their positions.

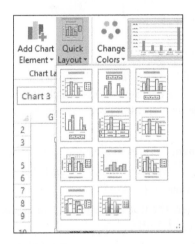

**FIGURE 3.26** Quick Layout Gallery

## Formatting Chart Elements

When you position the mouse pointer over the chart, Excel displays a ScreenTip with the name of that chart element. To select a chart element, click it when you see the ScreenTip, or click the Format tab, click the Chart Elements arrow in the Current Selection group, and then select the element from the list.

STEP 1 ≫  After you select a chart element, you can format it. For example, you might want to apply 18-pt font size to the chart title. In addition, you might want to change the fill color of a data series to red. You can apply these formats from the Home tab:

- Font for titles, axes, and labels
- Font Size for titles, axes, and labels
- Font Color for titles, axes, and labels
- Fill Color for column, bar, and line data series or background fill color behind titles and labels

## Format the Chart Area, Plot Area, and Data Series

STEP 4 » You can apply multiple settings, such as fill colors and borders, at once using a Format task pane. To display a chart element's task pane, double-click the chart element. Figure 3.27 displays the Format Chart Area, Format Plot Area, and Format Data Series task panes. All three task panes include the same fill and border elements. After you select a fill option, such as *Gradient fill*, the remaining options change in the task pane.

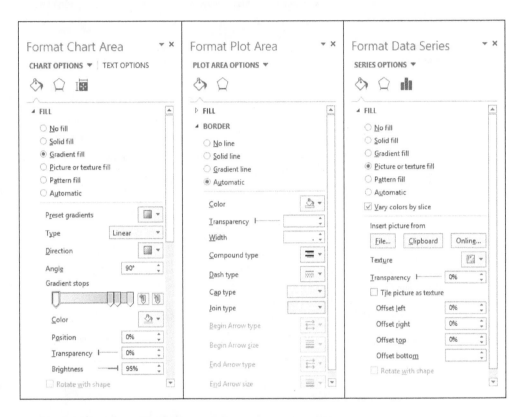

**FIGURE 3.27** Format Task Panes

---

### TIP  Use Images or Textures

For less formal presentations, you might want to use images or a texture to fill the data series, chart area, or plot area instead of a solid fill color. To use an image or a texture, click the Fill & Line icon at the top of the task pane, click Fill, and then click *Picture or texture fill* in the Format Data Series task pane. Click File or Online in the *Insert picture from* section and insert an image file or search online to insert an image. The image is stretched by default, but you can select the Stack option to avoid distorting the image. To add a texture, click *Picture or texture fill*, click Texture, and then select a textured background from the gallery of textures. Generally, do not mix images and textures.

---

## Format Axes

Based on the data source values and structure, Excel determines the starting, incremental, and stopping values that display on the value axis when you create the chart. You might want to adjust the value axis. For example, when working with large values such as 4,567,890, the value axis displays increments, such as 4,000,000 and 5,000,000. You can simplify the value axis by displaying values in millions, so that the values on the axis are 4 and 5 with the word *Millions* placed by the value axis to indicate the units. Figure 3.28 shows the Format Axis task pane. Diagonal black triangles, such as Axis Options, indicate all of a category's options are displayed (see the left task pane in Figure 3.28). Triangles with a white fill, such as Number, indicate the category options are not displayed (see the left task pane in Figure 3.28). You might need to scroll down and click a category name, such as Number, to see additional options. The task pane on the right side of Figure 3.28 shows the Number options after clicking the triangle.

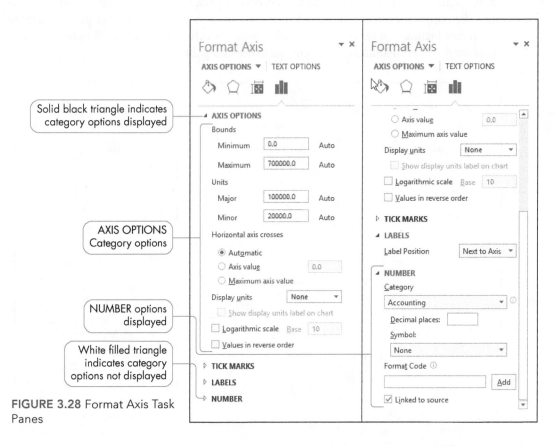

Solid black triangle indicates category options displayed

AXIS OPTIONS Category options

NUMBER options displayed

White filled triangle indicates category options not displayed

FIGURE 3.28 Format Axis Task Panes

## Insert and Format Data Labels

When you select a data label, Excel selects all data labels in that data series. To format the labels, double-click a data label to open the Format Data Labels task pane (see Figure 3.29). The Format Data Labels task pane enables you to specify what to display as the label. The default setting for Label Contains options is Value, but you can display additional label contents, such as the Category Name. However, displaying too much label content can clutter the chart. You can also specify the Label Position, such as Center or Outside End. If the numeric data labels are not formatted, click Number and apply number formats.

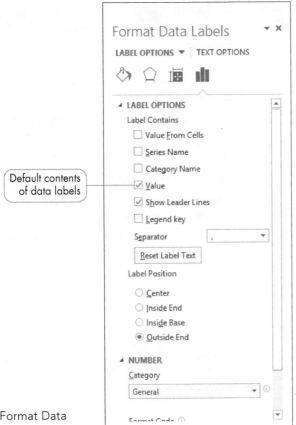

Default contents of data labels

**FIGURE 3.29** Format Data Labels Task Pane

## Use the Chart Tools Format Tab

The Format tab contains options to select a chart element, insert shapes, apply shape styles, apply WordArt styles, arrange objects, and specify the size of an object. Table 3.4 lists and describes the groups on the Format tab.

| TABLE 3.4 Chart Tools Format Tab | |
|---|---|
| **Group** | **Description** |
| Current Selection | Select a chart element, display the task pane to format the selected element, and clear custom formatting of the selected element. |
| Insert Shapes | Insert a variety of shapes in a chart. |
| Shape Styles | Specify a chart style, fill color, outline color, and shape effect. |
| WordArt Styles | Add artistic style, text fill, and text effects to an object. |
| Arrange | Bring an object forward or backward to layer multiple objects; align, group, and rotate objects. |
| Size | Adjust the height and width of the selected object. |

*Quick* Concepts

1. List at least four types of appropriate labels that describe chart elements. What types of things can you do to customize these labels? ***pp. 123–125***

2. How can you change the fill color of a data series in a column chart? ***p. 127***

3. What types of formats can you apply by using a Format task pane for a chart element? ***p. 127***

# Hands-On Exercises

## 2 Chart Elements

You want to enhance the computer job column, bar, and pie charts by adding some chart elements. In particular, you need to enter a descriptive chart title for each chart, add and format axis titles for the bar chart, add and format data labels for the pie chart, and change fill colors in the pie chart.

**Skills covered:** Add and Format Chart Titles • Add and Format Axis Titles • Add and Format Data Labels • Apply Fill Colors

---

### STEP 1 ≫ ADD AND FORMAT CHART TITLES

When you created the column, bar, and pie charts in Hands-On Exercise 1, Excel displayed *Chart Title* at the top of each chart. You need to type chart titles that appropriately describe each chart. In addition, you want to format the chart titles by applying bold to them and enlarging their font sizes. Refer to Figure 3.30 as you complete Step 1.

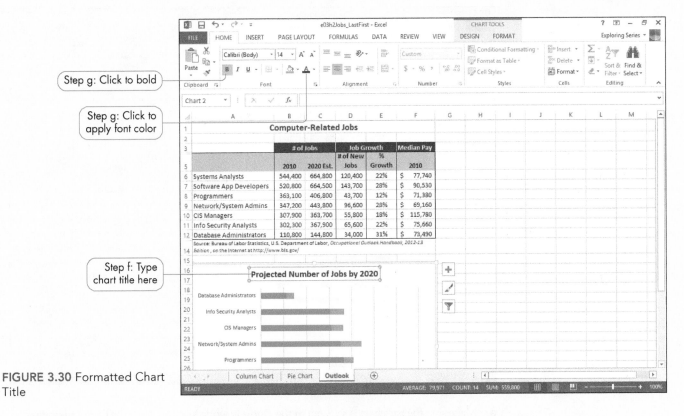

**FIGURE 3.30** Formatted Chart Title

a. Open *e03h1Jobs_LastFirst* if you closed it at the end of Hands-On Exercise 1 and save it as **e03h2Jobs_LastFirst**, changing *h1* to *h2*.

b. Make sure the Pie Chart sheet is the active sheet, select the **Chart Title placeholder**, type **New Computer-Related Jobs by 2020** in the Formula Bar, and then press **Enter**.

Excel displays the text you typed in the chart title.

> **TROUBLESHOOTING:** If you double-click a title and type directly into the title placeholder, do *not* press Enter after typing the new title. Doing so will add a blank line. If you select the title placeholder only and type text, the text will appear in the Formula Bar.

**c.** Click the **HOME tab**, click **Bold**, click the **Font Size arrow**, and then select **18**.

You formatted the pie chart's title so that it stands out better.

**d.** Click the **Column Chart sheet tab**, select the **Chart Title placeholder**, type **Number of Computer-Related Jobs 2010 and 2020** in the Formula Bar, and then press **Enter**.

**e.** Click **Bold**, click the **Font Size arrow**, and then select **18**.

**f.** Click the **Outlook sheet tab**, select the **Chart Title placeholder**, type **Projected Number of Jobs by 2020**, and then press **Enter**.

**g.** Click **Bold**, click the **Font Size arrow**, and then select **14**. Click the **Font Color arrow** and click **Dark Blue** in the *Standard Colors* section. Save the workbook.

You formatted the bar chart title to be consistently formatted with the worksheet title.

## STEP 2 ›› ADD AND FORMAT AXIS TITLES

For the bar chart, you want to add and format a title to describe the job titles on the vertical axis. In addition, you want to simplify the horizontal axis values to avoid *,000* for each increment and add the title *Thousands*. Refer to Figure 3.31 as you complete Step 2.

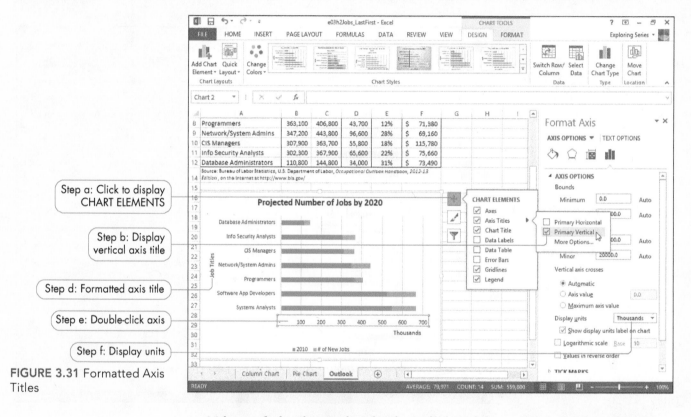

**FIGURE 3.31** Formatted Axis Titles

**a.** Make sure the bar chart is selected in the Outlook worksheet and click the **Chart Elements button** to the right of the chart.

Excel displays the CHART ELEMENTS menu.

**b.** Position the mouse pointer over *Axis Titles*, click the **Axis Titles arrow**, and then click the **Primary Vertical check box**.

Excel displays *Axis Title* on the left side of the vertical axis.

**c.** Make sure the *Axis Title* placeholder is selected, type **Job Titles** in the Formula Bar, and then press **Enter**.

**d.** Click **Font Color** to apply the default Dark Blue font color to the selected axis title.

**e.** Double-click the values on the horizontal axis.

Excel displays the Format Axis task pane so that you can format the value axis.

**f.** Click **AXIS OPTIONS**, if necessary, click the **Display units arrow,** and then select **Thousands**.

The axis now displays values such as 700 instead of 700,000. The title *Thousands* displays in the bottom-right corner of the horizontal axis.

**g.** Click the **HOME tab**, make sure the title *Thousands* is selected, and then apply **Dark Blue font color** in the Font group. Close the task pane. Save the workbook.

## STEP 3 ≫ ADD AND FORMAT DATA LABELS

The pie chart includes a legend to identify which color represents which computer-related job; however, it does not include numerical labels to help you interpret what percentage of all computer-related jobs will be hired for each position. You want to insert and format percentage value labels. Refer to Figure 3.32 as you complete Step 3.

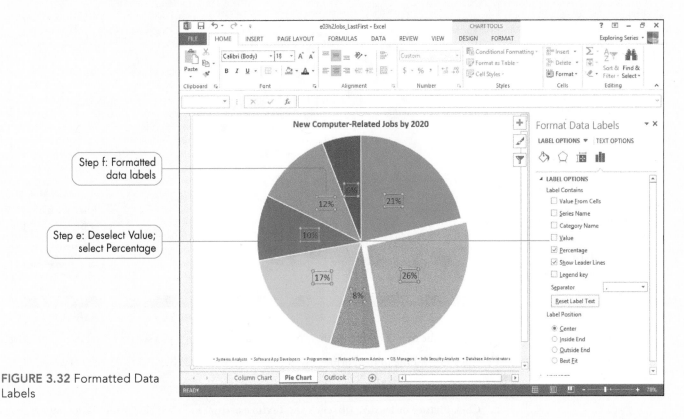

**FIGURE 3.32** Formatted Data Labels

**a.** Click the **Pie Chart Sheet tab** and click the **Chart Elements button**.

**b.** Click the **Data Labels arrow** and select **Center**.

You added data labels to the pie slices.

> **TROUBLESHOOTING:** If the Chart Elements menu remains open, click the Chart Elements button to close the menu.

**c.** Double-click one of the data labels to display the Format Data Labels task pane.

**d.** Click the **Label Options icon** in the Format Data Labels task pane, if necessary.

e. Click the **LABEL OPTIONS triangle**, if necessary, click the **Percentage check box** to select it, and then click the **Value check box** to deselect it.

Typically, pie chart data labels show percentages instead of values.

f. Change the font size to **18** to make the data labels larger. Save the workbook.

## STEP 4 ≫ APPLY FILL COLORS

You want to apply a texture fill to the chart area and change the fill colors for the Software Apps Developers' and the Database Administrators' slices. Refer to Figure 3.33 as you complete Step 4.

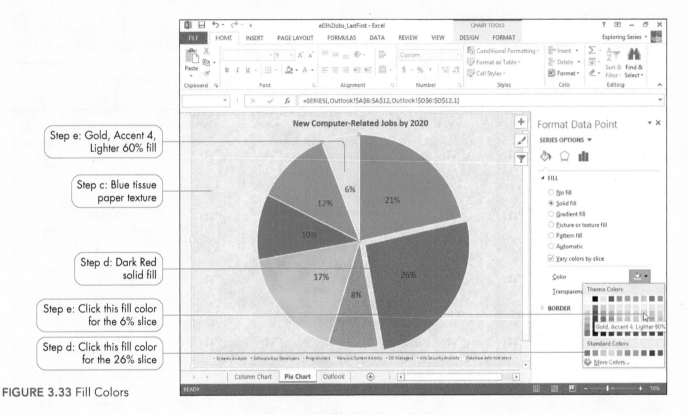

**FIGURE 3.33** Fill Colors

a. Position the mouse pointer in the white space and click when you see the Chart Area ScreenTip.

b. Click **Fill & Line** in the Format Chart Area task pane and click **FILL**, if necessary.

The task pane displays different fill options.

c. Click **Picture or texture fill**, click the **Texture arrow**, and then click **Blue tissue paper**.

The chart area now has the blue tissue paper texture fill.

d. Click the pie chart, pause, and then click the **26% orange slice**. Click **Solid fill**, click the **Color arrow**, and then click **Dark Red** in the *Standard Colors* section.

The Software Apps Developers slice is now dark red.

e. Click the **6% slice**, click **Solid fill**, click the **Color arrow**, and then click **Gold, Accent 4, Lighter 60%**.

The new color for the Database Administrators slice makes it easier to read the percentage data label.

f. Save the workbook. Keep the workbook open if you plan to continue with the next Hands-On Exercise. If not, close the workbook and exit Excel.

# Chart Design and Sparklines

After you add and format chart elements, you might want to experiment with other features to enhance a chart. The Chart Tools Design tab contains two other groups: Chart Styles and Data. These groups enable you to apply a different style or color scheme to a chart or manipulate the data that are used to build a chart. You can also click the Chart Styles and Chart Filters buttons to the right of a chart to change the design of a chart.

At times, you might want to insert small visual chart-like images within worksheet cells to illustrate smaller data series rather than a large chart to illustrate several data points. Excel enables you to create small chart-like images in close proximity to individual data points to help you visualize the data.

In this section, you will learn how to apply chart styles and colors, filter chart data, and insert and customize miniature charts (sparklines) within individual cells.

## Applying a Chart Style and Colors

**STEP 1 ▶** You can apply a different **chart style**, a collection of formatting that controls the color of the chart area, plot area, and data series. Styles also affect the look of the data series, such as flat, 3-D, or beveled. Figure 3.34 shows the options when you click the Chart Styles button to the right side of the chart, and Figure 3.35 shows the Chart Styles gallery when you click Chart Styles on the Design tab.

**FIGURE 3.34** Chart Styles

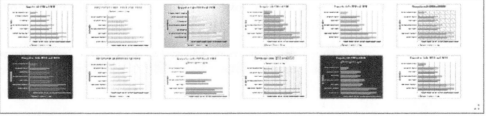

**FIGURE 3.35** Chart Styles Gallery

> **TIP** **Choosing Appropriate Chart Styles**
>
> When choosing a chart style, make sure the style complements the chart data and is easy to read. Also, consider whether you will display the chart onscreen in a presentation or print the chart. If you will display the chart in a presentation, consider selecting a style with a black background.

You can change the color scheme by clicking the Chart Styles button on the right side of the chart and clicking Color or click Change Colors in the Chart Styles group on the Design tab. You can select from the Colorful and Monochromatic sections.

# Modifying the Data Source

The data source is the range of worksheet cells that are used to construct a chart. Although you should select the data source carefully before creating a chart, you may decide to alter that data source after you create and format the chart. The Data group on the Design tab is useful for adjusting the data source.

## Create Chart Filters

**STEP 2 ❯❯** A *chart filter* controls which data series and categories are visible in a chart. By default, all the data you selected to create the chart are used to construct the data series and categories. However, you can apply a chart filter to hide extraneous data. Click the Chart Filter button to the right side of the chart to display the options (see Figure 3.36). A check mark indicates the data series or category currently displayed in the chart. Click a check box to deselect or hide a data series or category.

**FIGURE 3.36** Chart Filter Options

You can click Select Data in the Data group on the Design tab to open the Select Data Source dialog box (see Figure 3.37). This dialog box is another way to filter which categories and data series are visible in your chart.

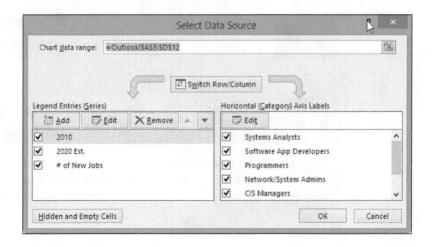

**FIGURE 3.37** Select Data Source Dialog Box

## Switch Row and Column Data

You can switch data used to create the horizontal axis and the legend. In Figure 3.38, the chart on the left uses the job titles to build the data series and legend, and the years display on the horizontal axis. The chart on the right shows the results after switching the data: the job titles build the horizontal axis, and the years build the data series and legend. To switch the data, click Switch Row/Column in the Data group on the Design tab.

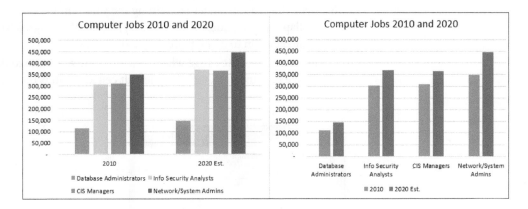

**FIGURE 3.38** Original Chart and Chart with Reversed Rows/Columns

# Creating and Customizing Sparklines

A *sparkline* is a small line, column, or win/loss chart contained in a single cell. The purpose of a sparkline is to present a condensed, simple, succinct visual illustration of data. Unlike a regular chart, a sparkline does not include a chart title or axis labels. Inserting sparklines next to data helps your audience understand data quickly without having to look at a full-scale chart.

Figure 3.39 shows three sample sparklines: line, column, and win/loss. The line sparkline shows trends over time, such as each student's trends in test scores. The column sparkline compares test averages. The win/loss sparkline depicts how many points a team won or lost each game.

**FIGURE 3.39** Sample Sparklines

## Create a Sparkline

STEP 3 >> Before creating a sparkline, identify which data you want to depict and where you want to place them. To create a sparkline, do the following:

1. Click the INSERT tab.
2. Click Line, Column, or Win/Loss in the Sparklines group. The Create Sparklines dialog box opens (see Figure 3.40).
3. Type the cell references containing the values in the Data Range box, or click the Collapse Dialog button (if necessary), select the range, and then click the Collapse Dialog button to display the dialog box again.
4. Enter or select the range where you want the sparkline to display in the Location Range box and click OK. The default cell location is the active cell unless you change it.

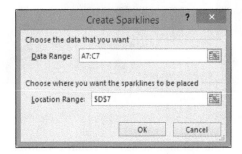

**FIGURE 3.40** Create Sparklines Dialog Box

## Customize a Sparkline

After you insert a sparkline, the Sparkline Tools Design tab displays (see Figure 3.41), with options to customize the sparkline.

**FIGURE 3.41** Sparkline Tools Design Tab

Table 3.5 lists and describes the groups on the Sparkline Tools Design tab.

| TABLE 3.5 | Sparkline Tools Design Tab |
|---|---|
| **Group** | **Description** |
| Sparkline | Edit the location and data source for a group or individual data point that generates a group of sparklines or an individual sparkline |
| Type | Change the selected sparkline type (line, column, win/loss) |
| Show | Display points, such as the high points, or markers within a sparkline |
| Style | Change the sparkline style, similar to a chart style, change the sparkline color, or change the marker color |
| Group | Specify the horizontal and vertical axis settings, group objects together, ungroup objects, and clear sparklines |

*Quick* Concepts

1. What are two ways to change the color scheme of a chart? *p. 135*
2. How can you change a chart so that the data in the legend are on the X-axis and the data on the X-axis are in the legend? *p. 137*
3. What is a sparkline, and why would you insert one? *pp. 137–138*

# Hands-On Exercises

## 3 Chart Design and Sparklines

Now that you have completed the pie chart, you want to focus again on the bar chart. You are not satisfied with the overall design and want to try a different chart style. In addition, you would like to include sparklines to show trends for all jobs between 2010 and 2020.

**Skills covered:** Apply a Chart Style • Apply Chart Filters • Insert and Customize Sparklines

### STEP 1 ➤➤ APPLY A CHART STYLE

You want to give more contrast to the bar chart. Therefore, you will apply the Style 2 chart style. That style formats the chart area with a dark fill color and helps highlight the data series. Refer to Figure 3.42 as you complete Step 1.

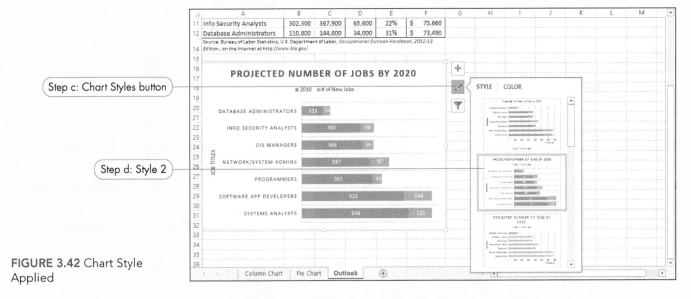

**FIGURE 3.42** Chart Style Applied

a. Open *e03h2Jobs_LastFirst* if you closed it at the end of Hands-On Exercise 2 and save it as **e03h3Jobs_LastFirst**, changing *h2* to *h3*.

b. Click the **Outlook Sheet tab** and click the bar chart to select it.

c. Click the **Chart Styles button** to the right of the chart.

The gallery of chart styles opens.

d. Click **Style 2**. Click the **Chart Styles button** to close the gallery. Save the workbook.

Excel applies the Style 2 chart style to the chart, which displays value data labels in white font color within each stack of the bar chart. The chart title and the category labels display in all capital letters. The legend displays above the plot area.

When you first created the clustered column chart, you included the number of new jobs as well as the number of 2010 jobs and the projected number of 2020 jobs. However, you decide that the number of new jobs is implied by comparing the 2010 to the 2020 jobs. Therefore, you want to set a chart filter to exclude the number of new jobs. Refer to Figure 3.43 as you complete Step 2.

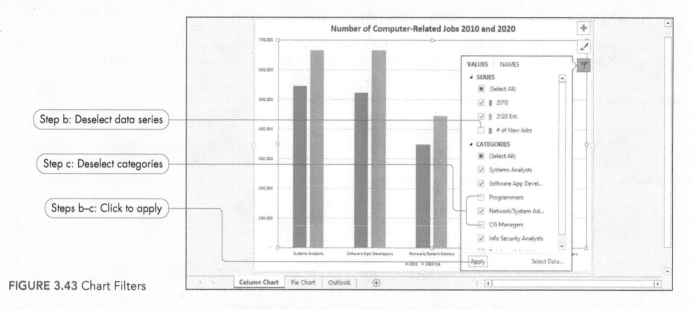

**FIGURE 3.43** Chart Filters

a. Click the **Column Chart Sheet tab** and click the **Chart Filters button** to the right of the chart.

b. Click the **# of New Jobs check box** in the SERIES group to deselect it and click **Apply** at the bottom of the filter window.

   The number of new jobs (gray) data series no longer displays in the clustered column chart.

c. Click the **Programmers check box** to deselect the category, click the **CIS Managers check box** to deselect it, and then click **Apply**. Click the **Chart Filters button** to close the menu. Save the workbook.

   The Programmers and CIS Managers categories no longer display in the clustered column chart.

You want to insert sparklines to show the trends between 2010 and 2020. After inserting the sparklines, you want to display the high points to show that all jobs will have major increases by 2020. Refer to Figure 3.44 as you complete Step 3.

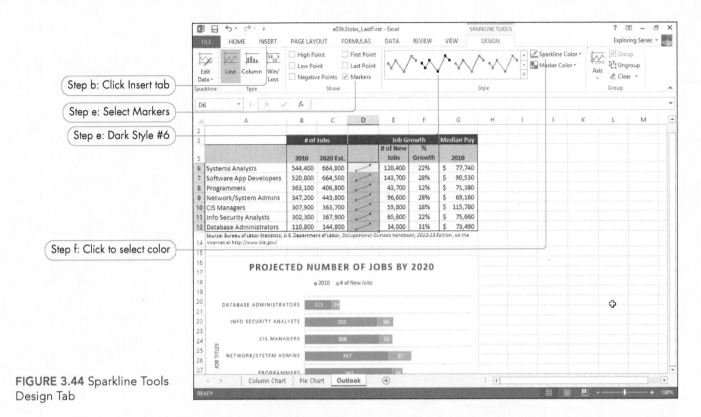

Step b: Click Insert tab

Step e: Select Markers

Step e: Dark Style #6

Step f: Click to select color

**FIGURE 3.44** Sparkline Tools Design Tab

a. Click the **Outlook sheet tab**, select **cell D6**, click the **HOME tab**, click the **Insert arrow** in the Cells group, and then select **Insert Sheet Columns**.

You inserted a new column to place the sparklines close to the data you want to visualize.

b. Click the **INSERT tab** and click **Line** in the Sparklines group.

c. Select the **range B6:C12** to enter that range in the Data Range box.

You can select multiple rows at one time to create a group of sparklines.

d. Press **Tab** and select the **range D6:D12** to enter that range in the Location Range box. Click **OK**.

Excel inserts sparklines in the range D6:D12 with each sparkline representing data on its respective row. The Sparkline Tools Design tab displays.

e. Click the **Markers check box** in the Show group to select it and click **Sparkline Style Dark #6** in the Style group.

f. Click **Sparkline Color** in the Style group and click **Red**.

g. Save and close the workbook, and submit based on your instructor's directions.

# Excel

# Statistical Functions

## CHAPTER 4

### Analyzing Statistics

Yuri Arcurs/Shutterstock

## OBJECTIVES  AFTER YOU READ THIS CHAPTER, YOU WILL BE ABLE TO:

1. Use conditional math and statistical functions p. 144

2. Calculate relative standing with statistical functions p. 147

## CASE STUDY | Education Evaluation

You are the superintendent of schools for Banton School System, a K–12 school district in Erie, Pennsylvania. You and your team have the task of evaluating student and teacher performance across schools in your district. As part of your evaluation you would like to perform several statistical calculations based on location, age, and test scores.

First, you will evaluate teachers' performance rankings and salary quartiles. You then plan to assess middle school students' standardized testing performance. As part of this analysis, you will perform basic descriptive statistical calculations. You will also compare performance to attendance and test the correlation between test scores and daily turnout. Last, you will perform more advanced evaluation of high school students' performance using the Analysis ToolPak.

# Math and Statistical Functions

Do not let the term *statistics* scare you. Every day, you rely on statistics to make routine decisions. When you purchase a car, you compare the miles per gallon (MPG) among several vehicles. The automobile manufacturer conducted multiple test drives, recorded the MPG under various driving conditions, and then calculated the MPG statistic. Statistics involves analyzing a collection of data and making inferences to draw conclusions about a dataset. You already have learned to use the SUM, AVERAGE, MIN, MAX, MEDIAN, and COUNT statistical functions.

However, sometimes you might want to calculate a statistic based on a particular condition. Excel's math and statistical function categories contain functions that enable you to perform conditional calculations, such as calculating a total only when a particular circumstance or set of circumstances exists. In addition, you might want to analyze individual values against others in a dataset to determine relative standing.

In this section, you will use math and statistical functions—SUMIF, AVERAGEIF, COUNTIF, SUMIFS, AVERAGEIFS, and COUNTIFS—to perform conditional statistical calculations. In addition, you will use relative-standing functions, such as RANK, PERCENTRANK, PERCENTILE, and QUARTILE.

## Using Conditional Math and Statistical Functions

When you use SUM, AVERAGE, and COUNT functions, Excel calculates the respective total, the mathematical average, and the number of values for all values in the range specified in the function's arguments. The math and statistical function categories contain related functions—SUMIF, AVERAGEIF, COUNTIF, SUMIFS, AVERAGEIFS, and COUNTIFS—that perform similar calculations but based on a condition. These functions are similar to the logical function IF. As you recall, the IF function evaluates a logical test to determine if it is true or false. If the logical test is true, Excel returns one result; if the logical test is false, it returns a different result. In a way, these conditional math and statistical functions are a hybrid of math/statistical and logical functionality. Figure 4.1 shows a salary table for educators in the district and the results of these math and statistical functions.

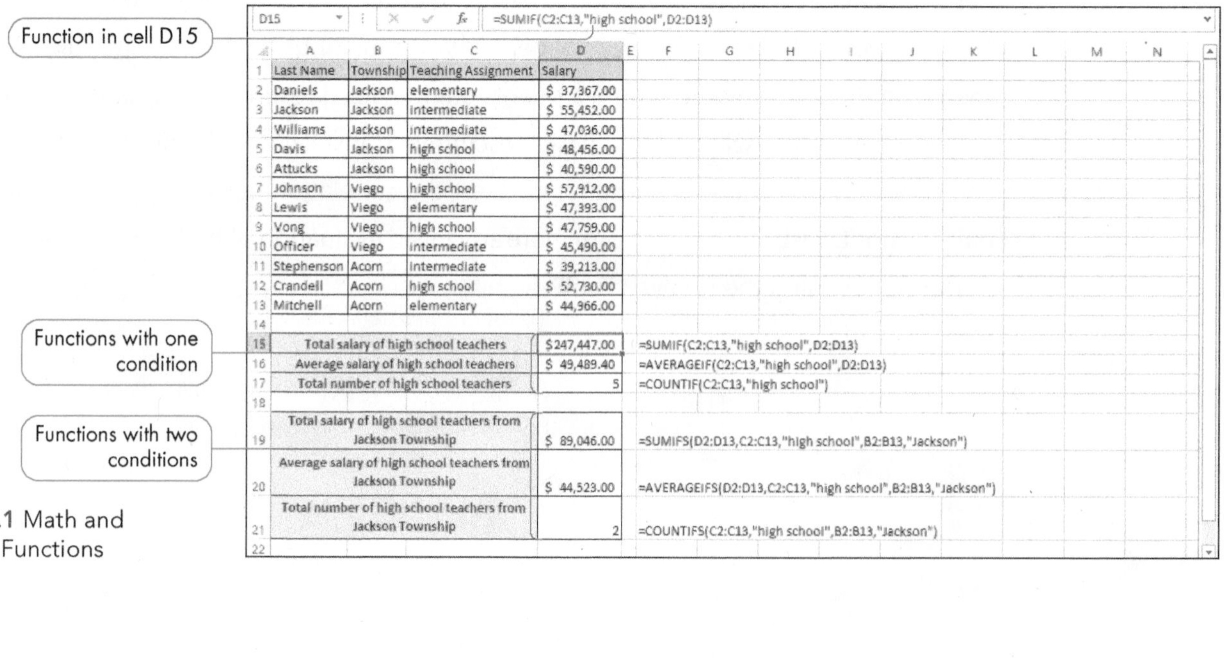

FIGURE 4.1 Math and Statistical Functions

# Use the SUMIF, AVERAGEIF, and COUNTIF Functions

**STEP 1 >>**  The ***SUMIF function*** is similar to the SUM function except that it calculates a sum of values in a range only when related data meet a specific condition instead of calculating the sum of an entire range. For example, in Figure 4.1, if you want to calculate the total salaries for all high school teachers in the district, you cannot use the SUM function because it would calculate the total salaries for teachers in the district's elementary and intermediate schools as well. However, you can complete the task using the SUMIF function. In Figure 4.1, cell D15 contains the results of the function =SUMIF(C2:C13,"high school",D2:D13) to sum the Salary column (D2:D13) if the Teaching Assignment column (C2:C13) contains the text *high school*. The total value of salaries for high school teachers is $247,447.00. The SUMIF function contains three required arguments:

=SUMIF(range,criteria,sum_range)

- **Range.** The range argument specifies the range of cells you want to evaluate to determine if the values meet a particular condition. In Figure 4.1, the SUMIF function's range is C2:C13, the range containing the job titles.

- **Criteria.** The criteria argument specifies the condition that imposes limitations on what values Excel sums. The criteria can be a value, date, text, or another cell containing a value, date, or text. In Figure 4.1, the SUMIF function's criterion is the text *high school*. Excel restricts the totaling to rows in which the range contains only *high school*. When you use text as a criterion, you must enclose it within quotation marks. When you use values as criteria, do not use quotation marks. You can also create an input range to specify the condition and then simply use a cell reference as the criteria argument in the SUMIF function.

- **Sum_range.** The sum_range argument designates the cells containing values to add if the condition is met. In Figure 4.1, the SUMIF function's sum_range is D2:D13, the range containing the salaries.

The ***AVERAGEIF function*** calculates the average, or arithmetic mean, of all cells in a range that meet a specific condition. In Figure 4.1, cell D16 contains =AVERAGEIF(C2:C13,"high school",D2:D13) to calculate the average value in the Salary column (D2:D13) when the Teaching Assignment column (C2:C13) contains the text *high school*. The average high school teacher's salary is $49,489.40.

=AVERAGEIF(range,criteria,average_range)

The AVERAGEIF function contains three required arguments: range, criteria, and average_range. The range and criteria arguments have the same meanings as the same arguments in the SUMIF function. The average_range argument specifies the range containing values that you want to average if the condition is met. In the AVERAGEIF function, the average_range is D2:D13.

 **TIP** **Referencing the Input Range**

When using the SUMIF, AVERAGEIF, and COUNTIF functions, you can create an input range to specify the condition and then simply use a cell reference as the criteria argument in the function. This allows the user the flexibility to change the criteria and receive instant calculation updates.

The ***COUNTIF function*** is similar to the COUNT function except that it calculates the number of cells in a range that meet a condition you specify instead of calculating the count of an entire range. In Figure 4.1, cell D17 contains =COUNTIF(C2:C13,"high school") to count the number of high school teachers, which is five.

=COUNTIF(range,criteria)

The COUNTIF function contains only two arguments: range and criteria. Similar to the SUMIF and AVERAGEIF functions, the range argument for the COUNTIF function specifies the range of cells you want to evaluate to see if the values meet a particular condition. The criteria argument specifies the condition to be met in order to count cells in the designated range.

## Use the SUMIFS, AVERAGEIFS, and COUNTIFS Functions

**STEP 2 »** Whereas the previously described functions enable you to perform conditional calculations, they can address only a single condition. Similar math and statistical functions enable you to specify more than one condition: SUMIFS, AVERAGEIFS, and COUNTIFS.

The *SUMIFS function* calculates the total value of cells in a range that meet multiple criteria. In Figure 4.1, cell D19 contains =SUMIFS(D2:D13,C2:C13,"high school",B2:B13,"Jackson"). This function sums the Salary range if the teaching assignment range contains *high school* and if the township range contains *Jackson*. The total salary of high school teachers in Jackson Township is $89,046.00. The SUMIFS function contains at least five arguments: sum_range, criteria_range1, criteria1, criteria_range2, and criteria2. Additional ranges and their criteria may be included. All conditions must be met in order to include values in the sum_range in the total.

=SUMIFS(sum_range,criteria_range1,criteria1,criteria_range2,criteria2...)

- **Sum_range.** The sum_range argument designates the cells containing values to add if the condition is met. In the SUMIFS function, the sum_range argument is the first argument instead of the last argument as in the SUMIF function. In Figure 4.1, the SUMIFS function's sum_range is D2:D13, the range containing the salaries.

- **Criteria_range1.** The range argument specifies the first range of cells you want to evaluate to see if the values meet a particular condition. The range must contain values, range names, arrays, or references that contain numbers, dates, or text. In Figure 4.1, the criteria_range1 is C2:C13, the range containing the teaching assignments.

- **Criteria1.** The criteria1 argument specifies the condition for the criteria_range1 argument that imposes limitations on what values are summed. In Figure 4.1, the SUMIFS function's criteria1 argument is *high school*.

- **Criteria_range2.** The range argument specifies the second range of cells you want to evaluate to see if the values meet a particular condition. The range must contain values, range names, arrays, or references that contain numbers, dates, or text. In Figure 4.1, the SUMIFS function's criteria_range2 is B2:B13, the range containing the township.

- **Criteria2.** The criteria2 argument specifies the condition that imposes limitations on what values are summed. In Figure 4.1, the SUMIFS function's criteria2 is *Jackson*.

The *AVERAGEIFS function* calculates the average value of cells in a range that meet multiple criteria. In Figure 4.1, cell D20 contains =AVERAGEIFS(D2:D13,C2:C13"high school",B2:B13,"Jackson"). This function calculates the average value in the Salary range if the teaching assignment is *high school* and if the township is *Jackson*. The average salary of high school teachers in Jackson Township is $44,523. The AVERAGEIFS function contains at least five arguments. The average_range argument specifies the range of cells containing values that will be averaged when multiple conditions specified by the criteria ranges and criteria are met.

=AVERAGEIFS(average_range,criteria_range1,criteria1,criteria_range2,criteria2...)

The *COUNTIFS function* counts the number of cells in a range that meet multiple criteria. In Figure 4.1, cell D21 contains =COUNTIFS(C2:C13,"high school",B2:B13,"Jackson"). This function counts the number of high school teachers in Jackson Township, which is two. The COUNTIFS function contains at least four arguments: two ranges and their respective criteria.

=COUNTIFS(criteria_range1,criteria1,criteria_range2,criteria2...)

Whereas the syntax shows only two criteria for SUMIFS, AVERAGEIFS, and COUNTIFS, you can continue adding criteria ranges and criteria. If you type the function in a cell, separate criteria ranges and criteria with commas. If you use the Function Arguments dialog box, it expands to display another Criteria box as you enter data in existing boxes, or you can press Tab within the dialog box to see additional criteria ranges and criteria boxes.

## Enter Math and Statistical Functions

Excel organizes the conditional functions in the math and statistical function categories. The SUMIF and SUMIFS functions are math functions. To enter these functions, click Math & Trig in the Function Library group on the Formulas tab and select either SUMIF or SUMIFS. Enter the arguments in the Function Arguments dialog box and click OK.

The AVERAGEIF, AVERAGEIFS, COUNTIF, and COUNTIFS functions are statistical functions. To enter these functions, click More Functions in the Function Library group on the Formulas tab, click Statistical, and then select the desired function name. Enter the arguments in the Function Arguments dialog box and click OK.

# Calculating Relative Standing with Statistical Functions

Often people analyze a dataset based on an individual value compared to the rest of the dataset. You do not have to be a statistician to need to use statistical calculations. For example, a professor might want to rank students in a chemistry class, or a medical doctor might want to identify diabetic patients' blood sugar levels based on what quartile they fall in. You can use the RANK.EQ, PERCENTRANK, QUARTILE, and PERCENTILE functions to analyze data.

## Use the RANK and PERCENTRANK Functions

STEP 3 >>

Excel 2013 contains two rank functions: RANK.EQ and RANK.AVG. The *RANK.EQ function* identifies a value's rank within a list of values. For example, the rank of 1, E7 in Figure 4.2, indicates that the $57,912.00 salary is the highest-ranking salary in the list, $55,452.00 is the second-highest-ranking salary, and so on. If the range of values contains duplicate numbers (such as $44,966.00 in cells D8 and D13), both values receive the same rank (8), the next ranking (9) is skipped, and the next value ($40,590) is assigned the ranking of 10.

The *RANK.AVG function* identifies the rank of a value but assigns an average rank when identical values exist. Column F shows the results of the RANK.AVG function in which both $44,966 values have a ranking of 8.5—the average of rankings 8 and 9—instead of a rank of 8. Some statisticians consider the RANK.AVG function results to be more accurate than the RANK.EQ function results.

PERCENTRANK.EXC identifies rank as a percentage, excluding 1 and 0

PERCENTRANK.EXC identifies rank as a percentage, excluding 1 and 0

PERCENTRANK.INC identifies rank as a percentage, with a top rank of 1.000 and a low rank 0.000

RANK.AVG identifies the average ranking for duplicate values

RANK.EQ identifies ranking with duplicate rankings

**FIGURE 4.2** RANK and PERCENTRANK Functions

| F2 | ▾ | : | × | ✓ | *fx* | =RANK.AVG(D2,$D$2:$D$13) |

| | A | B | C | D | E | F | G | H | I | J | K |
|---|---|---|---|---|---|---|---|---|---|---|---|
| 1 | Last Name | Township | Teaching Assignment | Salary | RANK.EQ | Rank.AVG | Percent Rank.INC | Percent Rank.EXC | | | |
| 2 | Daniels | Jackson | Elementary | $ 37,367.00 | 12 | 12 | 0.0% | 7.6% | | | |
| 3 | Jackson | Jackson | Intermediate | $ 55,452.00 | 2 | 2 | 90.9% | 84.6% | | | |
| 4 | Williams | Jackson | Intermediate | $ 47,096.00 | 6 | 6 | 54.5% | 53.8% | | | |
| 5 | Davis | Jackson | High School | $ 48,456.00 | 4 | 4 | 72.7% | 69.2% | | | |
| 6 | Attucks | Jackson | High School | $ 40,590.00 | 10 | 10 | 18.1% | 23.0% | | | |
| 7 | Johnson | Viego | High School | $ 57,912.00 | 1 | 1 | 100.0% | 92.3% | | | |
| 8 | Lewis | Viego | Elementary | $ 44,966.00 | 8 | 8.5 | 27.2% | 30.7% | | | |
| 9 | Vong | Viego | High School | $ 47,759.00 | 5 | 5 | 63.6% | 61.5% | | | |
| 10 | Officer | Viego | Intermediate | $ 45,490.00 | 7 | 7 | 45.4% | 46.1% | | | |
| 11 | Stephenson | Acorn | Intermediate | $ 39,213.00 | 11 | 11 | 9.0% | 15.3% | | | |
| 12 | Crandell | Acorn | High School | $ 52,730.00 | 3 | 3 | 81.8% | 76.9% | | | |
| 13 | Mitchell | Acorn | Elementary | $ 44,966.00 | 8 | 8.5 | 27.2% | 30.7% | | | |

Both the RANK.EQ and RANK.AVG functions contain two arguments (number and ref) and one optional argument (order).

`=RANK.EQ(number,ref,[order])`

`=RANK.AVG(number,ref,[order])`

- **Number.** The number argument specifies the cell containing the value you want to rank, such as cell D2.

- **Ref.** The ref argument specifies the range of values, such as D$2:D$13, that you want to use to identify their rankings. Mixed references are used so that the row numbers do not change as the formula is copied down the column.

- **Order.** The optional order argument enables you to specify how you want to rank the values. The implied default is 0, which ranks the values as if the values were listed in descending order. Because the order argument was omitted in Figure 4.2, the first-rank salary is the highest salary value of $57,912. If you enter any nonzero value for the order argument, Excel ranks the values as if the values were listed in ascending order (i.e., low to high). If the order argument were 2, the first-ranked salary would be the lowest value, which is $37,367.

Some functions have a descriptor added to the function name to further clarify the function's purpose and to distinguish functions that perform similar tasks but have subtle differences. The .INC descriptor indicates *inclusive* functions, that is, the functions *include* particular parameters. The .EXC descriptor indicates *exclusive* functions, that is, functions that *exclude* particular parameters. The **PERCENTRANK.INC** *function* displays a value's rank as a percentile of the range of data in the dataset. In other words, you can use this function to identify a value's relative standing compared to other values in the dataset. Excel displays ranks as decimal values between 0 and 1, but you can format the results with Percent Number Style. The first rank is 1.000, and the lowest percent rank is 0.000, because the .INC descriptor *includes* 0 and 1. The percent rank correlates with the rank of a value. For example, in Figure 4.2, the $57,912 salary is the highest-ranking salary; its percent rank is 1.00 or 100% percentile. The $55,452 value is the second-highest-ranking salary; its percent rank is 0.909, indicating that this salary is the 90.9% percentile.

Excel 2013 contains a similar function—PERCENTRANK.EXC. The **PERCENTRANK. EXC** *function* is similar in that it returns a value's rank as a percent. This function adheres to best practices in that a percent rank is between 0 and 1 because the .EXC descriptor *excludes* the 0 and 1. For this function, the $57,912 salary has a percent rank of 0.923 or is in the 92.3% percentile.

Both PERCENTRANK.INC and PERCENTRANK.EXC functions contain two required arguments (array and x) and one optional argument (significance).

`=PERCENTRANK.INC(array,x,[significance])`

`=PERCENTRANK.EXC(array,x,[significance])`

- **Array.** The array argument specifies the range that contains the values to compare, such as D$2:D$13.

- **x.** The x argument specifies an individual's salary, such as cell D2.

- **Significance.** The optional significance argument designates the number of significant digits for precision. If you omit the significance argument, Excel displays three significant digits.

## Use the QUARTILE and PERCENTILE Functions

STEP 4 >> A *quartile* is a value used to divide a range of numbers into four equal groups. The *QUARTILE.INC function* identifies the value at a specific quartile for a dataset, *including* quartile 0 for the lowest value and quartile 4 for the highest value in the dataset. The *QUARTILE.EXC function* is similar in that it returns the value at a specific quartile but *excluding* quartiles 0 and 4. These functions contain two required arguments: array and quart. The array argument specifies the range of values. The quart argument is a number that represents a specific quartile (see Table 4.1).

TABLE 4.1  **Quart Argument**

| Argument Value | Description |
|---|---|
| 0 | Lowest value in the dataset. Identical to using the MIN function. Allowed in QUARTILE.INC only. |
| 1 | First quartile of the dataset. Identifies the value at the 25th percentile. |
| 2 | Second quartile or median value within the dataset. Identifies the value at the 50th percentile. |
| 3 | Third quartile of the dataset. Identifies the value at the 75th percentile. |
| 4 | Fourth quartile or highest value within the dataset. Identical to using the MAX function. Allowed in QUARTILE.INC only. |

=QUARTILE.INC(array,quart)

=QUARTILE.EXC(array,quart)

In Figure 4.3, cell B24 contains =QUARTILE.INC(D$2:D$13,A24), where cell A24 contains the quartile of Salary. The function returns $37,367, which is the lowest salary in the range. Cell B25 contains =QUARTILE.INC(D$2:D$13,A25) to identify the top salary in the first quartile, which is $43,872. Look at column G, which contains the PERCENTRANK.INC function, and column H, which contains the PERCENTRANK.EXC function. Any salaries with 25% or less fall in the first quartile, salaries above 25% and up to 50% fall in the second quartile, salaries above 50% and up to 75% fall in the third quartile, and salaries above 75% fall in the fourth (or top) quartile. The dataset is sorted in ascending order by salary, and the data in columns D and H are color coded to help you identify values within each quartile.

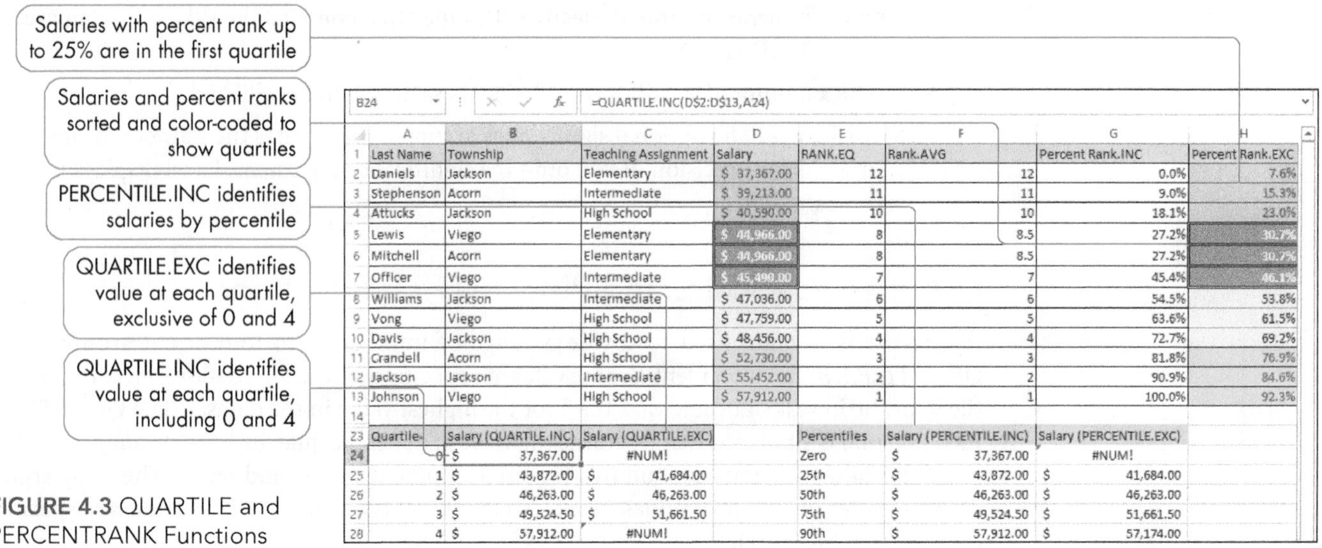

Salaries with percent rank up to 25% are in the first quartile

Salaries and percent ranks sorted and color-coded to show quartiles

PERCENTILE.INC identifies salaries by percentile

QUARTILE.EXC identifies value at each quartile, exclusive of 0 and 4

QUARTILE.INC identifies value at each quartile, including 0 and 4

**FIGURE 4.3** QUARTILE and PERCENTRANK Functions

Range C24:C28 contains the QUARTILE.EXC function. For example, cell C24 contains =QUARTILE.EXC(D$2:D$13,A24). Because QUARTILE.EXC excludes 0 and 4, the function returns #NUM! error messages when 0 and 4 are used as the quart argument in cells C24 and C28. The salaries at the first and second quartiles are identical for either QUARTILE function; however, the salaries for the third quartile differ based on which function you use. Table 4.2 summarizes the findings from the QUARTILE.EXC functions.

**TABLE 4.2  Quartile Grouping**

| Quartile | Salary at Top of Quartile | Salaries |
|---|---|---|
| 1 (0.25 or lower) | $41,684 | $37,367 |
| | | $39,213 |
| | | $40,590 |
| 2 (between 0.251 and 0.5) | $46,263 | $44,966 |
| | | $44,966 |
| | | $45,490 |
| 3 (between 0.501 and 0.75) | $51,661.50 | $47,036 |
| | | $47,759 |
| | | $48,456 |
| 4 (above 0.75) | $57,174.00 | $52,730 |
| | | $55,452 |
| | | $57,912 |

The **PERCENTILE.INC function** identifies the $k^{th}$ percentile of a specified value within a list of values, including the $0^{th}$ and $100^{th}$ percentiles. College admissions offices find this function helpful when identifying college applicants' percentiles to determine which candidates to admit to their college. For example, a college might have a policy to admit only candidates who fall within the $80^{th}$ percentile. The **PERCENTILE.EXC function** also identifies a value at a specified percentile; however, the .EXC *excludes* $0^{th}$ or $100^{th}$ percentiles.

The PERCENTILE functions contain two required arguments: array and k. The array argument specifies the range containing values to determine individual standing. For the PERCENTILE.INC function, the $k$ argument specifies the percentile value from 0 to 1.

For the PERCENTILE.EXC function, the *k* argument *excludes* values 0 and 1. For example, 0.25 represents the 25th percentile. In Figure 4.3, cell F25 contains =PERCENTILE.INC(D$2:D$13,0.25) to identify the value at the 25th percentile. Note that this salary ($43,872) is the same as the value returned by =QUARTILE.INC(D$2:D$13,A25). However, unlike the QUARTILE.INC function that has distinct quartiles (0, 1, 2, 3, 4), you can specify any decimal value for the *k* argument in the PERCENTILE functions, such as =PERCENTILE.INC(D$2:D$13,0.9) to find the value at the 90th percentile. The PERCENTILE.EXC returns different values than PERCENTILE.INC at the higher percentiles. Also, =PERCENTILE.EXC(D$2:D$13,0) returns an error since the .EXC descriptor excludes 0 as a legitimate parameter.

=PERCENTILE.INC(array,k)

=PERCENTILE.EXC(array,k)

*Quick*
Concepts

1. When would you use SUMIFS instead of SUMIF? *p. 146*

2. When would you use RANK.AVG instead of RANK.EQ? *p. 147*

3. What is the difference between PERCENTRANK.INC versus PERCENTRANK.EXC? *p. 148*

## 1 Math and Statistical Functions

For the first step of your assessment, you need to calculate summary statistics of the teachers' salaries. First, you want to calculate statistics, such as average salary for teachers hired before 2005. Then you will turn your attention to the Acorn Township, the township with the fewest teachers, as you perform statistical calculations. Finally, you want to rank each person's salary compared to the other salaries and identify the salary ranges for each quartile.

**Skills covered:** Use SUMIF, AVERAGEIF, and COUNTIF Functions • Enter SUMIFS, AVERAGEIFS, and COUNTIFS Functions • Calculate Salary Ranks • Identify Salary Ranges by Quartile

## STEP 1 >> USE SUMIF, AVERAGEIF, AND COUNTIF FUNCTIONS

You want to calculate the number of high school teachers that were hired before 1/1/2005. You also want to calculate the average salary and total payroll for all high school teachers hired before 1/1/2005. You will use SUMIF, COUNTIF, and AVERAGEIF to complete the calculations. Refer to Figures 4.4 and 4.5 as you complete Step 1.

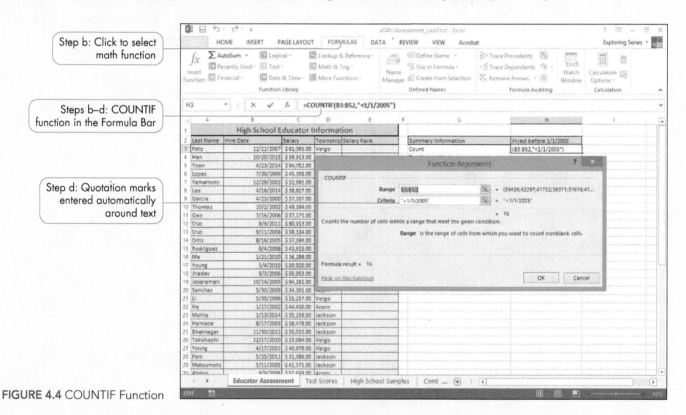

**FIGURE 4.4** COUNTIF Function

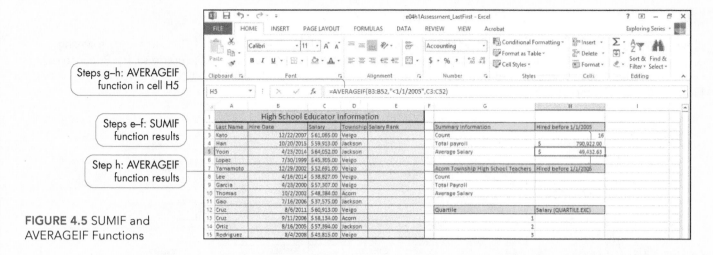

Steps g–h: AVERAGEIF
function in cell H5

Steps e–f: SUMIF
function results

Step h: AVERAGEIF
function results

**FIGURE 4.5** SUMIF and
AVERAGEIF Functions

a. Open *e04h1Assessment* and save it as **e04h1Assessment_LastFirst**. If necessary, click the
**Educator Assessment worksheet**.

> **TROUBLESHOOTING**: If you make any major mistakes in this exercise, you can close the
> file, open *e04h1Assessment* again, and then start this exercise over.

b. Click **cell H3**, click the **FORMULAS tab**, click **More Functions**, select **Statistical** in the
Function Library group, scroll through the list, and then select **COUNTIF**.

Cell H3 is the cell in which you want to calculate the total number of high school teachers
hired before 1/1/2005.

The Function Arguments dialog box opens so that you can enter the range and criteria
arguments.

c. Drag to select the **range B3:B52** to enter it in the Range box.

d. Click in the **Criteria box**, type **<1/1/2005**, and then click **OK**.

The newly created function indicates there are 16 teachers that meet the criteria
requirements.

e. Click **cell H4**, click **Math & Trig** in the Function Library group, and then select **SUMIF**.

The Function Arguments dialog box displays so that you can enter the range, criteria, and
sum_range arguments.

f. Type **B3:B52** in the **Range box**, type **<1/1/2005** in the **Criteria box**, type **C3:C52** in the
**Sum_range box**, and then click **OK**.

The total salaries paid to high school teachers hired before 1/1/2005 is $790,922.

g. Click **cell H5**, click **More Functions** in the Function Library group, click **Statistical**, and
then select **AVERAGEIF**.

h. Type **B3:B52** in the **Range box**, type **"<1/1/2005"** in the **Criteria box**, type **C3:C52** in the
**Average_range box**, and then click **OK**.

The average salary for high school teachers hired before 1/1/2005 is $49,432.63.

 **Quotation Marks**

When entering criteria that contain text, a date, or an operator such as <, you must surround the criteria with quotation marks. If you enter the criteria using the insert function
box, Excel will automatically add quotation marks. If you type the function from scratch
instead of using the insert function, you must type the quotation marks manually.

Now you want to focus on the summarizing data for high school teachers hired before 1/1/2005 in Acorn Township. Specifically, you want to calculate the total number of educators, total salary payroll, and average salary. Because each of these calculations requires two criteria, you will use the SUMIFS, AVERAGEIFS, and COUNTIFS functions. Refer to Figure 4.6 as you complete Step 2.

Steps a–c: COUNTIFS function in cell H8

Steps d–e: SUMIFS function results

Step f: AVERAGEIFS function results

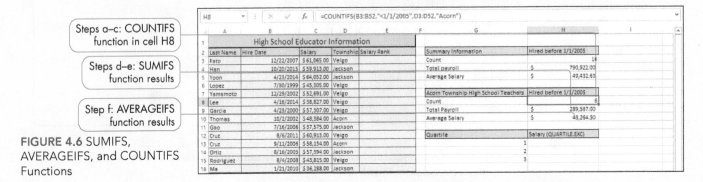

**FIGURE 4.6** SUMIFS, AVERAGEIFS, and COUNTIFS Functions

a. Click **cell H8**, click **More Functions – Statistical** in the Function Library group, scroll through the list, and then select **COUNTIFS**.

b. Type **B3:B52** in the **Criteria_range1 box**, click in the **Criteria1 box**, and then type **<1/1/2005**.

c. Click in the **Criteria_range2 box** and type **D3:D52**. Type **"Acorn"** in the **Criteria 2 box** and click **OK**.

   The function returns 6, the total number of high school teachers in Acorn Township hired before 1/1/2005, by using the criteria "<1/1/2005" and "Acorn" to filter the data ranges B3:B52 and D3:D32.

d. Click **cell H9**, click **Math & Trig** in the Function Library group, and then select **SUMIFS**.

e. Type **C3:C52** in the **Sum_range box**, type **B3:B52** in the **Criteria_range1 box**, type **"<1/1/2005"** in the **Criteria1 box**, type **D3:D52** in the **Criteria_range2 box**, type **"Acorn"** in the **Criteria2 box**, and then click **OK**.

   The total payroll for high school teachers in Acorn Township hired before 1/1/2005 is $289,587.00.

> **TROUBLESHOOTING:** If you misspell criterion text, such as the township name, the results will be inaccurate. Always check the criterion text to make sure it matches text in the respective column.

f. Click **cell H10** and type **=AVERAGEIFS(C3:C52,B3:B52,"<1/1/2005",D3:D52,"Acorn")** manually or by selecting the function from the More Functions list and entering the arguments similarly to how you entered the SUMIFS function in step e.

   The average salary of high school teachers in Acorn Township hired before 1/1/2005 is $48,264.50.

g. Save the workbook.

# STEP 3 >> CALCULATE SALARY RANKS

You want to identify the rank of each teacher's salary. Doing so will enable you to later compare salaries with classroom performance. Refer to Figure 4.7 as you complete Step 3.

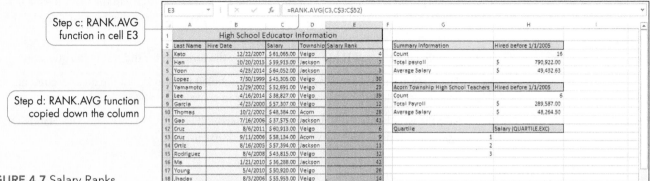

**FIGURE 4.7** Salary Ranks

- Step c: RANK.AVG function in cell E3
- Step d: RANK.AVG function copied down the column

a. Click **cell E3**, click **More Functions** in the Function Library group, click **Statistical**, and then select **RANK.AVG**.

b. Click **cell C3** to enter it in the Number box.

   Excel uses the individual salary to compare it to a list of salaries to identify its rank.

c. Click in the **Ref box**, type **C$3:C$52**, and then click **OK**.

   You use the mixed reference C$3:C$52 to prevent the row numbers from changing when you copy the functions down the column. You do not have to use absolute references since the column letters will be the same as you copy the function down the same column.

   Kato's salary of $61,065 is ranked fourth out of the entire list of salaries.

d. Double-click the **cell E3 fill handle** to copy the function down the rank column. Save the workbook.

# STEP 4 >> IDENTIFY SALARY RANGES BY QUARTILE

You want to see what salary ranges fall within each quartile. You will use the QUARTILE function to identify the ranges and to identify the lowest and highest salaries. Refer to Figure 4.8 as you complete Step 4.

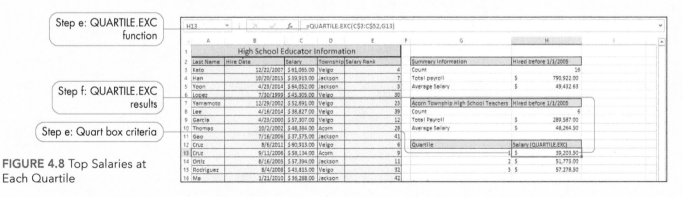

**FIGURE 4.8** Top Salaries at Each Quartile

- Step e: QUARTILE.EXC function
- Step f: QUARTILE.EXC results
- Step e: Quart box criteria

a. Click **cell H13**, the cell to contain the top salary for the first quartile.

b. Click **Insert Function** on the **FORMULAS tab** on the Ribbon. In the function Library group, click the **Or select a category arrow** and select **Statistical** if necessary.

c. Scroll through the *Select a function* list, select **QUARTILE.EXC**, and then click **OK**.

   The Function Arguments dialog box opens so that you can enter the array and quart arguments.

**d.** Drag to select the **range C3:C52** to enter it in the Array box. Edit the range to reflect mixed references so that the row numbers remain the same as you copy the function down: **C$3:C$52**.

**e.** Click in the **Quart box**, type **G13**, and then click **OK**.

Cell G13 contains 1, which reflects Quartile 1. The highest salary in the first quartile is $39,203.50. This would be the salary at the 25$^{th}$ percentile. Note that because QUARTILE. EXC was used, quartiles 0 and 4 were omitted.

**f.** Double-click the **cell H13 fill handle** to copy the function for the rest of the quartiles.

The array argument remains the same in the copied functions, but the quart argument changes to reflect the correct quartile values in column G.

**g.** Save the workbook. Keep the workbook onscreen if you plan to continue with Hands-On Exercise 2. If not, close the workbook and exit Excel.

# Specialized Functions

## Logical, Lookup, Databases, and Finances

## OBJECTIVES | AFTER YOU READ THIS CHAPTER, YOU WILL BE ABLE TO:

1. Create a nested logical function p. 158

2. Use MATCH and INDEX lookup functions p. 162

## CASE STUDY | Transpayne Filtration

You are an assistant accountant in the Human Resources (HR) Department for Transpayne Filtration, a company that sells water filtration systems to residential customers. Transpayne has locations in Atlanta, Boston, and Chicago, with a manager at each location who oversees several account representatives. You have an Excel workbook that contains names, locations, titles, hire dates, and salaries for the 20 managers and account representatives. To prepare for your upcoming salary analyses, you downloaded salary data from the corporate database into the workbook.

The HR manager wants you to perform several tasks based on locations and job titles. You will use logical functions to calculate annual bonus amounts and database functions to help analyze the data. Finally, you will review financial aspects of automobiles purchased for each manager.

# Logical and Lookup Functions

Logical functions enable you to test conditions to determine if the condition is true or false. You have used the IF function, which is the most popular logical function, to perform different actions based on whether the logical test is true or false. Lookup and reference functions are valuable when you need to look up a value contained elsewhere in a workbook. For example, the VLOOKUP and HLOOKUP functions enable you to take an identified value, such as the number of months for a certificate of deposit (CD) to mature, look up that value in a vertical or horizontal lookup table, and then obtain a related value, such as the annual percentage rate (APR). Excel contains additional logical and lookup functions to perform more complex calculations and analyses.

In this section, you will learn how to create a nested logical function using the IF function. In addition, you will learn how to use the MATCH and INDEX lookup functions.

## Creating a Nested Logical Function

The IF function contains three arguments: logical_test, Value_if_true, and Value_if_false. You can enter formulas within both the Value_if_true and Value_if_false arguments to perform calculations. For situations with multiple outcomes based on conditions, you can nest IF functions within the Value_if_true and Value_if_false arguments. A nested function is a function that is embedded within an argument of another function. Excel permits up to 64 IF statements in one formula.

### Nested IF Within an IF Function

STEP 1 » Figure 5.1 illustrates three bonus rates based on employee hire date. If a representative was hired before 1/1/2005, the rep receives 9% of her or his total salary as a bonus. If a representative was hired between 1/1/2005 and 1/1/2010, the rep earns a 5% bonus. Lastly, anyone hired after 1/1/2010 receives a 3% bonus.

**FIGURE 5.1** Nested IF Function Results

Figure 5.2 illustrates the process as a flowchart. Diamonds are logical_test arguments and rectangles are Value_if_true and Value_if_false arguments. The second IF function is stored in the outer Value_if_false argument. Figure 5.3 illustrates the process with cell references.

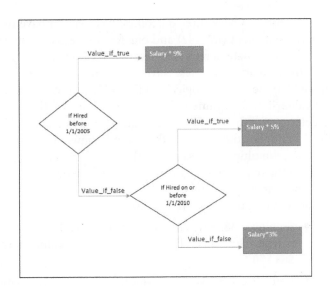

**FIGURE 5.2** Nested IF
Function Flowchart

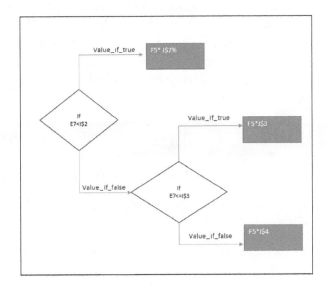

**FIGURE 5.3** Nested IF
Function Flowchart with Cell
References

Figure 5.4 shows the nested IF function as the argument in the Value_if_false box in the Function Arguments dialog box. The function uses relative cell references for the hire date (cell E7) so that the cell reference will change to the next sales rep's hire date when you copy the formula down the column. The formula uses mixed references for the date thresholds (I$2 and I$3) and for the bonus percentages (J$2, J$3, and J$4) so that the references will point to the same rows when you copy the formulas down the column. You could use absolute instead of mixed references, such as $J$4, but doing so creates a longer formula and makes it a little more difficult to read. In the Formula Bar, the nested IF statement looks like this:

=IF(E7<J$7, F5*K$7,IF(E7<=J$8,F5*K$8,F5*K$9))

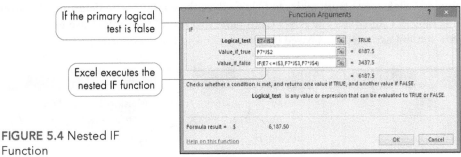

**FIGURE 5.4** Nested IF
Function

Because you have three outcomes, you need to have two logical tests: one for the primary IF statement (E7<I$2) and one for the nested IF statement (E7<=I$3). The primary logical test evaluates a rep's hire date in cell E7 against the first hire date cutoff stored in cell I2. If the primary logical test is true, Excel multiplies the salary in cell F7 by the rate stored in cell J2. If the primary logical test (E7<I$2) is false, Excel executes the nested IF function in the Value_if_false argument. The nested IF function then evaluates its logical test (E7<=I$3) to determine if the hire date meets the second bonus cutoff level. If that logical test is true, Excel multiplies the salary by the second bonus rate stored in cell J3. If that logical test is false, Excel multiples the salary by the third bonus rate stored in cell J4. You do not need a third logical test to execute the remaining outcome.

The following statements explain how the bonus is calculated for the individual representatives using the nested IF function:

- Employee 3824 was hired on 10/14/2002. In this situation, the logical test (E7<I$2) is true. This causes Excel to execute the Value_if_true argument J2*F$7, which is $68,750 * 9%.

- Employee 4955 was hired on 11/3/2013. In this situation, the logical test (E8<I$2) is false, as is the secondary logical test (E8<=I$3). This causes Excel to execute the Value_if_false argument F8*J$4, which is $49,575 * 3%.

- Employee 2521 was hired on 6/14/2009. In this situation, the logical test (E9<I$2) is false; however, the secondary logical test is true. This causes Excel to execute the Value_if_true argument F9*J$2, which is $46,000 * 5%.

**TIP   How Many Logical Tests?**

To determine how many logical tests you need, count the number of outcomes and subtract one. For example, if you have three outcomes (such as Exceeds Expectations, Meets Expectations, and Below Expectations), you need only two logical tests. The first logical test produces one outcome (Exceeds Expectations). The nested logical test produces a second outcome (Meets Expectations) if true or produces the third outcome (Below Expectations) if false. Therefore, you do not need a third logical test to produce the third outcome.

## Nest AND, OR, and NOT Functions

STEP 2>>
At times, you might need to evaluate *multiple* conditions *at the same time* to determine the result. For example, you might want to evaluate all employees that make less than $50,000 and who are managers for an equity-based salary increase. Excel contains three additional functions to determine whether certain conditions are true or false. These functions are AND, OR, and NOT. You can use these functions individually (which has limited usefulness) or nest them inside another function, such as inside an IF statement (which can increase the capabilities of the function).

The ***AND function*** accepts two or more logical tests and displays TRUE if *all* conditions are true or FALSE if *any* of the conditions are false. You can test up to 255 conditions. Programmers often create truth tables to help analyze the conditions to determine the overall result. Table 5.1 illustrates the AND truth table that a professor might use to determine whether a student earns a bonus based on attendance and homework submissions.

**TABLE 5.1   AND Truth Table**

|  | All Homework Submitted | Missing One or More Homework Scores |
| --- | --- | --- |
| **Perfect Attendance** | TRUE | FALSE |
| **Absent 1 or More Days** | FALSE | FALSE |

The bonus is awarded (TRUE) only when a student has perfect attendance *and* has completed all homework assignments, as shown in column D in Figure 5.5. Only Zach had perfect attendance and completed all assignments. All other combinations of attendance and homework submissions result in FALSE. Although Bill had perfect attendance, he missed one assignment, so he does not get the bonus.

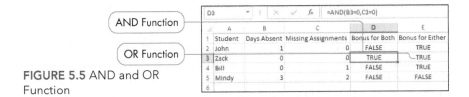

**FIGURE 5.5** AND and OR Function

=AND(logical1,logical2)

You can nest the AND function inside the logical_test argument of an IF function to test to see if multiple conditions are met. For example, =IF(AND(B2=0,C2=0),10,0) where B2 contains the number of days absent, C2 contains the number of homework assignments missed, 10 represents the number of bonus points if both conditions are met, and 0 represents that no bonus points are awarded if either condition is false.

---

### TIP | AND Results

If the logical argument contains text or empty cells, those values are ignored. If no values exist in the logical argument, the AND function returns the #VALUE! error.

---

The **OR function** also accepts two or more conditions and returns TRUE if any of the conditions are true. It returns FALSE only if all conditions are false. You can test up to 255 conditions. Table 5.2 illustrates the OR truth table that a professor might use to determine whether a student earns a bonus based on attendance and homework submissions.

**TABLE 5.2  OR Truth Table**

| | All Homework Submitted | Missing One or More Homework Scores |
| --- | --- | --- |
| **Perfect Attendance** | TRUE | TRUE |
| **Absent 1 or More Days** | TRUE | FALSE |

In column E in Figure 5.5, the bonus is awarded (TRUE) when the student had either perfect attendance *or* if the student completed all assignments. The only time the student does not earn a bonus is if the student is absent one or more days and is also missing one or more homework scores. Mindy was the only student who did not earn the bonus using the OR condition. See Table 5.3 for more detail on the differences between AND and OR functions.

=OR(logical1,logical2)

Table 5.3 displays the differences between AND and OR functions.

### TABLE 5.3 AND vs. OR

| | All conditions are true | At least one condition is true | At least one condition is false | All conditions are false |
|---|---|---|---|---|
| **AND** | TRUE | FALSE | FALSE | FALSE |
| **OR** | TRUE | TRUE | TRUE | FALSE |

The **NOT function** reverses the truth value of its argument. You use the NOT function when you want to make sure a value is not equal to a particular value. If the logical argument is false, the NOT function returns TRUE, and if the logical argument is true, the NOT function returns FALSE. Unlike the AND and OR functions that require two or more logical arguments, the NOT function contains only one logical argument.

=NOT(logical)

# Using MATCH and INDEX Lookup Functions

You have used the VLOOKUP and HLOOKUP functions to look up a value, compare it to a lookup table, and then return a result from the lookup table. Two other lookup functions that are helpful when the order of data is not conducive to VLOOKUP or HLOOKUP are MATCH and INDEX. Figure 5.6 demonstrates the MATCH, INDEX, and nested functions.

**FIGURE 5.6** MATCH, INDEX, and Nested Functions

## Use the MATCH Function

The **MATCH function** returns the position of a value in a list. Think of it like a reverse phone number lookup. Instead of using directory assistance to look up a person's phone number, it would be like using the phone number to look up the person. You should use the MATCH function, not the VLOOKUP function, when you have the value, such as $14,147, but want to identify its row position within a list, such as third row. Whereas the MATCH function is often nested inside other functions, you should understand how it works on its own. The MATCH function contains three arguments: lookup_value, lookup_array, and match_type. In Figure 5.6, the MATCH function in cell B9 returns 2, the position of $14,147 within the sales range. The following list explains the arguments of the MATCH function.

=MATCH(lookup_value,lookup_array,[match_type])

- **Lookup_value.** The lookup_value argument is the value that you want to find in the array or list. It can be a value, label, logical value, or cell reference that contains one of these items. In Figure 5.6, the lookup_value argument for the MATCH function in cell B9 refers to the cell containing the MAX function: B8.

- **Lookup_array.** This argument is a range of contiguous cells that contain potential lookup values. In Figure 5.6, the lookup_array argument for the MATCH function in cell B9 is the range of cells containing the sales values: B2:B5.

- **Match_type.** This argument is 1, 0, or -1 to indicate which value to return. Use 1 to find the largest value that is less than or equal to the lookup_value when the values in the lookup_array are arranged in ascending order. Use -1 to find the smallest value that is greater than or equal to the lookup_value when the values in the lookup_array are in descending order. Use 0 to find the first value that is identical to the lookup_value when the values in the lookup_array have no particular order. In Figure 5.6, the match_type is 0 to find an exact match of the highest sales amount.

## Use the Index Function

The *INDEX function* returns a value or the reference to a value within a range based on X and Y coordinates. So, for example, it will return the value in the intersection of a specific row and column such as the 3rd value in the 2nd column of a worksheet. When you select this function, the Select Arguments dialog box opens so that you can select an array form or a reference form. The array form is the more commonly used option. It displays the value of an element in a table based on either a row or column number.

`=INDEX(array,row_num,[column_num])`

- **Array.** This argument is one or more ranges. In Figure 5.6, the array argument in the INDEX function in cell B10 is the range containing the agents and their respective sales: A2:B5.
- **Row_num.** This argument identifies the row number within the array range. In the INDEX function in cell B10 in Figure 5.6, the row_num argument is B9, the cell containing the MATCH function results. Recall that the MATCH function in cell B8 determined the position of the highest sales amount from the list of Sales values in cells B2:B5. Therefore, the INDEX function refers to cell B10, which then uses the second row of the array in the range A2:B5.
- **Column_num.** This argument identifies the column within the reference that contains the value you want. In Figure 5.6, the column_num is 1 to identify the first column within the range A2:B5. The first column contains the agent names. So, after the MATCH function identifies the row (2) containing the highest sales value ($14,147.00), the column_num argument (1) identifies the name (Randy) in the first column that corresponds to the highest sales value.

The array in the range A2:B5 contains more than one row and column; therefore, row_num and column_num arguments were required. If an array contains only one row, the column_num is required, and if the array contains only one column, the row_num is required.

**TIP** **INDEX Function in Reference Form**

The reference form displays the cell reference of a row and column intersection. The syntax for the reference form is =INDEX(reference,row_num,[column_num],[area_num]). Use Help to learn about the arguments and to see an example of its usage.

You can reduce the number of cells containing functions by nesting the MATCH function inside the INDEX function. For example, cell B11 in Figure 5.6 contains a nested MAX function inside the MATCH function, which is then nested inside the INDEX function to identify which sales rep had the highest amount of sales.

## Nest Functions in Other Functions

**STEP 3»** You can use the Insert Function and Function Arguments dialog boxes to insert functions as arguments for another function instead of typing the entire nested function directly in the Formula Bar. For example, to create =INDEX(A2:B5,MATCH(MAX(B2:B5),B2:B5,0),1) in dialog boxes, do the following:

1. Click Insert Function, select the outer function, such as INDEX, and then click OK to display the Function Arguments dialog box.

2. Click in the argument box where the nested function is needed, click the Name Box arrow on the Formula Bar, and then select the desired function from the list of recently used functions, or select More Functions from the Name Box drop-down list, select the function, such as MATCH, in the Insert Function dialog box, and then click OK to open the Function Arguments dialog box for the nested function.

3. Enter the arguments for the nested function. Click in the outer function's name—INDEX—in the Formula Bar to display the Function Arguments dialog box for the outer function again.

4. Continue entering or nesting other arguments. When the entire function is complete, click OK in the outer function's Function Arguments dialog box.

*Quick*
Concepts

1. What is the difference between a single IF statement and a nested IF statement? *p. 158*

2. In what situation would you use an AND function over a nested IF statement? *p. 160*

3. What is the benefit of nesting the MATCH function inside the INDEX function? *p. 163*

# Hands-On Exercises

Watch the Video for this Hands-On Exercise!

MyITLab®
HOE1 Training

## 1 Logical and Lookup Functions

As the Transpayne accounting assistant, you have been asked to identify underpaid account representatives to bring their salaries up to a new minimum standard within the corporation. In addition, you want to calculate annual bonus amounts based on hire date as well as create a quick search lookup field to allow for instant access to individual information.

**Skills covered:** Create a Nested IF Function • Nest an AND Function Inside an IF Function • Create a Lookup Field Using INDEX and MATCH Functions

### STEP 1 ≫ CREATE A NESTED IF FUNCTION

Your first task is to calculate the annual bonus amount for each employee. The company uses a tiered bonus system that awards a specific percentage of salary based on hire date. Employees hired before 1/1/2005 receive 9%. Employees hired on or before 1/1/2010 receive 5%, and employees that were hired after 1/1/2010 receive 3%. You plan to use a nested IF function to calculate each employee's bonus. You will then use the fill handle to replace the function in the rest of the column. Refer to Figure 5.7 as you complete Step 1.

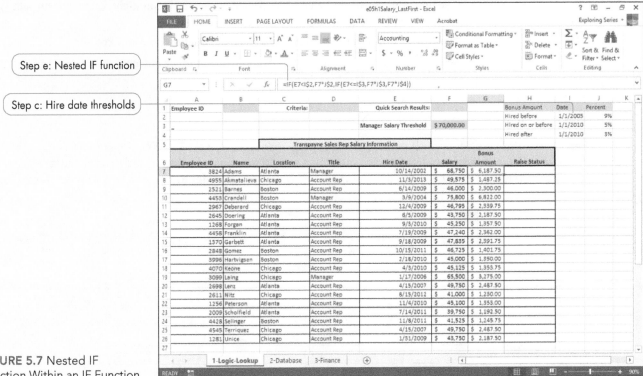

**FIGURE 5.7** Nested IF Function Within an IF Function

a. Open *e05h1Salary* and save it as **e05h1Salary_LastFirst**. Click the **1-Logic-Lookup worksheet tab**.

> **TROUBLESHOOTING:** If you make any major mistakes in this exercise, you can close the file, open *e05h1Salary* again, and then start this exercise over.

b. Click **cell G7**, click the **FORMULAS tab** if necessary, click **Logical** in the Function Library group, and then select **IF**.

c. Type **E7<I$2** in the **Logical_test box**.

The logical test compares the hire date to the first bonus threshold, 1/1/2005. Because you will copy the formula down the column and want to make sure the reference to the employee's hire date changes, use a relative cell reference to cell E7. To ensure that the reference to the date threshold remains constant, use a mixed cell reference to cell I$2. You could use an absolute reference, but because you are copying the formula down, the column letter I will remain the same. Using a mixed reference keeps the formula shorter and easier to read.

d. Type **F7*J$2** in the **Value_if_true box**.

This will multiply the salary by the bonus percentage if the logical test provided is true. If the logical test is not true, it will move on to the next argument created in step e.

e. Type **IF(E7<=I$3,F7*J$3,F7*J$4)** in the **Value_if_false box**.

By entering an IF statement in the Value_if_false box, you have created a nested function that evaluates the second threshold, 1/1/2010 (cell I3). If the hire date does not fall within the first or second thresholds defined by the primary and secondary logical tests, it will then by default trigger the Value_if_false, (F7*J$4). This will calculate the bonus based on the lowest bonus amount, 3% (cell J4). Use relative cell references for the employee's hire date (cell E7), because it should change when you copy the formula down the column. Use a mixed (or an absolute) reference for the threshold date (cell I$3) to ensure it does not change as you copy the formula down the column. Again, using mixed references keeps the formula shorter and easier to read than absolute references, but both produce the same results.

f. Click **OK** in the Function Arguments dialog box.

The function returns the value 6,188. This is calculated by multiplying the current salary, $68,750 (cell F7), by the bonus percentage rate of 9% (cell J2).

g. Double-click the **cell G7 fill handle** to copy the function down the column.

h. Select the **range G7:G26** and apply **Accounting Number Format**.

i. Save the workbook.

## STEP 2 ≫ NEST AN AND FUNCTION INSIDE AN IF FUNCTION

The Human Resources Director recommends that the company pay managers at least $70,000. You would like to nest an AND function inside an IF function to determine which managers should receive pay raises based on their current salary level. The salary threshold is located in cell F3 in the 1-Logic-Lookup worksheet. Refer to Figure 5.8 as you complete Step 2.

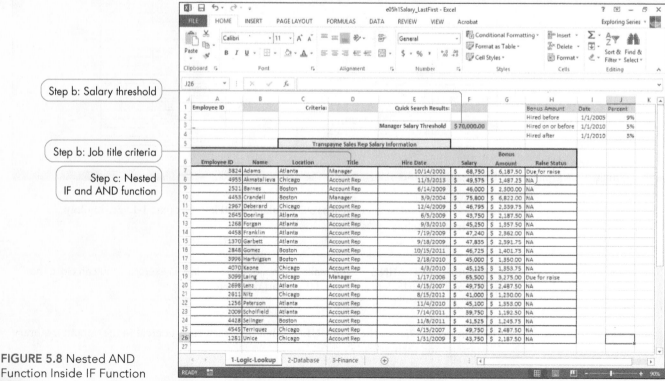

**FIGURE 5.8** Nested AND Function Inside IF Function

a. Click **cell H7**, click the **FORMULAS tab**, click **Logical** in the Function Library group, and then select **IF**.

b. Type **AND(D7="manager",F7<F$3)** in the **Logical_test box**.

Using the AND function nested in the logical test of the IF statement gives you the ability to add multiple arguments. In this scenario, you have the criteria if the employee is a manager (D7="manager" and makes less than $70,000 (F7<F$3).

c. Type **"Due for raise"** in the **Value_if_true box**.

If both conditions specified in the AND function are true, the employee is eligible for a raise. You use a mixed reference in cell F3 to ensure that row number 3 does not change when you copy the formula down the column.

d. Type **"NA"** in the **Value_if_false box**.

> **TROUBLESHOOTING:** Do not make cells D7 or F7 absolute or mixed. If you do, the function will use the incorrect values and return the first person's salary of $68,750, in the range H7:H26.

e. Click **OK**, double-click the **cell H7 fill handle** to copy the formula down the column, and then save the workbook.

The function now evaluates the employee's title and salary. If both arguments in the AND function are true, then *Due for raise* is displayed; if not, *NA* is displayed.

## STEP 3 ≫ CREATE A LOOKUP FIELD USING INDEX AND MATCH FUNCTIONS

You want to provide a simple search feature so that users can enter an employee number in cell B1 and then display employee title information in cell F1. For example, if Employee ID 4070 is entered in cell B1, cell F1 displays "Account Rep." Refer to Figure 5.9 as you complete Step 3.

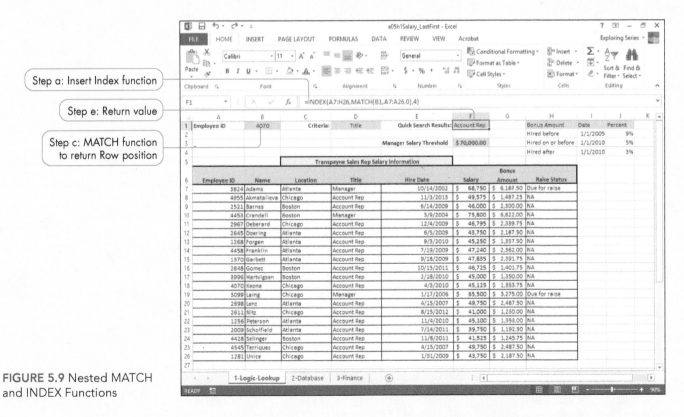

**FIGURE 5.9** Nested MATCH and INDEX Functions

a. Click **cell F1**, click **Lookup & Reference** in the Function Library group, and then select **INDEX**. Choose **array, row_num, column_num** from the Select Arguments dialog box and click **OK**.

**b.** Select **range A7:H26** in the Array box.

This defines the data pool from which Excel will pull information.

**c.** Type **MATCH(B1,A7:A26,0)** in the **Row_num box**.

If you nest the MATCH function in the Row_num box of the index function, Excel will look up the position of the employee number in cell B1 within the range A7:A26 and return the relative position, which for employee 4070 is 12. Currently, the function returns #N/A because cell B1 is blank.

**d.** Type **4** in the **Column_num box**. Click **OK**.

If you enter the number 4 in the Column_num box, the function returns information from the fourth column in the data set.

**e.** Type **4070** in **cell B1**.

Cell F1 now displays the current position of employee 4070. It does this by matching the Employee ID in column A to the Title in column D.

**f.** Save and leave the workbook open if you plan to continue with Hands-On Exercise 2. If not, save and close the workbook, and exit Excel.

# Excel

# Datasets and Tables

## CHAPTER 6

## Managing Large Volumes of Data

### OBJECTIVES | AFTER YOU READ THIS CHAPTER, YOU WILL BE ABLE TO:

1. Freeze rows and columns p. 171
2. Print large datasets p. 171
3. Design and create tables p. 179
4. Apply a table style p. 183
5. Sort data p. 190

6. Filter data p. 192
7. Use structured references and a total row p. 201
8. Apply conditional formatting p. 208
9. Create a new rule p. 212

## CASE STUDY | Reid Furniture Store

Vicki Reid owns Reid Furniture Store in Portland, Oregon. She divided her store into four departments: Living Room, Bedroom, Dining Room, and Appliances. All merchandise is categorized into one of these four departments for inventory records and sales. Vicki has four sales representatives: Chantalle Desmarais, Jade Gallagher, Sebastian Gruenewald, and Ambrose Sardelis. The sales system tracks which sales representative processed each transaction.

The business has grown rapidly, and Vicki hired you to analyze the sales data in order to increase future profits. For example, which department generates the most sales? Who is the leading salesperson? Do most customers purchase or finance? Are sales promotions necessary to promote business, or will customers pay the full price?

You downloaded March 2016 data from the sales system into an Excel workbook. To avoid extraneous data that is not needed in the analysis, you did not include customer names, accounts, or specific product numbers. The downloaded file contains transaction numbers, dates, sales representative names, departments, general merchandise description, total price, payment type, transaction type, and the total price.

# Large Datasets

So far you have worked with worksheets that contain small datasets, a collection of structured, related data in a limited number of columns and rows. In reality, you will probably work with large datasets consisting of hundreds or thousands of rows and columns of data. When you work with small datasets, you can usually view most or all of the data without scrolling. When you work with large datasets, you probably will not be able to see the entire dataset onscreen even on a large, widescreen monitor set at high resolution. You might want to keep the column and row labels always in view, even as you scroll throughout the dataset. Figure 6.1 shows the Reid Furniture Store's March 2016 sales transactions. Because it contains a lot of transactions, the entire dataset is not visible. You could decrease the zoom level to display more transactions; however, doing so decreases the text size onscreen, making it hard to read the data.

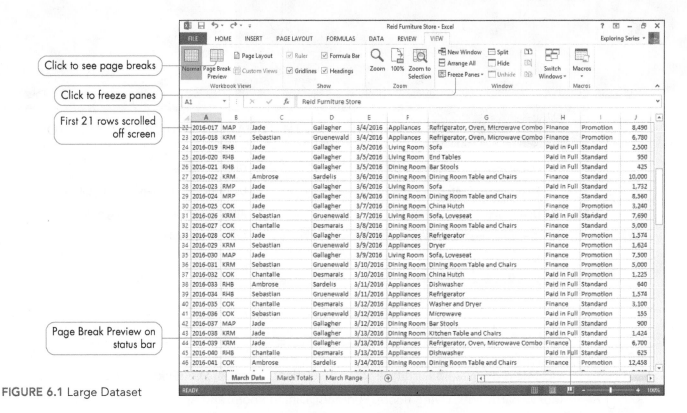

Click to see page breaks

Click to freeze panes

First 21 rows scrolled off screen

Page Break Preview on status bar

**FIGURE 6.1** Large Dataset

As you work with larger datasets, realize that the data will not always fit on one page. You will need to preview the automatic page breaks and probably insert some manual page breaks in more desirable locations, or you might want to print only a selected range within the large dataset to distribute to others.

In this section, you will learn how to keep labels onscreen as you scroll through a large dataset. In addition, you will learn how to manage page breaks, print only a range instead of an entire worksheet, and print column labels at the top of each page of a large dataset.

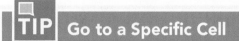

**TIP** Go to a Specific Cell

You can navigate through a large worksheet by using the Go To command. Click Find & Select in the Editing group on the Home tab and select Go To (or press F5 or Ctrl+G) to display the Go To dialog box, enter the cell address in the Reference box, and then press Enter to go to the cell.

You can also click in the Name Box, type the cell reference, and then press Enter to go to a specific cell.

# Freezing Rows and Columns

When you scroll to parts of a dataset not initially visible, some rows and columns disappear from view. When the row and column labels scroll off the screen, you may not remember what each column represents. You can keep labels onscreen by freezing them. *Freezing* is the process of keeping rows and/or columns visible onscreen at all times even when you scroll through a large dataset. Table 6.1 describes the three freeze options.

| TABLE 6.1 Freeze Options | |
|---|---|
| **Option** | **Description** |
| Freeze Panes | Keeps both rows and columns above and to the left of the active cell visible as you scroll through a worksheet. |
| Freeze Top Row | Keeps only the top row visible as you scroll through a worksheet. |
| Freeze First Column | Keeps only the first column visible as you scroll through a worksheet. |

**STEP 1 >>** To freeze labels, click the View tab, click Freeze Panes in the Window group, and then select a freeze option. To freeze one or more rows and columns, use the Freeze Panes option. Before selecting this option, make the active cell one row below and one column to the right of the rows and columns you want to freeze. For example, to freeze the first five rows and the first column, make cell B6 the active cell before clicking the Freeze Panes option. As Figure 6.2 shows, Excel displays a horizontal line below the last frozen row (row 5) and a vertical line to the right of the last frozen column (column A). Unfrozen rows (such as rows 6–14) and unfrozen columns (such as columns B and C) are no longer visible as you scroll down and to the right, respectively.

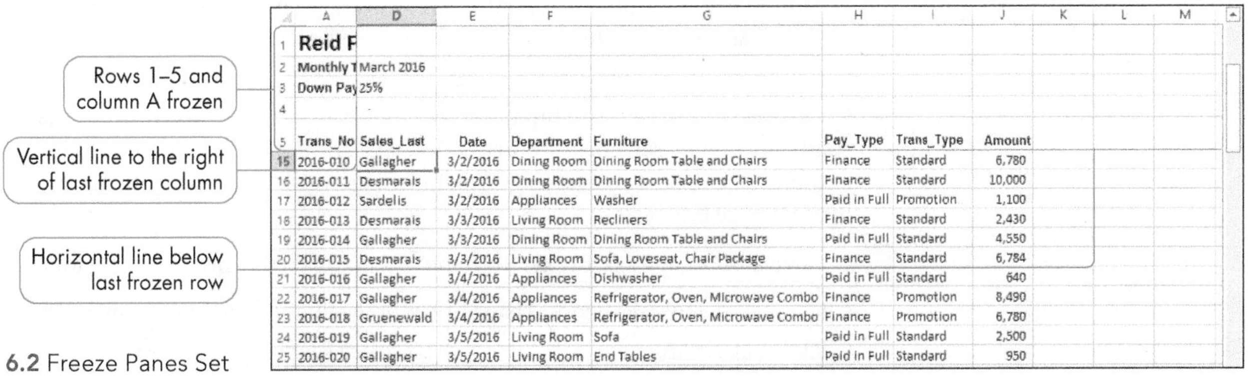

**FIGURE 6.2** Freeze Panes Set

To unlock the rows and columns from remaining onscreen as you scroll, click Freeze Panes in the Window group and select Unfreeze Panes, which only appears on the menu when you have frozen rows and/or columns. After you unfreeze the panes, the Freeze Panes option appears instead of Unfreeze Panes on the menu again.

When you freeze panes and press Ctrl+Home, the first unfrozen cell is the active cell instead of cell A1. For example, with column A and rows 1 through 5 frozen in Figure 6.2, pressing Ctrl+Home makes cell B6 the active cell. If you need to edit a cell in the frozen area, click the particular cell to make it active and edit the data.

# Printing Large Datasets

For a large dataset, some columns and rows may print on several pages. Analyzing the data on individual printed pages is difficult when each page does not contain column and row labels. To prevent wasting paper, always use Print Preview. Doing so enables you to adjust page settings until you are satisfied with how the data will print.

The Page Layout tab (see Figure 6.3) contains options to help you prepare large datasets to print. Previously, you changed the page orientation, set different margins, and adjusted the scaling. In addition, you can manage page breaks, set the print area, and print titles.

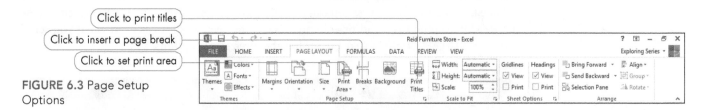

Click to print titles

Click to insert a page break

Click to set print area

**FIGURE 6.3** Page Setup Options

## Display and Change Page Breaks

Based on the paper size, orientation, margins, and other settings, Excel identifies how much data can print on a page. Then it displays a ***page break***, indicating where data will start on another printed page. To identify where these automatic page breaks will occur, click Page Break Preview on the status bar or in the Workbook Views group on the View tab. In Page Break Preview, Excel displays watermarks, such as *Page 1*, indicating the area that will print on a specific page. Blue dashed lines indicate where the automatic page breaks occur, and solid blue lines indicate manual page breaks.

If the automatic page breaks occur in undesirable locations, you can adjust the page breaks. For example, if you have a worksheet listing sales data by date, the automatic page break might occur within a group of rows for one date, such as between two rows of data for 3/14/2016. To make all rows for that date appear together, you can either insert a page break above the first data row for that date or decrease the margins so that all 3/14/2015 transactions fit at the bottom of the page. To do this, drag a page break line to the desired location.

**Manual Page Break:** Do the following to set a manual break at a specific location:

STEP 2 »

1. Click the cell that you want to be the first row and column on a new printed page. For example, click cell A50 if you want cell A50 to start a new page. If you click cell D50, you create a page for columns A through C, and then column D starts a new page.
2. Click the PAGE LAYOUT tab.
3. Click Breaks in the Page Setup group and select Insert Page Break. Excel displays a solid blue line in Page Break Preview or a dashed line in Normal view to indicate the manual page breaks you set. Figure 6.4 shows a worksheet with both automatic and manual page breaks.

**Remove a Manual Page Break:** To remove a manual page break, do the following:

1. Click a cell below a horizontal page break or a cell to the right of a vertical page break.
2. Click Breaks in the Page Setup group and select Remove Page Break.

**Reset Page Breaks:** To reset all page breaks back to the automatic page breaks, do the following:

1. Click Breaks in the Page Setup group.
2. Select Reset All Page Breaks.

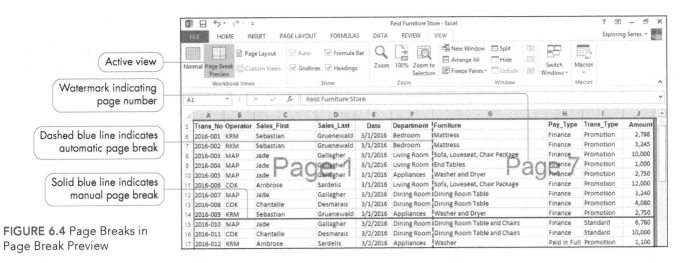

Active view

Watermark indicating page number

Dashed blue line indicates automatic page break

Solid blue line indicates manual page break

**FIGURE 6.4** Page Breaks in Page Break Preview

## Set and Clear a Print Area

The default Print settings send an entire dataset on the active worksheet to the printer. However, you might want to print only part of the worksheet data. If you display the worksheet in Page Break view, you can identify which page(s) you want to print. Then click the File tab and select Print. Type the number(s) of the page(s) you want to print. For example, to print page 2 only, type 2 in the Pages text box and in the *to* text box.

You can further restrict what is printed by setting the ***print area***, which is the range of cells that will print. For example, you might want to print only an input area or just the transactions that occurred on a particular date. To set a print area, do the following:

STEP 3»

1. Select the range you want to print.
2. Click the PAGE LAYOUT tab and click Print Area in the Page Setup group.
3. Select Set Print Area.

In Page Break Preview, the print area has a white background and solid blue border; the rest of the worksheet has a gray background (see Figure 6.5). In Normal view or Page Layout view, the print area is surrounded by thin gray lines.

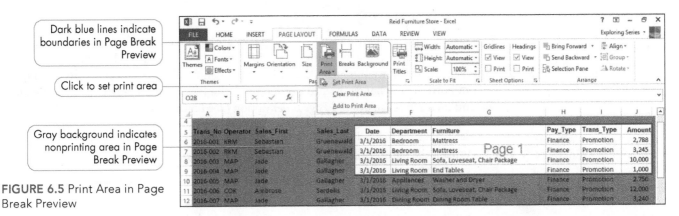

Dark blue lines indicate boundaries in Page Break Preview

Click to set print area

Gray background indicates nonprinting area in Page Break Preview

**FIGURE 6.5** Print Area in Page Break Preview

To add print areas where each print area will print on a separate page, select the range you want to print, click Print Area, and then select *Add to Print Area*. To clear the print area, click Print Area in the Page Setup group and select Clear Print Area.

**TIP** Print a Selection

Another way to print part of a worksheet is to select the range you want to print. Click the File tab and click Print. Click the first arrow in the *Settings* section and select Print Selection.

## Print Titles

STEP 4 » When you print large datasets, it is helpful that every page contains descriptive column and row labels. When you click Print Titles in the Page Setup group on the Page Layout tab, Excel opens the Page Setup dialog box with the Sheet tab active so that you can select which row(s) and/or column(s) to repeat on each printout (see Figure 6.6).

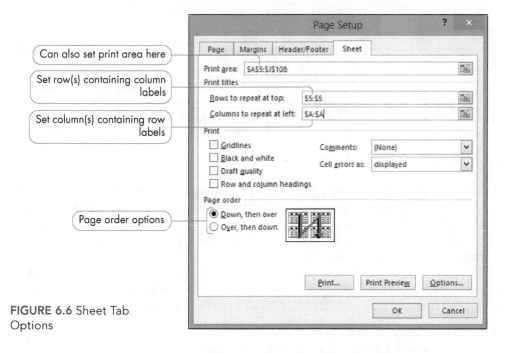

Can also set print area here

Set row(s) containing column labels

Set column(s) containing row labels

Page order options

**FIGURE 6.6** Sheet Tab Options

To print the column labels at the top of each page, select the row(s) that contain the labels or titles (such as row 5) in the *Rows to repeat at top* box to display $5:$5. To print the row labels at the left side of each page, select the column(s) that contain the labels or titles (such as column A) in the *Columns to repeat at left* box to display $A$A.

## Control Print Page Order

***Print order*** is the sequence in which the pages are printed. By default, the pages print in this order: top-left section, bottom-left section, top-right section, and bottom-right section. However, you might want to print the entire top portion of the worksheet before printing the bottom portion. To change the print order, open the Page Setup dialog box, click the Sheet tab, and then select the desired *Page order* option (see Figure 6.6).

*Quick* Concepts

1. What is the purpose of freezing panes in a worksheet? *p. 171*

2. Why would you want to insert page breaks instead of using the automatic page breaks? *p. 172*

3. What steps should you take to ensure that column labels display on each printed page of a large dataset? *p. 174*

# Hands-On Exercises

## 1 Large Datasets

You want to review the large dataset that shows the March 2016 transactions for Reid Furniture Store. You will need to view the data and adjust some page setup options so that you can print necessary labels on each page.

**Skills covered:** Freeze Rows and Columns • Manage Page Breaks • Set and Clear a Print Area • Print Titles

---

### STEP 1 ≫ FREEZE ROWS AND COLUMNS

Before printing the March 2016 transaction dataset, you want to view the data. The dataset contains more rows than will display onscreen at the same time. You decide to freeze the column and row labels to stay onscreen as you scroll through the transactions. Refer to Figure 6.7 as you complete Step 1.

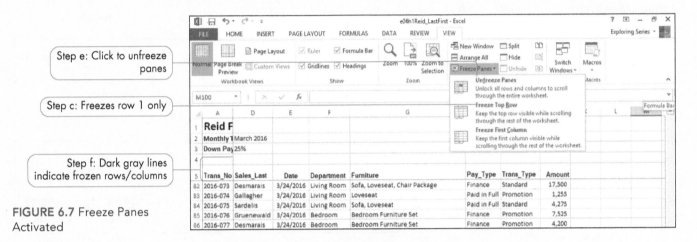

**FIGURE 6.7** Freeze Panes Activated

a. Open *e04h1Reid* and save it as **e04h1Reid_LastFirst**.

> **TROUBLESHOOTING:** If you make any major mistakes in this exercise, you can close the file, open *e04h1Reid* again, and then start this exercise over.

The workbook contains three worksheets: March Data (for Hands-On Exercises 1–3), March Totals (for Hands-On Exercise 4), and March Range (for Hands-On Exercise 5).

b. Press **Page Down** four times to scroll through the dataset. Then press **Ctrl+Home** to go back to the top of the worksheet.

After you press Page Down, the column labels in row 5 scroll off the screen, making it challenging to remember what type of data are in some columns.

c. Click the **VIEW tab**, click **Freeze Panes** in the Window group, and then select **Freeze Top Row**.

A dark gray horizontal line displays between rows 1 and 2.

d. Press **Page Down** to scroll down through the worksheet.

As rows scroll off the top of the Excel window, the first row remains frozen onscreen. The title by itself is not helpful; you need to freeze the column labels as well.

e. Click **Freeze Panes** in the Window group and select **Unfreeze Panes**.

**f.** Click **cell B6**, the cell below the row and one column to the right of what you want to freeze. Click **Freeze Panes** in the Window group and select **Freeze Panes**.

Excel displays a vertical line between columns A and B, indicating that column A is frozen, and a horizontal line between rows 5 and 6, indicating the first five rows are frozen.

**g.** Press **Ctrl+G**, type **M100** in the **Reference box** of the Go To dialog box, and then click **OK** to make cell M100 the active cell. Save the workbook.

Rows 6 through 81 and columns B and C are not visible because they scrolled off the screen.

> **TROUBLESHOOTING:** Your screen may differ from Figure 6.7 due to different Windows resolution settings. If necessary, continue scrolling right and down until you see columns and rows scrolling offscreen.

## STEP 2 ≫ MANAGE PAGE BREAKS

You plan to print the dataset so that you and Vicki Reid can discuss the transactions in your weekly meeting. Because the large dataset will not fit on one page, you want to see where the automatic page breaks are and then insert a manual page break. Refer to Figure 6.8 as you complete Step 2.

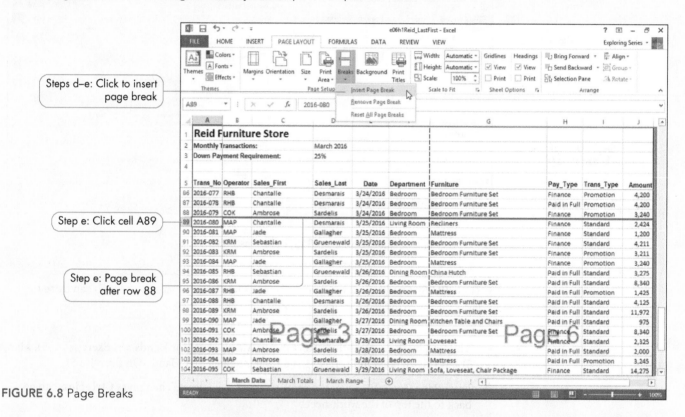

**FIGURE 6.8** Page Breaks

**a.** Press **Ctrl+Home** to move to **cell B6**, the first cell in the unfrozen area. Click the **VIEW tab**, if necessary, and click **Page Break Preview** in the Workbook Views group or on the status bar.

Excel displays blue dashed lines to indicate the automatic page breaks.

**b.** Scroll down until you see row 44 below the frozen column labels.

The automatic horizontal page break is between rows 46 and 47 (or between rows 45 and 46). You do not want transactions for a particular day to span between printed pages, so you need to move the page break up to keep all 3/13/2016 transactions together.

**c.** Click **cell A45**, the first cell containing 3/13/2016 data and the cell to start the top of the second page.

**d.** Click the **PAGE LAYOUT tab**, click **Breaks** in the Page Setup group, and then select **Insert Page Break**.

You inserted a page break between rows 44 and 45 so that the 3/13/2016 transactions will be on one page.

**e.** Click **cell A89**, click **Breaks** in the Page Setup group, and then select **Insert Page Break**. Save the workbook.

You inserted a page break between rows 88 and 89 to keep the 3/25/2016 transactions on the same page.

## TIP Using the Mouse Pointer to Move Page Breaks

To use the mouse pointer to adjust a page break, position the mouse pointer on the page break line to see the two-headed arrow and drag the line to where you want the page break to occur.

## STEP 3 ≫ SET AND CLEAR A PRINT AREA

You want to focus on the transactions for only March 1, 2016. To avoid printing more data than you need, you will set the print area to print transactions for only that day. Refer to Figure 6.9 as you complete Step 3.

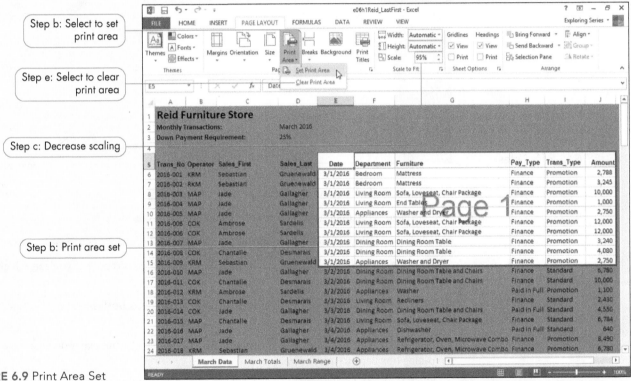

**FIGURE 6.9** Print Area Set

**a.** Scroll up to see the first row of March data. Select the **range E5:J15**, the range of data for March 1, 2016.

**b.** Click the **PAGE LAYOUT tab**, if necessary, click **Print Area** in the Page Setup group, and then select **Set Print Area**.

Excel displays the print area with a solid blue border. A dotted blue line displays between columns I and J, indicating an automatic page break. The rest of the worksheet displays with a gray background.

**c.** Click **cell E5** and click the **Scale arrow** down one time in the *Scale to Fit* group.

The selected print area will print on one page.

**d.** Press **Ctrl+P** to see that only the print area will print. Press **Esc**.

**e.** Click **Print Area** in the Page Setup group and select **Clear Print Area**. Save the workbook.

## STEP 4 >> PRINT TITLES

Only the first page will print both row and column labels. Pages 2 and 3 will print the remaining row labels, Page 4 will print the remaining column labels, and Pages 5 and 6 will not print either label. You want to make sure the column and row labels print on all pages. To do this, you will print titles. Refer to Figure 6.10 as you complete Step 4.

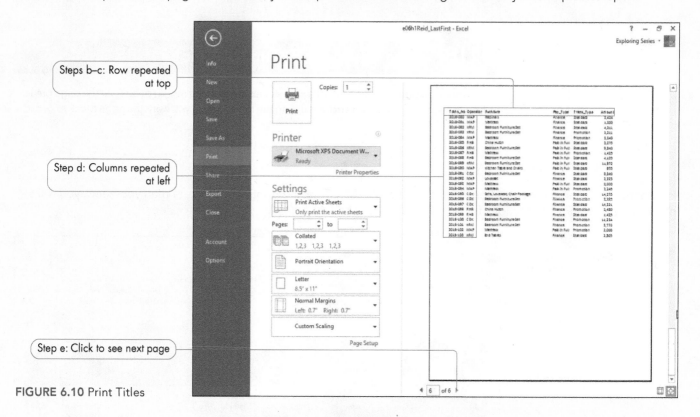

**FIGURE 6.10** Print Titles

**a.** Click **Print Titles** in the Page Setup group.

The Page Setup dialog box opens, displaying the Sheet tab.

**b.** Click the **Collapse Dialog box button** on the right side of the *Rows to repeat at top* box.

Clicking the *Collapse Dialog box* button reduces the dialog box so that you can select a range in the worksheet easily.

**c.** Click the **row 5 heading** and click the **Collapse Dialog box button** within the Page Setup: Rows to repeat at top dialog box.

You selected the fifth row, which contains the column labels, and expanded the Page Setup dialog box back to its full size.

**d.** Click in the **Columns to repeat at left box**, type **A:B**, and then click **Print Preview**.

**e.** Click **Next Page** at the bottom of the Microsoft Office Backstage view. Click **Next Page** until the sixth page displays.

Figure 6.10 shows a preview of the sixth page. The column labels and the first two columns appear on all pages.

**f.** Click the **Back arrow** in the top-left corner of the Microsoft Office Backstage view.

**g.** Save the workbook. Keep the workbook onscreen if you plan to continue with the next Hands-On Exercise. If not, close the workbook and exit Excel.

# Excel Tables

All organizations maintain lists of data. Businesses maintain inventory lists, educational institutions maintain lists of students and faculty, and governmental entities maintain lists of contracts. Although more complicated related data should be stored in a database-management program, such as Access, you can maintain structured lists in Excel tables. A *table* is a structured range that contains related data organized in such a way as to facilitate data management and analysis. Although you can manage and analyze a range of data, a table provides many advantages over a range of data:

- Column headings remain onscreen without having to use Freeze Panes.
- Filter arrows are available for efficient sorting and filtering.
- Table styles easily format table rows and columns with complementary fill colors.
- Calculated columns where the formulas copy down the columns automatically are available to create and edit.
- Calculated total row enables the user to implement a variety of summary functions.
- Structured references can be used instead of cell references in formulas.
- Table data can export to a SharePoint list.

In this section, you will learn table terminology and rules for structuring data. You will create a table from existing data, manage records and fields, and remove duplicates. Then you will apply a table style to format the table.

## Designing and Creating Tables

A table is a group of related data organized in a series of rows and columns that is managed independently from any other data on the worksheet. Each column represents a *field*, which is an individual piece of data, such as last names or quantities sold. Each field should represent the smallest possible unit of data. For example, instead of a Name field, separate name data into First Name and Last Name fields. Instead of one large address field, separate address data into Street Address, City, State, and ZIP Code fields. Separating data into the smallest units possible enables you to manipulate the data in a variety of ways for output. Each row in a table represents a *record*, which is a collection of related data about one entity. For example, all data related to one particular transaction form a record in the Reid Department Store worksheet.

You should plan the structure before creating a table. The more thoroughly you plan, the fewer changes you will have to make to the table after you create it. To help plan your table, follow these guidelines:

- Enter field (column) names on the top row.
- Keep field names short, descriptive, and unique. No two field names should be identical.
- Format the field names so that they stand out from the data.
- Enter data for each record on a row below the field names.
- Do not leave blank rows between records or between the field names and the first record.
- Delete any blank columns between fields in the dataset.
- Make sure each record has something unique, such as a transaction number or ID.
- Insert at least one blank row and one blank column between the table and other data, such as the main titles. When you need multiple tables in one workbook, a best practice is to place each table on a separate worksheet.

## Create a Table

STEP 1 » When your worksheet data are structured correctly, you can easily create a table. To create a table from existing data, do the following:

1. Click within the existing range of data.
2. Click the INSERT tab and click Table in the Tables group. The Create Table dialog box opens (see Figure 6.11), prompting you to enter the range of data.

   • If Excel does not correctly predict the range, select the range for the *Where is the data for your table?* box.
   • If the existing range contains column labels, select the *My table has headers* check box.

3. Click OK to create the table.

**FIGURE 6.11** Create Table Dialog Box

| **TIP** | **Quick Analysis Table Creation**

You can also create a table by selecting a range, clicking the Quick Analysis button, clicking TABLES (see Figure 6.12) in the Quick Analysis gallery, and then clicking Table. While Quick Analysis is efficient for tasks such as creating a chart, it may take more time to create a table because you have to select the entire range first. Some people find that it is faster to create a table from the Insert tab.

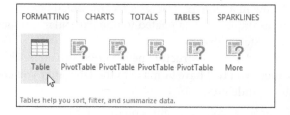

**FIGURE 6.12** Quick Analysis Gallery

After you create a table, the Table Tools Design tab displays. Excel applies the default Table Style Medium 2 style to the table, and each cell in the header row has arrows, also called *filtering arrows* or *filtering buttons* in Excel Help (see Figure 6.13). This book uses the term *filter arrows* for consistency. Excel assigns a name to each table, such as Table 1. You can change the table name by clicking in the Table Name box in the Properties group, typing a new name using the same rules you applied when assigning range names, and then pressing Enter.

- Table Tools contextual tab
- Table name
- Click to show or hide filtering arrows in the header row
- Filtering arrow
- Alternating fill colors applied

**FIGURE 6.13** Excel Table in Default Format

Instead of converting a range to a table, you can create a table structure first and add data to it later. Select an empty range and follow the previously listed steps to create the range for the table. The default column headings are Column1, Column2, and so on. Click each default column heading and type a descriptive label. Then enter the data into each row of the newly created table.

## TIP | Converting a Table to a Range

To convert a table back to a range, click within the table range, click the Table Tools Design tab, click *Convert to Range* in the Tools group, and then click Yes in the message box asking, *Do you want to convert the table to a normal range?*

## Add and Delete Fields

**STEP 2 »** After creating a table, you might want to add a new field. For example, you might want to add a field for product numbers to the Reid Furniture Store transaction table. To insert a field:

1. Click in any data cell (but not the cell containing the field name) in a field that will be to the right of the new field. For example, to insert a new field between the fields in columns A and B, click any cell in column B.
2. Click the HOME tab and click the Insert arrow in the Cells group.
3. Select *Insert Table Columns to the Left*.

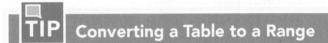

## TIP | Adding a New Field on the Right Side of a Table

If you want to add a field at the end of the right side of a table, click in the cell to the right of the last field name and type a label. Excel will extend the table to include that field and will format the cell as a field name.

You can also delete a field if you no longer need any data for that particular field. Although deleting records and fields is easy, you must make sure not to delete data erroneously. If you accidentally delete data, click Undo immediately. To delete a field, do the following:

1. Click a cell in the field that you want to delete.
2. Click the Delete arrow in the Cells group on the HOME tab.
3. Select Delete Table Columns.

## Add, Edit, and Delete Records

STEP 3» After you create a table, you might want to add new records, such as adding a new client or a new item to an inventory table. To add a record to a table, do the following:

1. Click a cell in the record below which you want the new record inserted. If you want to add a new record below the last record, click the row containing the last record.
2. Click the HOME tab and click the Insert arrow in the Cells group.
3. Select Insert Table Rows Above to insert a row above the current row, or select Insert Table Row Below if the current row is the last one and you want a row below it.

 **TIP Adding a New Record at the End of a Table**

You can also add a record to the end of a table by clicking in the row immediately below the table and typing. Excel will extend the table to include that row as a record in the table and will apply consistent formatting.

You might need to change data for a record. For example, when a client moves, you need to change the client's address and phone number. You edit data in a table the same way you edit data in a regular worksheet cell.

Finally, you can delete records. For example, if you maintain an inventory of artwork in your house and sell a piece of art, delete that record from the table. To delete a record from the table:

1. Click a cell in the record that you want to delete.
2. Click the HOME tab and click the Delete arrow in the Cells group.
3. Select Delete Table Rows.

## Remove Duplicate Rows

STEP 4» A table might contain duplicate records, which can give false results when totaling or performing other calculations on the dataset. For a small table, you might be able to detect duplicate records by scanning the data. For large tables, it is more difficult to identify duplicate records by simply scanning the table with the eye. To remove duplicate records, do the following:

1. Click within the table and click the DESIGN tab.
2. Click Remove Duplicates in the Tools group to display the Remove Duplicates dialog box (see Figure 6.14).
3. Click Select All to set the criteria to find a duplicate for every field in the record and click OK. If you select individual column(s), Excel looks for duplicates in the specific column(s) only and deletes all but one record of the duplicated data. Excel will display a message box informing you of how many duplicate rows it removed.

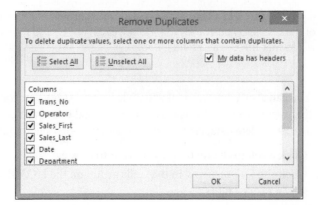

**FIGURE 6.14** Remove Duplicates Dialog Box

## Applying a Table Style

**STEP 5 >>**  Excel applies a table style when you create a table. ***Table styles*** control the fill color of the header row (the row containing field names) and rows of records. In addition, table styles specify bold and border lines. You can change the table style to a color scheme that complements your organization's color scheme or to emphasize data the header rows or columns. Click Quick Styles in the Table Styles group to display the Table Styles gallery (see Figure 6.15). To see how a table style will format your table using Live Preview, position the pointer over a style in the Table Styles gallery. After you identify a style you want, click it to apply it to the table.

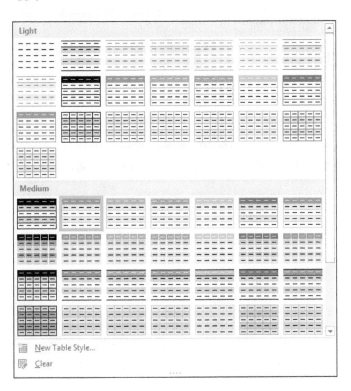

**FIGURE 6.15** Table Styles Gallery

After you select a table style, you can control what the style formats. The Table Style Options group contains check boxes to select specific format actions in a table. Table 6.2 lists the options and the effect of each check box. Avoid overformatting the table. It is not good to apply so many formatting effects that the message you want to present with the data is obscured or lost.

| TABLE 6.2 Table Style Options | |
|---|---|
| **Check Box** | **Action** |
| Header Row | Displays the header row (field names) when checked; removes field names when not checked. Header Row formatting takes priority over column formats. |
| Total Row | Displays a total row when selected. Total Row formatting takes priority over column formats. |
| First Column | Applies a different format to the first column so that the row headings stand out. First Column formatting takes priority over Banded Rows formatting. |
| Last Column | Applies a different format to the last column so that the last column of data stands out; effective for aggregated data, such as grand totals per row. Last Column formatting takes priority over Banded Rows formatting. |
| Banded Rows | Displays alternate fill colors for even and odd rows to help distinguish records. |
| Banded Columns | Displays alternate fill colors for even and odd columns to help distinguish fields. |
| Filter Button | Displays a filter button on the right side of each heading in the header row. |

*Quick*
Concepts

1. List at least four guidelines for planning a table in Excel. *p. 179*

2. Why would you convert a range of data into an Excel table? *p. 179*

3. What are six options you can control after selecting a table style? *p. 184*

# Hands-On Exercises

**Watch the Video for this Hands-On Exercise!**

**MyITLab®** HOE2 Training

## 2 Excel Tables

You want to convert the March data to a table. As you review the table, you will delete the unnecessary Operator field, add two new fields, insert a missing furniture sale transaction, and remove duplicate transactions. Finally, you will enhance the table appearance by applying a table style.

**Skills covered:** Create a Table • Add and Delete Fields • Add Records • Remove Duplicate Rows • Apply a Table Style

---

### STEP 1 ≫ CREATE A TABLE

Although the Reid Furniture Store's March transaction data are organized in an Excel worksheet, you know that you will have additional functionality if you convert the range to a table. Refer to Figure 6.16 as you complete Step 1.

**FIGURE 6.16** Range Converted to a Table

**a.** Open *e04h1Reid_LastFirst* if you closed it at the end of Hands-On Exercise 1 and save it as **e04h2Reid_LastFirst**, changing *h1* to *h2*. Click **Normal** on the status bar.

**b.** Click in any cell within the transactional data, click the **INSERT tab**, and then click **Table** in the Tables group.

The Create Table dialog box opens. The *Where is the data for your table?* box displays =$A$5:$I$112. Keep the *My table has headers* check box selected so that the headings on the fifth row become the field names for the table.

**c.** Click **OK** and click **cell A5**.

Excel creates a table from the data range and displays the DESIGN tab, filter arrows, and alternating fill colors for the records. The columns widen to fit the field names, although the wrap text option is still applied to those cells.

**d.** Set column width to **11** for the Sales_First, Sales_Last, Department, Pay_Type, and Trans_Type fields.

**e.** Unfreeze the panes and scroll through the table. Save the workbook.

With a regular range of data, column labels scroll off the top of the screen if you do not freeze panes. When you scroll within a table, the table's header row remains onscreen by moving up to where the Excel column (letter) headings usually display (see Figure 6.16).

# STEP 2 ›› ADD AND DELETE FIELDS

The original range included a column for the data entry operators' initials. You will delete this column because you do not need it for your analysis. In addition, you want to add a field to display down payment amounts in the future. Refer to Figure 6.17 as you complete Step 2.

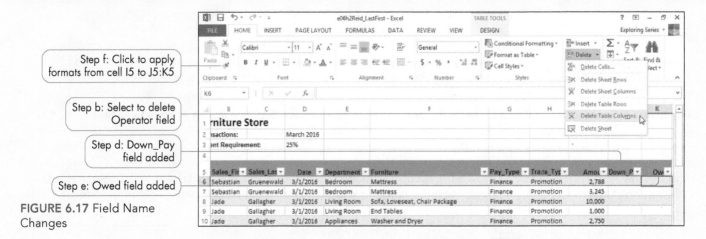

**Step f:** Click to apply formats from cell I5 to J5:K5

**Step b:** Select to delete Operator field

**Step d:** Down_Pay field added

**Step e:** Owed field added

**FIGURE 6.17** Field Name Changes

a. Click **cell B25** or any cell containing a value in the Operator column.

You need to make a cell active in the field you want to remove.

b. Click the **HOME tab**, click the **Delete arrow** in the Cells group, and then select **Delete Table Columns**.

Excel deletes the Operator column and may adjust the width of other columns.

c. Adjust the widths of columns E, F, and G as necessary. Click **cell J5**, the first blank cell on the right side of the field names.

d. Type **Down_Pay** and press **Ctrl+Enter**.

Excel extends the table formatting to column J automatically. A filter arrow appears for the newly created field name, and alternating fill colors appear in the rows below the field name. The fill color is the same as the fill color for other field names; however, the font color is White, Background 1, instead of Black Text 1.

e. Click **cell K5**, type **Owed**, and then press **Ctrl+Enter**.

f. Click **cell I5**, click **Format Painter** in the Clipboard group, and then select the **range J5:K5** to copy the format. Save the workbook.

As you review the March 2016 transaction table, you notice that two transactions are missing: 2016-68 and 2016-104. After finding the paper invoices, you are ready to add records with the missing transaction data. Refer to Figure 6.18 as you complete Step 3.

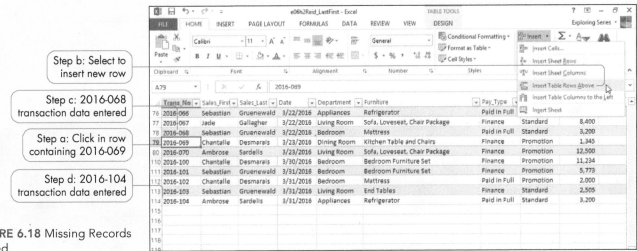

**FIGURE 6.18** Missing Records Added

a. Click **cell A78** or any cell within the table range on row 78.

The missing record 2016-68 needs to be inserted between 2016-67 on row 77 and 2016-69 on row 78.

b. Click the **HOME tab**, click the **Insert arrow** in the Cells group, and then select **Insert Table Row Above**.

Excel inserts a new table row on row 78, between the 2016-67 and 2016-69 transactions.

c. Enter the following data in the respective fields on the newly created row.

**2016-68, Sebastian, Gruenewald, 3/22/2016, Bedroom, Mattress, Paid in Full, Standard, 3200**

d. Click **cell A114** and enter the following data in the respective fields. Save the workbook.

**2016-104, Ambrose, Sardelis, 3/31/2016, Appliances, Refrigerator, Paid in Full, Standard, 1500**

When you start typing 2016-104 in the row immediately below the last record, Excel immediately includes and formats row 114 as part of the table. Review Figure 6.18 to ensure you inserted the records in the correct locations. Rows 81–109 are hidden to display both new records in one screenshot.

# STEP 4 >> REMOVE DUPLICATE ROWS

You noticed that the 2016-006 transaction is duplicated on rows 11 and 12 and that the 2016-118 transaction is duplicated on rows 24 and 25. You think the table may contain other duplicate rows. To avoid having to look at the entire table row by row, you want to have Excel find and remove the duplicate rows for you. Refer to Figure 6.19 as you complete Step 4.

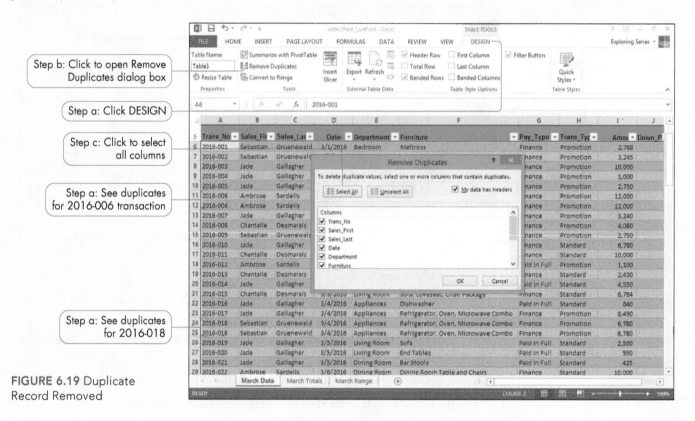

Step b: Click to open Remove Duplicates dialog box

Step a: Click DESIGN

Step c: Click to select all columns

Step a: See duplicates for 2016-006 transaction

Step a: See duplicates for 2016-018

**FIGURE 6.19** Duplicate Record Removed

a. Scroll to see rows 11 and 12. Click the **DESIGN tab**.

   The records on rows 11 and 12 are identical. Rows 24 and 25 are also duplicates. You need to remove the extra rows.

b. Click **Remove Duplicates** in the Tools group.

   The Remove Duplicates dialog box opens.

c. Click **Select All**, make sure the **My data has headers check box** is selected, and then click **OK**.

   Excel displays a message box indicating *5 duplicate records found and removed; 104 unique values remain.*

d. Click **OK** in the message box. Press **Page Down** until you see the last record. Save the workbook.

   Transaction 2016-104 is located on row 109 after the duplicate records are removed.

# STEP 5 ≫ APPLY A TABLE STYLE

Now that you have finalized the fields and added missing records to the March 2016 transaction table, you want to apply a table style to format the table. Refer to Figure 6.20 as you complete Step 5.

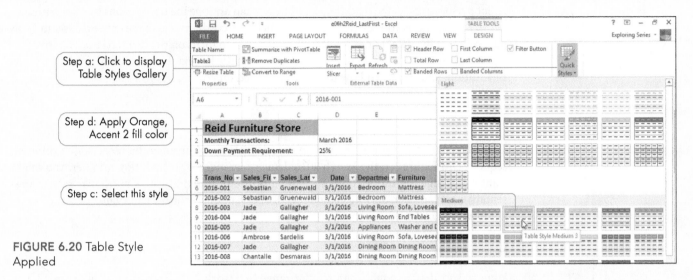

**Step a:** Click to display Table Styles Gallery

**Step d:** Apply Orange, Accent 2 fill color

**Step c:** Select this style

**FIGURE 6.20** Table Style Applied

a. Click the **DESIGN tab** and click **Quick Styles** in the Table Styles group to open the Table Styles gallery.

b. Position the mouse pointer over the fourth style on the second row in the *Light* section.

Live Preview shows the table with the Table Style Light 10 style but does not apply it.

c. Click **Table Style Medium 3**, the third style on the first row in the *Medium* section.

Excel formats the table with the Table Style Medium 3, which applies Orange, Accent 2 fill color to the header row and Orange, Accent 2, Lighter 80% fill color to every other record.

d. Press **Ctrl_Home** to go to cell A1. Select the **range A1:C1**, click the **Fill Color arrow** in the Font group on the HOME tab, and then click **Orange, Accent 2**.

You applied a fill color for the title to match the fill color of the field names on the header row in the table.

e. Save the workbook. Keep the workbook onscreen if you plan to continue with the next Hands-On Exercise. If not, close the workbook and exit Excel.

# Table Manipulation

You have a variety of options to manipulate table data, in addition to managing fields, adding records, and applying table styles. You can arrange the records in different sequences to get different perspectives on the data. For example, you can arrange the transactions by sales representative. Furthermore, you can display only particular records instead of the entire dataset to focus on a subset of the data. For example, you might want to focus on the financed transactions.

In this section, you will learn how to sort records by text, numbers, and dates in a table. In addition, you will learn how to filter data based on conditions you set.

## Sorting Data

Table data are easier to understand and work with if you arrange the records in a different sequence. In Figure 6.1, the March 2016 data are arranged by transaction number. You might want to arrange the transactions so that all of the transactions for a particular sales representative are together. *Sorting* is the process of arranging records by the value of one or more fields within a table.

### Sort One Field

STEP 1 ›› You can sort data in a table or a regular range in a worksheet. To sort by only one field, you can use any of the following methods for either a range of data or a table:

- Click in a cell within the field you want to sort and click Sort & Filter in the Editing group on the HOME tab.
- Click in a cell within the field you want to sort and click *Sort A to Z*, *Sort Z to A*, or Sort in the Sort & Filter group on the DATA tab.
- Right-click the field to sort, point to Sort on the shortcut menu, and then select the type of sort you want.
- Click the filter arrow in the header row and select the desired sort option.

Table 6.3 lists sort options by data type.

| TABLE 6.3 Sort Options | | |
| --- | --- | --- |
| Data Type | Options | Explanation |
| Text | Sort A to Z | Arranges data in alphabetical order. |
| | Sort Z to A | Arranges data in reverse alphabetical order. |
| Dates | Sort Oldest to Newest | Displays data in chronological order, from oldest to newest. |
| | Sort Newest to Oldest | Displays data in reverse chronological order, from newest to oldest. |
| Values | Sort Smallest to Largest | Arranges values from the smallest value to the largest. |
| | Sort Largest to Smallest | Arranges values from the largest value to the smallest. |
| Color | Sort by Cell Color | Arranges data together for cells containing a particular fill color. |
| | Sort by Font Color | Arranges data together for cells containing a particular font color. |

### Sort Multiple Fields

STEP 2 ›› At times, sorting by only one field yields several records that have the same information. For example, the same last name or the same department could display several times. In those instances, you may want to add a sort on a second field. A second sort will help to uniquely identify a record. You might need both last name and first name to identify an individual. Using multiple level sorts enables like records in the primary sort to be further organized by additional sort levels. For example, you might want to sort by department, then by sales representative, and finally by sales amount. Excel enables you to sort data on 64 different levels. To perform a multiple level sort:

1. Click in any cell in the table.
2. Click Sort in the Sort & Filter group on the Data tab to display the Sort dialog box.
3. Select the primary sort level by clicking the *Sort by* arrow, selecting the field to sort by, and then clicking the Order arrow and selecting the sort order from the list.
4. Click Add Level, select the second sort level by clicking the *Then by* arrow, select the column to sort by, click the Order arrow, and then select the sort order from the list.
5. Continue to click Add Level and add sort levels until you have entered all sort levels. See Figure 6.21. Click OK.

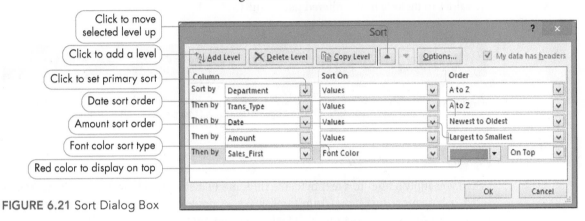

FIGURE 6.21 Sort Dialog Box

## Create a Custom Sort

Excel arranges data in defined sequences, such as alphabetical order. For example, days of the week are sorted alphabetically: Friday, Monday, Saturday, Sunday, Thursday, Tuesday, and Wednesday. However, you might want to create a custom sort sequence. For example, you can create a custom sort to arrange days of the week in order from Sunday to Saturday.

To create a custom sort sequence:

1. Click Sort in the Sort & Filter group on the DATA tab.
2. Click the Order arrow and select Custom List to display the Custom Lists dialog box (see Figure 6.22).
3. Select an existing sort sequence in the *Custom lists* box, or select NEW LIST.
4. Click Add and type the entries in the desired sort sequence in the *List entries* box, pressing Enter between entries.
5. Click Add and click OK.

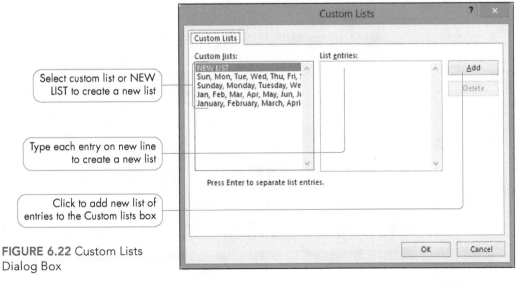

FIGURE 6.22 Custom Lists Dialog Box

# Filtering Data

***Filtering*** is the process of specifying conditions to display only those records that meet certain conditions. For example, you might want to filter the data to show transactions for only a particular sales representative. To filter records by a particular field, click the filter arrow for that field. The list displays each unique label, value, or date contained in the column. Deselect the (Select All) check box and click the check box for each value you want to include in the filtered results.

Often you will need to apply more than one filter to display the needed records. You can filter more than one field. Each additional filter is based on the current filtered data and further reduces a data subset. To apply multiple filters, click each field's filter arrow and select the values to include in the filtered data results.

## TIP | Copying Before Filtering Data

Often, you need to show different filters applied to the same dataset. You can copy the worksheet and filter the data on the copied worksheet to preserve the original dataset.

## Apply Text Filters

**STEP 3 ≫** When you apply a filter to a text field, the filter menu displays each unique text item. You can select one or more text items from the list. For example, select Gallagher to show only her records. To display records for both Gallagher and Sardelis, deselect the (Select All) check mark and click the Gallagher and Sardelis check boxes. You can also select Text Filters to see a submenu of additional options, such as *Begins With*, to select all records for which the name begins with the letter G, for example.

Figure 6.23 shows the Sales_Last filter menu with two names selected. Excel displays records for these two reps only. The records for the other sales reps are hidden but not deleted. The filter arrow displays a filter icon, indicating which field is filtered. Excel displays the row numbers in blue, indicating that you applied a filter. The missing row numbers indicate hidden rows of data. When you remove the filter, all the records display again.

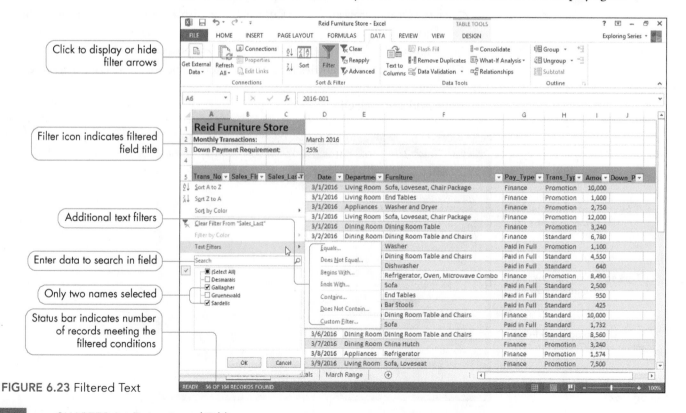

**FIGURE 6.23** Filtered Text

Click the Filter Button check box in the Table Style Options group on the Design tab to display or hide the filter arrows. For a range of data instead of a table, click Filter in the Sort & Filter group on the Data tab to display or hide the filter arrows.

## Apply Number Filters

STEP 4»

When you filter a field of numbers, you can select specific numbers. You might want to filter numbers by a range, such as numbers greater than $5,000 or numbers between $4,000 and $5,000. The submenu enables you to set a variety of number filters. In Figure 6.24, the amounts are filtered to show only those that are above the average amount. In this situation, Excel calculates the average amount as $4,512. Only records above that amount display.

If the field contains a large number of unique entries, you can click in the Search box and then type a value, text label, or date. Doing so narrows the visible list so that you do not have to scroll through the entire list. For example, if you enter $7, the list will display only values that start with $7.

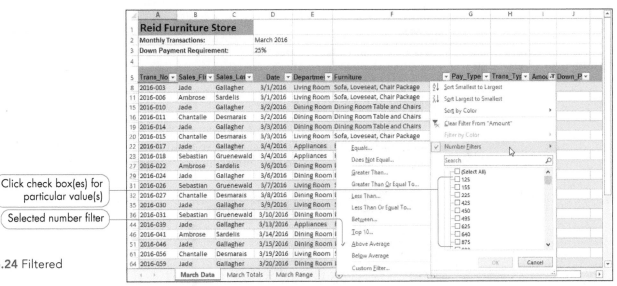

Click check box(es) for particular value(s)

Selected number filter

**FIGURE 6.24** Filtered Numbers

The Top 10 option enables you to specify the top records. Although the option name is Top 10, you can specify the number or percentage of records to display. For example, you can filter the list to display only the top five or the bottom 7%. Figure 6.25 shows the Top 10 AutoFilter dialog box. Click the first arrow to select either Top or Bottom, click the spin arrows to indicate a value, and then click the last arrow to select either Items or Percent.

**FIGURE 6.25** Top 10 AutoFilter Dialog Box

## Apply Date Filters

When you filter a field of dates, you can select specific dates or a date range, such as dates after 3/15/2016 or dates between 3/1/2016 and 3/7/2016. The submenu enables you to set a variety of date filters. For more specific date options, point to Date Filters, point to *All Dates in the Period*, and then select a period, such as Quarter 2 or October. Figure 6.26 shows the Date Filter menu.

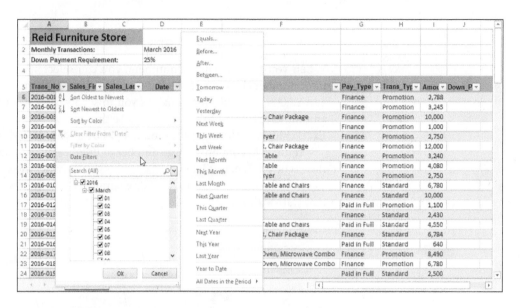

**FIGURE 6.26** Filtered Dates

## Apply a Custom Filter

If you select options such as *Greater Than* or *Before*, Excel displays the Custom AutoFilter dialog box (see Figure 6.27). You can also select Custom Filter from the menu to display this dialog box, which is designed for more complex filtering requirements.

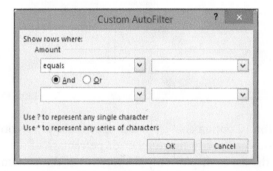

**FIGURE 6.27** Custom AutoFilter Dialog Box

The dialog box indicates the column being filtered. To set the filters, click the arrows to select the comparison type, such as equals or contains. Click the arrow on the right to select a specific text, value, or date entry, or type the data yourself. For ranges of dates or values, click And, and then specify the comparison operator and value or date for the next condition row. For text, click Or. For example, if you want both Gallagher and Desmarais, you must select Or because each data entry contains either Gallagher or Desmarais but not both at the same time.

You can use wildcards to represent characters. For example, to select all states starting with New, type *New* * in the second box to obtain results such as New York or New Mexico. The asterisk (*) represents any number of characters. If you want a wildcard for only a single character, type the question mark (?).

## Clear Filters

You can remove the filters from one or more fields to expand the dataset again. To remove only one filter and keep the other filters, click the filter arrow for the field from which you wish to clear the filter and select Clear Filter From.

To remove all filters and display all records in a dataset, do one of the following:

- Click Filter in the Sort & Filter group on the DATA tab.
- Click Sort & Filter in the Editing group on the HOME tab and select Filter.

*Quick*
Concepts

1. What is the purpose of sorting data in a table? *p. 190*

2. What are two ways to arrange (sort) dates? *p. 190*

3. List at least five ways you can filter numbers. *p. 193*

4. Assume you are filtering a list and want to display records for people who live in Boston or New York. What settings do you enter in the Custom AutoFilter dialog box for that field? *p. 194*

## 3 Table Manipulation

You want to start analyzing the March 2016 transactions for Reid Furniture Store by sorting and filtering data in a variety of ways to help you understand the transactions better.

**Skills covered:** Sort One Field • Sort Multiple Fields • Apply Text Filters • Apply a Number Filter • Apply a Date Filter

### STEP 1 ≫ SORT ONE FIELD

First, you want to compare the number of transactions by sales rep, so you will sort the data by the Rep_Last field. After reviewing the transactions by sales reps, you want to arrange the transactions from the one with the largest purchase first to the smallest purchase last. Refer to Figure 6.28 as you complete Step 1.

Step b: Click to sort alphabetically by last name

Step c: Click to sort amount from largest to smallest

**FIGURE 6.28** Sorted Data

a. Open *e04h2Reid_LastFirst* if you closed it at the end of Hands-On Exercise 2. Save it as **e04h3Reid_LastFirst**, changing *h2* to *h3*.

b. Click the **Sales_Last filter arrow** and select **Sort A to Z**.

Excel arranges the transactions in alphabetical order by last name, starting with Desmarais. Within each sales rep, records display in their original sequence by transaction number. If you scan the records, you can see that Gallagher completed the most sales transactions in March. The up arrow icon on the Sales_Last filter arrow indicates records are sorted in alphabetical order by that field.

**TIP Name Sorts**

Always check the data to determine how many levels of sorting you need to apply. If your table contains several people with the same last name but different first names, you would first sort by the Last Name field, then sort by First Name field. All the people with the last name Desmarais would be grouped together and further sorted by first name, such as Amanda and then Bradley.

**c.** Click the **Amount filter arrow** and select **Sort Largest to Smallest**. Save the workbook.

The records are no longer sorted by Sales_Last. When you sort by another field, Excel arranges the data for that field. In this case, Excel arranges the transactions from the one with the largest amount to the smallest amount, indicated by the down arrow icon in the Amount filter arrow.

## STEP 2 >> SORT MULTIPLE FIELDS

You want to review the transactions by payment type (financed or paid in full). Within each payment type, you want to further compare the transaction type (promotion or standard). Finally, you want to compare costs within the sorted records by displaying the highest costs first. You will use the Sort dialog box to perform a three-level sort. Refer to Figure 6.29 as you complete Step 2.

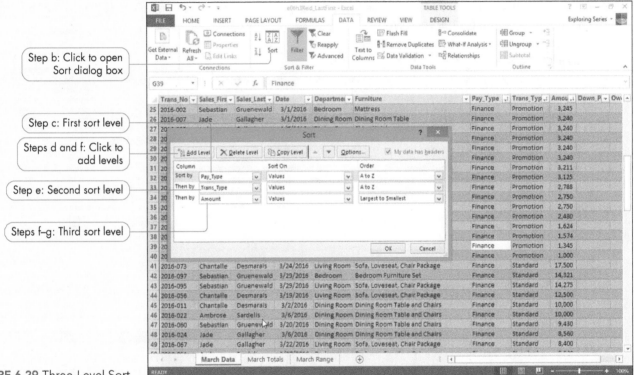

**FIGURE 6.29** Three-Level Sort

**a.** Click inside the table and click the **DATA tab**.

Both the DATA and HOME tabs contain commands to open the Sort dialog box.

**b.** Click **Sort** in the Sort & Filter group to open the Sort dialog box.

**c.** Click the **Sort by arrow** and select **Pay_Type**. Click the **Order arrow** and select **A to Z**.

You start by specifying the column for the primary sort. In this case, you want to sort the records first by the Payment Type column.

**d.** Click **Add Level**.

The Sort dialog box adds the *Then by* row, which adds a secondary sort.

**e.** Click the **Then by arrow** and select **Trans_Type**.

The default order is A to Z, which will sort in alphabetical order by Trans_Type. Excel will first sort the records by the Pay_Type (Finance or Paid in Full). Within each Pay_Type, Excel will further sort records by Trans_Type (Promotion or Standard).

**f.** Click **Add Level** to add another *Then by* row. Click the second **Then by arrow** and select **Amount**.

g. Click the **Order arrow** for the Amount sort and select **Largest to Smallest**.

Within the Pay_Type and Trans_Type sorts, this will arrange the records with the largest amount first in descending order to the smallest amount.

h. Click **OK** and scroll through the records. Save the workbook.

Most customers finance their purchases instead of paying in full. For the financed transactions, more than half were promotional sales. For merchandise paid in full, a majority of the transactions were standard sales, indicating that people with money don't necessarily wait for a promotional sale to purchase merchandise.

## STEP 3 ≫ APPLY TEXT FILTERS

Now that you know Jade Gallagher had the most transactions for March, you will filter the table to focus on her sales. You notice that she sells more merchandise from the Dining Room department, so you will filter out the other departments. Refer to Figure 6.30 as you complete Step 3.

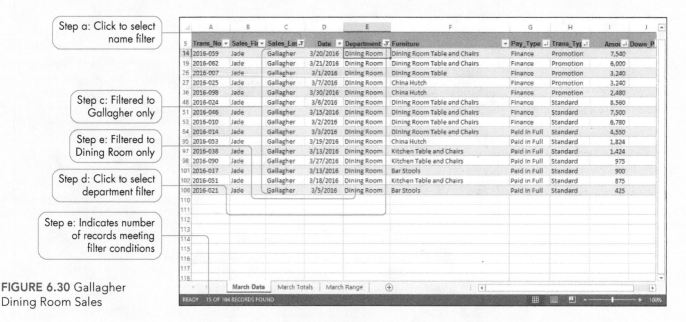

**FIGURE 6.30** Gallagher Dining Room Sales

a. Click the **Sales_Last filter arrow**.

The (Select All) check box is selected.

b. Click the **(Select All) check box** to deselect all last names.

c. Click the **Gallagher check box** and click **OK**.

The status bar indicates that 33 out of 104 records meet the filtering condition. The Sales_Last filter arrow includes a funnel icon, indicating that this column is filtered.

d. Click the **Department filter arrow**.

e. Click the **(Select All) check box** to deselect all departments, click the **Dining Room check box** to focus on that department, and then click **OK**. Save the workbook.

The remaining 15 records show Gallagher's dining room sales for the month. The Department filter arrow includes a funnel icon, indicating that this column is also filtered.

# STEP 4 >> APPLY A NUMBER FILTER

Vicki is considering giving a bonus to employees who sold the high-end dining room furniture during a specific time period (3/16/2016 to 3/31/2016). You want to determine if Jade Gallagher qualifies for this bonus. In particular, you are interested in how much gross revenue she generated for dining room furniture that cost at least $5,000 or more. Refer to Figure 6.31 as you complete Step 4.

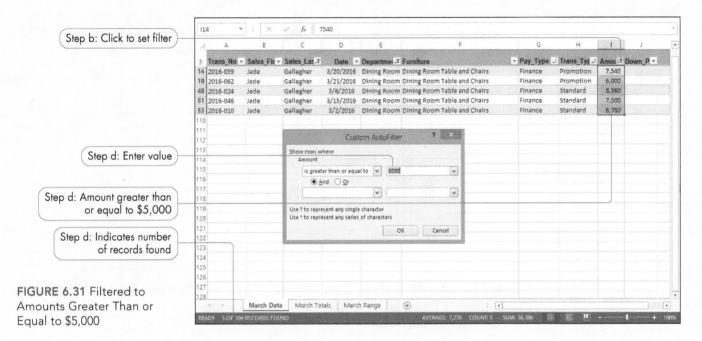

**FIGURE 6.31** Filtered to Amounts Greater Than or Equal to $5,000

a. Select the **range I14:I108** of the filtered list and then view the status bar.

   The average transaction amount is $3,754 with 15 transactions (i.e., 15 filtered records).

b. Click the **Amount filter arrow**.

c. Point to **Number Filters** and select **Greater Than Or Equal To**.

   The Custom AutoFilter dialog box opens. The default comparison *is greater than or equal to* is displayed.

d. Type **5000** in the box to the right of *is greater than or equal to* and click **OK**. Save the workbook.

   When typing numbers, you can type raw numbers such as 5000 or formatted numbers such as $5,000. Out of Gallagher's original 15 dining room transactions, only 5 transactions (one-third of her sales) were valued at $5,000 or more.

> **TROUBLESHOOTING:** If no records display or if too many records display, you might have entered 500000 or 500. Repeat steps b through d.

Finally, you want to study Jade Gallagher's sales records for the last half of the month. You will add a date filter to identify those sales records. Refer to Figure 6.32 as you complete Step 5.

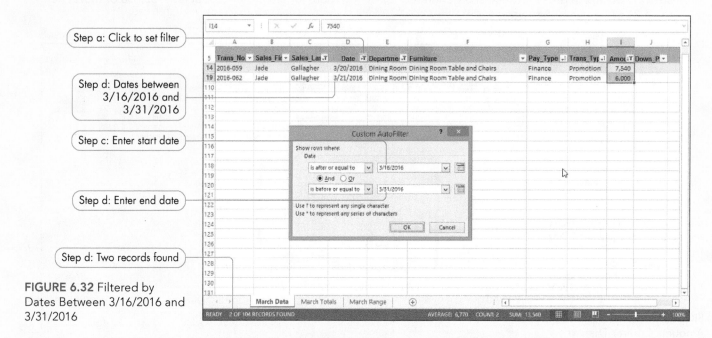

Step a: Click to set filter

Step d: Dates between 3/16/2016 and 3/31/2016

Step c: Enter start date

Step d: Enter end date

Step d: Two records found

**FIGURE 6.32** Filtered by Dates Between 3/16/2016 and 3/31/2016

a. Click the **Date filter arrow**.

b. Point to **Date Filters** and select **Between**.

The Custom AutoFilter dialog box opens. The default comparisons are *is after or equal to* and *is before or equal to*, ready for you to enter the date specifications.

c. Type **3/16/2016** in the box on the right side of *is after or equal to*.

You specified the starting date of the range of dates to include. You will keep the *And* option selected.

d. Type **3/31/2016** in the box on the right side of *is before or equal to*. Click **OK**.

Gallagher had only two dining room sales greater than $5,000 during the last half of March.

e. Save the workbook. Keep the workbook onscreen if you plan to continue with the next Hands-On Exercise. If not, close the workbook and exit Excel.

# Table Aggregation

In addition to sorting and filtering tables to analyze the data, you might want to add fields that perform calculations using existing fields. For example, you might want to calculate a required down payment on the amount purchased. Furthermore, you might want to perform aggregate calculations, such as AVERAGE, for a field of numeric data.

In this section, you will learn how to insert structured references to build formulas within a table. In addition, you will learn how to add a row at the end of the table to display basic statistical calculations.

## Using Structured References and a Total Row

Excel aids you in quantitative analysis. Your value to an organization increases with your ability to create sophisticated formulas, aggregate data in a meaningful way, and interpret those results. Although you can create complex formulas that you understand, you should strive to create formulas that other people can understand. Creating easy-to-read formulas helps you present self-documenting formulas that require less explanation on your part. When you create formulas for tables, you can use built-in functionality (such as structured references and a total row) that assists you in building understandable formulas.

### Create Structured References in Formulas

Your experience in building formulas involves using cell references, such as =SUM(B1:B15) or =H6*$B$3, or range names, such as grades in =VLOOKUP(E5,grades,2). You can use cell references and range names in formulas to perform calculations in a table, as well as another type of reference for formulas in tables: structured references. A *structured reference* is a tag or use of a table element, such as a field heading, as a reference in a formula. Structured references in formulas clearly indicate which type of data is used in the calculations.

STEP 1 ⟫    A structured reference requires brackets around column headings or field names, such as =[Amount]–[Down_Pay]. The use of field headings without row references in a structured formula is called an *unqualified reference*. Formula AutoComplete displays a list of field headings after you type the equal sign and the opening bracket (see Figure 6.33). Type or double-click the column name from the list and type the closing bracket. Excel displays a colored border around the referenced column. When you enter a formula using structured references, Excel copies the formula down the rest of the table column automatically, compared to typing references in formulas and manually copying the formula down a column.

| | Date | Department | Furniture | Pay_Type | Trans_Type | Amount | Down_P | Owed |
|---|---|---|---|---|---|---|---|---|
| 98 | 3/28/2016 | Bedroom | Mattress | Paid in Full | Standard | 2,000 | =[ | |
| 99 | 3/28/2016 | Bedroom | Mattress | Paid in Full | Promotion | 3,245 | | |
| 100 | 3/29/2016 | Living Room | Sofa, Loveseat, Chair Package | Finance | Standard | 14,275 | | |
| 101 | 3/29/2016 | Bedroom | Bedroom Furniture Set | Finance | Promotion | 3,285 | | |
| 102 | 3/29/2016 | Bedroom | Bedroom Furniture Set | Finance | Standard | 14,321 | | |
| 103 | 3/30/2016 | Dining Room | China Hutch | Finance | Promotion | 2,480 | | |
| 104 | 3/30/2016 | Bedroom | Mattress | Finance | Standard | 1,425 | | |
| 105 | 3/30/2016 | Bedroom | Bedroom Furniture Set | Finance | Promotion | 11,234 | | |
| 106 | 3/31/2016 | Bedroom | Bedroom Furniture Set | Finance | Promotion | 5,773 | | |
| 107 | 3/31/2016 | Bedroom | Mattress | Paid in Full | Promotion | 2,000 | | |
| 108 | 3/31/2016 | Living Room | End Tables | Finance | Standard | 2,505 | | |
| 109 | 3/31/2016 | Appliances | Refrigerator | Paid in Full | Standard | 1,500 | | |

Type =[ to start structured reference

Formula AutoComplete displays field names

AutoComplete list: Trans_No, Sales_First, Sales_Last, Date, Department, Furniture, Pay_Type, Trans_Type, Amount, Down_Pay, Owed

**FIGURE 6.33** Structured Reference Creation

You can also use the semiselection process to create a formula. As you point to cells to enter a formula in a table, Excel builds a formula like this: =[@Amount]–[@Down_Pay], where the @ indicates the current row. If you use the semiselection process to create a formula outside the table, the formula includes the table and field names, such as =Table1 [@Amount]–Table1[@Down_Pay]. Table1 is the name of the table; Amount and Down_Pay are field names. This structured formula that includes references, such as table numbers, is called a *fully qualified structured reference*. When you build formulas *within* a table, you can use either unqualified or fully qualified structured references. If you need to use table data in a formula *outside* the table boundaries, you must use fully qualified structured references.

## Add a Total Row

At times, aggregating data provides more meaningful quantitative interpretation than individual values. For regular ranges of data, you use basic statistical functions, such as SUM, AVERAGE, MIN, and MAX, to provide meaning for a dataset. An Excel table provides the advantage of being able to display a total row automatically without creating the aggregate function yourself. A **total row** displays below the last row of records in an Excel table and enables you to display summary statistics, such as a sum of values displayed in a column.

To display and use the total row:

STEP 2 ›› 1. Click the DESIGN tab.

2. Click Total Row in the Table Style Options group. Excel displays the total row below the last record in the table. Excel displays *Total* in the first column of the total row. Excel either sums or counts data for the last field, depending on the type of data stored in that field. If the last field consists of values, Excel sums the values. If the last field is text, Excel counts the number of records.

3. Click a cell in the total row, click that cell's total row arrow, and then select the function results that you desire. To add a summary statistic to another column, click in the empty cell for that field in the total row and click the arrow to select the desired function. Select None to remove the function.

Figure 6.34 shows the active total row with totals applied to the Amount, Down_Pay, and Owed fields. A list of functions displays to change the function for the last field.

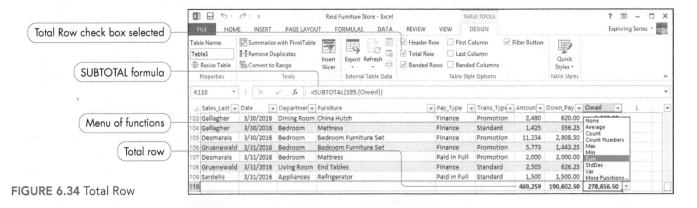

FIGURE 6.34 Total Row

---

## TIP | Filtering Data and Subtotals

If you filter the data and display the total row, the SUBTOTAL function's 109 argument ensures that only the displayed data are summed; data for hidden rows are not calculated in the aggregate function.

---

The calculations on the total row use the SUBTOTAL function. The **SUBTOTAL function** calculates an aggregate value, such as totals or averages, for values in a range or database. If you click in a calculated total row cell, the SUBTOTAL function displays in the Formula Bar. The function for the total row looks like this: =SUBTOTAL(function_num,ref1). The function_num argument is a number that represents a function (see Table 6.4). The ref1 argument indicates the range of values to calculate. The SUBTOTAL function to total the values in the Owed field would be =SUBTOTAL(109,[Owed]), where the number 109 represents the SUM function, and [Owed] represents the Owed field. A benefit of the SUBTOTAL function is that it subtotals data for filtered records, so you have an accurate total for the visible records.

=SUBTOTAL(function_num,ref1,...)

### TABLE 6.4 SUBTOTAL Function Numbers

| Function | Database Number | Table Number |
|----------|-----------------|--------------|
| AVERAGE | 1 | 101 |
| COUNT | 2 | 102 |
| COUNTA | 3 | 103 |
| MAX | 4 | 104 |
| MIN | 5 | 105 |
| PRODUCT | 6 | 106 |
| STDEV | 7 | 107 |
| STDEVP | 8 | 108 |
| SUM | 9 | 109 |
| VAR | 10 | 110 |
| VARP | 11 | 111 |

Quick
Concepts

1. What is a structured reference? What is the general format for including a field name in a formula? Give an example. *p. 201*

2. What are the benefits of displaying a total row and selecting functions instead of adding functions yourself below a table? *p. 202*

# Hands-On Exercises

## 4 Table Aggregation

You further analyze the March 2016 transactions for Reid Furniture Store: You want to calculate the required down payment amount and how much customers owe for their purchases. Finally, you will convert the table back to a range.

**Skills covered:** Create Structured References in Formulas • Add a Total Row • Convert a Table to a Range

### STEP 1 ⟫ CREATE STRUCTURED REFERENCES IN FORMULAS

To continue reviewing the March transactions, you need to calculate the required down payment for customers who financed their purchases. The required down payment is located above the table data so that you can change that value if needed. In addition, you want to calculate how much customers owe on their purchases if they did not pay in full. You will use structured formulas to perform these calculations. Refer to Figure 6.35 as you complete Step 1.

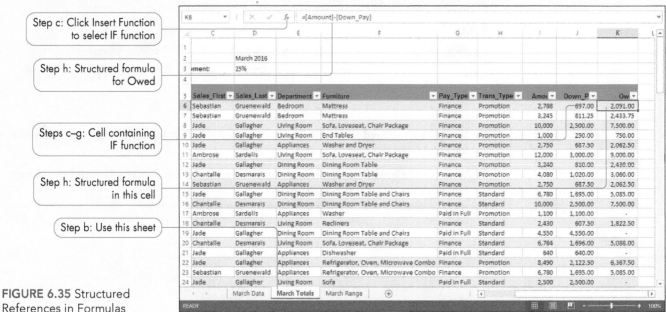

**FIGURE 6.35** Structured References in Formulas

a. Open *e04h3Reid_LastFirst* if you closed it at the end of Hands-On Exercise 3. Save it as **e04h4Reid_LastFirst**, changing *h3* to *h4*.

b. Click the **March Totals worksheet tab** and make **cell J6** the active cell.

To preserve the integrity of the sorting and filtering in case your instructor wants to verify your work, you will continue with an identical dataset on another worksheet.

c. Click **Insert Function** to open the Insert Function dialog box, select **IF** in the **Select a function list**, and then click **OK**.

d. Type **[Pay_Type]="Paid in Full"** in the **Logical_test box**.

The logical test evaluates whether a customer paid in full, indicated in the Pay_Type field. Remember to type the brackets around the column label.

e. Type **[Amount]** in the **Value_if_true box**.

If a customer pays in full, the down payment is the full amount.

**f.** Type [**Amount**]*$D$3 in the **Value_if_false box**.

If a customer does not pay in full, he or she must pay a required down payment. You use [Amount] to refer to the Amount field in the table. Enclose the field labels in brackets. The amount is multiplied by the absolute reference to D3, the cell containing the required down payment percentage. Make this cell reference absolute so that it does not change when Excel copies the formula down the Down_Pay column.

**g.** Click **OK** to enter the formula.

The formula looks like this in the Formula Bar: =IF([Pay_Type]= "Paid in Full",[Amount],[Amount]*$D$3). Because you are entering formulas in a table, Excel copies the formula down the column automatically. The first customer must pay a $697 down payment (25% of $2,788). The columns in the current worksheet have been formatted as Comma Style for you.

> **TROUBLESHOOTING:** If the results seem incorrect, check your function. Errors will result if you do not enclose the field names in brackets, if you have misspelled a field name, if you omit the quotation marks around *Paid in Full*, and so on. Correct any errors.

**h.** Click **cell K6**. Type the formula =[**Amount**]–[**Down_Pay**] and press **Enter**. Save the workbook.

The formula calculates how much customers owe if they finance their purchases. Excel copies the formula down the column.

## STEP 2 ≫ ADD A TOTAL ROW

You want to see the monthly totals for the Amount, Down_Pay, and Owed columns. Instead of entering SUM functions yourself, you will add a total row. Refer to Figure 6.36 as you complete Step 2.

**FIGURE 6.36** Totals for Filtered Table

a. Click the **DESIGN tab** and click **Total Row** in the Table Style Options group.

Excel displays the total row after the last record. It sums the last field of values automatically. The total amount customers owe is $278,656.50.

b. Click the **Down_Pay cell** in row 110, click the **total arrow**, and then select **Sum**.

You added a total to the Down_Pay field. The total amount of down payment collected is $190,602.50. The formula displays as =SUBTOTAL(109,[Down_Pay]) in the Formula Bar.

c. Click the **Amount cell** in row 110, click the **total arrow**, and then select **Sum**.

You added a total to the Amount column. The total amount of merchandise sales is $469,259. The formula displays as =SUBTOTAL(109,[Amount]) in the Formula Bar.

d. Filter by Gallagher again. Save the workbook.

The total row values change to display the totals for only Gallagher: $120,374 (Amount), 47,159.75 (Down_Pay), and 73,214.25 (Owed). This is an advantage of using the Total Row, which uses the SUBTOTAL function, as opposed to if you had inserted the SUM function manually. The SUM function would provide a total for all data in the column, not just the filtered data.

## STEP 3 ≫ CONVERT A TABLE TO A RANGE

Your last task for now is to convert a copy of the table to a range again so that you can apply other formats. Refer to Figure 6.37 as you complete Step 3.

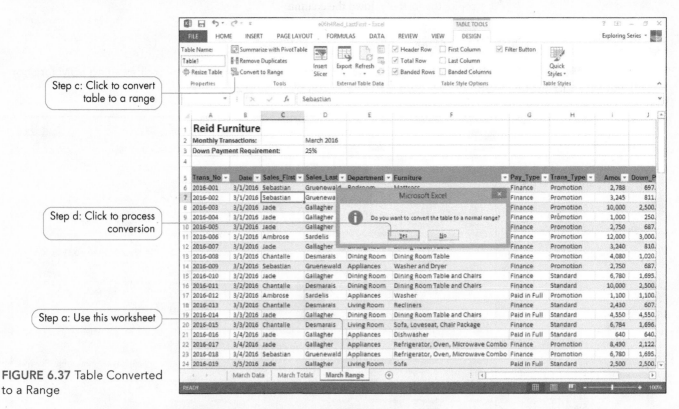

**FIGURE 6.37** Table Converted to a Range

a. Click the **March Range worksheet tab**.

To preserve the integrity of the sorting and filtering in case your instructor wants to verify your work, you will continue with an identical dataset on another worksheet.

b. Click within the table and click the **DESIGN tab**, if necessary.

**c.** Click **Convert to Range** in the Tools group.

Excel displays a message box asking if you want to convert the table to a range.

**d.** Click **Yes**.

Excel converts the table to a range. The filter arrows disappear, and the Design tab no longer displays. The range is still formatted using a table style. The structured formula =[Amount]-[Down_Pay] in cell K6 changes to ='March Range'!$I$6:$I$109-'March Range'!$J$6:$J$109.

**e.** Save the workbook. Keep the workbook onscreen if you plan to continue with the next Hands-On Exercise. If not, close the workbook and exit Excel.

# Conditional Formatting

You use table styles, or a variety of font, alignment, and number formats on the Home tab, to format a worksheet. You can also apply special formatting to cells that contain particular values or text using conditional formatting. ***Conditional formatting*** applies special formatting to highlight or emphasize cells that meet specific conditions. For example, a sales manager might want to highlight cells containing the top 10 sales amounts, or a professor might want to highlight test scores that fall below the average. You can also apply conditional formatting to point out data for a specific date or duplicate values in a range.

In this section, you will learn about the five conditional formatting categories and how to apply conditional formatting to a range of values based on a condition you set.

## Applying Conditional Formatting

Conditional formatting helps you and your audience understand a dataset better because it adds a visual element to the cells. The term is called *conditional* because the formatting occurs when a condition is met. This is similar logic to the IF function you have used. Remember with an IF function, you create a logical test that is evaluated. If the logical or conditional test is true, the function produces one result. If the logical or conditional test is false, the function produces another result. With conditional formatting, if the condition is true, Excel formats the cell automatically based on that condition. If the condition is false, Excel does not format the cell. If you change a value in a conditionally formatted cell, Excel examines the new value to see if it should apply the conditional format.

### Apply Conditional Formatting with the Quick Analysis Tool

When you select a range and click the Quick Analysis button, the FORMATTING options display in the Quick Analysis gallery. Position the mouse over a thumbnail to see how it will affect the selected range (see Figure 6.38). You can also apply conditional formatting by clicking Conditional Formatting in the Styles group on the Home tab.

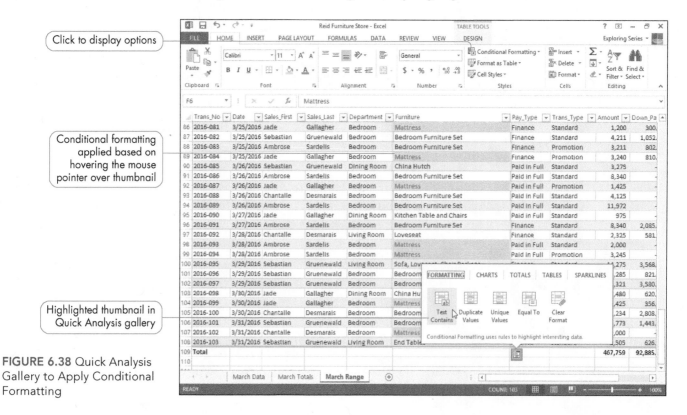

**FIGURE 6.38** Quick Analysis Gallery to Apply Conditional Formatting

Table 6.5 describes the conditional formatting options in the Quick Analysis gallery.

| TABLE 6.5 | Conditional Formatting Options in Quick Analysis Gallery |
|---|---|
| **Options** | **Description** |
| Text Contains | Formats cells that contain the text in the first selected cell. In Figure 6.38, the first selected cell contains Mattress. If a cell contains Mattress and Springs, Excel would format that cell also because it *contains* Mattress. |
| Duplicate Values | Formats cells that are duplicated in the selected range. |
| Unique Values | Formats cells that are unique; that is, no other cell in the selected range contains the same data. |
| Equal To | Formats cells that are exactly like the data contained in the first selected cell. |
| Clear Format | Removes the conditional formatting from the selected range. |

Table 6.6 lists and describes a number of different conditional formats that you can apply if you want more specific rules.

| TABLE 6.6 | Conditional Formatting Options |
|---|---|
| **Options** | **Description** |
| Highlight Cells Rules | Highlights cells with a fill color, font color, or border (such as Light Red Fill with Dark Red Text) if values are greater than, less than, between two values, equal to a value, or duplicate values; text that contains particular characters; or dates when a date meets a particular condition, such as *In the last 7 days.* |
| Top/Bottom Rules | Formats cells with values in the top 10 items, top 10%, bottom 10 items, bottom 10%, above average, or below average. You can change the exact values to format the top or bottom items or percentages, such as top 5 or bottom 15%. |
| Data Bars | Applies a gradient or solid fill bar in which the width of the bar represents the current cell's value compared to other cells' values. |
| Color Scales | Formats different cells with different colors, assigning one color to the lowest group of values and another color to the highest group of values, with gradient colors to other values. |
| Icon Sets | Inserts an icon from an icon palette in each cell to indicate values compared to each other. |

To apply a conditional format, select the cells for which you want to apply a conditional format, click the Home tab, click Conditional Formatting in the Styles group, and then select the conditional formatting category you want to apply.

## Apply the Highlight Cells Rules

STEP 1 ≫ The Highlight Cells Rules category enables you to apply a highlight to cells that meet a condition, such as a value greater than a particular value. This option contains predefined combinations of fill colors, font colors, and/or borders. This category is useful because it helps you identify and format automatically values of interest. For example, a weather tracker who developed a worksheet containing the temperatures for each day of a month might want to apply a conditional format to cells that contain temperatures between 70 and 75 degrees. To apply this conditional formatting, she would select Highlight Cells Rules and then select

Between. In the Between dialog box (see Figure 6.39), the weather tracker would type 70 in the *Format cells that are BETWEEN* box and 75 in the *and* box, select the type of conditional formatting, such as *Light Red Fill with Dark Red Text*, and then click OK to apply the formats.

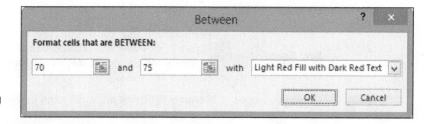

**FIGURE 6.39** Between Dialog Box

Figure 6.40 shows two columns of data that contain conditional formats. The Department column is conditionally formatted to highlight text with a Light Red Fill with Dark Red Text for cells that contain *Living Room*, and the Amount column is conditionally formatted to highlight with Red Border values between $5,000 and $10,000.

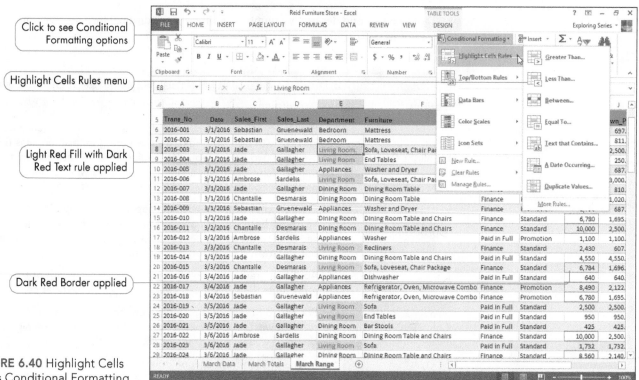

**FIGURE 6.40** Highlight Cells Rules Conditional Formatting

## Specify Top/Bottom Rules

**STEP 2** You might be interested in identifying the top five sales to reward the sales associates, or want to identify the bottom 15% of automobile dealers so that you can close underperforming locations. The Top/Bottom Rules category enables you to specify the top or bottom number, top or bottom percentage, or values that are above or below the average value in that range. In Figure 6.41, the Amount column is conditionally formatted to highlight the top five amounts. (Some rows are hidden so that all top five values display in the figure.) Although the menu option is Top 10 Items, you can specify the exact number of items to format.

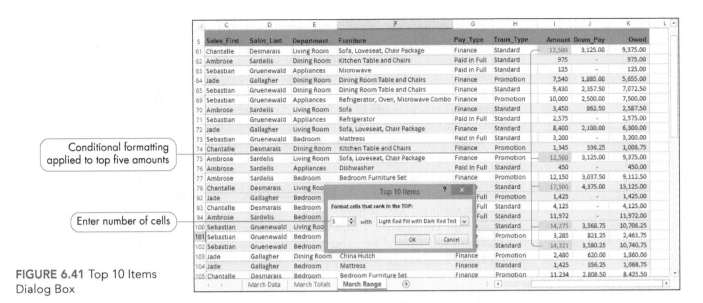

Conditional formatting applied to top five amounts

Enter number of cells

**FIGURE 6.41** Top 10 Items Dialog Box

## Display Data Bars, Color Scales, and Icon Sets

**STEP 3** *Data bars* indicate the value of a cell relative to other cells (see Figure 6.42). The width of the data bar represents the value in a cell, with a wider bar representing a higher value and a narrower bar a lower value. Use data bar conditional formatting to identify high and low values. Excel locates the largest value and displays the widest data bar in that cell. Excel then finds the smallest value and displays the smallest data bar in that cell. Excel sizes the data bars for the remaining cells based on their values relative to the high and low values in the column. If you change the values, Excel updates the data bar widths. Excel uses the same color for each data bar, but each bar differs in size based on the value in the respective cells.

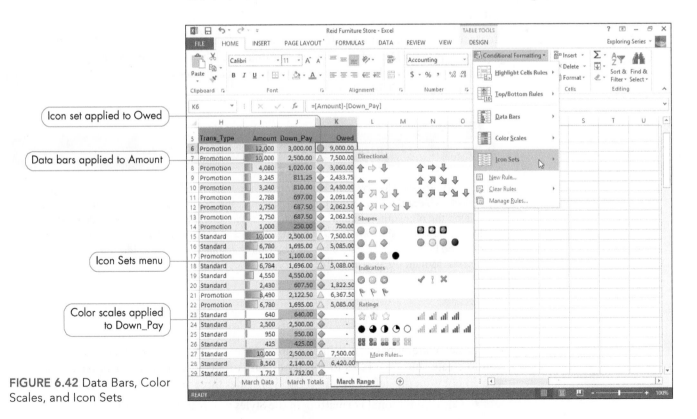

Icon set applied to Owed

Data bars applied to Amount

Icon Sets menu

Color scales applied to Down_Pay

**FIGURE 6.42** Data Bars, Color Scales, and Icon Sets

*Color scales* format cells with different colors based on the relative value of a cell compared to other selected cells. You can apply a two- or three-color scale. This scale assists in comparing a range of cells using gradations of those colors. The shade of the color represents higher or lower values. In Figure 6.42, for example, the red color scales display for the lowest values, the green color displays for the highest values, and gradients of yellow and orange represent the middle range of values in the Down_Pay column. Use color scales to understand variation in the data to identify trends, for example, to view good stock returns and weak stock returns.

*Icon sets* are symbols or signs that classify data into three, four, or five categories, based on the values in a range. Excel determines categories of value ranges and assigns an icon to each range. In Figure 6.42, a three-icon set was applied to the Owed column. Excel divided the range of values between the lowest value $0 and the highest value of $13,125 into thirds. The red diamond icon displays for the cells containing values in the lowest third ($0 to $4,375), the yellow triangle icon displays for cells containing the values in the middle third ($4,376 to $8,750), and the green circle icon displays for cells containing values in the top third ($8,751 to $13,125). Most purchases fall into the lowest third.

 **TIP | Don't Overdo It!**

Although conditional formatting helps identify trends, you should use this feature wisely. Apply conditional formatting when you want to emphasize important data. When you decide to apply conditional formatting, think about which category is best to highlight the data. Sometimes simple highlighting will suffice when you want to point out data meeting a particular condition; other times, you might want to apply data bars to point out relative differences among values. Finally, do not apply conditional formatting to too many columns.

## Clear Rules

To clear conditional formatting from the entire worksheet, click Conditional Formatting in the Styles group on the Home tab, point to Clear Rules, and then select *Clear Rules from Entire Sheet*. To remove conditional formatting from a range of cells, select cells. Then click Conditional Formatting, point to Clear Rules, and then select *Clear Rules from Selected Cells*.

 **TIP | Sort and Filter Using Conditional Formatting**

You can sort and filter by conditional formatting. For example, if you applied the Highlight Cells Rules conditional formatting, you can sort the column by color so that all cells containing the highlight appear first or last. To do this, display the filter arrows, click the arrow for the conditionally formatted column you wish to sort, point to Sort by Color, and then click the fill color or No Fill in the *Sort by Cell Color* area. If you applied the Icon Sets conditional formatting, you can filter by icon.

## Creating a New Rule

The default conditional formatting categories provide a variety of options. Excel also enables you to create your own rules to specify different fill colors, borders, or other formatting if you do not want the default settings. Excel provides three ways to create a new rule:

- Click Conditional Formatting in the Styles group and select New Rule.
- Click Conditional Formatting in the Styles group, select Manage Rules to open the Conditional Formatting Rules Manager dialog box, and then click New Rule.
- Click Conditional Formatting in the Styles group, select a rule category such as Highlight Cells Rules, and then select More Rules.

The New Formatting Rule dialog box opens (see Figure 6.43) so that you can define your new conditional formatting rule. First, select a rule type, such as *Format all cells based on their values*. The *Edit the Rule Description* section changes, based on the rule type you select. With the default rule type selected, you can specify the format style (2-Color Scale, 3-Color Scale, Data Bar, or Icon Sets). You can then specify the minimum and maximum values, the fill colors for color sets or data bars, or the icons for icon sets. After you edit the rule description, click OK to save your new conditional format.

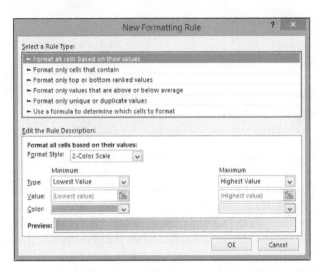

**FIGURE 6.43** New Formatting Rule Dialog Box

If you select any rule type except the *Format all cells based on their values* rule, the dialog box contains a Format button. When you click Format, the Format Cells dialog box opens so that you can specify number, font, border, and fill formats to apply to your rule.

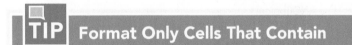

### TIP | Format Only Cells That Contain

This option provides a wide array of things you can format: values, text, dates, blanks, no blanks, errors, or no errors. Formatting blanks is helpful to see where you are missing data, and formatting cells containing errors helps you find those errors quickly.

## Use Formulas in Conditional Formatting

**STEP 4 »** If you need to create a complex conditional formatting rule, you can select a rule that uses a formula to format cells. For example, you might want to format merchandise amounts of financed items *and* amounts that are $10,000 or more. Figure 6.44 shows the Edit Formatting Rule dialog box and the corresponding conditional formatting applied to cells.

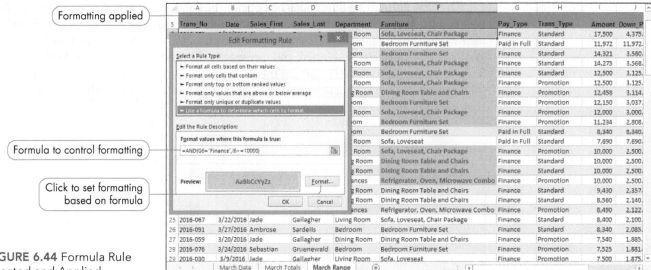

**Formatting applied**

**Formula to control formatting**

**Click to set formatting based on formula**

**FIGURE 6.44** Formula Rule Created and Applied

To create a formula-based conditional formatting rule, select the data and create a new rule. In the New Formatting Rule dialog box, select *Use a formula to determine which cells to format* and type the formula, using cell references in the first row, in the *Format values where this formula is true* box. Excel applies the general formula to the selected range, substituting the appropriate cell reference as it makes the comparisons. In the Figure 6.44 example, =AND(G6="Finance",I6>=10000) requires that the text in the Pay_Type column (column F) contain *Finance* and the Amount column (column I) contain a value that is greater than or equal to $10,000. The AND function requires that both logical tests be met to apply the conditional formatting. Two logical tests are required; however, you can include additional logical tests. Note that *all* logical tests must be true to apply the conditional formatting.

= AND(logical1,logical2,... )

## Manage Rules

To edit or delete conditional formatting rules you create, click Conditional Formatting in the Styles group and select Manage Rules. The Conditional Formatting Rules Manager dialog box opens (see Figure 6.45). Click the *Show formatting rules for* arrow and select from current selection, the entire worksheet, or a specific table. Select the rule and click Edit Rule or Delete Rule.

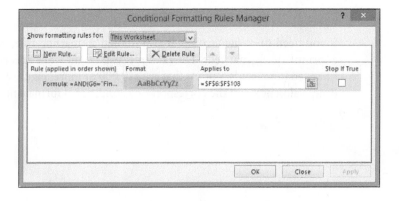

**FIGURE 6.45** Conditional Formatting Rules Manager Dialog Box

*Quick Concepts* ✓

1. How is conditional formatting similar to an IF function? *p. 208*

2. What conditional formatting would be helpful to identify the three movies with the highest revenue playing at theaters? *p. 210*

3. How is data bar conditional formatting helpful when reviewing a column of data? *p. 211*

MyITLab®
HOE5 Training

# 5 Conditional Formatting

Vicki Reid wants to review the transactions with you. She is interested in Sebastian Grunewald's sales record and the three highest transaction amounts. In addition, she wants to compare the down payment amounts visually. Finally, she wants you to analyze the amounts owed for sales completed by Sebastian.

**Skills covered:** Highlight Cells Rules • Specify Top/Bottom Rules • Display Data Bars • Use a Formula in Conditional Formatting

## STEP 1 ≫ HIGHLIGHT CELLS RULES

You want to identify Sebastian's sales for March 2016 without filtering the data. You will apply a conditional format to apply a fill and font color so that cells containing his first name stand out. Refer to Figure 6.46 as you complete Step 1.

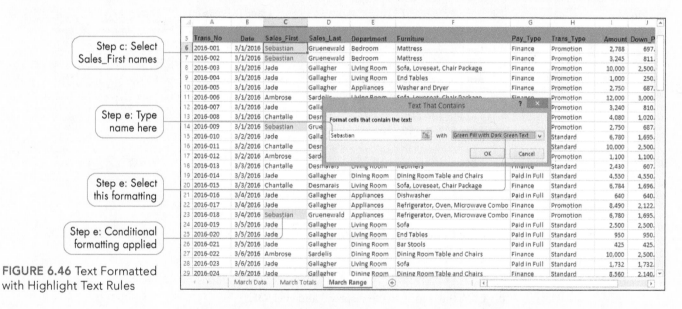

**FIGURE 6.46** Text Formatted with Highlight Text Rules

a. Open *e04h4Reid_LastFirst* if you closed it at the end of Hands-On Exercise 4. Save the workbook as **e04h5Reid_LastFirst**, changing *h4* to *h5*.

b. Select **row headings 6 through 109** in the March Range worksheet. Click the **HOME tab**, if necessary, click the **Fill Color arrow**, and then select **No Fill**.

   You removed the previous table style with banded rows. This will avoid having too many fill colors when you apply conditional formatting rules.

c. Select the **range C6:C109**, which is the column containing the sales representatives' first names.

d. Click **Conditional Formatting** in the Styles group, point to *Highlight Cells Rules*, and then select **Text that Contains**.

   The Text That Contains dialog box opens.

e. Type **Sebastian** in the box, click the **with arrow**, and then select **Green Fill with Dark Green Text**. Click **OK**. Deselect the range and save the workbook.

   Excel formats only cells that contain Sebastian with the fill and font color.

**Apply Multiple Formats to One Column**

While the range is selected, you can apply another conditional format, such as Light Yellow with Dark Yellow text for another first name.

## STEP 2 ›› SPECIFY TOP/BOTTOM RULES

Vicki is now interested in identifying the highest three sales transactions in March. Instead of sorting the records, you will use the Top/Bottom Rules conditional formatting. Refer to Figure 6.47 as you complete Step 2.

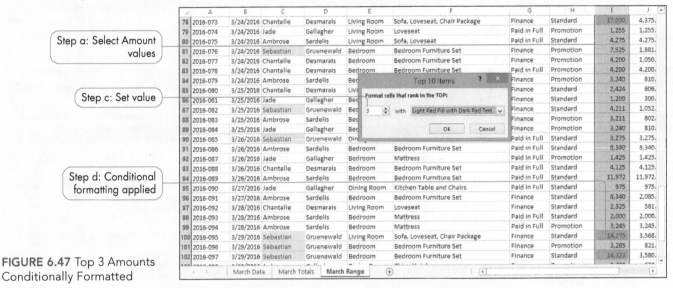

**FIGURE 6.47** Top 3 Amounts Conditionally Formatted

a. Select the **range I6:I109**, the range containing the amounts.

b. Click **Conditional Formatting** in the Styles group, point to *Top/Bottom Rules*, and then select **Top 10 Items**.

   The Top 10 Items dialog box opens.

c. Click the spin arrow to display 3 and click **OK**.

d. Scroll through the worksheet to see the top three amounts. Save the workbook.

## STEP 3 ›› DISPLAY DATA BARS

Vicki wants to compare all of the down payments. Data bars would add a nice visual element as she compares down payment amounts. Refer to Figure 6.48 as you complete Step 3.

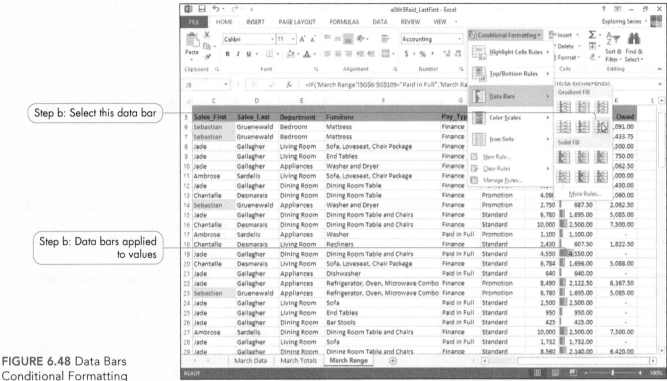

**FIGURE 6.48** Data Bars Conditional Formatting

Step b: Select this data bar

Step b: Data bars applied to values

a. Select the **range J6:J109**, which contains the down payment amounts.

b. Click **Conditional Formatting** in the Styles group, point to *Data Bars*, and then select **Purple Data Bar** in the *Gradient Fill* section. Scroll through the list and save the workbook.

Excel displays data bars in each cell. The larger bar widths help Vicki quickly identify the largest down payments. However, the largest down payments are identical to the original amounts when the customers pay in full. This result illustrates that you should not accept the results at face value. Doing so would provide you with an inaccurate analysis.

## STEP 4 ›› USE A FORMULA IN CONDITIONAL FORMATTING

Vicki's next request is to analyze the amounts owed by Sebastian's customers. In particular, she wants to highlight the merchandise for which more than $5,000 is owed. To do this, you realize you need to create a custom rule that evaluates both the Sales_First column and the Owed column. Refer to Figure 6.49 as you complete Step 4.

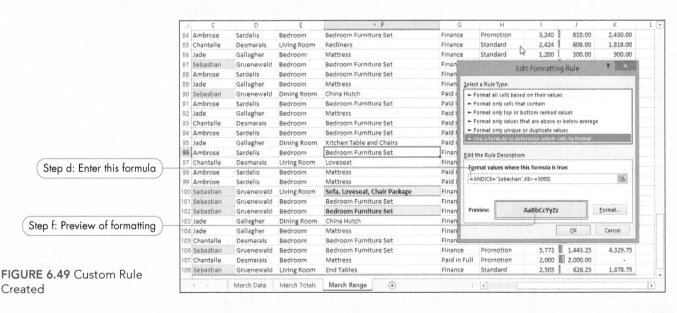

Step d: Enter this formula

Step f: Preview of formatting

**FIGURE 6.49** Custom Rule Created

a. Select the **range F6:F109**, which contains the merchandise.

b. Click **Conditional Formatting** in the Styles group and select **New Rule**.

The New Formatting Rule dialog box opens.

c. Select **Use a formula to determine which cells to format**.

d. Type **=AND(C6="Sebastian",K6>5000)** in the **Format values where this formula is true box**.

Because you are comparing the contents of cell C6 to text, you must enclose the text within quotation marks.

e. Click **Format** to open the Format Cells dialog box.

f. Click the **Font tab**, if necessary, and then click **Bold** in the **Font style list**. Click the **Border tab**, click the **Color arrow**, select **Blue, Accent 5**, and then click **Outline**. Click the **Fill tab**, click **Blue, Accent 5, Lighter 80% background color** (the second color from the right on the first row below the first horizontal line), and then click **OK**.

Figure 6.49 shows the Edit Formatting Rule dialog box, but the options are similar to the New Formatting Rule dialog box.

g. Click **OK** in the New Formatting Rule dialog box and scroll through the list to see which amounts owed are greater than $5,000 for Sebastian only.

---

**TROUBLESHOOTING:** If the results seem incorrect, click Conditional Formatting and select Manage Rules. Edit the rule you just created and make any corrections to the formula.

---

h. Save and close the workbook and submit based on your instructor's directions.

# Chapter Objectives Review

After reading this chapter, you have accomplished the following objectives:

## 1. Freeze rows and columns.

- The Freeze Panes setting freezes the row(s) above and the column(s) to the left of the active cell. When you scroll, those rows and columns remain onscreen.
- Use Unfreeze Panes to clear the frozen rows and columns.

## 2. Print large datasets.

- Display and change page breaks: Display the data in Page Break Preview to see the automatic page breaks. Dashed blue lines indicate automatic page breaks. You can insert manual page breaks, indicated by solid blue lines.
- Set and clear a print area: If you do not want to print an entire worksheet, select a range and set a print area.
- Print titles: Select rows to repeat at top and/or columns to repeat at left to print the column and row labels on every page of a printout of a large dataset.
- Control print page order: You can control the sequence in which the pages will print.

## 3. Design and create tables.

- A table is a structured range that contains related data. Tables have several benefits over regular ranges. The column labels, called *field names*, display on the first row of a table. Each row is a complete set of data for one record.
- You should plan a table before you create it. Create unique field names on the first row of the table and enter data below the field names, avoiding blank rows.
- Create a table: You can create a table from existing data. Excel applies the Table Style Medium 2 format and assigns a name, such as Table1, to the table. When the active cell is within a table, the Table Tools Design tab displays.
- Add and delete fields: You can insert and delete table rows and columns to adjust the structure of a table.
- Add, edit, and delete records: You can add table rows, edit records, and delete table rows.
- Remove duplicate rows: Use the Remove Duplicates dialog box to remove duplicate records in a table. Excel will display a dialog box telling you how many records are deleted.

## 4. Apply a table style.

- Table styles control the fill color of the header row and records within the table.

## 5. Sort data.

- Sort one field: You can sort text in alphabetical or reverse alphabetical order, values from smallest to largest or largest to smallest, and dates from oldest to newest or newest to oldest. Click the filter arrow and select the sort method from the list.
- Sort multiple fields: Open the Sort dialog box and add column levels and sort orders.

- Create a custom sort: You can create a custom sort for unique data, such as ensuring the months sort in sequential order rather than alphabetical order.

## 6. Filter data.

- Filtering is the process of specifying conditions for displaying records in a table. Only records that meet those conditions display; the other records are hidden.
- Apply text filters: A text filter can find exact text, text that does not equal a condition, text that begins with a particular letter, and so forth.
- Apply number filters: A number filter can find exact values, values that do not equal a particular value, values greater than or equal to a value, and so on.
- Apply date filters: You can set filters to find dates before or after a certain date, between two dates, yesterday, next month, and so forth.
- Clear filters: If you do not need filters, you can clear the filters.

## 7. Use structured references and a total row.

- Create structured references in formulas: A structured reference uses field names instead of cell references, such as =[Amount]–[Down Payment]. Field names must display in brackets within the formula.
- Add a total row: You can display a total row after the last record. You can add totals or select a different function, such as Average.

## 8. Apply conditional formatting.

- Apply conditional formatting with the Quick Analysis Tool: After selecting text, click FORMATTING on the Quick Analysis gallery to apply a conditional format.
- Apply the highlight cells rules: This rule highlights cell contents with a fill color, font color, and/or border color where the contents match a particular condition.
- Specify top/bottom rules: This rule enables you to highlight the top *x* number of items or percentage of items.
- Display data bars, color scales, and icon sets: Data bars compare values within the selected range. Color scales indicate values that occur within particular ranges. Icon sets display icons representing a number's relative value compared to other numbers in the range.
- Clear rules: If you no longer want conditional formatting applied, you can clear a rule.

## 9. Create a new rule.

- You can create conditional format rules. The New Formatting Rule dialog box enables you to select a rule type.
- Use formulas in conditional formatting: You can create rules based on content in multiple columns.
- Manage rules: Use the Conditional Formatting Rules Manager dialog box to edit and delete rules.

# Key Terms Matching

Match the key terms with their definitions. Write the key term letter by the appropriate numbered definition.

a. Color scale
b. Conditional formatting
c. Data bar
d. Field
e. Filtering
f. Freezing
g. Icon set
h. Page break
i. Print area

j. Print order
k. Record
l. Sorting
m. Structured reference
n. SUBTOTAL function
o. Table
p. Table style
q. Total row

1. _____ A conditional format that displays horizontal gradient or solid fill indicating the cell's relative value compared to other selected cells. **p. 211**

2. _____ The process of listing records or text in a specific sequence, such as alphabetically by last name. **p. 190**

3. _____ The process of specifying conditions to display only those records that meet those conditions. **p. 192**

4. _____ A set of rules that applies specific formatting to highlight or emphasize cells that meet specifications. **p. 208**

5. _____ A group of related fields representing one entity, such as data for one person, place, event, or concept. **p. 179**

6. _____ The rules that control the fill color of the header row, columns, and records in a table. **p. 183**

7. _____ An indication of where data will start on another printed page. **p. 172**

8. _____ A table row that appears below the last row of records in an Excel table and displays summary or aggregate statistics, such as a sum or an average. **p. 202**

9. _____ A conditional format that displays a particular color based on the relative value of the cell contents to the other selected cells. **p. 213**

10. _____ The sequence in which the pages are printed. **p. 174**

11. _____ A tag or use of a table element, such as a field label, as a reference in a formula. Field labels are enclosed in square brackets, such as [Amount] within the formula. **p. 201**

12. _____ A conditional format that displays an icon representing a value in the top third, quarter, or fifth based on values in the selected range. **p. 212**

13. _____ The range of cells within a worksheet that will print. **p. 173**

14. _____ A predefined formula that calculates an aggregate value, such as totals, for values in a range, a table, or a database. **p. 202**

15. _____ The smallest data element contained in a table, such as first name, last name, address, and phone number. **p. 179**

16. _____ A structure that organizes data in a series of records (rows), with each record made up of a number of fields (columns). **p. 179**

17. _____ The process of keeping rows and/or columns visible onscreen at all times even when you scroll through a large dataset. **p. 171**

# Multiple Choice

1. You have a large dataset that will print on several pages. You want to ensure that related records print on the same page with column and row labels visible and that confidential information is not printed. You should apply all of the following page setup options *except* which one to accomplish this?

   (a) Set a print area.

   (b) Print titles.

   (c) Adjust page breaks.

   (d) Change the print page order.

2. You are working with a large worksheet. Your row headings are in column A. Which command(s) should be used to see the row headings and the distant information in columns X, Y, and Z?

   (a) Freeze Panes command

   (b) Hide Rows command

   (c) New Window command and cascade the windows

   (d) Split Rows command

3. Which statement is *not* a recommended guideline for designing and creating an Excel table?

   (a) Avoid naming two fields with the same name.

   (b) Ensure no blank columns separate data columns within the table.

   (c) Leave one blank row between records in the table.

   (d) Include field names on the first row of the table.

4. You have a list of all the employees in your organization. The list contains employee name, office, title, and salary. You want to list all employees in each office branch. The branches should be listed alphabetically, with the employee earning the highest salary listed first in each office. Which is true of your sort order?

   (a) Branch office is the primary sort and should be in A to Z order.

   (b) Salary is the primary sort and should be from highest to lowest.

   (c) Salary is the primary sort and should be from lowest to highest.

   (d) Branch office is the primary sort and should be in Z to A order.

5. You suspect a table has several identical records. What should you do?

   (a) Do nothing; a logical reason probably exists to keep identical records.

   (b) Use the Remove Duplicates command.

   (c) Look at each row yourself and manually delete duplicate records.

   (d) Find the duplicate records and change some of the data to be different.

6. Which check box in the Table Style Options group enables you to apply different formatting to the records in a table?

   (a) Header Row

   (b) Banded Rows

   (c) Banded Columns

   (d) Total Row

7. Which date filter option enables you to specify criteria for selecting a range of dates, such as between 3/15/2016 and 7/15/2016?

   (a) Equals

   (b) Before

   (c) All Dates in the Period

   (d) Between

8. You want to display a total row that identifies the oldest date in a field in your table. What function do you select from the list?

   (a) Max

   (b) Sum

   (c) Min

   (d) Count

9. What type of conditional formatting displays horizontal colors in which the width of the bar indicates relative size compared to other values in the selected range?

   (a) Color Scales

   (b) Icon Sets

   (c) Data Bars

   (d) Sparklines

10. When you select the _____ rule type, the New Formatting Rule dialog box does not show the Format button.

    (a) Format all cells based on their values

    (b) Format only cells that contain

    (c) Use a formula to determine which cells to format

    (d) Format only unique or duplicate values

# Practice Exercises

## 1 Fiesta® Items and Replacement Values

Marie Maier has collected Fiesta dinnerware, manufactured by the Homer Laughlin China Company, since 1986. Between 1986 and 2012, the company produced 30 colors, each with a unique name. Marie created a table in Word that lists the name, number, year introduced, and year retired (if applicable) for each color. She created another table in Word that lists the item number, item, replacement value, and source of information for each item in her collection. Her main sources for replacement values are Homer Laughlin (www.fiestafactorydirect.com), Replacements, Ltd. (www.replacements.com), eBay (www.ebay.com), and two local antique stores. She needs your help to convert the data to Excel tables, apply table formatting, delete duplicate records, insert functions, and sort and filter the data. This exercise follows the same set of skills as used in Hands-On Exercises 1–3 in the chapter. Refer to Figure 6.50 as you complete this exercise.

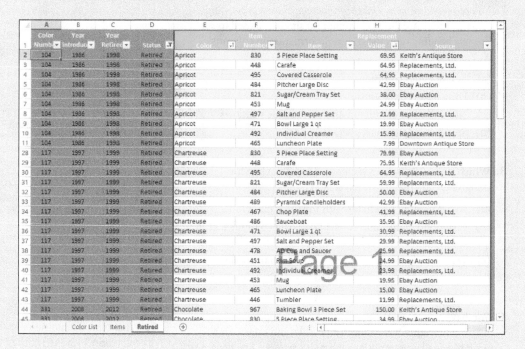

**FIGURE 6.50** Fiesta® Collection

a. Open *e04p1Colors* in Word. Do the following to copy the Word table data into Excel and prepare the data to be used as a lookup table:
- Click the **table icon** in the top-left corner of the table and click **Copy** in the Clipboard group.
- Start a new Excel workbook, click the **Paste arrow** in the Clipboard group in Excel, and then select **Match Destination Formatting (M)**.
- Bold and horizontally center the labels on the first row. Center the data in the first, third, and fourth columns. Widen the second and third columns to fit the data.
- Select the **range A2:D31**, click in the **Name Box**, type **colors**, and then press **Enter** to assign a name to the selected range.
- Click **cell A2**, click **Sort & Filter** in the Editing group, and then select **Sort Smallest to Largest**. Remember that you must sort the first column in ascending order to use the table for an exact match for a VLOOKUP function.
- Save the Excel workbook as **e04p1Collection_LastFirst**. Close the Word document.

b. Open *e04p1Items* in Word. Select and copy the table, display the Excel workbook, add a new sheet, make sure **cell A1** is the active cell in the new sheet, and then paste the table in the same way you did in step a. Widen column E. Rename *Sheet2* **Items**. Close the Word document.

c. Click **cell A2** in the Items sheet, click the **VIEW tab**, click **Freeze Panes** in the Window group, and then select **Freeze Top Row**.

**d.** Press **Ctrl+End** to go to the last data cell. The first row is frozen so that the column labels remain onscreen. Press **Ctrl+Home** to go back to **cell A2**.

**e.** Click the **INSERT tab**, click **Table** in the Tables group, and then click **OK** in the Create Table dialog box.

**f.** Click **Quick Styles** in the Table Styles group and click **Table Style Medium 5**.

**g.** Click the **DATA tab**, click **Remove Duplicates** in the Data Tools group, and then click **OK** in the Remove Duplicates dialog box. Click **OK** in the message box that informs you that *12 duplicate values were found and removed; 356 unique values remain.*

**h.** Click **cell B2**, click the **HOME tab**, click the **Insert arrow** in the Cells group, and then select **Insert Table Columns to the Left**. Then insert two more columns to the left. Do the following to insert functions and customize the results in the three new table columns:

- Type **Year Introduced** in **cell B1**, **Year Retired** in **cell C1**, and **Color** in **cell D1**.
- Click **cell B2**, type **=VLOOKUP([Color Number],colors,3,False)**, and then press **Enter**. Excel copies the function down the Year Introduced column. This function looks up each item's color number using the structured reference [Color Number], looks up that value in the colors table, and then returns the year that color was introduced, which is in the third column of that table.
- Click **cell B2**, click **Copy**, click **cell C2**, and then click **Paste**. Change the *3* to *4* in the col_index_num argument of the pasted function. Excel copies the function down the Year Retired column. This function looks up each item's color number using the structured reference [Color Number], looks up that value in the colors table, and then returns the year that color was retired, if applicable, which is in the fourth column of that table. The function returns 0 if the retired cell in the lookup table is blank.
- Click the **FILE tab**, click **Options**, click **Advanced**, scroll down to the *Display options for this worksheet* section, click the **Show a zero in cells that have zero value check box** to deselect it, and then click **OK**. The zeros disappear. (This option hides zeros in the active worksheet. While this is not desirable if you need to show legitimate zeros, this worksheet is designed to avoid that issue.)
- Click **cell C2**, click **Copy**, click **cell D2**, and then click **Paste**. Change the *4* to *2* in the col_index_num argument of the pasted function. Excel copies the function down the Color column. This function looks up each item's color number using the structured reference [Color Number] to look up that value in the colors table and returns the color name, which is in the second column of that table.

**i.** Apply wrap text, horizontal centering, and **30.75 row height** to the column labels row. Adjust column widths. Center data horizontally in the Color Number, Year Introduced, Year Retired, and Item Number columns. Apply **Comma Style** to the Replacement Values. Deselect the data.

**j.** Click **Sort & Filter** in the Editing group and select **Custom Sort** to display the Sort dialog box. Do the following in the Sort dialog box:

- Click the **Sort by arrow** and select **Color**.
- Click **Add Level**, click the **Then by arrow**, and then select **Replacement Value**.
- Click the **Order arrow** and select **Largest to Smallest**. Click **OK**.

**k.** Right-click the **Items sheet tab**, select **Move or Copy**, click **(move to end)**, click the **Create a copy check box**, and then click **OK**. Rename the copied sheet **Retired**.

**l.** Make sure the active sheet is Retired. Insert a table column between the Year Retired and Color columns.

- Type **Status** in **cell D1** as the column label.
- Click **cell D2**, type **=IF([Year Retired]=0, "Current","Retired")**, and then press **Enter**. This function determines that if the cell contains a 0 (which is hidden), it will display the word *Current*. Otherwise, it will display *Retired*.

**m.** Click the **Status filter arrow**, deselect the **Current check box**, and then click **OK** to filter out the current colors and display only retired colors.

**n.** Click the **DESIGN tab** and click **Total Row** in the Table Style Options group. Press **Ctrl+End** to go to the total row, click the **Source total cell** (which contains a count of visible items), click the

DISCOVER

**Source total arrow**, and then select **None**. Click **cell H358**, the *Replacement Value total* cell, click the **Replacement Value total arrow**, and then select **Sum**.

o. Prepare the Retired worksheet for printing by doing the following:
   - Set **0.2"** left and right page margins.
   - Select the **range E1:I358**, click the **PAGE LAYOUT tab**, click **Print Area** in the Page Setup group, and then select **Set Print Area**.
   - Click **Print Titles** in the Page Setup group, click the **Rows to repeat at top Collapse Dialog box button**, click the **row 1 header**, and then click the **Collapse Dialog box button**. Click **OK**.
   - Click the **VIEW tab** and click **Page Break Preview** in the Workbook Views group. Decrease the top margin to avoid having only one or two records print on the last page.

p. Create a footer with your name on the left side, the sheet name code in the center, and the file name code on the right side of each worksheet.

q. Save and close the workbook and submit based on your instructor's directions.

## 2 Dentist Association Donation List

The Midwest Regional Dentist Association is planning its annual meeting in Lincoln, Nebraska, this spring. Several members donated items for door prizes at the closing general session. You will organize the list of donations and format it to highlight particular data for your supervisor, who is on the conference board of directors. This exercise follows the same set of skills as used in Hands-On Exercises 2–5 in the chapter. Refer to Figure 6.51 as you complete this exercise.

FIGURE 6.51 Donation List

a. Open *e04p2Donate* and save it as **e04p2Donate_LastFirst**.

b. Click the **DESIGN tab**, click **Remove Duplicates** in the Tools group, and then click **OK**. Click **OK** in the message box that tells you that Excel removed three duplicate records.

c. Click **Convert to Range** in the Tools group and click **Yes** in the message box.

d. Select the **range A2:J35**, click the **HOME tab**, click the **Fill Color arrow** in the Font group, and then select **No Fill** to remove the table fill colors.

e. Select the **range I2:I35**. Click **Conditional Formatting** in the Styles group, point to *Highlight Cells Rules*, and then select **Greater Than**. Type **99** in the **Format cells that are GREATER THAN box** and click **OK**.

**f.** Select **cells H2:H35**. Create a custom conditional format by doing the following:

- Click **Conditional Formatting** in the Styles group and select **New Rule**.
- Click **Use a formula to determine which cells to format**.
- Type **=(J2="Equipment")** in the **Format values where this formula is true box**. The basic condition is testing to see if the contents of cell J2 equal the word *Equipment*. You type *Equipment* in quotation marks because you are comparing text instead of a value.
- Click **Format**, click the **Fill tab** if necessary, and then click **Red, Accent 2, Lighter 60%** (sixth background color on the second row below the first horizontal line).
- Click the **Border tab**, click the **Color arrow**, click **Dark Red**, and then click **Outline**.
- Click **OK** in each dialog box.

DISCOVER

**g.** Click in the table to deselect the range. Click **Sort & Filter** in the Editing group and select **Custom Sort**. The dialog box may contain existing sort conditions for the State and City fields, which you will replace. Set the following sort conditions:

- Click the **Sort by arrow** and select **Item Donated**. Click the **Sort On arrow** and select **Cell Color**. Click the **Order arrow** and select the **RGB(146, 205, 220) fill color**. The fill color displays for the Order.
- Click the **Then by arrow** and select **Value**. Click the **Order arrow** and select **Largest to Smallest**.
- Click **OK**.

**h.** Select **Landscape orientation**, set appropriate margins, and then adjust column widths so that all the data will print on one page. Do not decrease the scaling.

**i.** Create a footer with your name on the left side, the sheet name code in the center, and the file name code on the right side.

**j.** Save and close the workbook and submit based on your instructor's directions.

# Mid-Level Exercises

## 1 Biology Department Teaching Schedule

As the department head of the biology department at a university, you prepare and finalize the faculty teaching schedule. Scheduling preparation takes time because you must ensure that you do not book faculty for different courses at the same time or double-book a classroom with two different classes. You downloaded the Spring 2015 schedule as a starting point and edited it to prepare the Spring 2016 schedule, and now you need to sort and filter the schedule to review it from several perspectives.

**DISCOVER**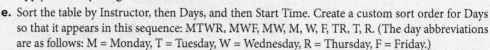

a. Open *e04m1Classes* and save it as **e04m1Classes_LastFirst**.

b. Freeze the panes so that the column labels do not scroll offscreen.

c. Convert the data to a table and name the table **Spring2016**.

d. Apply **Table Style Light 14** to the table.

e. Sort the table by Instructor, then Days, and then Start Time. Create a custom sort order for Days so that it appears in this sequence: MTWR, MWF, MW, M, W, F, TR, T, R. (The day abbreviations are as follows: M = Monday, T = Tuesday, W = Wednesday, R = Thursday, F = Friday.)

f. Remove duplicate records from the table. Excel should find and remove three duplicate records.

g. Copy the Faculty sheet, place the copied worksheet to the right of the Faculty sheet, and then rename the duplicate worksheet **Rooms**. Sort the data in the Rooms sheet by Room in ascending order, then by Days using the custom sort order you created in step e, and finally by Start Time from earliest to latest time.

h. Copy the Rooms sheet, place the copied worksheet to the right of the Rooms sheet, and then rename the duplicate worksheet **Prime Time**.

i. Filter the table in the Prime Time sheet to show only classes scheduled on any combination of Monday, Wednesday, and Friday. Include classes that meet four days a week (MTWR). Do not include any other combination of Tuesday or Thursday classes, though. Also filter the table by classes that start between 9:00 AM and 12:00 PM. The status bar indicates 20 of 75 records found.

j. Insert a field on the right side of the Credits field in the Faculty sheet. Type the label **Capacity**. Insert a lookup function that looks up the room number, compares it to the lookup table in the Room Capacity worksheet, and returns the room capacity. Make sure the function copies down the entire column.

k. Select the first three sheet tabs and set **0.2"** left and right margins, **Landscape orientation**, and **95% scaling**. Repeat the column labels on all pages. On the Faculty sheet, decrease some column widths so that the Capacity column will print on the same page as the other columns.

l. Display the Faculty sheet in Page Break Preview. Adjust any page breaks so that classes for a particular instructor do not split between pages.

m. Display the Rooms sheet in Page Break Preview. Adjust any page breaks so that classes for a particular room do not split between pages, if necessary. Set the worksheet to print 1 page wide and 3 pages tall.

n. Insert a footer with your name on the left side, the sheet name code in the center, and the file name code on the right side of all four sheets.

o. Save and close the workbook and submit based on your instructor's directions.

## 2 Artwork

**ANALYSIS CASE**

You work for a gallery that is an authorized Greenwich Workshop fine art dealer (www .greenwichworkshop.com). Customers in your area are especially fond of James C. Christensen's art. Although customers can visit the Web site to see images and details about his work, they have requested a list of all his artwork. Your assistant prepared a list of artwork: art, type, edition size, release date, and issue price. In addition, you included a column to identify which pieces are sold out at the publisher, indicating the rare, hard-to-obtain artwork that is available on the secondary market. You now want to convert the data to a table so that you can provide information to your customers.

a. Open *e04m2FineArt* and save it as **e04m2FineArt_LastFirst**.

b. Convert the data to a table and apply **Table Style Medium 5**.

c. Add a row (below the *The Yellow Rose* record) for this missing piece of art: **The Yellow Rose**, **Masterwork Canvas Edition**, **50** edition size, **May 2009** release date, **$895** issue price. Enter **Yes** to indicate the piece is sold out.

d. Sort the table by Type in alphabetical order and then by release date from newest to oldest.

e. Add a total row that shows the largest edition size and the most expensive issue price. Delete the Total label in **cell A205**. Add a descriptive label in **cell C205** to reflect the content on the total row.

DISCOVER

f. Create a custom conditional format for the Issue Price column with these specifications:
  - 4 Traffic Lights icon set (Black, Red, Yellow, Green)
  - Red icon when the number is greater than 1000
  - Yellow icon when the number is less than or equal to 1000 and greater than 500
  - Green icon when the number is less than or equal to 500 and greater than 250
  - Black icon when the number is less than or equal to 250.

DISCOVER

g. Filter the table by the Red Traffic Light conditional formatting icon.

h. Answer the questions in the range D211:D215 based on the filtered data.

i. Set the print area to print the **range C1:H205**, select the **first row to repeat at the top of each printout**, set **1"** top and bottom margins, set **0.3"** left and right margins, and then select **Landscape orientation**. Set the option to fit the data to 1 page.

j. Wrap text and horizontally center column labels and adjust column widths and row heights as needed.

k. Create a footer with your name on the left side, the sheet name code in the center, and the file name code on the right side.

l. Save and close the workbook and submit based on your instructor's directions.

---

## 3 Party Music

COLLABORATION CASE

FROM SCRATCH

You are planning a weekend party and want to create a mix of music so that most people will appreciate some of the music you will play at the party. To help you decide what music to play, you have asked five classmates to help you create a song list. The entire class should decide on the general format, capitalization style, and sequence: song, musician, genre, year released, and approximate song length.

a. Conduct online research to collect data for your favorite 25 songs.

b. Enter the data into a new workbook in the format, capitalization style, and sequence that was decided by the class.

c. Save the workbook as **e04m3PlayList_LastFirst**.

d. Upload the file to a shared folder on OneDrive or Dropbox that everyone in the class can access.

e. Download four workbooks from friends and copy and paste data from their workbooks into yours.

f. Convert the data to a table and apply a table style of your choice.

g. Detect and delete duplicate records. Make a note of the number of duplicate records found and deleted.

h. Sort the data by genre in alphabetical order, then by artist in alphabetical order, and then by release date with the newest year first.

i. Set a filter to hide songs that were released before 2000.

j. Display the total row and select the function to count the number of songs displayed.

k. Insert comments in the workbook to indicate which student's workbooks you used, the number of duplicate records deleted, and number of filtered records.

l. Save and close the workbook. Submit the workbook based on your instructor's directions.

## Flight Arrival Status

As an analyst for an airport, you want to study the flight arrivals for a particular day. Select an airport and find its list of flight arrival data. Some airport websites do not list complete details, so search for an airport that does, such as Will Rogers World Airport or San Diego International Airport. Copy the column labels and arrival data (airline, flight number, city, gate, scheduled time, status, etc.) for one day and paste them in a new workbook. The columns may be in a different sequence from what is listed here. However, you should format the data as needed. Leave two blank rows below the last row of data and enter the URL of the Web page from which you got the data, the date, and the time. Save the workbook as **e04b2Flights_LastFirst**. Convert the list to a table and apply a table style.

Sort the table by scheduled time and then by gate number. Apply conditional formatting to the Status column to highlight cells that contain the text *Delayed* (or similar text). Add a total row to calculate the MODE for the gate number and arrival time. You must select **More Functions** from the list of functions in the total row and search for and select **MODE**. Change the label in the first column from *Total* to **Most Frequent**. Use Help to refresh your memory on how to nest an IF function inside another IF function. Add a calculated column on the right side of the table using a nested IF function and structured references to display *Late* if the actual time was later than the scheduled time, *On Time or Early* if the actual time was earlier or equal to the scheduled time, or *Incomplete* if the flight has not landed yet.

Name the worksheet **Arrival Time**. Copy the worksheet and name the copied worksheet **Delayed**. Filter the list by delayed flights. Include a footer with your name on the left side, the sheet name code in the center, and the file name code on the right side of both worksheets. Adjust the margins on both worksheets as necessary. Save and close the workbook, and submit based on your instructor's directions.

## U.S. Population

A colleague at an advertising firm downloaded U.S. population information from the government Web site. In the process of creating tables, he made some errors and needs your help. Open *e04b3Populate* and save it as **e04b3Populate_LastFirst**. As you find the errors, document them on the Errors worksheet and make the corrections. Your documentation should include these columns: Error Number, Location, Problem, and Solution. Both tables in the U.S. Population worksheet should show grand total populations per year. The state table should be sorted by region and then by state. Your colleague wants to emphasize the top 15% state populations for the most recent year in the state table. The last column should show percentage changes from year to year, such as 0.6%. Your colleague wants to print only the state data. Select the sorted data population for one region at a time to compare to the regional totals in the first table to crosscheck the totals. For example, when you select the July 1, 2008, Midwest values in the second table, the status bar should display the same value as shown for the Midwest July 1, 2008, values in the first table. Create a footer with your name, the sheet name code, and the file name code. Save and close the workbook, and submit based on your instructor's directions.

## Performance Evaluation

**SOFT SKILLS CASE**

**FROM SCRATCH**

After watching the Performance Evaluation video, create a workbook that lists at least 10 performance traits mentioned in the video or other common performance traits, such as "arriving to work on time." Use the second column for a self-evaluation and the third column for manager evaluation. Below the list, create a description to describe ratings 1 through 5. For example, Exemplary—exceeds expectations is a 5, and Unacceptable—grounds for probation is a 1. Enter your own scores for each performance trait and enter scores based on your manager's review. Save the workbook as **e04b4Performance_LastFirst**.

Convert the list to a table and sort the table alphabetically by performance trait descriptions. Add a total row and select the AVERAGE function for the two ratings columns. Create a conditional formatting rule to highlight cells in the ratings columns for values less than 3. Insert three rows at the top for a title, your name, and the current date. Create a footer with your name on the left side, the date code in the center, and the filename code on the right side. Save and close the workbook, and submit based on your instructor's directions.

# Capstone Exercise

You work at Mountain View Realty. A coworker developed a spreadsheet listing houses listed and sold during the past several months. She included addresses, location, list price, selling price, listing date, and date sold. You need to convert the data to a table. You will manage the large worksheet, prepare the worksheet for printing, sort and filter the table, include calculations, and then format the table.

## Prepare the Large Worksheet as a Table

You will freeze the panes so that labels remain onscreen. You also want to convert the data to a table so that you can apply table options.

a. Open the *e04c1Houses* workbook and save it as **e04c1Houses_LastFirst**.

b. Freeze the first row on the Sales Data worksheet.

c. Convert the data to a table and apply the **Table Style Medium 17**.

d. Remove duplicate records.

## Add Calculated Fields and a Total Row

The office manager asked you to insert a column to display the percentage of list price. The formula finds the sale price percentage of the list price. For example, if a house was listed at $100,000 and sells for $75,000, the percentage of list price is 75%. In some cases, the percentage is more than 100%. This happens when a bidding war occurs and buyers increase their offers, which results in the seller getting more than the list price.

a. Insert a new field to the right of the Selling Price field. Name the new field **Percent of List Price**.

b. Create a formula with structured references to calculate the percentage of the list price.

c. Format the field with **Percent Style** with one decimal place.

d. Insert a new field to the right of the Sale Date field. Name the new field **Days on Market**.

e. Create a formula with structured references to calculate the number of days on the market. Apply the **General number format** to the values.

f. Add a total row to display the average percentage of list price and average number of days on market. Format the average number of days on market as a whole number. Use an appropriate label for the total row.

## Sort and Print the Table

To help the office manager compare house sales by city, you will sort the data. Then you will prepare the large table to print.

a. Sort the table by city in alphabetical order and add a second level to sort by days on market with the houses on the market the longest at the top within each city.

b. Adjust column widths so that the data are one page across (three pages total). Wrap the column labels.

c. Repeat the field names on all pages.

d. Change page breaks so that city data do not span between pages and change back to Normal view.

e. Add a footer with your name on the left side, the sheet name code in the center, and the file name code on the right side.

## Copy and Filter the Data

The office manager needs to focus on houses that took longer than 30 days to sell within three cities. To keep the original data intact for the agents, you will copy the table data to a new sheet and use that sheet to display the filtered data.

a. Copy the Sales Data sheet and place the duplicate sheet to the right of the original sheet tab. Convert the table to a range of data and delete the average row.

b. Rename the duplicate worksheet **Filtered Data**.

c. Display the filter arrows for the data.

d. Filter the data to display the cities of Alpine, Cedar Hills, and Eagle Mountain.

e. Filter the data to display records for houses that were on the market 30 days or more.

## Apply Conditional Formatting

To highlight housing sales to illustrate trends, you will apply conditional formatting. Because data are sorted by city, you will use an icon set to color-code the number of days on market. You will also apply data bar conditional formatting to the sale prices to help the office manager visualize the differences among the sales.

a. Apply the **3 Arrows (Colored) icon set** to the *Days on Market* values.

b. Apply the **Light Blue Data Bar conditional formatting** in the *Gradient Fill* section to the selling prices.

c. Create a new conditional format that applies yellow fill and bold font to values that contain 95% or higher for the *Percent of List Price* column.

d. Edit the conditional format you created so that it formats values 98% or higher.

## Finalize the Workbook

You are ready to finalize the workbook by adding a footer to the new worksheet and saving the final workbook.

a. Add a footer with your name on the left side, the sheet name code in the center, and the file name code on the right side.

b. Remove all page breaks in the Filtered Data worksheet.

c. Select **Landscape orientation** and set appropriate margins so that the data will print on one page.

d. Save and close the workbook and submit based on your instructor's directions.

# Multiple-Sheet Workbook Management

## Ensuring Quality Control

## OBJECTIVES | AFTER YOU READ THIS CHAPTER, YOU WILL BE ABLE TO:

1. Work with grouped worksheets p. 232

2. Manage windows and workspaces p. 235

3. Insert hyperlinks p. 237

4. Insert a 3-D formula p. 245

5. Link workbooks p. 247

6. Audit formulas p. 255

7. Set up a Watch Window p. 257

8. Validate data p. 258

## CASE STUDY | Circle City Sporting Goods

You are the regional manager of Circle City Sporting Goods (CSG), which has locations in Indianapolis, Bloomington, and South Bend. CSG is a comprehensive retailer that sells athletic apparel, exercise equipment, footwear, camping gear, sports gear, and sports nutrition items. Each store manager gathers data for every department monthly and prepares a quarterly worksheet. Because each store contains the same departments, the worksheets are identical. Having an identical structure helps you consolidate sales data for all three locations.

You want to review sales data for the past fiscal year. Before consolidating data, you need to format the worksheets, copy data to the summary sheet, and then insert hyperlinks from the summary sheet back to the individual quarterly sheets in the Indianapolis workbook. Later, you will consolidate data from the Indianapolis, Bloomington, and South Bend workbooks into a regional workbook. Finally, you will use auditing tools to identify errors in the Bloomington workbook and add validation to ensure users enter correct data.

# Multiple Worksheets

A workbook can contain one or more worksheets of related data. Deciding how to structure data into multiple worksheets and how to manage these worksheets is important. You should determine how much data to enter on each worksheet, when to divide data among several worksheets, and how to format worksheets efficiently. You might also want to create links among the worksheets to enable efficient navigation. For example, you can create a documentation worksheet and then insert links to each worksheet.

After you design multiple worksheets in a workbook, you might want to display worksheets side by side or in a particular arrangement. You can also save the worksheet view layout so that it retains a specific view when you open the workbook again.

In this section, you will work with multiple worksheets and insert hyperlinks from one worksheet to other worksheets. In addition, you will group worksheets together to enter data and apply formatting. Finally, you will manage windows by controlling worksheet visibility, opening and arranging windows, splitting a window, and saving a workspace.

## Working with Grouped Worksheets

You often work with workbooks that contain several worksheets. For example, a workbook might contain sales data on one worksheet, a column chart on another sheet, and a PivotTable on a third sheet. In addition, you might create scenarios with Scenario Manager, generate a scenario summary report on a new worksheet or create a Solver model, and then generate a Solver answer report on a new worksheet. In these situations, in order to organize data, the original data are separated into separate worksheets from the consolidated analysis.

Worksheets within a workbook often contain similar content and formatting. For example, a budget workbook might contain detailed monthly data on separate worksheets. By placing monthly data on separate worksheets, you can focus on one month's data at a time instead of presenting the entire year's worth of data on only one worksheet. When worksheets contain similar data but for different time periods—such as months—or different company locations—such as department store locations in various states—you should structure and format the data the same on all worksheets. For example, each monthly worksheet in the yearly budget workbook should contain an identical structure and format for the list of income and expenses. The only differences among the worksheets are the actual values and the column labels that identify the respective months.

Creating worksheets with identical structure and formatting provides consistency and continuity when working with the same type of data on multiple worksheets. In addition, it helps you locate particular items quickly on all worksheets because you know the structure is identical.

### Group and Ungroup Worksheets

STEP 1 >> Although you can design and format worksheets individually, you can improve your productivity by designing and formatting the worksheets as a group. *Grouping* is the process of selecting two or more worksheets so that you can perform the same action at the same time on all selected worksheets. Table 7.1 describes how to group worksheets. Excel displays grouped worksheet tabs with a white background color and green line spanning the length of all grouped worksheets, and [Group] appears in the title bar.

| TABLE 7.1 Grouping Worksheets | |
|---|---|
| **To Group:** | **Do This:** |
| All worksheets | Right-click a worksheet tab and select Select All Sheets. |
| Adjacent worksheets | Click the first worksheet tab, press and hold Shift, and then click the last worksheet tab. |
| Nonadjacent worksheet tabs | Click the first worksheet tab, press and hold Ctrl, and then click each additional worksheet tab. |

*Ungrouping* is the process of deselecting grouped worksheets so that actions performed on one sheet do not affect other worksheets. To ungroup worksheets, click a worksheet tab for a sheet that is not grouped. If you grouped all worksheets, right-click a worksheet tab and select Ungroup Sheets.

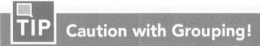

**TIP**  **Caution with Grouping!**

Make sure that you ungroup worksheets when you want to perform a task on only one worksheet. If you forget to ungroup sheets, you could potentially ruin several worksheets by overwriting data on all worksheets instead of just the active worksheet.

## Enter Data and Format Grouped Worksheets

STEP 2 >> Grouping worksheets enables you to improve your productivity by performing the same tasks on the grouped worksheets at the same time instead of performing the tasks individually on each worksheet. Grouping worksheets helps you enter data, change the worksheet structure, apply page layouts, and print worksheets. Whatever you do to the active worksheet also affects the other grouped worksheets.

### Data Entry

You can enter labels, values, dates, and formulas efficiently on grouped worksheets, saving you from entering the same data on each worksheet individually. For example, if you enter row labels in the range A5:A10 to describe the different types of monthly income and expenses, Excel enters the same data in the same location (the range A5:A10) on the other grouped worksheets. When you enter a formula on grouped worksheets, Excel enters the formula in the same cell address on all grouped worksheets. For example, if you enter =A4-B4 in cell C4 on the active worksheet, Excel enters =A4-B4 in cell C4 on all grouped worksheets. The formulas use the values on the respective worksheets.

### Structural Changes

If you insert a row between rows 4 and 5 and widen column B on the active worksheet, Excel inserts a row between rows 4 and 5 and widens column B on all grouped worksheets. You can cut, copy, and paste data to the same locations and delete cell contents, rows, and columns on grouped worksheets. You can also copy, delete, or hide a group of worksheets.

### Formatting

You can apply font formats (e.g., font, font size, bold, font color), alignment settings (e.g., top-left vertical alignment, center horizontal alignment, wrap text), and number formats (e.g., Accounting Number Format, Percent Style, and decimal points) in the same cells on grouped worksheets. Figure 7.1 shows worksheets that were grouped to enter and format data.

### Page Layouts and Printing

You can group worksheets, and then apply identical headers, set the page orientation, set the print areas, and adjust the scaling all at one time instead of applying these page layouts individually to each worksheet. After grouping worksheets, you can display them in Print Preview, select print settings, and then finally print the grouped worksheets.

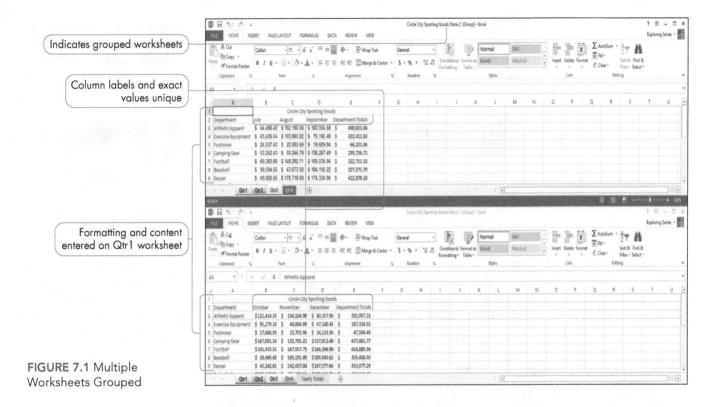

Indicates grouped worksheets

Column labels and exact values unique

Formatting and content entered on Qtr1 worksheet

**FIGURE 7.1** Multiple Worksheets Grouped

**Unavailable Tasks**

Some tasks are not available on grouped worksheets. These tasks appear grayed out on the Ribbon or in menus. For example, you cannot apply conditional formatting or format data as a table on grouped worksheets. Most commands such as PivotTable on the Insert tab are unavailable for grouped worksheets.

## Fill Across Worksheets

The previous discussion assumes you are entering new data or formatting existing data across several worksheets at the same time. However, you might have created and formatted only one worksheet, and now you want to copy the data and formats to other worksheets. Instead of using the Copy and Paste commands or copying the entire worksheet, you can fill the data to other worksheets to save time and reduce potential errors, such as formatting the wrong area or forgetting to format a worksheet. To fill data and/or formats from one sheet to other sheets, do the following:

1. Click the worksheet tab that contains the data and/or formats you want to copy. Select the range that you want to fill across the worksheets.
2. Press Ctrl while you click the destination worksheet tabs—the worksheets that you want the data and/or formats applied to.
3. Click the HOME tab, click Fill in the Editing group, and then select Across Worksheets to open the Fill Across Worksheets dialog box (see Figure 7.2).
4. Click All to copy data and formats, click Contents to copy the data only without the formatting, or click Formats to copy only the formatting to the other grouped worksheets. Click OK.

**FIGURE 7.2** Fill Across
Worksheet Dialog Box

Excel copies the data and/or formatting to the same cells in the other worksheets. For example, if cell A1 in the original worksheet contains the text *Heartland Department Store* bold, centered, and in 14-pt font, Excel copies this text and formatting to cell A1 in the grouped worksheets.

## TIP Conditional Formatting

Excel disables the Conditional Formatting feature when you group worksheets. You cannot group worksheets and then create and manage conditional formats. However, you can create a conditional formatting rule on one worksheet, group the worksheets, and then use the Fill Across Worksheets command to replicate the conditional formatting rule to a range on other worksheets.

# Managing Windows and Workspaces

Because a workbook may contain several worksheets, you need to be able to manage the worksheets onscreen to help you focus on particular worksheets and reduce information overload. To help you manage worksheet windows, you can control worksheet visibility, open and arrange windows for ease of use, split a window to see different parts of a worksheet, and save the layout of the worksheet windows.

## Control Visibility of Worksheets

**STEP 4 >>** If a workbook contains so many worksheets that each corresponding tab is not visible, use the worksheet scroll buttons on the left side of the worksheet tabs to find the worksheet you need. If you do not need to view a worksheet, you can hide it. Hiding worksheets is helpful to keep visible only those worksheet tabs that you are currently working on to minimize scrolling through worksheet tabs or when you want to display worksheets on a projector in a meeting but you do not want to accidently click a worksheet containing confidential data. To hide a worksheet, right-click a worksheet tab and select Hide, or do the following:

1. Select the worksheet or worksheets you want to hide. If you want to hide a single worksheet, click the respective worksheet tab. If you want to hide two or more worksheets, select their tabs in a similar way to that with which you group worksheets.
2. Click the HOME tab and click Format in the Cells group.
3. Point to Hide & Unhide and select Hide Sheet.

When you need to display a hidden worksheet again, click Format in the Cells group, point to Hide & Unhide, and then select Unhide Sheet. Excel then opens the Unhide dialog box (see Figure 7.3). Select the worksheet that you want to display and click OK.

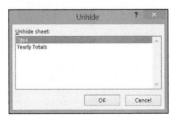

**FIGURE 7.3** Unhide
Dialog Box

## Open and Arrange Windows

You might want to see the contents of two worksheets in the same workbook at the same time. For example, you might want to compare the Qtr1 and Qtr2 worksheets simultaneously. Instead of clicking back and forth between worksheet tabs, you can open another window of the same workbook, and then display different worksheets within each window.

**Open Another Window.** To open another window of the current workbook, click the View tab, and then click New Window in the Window group. Excel opens another window of the workbook. The title bar adds *:1* to the original workbook view and *:2* to the second window. Although only one window appears maximized, both windows are open. There is no limit to the number of windows that can be opened.

**Arrange the Windows.** To see all windows of the same workbook, click Arrange All in the Window group. Select one of the options from the Arrange Windows dialog box (see Figure 7.4). You can display windows in a tiled arrangement, horizontally, vertically, or in a cascaded view. If you have other workbooks open when you click Arrange All, Excel includes those workbook windows. To display windows for the current workbook only, click the *Windows of active workbook* check box.

**FIGURE 7.4** Arrange Windows Dialog Box

## Split a Window

When you work with very large, complex worksheets, you may need to view different sections at the same time. For example, you may need to look at input data on rows 5 and 6 and see how changing the data affects overall results on row 150. To see these different worksheet sections at the same time, split the worksheet window. *Splitting* is the process of dividing a worksheet window into two or four resizable panes so you can view separate parts of a worksheet at the same time (see Figure 7.5). All panes are part of the one worksheet. Any changes you make to one pane affect the entire worksheet.

To divide a worksheet into panes, click Split in the Window group on the View tab. Depending on which cell is the active cell, Excel splits the worksheet into two or four panes with *split bars*—vertical and horizontal lines that frame the panes—above and to the left of the active cell. If the active cell is in row 1, the worksheet appears in two *vertical* panes. If the active cell is in column A, the worksheet appears in two *horizontal* panes. If the active cell is cell A1 or any cell besides in the first row or first column, the worksheet appears in four panes.

Once the window is split, you can further customize the display by dragging the horizontal or vertical line that appears. Drag the vertical split bar to divide the worksheet into left and right (vertical) panes. Drag the horizontal split bar to divide the worksheet into upper and lower (horizontal) panes. While the active cell will be mirrored across all split panes, you can scroll each pane to the desired range you wish to see.

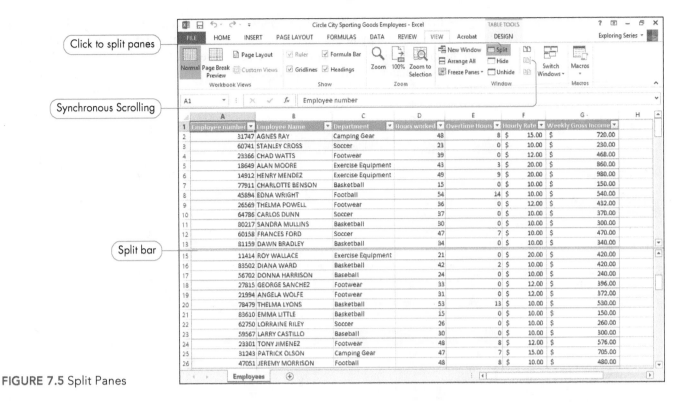

Click to split panes

Synchronous Scrolling

Split bar

**FIGURE 7.5** Split Panes

To remove panes, click Split in the Window group, or double-click the split bar, or drag a vertical split bar to the left or right edge of the worksheet window or a horizontal split bar to the top or bottom of the worksheet window.

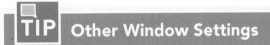

## TIP   Other Window Settings

The Window group on the View tab contains options to enable you to view two worksheet windows side by side and synchronize the scrolling for both windows or enable separate scrolling. If you have adjusted the window sizes, you can reset the open worksheet windows to share the screen equally. In addition, you can hide a worksheet if you do not want to display it, or you can display a previously hidden worksheet window. However, you cannot use the Freeze Panes settings and split bars at the same time.

# Inserting Hyperlinks

**STEP 3 >>** When you create a workbook that has multiple worksheets, you might want to include a documentation worksheet that is similar to a table of contents. On the documentation worksheet, enter labels to describe each worksheet, and then create hyperlinks to the respective worksheets. A *hyperlink*, or link, is an electronic marker that, when clicked, connects to another location in the same or a different worksheet, another file, a Web page, or an e-mail. To create a hyperlink, click the cell that will contain the hyperlink or select an object, such as an image, that you want to use as the hyperlink, and then do one of the following:

1. Click the INSERT tab and click Hyperlink in the Links group.
2. Right-click the cell or object and select Hyperlink.
3. Click a cell or object and press Ctrl+K.

The Insert Hyperlink dialog box opens so that you can specify the conditions of the hyperlink. In addition, you can click ScreenTip and enter the text to appear as a ScreenTip when the mouse pointer hovers over a hyperlink. Based on the type of link you select on the left side of the dialog box, the options change to complete the hyperlink specifications (see Figures 7.6 and 7.7).

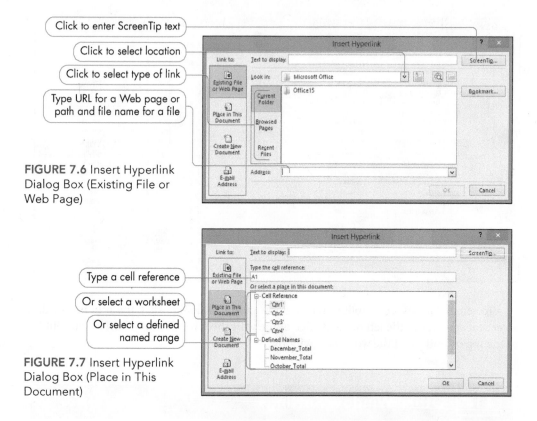

**FIGURE 7.6** Insert Hyperlink Dialog Box (Existing File or Web Page)

**FIGURE 7.7** Insert Hyperlink Dialog Box (Place in This Document)

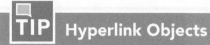

**TIP   Hyperlink Objects**

You have the ability to add hyperlinks to more than just text. You have the ability to add links to inserted images and objects as well.

Workbook hyperlinks are similar to Web page hyperlinks. Textual hyperlinks appear blue with a blue underline. When you position the mouse pointer over a hyperlink, the pointer looks like a hand, and Excel displays a default ScreenTip indicating where the link will take you or the custom ScreenTip if you created one in the Set Hyperlink ScreenTip dialog box (see Figure 7.8). Click the link to jump to the link's destination. After you click a hyperlink, the color changes to purple so that you can distinguish between links you have clicked and links you have not clicked. The hyperlink color changes back to blue after a period of time.

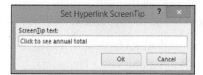

**FIGURE 7.8** Set Hyperlink ScreenTip Dialog Box

**TIP** **Edit or Remove a Hyperlink**

To modify a hyperlink, right-click it, and then select Edit Hyperlink to open the Edit Hyperlink dialog box, which is similar to the Insert Hyperlink dialog box. Make the desired changes and click OK. To remove a hyperlink, right-click it and select Remove Hyperlink. This action removes the hyperlink but does not delete the cell contents or object.

*Quick* **Concepts**

1. What are the benefits of grouping worksheets? *p. 232*

2. What are the benefits of using Split window? *p. 236*

3. Besides linking inside a worksheet, where else can hyperlinks lead the user? *p. 237*

## 1 Multiple Worksheets

After reviewing last year's fiscal data, you need to improve the appearance of the worksheets for Circle City Sporting Goods. You need to enter a missing heading on the summary worksheet and enter formulas across the quarterly worksheets. To save time, you will group the worksheets to perform tasks to all grouped worksheets at the same time. After you complete the quarterly worksheets, you will insert hyperlinks from the yearly worksheet to the quarterly worksheets.

**Skills covered:** Group and Fill Across Worksheets • Enter and Format Data Across Worksheets • Insert Hyperlinks • Open and Arrange Worksheets

### STEP 1 » GROUP AND FILL ACROSS WORKSHEETS

You noticed that the main title and the row headings are displayed only in the Qtr1 worksheet in the Indianapolis workbook. You need to fill in the title and row headings for the other three quarterly and the yearly worksheets. Refer to Figure 7.9 as you complete Step 1.

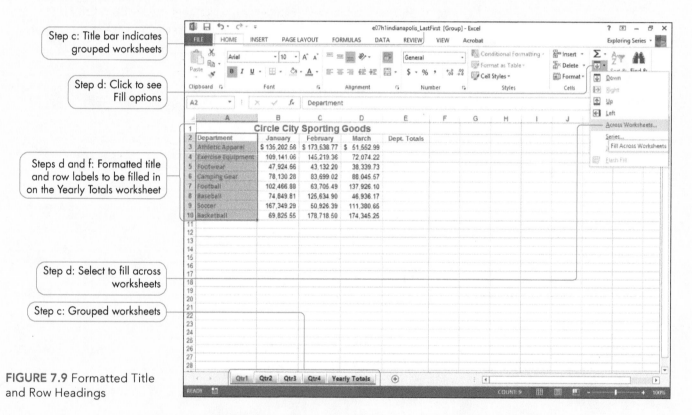

**FIGURE 7.9** Formatted Title and Row Headings

a. Open *e07h1Indianapolis* and save it as **e07h1Indianapolis_LastFirst**.

> **TROUBLESHOOTING:** If you make any major mistakes in this exercise, you can close the file, open *e07h1Indianapolis* again, and then start this exercise over.

b. Click the **Qtr1 worksheet tab** and click each worksheet tab to see the differences.

   The Qtr1 worksheet contains a title and row labels, whereas the Qtr2, Qtr3, and Qtr4 worksheets are missing the title, row labels, and number formatting. The Yearly Totals worksheet is empty.

c. Click the **Qtr1 worksheet tab**, press and hold **Shift**, and then click the **Yearly Totals worksheet tab**.

You grouped all worksheets together. Anything you do now affects all grouped worksheets. The title bar displays *[Group]* after the file name.

d. Click **cell A1** in the Qtr1 worksheet to select it, click **Fill** in the Editing group on the HOME tab, and then select **Across Worksheets**.

The Fill Across Worksheets dialog box opens so that you can select what to fill from the active worksheet to the other grouped worksheets. The default option is All, which will fill in both the content and the formatting.

e. Click **OK**.

Excel fills in the formatted title from the Qtr1 worksheet to the other worksheets.

f. Select the **range A2:A10** on the Qtr1 worksheet, click **Fill** in the Editing group on the HOME tab, select **Across Worksheets**, and then click **OK**.

> **TROUBLESHOOTING:** Do not select the range A1:D9 to fill across worksheets. If you do, you will overwrite the other worksheet data with the January, February, and March labels and data. If this happens, click Undo to restore data in the other worksheets.

g. Right-click the **Yearly Totals worksheet tab** and select **Ungroup Sheets**. Click each worksheet to review the results. Save the workbook once review is complete.

You ungrouped the worksheets. Now all grouped worksheets contain the formatted title and row labels that were copied across worksheets.

## STEP 2 » ENTER AND FORMAT DATA ACROSS WORKSHEETS

You need to regroup the worksheets so that you can increase the width of column A. In addition, you want to insert monthly and department totals for the quarterly worksheets. Refer to Figure 7.10 as you complete Step 2.

**FIGURE 7.10** Data and Formatting Filled in Qtr4 Worksheet

a. Right-click the **Yearly Totals worksheet tab** and select **Select All Sheets**.

b. Click **cell A2**, click **Format** in the Cells group, select **Column Width**, type **18** in the **Column width box**, and then click **OK**.

You set the column width to 18 for the first column in the grouped worksheets, ensuring that column A's width is identical among the worksheets.

c. Right-click the **Qtr1 worksheet tab** and select **Ungroup Sheets**.

d. Press and hold **Shift** and click the **Qtr4 worksheet tab**.

You have to ungroup sheets and group only the four quarterly worksheets to perform the next few steps.

**e.** Do the following to the grouped quarterly worksheets:

- Select the **range B3:E11** and click **AutoSum** in the Editing group to insert department totals in column E and monthly totals in row 11.
- Apply **Accounting Number Format** to the **ranges B3:E3** and **B11:E11** to display $ and commas for the first and total rows.
- Type **Monthly Totals** in **cell A11**. Apply bold, increase indent, and **Purple font color**.
- Type **Dept. Totals** in **cell E2**. Use Format Painter to copy the formats from **cell D2** to **cell E2**.
- Select the **range B11:E11**, click the **Border arrow** in the Font group, and then select **Top and Double Bottom Border**.

You applied the Top and Double Bottom Border style to the monthly totals to conform to standard accounting formatting practices.

**f.** Right-click the **Qtr4 worksheet tab**, select **Ungroup Sheets**, click each quarterly worksheet tab to ensure the formats were applied to each worksheet, and then save the workbook.

## STEP 3 ≫ INSERT HYPERLINKS

You want to insert hyperlinks on the Yearly Totals worksheet so that you can click a hyperlink to jump back to the respective quarterly worksheet quickly. Refer to Figure 7.11 as you complete Step 3.

**FIGURE 7.11** Hyperlinks

**a.** Click the **Yearly Totals worksheet tab**, type **Qtr1** in **cell B2**, and then use the fill handle to fill in the remaining quarter labels in the **range C2:E2**. Type **Dept. Totals** in **cell F2**. Center the labels. Increase the width of column F to **12**.

**b.** Click **cell B2**, click the **INSERT tab**, and then click **Hyperlink** in the Links group.

The Insert Hyperlink dialog box opens so that you can specify the destination when the user clicks the hyperlink.

**c.** Click **Place in This Document** in the *Link to* section on the left side of the dialog box.

**d.** Type **E2:E11** in the **Type the cell reference box**, click **'Qtr1'** in the **Or select a place in this document list**, and then click **OK**.

You created a hyperlink to the range E2:E11 in the Qtr1 worksheet. Note that if you do not specify a reference cell for the link it will default to cell A1.

**e.** Create the following hyperlinks by adapting steps b through d:

- **Cell C2**: Create a hyperlink to the **range E2:E11** in the Qtr2 worksheet.
- **Cell D2**: Create a hyperlink to the **range E2:E11** in the Qtr3 worksheet.
- **Cell E2**: Create a hyperlink to the **range E2:E11** in the Qtr4 worksheet.

**f.** Position the mouse pointer over cell E2.

The ScreenTip informs you where the hyperlink's destination is (see Figure 7.11). The path and file name shown on your screen will differ from those shown in the figure. If you had created a ScreenTip in the Insert Hyperlink dialog box, that text would appear instead of the destination.

**g.** Click the hyperlink in **cell E2**.

The hyperlink jumps to the destination: the range E2:E11 in the Qtr4 worksheet.

**h.** Click the **Yearly Totals worksheet tab** and click the other hyperlinks to ensure they work. When you are done, click the **Yearly Totals worksheet tab** and save the workbook.

> **TROUBLESHOOTING:** If a hyperlink does not jump to the correct range and worksheet, right-click the cell containing the wrong hyperlink, click Edit Hyperlink, and then edit the hyperlink in the Edit Hyperlink dialog box.

## STEP 4 ≫ OPEN AND ARRANGE WORKSHEETS

You want to see the four quarterly sales data worksheets at the same time. To do this, you need to open additional windows of the workbook, and then arrange them. Refer to Figure 7.12 as you complete Step 4.

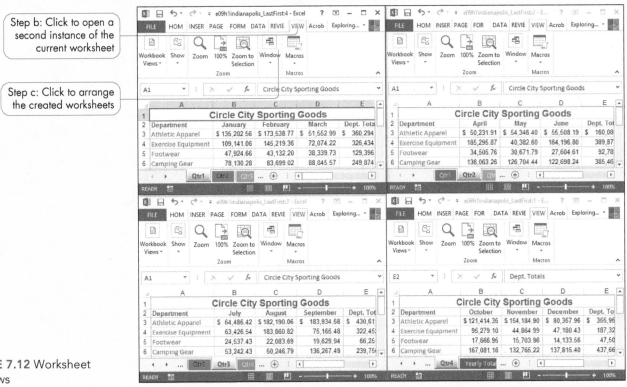

Step b: Click to open a second instance of the current worksheet

Step c: Click to arrange the created worksheets

**FIGURE 7.12** Worksheet Windows

**a.** Click the **VIEW tab** and click **New Window** in the Window group.

You opened another window of the same workbook. The title bar displays the same file name with *:2* at the end of the name.

**b.** Click **New Window** on the **VIEW tab** in the Window group twice.

Two new windows open with *:3* and *:4* at the end of each file name. You now have four windows open.

**c.** Click **Arrange All** in the Window group on the VIEW tab.

The Arrange Windows dialog box opens so you can specify how you want to arrange the open worksheet windows.

**d.** Click **Tiled**, if necessary, click the **Windows of active workbook check box**, and then click **OK**.

Clicking the *Windows of active workbook* check box ensures that the windows display for the active workbook. If you have other workbooks open, those windows do not display.

Excel arranges the four windows of the same workbook. Currently, all the windows display the Yearly Totals worksheet, but you will display a different worksheet in each window.

**e.** Click the **Qtr1 worksheet tab** twice in the top-left window, click the **Qtr2 worksheet tab** twice in the top-right window, click the **Qtr3 worksheet tab** twice in the bottom-left window, and click the **Qtr4 worksheet tab** twice in the bottom-right window.

**f.** Save the workbook. Keep the workbook open if you plan to continue with Hands-On Exercise 2. If not, close the workbook and exit Excel.

# 3-D Formulas and Linked Workbooks

Excel workbooks often contain data from different time periods, geographic regions, or products. For example, a workbook might contain a worksheet to store data for each week in a month, data for each location of a chain of department stores, or data for sales of each type of automobile produced by one manufacturer. While you have experience creating formulas and functions to perform calculations within one worksheet, you need to be able to consolidate, or combine, data from multiple worksheets into one. For example, you might want to consolidate sales data from all of your department store locations into one worksheet for the year.

Additional data analysis occurs over time. To avoid overloading a workbook with detailed sales data for several years, you might have detailed sales data in individual worksheets in one workbook for a specific year. You then might want to determine the average yearly sales for the past 10 years.

In this section, you will create a 3-D formula to consolidate data from several worksheets. In addition, you will learn how to link data from several workbooks to one workbook.

## Inserting a 3-D Formula

**STEP 1 >>** You have referenced other cells in the same worksheet. For example, when you created a one-variable data table, you entered a reference, such as =B12, to display the contents of a formula in cell B12 instead of performing the calculation again in the one-variable data table. At times, you need to consolidate data from multiple worksheets into one worksheet. For example, you might want to create a yearly budget by consolidating values from monthly worksheets, or you might want to calculate average daily occupancy rates for a hospital from detailed weekly occupancy worksheets. When you create formulas that involve reference cells on different worksheets, you include worksheet references. A ***3-D reference,*** is a pointer to a cell in another worksheet, such as October!E3, which references cell E3 in the October worksheet. An exclamation point separates the worksheet name and the cell reference. If the value in cell E3 in the October worksheet changes, you do not have to edit the value in another worksheet; the reference does that for you automatically.

'Worksheet Name'!RangeOfCells

You can use worksheet references in formulas. For example, a formula that adds the values of cell E3 in the October, November, and December worksheets looks like this: =October!E3+November!E3+December!E3. If a worksheet name contains words separated by a space such as *October Sales*, single quotation marks surround the worksheet name, such as ='October Sales'!E3+'November Sales'!E3+'December Sales'!E3.

 **TIP** | **CamelCase Notation**

CamelCase notation is a file naming convention that eliminates spaces and capitalizes compound words—for example, OctoberSales.xlsx versus October sales.xlsx. By using a naming convention such as CamelCase, you can reduce some of the complexity of a 3-D formula by eliminating the need for single quotation marks.

Entering this type of formula manually or by using the semi-selection process is time-consuming to ensure you click every worksheet and every cell within the respective worksheets. When individual worksheets have an identical structure (i.e., totals for the Jewelry Department are in cell E7 in each quarterly worksheet), you can improve your efficiency in creating formulas by using a *3-D formula*, which is a formula or function that refers to the same cell or range in multiple worksheets. The term *3-D formula* comes from having a reference with three dimensions: worksheet name, column letter, and row number. It is a convenient way to reference several identically structured worksheets in which the cells in each worksheet contain the same type of data, such as when you consolidate sales information from different branches into the Summary worksheet. For example, =SUM('Qtr1:Qtr4'!E3) is a 3-D formula that adds the values in cell E3 in each worksheet, starting in the Qtr1 worksheet and ending in the Qtr4 worksheet, including worksheets between those two. You can type a 3-D reference directly into a cell formula or function, but using the semi-selection method is more efficient. To create a 3-D formula, do the following:

1. Click the cell in which you will enter the 3-D formula.
2. Type =, type the name of the function, such as SUM, and then type an opening parenthesis.
3. Click the first worksheet tab, such as Qtr1.
4. Press and hold Shift as you click the last worksheet tab for adjacent worksheets, or press and hold Ctrl as you click nonadjacent worksheet tabs.
5. Click the cell or select the range that contains the value(s) you want to use in the function argument and press Enter. Figure 7.13 shows the process of creating a 3-D formula before you press Enter.

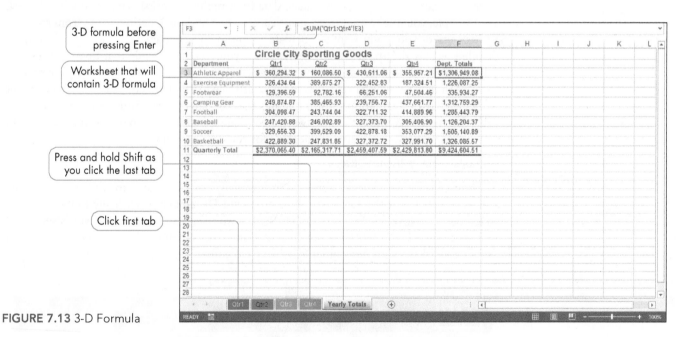

**FIGURE 7.13** 3-D Formula

=SUM('First Worksheet:Last Worksheet'!RangeOfCells)

You can use a variety of functions for 3-D formulas. Some of these functions include SUM, AVERAGE, COUNT, MIN, and MAX. You can create 3-D formulas using some standard deviation and variance functions. Other functions, such as PMT, VLOOKUP, and COUNTIF, do not work with 3-D formulas.

When you have a function such as =SUM(B1:B5) and insert a new fourth row, Excel modifies the SUM function to include the new row: =SUM(B1:B6). Similarly, if you insert or copy a worksheet between the beginning and ending worksheet references, the 3-D formula automatically includes those worksheet data points in the calculation. If you move a worksheet out of the range, Excel excludes that worksheet's values from the 3-D formula calculations. Finally, if you move or delete an endpoint worksheet, Excel adjusts the 3-D formula for you.

# Linking Workbooks

Workbook linking is another way of consolidating data. When you link workbooks, you consolidate the data from several workbooks into another workbook. *Linking* is the process of creating external cell references from worksheets in one workbook to cells on a worksheet in another workbook. For example, you might have three workbooks—Indianapolis, Bloomington, and South Bend—one for each store location. Each store manager maintains a workbook to record sales by department—such as exercise equipment, footwear, and camping gear—for a particular time period. As district manager, you want to consolidate the data from each workbook into one workbook. Instead of reentering the data, you can create links from specific cells of data in the individual workbooks to your active workbook.

Before creating links, identify the source and destination files. A *source file* is one that contains original data that you need elsewhere. For example, the individual department store workbooks—Indianapolis, Bloomington, and South Bend—are source files. The *destination file* is a file containing a pointer to receive data from the source files—that is, the target file that needs the data. When you link workbooks, you create a connection between the source and destination files. If data change in the source file, the destination file's data update also. Linking ensures that the destination file always contains the most up-to-date data.

## Create an External Reference

STEP 3>> When you create a link between source and destination files, you establish an external reference or pointer to one or more cells in another workbook. The external reference is similar to the worksheet reference that you created for 3-D formulas. However, an external reference must include the workbook name to identify which workbook contains the linked worksheet and cell reference. For example, to create a link to cell E3 in the Qtr3 worksheet in the Indianapolis file, type =[Indianapolis.xlsx]Qtr3!E3. You must type the workbook name, including the file name extension, between brackets, such as [Indianapolis.xlsx]. After the closing bracket, type the worksheet name, such as Qtr3, followed by an exclamation mark and the cell reference, such as E3. Table 7.2 lists additional rules to follow when entering external references.

[WorkbookName]WorksheetName!RangeOfCells

## TABLE 7.2 External References

| Situation | Rule | Example |
|---|---|---|
| Workbook and worksheet names do not contain spaces; source and destination files are in the same folder. | Type brackets around the workbook name and an exclamation mark between the worksheet name and range. | [Indianapolis.xlsx]Qtr3!A1 |
| Workbook or worksheet name contains spaces; source and destination files are in the same folder. | Type single quotation marks on the left side of the opening bracket and the right side of the worksheet name. | '[South Bend.xlsx]Qtr3'!A1 |
| Worksheet name contains spaces; source and destination files are in the same folder. | Type single quotation marks on the left side of the opening bracket and the right side of the worksheet name. | '[Bloomington.xlsx]Qtr 3 Sales'!A1 |
| Source workbook is in a different folder than the destination workbook. | Type a single quotation mark, and then the full path—drive letter and folder name—before the opening bracket and a single quotation mark after the worksheet name. | 'C:\Data[Indianapolis.xlsx] Sheet1'!A1 |

Excel displays formulas with external references in two ways, depending on whether the source workbook is open or closed. When the source is open, the external reference shows the file name, worksheet, and cell reference. When the source workbook is closed, the external reference shows the full path name in the Formula Bar. By default, Excel creates absolute cell references in the external reference. However, you can edit the external reference to create a relative or mixed cell reference. To create an external reference between cells in different workbooks:

1. Open the destination workbook and all source workbooks.
2. Select the cell or cells to hold the external reference.
3. Type =. If you want to perform calculations or functions on the external references, type the operator or function.
4. Switch to the source workbook and click the worksheet that contains the cells to which you want to link.
5. Select the cells you want to link to and press Enter.

 **Drive and Folder Reference**

Excel updates an external reference regardless of whether the source workbook is open. The source workbooks must be in the same folder location as when you created the link to update the destination workbook. If the location of the workbooks changes, as may happen if you copy the workbooks to a different folder, click Edit Links in the Connections group on the Data tab.

## Manage and Update Linked Workbooks

 If you create an external reference when both the source and destination files are open, changes you make to the source file occur in the destination file as well. However, if the destination file is closed when you change data in the source file, the destination file does not automatically update to match the source file. Excel does not update linked data in a destination workbook automatically to protect the workbook against malicious activity, such as viruses.

When you open the destination file the first time, Excel displays the Security Warning Message Bar between the Ribbon and Formula Bar with the message *Automatic updates of links has been disabled*. If you are confident that the source files contain safe data, enable the links in the destination file. Click Enable Content to update the links and save the workbook. The next time you open the destination file, Excel displays a message box that prompts the user to update, do not update, or select help. Click Update to update the links. Figure 7.14 has been contrived to show you both ways of updating links.

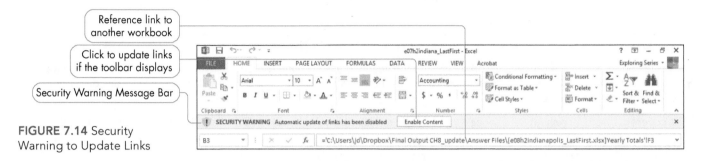

**FIGURE 7.14** Security Warning to Update Links

External references identify the workbook names and locations. If you rename or move the source workbook, you must ensure that the external reference in the destination file matches the name of the new source workbook. Otherwise, when you open a destination file that contains external links that cannot be updated, Excel displays an error message, *This workbook contains one or more links that cannot be updated.* Click Edit Links to display the Edit Links dialog box and modify the source links (see Figure 7.15).

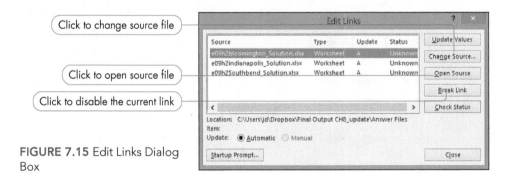

**FIGURE 7.15** Edit Links Dialog Box

The Status column displays OK if the external reference link to the source file still works. If a problem exists, the Status column indicates the type of error, such as *Error: Source not found.* Click the source that contains an error and click Change Source to find and select the renamed or moved source file.

*Quick Concepts*

1. What is a 3-D formula? *p. 246*

2. What are the benefits of 3-D formulas? *p. 246*

3. How do you create an external reference? *pp. 247–248*

# Hands-On Exercises

Watch the Video
for this Hands-
On Exercise!

MyITLab®
HOE2 Training

## 2 3-D Formulas and Linked Workbooks

Previously, you set up the four quarterly worksheets and the yearly total worksheet for Circle City Sporting Goods. Next, you want to calculate total yearly sales for each department as well as the overall total sales. In addition, you want to link sales data from all three locations into one workbook.

**Skills covered:** Insert Worksheet References • Insert 3-D Formulas • Link Workbooks • Complete the Linked Workbook

### STEP 1 ≫ INSERT WORKSHEET REFERENCES

Each quarterly worksheet calculates the quarterly sales totals for a three-month period for each department. You want to insert references from each quarterly worksheet to consolidate the quarterly sales on the Yearly Totals worksheet. Refer to Figure 7.16 as you complete Step 1.

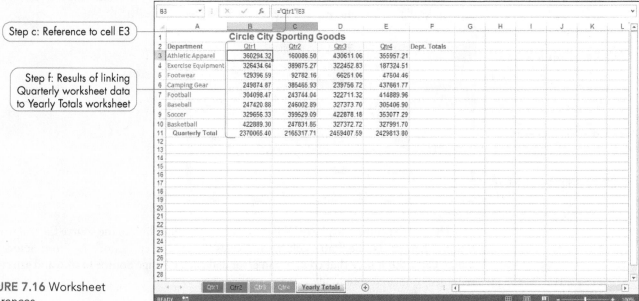

**FIGURE 7.16** Worksheet References

a. Open *e07h1Indianapolis_LastFirst* and save it as **e07h2Indianapolis_LastFirst**, changing *h1* to *h2*.

b. Click the **Yearly Totals worksheet tab**. Type **Quarterly Total** in **cell A11**. Bold, indent, and apply **Purple font color** to the label.

c. Click **cell B3**, type **=**, click the **Qtr1 worksheet tab**, click **cell E3** in that worksheet, and then press **Ctrl+Enter**.

   Look at the Formula Bar. The formula is ='Qtr1'!E3, where Qtr1 refers to the worksheet, and E3 refers to the cell within that worksheet.

d. Double-click the **cell B3 fill handle** to copy the formula down the column.

   The formula's cell reference is relative, so it changes as you copy the formula down the column. The formula in cell B4 is ='Qtr1'!E4.

e. Click **cell C3** in the Yearly Totals worksheet, type =, click the **Qtr2 worksheet tab**, click **cell E3** in that worksheet, and then press **Ctrl+Enter**. Double-click the **cell C3 fill handle** to copy the formula down the column.

   Look at the Formula Bar. The formula is ='Qtr2'!E3, where Qtr2 refers to the worksheet and E3 refers to the cell within that worksheet.

f. Adapt step e to enter references to the appropriate totals in the Qtr3 and Qtr4 worksheets.

g. Increase the four quarterly column widths to **13**. Save the workbook.

## STEP 2 » INSERT 3-D FORMULAS

You want to calculate the total annual sales by department. Although you could simply sum the values in the Yearly Totals worksheet, you want to use a 3-D formula to provide a cross-check that the totals are correct. Refer to Figure 7.17 as you complete Step 2.

Step d: 3-D Formula

Step e: 3-D Formulas completed by the fill handle

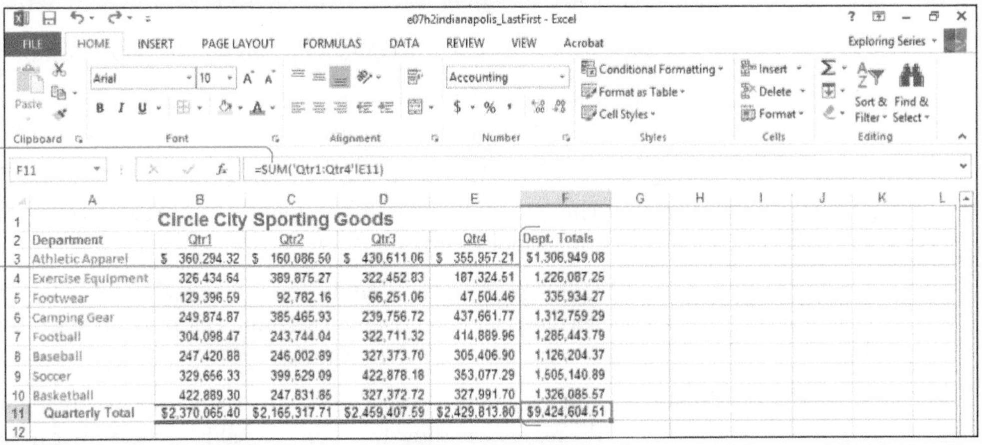


**FIGURE 7.17** 3-D Formulas

a. Click **cell F3** in the Yearly Totals worksheet.

   This cell needs to calculate the total yearly sales for the Men's Clothing Department.

b. Type **=SUM(**

   You start the 3-D formula with =, the function name, and the opening parenthesis.

c. Click the **Qtr1 worksheet tab**, press and hold **Shift**, and then click the **Qtr4 worksheet tab**.

   You grouped the worksheets together so that you can use a common cell reference for the range of cells to sum.

d. Click **cell E3**, the cell containing the quarterly sales, and press **Ctrl+Enter**.

   Look at the Formula Bar. The formula is =SUM('Qtr1:Qtr4'!E3). If you select the range B3:E3, the status bar shows that the sum is $1,306,949.08, the same value that appears when you inserted the 3-D formula.

e. Double-click the **cell F3 fill handle** to copy the formula down the column.

   The cell reference is relative, so it changes as you copy the 3-D formula.

f. Apply **Accounting Number Format** to the **ranges B3:F3** and **B11:F11**. Apply **Comma Style** to the **range B4:F10**. Increase the width of column F to **13**. Apply the **Top and Double Bottom Border** to the **range B11:F11**. Bold **cell F2** and change the color to **purple**. Save the workbook.

## STEP 3 » LINK WORKBOOKS

You need to link the Indianapolis, Bloomington, and South Bend workbooks to display their totals in the Indiana workbook. The South Bend and Bloomington workbooks have the same structure as the Indianapolis workbook on which you have been working. Refer to Figure 7.18 as you complete Step 3.

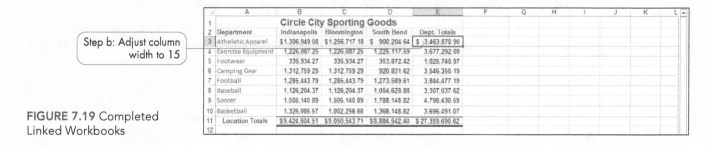

Step d: Linked data from Bloomington worksheet

Step c: Linked data from Indianapolis worksheet

Step e: Linked data from South Bend worksheet

FIGURE 7.18 Linked Workbooks

| | Circle City Sporting Goods | | | |
|---|---|---|---|---|
| Department | Indianapolis | Bloomington | South Bend | Dept. Totals |
| Atheletic Apparel | $1,306,949.08 | $1,256,717.18 | $ 900,204.64 | |
| Exercise Equipment | 1,226,087.25 | 1,226,087.25 | 1,225,117.59 | |
| Footwear | 335,934.27 | 335,934.27 | 353,872.42 | |
| Camping Gear | 1,312,759.29 | 1,312,759.29 | 920,631.62 | |
| Football | 1,285,443.79 | 1,285,443.79 | 1,273,589.61 | |
| Baseball | 1,126,204.37 | 1,126,204.37 | 1,054,628.88 | |
| Soccer | 1,505,140.89 | 1,505,140.89 | 1,788,148.82 | |
| Basketball | 1,326,085.57 | 1,002,256.68 | 1,368,148.82 | |
| Location Totals | $9,424,604.51 | $9,050,543.71 | $8,884,542.40 | |

a. Open *e07h2Bloomington* and save it as **e07h2Bloomington_LastFirst**; open *e07h2SouthBend* and save it as **e07h2SouthBend_LastFirst**; and then open *e07h2Indiana* and save it as **e07h2Indiana_LastFirst**, making sure you save the workbooks in the same folder as your *e07h2Indianapolis_LastFirst* workbook.

b. Click *e07h2Indiana_LastFirst* on the taskbar to make it the active workbook.

This workbook will contain the links to the three location workbooks.

c. Click **cell B3**, type =, point to the Excel icon on the Windows taskbar, select the *e07h2Indianapolis_LastFirst* workbook, click the **Yearly Totals worksheet tab**, click **cell F3** containing the yearly department totals, and then press **Ctrl+Enter**.

The formula =‘[e07h2Indianapolis_LastFirst.xlsx]Yearly Totals’!$F$3 creates a link to the Indianapolis workbook.

d. Edit the cell reference in the formula to make cell F3 relative by removing the $ signs in the Formula Bar and pressing **Ctrl+Enter** or placing the cursor after the formula in the Formula Bar and pressing **F4** three times.

You must make this cell reference relative before copying it down the column. Otherwise, the results will show the value for cell F3 for the other Indianapolis departments.

e. Click **cell C3**, type =, point to the Excel icon on the Windows taskbar, select the *e07h2Bloomington_LastFirst* workbook, click the **Yearly Totals worksheet tab**, click **cell F3**, and then press **Ctrl+Enter**.

You created a link to the Bloomington workbook. The formula appears as =‘[e07h2Bloomington_LastFirst.xlsx]Yearly Totals’!$F$3.

f. Edit the cell reference in the formula to make cell F3 relative.

g. Adapt steps e and f to create a link to the South Bend workbook's yearly totals.

h. Copy the formulas down the columns in the *e07h2Indiana_LastFirst* workbook. Save the workbook.

## STEP 4 ≫ COMPLETE THE LINKED WORKBOOK

You need to insert department totals for all three locations and format the linked workbook. Refer to Figure 7.19 as you complete Step 4.

Step b: Adjust column width to 15

FIGURE 7.19 Completed Linked Workbooks

| | Circle City Sporting Goods | | | |
|---|---|---|---|---|
| Department | Indianapolis | Bloomington | South Bend | Dept. Totals |
| Atheletic Apparel | $1,306,949.08 | $1,256,717.18 | $ 900,204.64 | $ 3,463,870.90 |
| Exercise Equipment | 1,226,087.25 | 1,226,087.25 | 1,225,117.59 | 3,677,292.09 |
| Footwear | 335,934.27 | 335,934.27 | 353,872.42 | 1,025,740.97 |
| Camping Gear | 1,312,759.29 | 1,312,759.29 | 920,631.62 | 3,546,350.19 |
| Football | 1,285,443.79 | 1,285,443.79 | 1,273,589.61 | 3,844,477.19 |
| Baseball | 1,126,204.37 | 1,126,204.37 | 1,054,628.88 | 3,307,037.62 |
| Soccer | 1,505,140.89 | 1,505,140.89 | 1,788,148.82 | 4,798,430.59 |
| Basketball | 1,326,085.57 | 1,002,256.68 | 1,368,148.82 | 3,696,491.07 |
| Location Totals | $9,424,604.51 | $9,050,543.71 | $8,884,542.40 | $ 27,359,690.62 |

a. Click **cell E3** in the *e07h2Indiana_LastFirst* workbook.

b. Insert the SUM function to enter **=SUM(B3:D3)**. Copy the formula down column E. Adjust the width of column E to **15**.

You calculated the total yearly sales across all three locations by department.

c. Format the **range B4:E10** with **Comma Style**.

d. Apply **Top and Double Bottom Border** to the **range B11:E11**.

e. Save and close all open workbooks, and submit based on your instructor's directions.

# Formula Audits and Data Validation

Errors can occur in a worksheet in several ways. Sometimes, an error may occur with a function name, such as =AVG(B1:E1) when the formula should be =AVERAGE(B1:E1). A *syntax error* is an error that occurs because a formula or function violates correct construction, such as a misspelled function name or illegal use of an operator. Syntax errors also include illegal mathematical construction, such as attempting to divide a value by zero. You must correct syntax errors to obtain a viable result. Excel helps you detect and correct syntax errors. For example, Excel displays #DIV/0! if the formula divides a value by zero to inform you that a result cannot be calculated. Table 7.3 lists some common syntax errors and the reasons for those errors.

| TABLE 7.3 Syntax Errors Explained | |
|---|---|
| **Error** | **Reasons** |
| #DIV/0! | Formula attempts to divide a value by zero or an empty cell |
| #NAME? | Misspelled or invalid range name or function name, such as VLOKUP instead of VLOOKUP |
| | Parentheses missing for function, such as =TODAY instead of =TODAY( ) |
| | Omitted quotation marks around text, such as using *text* instead of *"text"* in the function =IF(A4="text",A5,A6) |
| | Missing colon in a range reference, such as =SUM(A1A8) |
| #N/A | Function is missing one or more required arguments, or VLOOKUP, HLOOKUP, or MATCH functions do not return a match |
| #NULL! | Incorrect range separator |
| | Formula requires cell ranges to intersect and they do not |
| #NUM! | Invalid arguments used in a function |
| #REF! | Reference to cell that contains no data or deleted data |
| #VALUE! | Incorrect type of data used in an argument, such as referring to a cell that contains text instead of a value |

More difficult to detect are errors that appear to be correct but are not because an incorrect range was entered, such as =AVERAGE(B1:D1) when the range should be =AVERAGE(B1:E1). *Logic errors* are the result of a syntactically correct formula but logically incorrect construction, which produces inaccurate results. Logic errors occur when a formula contains the wrong operator or cell reference.

You can design worksheets to help facilitate correct data entry, such as ensuring that a user enters a value, not text. Doing so helps prevent formula errors because the user must enter valid data. Although you can design workbooks to require valid data, you might work with workbooks that other people created that contain errors in the formulas.

In this section, you will learn how to use formula auditing tools to detect errors. In addition, you will apply data validation rules to make sure users enter correct data into input cells.

# Auditing Formulas

Recall that you can press Ctrl+` (grave accent key) to display cell formulas instead of cell results. Displaying the formulas may help you identify some errors, but you might not be able to detect all errors immediately. Especially challenging to detect are errors in 3-D formulas or formulas that link workbooks. To help you detect and correct formula errors, you can use *formula auditing*, a set of tools that enable you to display or trace relationships for formula cells, show formulas, check for errors, and evaluate formulas. The Formula Auditing group on the Formulas tab contains commands to help you audit a workbook (see Figure 7.20).

**FIGURE 7.20** Formula Auditing Group

> ## TIP | Green Triangle
>
> Excel detects potential logic errors even if the formula does not contain a syntax error. For example, Excel might detect that =SUM(B2:B5) contains a potential error if cell B1 contains a value, assuming the possibility that the function might need to include B1 in the range of values to add. When this occurs, Excel displays a green triangle in the top-left corner of the cell. Click the cell containing the green triangle and click the error icon, the yellow diamond with the exclamation mark, to see a list of options to correct the error.

## Trace Precedents and Dependents

**STEP 1** Although Excel displays error messages, you might not know what cell is causing the error to appear in the formula cell. Even if your worksheet does not contain errors, you might want to use formula auditing tools to identify which cells are used in formulas. Formulas involve both precedent and dependent cells. *Precedent cells* are cells that are referenced in a formula. For example, assume an hourly pay rate ($10.25) is stored in cell A1, hours worked (40) is stored in cell A2, and the formula =A1*A2 is stored in cell A3 to calculate the gross pay. Cells A1 and A2 are precedent cells to the formula in cell A3. *Dependent cells* contain formulas that refer to other cells. These cells *depend* on other cells to generate their values. For example, if cell A3 contains the formula =A1*A2, cell A3 is a dependent of cells A1 and A2.

You use Trace Precedents and Trace Dependents to display *tracer arrows* that show the relationship between cells and formulas (see Figure 7.21). The tracer starts in a precedent cell with the arrowhead ending in the dependent cell. To trace precedents, select the cell that contains the formula for which you will find precedent cells and click Trace Precedents in the Formula Auditing group. To trace dependent cells, click the cell for which you will find dependents and click Trace Dependents in the Formula Auditing group. The tracer arrows help you identify cells that cause errors. Blue arrows show cells with no errors. Red arrows show cells that cause errors.

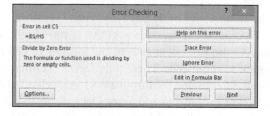

**FIGURE 7.21** Trace Precedents

Red indicates error

---

<blockquote>
**TIP** | **Remove Tracer Arrows**

Click Remove Arrows in the Formula Auditing group on the Formulas tab to remove all tracer arrows, or click the Remove Arrows arrow and select Remove Arrows, Remove Precedent Arrows, or Remove Dependent Arrows.
</blockquote>

## Check For and Repair Errors

**STEP 2»** When the tracing of precedents or dependents shows errors in formulas, or if you want to check for errors that have occurred in formulas anywhere in a worksheet, you can use Error Checking in the Formula Auditing group. When Excel identifies an error, the Error Checking dialog box opens (see Figure 7.22) and identifies the cell containing an error and describes the error.

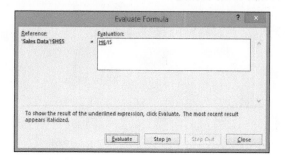

**FIGURE 7.22** Error Checking Dialog Box

Click *Help on this error* to see a description of the error. Click Show Calculation Steps to open the Evaluate Formula dialog box (see Figure 7.23), which provides an evaluation of the formula and shows which part of the evaluation will result in an error. Clicking Ignore Error either moves to the next error or indicates that Error Checking is complete. When you click *Edit in Formula Bar*, you can correct the formula in the Formula Bar.

**FIGURE 7.23** Evaluate Formula Dialog Box

## Evaluate a Formula

Using nested formulas can make it difficult to understand the formula evaluation. Understanding how a nested formula calculates is hard because intermediate calculations and logical tests exist. You can use the Evaluate Formula dialog box to view different parts of a nested formula and evaluate each part. To use the Evaluate Formula dialog box, do the following:

1. Select the cell you want to evaluate.
2. Click Evaluate Formula in the Formula Auditing group to see the Evaluate Formula dialog box (see Figure 7.23).
3. Click Evaluate to examine the value of the reference that is underlined.
4. If the underlined part of the formula is a reference to another formula, click Step In to display the other formula in the Evaluation box.
5. Click Step Out to return to the previous cell and formula.
6. Continue until you have evaluated the entire formula and click Close.

## Use the IFERROR Function to Detect Errors

If you create a workbook for others to use, you should anticipate errors the users will introduce so that you can provide a way to identify and correct those errors. The **IFERROR function** is a logical function that checks a cell to determine if that cell contains an error or if a formula will result in an error. If no error exists, the IFERROR function returns the value of the formula. The *value* argument contains the value being checked for an error, and the *value_if_error* argument is the value to return if the formula evaluates to an error. IFERROR detects the following types of errors: #N/A, #VALUE!, #REF!, #DIV/0!, #NUM!, #NAME?, and #NULL, although the output does not indicate the type of error.

Typically, you use a text string enclosed in quotation marks to return an error message. For example, if you divide the contents of cells in row 2 by cell B1 and anticipate that a #DIV/0! error might occur when copying the formula, you can use =IFERROR(A2/B1,"You cannot divide by zero. Change the value of cell B1 to a value higher than 0.").

=IFERROR(value,value_if_error)

### TIP | Information Functions

The Information functions contain additional functions you can use for error checking. Of particular interest are the ERROR.TYPE and ISERROR functions. Use Help to learn how to incorporate these functions in error-checking tasks.

# Setting Up a Watch Window

When you are working with a worksheet containing a large dataset, formulas in cells that are not visible can be "watched" using the Watch Window. You do not need to keep scrolling to different parts of the worksheet if you are using a Watch Window. The **Watch Window** enables you to create a small window so you can conveniently inspect, audit, or confirm formula calculations involving cells not immediately visible on the screen. You can double-click a cell in the Watch Window to jump to that cell quickly. To add cells to the Watch Window, do the following:

1. Click Watch Window in the Formula Auditing group.
2. Click Add Watch in the Watch Window toolbar.
3. Select the cells to watch in the Add Watch dialog box and click Add. The Watch Window shows the cells and formulas you selected to watch (see Figure 7.24).

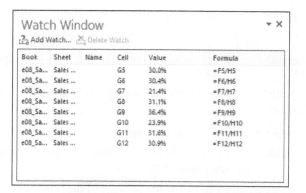

**FIGURE 7.24** Watch Window

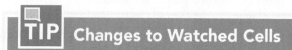

> **TIP** **Changes to Watched Cells**
>
> Any time you make a change to the watched cell(s), the Watch Window shows you the current value of the watched cell(s).

# Validating Data

**STEP 4 >>** ***Data validation*** enables you to control the data that can be entered into a cell. It warns and prevents people from entering "wrong" data in a cell, or it can provide a list of valid data from which to choose. Data validation enables you to specify and correct the kind of data that can be entered, specify an input message alerting users when they click a cell that only specific types of data can be entered in that cell, and specify error messages that appear when others persist and attempt to enter incorrect data. To set up a data validation rule, click the cell for which the rule will be applied, and then click Data Validation in the Data Tools group on the Data tab.

## Specify Data Validation Criteria

In the Data Validation dialog box, use the Settings tab to specify the ***validation criteria***—the rules that dictate the type of data that can be entered in a cell. Click the Allow arrow to specify what type of data you will allow the user to enter, such as a whole number, a value that is part of a specific list, or a date that is within a particular date range. For example, if you specify whole number and the user attempts to enter a decimal, Excel displays an error message. You can also specify that the data must be between two values and specify the minimum and maximum values permitted. Figure 7.25 shows a validation rule in which the cell contents must be (a) a whole number and (b) between a minimum and maximum value, which are stored respectively in cells G5 and G6.

**FIGURE 7.25** Data Validation Settings Tab: Criteria

To make data entry easier or to limit items to certain defined items and thereby be more accurate, you can create a list of valid entries from data contained in cells. When you create a list, Excel displays an arrow in the cell. The user clicks the arrow, and then selects the desired entry. The user cannot enter invalid data. To create a list, do the following:

1. Create a list of valid entries in a single column or row without blank cells.
2. Click the cell for which you want to create a validation rule.
3. Click the DATA tab and select Validation in the Data Tools group to show the Data Validation dialog box.
4. Click the Settings tab, click the Allow arrow, and then select List.
5. Enter a reference to the list in the Source box (see Figure 7.26).
6. Make sure that the *In-cell dropdown* check box is selected and that the *Ignore blank* check box is clear and click OK.

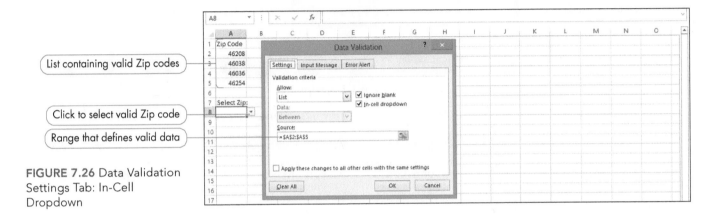

**FIGURE 7.26** Data Validation Settings Tab: In-Cell Dropdown

## Create an Input Message

STEP 5» *Input messages* are descriptive text or instructions for data entry that can be entered in the Data Validation dialog box. You add input messages to cells, and Excel displays these messages when a user moves to a cell that has a data-entry restriction. Input messages consist of two parts: a title and an input message (see Figure 7.27). These messages should describe the data validation and explain or show how to enter data correctly. For example, an input message might be *Enter hire date in the form: mm/dd/yyyy* or *Enter Employee name: last name, first name.*

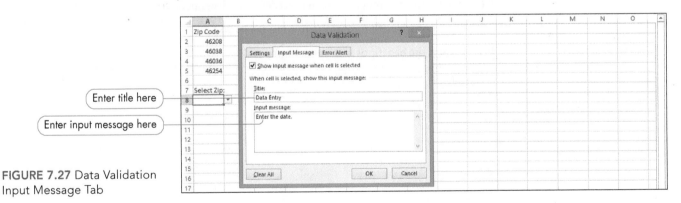

**FIGURE 7.27** Data Validation Input Message Tab

## Create an Error Alert

Sometimes, no matter how descriptive you are with an input message, users will attempt to enter invalid data in a cell. Instead of using Excel's default error message, you can create an *error alert*, a message that displays when a user enters invalid data in a cell that has a validation rule applied to it. To create an error alert, specify the style, title, and error message on the Error Alert tab (see Figure 7.28). The error alert message should be polite and clearly state what the error is. Cryptic, nondescriptive alert messages do not help users understand the data-entry problem. Table 7.4 shows the error styles that control the icon that appears with the error message.

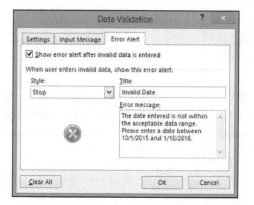

**FIGURE 7.28** Data Validation Error Tab

### TABLE 7.4 Error Style

| Icon | Style | Description |
|------|-------|-------------|
| | Stop | Prevents the user from entering invalid data |
| | Warning | Accepts invalid data but warns user that data are invalid |
| | Information | Accepts invalid data but provides information to user |

## TIP Circle Text

After defining data validation rules, you can display circles around invalid text. To display circles for invalid data, click the Data Validation arrow in the Data Tools group and select Circle Invalid Data. When the user corrects the invalid data, the circles disappear.

*Quick* Concepts

1. What is the difference between precedent and dependent cells? *p. 255*

2. What is the benefit of the Watch Window? *p. 257*

3. What is the benefit of data validation? *p. 258*

## 3 Formula Audits and Data Validation

A colleague prepared a worksheet based on projected data if the company opened a store in Fort Wayne. Unfortunately, your colleague introduced several errors. You will use auditing tools to identify and correct the errors. In addition, you will insert validation rules to ensure only valid data are entered in the future.

**Skills covered:** Trace Precedents and Dependents • Check for Errors • Set Up a Watch Window • Create a Validation Rule • Specify Inputs and Alerts

### STEP 1 ≫ TRACE PRECEDENTS AND DEPENDENTS

You want to display precedent and dependent arrows to identify sources and destinations for cells being used in formulas in the Fort Wayne workbook. Refer to Figure 7.29 as you complete Step 1.

**FIGURE 7.29** Dependent and Precedent Arrows

a. Open *e07h3FortWayne*, click **OK** when prompted to fix a circular error, and then save it as **e07h3FortWayne_LastFirst**.

b. Click **cell B3**, click the **FORMULAS tab**, and then click **Trace Dependents** in the Formula Auditing group.

Excel displays a tracer arrow from cell B3 to cells E3 and B11, indicating that cell B3's value is used in formulas in cells E3 and B11.

c. Click **cell E11** and click **Trace Precedents** in the Formula Auditing group.

Excel displays a tracer error showing that the values in the range B11:D11 are used within the current cell's formula.

d. Click **Remove Arrows** in the Formula Auditing group. Save the workbook.

### STEP 2 ≫ CHECK FOR ERRORS

The Qtr2 worksheet contains errors. You will use the Error Checking dialog box and trace precedents to identify the errors. Refer to Figure 7.30 as you complete Step 2.

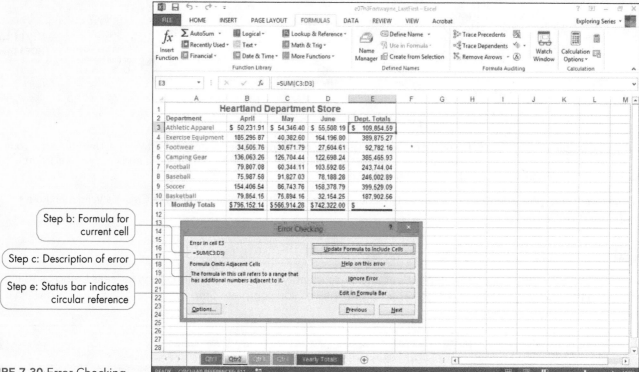

Step b: Formula for current cell

Step c: Description of error

Step e: Status bar indicates circular reference

**FIGURE 7.30** Error Checking

a. Click the **Qtr2 worksheet tab**, look for the green error checking error in cell E3, and then click **cell A1**.

b. Click the **Error Checking arrow** in the Formula Auditing group and select **Error Checking**.

The Error Checking dialog box opens, indicating an error in cell E3. Excel detects that the formula omits an adjacent cell.

c. Click **Update Formula to Include Cells**.

Excel modifies the formula from =SUM(C3:D3) to =SUM(B3:D3) to include the April sales.

d. Click **OK** in the message box that informs you that error checking is complete.

When you opened the workbook, an error message stated that the workbook contains a circular reference. However, the Error Checking dialog box did not locate that circular reference. The status bar still indicates that a circular reference exists.

e. Click the **Error Checking arrow** in the Formula Auditing group, point to *Circular References*, and then select **$E$11**.

A circular reference occurs when a formula refers to itself. In this case, cell E11's formula includes itself in the function argument.

f. Edit the formula to be **=SUM(B11:D11)**. Save the workbook.

The circular reference notation on the status bar disappears.

## STEP 3 ⟫ SET UP A WATCH WINDOW

You want to set up a Watch Window to watch the results of formulas in the Yearly Totals worksheet when you change values in another worksheet. Refer to Figure 7.31 as you complete Step 3.

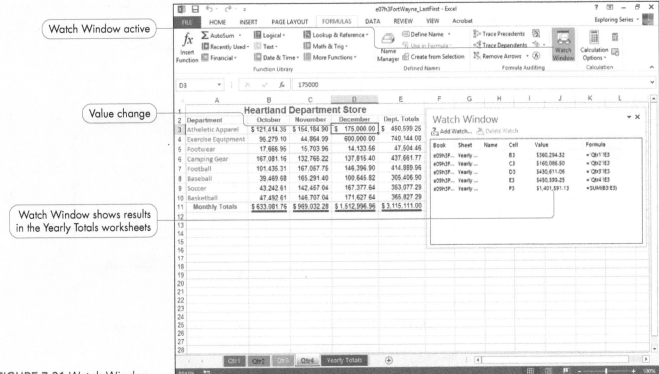

**FIGURE 7.31** Watch Window

a. Click the **Yearly Totals worksheet tab**.

b. Select the **range B3:F3**.

You selected the range you want to watch to ensure formulas work correctly.

c. Click **Watch Window** in the Formula Auditing group and click **Add Watch** in the Watch Window.

The Add Watch dialog box opens, indicating the worksheet and cells you selected.

d. Click **Add**.

The Watch Window adds a watch for every cell in the selected range. It shows the workbook name, worksheet name, cell address, current value, and formula.

e. Click the **Qtr4 worksheet tab**.

The Watch Window remains onscreen. The current Athletic apparel total is $355,957.21, shown in cell E3 and in the Watch Window. The Watch Window also shows the total Athletic Apparel sales to be $1,306,949.08.

f. Click **cell D3**, enter **175000**, and then press **Ctrl+Enter**.

The Qtr4 Athletic Apparel total changed to $450,599.25 in cell E3 and in the Watch Window. The Watch Window also shows that the total Athletic Apparel sales are now $1,401,591.13.

g. Click **Watch Window** in the Formula Auditing group to hide the Watch Window. Save the workbook.

## STEP 4 ≫ CREATE A VALIDATION RULE

You want to insert a validation rule for the Exercise Equipment, Footwear, and Camping Gear values on the Qtr4 worksheet. Based on projections, you believe the maximum revenue would be no more than $500,000. Refer to Figure 7.32 as you complete Step 4.

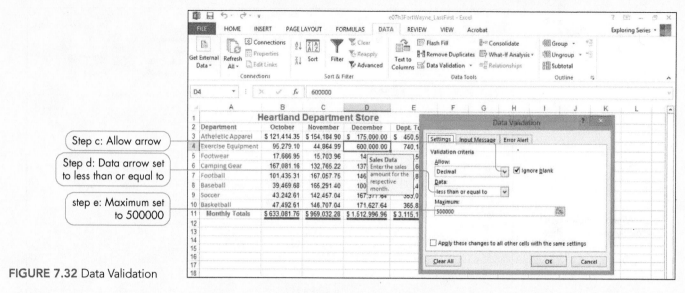

**FIGURE 7.32** Data Validation

a. Select the **range B4:D4** on the Qtr4 worksheet.

b. Click the **DATA tab** and click **Data Validation** in the Data Tools group.

The Data Validation dialog box opens.

c. Click the **Allow arrow** and select **Decimal** to allow for dollar-and-cent entries.

The dialog box displays Data, Minimum, and Maximum options.

d. Click the **Data arrow** and select **less than or equal to**.

e. Type **500000** in the **Maximum box**. Keep the Data Validation dialog box open for the next step.

## STEP 5 ≫ SPECIFY INPUTS AND ALERTS

You will specify the input message and an alert if a user enters more than 500,000 however, you will let the incorrect value be entered. Refer to Figure 7.33 as you complete Step 5.

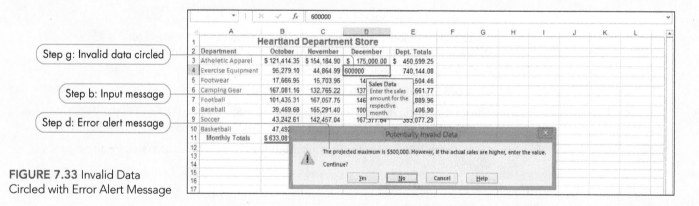

**FIGURE 7.33** Invalid Data Circled with Error Alert Message

a. Click the **Input Message tab** in the Data Validation dialog box.

> **TROUBLESHOOTING:** If you wish to edit the validation message that was set up after completing the prior step, you can edit the validation rule by reentering the data validation menu.

b. Type **Sales Data** in the **Title box** and type **Enter the sales amount for the respective month.** in the **Input message box**.

c. Click the **Error Alert tab** in the Data Validation dialog box, click the **Style arrow**, and then select **Warning**.

The stop style would prevent values outside the acceptable maximum from being entered. However, your sales projections might be wrong, so you want to allow values over the maximum.

d. Type **Potentially Invalid Data** in the **Title box** and type **The projected maximum is $500,000. However, if actual sales are higher, enter the actual value.** in the **Error message box**. Click **OK**.

e. Click **cell D4**, notice the input message you created from step b, type **600000**, and then press **Enter**.

The error message you created appears (see Figure 7.33).

f. Click **Yes**. Note that even though 600000 is beyond the validation limit, the user is still able to enter the number by clicking **Yes**.

g. Click the **Data Validation arrow** in the Data Tools group and select **Circle Invalid Data**.

Excel circles the value in cell D4, indicating that the value violates the validation rule.

h. Save and close the workbook, and submit it based on your instructor's directions.

# Imports, Web Queries, and XML

## Managing Data

## OBJECTIVES   AFTER YOU READ THIS CHAPTER, YOU WILL BE ABLE TO:

1. Import data from external sources p. 268

2. Create a Web query p. 272

3. Manage connections p. 274

4. Convert text to columns p. 282

5. Manipulate text with functions p. 283

6. Use Flash Fill p. 285

## CASE STUDY | Stock Analysis

You are a junior financial analyst for a stockbroker. One of your new clients, Angie Warner, wants you to analyze stock patterns for 10 companies in which she is interested. She e-mailed you a list of the company names and stock symbols, which you will import into an Excel worksheet. You need to create links to stock data on the Web so that you can prepare a thorough analysis for her next week. However, you do not want to simply create hyperlinks to a Web site; you want to import current data into an Excel worksheet so that the data are always up to date. Angie wants a comparison table of basic stock data, which you can import from a Web site. In addition, you need to do in-depth research on two particular stocks by connecting to a Web site containing historical stock data. Your assistant compiled some historical data and saved it in an XML format. You will import those data into your workbook for additional analysis.

In addition to creating links to external data, you need to format the worksheet data. One challenge you will face is to separate the company names (such as BEST BUY CO., INC.) from the stock symbols (such as BBY) that currently share one column into two columns. After separating the data, you will use text functions to display the data in title or proper case, such as Best Buy Co., Inc., because title case is easier to read than all capital letters. Using text functions will save time so that you do not have to retype the data in the desired format. Finally, you will import data containing open, high, low, and close stock prices from an XML file.

# External Data

Data originate from and are stored in a variety of locations and formats. When you use Excel to manipulate data and perform quantitative analyses, you might obtain data that originate in an external source—somewhere besides an Excel workbook. For example, you might download customer data from a large database stored on your organization's server, or you want to receive a text file containing data you need to manipulate in Excel.

External data may not be properly formatted for your Excel worksheet, but importing external data and formatting them in Excel maintains greater accuracy than if you manually enter the data. Furthermore, importing external data into a worksheet enables you to update the worksheet data based on changes from the external source.

In this section, you will learn how to import external data into an Excel workbook. Specifically, you will learn how to import text files and Access database tables. In addition, you will learn how to create Web queries.

## Importing Data from External Sources

**Importing** is the process of inserting external data—data created or stored in another format—into the current application. Excel enables you to import a variety of data formats directly into Excel either by opening the file using the Open dialog box or by creating a connection or a link to the original data source. Two of the most common file types you can easily import into Excel are text files and Access database files.

When you import external data into Excel but do not maintain a link to the original data source, you **embed** the data within the Excel worksheet. That is, you can edit the data directly within Excel because they do not have a connection to the original data source. Changes in the original data source or the embedded data in Excel do not change the other data; they are two separate datasets.

When you import external data as a connection, you create a link to the original data source. You can refresh the Excel worksheet so that the imported data are updated if any changes are made to the original data source. Before importing data into Excel, decide whether you need to manage the data as a separate dataset in Excel or if you want to maintain a connection to the original data source.

### Import a Text File

A **text file** (indicated by the .txt file extension) is a data file that contains characters, such as letters, numbers, and symbols, including punctuation and spaces. However, a text file does not contain formatting, sound, or video. You can use a text editor, such as Notepad, to create a text file, or you can download data from an organization's database or Web server as a text file. The benefit of a text file is that you can import a text file easily into a variety of programs, such as Excel or Access. After importing data from a text file, you can format the data within Excel.

Text files contain **delimiters**, special characters (such as a tab or space) that separate data. A **tab-delimited file** uses tabs to separate data into columns; a **newline character** is a special character that designates the end of a line and separates data for the next line or row. Figure 8.1 shows a tab-delimited file in Notepad and the imported data in Excel. In the tab-delimited file, the columns do not align; only one tab separates columns. If the user had pressed Tab multiple times to align the data, the data would not have imported correctly into Excel because Excel counts the number of tabs to determine what column the data imports into. An extra tab in a text file imports as a blank cell in Excel.

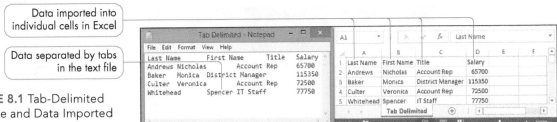

Data imported into individual cells in Excel

Data separated by tabs in the text file

**FIGURE 8.1** Tab-Delimited Text File and Data Imported into Excel

The **comma separated values (CSV) file** uses commas to separate data into columns and a newline character to separate data into rows. Many Web sites, such as census.gov, contain links to download a text file directly into Excel. When you click the download link from a Web site, the data download into a new Excel workbook or the File Download dialog box opens so that you can open the data in Excel or save the dataset. Figure 8.2 shows a CSV file in Notepad and the imported data in Excel. In the CSV file, commas are used only to separate data; commas are *not* used as the thousands separators in values or as punctuation marks. Otherwise, Excel would separate data at the commas used for punctuation or in values.

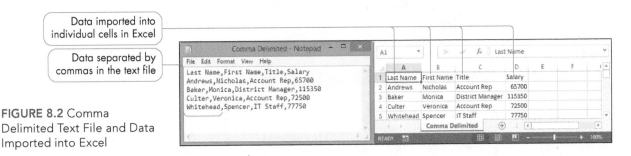

Data imported into individual cells in Excel

Data separated by commas in the text file

**FIGURE 8.2** Comma Delimited Text File and Data Imported into Excel

To import data from a text file into a new Excel workbook, do the following:

**STEP 1**

1. Open the Open dialog box.
2. Click the File Type arrow that currently displays *All Excel Files* and select Text Files.
3. Navigate to the folder that contains the text file, select it, and then click Open.

If you open a file with the .CSV file extension, Excel opens the data immediately in Excel. Because commas delimit the data, data between commas in the CSV file import into individual cells in Excel. Each line within the CSV file becomes a row within Excel.

If you open a file with the .txt file extension, the Text Import Wizard opens, prompting you to specify the data type and other instructions for importing the data during these three major steps:

**Step 1:** Select Delimited or *Fixed width* based on how the data are structured in the text file. Most text files use delimiters to separate data; therefore, you usually select Delimited to import text data. If data in each column contain the same number of characters and spaces are used only to separate columns, you can choose *Fixed width*. A **fixed-width text file** is a file in which each column contains a specific number of characters, such as 5 characters for the first column, 20 for the second column, and so on, to separate the fields.

Set the *Start import at row* value to where you want the data to begin (see Figure 8.3). Look at the *Preview of file* section to see the data in the text file and how they will import based on the *Start import at row* setting. If the text file contains a title or extraneous data extending across multiple columns, do not import from row 1; start importing from the row that contains the actual data.

If the text file contains column headings that describe the contents of each column, click the *My data has headers* check box.

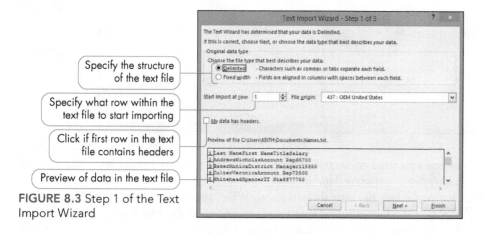

**Specify the structure of the text file**

**Specify what row within the text file to start importing**

**Click if first row in the text file contains headers**

**Preview of data in the text file**

**FIGURE 8.3** Step 1 of the Text Import Wizard

**Step 2:** Do one of the following in the Text Import Wizard (see Figure 8.4).

- If the text file is delimited, click the appropriate delimiter check box, such as Tab. If the text file contains a different delimiter, click the Other check box and type the specific character in the box.

- If the text file contains fixed-width columns, move the column break lines to where the columns begin and end.

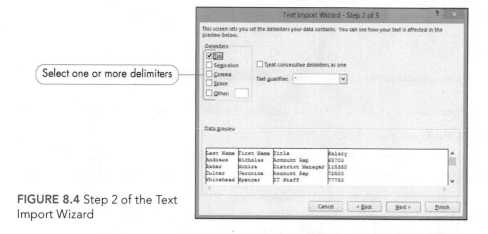

**Select one or more delimiters**

**FIGURE 8.4** Step 2 of the Text Import Wizard

**Step 3:** Select an option in the *Column data format* section for each column you want to import in the Text Import Wizard (see Figure 8.5).

Click the column heading in the *Data preview* window and select an option in the *Column data format* section. If you do not want to import a column, select it and click *Do not import column (skip)*. The default column data format is General, but you can apply a different format. For example, you might want a column of dates to have the Date format.

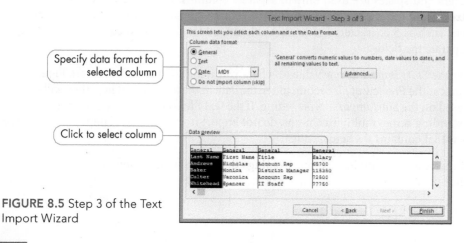

**Specify data format for selected column**

**Click to select column**

**FIGURE 8.5** Step 3 of the Text Import Wizard

After you import data from a text file, review the data in Excel. Typically, you will need to adjust column widths and format the data, such as centering column labels and applying Accounting Number Format to monetary data. Check for and correct any data errors if the data did not import correctly.

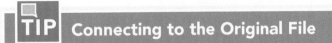

## TIP Connecting to the Original File

When you select an import type, such as From Text, in the Get External Data group on the Data tab, you create a connection to the original data file. This approach enables you to refresh the data in Excel to match any changes made to the original file, as long as the original source file is in the same location.

## Import an Access Database Table or Query

Large amounts of data are often stored in databases, such as an Access database table. However, database programs are less intuitive about manipulating data for quantitative analyses or do not contain the capabilities to do so. For example, Access 2013 does not contain a PivotTable feature. However, you can import database tables or queries into Excel for further analysis. For example, a car dealership uses a database to maintain an inventory of new cars on the lot, but to analyze monthly sales by car model, the manager uses Excel and creates a PivotTable.

When importing an Access database table or query into Excel, you can maintain a connection to the Access data so that the Excel worksheet data are always current. To import an Access database table or query into Excel:

**STEP 2>>**

1. Start Excel, start a new workbook or open an existing workbook, and then click the appropriate worksheet tab to which you want to import the data.
2. Click the DATA tab and click From Access in the Get External Data group to open the Select Data Source dialog box.
3. Select the Access database file that contains data you need to import and click Open.
4. Choose a table or query from the list in the Select Table dialog box (see Figure 8.6). A rectangle icon in the Name column and TABLE in the Type column indicate a table object. The two overlapping rectangles icon in the Name column and VIEW in the Type column indicate a query object. If you want to import more than one table or query, click the *Enable selection of multiple tables* check box and click the check box for each table and query you want to import. Click OK to display the Import Data dialog box (see Figure 8.7).
5. Select how you want to view the data in your workbook, such as Table or PivotTable Report. Select where you want to import the data, such as starting in cell A1 in an existing worksheet or in a new worksheet. Click OK.

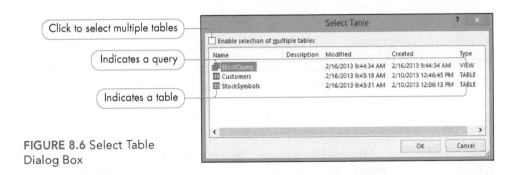

**FIGURE 8.6** Select Table Dialog Box

**FIGURE 8.7** Import Data Dialog Box

If you import the data as a table, Excel formats the data using a default Excel table style. In addition, Excel displays the Table Tools Design tab as well as the filter arrows so that you can sort and filter data. The Table Name box indicates the data type, such as Table, an underscore, and the name of the Access object (see Figure 8.8).

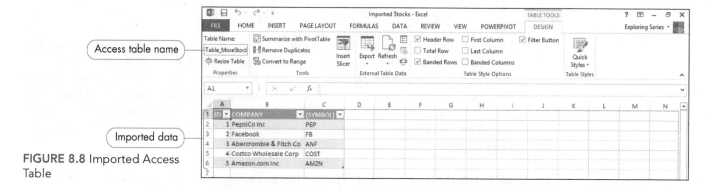

**FIGURE 8.8** Imported Access Table

---

**TIP** **Copying Data from an Access Table**

If you do not want to create a link to the Access database table, you can open the table in Access, select the table including field names, copy it, and then paste the data in Excel.

## Import Data from Other Sources

You can import data from sources other than text files and Access databases. Click From Other Sources in the Get External Data group to display a list of additional sources:

- SQL Server
- Analysis Services
- Windows Azure Marketplace
- OData Data Feed
- XML Data Import
- Data Connection Wizard
- From Microsoft Query

Use Help to learn about each source and the type of data you can import. Some services require a username and password. Some marketplace datasets require a fee to obtain.

## Creating a Web Query

You might need to frequently update worksheet data you imported from a particular Web page. For example, you might want to analyze daily stock prices, traffic accident reports, or airport delays. You can create a *Web query* to set up a connection to a table on a Web page.

The Web query creates a link to the Web page so that you can update the results in Excel without importing the data again. To create a Web query, do the following:

STEP 3 »
1. Click the DATA tab in Excel and click From Web in the Get External Data group to display the New Web Query dialog box (see Figure 8.9).

STEP 4 »
2. Type or paste the URL in the Address box and click Go to display the Web page. Click Yes if the Script Error dialog box opens. If a Security Warning message box opens, click the appropriate button to respond.

3. Scroll within the Web page to the specific data you want.

4. Click the yellow selection icon with a right-pointing arrow to select the table you want. The icon changes to a green box with a check mark, and the table data are selected.

5. Click Options to display the Web Query Options dialog box. Select desired formatting. *None* imports the data without any formatting. Select *Rich text formatting only* or *Full HTML formatting* to maintain formatting, such as bold for the imported data. Click OK.

6. Click Import at the bottom-right corner of the New Web Query dialog box to open the Import Data dialog box.

7. Click either *Existing worksheet* and enter a cell reference of the top-left cell where you want the data to import or click *New worksheet* and click OK.

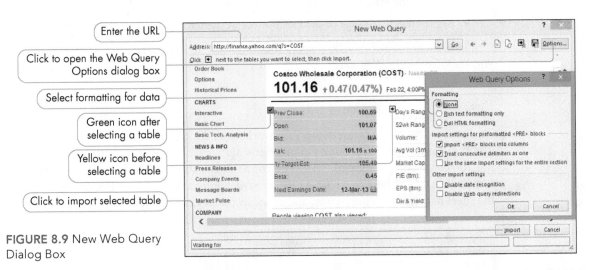

**FIGURE 8.9** New Web Query Dialog Box

---

 **TIP** **Limitations of a Web Query**

Before setting up a Web query, you should be aware of its limitations. First, not all Web pages contain data that are structured as a table. Data may *appear* to be in a table format, but if they are not formatted a particular way, you will not be able to create a Web query to the data. Second, Excel connects a Web query to a specific URL. If the URL changes, you must change the URL specified in your Web query to prevent errors. Third, if you have to log in to a Web site, the query generally will not work because it has no built-in feature to store your login and password.

---

**TIP** **Copying or Downloading Data from a Web Page**

If you do not want to create a link to a Web page, you can select the data on the Web page in a Web browser, copy them, and then paste the data in Excel. Some Web pages have links that will download a CSV file that directly opens into Excel or one you can save to your computer and then open from within Excel.

# Managing Connections

When you import data using the options in the Get External Data group, Excel creates a link to the original data source so that you can update the data quickly in Excel. After you create the initial connection, you might want to view or modify the connection. The Connections group on the Data tab contains options to manage your external data connections.

## Refresh Connections

Data on a Web page or data in an external database may change periodically. Although you created a connection to the external data within Excel, the data in the database or on a Web page may have changed. For example, if you created a connection to a Web page containing hourly weather, the weather may have changed after you created the connection. To ensure that the Excel data are current, you need to *refresh* the connections to the original external data source periodically. Do one of the following to refresh data:

**STEP 5》**

- Click Refresh All in the Connections group to refresh all connections in the active workbook.
- Click the Refresh All arrow in the Connections group and select Refresh to update data for the range containing the active cell.
- Right-click in a range of data and select Refresh to update that data only.

The status bar will briefly display *Running background query...(Click here to cancel)* if you are refreshing a Web query.

## Display Connections

To display a list of all connections in a workbook, click Connections in the Connections group to display the Workbook Connections dialog box (see Figure 8.10). To see where a specific connection is located, select the connection name in the top portion of the dialog box and click *Click here to see where the selected connections are used.* The dialog box shows the sheet name, connection name, and range in the worksheet.

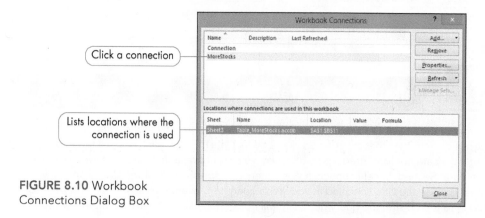

**FIGURE 8.10** Workbook Connections Dialog Box

You can remove a connection if you no longer want to link the data to the external data source. After you disconnect the data in Excel from the external data source, you will not be able to refresh the data. To remove a connection, do the following:

1. Select it in the Workbook Connections dialog box.
2. Click Remove.
3. Click OK in the warning message box and click Close in the Workbook Connections dialog box.

## Set Connection Properties

***Data range properties*** are settings that control how imported data in cells connect to their source data. These properties also specify how the data display in Excel, how often the data are refreshed, and what happens if the number of rows in the data range changes based upon the current data in the external data source. To display the properties, do one of the following:

- Click Properties in the Connections group.
- Click the Refresh All arrow and select Connection Properties.
- Click Connections in the Connections group and click Properties.

When you click Properties in the Connections group, the External Data Range Properties dialog box displays (see Figure 8.11). This dialog box looks slightly different based on the type of external data you imported and based on which option you use to display the dialog box. For example, the dialog box has fewer options for a connection to an Access database table than it does for a Web query.

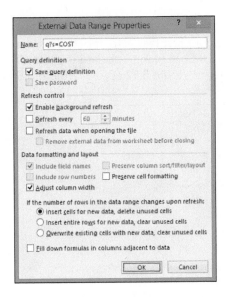

**FIGURE 8.11** External Data Range Properties Dialog Box

*Quick* Concepts

1. What is the purpose of delimiters in a text file? Name two common text file delimiters. ***pp. 268–269***

2. What is the difference in opening a text file directly in Excel and using the Get External Data option to import text file data? ***p. 271***

3. What is the purpose in creating a Web query? Give two examples of Web pages for which it would make sense to create a Web query. ***pp. 272–273***

Watch the Video for this Hands-On Exercise!

MyITLab®
HOE1 Training

## 1 External Data

Angie e-mailed a list of 10 companies for you to research. In addition, you want to include a list of 10 other companies that is stored in an Access database table for her further consideration. You will research five companies on each list and then create a Web query to a specific company's historical stock information. Each day, you will need to refresh the connection to import the most up-to-date data into your worksheet.

**Skills covered:** Import a Text File • Import an Access Database Table • Create Web Queries for Multiple Stocks • Create a Web Query for Historical Stock Data • Maintain Connections

### STEP 1 >> IMPORT A TEXT FILE

Angie created her list of companies in Notepad, so your first task is to import the data into Excel. You do not need to create a connection to the text file because Angie does not plan to update the text file, so you will simply open the file directly from the Open dialog box in Excel. Refer to Figure 8.12 as you complete Step 1.

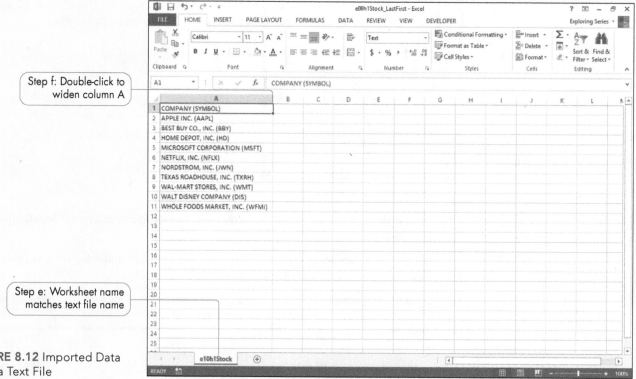

Step f: Double-click to widen column A

Step e: Worksheet name matches text file name

**FIGURE 8.12** Imported Data from a Text File

a.  Start Excel, click **Open Other Workbooks** in the bottom-left corner of the start window, and then double-click **Computer** to display the Open dialog box.

b.  Click the **File Type arrow** that currently displays *All Excel Files*, select **Text Files**, select *e08h1Stock*, and then click **Open**.

 The Text Import Wizard dialog box opens. Accept the defaults: Delimited and 1 as *Start at row number*.

**c.** Click the **My data has headers check box** and click **Next**.

The *Text Import Wizard – Step 2 of 3* dialog box contains options to specify the type of delimiter(s) contained in the text file. This text file does not contain delimiters. You could use the opening parenthesis as a delimiter, but you will use text functions in Hands-On Exercise 2 to separate the company names from the stock symbols.

> **TROUBLESHOOTING**: If you select Space as a delimiter, you will import company names into separate columns. For example, the text *Home Depot, Inc.*, will appear in three separate cells. You cannot use the comma as a delimiter for a similar reason: Home Depot will appear in one cell and Inc. will appear in a separate cell.

**d.** Deselect all check boxes in the *Delimiters* section and click **Next**.

The *Text Import Wizard – Step 3 of 3* dialog box lets you select each column and specify its data type.

**e.** Click **Text** in the *Column data format* section and click **Finish**.

Excel imports the data from the text file into the first column of the worksheet. The worksheet name matches the name of the text file: *e08h1Stock*.

**f.** Double-click between the column A and B headings to widen column A.

**g.** Click the **FILE tab**, click **Save As**, double-click **Computer**, type **e08h1stock_LastFirst** in the **File name box**, click the **Save as type arrow**, select **Excel Workbook**, and then click **Save**.

## STEP 2 ≫ IMPORT AN ACCESS DATABASE TABLE

You created an Access database table that contains additional company names and their stock symbols. You want to import that into the Excel workbook so that you will be able to analyze more stock options for Angie. Refer to Figure 8.13 as you complete Step 2.

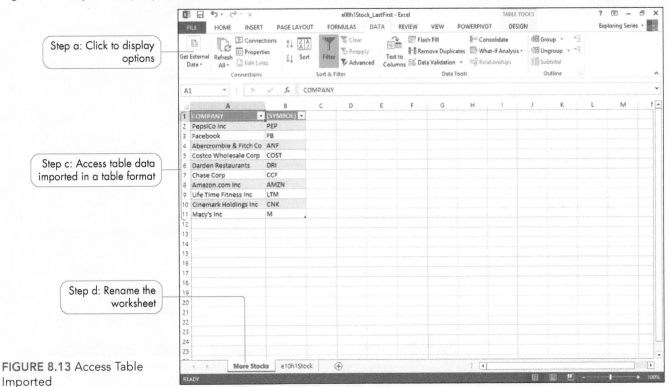

**FIGURE 8.13** Access Table Imported

**a.** Click the **DATA tab**, click **Get External Data** (if necessary), and then click **From Access**.

**b.** Select **e08h1MoreStocks** in the Select Data Source dialog box and click **Open**.

The Import Data dialog box opens so that you can specify how to the view data and where to place it.

**c.** Make sure *Table* is selected, click **New worksheet**, and then click **OK**.

You imported the Access data in a new worksheet. Notice that when you import data from a text file, the data import into a range of cells, whereas the Access import formats data as a table.

---

**TROUBLESHOOTING**: If you accepted the default set to *Existing worksheet* and *=$A$1*, Excel will import the data starting in cell A1 and move the existing data to the right. If this happens, select columns A and B, delete them, and then start step a over again.

---

**d.** Double-click the **Sheet1 tab**, type **More Stocks**, and then press **Enter** to rename the worksheet.

**e.** Save the workbook.

## STEP 3 ➤➤ CREATE WEB QUERIES FOR MULTIPLE STOCKS

Based on your past analysis, you selected five stocks from Angie's list and five stocks from your list for further analysis. You want to create a worksheet that compares data for these 10 stocks. However, you will create two separate Web queries of five stocks each. You know from experience that if you try to enter more than five stock symbols at a time, the results will show fewer details than if you limit the Web query to five queries. Refer to Figure 8.14 as you complete Step 3.

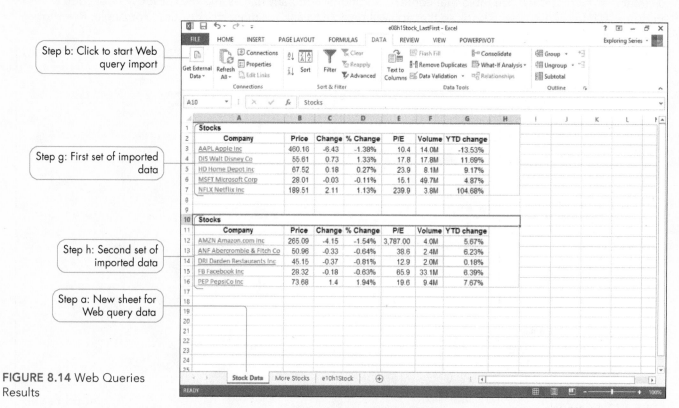

**FIGURE 8.14** Web Queries Results

**a.** Click **New sheet** to the right of the e08h1_Stock sheet tab and drag the sheet tab to the left of More Stocks. Rename it **Stock Data**. Make sure **cell A1** is the active cell.

**b.** Click the **DATA tab**, click **Get External Data** (if necessary), and then click **From Web**.

The New Web Query dialog box opens, similar to a Web browser window. Maximize the dialog box if you want.

**c.** Type **www.money.cnn.com** in the **Address box** and click **Go**.

The Web page loads within the New Web Query dialog box.

**d.** Type **AAPL,DIS,HD,MSFT,NFLX** in the **Enter symbol or keyword box** on the right side of the Web page and click **Search**.

> **TROUBLESHOOTING**: Make sure you spell the symbol names correctly and separate them with commas. If you mistype a stock symbol or leave out a comma, the results will be inaccurate or will produce an error message.

The Web page loads the stock results below the heading *Multiquote results*. A yellow selection icon with a right-pointing arrow displays to the left of the subheading *Stocks*.

**e.** Click the **yellow selection icon** to the left of the *Stocks* subheading to select the table of multistock data.

The icon is now green with a check mark, indicating you selected this table to import.

**f.** Click **Options** in the top-right corner of the dialog box to open the Web Query Options dialog box, click **Full HTML formatting**, and then click **OK**.

The Full HTML formatting option maintains hyperlinks to individual company data, header formatting, and other Web page formatting.

**g.** Click **Import** in the bottom-right corner of the dialog box and click **OK** in the Import Data dialog box.

The headings and table data are imported into the range A1:H7, with column H appearing empty.

**h.** Click **cell A10**. Repeat steps b through g, substituting **AMZN,ANF,DRI,FB,PEP** in step d. Save the workbook.

The headings and table data are imported into the range A10:H16, with column H appearing empty. Figure 8.14 shows that Netflix had the highest positive year-to-date (YTD) change. (Note: Your results will differ based on the day you perform the Web query.)

## STEP 4 ≫ CREATE A WEB QUERY FOR HISTORICAL STOCK DATA

You want to create a Web query to display historical data for Netflix since it has the highest positive year-to-date (YTD) change. The money.cnn.com Web site does not have a built-in table to display historical data for a particular stock, so you will use finance.yahoo.com. Refer to Figure 8.15 as you complete Step 4.

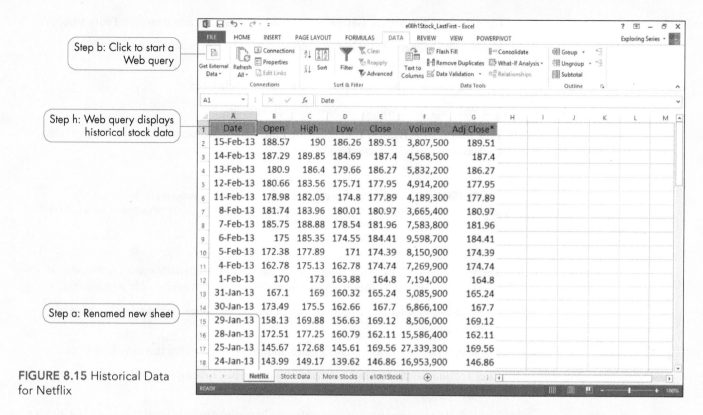

Step b: Click to start a Web query

Step h: Web query displays historical stock data

Step a: Renamed new sheet

**FIGURE 8.15** Historical Data for Netflix

a. Click **New sheet**, move it to the left of Stock Data, and rename it **Netflix**. Make sure **cell A1** is the active cell.

b. Click **Get External Data** and click **From Web**.

   The New Web Query dialog box opens.

c. Select any existing text in the **Address box**, type **www.finance.yahoo.com**, and then click **Go**.

> **TROUBLESHOOTING**: If a Script Error dialog box opens, click Yes to continue running scripts on this page. This error may occur several times.

d. Click in the box to the left of *Get Quotes*, type **NFLX**, and then click **Get Quotes**.

   A Web page containing information about Netflix, Inc. displays.

e. Scroll down and click **Historical Prices** on the left side.

f. Scroll down to see the *Prices* section and click the **yellow selection icon** next to the Date column heading to select the table containing the data.

   The icon changes to a green box with a check mark.

> **TROUBLESHOOTING**: Make sure you click the yellow selection arrow to the top-left of the Date column heading; do not click the yellow selection arrow to the left of the PRICES heading.

g. Click **Options** in the top-right corner of the dialog box to open the Web Query Options dialog box, click **Full HTML formatting**, and then click **OK**.

h. Click **Import** in the bottom-right corner of the dialog box and click **OK** in the Import Data dialog box. Save the workbook.

   You will review the historical stock data with Angie during your next meeting.

# STEP 5 >> MAINTAIN CONNECTIONS

You want to change the refresh property so that it will refresh every 30 minutes for the Web queries you imported for Angie's potential stock investment. This change will enable you to monitor stock price changes throughout the day. Refer to Figure 8.16 as you complete Step 5.

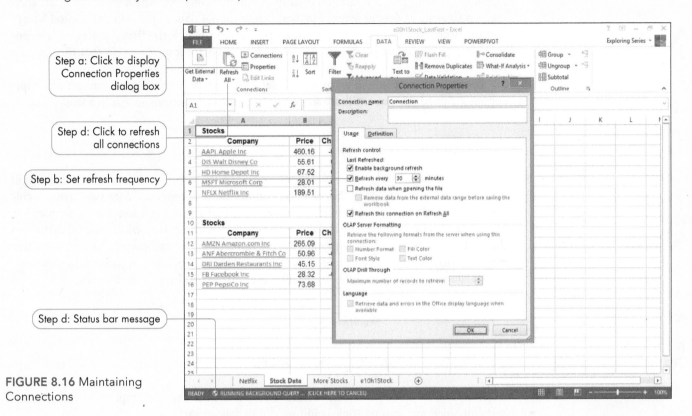

Step a: Click to display Connection Properties dialog box

Step d: Click to refresh all connections

Step b: Set refresh frequency

Step d: Status bar message

**FIGURE 8.16** Maintaining Connections

a. Click the **Stock Data worksheet** and click **cell A10**, if necessary. Click the **DATA tab** (if necessary) and click **Properties** in the Connections group.

   A dialog box opens so that you can modify the properties for the Web query.

b. Click the **Refresh every check box**, type **30** in the **minutes box**, and then click **OK**.

   The second Web query should update every 30 minutes to reflect any changes that occur on the Web page.

c. Click **cell A1**, set its refresh setting to **30** minutes, and then click **OK**.

   The first Web query should update every 30 minutes to reflect any changes that occur on the Web page.

d. Click **Refresh All** in the Connections group.

   The status bar displays *Running background query* and the connected data update.

e. Save the workbook. Keep the workbook open if you plan to continue with Hands-On Exercise 2. If not, close the workbook and exit Excel.

# Text Manipulation

When you import data from external sources or need to modify a workbook created by someone else, the data may not be structured in a way that meets your needs. For example, data might import into one column instead of multiple columns, which would facilitate sorting and filtering at deeper levels. Furthermore, external data might be in all capital letters, and you want to display the data in title case—text in which the first letter of each major word is capitalized but prepositions such as *in* and *on* are lowercase—so that the data are easier to read. Excel contains features to help you manipulate text to fit your needs.

In this section, you will learn how to separate text stored in one column into multiple columns. In addition, you will use some text functions to manipulate text in a worksheet.

## Converting Text to Columns

Whether you use someone else's workbook or import data from external sources, data might display in one column when they would be more useful if separated into two or more columns. For example, a column might contain titles, first names, and last names, such as Mr. John Doe. You need to sort the list alphabetically by last name, but you cannot do that when the first and last names are combined in the same cell. You can use the Text to Columns command to split the contents in one column into separate columns. Figure 8.17 shows combined data in column A and the results after converting text into three columns.

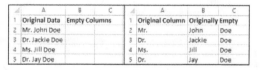

**FIGURE 8.17** Combined and Separated Data

The *Convert Text to Columns* Wizard is very similar to the Text Import Wizard. To convert combined text into multiple columns, do the following:

1. Select the column containing the text you want to separate.
2. Click the DATA tab and click *Text to Columns* in the Data Tools group.
3. Use the *Convert Text to Columns* Wizard to distribute the data. Specify the file type, such as Delimited or *Fixed width*, and click Next.
4. Specify the delimiters, such as a Tab or Space, in the *Convert Text to Columns* Wizard—Step 2 of 3. The data shown in Figure 8.17 are delimited by spaces. The wizard can use the space to separate the title and first and last names in this example. Click Next.
5. Select the column data format, such as Text, in the *Convert Text to Columns* Wizard—Step 3 of 3, and click Finish.

> **TIP** Allow Room for Separation
>
> Allow enough columns to the right of the column containing text to separate to avoid overwriting data. Excel does *not* insert new columns. It separates data by placing them into adjoining columns. If you have a first name, middle name, and last name all in one column and you separate to get a first name column, middle name column, and last name column, you must have two empty columns. If the columns on the right side of the original column to split are not empty, Excel will overwrite existing data.

# Manipulating Text with Functions

Excel has 24 functions that are specifically designed to change or manipulate text strings. The Function Library group on the Formulas tab contains a Text command that, when clicked, displays a list of text functions. You can also access the text functions from the Insert Function dialog box. Some of the most commonly used text functions are CONCATENATE, PROPER, UPPER, LOWER, and SUBSTITUTE.

## Combine Text with the CONCATENATE Function

Text labels are often called text strings. A text string is not used for calculation. You can combine text strings stored in two or more cells into one cell. For example, you might want to combine a last name (e.g., Doe) and first name (e.g., John) stored in two cells into one text string to look like this: *Doe, John*. In this example, you included a comma and a space after the last name. The ***CONCATENATE function*** joins between 2 and 255 individual text strings into one text string. In Figure 8.18, the first name is in cell B2, the last name is in cell C2, and cell E2 contains the =CONCATENATE(C2," ",B2) function. The comma and space included inside quotes produce *Doe, John*. When constructing a CONCATENATE function, place any data (such as commas and spaces) correctly within quotation marks so that you get the desired result. The text items can be strings of text, numbers, or single-cell references.

=CONCATENATE(text1,text2)

**FIGURE 8.18** Concatenation: Join Text Strings

**TIP** **Another Way to Concatenate**

Use the ampersand (&) operator instead of the CONCATENATE function to join text items. For example, =A4&B4 returns the same value as =CONCATENATE(A4,B4).

## Change Text Case with Text Functions

Data come in a variety of case or capitalization styles, such as ALL CAPS, Title Case, and lowercase. Depending on your usage of data, you may need to change the case in a worksheet. Excel contains three functions to change the case or capitalization of text: PROPER, UPPER, and LOWER. Figure 8.19 illustrates the results of these three functions.

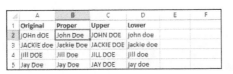

**FIGURE 8.19** Results of Text Functions

**STEP 2》** Large amounts of capitalized text are difficult to read. Use the ***PROPER function*** to capitalize the first letter of each word in a text string, including the first letter of prepositions (such as *of*) and articles (such as *a*). The PROPER function converts all other letters to lowercase. The text argument is a text string that must be enclosed in quotation marks, a formula that returns text, or a reference to a cell that contains text that you want to partially capitalize. In Figure 8.19, cell B2 contains =PROPER(A2) to change the case to proper case, such as *John Doe*.

=PROPER(text)

The **UPPER function** converts text strings to uppercase letters. The text argument is the text to be converted to all capitals and can be a reference or text string. Use this function when a cell or range contains text in lowercase letters and you need the text to be formatted in all uppercase letters. In Figure 8.19, cell C2 contains =UPPER(A2) to change the case to uppercase letters, such as *JOHN DOE*.

=UPPER(text)

The **LOWER function** converts all uppercase letters in a text string to lowercase. The text argument is text you want to convert to lowercase. In Figure 8.19, cell D2 contains =LOWER(A2) to change the case to lowercase letters, such as *john doe*.

=LOWER(text)

## Use the SUBSTITUTE Function

**STEP 3 »** The **SUBSTITUTE function** substitutes or replaces new text for old text in a text string. For example, if a company changes its name, you can use the SUBSTITUTE function to replace the old company name with the new company name.

=SUBSTITUTE(text,old_text,new_text,instance_num)

*Text* is the original text or reference to a cell that is to be substituted, *old_text* is the text to be replaced, and *new_text* is the text you want to replace old_text with. *Instance_num* specifies which occurrence of old_text you want to replace with new_text. When instance_num is specified, only that instance is changed. If you do not include instance_num, all occurrences are changed.

## Use Other Text Functions

Other text functions help you achieve a variety of text manipulations. Table 8.1 lists a few other common text functions and their descriptions.

| TABLE 8.1  Additional Text Functions | |
| --- | --- |
| **Function** | **Description** |
| TRIM(Text) | Removes leading and trailing spaces in a text string but maintains spaces between words in a text string |
| LEFT(Text,Num_chars) | Returns the specified number of characters from the start of a text string |
| RIGHT(Text, Num_chars) | Returns the specified number of characters from the end of a text string |
| MID(Text,Start_num,Num_chars) | Returns the specified number of characters from the middle of a text string, based on a starting position and length |

### Nested Text Functions

Text functions are often used in nested functions. You can nest text functions, such as nesting the CONCATENATE function inside an UPPER function argument. For example, =UPPER((CONCATENATE(A2," ",A3)) concatenates the contents of cells A2, a comma and a space, and the contents of cell A3. The concatenated result is then converted to uppercase.

# Using Flash Fill

**Flash Fill** enables you to enter data in one or two cells to set an example, and Excel completes the data entry for you. Often, you use Flash Fill in conjunction with data in existing columns. Data within a column must be structured in a similar way for Flash Fill to recognize data patterns. For example, in Figure 8.20, column A contains cities and state abbreviations. Instead of using Text to Columns, you can type the first city name in a column adjacent to the dataset and use Flash Fill to create a column of city names only. To use Flash Fill, do the following:

STEP 4 »

1. Enter data that use part of existing data in a column in the dataset.
2. Press Enter and start typing the second sample data. Flash Fill should identify the pattern and complete the column.

If you type only one sample entry and leave that as the active cell, you can click Fill in the Editing group on the Home tab and select Flash Fill to complete the rest of the column. If Excel can detect a pattern, it will fill in the data in the rest of the column. If Excel cannot detect a pattern, it displays an error message. In order for Flash Fill to work, the existing data must be structured in some pattern Excel can recognize. Flash Fill can often perform the same tasks as some of the text functions, such as PROPER and CONCATENATE.

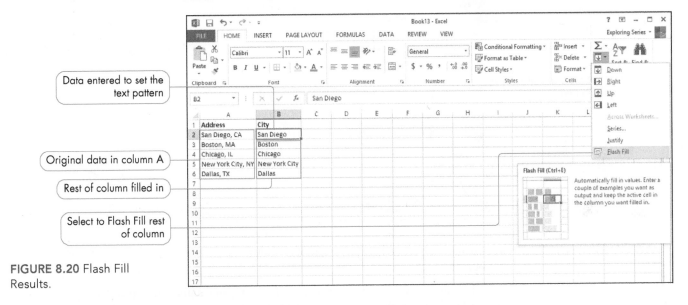

**Data entered to set the text pattern**

**Original data in column A**

**Rest of column filled in**

**Select to Flash Fill rest of column**

**FIGURE 8.20** Flash Fill Results.

*Quick* Concepts

1. What is the purpose of the Text to Columns feature? Provide one example of when it would be useful. **p. 282**

2. What is the difference among the PROPER, UPPER, and LOWER functions? **pp. 283–284**

3. How must data be structured in order for Flash Fill to work? **p. 285**

# Hands-On Exercises

Watch the Video for this Hands-On Exercise!

MyITLab®
HOE2 Training

## 2 Text Manipulation

After importing the stock data from the text file that Angie gave you, you want to use text functions to manipulate the text within the worksheet. You want to make the data easier to access and display in multiple formats for future usage.

**Skills covered:** Convert Text to Columns • Use the PROPER Function • Use the SUBSTITUTE Function • Use Flash Fill

---

### STEP 1 ≫ CONVERT TEXT TO COLUMNS

Currently, the e08h1Stock worksheet contains the company name and stock symbol in the same column. You want to separate the company names and stock symbols so that you can sort or filter by stock symbols more easily in the future. Refer to Figure 8.21 as you complete Step 1.

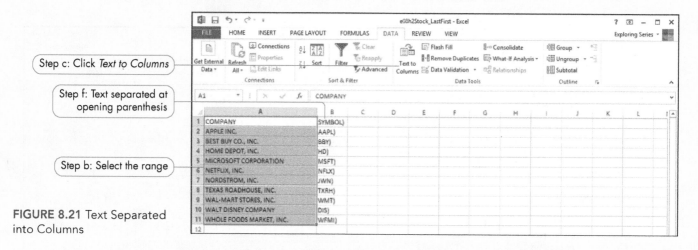

Step c: Click *Text to Columns*

Step f: Text separated at opening parenthesis

Step b: Select the range

**FIGURE 8.21** Text Separated into Columns

a. Open *e08h1Stock_LastFirst* and save it as **e08h2Stock_LastFirst**. Click the **e08h1stock worksheet tab**.

b. Select the **range A1:A11**, which contains the company names and stock symbols. Copy the data and paste them starting in **cell A20**. Press **Esc** and select the **range A1:A11** again.

   Before using Text to Columns, you copied the data so that you can use Flash Fill later in this exercise.

c. Click the **DATA tab** if necessary and click **Text to Columns** in the Data Tools group.

   The Convert Text to Columns Wizard dialog box opens.

d. Leave *Delimited* selected and click **Next**.

   Because the selected text has multiple-word company names with spaces and commas such as *Home Depot, Inc.*, you cannot use the space or comma as a delimiter. The best option is to create a custom delimiter character: the opening parenthesis.

e. Deselect all check boxes, click the **Other check box**, and then type ( in the **Other box**.

   The *Data preview* shows the data in two columns: company names and symbols. Because you used the opening parenthesis as the delimiter, Excel removes that symbol from the text. The closing parenthesis remains at the end of the stock symbol.

> **TROUBLESHOOTING:** If you do not deselect all but the Other check box, the data may not separate correctly into columns.

f. Click **Next**, click **Text** in the *Column data format* section, click the **second column** in the *Data preview* section, click **Text**, and then click **Finish**.

g. Save the workbook.

## STEP 2 ≫ USE THE PROPER FUNCTION

You want to improve the readability of the company names by displaying the data in title case using the PROPER function. Refer to Figure 8.22 as you complete Step 2.

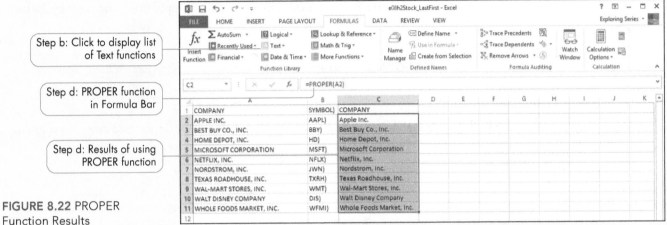

**FIGURE 8.22** PROPER Function Results

a. Type **COMPANY** in all capital letters in **cell C1** and press **Enter**.

b. Click the **FORMULAS tab**, click **Text** in the Function Library group, and then select **PROPER**.

   The Function Arguments dialog box opens.

c. Click **cell A2** to enter it in the Text box and click **OK**.

   The results of the PROPER function return the proper case of APPLE INC. as Apple Inc.

d. Double-click the **cell C2 fill handle** to copy the formula down the column.

e. Increase the width of column C. Save the workbook.

## STEP 3 ≫ USE THE SUBSTITUTE FUNCTION

You notice that the second column containing the stock symbols still shows the closing parenthesis. The opening parenthesis was removed when you used it as the delimiter to separate the company names from the symbols in Step 1. Now you will use the SUBSTITUTE function to remove the closing parenthesis. Refer to Figure 8.23 as you complete Step 3.

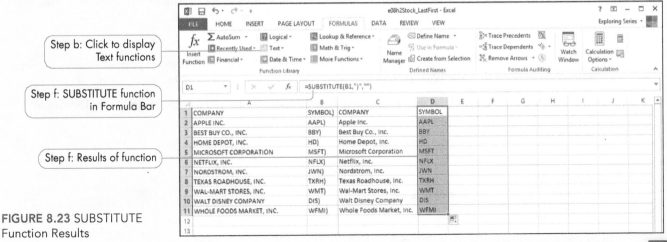

**FIGURE 8.23** SUBSTITUTE Function Results

**a.** Click **cell D1**.

**b.** Click **Text** in the Function Library group and select **SUBSTITUTE**.

The Function Arguments dialog box opens so that you can specify the arguments for the SUBSTITUTE function.

**c.** Click **cell B1** to enter it in the Text box.

**d.** Press **Tab** and type ) in the **Old_text box**.

**e.** Press **Tab** and type "" in the **New_text box**.

You are replacing the closing parenthesis with a null or empty string, indicated by the two double quotation marks.

> **TROUBLESHOOTING:** If you attempt to leave the New_text argument blank, an error will occur.

**f.** Click **OK** and double-click the **cell D1 fill handle** to copy the formula down the column. Save the workbook.

## STEP 4 >> USE FLASH FILL

While you have been using text functions, you want to experiment with using Flash Fill on the company names and stock symbols. Refer to Figure 8.24 as you complete Step 4.

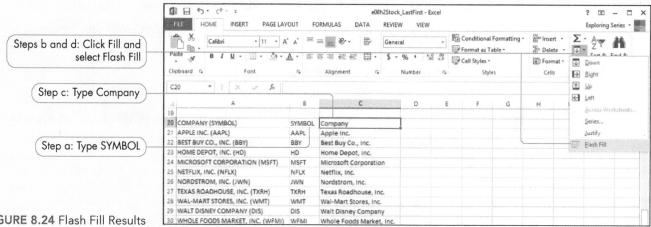

**FIGURE 8.24** Flash Fill Results

**a.** Type **SYMBOL** in **cell B20** and press **Ctrl+Enter**.

**b.** Click the **HOME tab**, click **Fill** in the Editing group, and then select **Flash Fill**.

Excel detects that you entered SYMBOL without the parentheses and was able to use that data entry to fill in the stock symbols without parentheses.

**c.** Type **Company** in **cell C20** and press **Ctrl+Enter**.

**d.** Click **Fill** in the Editing group and select **Flash Fill** to fill in the company names in proper case. Widen column C so that the company names fit within the column.

**e.** Save the workbook. Keep the workbook open if you plan to continue with Hands-On Exercise 3. If not, close the workbook and exit Excel.

# Templates, Styles, and Macros

## Standardizing Workbooks

## OBJECTIVES AFTER YOU READ THIS CHAPTER, YOU WILL BE ABLE TO:

1. Select a template p. 290
2. Apply themes and backgrounds p. 291
3. Apply cell styles p. 293
4. Create and use a template p. 299
5. Protect a cell, a worksheet, and a workbook p. 300

6. Create a macro p. 309
7. Create macro buttons p. 312
8. Set macro security p. 313
9. Create a sub procedure p. 319
10. Create a custom function p. 321

## CASE STUDY | Staff Accounting Services

Recently, you took a position as the manager of staff accounting at EBL, Ltd., a regional information technology (IT) company based in Denver, Colorado, with additional offices in Salt Lake City, Utah, and Reno, Nevada. The company provides computer and data network consultation services to individuals, small businesses, and nonprofits. The previous manager used a paper-based system to prepare expense reports, invoices, and payroll statements. However, this was a time-consuming process and required manual recalculation when any values changed.

Because of your extensive experience using Excel, you want to start automating these tasks. You decide to start with the monthly travel expense report form. Because each office utilizes the same procedures, you want to adapt an Excel template to use as a model for travel expense documentation. The template needs to be generic enough to accommodate a range of options, but it also needs to maintain a standard design to facilitate easy data entry.

You will customize the template by applying cell styles to give the form a more polished look and then create macros to perform a series of tasks, such as clearing the values to reset the form if needed and printing the expense report worksheet for management approval.

# Templates, Themes, and Styles

Designing the perfect workbook can be time consuming. By now, you know you have to plan the layout before you enter data to minimize data-entry changes later. You decide what column and row labels are needed to describe the data, where to place the labels, and how to format the labels. In addition, you enter and format quantitative data, such as applying Accounting Number Format and decreasing the number of decimal places. The longer you work for the same department or organization, the more you will notice that you create the same types of workbooks. Excel has the right tools to improve your productivity in developing consistently formatted workbooks. Some of these tools include templates, themes, backgrounds, and styles.

In this section, you will select an Excel template. After opening the template, you will apply a theme, display a background, and apply cell styles.

## Selecting a Template

**STEP 1** A ***template*** is a partially completed document that you use as a model to create other documents that have the same structure and purpose. A template typically contains standard labels, formulas, and formatting but may contain little or no quantitative data. Templates help ensure consistency and standardization for similar workbooks, such as detailed sales reports for all 12 months of a year. When you start Excel, you are presented with a gallery of templates. If you are already working within a workbook, click the File tab and click New. The Backstage view displays a gallery of featured templates (see Figure 9.1). You can select from templates you have recently used, sample templates that were installed with the software, or templates you created, or download new templates. To create a workbook based on a template, do the following:

1. Click a sample template, such as *Travel expense report*.
2. A pop-up window will display a sample of the selected template (see Figure 9.2).
3. Click Create to load the template data as a new workbook.

**FIGURE 9.1** Template Thumbnails

The *Search for online templates* box allows you to search Office.com for a particular template by entering your search conditions and pressing Enter. Start searching, or you can select a template from a category, such as Budgets. These templates are created by Microsoft, a Microsoft partner, or a member of the Microsoft community. To download an Office.com template, do the following:

1. Click a template category, such as Expense. The Backstage view then displays thumbnails representing the various templates in that category.
2. Click the template thumbnail representing the template you want to download. A pop-up window displays information about the selected template, such as the template name and creator and the download size (see Figure 9.2).
3. Click Create. The Download Template message box displays briefly, after which the template is opened as a workbook in Excel.

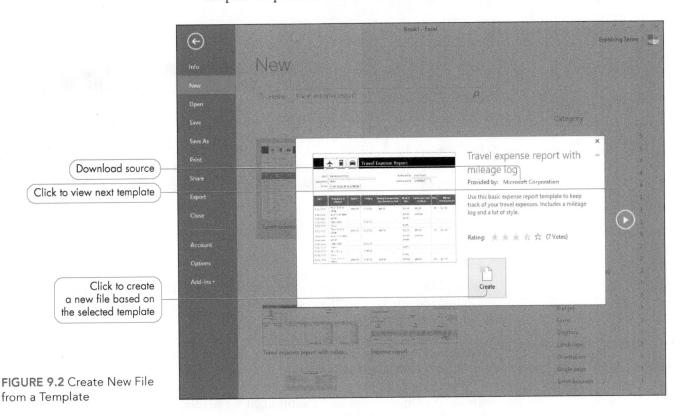

**FIGURE 9.2** Create New File from a Template

Downloading the template does not save it to a storage location. You must save the workbook on a storage device. When you save a workbook from a downloaded template for the first time, the Save As dialog box defaults to SkyDrive in Windows 8; however, you can select another location in which to save the workbook.

## Applying Themes and Backgrounds

**STEP 2**>> In addition to selecting a template, you might want to apply a theme or insert a background to create a consistent look with the workbooks you create. A *theme* is a collection of formats that include coordinating colors, fonts, and special effects to provide a stylish appearance. You can apply a theme to a workbook to give it a consistent look with other workbooks used in your department or organization. Most organizations have a style that encompasses particular fonts, colors, and a logo or trademark on corporate stationery, advertisements, and Web pages. You can use themes in Excel workbooks to match the corporate "look and feel." Some of the Excel theme names match theme names in other Office applications so that you can provide continuity and consistency in all of your documents. To apply a theme to all worksheets in a workbook, do the following:

1. Click the PAGE LAYOUT tab.
2. Click Themes in the Themes group. The Office theme is presented first; the other built-in themes are listed alphabetically in the Themes gallery (see Figure 9.3).
3. Position the pointer over each theme to display a Live Preview of how the theme would format existing data on the current worksheet.
4. Click a theme to make it active.

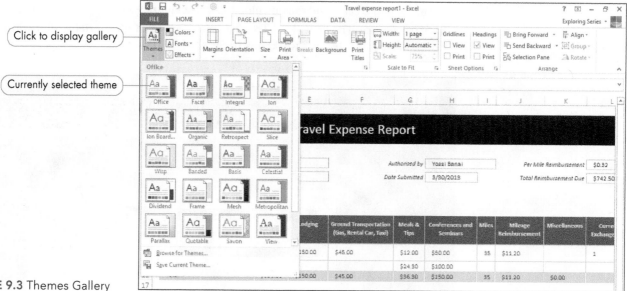

**FIGURE 9.3** Themes Gallery

## Customize a Theme

After applying a theme, you can customize the three elements that comprise the theme: colors, fonts, and effects. The Themes group on the Page Layout tab contains commands to customize your theme. When you click Colors, you can select from a gallery of colors, or you can select Customize Colors to define the text, background, accent, hyperlink, and followed hyperlink colors. If you create and name your own color theme, that theme name will appear in the *Custom* section of the Colors menu.

Theme fonts contain a coordinating heading and body text font for each theme. For example, the Office theme uses Calibri Light for headings and Calibri for cell entries. To select a theme font, click Fonts in the Themes group and select a theme font, or select Customize Fonts to define your own theme fonts.

Theme effects are special effects that control the design differences in objects, such as shapes, SmartArt, and object borders. To select a theme effect, click Effects in the Themes group, position the mouse pointer over an effect to see a Live Preview of how that effect will affect objects, and click the desired effect to apply it to your workbook.

## Apply a Background

**STEP 3** Excel enables you to use graphics as the background of a worksheet. The effect is similar to placing a background on a Web page. A ***background*** is an image placed behind the worksheet data. For example, you might want to use the corporate logo as your background, or you might want a "Confidential" graphic image to remind onscreen viewers that the worksheet contains corporate trade secrets. (If you want an image to appear behind data on a printed worksheet, insert the image as a watermark in a header.) Be careful in selecting and using backgrounds, because the images can distract users from comprehending the quantitative data. A subtle, pale image is less likely to distract a workbook user than a bright, vividly colored image. To add a background to a worksheet, do the following:

1. Click Background in the Page Setup group on the PAGE LAYOUT tab to open the Insert Pictures dialog box.

2. Select the picture file, such as a jpeg or bitmap file, that you want to use as a background.

3. Click Insert.

The image, like background images in Web pages, is tiled across your worksheet (see Figure 9.4). The background image displays only in the worksheet onscreen; it does not print. Notice that Delete Background replaces Background in the Page Setup group after you insert a background for a specific worksheet.

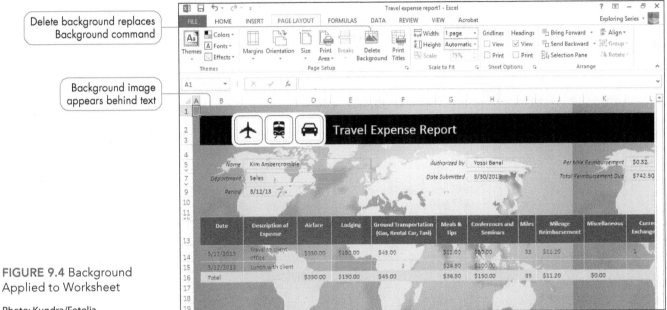

FIGURE 9.4 Background Applied to Worksheet

Photo: Kundra/Fotolia

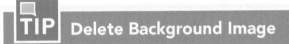 **Background Visibility**

You can turn off the gridlines to increase the visibility of the background image and the worksheet data. Click the Page Layout tab and deselect the Gridlines View check box in the Sheet Options group.

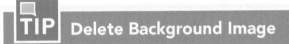 **Delete Background Image**

To delete a background picture, click Delete Background in the Page Setup group on the Page Layout tab.

## Applying Cell Styles

STEP 4 ⟩⟩ Different areas of a worksheet have different formatting. For example, titles may be centered in 16-pt size; column labels may be bold, centered, and dark blue font; and input cells may be formatted differently from output cells. A *cell style* is a collection of format settings based on the currently selected theme to provide a consistent appearance within a worksheet and among similar workbooks. Cell styles control the following formats:

• Font attributes, such as font and font size

• Borders and fill styles and colors

• Vertical and horizontal cell alignment

- Number formatting, such as Currency and number of decimal places
- Cell-protection settings

The currently selected theme controls cell styles. If you change the theme, Excel updates cells formatted by cell styles to reflect the new theme. For example, if you change from Facet theme to Integral, particular fill colors change from shades of green to blue. To apply a style to a cell or range of cells, do the following:

1. Click the HOME tab and click Cell Styles in the Styles group to display the Cell Styles gallery (see Figure 9.5).
2. Position the mouse pointer over a style name to see a Live Preview of how that style will affect the active cell.
3. Click a style to apply it to the active cell or range.

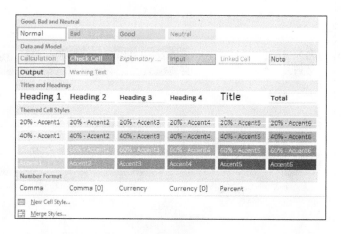

**FIGURE 9.5** Cell Styles

The gallery contains the following five predefined cell categories:

- **Good, Bad, and Neutral:** Use to emphasize bad, good, or neutral results, or click Normal to reset a cell to its original default setting.

- **Data and Model:** Use to indicate special cell contents, such as a calculated result, input cell, output cell, or warning.

- **Titles and Headings:** Use to format titles and headings, such as column and row labels, for emphasis.

- **Themed Cell Styles:** Use Accent styles for visual emphasis. These cell styles are dependent on the currently selected theme.

- **Number Format:** Provide the same formatting as commands in the Number group on the Home tab.

## Create Custom Cell Styles

You can create your own custom cell styles if the predefined cell styles do not meet your needs. For example, you might want to create custom cell styles that match the color, font, and design of your corporate logo or stationery to help brand your workbooks with the company image. After you create custom cell styles, you can apply them in multiple workbooks instead of formatting each workbook individually. To create a custom cell style do the following:

1. Click the cell that contains the desired formatting.
2. Click the HOME tab and click Cell Styles in the Styles group.
3. Select New Cell Style at the bottom of the gallery to open the Style dialog box (see Figure 9.6).
4. Type the name for your new style in the *Style name* box.

5. Click the check boxes to select the style options you want in the *Style Includes (By Example)* section. (If you are not creating a style using the active cell as an example, click Format to open the Format Cells dialog box and select the formats just as you would format an individual cell.)

6. Click OK to close the Style dialog box.

After you create a custom style, Excel displays another section, *Custom*, at the top of the Cell Styles gallery. This section lists the custom styles you create.

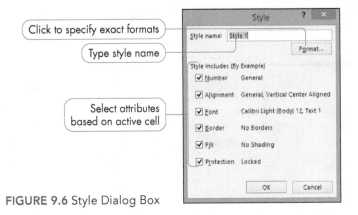

FIGURE 9.6 Style Dialog Box

## Modify and Remove Custom Cell Styles

After you create and apply custom styles to worksheet cells, you might decide to change the format. For example, you might want to change the font size or fill color. The primary advantage to creating and applying styles is that you can modify the style, and Excel updates all cells for which you applied the style automatically. To modify a style, do the following:

1. Right-click the style in the *Custom* section of the Cell Styles palette.

2. Select Modify to open the Style dialog box.

3. Make the desired format changes and click OK.

If you no longer need a cell style, you can delete it. However, if you delete a cell style that has been applied to worksheet cells, Excel will remove all formatting from those cells. To delete a cell style, right-click the style name in the *Custom* section of the Cell Styles palette and select Delete. Excel does not ask for confirmation before deleting the style.

### TIP | Use Styles in Other Workbooks

When you create your own cell styles, the styles are saved with the workbook in which you created the styles. However, you may want to apply those styles in other workbooks as well. To do this, open the workbook that contains the custom cell styles (the source) and open the workbook in which you want to apply those custom styles (the destination). In the destination workbook, click Cell Styles in the Styles group on the Home tab. Select Merge Styles at the bottom of the Cell Styles gallery to open the Merge Styles dialog box. In the *Merge styles from* list, select the name of the workbook that contains the styles you want and click OK. When you click Cell Styles again, the custom styles appear in the gallery.

*Quick* Concepts

1. What are the benefits of using templates? *p. 290*

2. How do you print worksheets with background images? *p. 292*

3. Why would you create a custom cell style? *p. 294*

# Hands-On Exercises

 Watch the Video for this Hands-On Exercise!

 MyITLab®
HOE1 Training

## 1 Templates, Themes, and Styles

You need to get up and running quickly since you took over at EBL, Ltd. You decide to use the Travel Expense Report template that is part of the Office 2013 template downloads. After opening the template, you will modify it by applying a theme, theme color, background, and cell styles.

**Skills covered:** Select a Template • Apply a Theme • Apply a Background • Apply Cell Styles

---

### STEP 1 >> SELECT A TEMPLATE

To save time, you would like to create a new report using a template. After reviewing the templates available in the template gallery, you decided the Travel Expense Report template shown in Figure 9.7 was sufficient to build your company's report. Your first step is to download the Travel Expense Report template. Refer to Figure 9.7 as you complete Step 1.

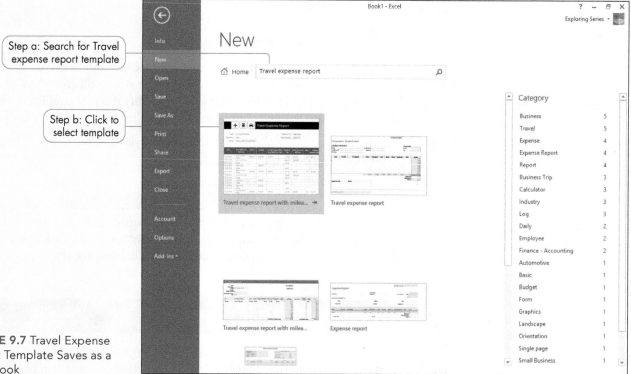

**FIGURE 9.7** Travel Expense Report Template Saves as a Workbook

a. Open Excel, type **Travel expense report** in the **Search for online templates box**, and then press **Enter**.

b. Click **Travel expense report with mileage log** to select it; a pop-up window will appear with a brief description of the template.

Since there are several templates with the same name, choose the template that is the same format as the template shown in Figure 9.7.

> **TROUBLESHOOTING:** Any Microsoft Office user has the ability to submit personally created templates to Office.com. If when searching you discover several templates with the name *Travel Expense Report*, be sure to select the option that resembles the image in Figure 9.7.
> If you are unable to locate the required template, a copy of the file *e09h1ExpenseReport* is included with the start files for this chapter.

**c.** Click **Create** below the preview on the right side of the Backstage view.

Excel opens a copy of the Travel Expense Report as a new workbook. The template contains labels, fill colors, sample data, and formulas.

**d.** Save the workbook as **e09h1ExpenseReport_LastFirst**.

## STEP 2 >> APPLY A THEME

The Travel Expense Report template provides the basic design you need, but you want to apply a different theme to the workbook. Refer to Figure 9.8 as you complete Step 2.

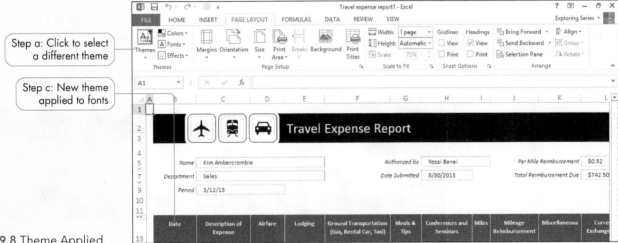

**FIGURE 9.8** Theme Applied

**a.** Click the **PAGE LAYOUT tab** and click **Themes** in the Themes group.

**b.** Move the pointer over the Banded and Office themes to see the Live Preview of how those themes will affect the workbook.

**c.** Click **Basis** to apply that theme to the workbook. Save the workbook.

## STEP 3 >> APPLY A BACKGROUND

To enhance the professional look and feel of the Travel Expense Report, you will add a clip art background image. Refer to Figure 9.9 as you complete Step 3.

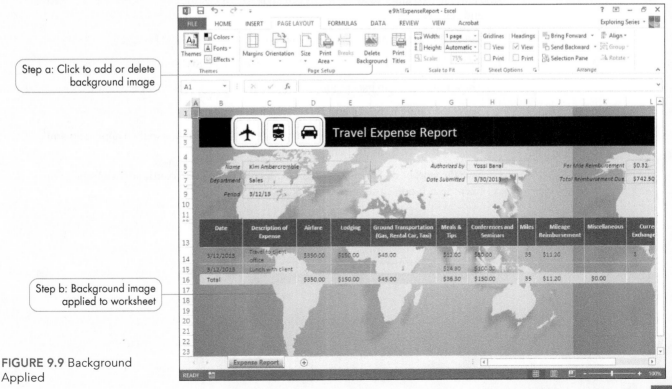

**FIGURE 9.9** Background Applied

a. Click the **PAGE LAYOUT tab**, if necessary, and click **Background** in the Page Setup group.

b. Select *e09h1Map.jpg* from the student data file folder and click **Insert**.

   The image is tiled across and down the worksheet and appears behind the worksheet data. Because the original template did not include fill colors, the background image can be seen underneath the cells in the worksheet.

c. Save the workbook.

## STEP 4 ≫ APPLY CELL STYLES

You want to further customize the Travel Expense Report workbook by applying different cell styles. For example, you want fill colors in the cells that contain data labels for rows 4:9. You also would like an accent color for rows 14:15 to make the data easier to view. Refer to Figure 9.10 as you complete Step 4.

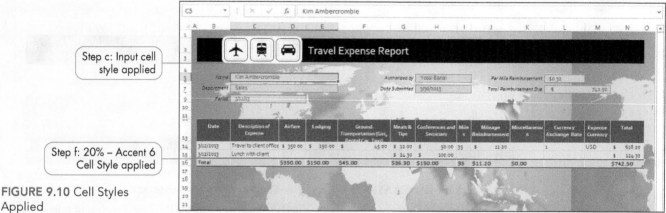

**FIGURE 9.10** Cell Styles Applied

a. Select **cell C5**, press and hold **Ctrl**, and then select **cell C7**.

b. Click the **HOME tab** and click **Cell Styles** in the Styles group.

   The Cell Styles gallery opens so that you can apply a cell style to the selected cells.

c. Click **Input** in the *Data and Model* section.

d. Adapt steps b and c to apply **Input cell style** to **cell C9**, the **range H5:I5**, **cell H7**, **cell L5**, and **cell L7**.

e. Apply **Short Date number format** to **cell C9**.

f. Select the **range B14:N15**. Apply **20% – Accent 6 Cell Style**.

   These ranges had no background. With the cell styles applied, they are now easier to read.

g. Select the **range B16:N16** and apply **Bold** font format.

h. Select the **range B16:N16**, if necessary, click the **HOME tab**, and then apply **Top and Bottom Border** from the Font group.

i. Save the workbook. Keep the workbook open if you plan to continue with Hands-On Exercise 2. If not, close the workbook and exit Excel.

# Custom Templates and Workbook Protection

Using Excel templates helps save time when designing workbooks, but these templates will not always meet your needs. When this is the case, you can create a workbook with the specifications you need and save it as a template so that you can use it as a model to create identically structured workbooks for unique data. For example, after downloading the Travel Expense Report template, you applied a theme, a background, and several cell styles. You want the company's employees to be able to use this modified workbook to create individual reports. However, creating a new workbook from scratch for each employee is time consuming. When you find yourself needing the same workbook design for several unique workbooks, you should develop and use a template that can be accessed by each employee and modified as needed.

You can protect cells or worksheets from unauthorized or accidental changes. Doing so ensures that people do not change areas of a worksheet, such as formulas, when you distribute the worksheet on an organization's server.

In this section, you will learn how to save a workbook as a template. In the process, you will learn how to protect cells and worksheets from being changed.

## Creating and Using a Template

The Travel Expense Report template you used contains labels, sample values, and formulas. The formulas calculate category totals, such as the total airfare and total of the lodging category expenses. You can remove the sample expenses from the workbook and save it as a template so that you have an empty report for each employee to fill out.

When you create a template from scratch instead of starting with an existing template, adhere to the following guidelines:

- Keep in mind that a template should contain formatted, descriptive labels, empty cells, and formulas.
- Avoid values when possible in formulas; use cell references instead.
- Use an appropriate function to trap errors.
- Include data-validation settings (valid data rules, warning messages, input messages).
- Include instructions for the template.
- Turn off worksheet gridlines, if desired, for clarity.
- Apply appropriate formatting to the template.
- Give worksheets meaningful names and delete worksheets that are not used.

 **TIP** **Trap Errors with the IFERROR Function and Set Data Validation**

Formulas used in workbooks display zeros or error messages when you remove values to create a template. You can use the IFERROR function to check a cell to see if it contains errors or if a formula will result in an error. If no error exists, the IFERROR function returns the value of the formula. You can enter an argument in the function to display a customized error message instead of a default error, such as #DIV/0! In addition, you can set validation rules so template users will enter correct data.

After you finalize your workbook, you need to save it. To save a workbook as a template, do the following:

1. Click the FILE tab and click Export.
2. Click Change File Type.
3. Click Template in the Change File Type scrollable list and click Save As at the bottom of the Backstage view to open the Save As dialog box. Notice that the *Save as type* is set to Excel Template.
4. Select the desired location, type a name in the *File name* box, and then click Save. **Note: This method does not default to the "correct" Template folder to provide easy access.**

To save the template so that it automatically is included in the Templates gallery, do the following:

1. From the Backstage view, click Save As and click Computer to open the Save As dialog box.
2. Click the *Save as type* arrow and select Excel Template. Excel then selects the C:\Users\ username\Documents\CustomOfficeTemplates folder automatically.
3. Type a name in the *File name* box and click Save.

---

 **TIP** **Templates Folder**

Templates use a different file extension (.xltx) than Excel workbooks (.xlsx). In order for your template to appear in the Template gallery in the Backstage view, be sure to save it in the correct folder, C:\Users\username\Documents\CustomOfficeTemplates in Windows 8 and Windows 7. If you use File Explorer to find the Templates folder, you will need to display hidden folders to do so. If you save your custom templates in the correct location, you can use them to create new workbooks by clicking the File tab, clicking New, and then clicking Personal in the Templates gallery of the Backstage view. The New dialog box displays thumbnails and names for the templates you created.

## Protecting a Cell, a Worksheet, and a Workbook

Most templates protect worksheets by enabling users to change only particular cells in a worksheet. For example, users are permitted to enter data in input cells, but they cannot change formulas or alter formatting or worksheet structure. In Hands-On Exercise 2, you will protect the formula cells in the Travel Expense Report template. This will prevent users from changing the formulas. Protecting worksheets prevents modification of formulas and text but enables you to change values in unprotected cells.

### Lock and Unlock Cells

STEP 1 ≫  A *locked cell* is one that prevents users from editing the contents or formatting of that cell in a protected worksheet. By default, all cells are locked as indicated by the blue border around the padlock icon for the Lock Cell option on the Format menu in the Cells group on the Home tab. Locked cells are not enforced until you protect the worksheet. Locking or unlocking cells has no effect if the worksheet has not been protected. Before protecting the worksheet, you should unlock the cells that you want users to be able to edit. For example, you will unlock the Per Mile Reimbursement and Date Submitted cells in the Travel Expense Report template so that users can enter unique values. However, you will keep the cells containing formulas locked. To unlock input cells, do the following:

1. Select the cells in which you want users to be able to enter or edit data.
2. Click the HOME tab and click Format in the Cells group (see Figure 9.11). Note that Lock Cell is active by default.
3. Select Lock Cell in the *Protection* section to unlock the active cell or selected range of cells.

To relock cells, repeat the above process.

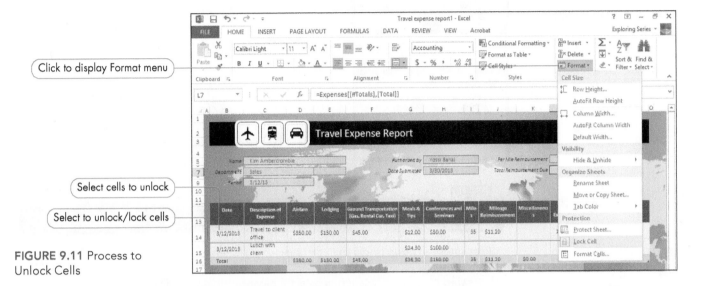

**Click to display Format menu**

**Select cells to unlock**

**Select to unlock/lock cells**

**FIGURE 9.11** Process to Unlock Cells

---

### TIP  Using the Format Cells Dialog Box

Alternatively, after selecting a cell or range of cells to unlock, you can open the Format Cells dialog box, click the Protection tab, deselect the Locked check box, and then click OK.

## Protect a Worksheet

**STEP 2**  After unlocking cells that you want the users to be able to modify, you are ready to protect the worksheet. When you protect a worksheet, you prevent users from altering the locked cells. During the process of protecting a worksheet, you can enter a password to ensure that only those who know the password can unprotect the worksheet. Protecting the template is typically the final step in the creation of a custom template because you need to enter standard labels, create formulas, and unprotect input cells first. If you protect the worksheet before finalizing the content, you will have to unprotect the worksheet, make content changes, and then protect the worksheet again. To protect a worksheet, do the following:

**STEP 3**
1. Click the HOME tab and click Format in the Cells group.
2. Select Protect Sheet in the *Protection* section (or click Protect Sheet in the Changes group on the REVIEW tab) to open the Protect Sheet dialog box (see Figure 9.12).
3. Select the check boxes for actions you want users to be able to do in the *Allow all users of this worksheet to* list.
4. Type a password in the *Password to unprotect sheet* box and click OK. The Confirm Password dialog box opens (see Figure 9.13). Type the same password in the *Reenter password to proceed* box.
5. Read the caution statement and click OK.

**FIGURE 9.12** Protect Sheet Dialog Box

**FIGURE 9.13** Confirm Password Dialog Box

---

**TIP  Passwords**

Passwords can be up to 255 characters, including letters, numbers, and symbols. Passwords are case sensitive, so *passWORD* is not the same as *Password*. Make sure you record your password in a secure location or select a password that you will always remember. If you forget the password, you will not be able to unprotect the worksheet.

---

After you protect a worksheet, most commands on the Ribbon are dimmed, indicating that they are not available. If someone tries to enter or change data in a locked cell on a protected workbook, Excel displays the warning message and instructs the user how to remove the protection (see Figure 9.14). To unprotect a worksheet, do the following:

1. Click Unprotect Sheet in the Changes group on the REVIEW tab, or click Format in the Cells group on the HOME tab and select Unprotect Sheet. The Unprotect Sheet dialog box opens.

2. Type the password in the Password box and click OK. The worksheet is then unprotected so that you can make changes.

**FIGURE 9.14** Warning Message

## Protect a Workbook

Although locking cells and protecting a worksheet prevents unauthorized modifications, users might make unwanted changes to other parts of the workbook. You can prevent users from inserting, deleting, renaming, moving, copying, and hiding worksheets within the workbook by protecting the workbook with a password. Protecting an entire workbook does not disable the unlocked cells within a workbook; it merely prevents worksheet manipulation from occurring. That is, individual cells must still be unlocked even if a workbook is unprotected. To protect a workbook, do the following:

1. Click the REVIEW tab and click Protect Workbook in the Changes group. The Protect Structure and Windows dialog box opens (see Figure 9.15).
2. Click the check boxes for the desired action in the *Protect workbook for* section.
3. Type a password in the *Password (optional)* box and click OK. The Confirm Password dialog box opens.
4. Type the same password in the *Reenter password to proceed* box and click OK.

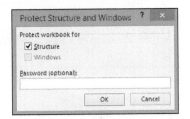

**FIGURE 9.15** Protect Structure and Windows Dialog Box

## TIP Unprotect a Workbook

To unprotect a workbook, click the Review tab, click Protect Workbook, type the password in the Password box in the Unprotect Workbook dialog box, and then click OK.

**STEP 4 >>** Once a workbook is completed and the appropriate cells are locked, the last step is to save the file as a template. Saving the file as a template not only stores the files as a template in the Custom Office Templates folder on your computer, it also displays the file as a personal template in the Backstage gallery. To save a workbook as a template, do the following:

**STEP 5 >>**
1. Click the FILE tab.
2. Click Save As, click Computer, and then click Browse.
3. Select Excel Template from the *Save as type* menu.
4. Click Save.

*Quick Concepts*

1. What is the default file extension for a template? *p. 300*
2. Where are templates saved in Windows 8? *p. 300*
3. Why would you protect a workbook? *p. 302*

# Hands-On Exercises

Watch the Video
for this Hands-
On Exercise!

MyITLab®
HOE2 Training

## 2 Custom Templates and Workbook Protection

After customizing the Travel Expense Report, you want to ensure consistency of use within the company by saving the workbook as a template. As the manager, you do not want your staff deleting formulas or other imperative sections of the expense form you have created. Your next set of steps will include protecting the workbook and then saving it as a template.

**Skills covered:** Unlock Input Cells • Delete Sample Values • Protect the Worksheet • Save the Workbook as a Template • Use the Template to Create a Sample Expense Report

### STEP 1 ≫ UNLOCK INPUT CELLS

Before protecting the worksheet, you will unlock input cells. You need to ensure the input cells are unlocked so that each employee can enter specific lodging, mileage, and miscellaneous costs. Refer to Figure 9.16 as you complete Step 1.

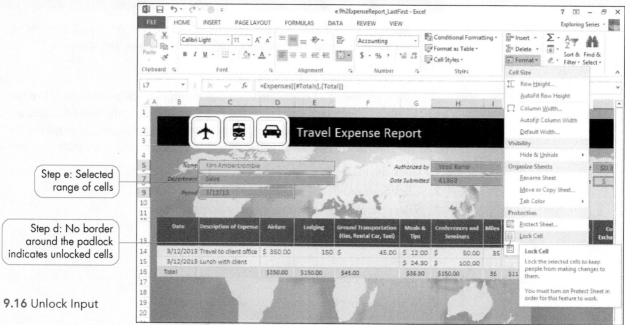

Step e: Selected range of cells

Step d: No border around the padlock indicates unlocked cells

**FIGURE 9.16** Unlock Input Cells

a. Open the *e09h1ExpenseReport_LastFirst* workbook and save it as **e09h2ExpenseReport_LastFirst**, changing *h1* to *h2*.

b. Select **cell C5**.

   This cell will be the input area for the name of the creator of the report.

c. Click the **HOME tab**, if necessary, and click **Format** in the Cells group.

   The Format menu opens.

**d.** Select **Lock Cell** in the *Protection* section.

The Lock Cell option does not change to Unlock Cell. However, when you unlock a cell, the Lock Cell command does not have a blue border around the padlock icon on the menu. The selected range of cells is unlocked and will remain unlocked when you protect the worksheet later.

**e.** Press **Ctrl** while selecting the following cells and range and repeat steps c and d to unlock the cells and range:

- **Cell C7**
- **Cell C9**
- **Cell H5**
- **Cell H7**
- **Cell L5**
- **Range B14:M15**

> **TROUBLESHOOTING**: If you unlock too many cells, select the cells that should be locked, click Format, and then select Lock Cell to lock them again.

**f.** Save the workbook.

## STEP 2 ≫ DELETE SAMPLE VALUES

Although you unlocked the input cells for Name, Department, Period, Authorized by, Date Submitted, Per Mile Reimbursement, and Total Reimbursement, you need to delete the sample values to create a ready-to-use empty form before you protect the worksheet and save it as a template. Refer to Figure 9.17 as you complete Step 2.

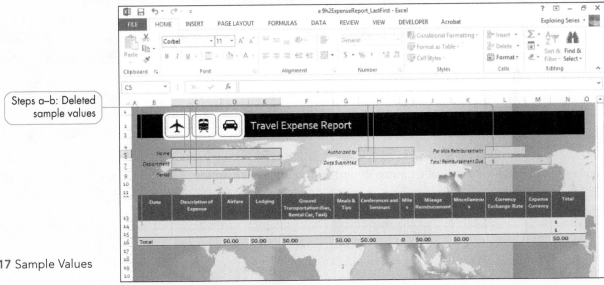

**FIGURE 9.17** Sample Values Removed

**a.** Select **cell C5** and press **Delete**.

**b.** Delete the sample values in the following cells and range:

- **Cell C7**
- **Cell C9**
- **Cell H5**
- **Cell H7**
- **Cell L5**
- **Range B14:M15**

**c.** Save the workbook.

## STEP 3 >> PROTECT THE WORKSHEET

Now that you have unlocked input cells and deleted sample expense values, you are ready to protect the Expense Report worksheet. The other cells in the worksheet still have the Lock Cell property enabled. So, after you protect the worksheet, those cells will not be able to be modified.

a. Press **Ctrl+Home**.

b. Click **Format** in the Cells group and select **Protect Sheet**. If not already checked, check *Select locked cells* and *Select unlocked cells*.

The Protect Sheet dialog box opens. The *Protect worksheet and contents of locked cells* check box is selected by default. In addition, the users are allowed to *Select locked cells* and *Select unlocked cells*. Although they can select locked cells, they will not be able to change those cells. Notice that users are not allowed to format data, insert columns or rows, or delete columns or rows.

c. Type **eXploring** in the **Password to unprotect sheet box**.

Remember that passwords are case sensitive and that you must remember the password. If you forget it, you will not be able to unprotect the sheet.

d. Click **OK**.

The Confirm Password dialog box opens with a caution.

e. Read the caution, type **eXploring** in the **Reenter password to proceed box**, and then click **OK**.

f. Click **cell N14** and try to type **1000**.

Excel displays the warning box that the cell is protected with instructions on how to unprotect the worksheet.

> **TROUBLESHOOTING**: If you are allowed to enter the new value without the warning box, the cell is not locked. Click Undo to restore the formula, review Step 1, and then lock this cell.

g. Click **OK** to close the warning box and save the workbook.

## STEP 4 >> SAVE THE WORKBOOK AS A TEMPLATE

You are ready to save the Travel Expense Report workbook as a template. Refer to Figure 9.18 as you complete Step 4.

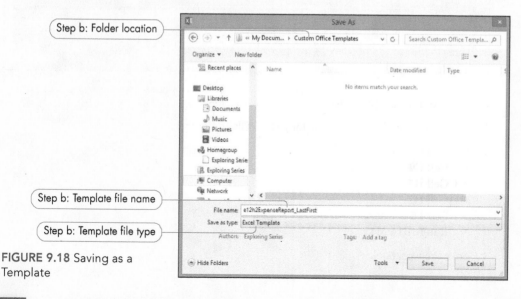

**FIGURE 9.18** Saving as a Template

a. Click the **FILE tab**, click **Save As**, click **Browse**, and then click the **Save as type arrow**.

b. Select **Excel Template** and save the file to the default folder, Custom Office Templates, as **e09h2ExpenseReportTemplate_LastFirst**.

The Save As dialog box opens, displaying the current workbook name and Excel Workbook as the default file type.

> **TROUBLESHOOTING**: When saving a template, Excel changes the file location to C:\Users\ Username\My Documents\CustomOfficeTemplates. You may not have the ability to save a template to the hard drive of your school's computer lab, or your instructor may request you submit the file. To ensure you do not lose the template, be sure to change the save location to your student data folder. Note that if you do change the default location, the template will not display in the Personal template gallery and you will need to manually open the file from your student data folder to continue.

c. Click **Save**.

This will save the workbook as a template and exit the backstage area.

d. Click the **FILE tab** and click **Close**.

## STEP 5 ≫ USE THE TEMPLATE TO CREATE A SAMPLE EXPENSE REPORT

Now that you have created a Travel Expense Report template, you are ready to enter data for one of your coworkers. Refer to Figure 9.19 as you complete Step 5.

**FIGURE 9.19** Create a New Workbook from a Personal Template

a. Click the **FILE tab** and click **New**.

The Backstage view displays a gallery of available templates.

b. Click **PERSONAL** in the *gallery* section.

This displays personal templates saved on your computer.

> **TROUBLESHOOTING**: If you were not able to save the template to the Custom Office Templates folder in Step 4, you will not see the template in the Personal template gallery. If this is the case, the file can be located by searching Recent Workbooks from the Open menu in the Backstage view.

c. Click *e09h2ExpenseReportTemplate_LastFirst* and click **OK**.

The template creates a new workbook based on the same file name but with a number appended to the end, such as *e09h2ExpenseReportTemplate_LastFirst1*.

d. Type **Your Name** in **cell C5**.

e. Type the following values in the appropriate cells:

| Cell | Value |
|------|-------|
| C7 | Finance |
| H7 | 1/28/2015 |
| L5 | .35 |
| B14 | 1/3/2015 |
| C14 | Sales Conference |
| D14 | 250.00 |
| E14 | 125.00 |
| F14 | 35.00 |

f. Press **Ctrl+Home** and save the workbook as **e09h2Sample_LastFirst** in the Excel Workbook file format. Close the workbook and submit based on your instructor's directions.

# Macros

By now, you have used most of the tabs on the Ribbon to perform a variety of tasks. Often, you repeat the execution of the same commands as you develop and modify workbooks. Although the sequence to execute commands is easy, you lose productivity when you repeat the same procedures frequently. Previously, you learned how to apply styles and themes and how to create and use templates as models to develop similar workbooks. However, you can automate other routine tasks to increase your productivity. For example, think about how often you set a print range, adjust scaling, set margins, insert a standard header or footer, and specify other page setup options.

You can automate a series of routine or complex tasks by creating a macro. A *macro* is a set of instructions that execute a sequence of commands to automate repetitive or routine tasks. While the term *macro* often intimidates people, you should view macros as your personal assistants that do routine tasks for you! After you create a macro, you can execute the macro to perform all the tasks with minimal work on your part. When you run a macro, the macro executes all of the tasks the same way each time, and faster than you could execute the commands yourself, thus reducing errors while increasing efficiency.

The default Excel Workbook file format (.xlsx) cannot store macros. When you save a workbook containing macros, click the *Save as type* arrow in the Save As dialog box, and select one of the following file formats that support macros:

- Excel Macro-Enabled Workbook (.xlsm)
- Excel Binary Workbook (.xlsb)
- Excel Macro-Enabled Template (.xltm)

In this section, you will learn how to use the Macro Recorder to record a macro. You will also learn how to run a macro, edit a macro, create macro buttons, and review macro security issues.

## Creating a Macro

Excel provides two methods for creating macros. You can use the Macro Recorder or type instructions using *Visual Basic for Applications (VBA)*. VBA is a robust programming language that is the underlying code of all macros. While programmers use VBA to create macros, you do not have to be a programmer to write macros. It is relatively easy to use the *Macro Recorder* within Excel to record your commands, keystrokes, and mouse clicks to store Excel commands as VBA code within a workbook. Before you record a macro, keep the following points in mind:

- Remember that once you begin recording a macro, most actions you take are recorded in the macro. If you click something in error, you have to edit the code or undo the action to correct it.
- Practice the steps before you start recording the macro so that you will know the sequence in which to perform the steps when you record the macro.
- Ensure your macros are broad enough to apply to a variety of situations or an action you perform often for the workbook.
- Determine whether cell references should be relative, absolute, or mixed if you include cell references in the macro.

### Use the Macro Recorder

You can access the Macro Recorder in a variety of ways: from the View tab, from the Developer tab, or from the status bar. The following list briefly describes what each method includes:

- The View tab contains the Macros group with the Macros command. You can click the Macros arrow to view macros, record a macro, or use relative references.

- The Developer tab, when displayed, provides more in-depth tools that workbook developers use. The Code group contains the same commands as the Macros arrow on the View tab, but it also includes commands to open the Visual Basic editor and set macro security.

- The status bar displays the Macro Recording button so that you can quickly click it to start and stop recording macros.

To display the Developer tab on the Ribbon, do the following:

1. Click the FILE tab and click Options to open the Excel Options dialog box.
2. Click Customize Ribbon on the left side to display the *Customize the Ribbon* options.
3. Click the Developer check box in the Main Tabs list to select it and click OK. Figure 9.20 shows the DEVELOPER tab.

**FIGURE 9.20** Developer Tab

## Record a Macro

Recording a macro is relatively straightforward: You initiate the macro recording, perform a series of commands as you normally do, then stop the macro recording. Be careful and thorough when recording a macro to ensure that it performs the task it is designed to do and to avoid the need to edit the macro in the VBA Editor. Before recording a macro, you should practice it first and make sure you know the sequence of tasks you want to perform. After planning a macro, you are ready to record it. To record a macro, do the following:

1. Click the VIEW tab, click the Macros arrow in the Macros group, and then select Record Macro; or click the DEVELOPER tab and click Record Macro in the Code group; or click Macro Recording on the status bar. The Record Macro dialog box opens (see Figure 9.21 and Figure 9.22).
2. Type a name for the macro in the *Macro name* box. Macro names cannot include spaces or special characters and must start with a letter. Use CamelCasing (capitalize the first letter of each word but without a space), a programming naming convention, to increase readability of the macro name.
3. Assign a keyboard shortcut, if desired, for your macro in the *Shortcut key* box. Use caution, because many Ctrl+ shortcuts are already assigned in Excel. To be safe, it is best to use Ctrl+Shift+, such as Ctrl+Shift+C instead of Ctrl+C, because Ctrl+C is the existing keyboard shortcut for the Copy command.
4. Click the *Store macro in* arrow and select a storage location, such as This Workbook.
5. Type a description of the macro and its purpose in the Description box and click OK to start recording the macro.
6. Perform the commands that you want to record.
7. Click the VIEW tab, click Macros in the Macros group, and then select Stop Recording; or click the DEVELOPER tab and click Stop Recording in the Code group; or click Stop Recording on the status bar.

Click to record Macro

**FIGURE 9.21** Status Bar

**FIGURE 9.22** Record Macro
Dialog Box

## Use Relative References

It is important to determine if your macro should use relative, absolute, or mixed references as you record the macro. By default, when you select cells when recording a macro, the macro records the cells as absolute references. When you run the macro, the macro executes commands on the absolute cells, regardless of which cell is the active cell when you run the macro. If you want flexibility in that commands are performed relative to the active cell when you run the macro, click the Macros arrow in the Macros group on the View tab and select Use Relative References *before* you perform the commands. Relative references look like this in the VBA Editor:

ActiveCell.Offset(3,-2).Range("A1").Select

This code moves the active cell down three rows and back to the left by two cells. If the active cell is D1 when you run the macro, the active cell becomes B4 (down three rows; to the left by two cells).

## Run a Macro

**STEP 3 >>** After you record a macro, you should run a test to see if it performs the commands as you had anticipated. When you run a macro, Excel performs the tasks in the sequence in which you recorded the steps. To run a macro, do the following:

1. Select the location where you will test the macro. It is recommended to test a macro in a new, blank workbook if you recorded it so that it is available for multiple workbooks. If you saved it to the current workbook only, insert a new worksheet to test the macro.
2. Click the VIEW tab, click the Macros arrow in the Macros group, and then select View Macros; or click the DEVELOPER tab and click Macros in the Code group. The Macro dialog box opens (see Figure 9.23).
3. Select the macro from the *Macro name* list and click Run.

### TIP Delete a Macro

If you no longer need a macro, use the Macro dialog box to select the macro and click Delete. Excel will prompt you with a message box asking if you want to delete the selected Macro. Click Yes to confirm the deletion.

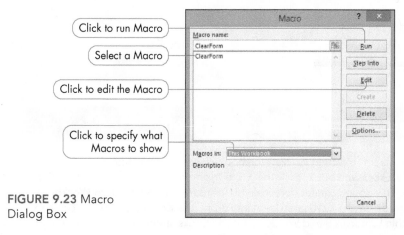

**FIGURE 9.23** Macro Dialog Box

## Creating Macro Buttons

**STEP 4 >>** For the most part, it will be a rare macro that is so all-encompassing that it would rate a place on the Quick Access Toolbar. On the other hand, you may create a macro that is frequently used in a particular workbook. The easiest way to access frequently used macros within a workbook is to assign a macro to a button on a worksheet. That way, when you or other people use the workbook, it is easy to click the button to run the macro. To add a macro button to a worksheet, do the following:

1. Click the DEVELOPER tab, click Insert in the Controls group, and then click Button (Form Control) in the *Form Controls* section of the Insert gallery. See Figure 9.24.
2. Drag the crosshair pointer to draw the button on the worksheet. When you release the mouse button, the Assign Macro dialog box opens (see Figure 9.25).
3. Select the macro to assign to the button and click OK.
4. Right-click the button, select Edit Text, delete the default text, and then type a more descriptive name for the button.
5. Click the worksheet to complete the button.
6. Click a cell, if necessary, that should be the active cell when the macro runs and click the button to execute the macro assigned to the button.

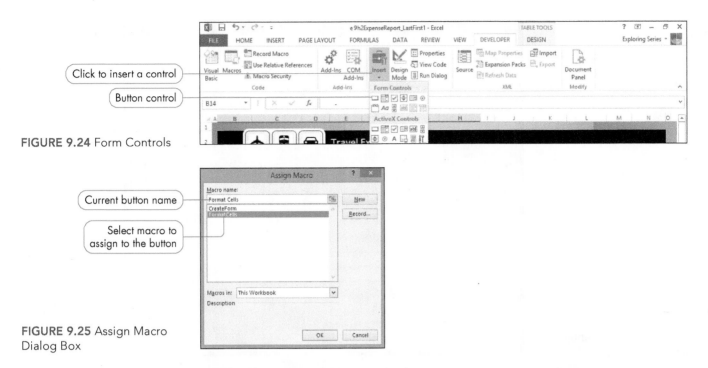

Click to insert a control

Button control

**FIGURE 9.24** Form Controls

Current button name

Select macro to
assign to the button

**FIGURE 9.25** Assign Macro
Dialog Box

---

### TIP Other Controls

You can insert other controls in a worksheet such as images and artwork and then assign macros to them. For example, you can insert combo boxes, check boxes, and option buttons by clicking Insert in the Controls group on the Developer tab and selecting the desired control. Drag an area on the worksheet to draw the control, right-click the object, and then select Assign Macro to assign a macro action for that particular control.

## Setting Macro Security

Macro security is a concern for anyone who uses files containing macros. A macro virus is nothing more than actions written in VBA set to perform malicious actions when run. The proliferation of macro viruses has made people more cautious about opening workbooks that contain macros. By default, Excel automatically disables the macros and displays a security warning that macros have been disabled (see Figure 9.26). Click Enable Content to use the workbook and run macros.

Excel Security Warning

**FIGURE 9.26** Security
Warning Message Bar

You can use the Trust Center dialog box to change settings to make it easier to work with macros. The Trust Center can direct Excel to trust files in particular folders, trust workbooks created by a trusted publisher, and lower the security settings to allow macros. To open the Trust Center, do the following:

1. Click the FILE tab and click Options.
2. Click Trust Center on the left side of the Excel Options dialog box.
3. Click Trust Center Settings. The Trust Center dialog box displays the sections described in Table 9.1 on the left side of the dialog box (see Figure 9.27).

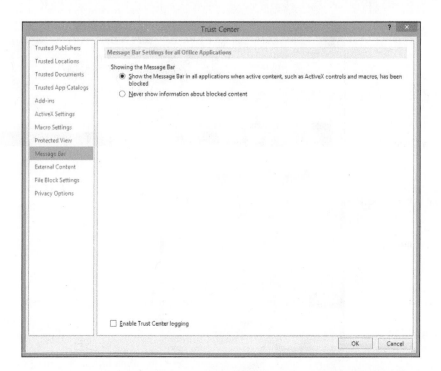

**FIGURE 9.27** Trust Center Dialog Box

| TABLE 9.1 | Trust Center Options |
|---|---|
| **Item** | **Description** |
| Trusted Publishers | Directs Excel to trust digitally signed workbooks by certain creators. |
| Trusted Locations | Enables you to select places on your computer to store workbooks securely. |
| Trusted Documents | Enables you to trust network documents to open without Excel displaying any security warnings. |
| Trusted App Catalogs | Enables you to trust third-party Office Apps that run inside Excel. |
| Add-Ins | Enables you to specify which add-ins will be allowed to run given the desired level of security. |
| ActiveX Settings | Enables you to adjust how Excel deals with ActiveX controls. |
| Macro Settings | Enables you to specify how Excel deals with macros. |
| Protected View | Opens potentially dangerous files in a restricted mode but without any security warnings. |
| Message Bar | Enables you to specify when Excel shows the message bar when it blocks macros. |
| External Content | Enables you to specify how Excel deals with links to other workbooks and data from other sources. |
| File Block Settings | Enables you to select which types of files, such as macros, to open in Protected View or which file type to prevent saving a file in. |
| Privacy Options | Enables you to deal with nonmacro privacy issues. |

*Quick* Concepts

1. What is the purpose of a macro? *p. 309*

2. How are macros accessed after they have been recorded? *p. 312*

3. What potential risks are associated with macros? *p. 313*

# 3 Macros

Because you want all employees to use the Travel Expense Report template to report expenditures each month, you want to create a macro to clear the form. In addition, you want to create a button to run the macro so that other users can easily clear the form if they do not know what a macro is or how to run it.

**Skills covered:** Display Developer Tab • Record a Macro • Run a Macro • Add a Macro Button

## STEP 1 ≫ DISPLAY DEVELOPER TAB

The average employee at your company does not use developer tools; therefore, they are not enabled on your workstation. You would like to display the Developer tab so that you can record the macro.

> a. Open *e09h2ExpenseReportTemplate_LastFirst* and save it with the file name **e09h3ExpenseReportTemplate_LastFirst**, changing *h2* to *h3*.
>
> When you use Open or Recent to open a template, you open it as a template to edit. When you use New, you make a copy of the template as a workbook.
>
> ---
> **TROUBLESHOOTING**: If you do not see Templates in Recent Places, click Open and navigate to the local directory that contains your student files.
> ---
>
> b. Click the **FILE tab** and click **Options** to open the Excel Options dialog box.
>
> c. Click **Customize Ribbon**, click the **Developer check box** in the Main Tabs list, and then click **OK**.
>
> The Developer tab is added to the Ribbon.

## STEP 2 ≫ RECORD A MACRO

You do not want to assume the level of Excel expertise throughout your company; therefore, you want to craft a macro that will automate as much as possible. The macro you would like to create needs to automatically clear existing values and then display an instruction for users to enter specific data. Although the template is empty to start, users might open the template, save a workbook, and then want to use that workbook to prepare future months' reports. Therefore, you need the macro to clear cells even though the original template has no values. Refer to Figure 9.28 as you complete Step 2.

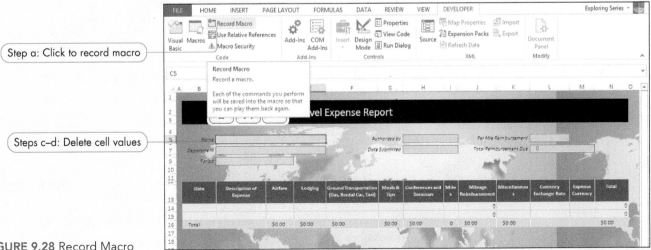

**Step a:** Click to record macro

**Steps c–d:** Delete cell values

**FIGURE 9.28** Record Macro

a. Click the **DEVELOPER tab** and click **Record Macro** in the Code group.

The Record Macro dialog box opens so that you can name and describe the macro.

b. Type **ClearForm** in the **Macro name box**, click in the **Description box**, type **This macro clears existing values in the current Travel Expense Report**, and then click **OK**.

> **TROUBLESHOOTING**: Read through steps c–g in advance before you proceed. Remember most actions taken in Excel are recorded by the macro recorder. Practice the steps below before activating the recorder. If you make a major mistake, delete the macro and repeat steps b through j.

c. Select **cell C5** and press **Delete**.

Even though the cells are empty now, they may contain values at some point. You want the macro to delete any values that might exist in this range.

d. Adapt step c for the following cells and ranges:

- **Cell C7**
- **Cell C9**
- **Cell H5**
- **Cell H7**
- **Cell L5**
- **Range B14:I15**
- **Range K14:M15**

You deleted ranges that might contain values after the user enters data into any workbooks created from the template. It is always good to plan for various possibilities in which data might be entered even if those ranges do not contain values now.

e. Press **Ctrl+G**, type **C5** in the **Reference box** of the Go To dialog box, and then click **OK**.

f. Type **Enter Name Here** in **cell C5** and press **Ctrl+Enter**.

Pressing Ctrl+Enter keeps cell C5 the active cell so that users can immediately enter the label when they open a workbook from the template.

g. Click **cell C7**, type **Enter Department Name**, and then press **Ctrl+Enter**.

h. Click **Stop Recording** in the Code group on the DEVELOPER tab.

i. Save the *e09h3ExpenseReportTemplate_LastFirst* template; click **No** when prompted that the workbook cannot be saved with the macro in it.

Excel opens the Save As dialog box so that you can select the file type.

j. Click the **Save as type arrow**, select **Excel Macro-Enabled Template**, and then click **Save**.

> **TROUBLESHOOTING**: Make sure you select Excel Macro-Enabled Template, not Excel Macro-Enabled Workbook, because you want the file saved as a template, not a workbook. Because the template contains macros, you must save it as an Excel Macro-Enabled Template, not just a template.

## STEP 3 ›› RUN A MACRO

You want to make sure the ClearForm macro does what you want it to do. First, you will add some sample data and run the macro.

a. Type your name in **cell C5**, type **Finance** in **cell C7**, type **1/25/2015** in **cell H7**, type **1/5/2015** in **cell B14**, type **Sales Meeting** in **cell C14**, and then type **$75.00** in **cell G14**.

You entered some sample values in various cells to test the ClearForm macro to verify if it will delete those values.

**b.** Click the **DEVELOPER tab**, if necessary, and click **Macros** in the Code group.

The Macro dialog box opens and displays the ClearForm macro, which should be selected in the Macro name box.

**c.** Select **ClearForm**, if necessary, and click **Run**.

The ClearForm macro quickly goes through the worksheet, erasing the values in the specified ranges, goes to cells C5 and C7, enters descriptive labels, and then stops.

> **TROUBLESHOOTING**: If the macro does not delete sample values, delete the macro and rerecord it.

## STEP 4 >> ADD A MACRO BUTTON

Your colleagues are probably not Excel experts and do not know how to run a macro. To make it easier to clear values from the form, you want to assign the ClearForm macro to a button. The users can then click the button to clear the form to use it for another month. Refer to Figure 9.29 as you complete Step 4.

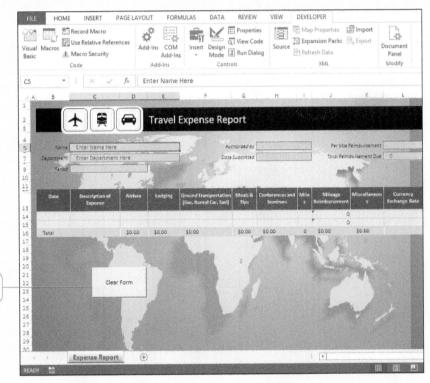

Steps b–d: Create macro button

**FIGURE 9.29** Macro Button

**a.** Click the **HOME tab**, click **Format** in the Cells group, select **Unprotect Sheet**, type **eXploring** in the **Password box** in the Unprotect Sheet dialog box, and then click **OK**.

You have to unprotect the worksheet before you can insert a macro button.

**b.** Click the **DEVELOPER tab**, click **Insert** in the Controls group, and then click **Button (Form Control)** in the *Form Controls* section of the gallery.

**c.** Click the top of **cell C20** and drag down and to the right to the bottom of **cell D23** to create the area where the button will be placed.

The Assign Macro dialog box opens.

**d.** Select **ClearForm** in the Macro name list and click **OK**.

This action assigns the ClearForm macro to the button. The button appears in cells C20:D23, is selected, and displays *Button 1*. You will provide descriptive text to appear on the button.

**e.** Right-click **Button 1** and select **Edit Text**. Select the **Button 1 text**, type **Clear Form**, and then click any cell on the worksheet outside the button.

The button now shows *Clear Form*, which is more descriptive of the button's purpose than *Button 1*.

**f.** Right-click the **Expense Report worksheet tab**, select **Protect Sheet**, type **eXploring** in the **Password to protect sheet box**, click **OK**, type **eXploring** in the **Reenter password to proceed box**, and then click **OK**.

You need to protect the worksheet after creating the macro button.

**g.** Type **6/1/2015** in cell **B14** and type **6/29/2015** in cell **B15** to enter sample data.

**h.** Click **Clear Form** in the worksheet.

When you click Clear Form, Excel runs the ClearForm macro.

**i.** Save the Macro-Enabled Template. Keep the workbook open if you plan to continue with Hands-On Exercise 4. If not, close the workbook and exit Excel.

# Visual Basic for Applications

As you perform commands while recording a macro, those commands are translated into programming code called Visual Basic for Applications (VBA). VBA is a robust programming language that can be used within various software packages to enhance and automate functionality. While many casual users will be able to complete required tasks using just the macro recorder, more advanced VBA macros can be created by authoring code directly into modules within the Visual Basic Editor. A **module** is a file in which macros are stored. The ***Visual Basic Editor*** is an application used to create, edit, execute, and debug Office application macros using programming code. These macros can then be used within a Macro-Enabled Workbook or Template. The two types of VBA macros are sub procedures and custom functions. ***Sub procedures***, which are also created when using the macro recorder, perform actions on a workbook, such as the ClearForm example earlier in the chapter. For example, you can create a sub procedure to insert the current date in a worksheet. Similar to the hundreds of built-in functions in Excel, custom functions have the ability to manipulate input variables and return a value.

## Creating a Sub Procedure

STEP 1 >> The first step to creating a sub procedure is inserting a new module or editing data in an existing module within the VBA editor. To access the VBA Editor, press Alt+F11 on your keyboard. The left side of the VBA window contains the Project Explorer, which is similar in concept and appearance to the File Explorer except that it displays only open workbooks and/or other Visual Basic projects (see Figure 9.30).

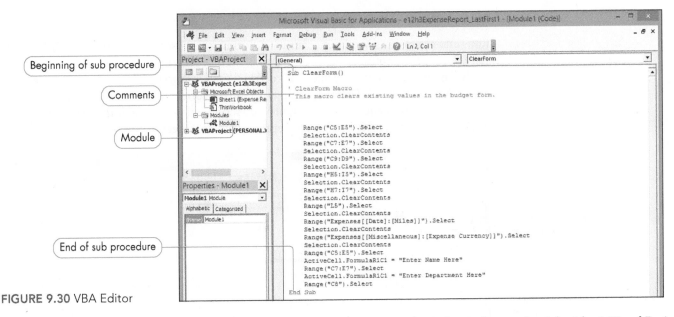

**FIGURE 9.30** VBA Editor

The Visual Basic statements appear in the Code window on the right side. A Visual Basic module consists of at least one **procedure**, which is a named sequence of statements stored in a macro. In this example, Module1 contains the ClearForm procedure, which is also the name of the macro created in Excel. Module1 is stored in the Travel Expense Report workbook.

A procedure or macro always begins and ends with the Sub and End Sub statements. The Sub statement contains the name of the macro, such as Sub ClearForm() in Figure 9.30. The End Sub statement is the last statement and indicates the end of the macro. Sub and End Sub are Visual Basic keywords and appear in blue. **Keywords** are special programming syntax that have special meaning with the programming language and must be used for their intended purposes.

**Comments**, which are indicated by an apostrophe and appear in green, provide information about the macro but do not affect its execution and are considered documentation. Comments can be entered manually or are inserted automatically by the macro recorder to document the macro name, its author, and shortcut key (if any). You can add, delete, or modify comments. To create a basic sub procedure that would enter a date into a cell, complete the following steps:

1. From the VBA Editor, select Module from the Insert menu.
2. Type *sub currentdate()* and press Enter.
3. Type '*This macro will insert the current date in cell H7.*
4. Type *range("H7") = date* and press Enter.
5. Type *range("H7").font.bold = true.*
6. Save and exit the Visual Basic Editor.

Table 9.2 explains some of the lines of code used to create the previous sub procedure. The first word, *range*, refers to an object. An **object** is a variable that contains both data and code and represents an element of Excel such as Range or Selection. A period follows the object name, and the next word is often a behavior or attribute, such as Select or ClearContents, that describes a behavior or action performed on the object.

## TABLE 9.2  VBA Editor Code

| Code | Explanation |
|---|---|
| range("H7") | Identifies the range H7 |
| = date | Applies the current date to the cell |
| font.bold = true | Applies object property, setting the font to bold. To disable, change *true* to *false*. |

## Use VBA with Protected Worksheets

Run time errors can sometimes occur when running VBA scripts on protected worksheets. A **run time error** is a software or hardware problem that prevents a program from working correctly. This is most commonly due to a procedure such as *range("H7").font.bold = true*, attempting to alter a locked cell. There are several methods to correct this issue. The simplest, as shown in Figure 9.31, is to encase your current VBA script with a statement that will unprotect the worksheet, run the current script, and reprotect the worksheet before ending the procedure.

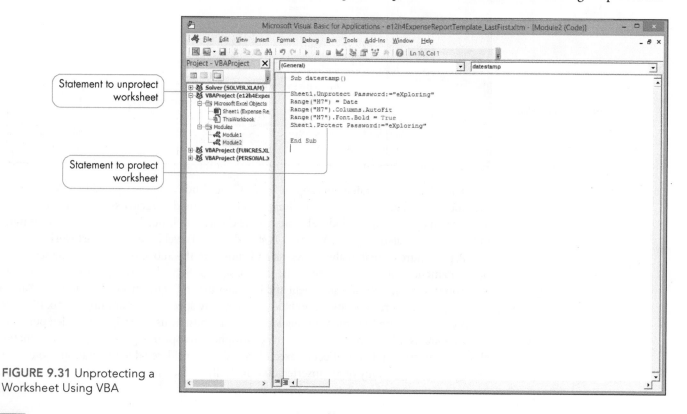

**FIGURE 9.31** Unprotecting a Worksheet Using VBA

In the example given, cell H7 is formatted and the column size is altered. However, this will create a run time error because the worksheet is protected. The statement *Sheet1.Unprotect Password:= "eXploring"* unprotects the worksheet to allow the format changes to occur. The statement *Sheet1.Protect Password:= "eXploring"* then reprotects the worksheet.

### Edit a Macro in the Visual Basic Editor

STEP 2 »

If you work with a workbook that has macros that were created by a coworker or you used the macro recorder, you can edit the existing macro using the Visual Basic Editor. For example, if you record a macro to apply bold, Arial font, 12-pt size, and Red font color, each command appears in a separate statement (see Figure 9.32). The two statements to apply bold and italic start with Selection.Font, indicating that a font attribute will be applied to the current selection. The statement continues with a period and behavior, such as *Bold = True*, indicating that bold is activated. If the sub procedure is turning off bold, the statement looks like this:

```
Selection.Font.Bold = False
```

The With statement enables you to perform multiple actions on the same object. All commands between the With and the corresponding End With statement are executed collectively. Although the font and font size were changed in the macro, the macro also indicates that other attributes, such as superscript and subscript, are turned off. You can delete those lines of code if you want.

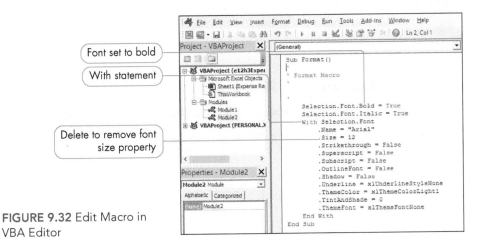

**FIGURE 9.32** Edit Macro in VBA Editor

## Creating a Custom Function

STEP 4 »

There are several hundred built-in functions in Excel that can perform tasks as simple as capitalizing the first letter of a word, such as the Proper function, or as complex as a multiconditional sum, as created with SumIFs. In the event that one of the numerous built-in functions does not meet your needs, you have the ability to create your own custom function using VBA. Custom functions are virtually limitless. However, like sub procedures, they are still saved in modules. This means that if they are not saved to a Personal Macro Workbook, they will only be available within the Macro-Enabled Workbook in which they were created.

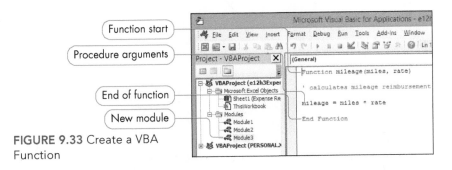

**FIGURE 9.33** Create a VBA Function

When creating a custom function in VBA, you must start by creating a new module and typing *function* followed by the name of the function you are creating and the arguments that the function will use inside parentheses (see Figure 9.32).

After entering arguments on the next line, you have the ability to add comments in the same manner they were added to sub procedures. Your next step is to enter the statement that defines your function such as:

`Mileage = miles * rate`

After completing the statement, you end the function by typing End Function. However, this step should automatically be completed by the VBA editor.

Once a custom function is completed, it can be viewed within Excel under User Defined functions within the Insert Function command in the Function Library. Furthermore, you can access the function by simply typing = in the cell of your choice and the name of the function. This will allow you to use the custom function in the same manner as any of the built-in Excel functions. To create the VBA function described above, complete the following steps:

1. Press Alt+F11 to open the VBA Editor.
2. From the INSERT tab, select Module.
3. Type *Function mileage (rate, miles)* and press Enter.
4. Type *mileage = rate * miles*.
5. Type End Function.
6. Save the module and return to the workbook to access the newly created custom function.

*Quick Concepts*

1. When using Excel, why would you want to access the VBA editor? *p. 319*
2. What are the two types of VBA macros that can be created in the VBA editor? *p. 319*
3. Why would it be necessary to create a custom function? *p. 321*

# Hands-On Exercises

**Watch the Video for this Hands-On Exercise!**

MyITLab®
HOE4 Training

## 4 Visual Basic for Applications

You would like to automate as much of the Travel Expense Report as possible. Therefore, you will create a sub procedure assigned to a macro button to automatically insert the current date into the worksheet. You would also like to add an additional function that will allow the user to estimate mileage reimbursement prior to submission.

**Skills covered:** Create a Sub Procedure • Edit a Macro • Assign a Macro to an Image • Create a Custom Function

### STEP 1 ⟫ CREATE A SUB PROCEDURE

Before you create the sub procedure, you will open the template you created in Hands-On Exercise 3 and save it as a template with another name to preserve the original template in case you make any mistakes.

   **a.** Open the Macro-Enabled Template *e09h3ExpenseReportTemplate_LastFirst*, click **Enable Content** to activate the prior macro, and save it as **e09h4ExpenseReportTemplate_LastFirst**, changing *h3* to *h4*.

   When you use Open or Recent to open a template, you open it as a template to edit. When you use New, you make a copy of the template as a workbook.

   **b.** Press **Alt+F11** on your keyboard to open the Visual Basic Editor.

   **c.** Click the **Insert menu** and select **Module**.

   **d.** Type *sub datestamp ()* on the first line of the newly created module and press **Enter**.

   **e.** Type **Sheet1.Unprotect Password:= "eXploring"** and press **Enter**.

   This unprotects the workbook to allow the remaining changes to take place.

   **f.** Type **range("H7") = date** and press **Enter**.

   This enters the current date.

   **g.** Type **range("H7").columns.autofit** and press **Enter**.

   This sets the selected column to autofit, which will ensure proper display of the date.

   **h.** Type **range("H7").Font.Bold = True**.

   This sets the newly entered date to bold.

   **i.** Type **Sheet1.Protect Password:= "eXploring"** and press **Enter**.

   **j.** Save the macro and press **F5** to test the newly created macro.

   When run, the newly created sub procedure unprotects the worksheet, adds and formats the current date, sets the column width to auto, and reprotects the document.

### STEP 2 ⟫ EDIT A MACRO

After running the created sub procedure, you have decided that the newly inserted date should be italicized instead of bold. You will make this change in the VBA Editor by editing the bold property.

   **a.** Press **Alt+F11** on your keyboard if the VBA Editor is not open.

   Excel opens the VBA Editor so that you can edit the macro programming language.

   **b.** Click **module 2**, if it is not already selected, to display the sub procedure created in Step 1. Select the line **Range("H7").Font.Bold = True** and replace the word *Bold* with **Italic**.

   This edits the command to set the inserted date to italics instead of bold.

   **c.** Save and exit the VBA Editor.

# STEP 3 >> ASSIGN A MACRO TO AN IMAGE

After creating the sub procedure to insert the current date in the worksheet, you would like to enhance the usability of the document by creating a calendar icon to activate the macro. Refer to Figure 9.34 as you complete Step 3.

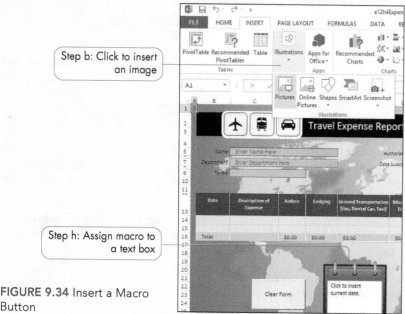

Step b: Click to insert an image

Step h: Assign macro to a text box

**FIGURE 9.34** Insert a Macro Button

**a.** Right-click the **Expense Report worksheet tab**, select **Unprotect Sheet**, type **eXploring** in the **Password to unprotect sheet box**, and then click **OK**.

**b.** Click the **INSERT tab** and select **Pictures** from the Illustrations group.

**c.** Insert the image **e09h4Calendar.png** and position the image to the right of Clear Form.

**d.** Right-click the inserted image and click **Assign Macro**. Click the **datestamp macro**.

**e.** Click the **INSERT tab**, if necessary, and click **Text Box** in the Text group.

**f.** Draw a text box inside the image inserted in step b.

**g.** Type **Click to insert current date** in the text box.

**h.** Right-click the text box and click **Assign Macro**. Click the **datestamp macro box**.

You decided to assign the macro to both the inserted image and the text box to make sure that the macro activates no matter where the end user clicks on the image.

**i.** Click the newly created button to verify the current date. Once the date is verified, click **Clear Form** and save the template.

# STEP 4 >> CREATE A CUSTOM FUNCTION

Even though the Travel Expense Report has the ability to automatically calculate travel mileage reimbursement, you have decided to create a custom function to allow users to manually calculate their mileage reimbursement if they choose.

**a.** Press **Alt +F11** on your keyboard to open the Visual Basic Editor.

**b.** Click the **Insert menu** and select **Module**.

**c.** Type **function mileage(miles,rate)** on the first line of the newly created module and press **Enter**.

**d.** Type **This function will calculate mileage reimbursement**. Press **Enter**.

This will appear as a comment in the module. However, it will not impact the calculation of the function.

**e.** Type the statement **mileage = miles * rate** and press **Enter**.

**f.** Save and exit the VBA Editor.

This creates a custom function that can be used in a similar fashion to any built-in function within Excel.

**g.** Click **cell H21** and type **=mileage(32,0.75)**. This returns the value 24.

You entered 32 miles at the rate of $.75 per mile to test the newly created function.

**h.** Delete the contents of **cell H21**.

**i.** Right-click the **Expense Report worksheet tab**, select **Protect Sheet**, type **eXploring** in the **Password to protect sheet box**, click **OK**, type **eXploring** in the **Reenter password to proceed box**, and then click **OK**.

**j.** Save the workbook and submit based on your instructor's directions.

# Excel

## CHAPTER 10

# Subtotals, PivotTables, and PivotCharts

## Summarizing and Analyzing Data

## OBJECTIVES  AFTER YOU READ THIS CHAPTER, YOU WILL BE ABLE TO:

1. Subtotal data p. 328

2. Group and ungroup data p. 331

3. Create a PivotTable p. 336

4. Modify a PivotTable p. 339

5. Filter and slice a PivotTable p. 349

6. Create a calculated field p. 352

7. Format a PivotTable p. 359

8. Use PowerPivot Functionality p. 360

9. Create a PivotChart p. 362

## CASE STUDY | Ivory Halls Publishing Company

You are the new Vice President of the Sociology Division at Ivory Halls Publishing Company. The sociology domain has many disciplines, such as introductory sociology, family, research, gender issues, and more. Ivory Halls publishes several textbooks in each discipline to appeal to a vast array of university professors and students.

Your assistant prepared a list of books, their disciplines, and other pertinent data. The current list is not easy to analyze. You need to organize the data so that you can study the sales trends by discipline and area. The list contains current editions of all sociology textbooks. Some books are brand new—in their first edition—while other books are in their 10th edition. All of the books on the list have publication dates between 2014 and 2017.

One of your first tasks in your new position is to analyze sales for all books published in the Sociology Division. To do this, you need to organize data so that you can group data by discipline and then insert subtotal rows. You will also use Excel's PivotTable tool to gain a variety of perspectives of aggregated data. Finally, you will create a PivotChart to depict the aggregated data visually.

# Subtotals and Outlines

When you use large datasets, you develop an appreciation for functionality that enables you to manage the data and quickly provide answers to imperative questions. Data alone are meaningless; data translated into meaningful information increase your knowledge so that you can make well-informed decisions. Previously, you used analytical tools such as sorting, filtering, conditional formatting, tables, and charts. These tools help translate raw data into information so that you can identify trends, patterns, and anomalies in a dataset. Now you are ready to explore other functionalities that help you consolidate and analyze large amounts of data.

In this section, you will learn how to insert subtotals for categories. Then you will learn how to group data to create an outline, collapse and expand groups within the outline, and ungroup data to return them to their original state.

## Subtotaling Data

Decision makers often want to calculate subtotals by groups within large dataset. You can use the Subtotal feature to insert subtotal rows by categories for a regular data range.

For example, the Ivory Halls Publishing Company's dataset contains a list of sociology textbooks organized by discipline, such as Family. Textbooks are further classified by a specific area within the discipline. For example, the Family discipline contains specific areas such as *Family Interaction* and *Marriage and Family*. You can calculate the number of books sold and the total sales per area. Adding subtotals can help you identify which disciplines and which areas contribute the highest revenue for the company and which disciplines and areas produce the lowest revenue. You can then analyze the data to determine to continue publishing books in high-revenue–generating areas or discontinue the publication of books in low-selling areas. To add subtotals to a dataset, do the following:

**STEP 1 »**

1. Sort the data on a primary category (such as Discipline in the sociology textbook example) that has the same values, such as the same city, state, or department name for several records in one column. **NOTE: If the data are not sorted by a major category, the subtotaled results will not be correct.**
2. Convert the table to range (if the dataset is a table).
3. Click in the dataset and click the DATA tab.
4. Click Subtotal in the Outline group to open the Subtotal dialog box.
5. Click the *At each change in* arrow and select the column by which the data are sorted (see Figure 10.1). **NOTE: You must select the column by which you sorted data in Step 1.**
6. Click the *Use function* arrow and select the function you want to apply.
7. Select the appropriate column heading check boxes in the *Add subtotal to* list for each field you want to subtotal. You can use all functions for columns that contain numeric data. For text columns, you can only count the number of rows within the group.
8. Select any other check boxes you want to use and click OK.

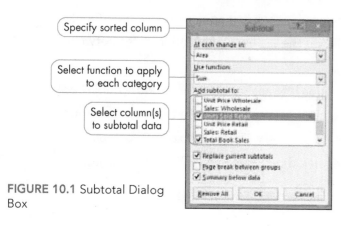

**FIGURE 10.1** Subtotal Dialog Box

The dataset must be sorted by categorical labels. For example, the Sociology Textbooks dataset is sorted first by discipline. When you use the Subtotal feature, Excel inserts a *subtotal*, a row within the dataset containing at least one aggregated value when the category you specified in the *At a change in* option changes. For example, when Excel detects a change from Family to Introductory, a subtotal row is inserted on row 35 (see Figure 10.2). (NOTE: Subtotal rows for discipline are highlighted in yellow in the figure; however, the Subtotal feature does not add highlighting.) The subtotal of the number of Family discipline books sold at wholesale was 76,710, and the subtotal of the number of Introductory discipline books sold at wholesale was 179,415, indicating that the number of Introductory books sold is more than double the number of Family books sold. A grand total row is inserted at the end of the dataset to indicate the grand total values (not shown in the figure).

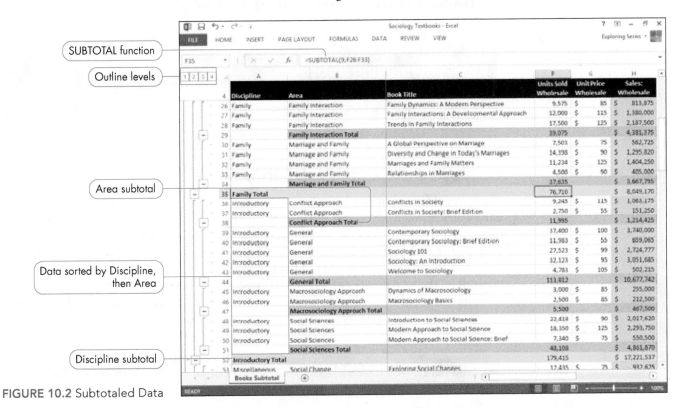

FIGURE 10.2 Subtotaled Data

Excel uses the SUBTOTAL function to calculate the subtotals. Cell F35 contains =SUBTOTAL(9,F26:F33) to sum the values in the range F26:F33. The first argument indicates which summary function is used to calculate the subtotal. Use 1-11 to summarize data including hidden values; use 101-111 to summarize visible data only. Table 10.1 lists some of the summary functions and their respective argument values. For example, 9 sums all values in the range specified in the second argument. If you create a subtotal to average the gross sales, the first argument in the function would be 1 instead of 9.

## TABLE 10.1  SUBTOTAL Function_Num Argument

| Summary Function | Argument to Include Hidden Values | Argument to Ignore Hidden Values |
| --- | --- | --- |
| AVERAGE | 1 | 101 |
| COUNT | 2 | 102 |
| COUNTA | 3 | 103 |
| MAX | 4 | 104 |
| MIN | 5 | 105 |
| SUM | 9 | 109 |

## Add a Second Level of Subtotals

You can add a second level of subtotals to a dataset. Adding a second level preserves the primary subtotals and adds another level of subtotals for subcategories. In the Sociology Textbook example, Figure 10.2 shows the discipline subtotals as well as the areas subcategory subtotals. To add a second level of subtotals while maintaining the existing subtotals, do the following:

1. Perform a two-level sort based on primary and secondary categorical data.
2. Click the DATA tab and click Subtotal in the Outline group.
3. Click the *At a change in* arrow and specify the column that was used for the secondary sort.
4. Select the function and columns to be subtotaled.
5. Deselect the *Replace current subtotals* check box and click OK.

> **TIP | Removing Subtotals**
>
> The subtotal rows are temporary. To remove them, display the Subtotals dialog box and click Remove All.

## Collapse and Expand the Subtotals

**STEP 3**》 The Subtotal feature creates an *outline*, a hierarchical structure of data. When a dataset contains a structured list, you can collapse or expand the categories after using the Subtotal feature. Table 10.2 explains the outline buttons that appear on the left side of the subtotaled data. Figure 10.3 shows a dataset that is collapsed to display the discipline subtotals and the grand total after the user clicked the outline button 2. The number of outline buttons depends on the total number of subtotals created. Because the data in Figure 10.2 contained discipline and area subtotals, four outline buttons appear in Figure 10.3. If the dataset contained only one level of subtotals, only three outline buttons would appear.

### TABLE 10.2  Outline Buttons

| Button | Description |
| --- | --- |
| 1 | Collapse outline to display the grand total only. |
| 2 | Display subtotals by the main subtotal category and the grand total. |
| 3 | Displays subtotals by the main subtotal category, the secondary subtotal category, and the grant total. |
| 4 | Display the entire list. |
| + | Expand an outline group to see its details. |
| − | Collapse an outline group to see its category name only. |

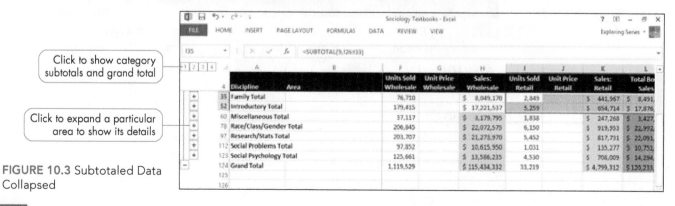

**FIGURE 10.3** Subtotaled Data Collapsed

# Grouping and Ungrouping Data

STEP 4 >> The Subtotals feature outlines data into categories by rows. You can create outlines by columns of related data as well. For Excel to outline by columns, the dataset must contain formulas or aggregate functions. If Excel cannot create the outline, it displays the message box *Cannot create an outline*. To create an outline by columns, do the following:

1. Click the DATA tab.
2. Click the Group arrow in the Outline group.
3. Select Auto Outline.

For more control in creating an outline, you can create groups. *Grouping* is the process of joining rows or columns of related data together into a single entity. After you create groups in the dataset, you can click a collapse button (–) to collapse a group to show the outsider column or click the expand button (+) to expand groups of related columns to view the internal columns of data. Grouping enables you to hide raw data while you focus on key calculated results. To group data, do the following:

1. Select the rows or columns you want to group. For column groups, you often select columns containing details but not aggregate columns, such as totals or averages. (Rows are automatically grouped if you use the Subtotals feature.)
2. Click the DATA tab.
3. Click Group in the Outline group. If the Group dialog box opens, choose the option to group by columns or rows and click OK.

In Figure 10.4, Excel grouped the data by columns. Because the Units Sold Retail and Unit Price Retail columns are grouped, you can click the collapse button above Sales Retail to collapse the columns and focus on the Sales Retail column. Currently, some of the wholesale columns are hidden, showing only the Sales: Wholesale column. You can click the expand button above the Sales: Wholesale column to display the related wholesale columns.

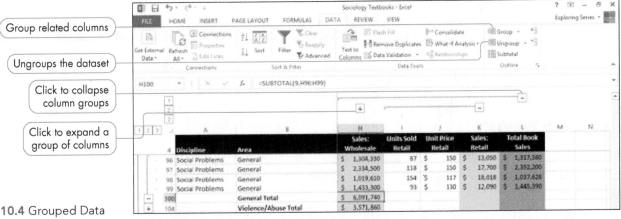

**FIGURE 10.4** Grouped Data

> **TIP** Removing Groups
>
> To remove groups, select all grouped columns or rows and click Ungroup in the Outline group.

**Quick Concepts**

1. Why must a dataset be sorted by a category before using the Subtotal feature? Within the Subtotal dialog box, which option do you set to match the column you used to sort the data? *p. 328*

2. Explain the SUBTOTAL function as it is used by the Subtotal feature. *p. 329*

3. How can you expand or collapse outlined groups of columns? *p. 331*

# Hands-On Exercises

## 1 Subtotals and Outlines

As VP of the Sociology Division at Ivory Halls Publishing Company, you want to conduct a preliminary analysis of your current textbook offerings. Each textbook falls within a general discipline, and each discipline is divided into several areas. Details for each textbook include the title, current edition, and copyright year. The company tracks units sold, unit prices, and gross sales by two major types of sales: (1) wholesale sales to bookstores and (2) retail sales to individual consumers. You will organize the data and include area subtotals. Your assistant applied Freeze Panes to keep the column headings in row 4 and the disciplines and areas in columns A and B visible regardless of where you scroll.

**Skills covered:** Subtotal the Data • Add a Second Subtotal • Collapse and Expand the Subtotals • Group and Ungroup Data

### STEP 1 ›› SUBTOTAL THE DATA

Before you use the Subtotal feature, you must sort the data by discipline and then by area. After sorting the data, you will insert subtotals for each discipline. You want to see the totals for the wholesale sales, retail sales, and combined book sales. Refer to Figure 10.5 as you complete Step 1.

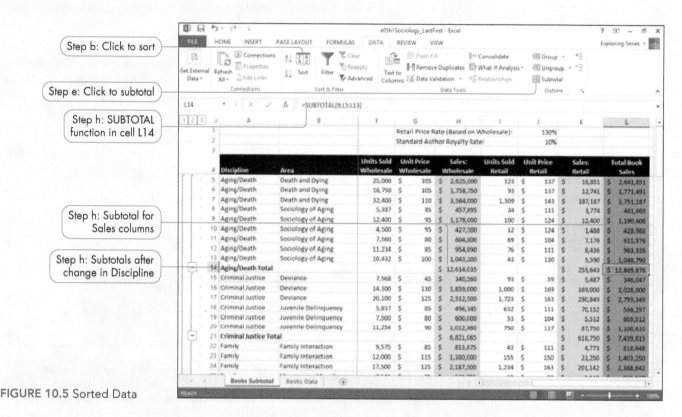

**FIGURE 10.5** Sorted Data

**a.** Open *e10h1Sociology* and save it as **e10h1Sociology_LastFirst**.

> **TROUBLESHOOTING:** If you make any major mistakes in this exercise, you can close the file, open *e10h1Sociology* again, and then start this exercise over.

The workbook contains two worksheets: Books Subtotal for Hands-On Exercise 1 and Books Data for Hands-On Exercises 2–4.

b. Click the **DATA tab** and click **Sort** in the Sort & Filter group.

c. Click the **Sort by arrow** and select **Discipline** in the Sort dialog box.

d. Click **Add Level**, click the **Then by arrow**, and then select **Area**. Click **OK**.

Excel sorts the data by discipline in alphabetical order. Within each discipline, Excel sorts the data further by area. The data are sorted first by disciplines so that you can apply subtotals to each discipline.

e. Click **Subtotal** in the Outline group.

The Subtotal dialog box opens. The default *At each change in* is the Discipline column, and the default *Use function* is Sum. These settings are correct.

f. Click the **Sales: Wholesale check box** in the *Add subtotal to* section.

g. Click the **Sales: Retail check box** in the *Add subtotal to* section.

Excel selected the last column—Total Book Sales—automatically. You selected the other two sales columns to total. You will leave the *Replace current subtotals* and *Summary below data* check boxes selected.

h. Click **OK**. Scroll to the right to see the subtotals and click **cell L14** to see the SUBTOTAL function for the total book sales for the Aging/Death discipline. Save the workbook.

Excel inserts subtotal rows after each discipline category. The subtotal rows include labels and subtotals for the wholesale sales, retail sales, and book sales columns.

> **TROUBLESHOOTING**: If your subtotals do not match the totals in Figure 10.5, open the Subtotal dialog box, click Remove All, click OK, and repeat steps b through h again.

## STEP 2 ≫ ADD A SECOND SUBTOTAL

Displaying subtotals by discipline helps you compare sales data better; however, you want to add another level to see subtotals for each area within each discipline. To insert two levels of subtotals, you must subtotal the primary category first (Discipline) and then add a subtotal to the second category (Area). As you use the Subtotal dialog box, you want to keep the original subtotals intact. Refer to Figure 10.6 as you complete Step 2.

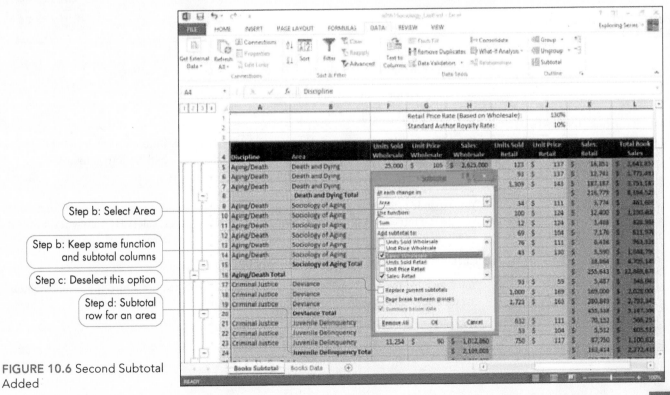

Step b: Select Area

Step b: Keep same function and subtotal columns

Step c: Deselect this option

Step d: Subtotal row for an area

**FIGURE 10.6** Second Subtotal Added

**a.** Click **Subtotal** in the Outline group to open the Subtotal dialog box again.

**b.** Click the **At each change in arrow** and select **Area**.

The *Use function* is still Sum, and Excel remembers the last columns you selected in the *Add subtotal to* section—Sales: Wholesale, Sales: Retail, and Total Book Sales.

**c.** Click the **Replace current subtotals check box** to deselect it.

Deselecting this check box will keep the discipline subtotals.

**d.** Click **OK** and click **cell L15**. Save the workbook.

Excel inserts subtotal rows after each area. The Formula Bar displays =SUBTOTAL(9,L9:L14). Your data have discipline subtotals and area subtotals within each discipline.

---

**TROUBLESHOOTING**: If you subtotal the area first and then discipline, Excel adds several discipline subtotals, which repeat the area subtotals. That is why you must subtotal by the primary category first and then subtotal by the secondary category.

---

## STEP 3 ≫ COLLAPSE AND EXPAND THE SUBTOTALS

You want to compare wholesale, retail, and book sales among the disciplines and then among areas within a discipline. Refer to Figure 10.7 as you complete Step 3.

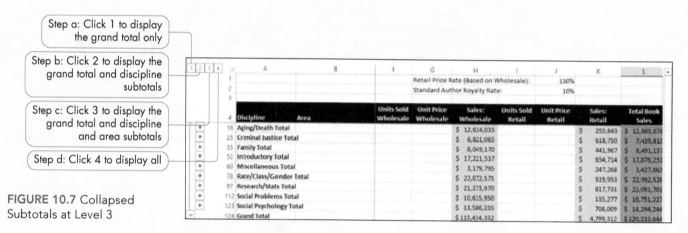

Step a: Click 1 to display the grand total only

Step b: Click 2 to display the grand total and discipline subtotals

Step c: Click 3 to display the grand total and discipline and area subtotals

Step d: Click 4 to display all

**FIGURE 10.7** Collapsed Subtotals at Level 3

**a.** Click the **1** in the top-left outline area (to the left of the column headings).

You collapsed the outline to show the grand totals only.

**b.** Click the **2** in the top-left outline area.

You expanded the outline to show the grand and discipline subtotals. Which two disciplines had the highest wholesale and retail sales? Which discipline had the lowest total sales?

**c.** Click the **3** in the top-left outline area.

You expanded the outline to show the grand, discipline, and area subtotals (see Figure 10.7). Within the Introductory discipline, which area had the lowest sales? How do wholesale and retail sales compare? Are they proportionally the same within each area?

**d.** Click the **4** in the top-left outline area. Save the workbook.

You expanded the outline to show all details again. If you had not added the second subtotal, the outline would have had three levels instead of four.

# STEP 4 ≫ GROUP AND UNGROUP DATA

You want to apply an outline to the columns so that you can collapse or expand the units sold and unit prices columns. Refer to Figure 10.8 as you complete Step 4.

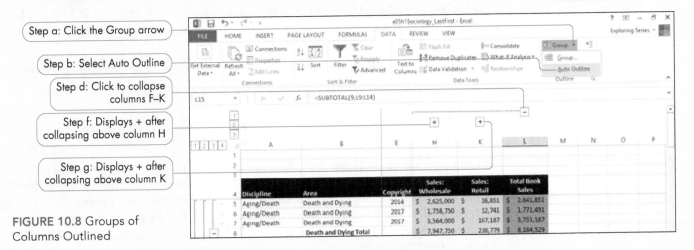

**FIGURE 10.8** Groups of Columns Outlined

Callouts:
- Step a: Click the Group arrow
- Step b: Select Auto Outline
- Step d: Click to collapse columns F–K
- Step f: Displays + after collapsing above column H
- Step g: Displays + after collapsing above column K

a. Click the **Group arrow** in the Outline group on the DATA tab.

> You want to see if Excel can create a column outline for you so that you do not have to select columns and group them individually.

b. Select **Auto Outline**.

> Excel displays the message box *Modify existing outline?* because it recognizes that an existing outline exists—the row subtotals outline.

c. Click **OK**.

> Excel maintains the outlined subtotals and adds column subtotals. Horizontal lines and collapse buttons appear above the columns. The formula in column H is =F5*G5, so Excel creates an outline for these columns. The formula in column K is =I5*J5, so Excel creates an outline for these columns. It also creates a hierarchical outline of columns F through K, since the formula in column L sums the values in columns H and K.

d. Click the **collapse (–) button** above column L.

> You collapsed columns F through K to display disciplines, areas, and total sales by title.

e. Click the **expand (+) button** above column L.

> You expanded the outline to show columns F through K again.

f. Click the **collapse (–) button** above column H.

> You collapsed the outline to hide columns F and G so you can focus on the wholesale sales without the distraction of the Units Sold or Unit Price columns.

g. Click the **collapse (–) button** above column K.

> You collapsed the outline to hide columns I and J so you can focus on the retail sales without the distraction of the Units Sold or Unit Price columns.

h. Save the workbook. Keep the workbook open if you plan to continue with Hands-On Exercise 2. If not, close the workbook and exit Excel.

# PivotTable Basics

Analyzing large amounts of data is important for making solid decisions. Entering data is the easy part; retrieving data in a structured, meaningful way is more challenging. ***Data mining*** is the process of analyzing large volumes of data, using advanced statistical techniques, and identifying trends and patterns in the data. Managers use data-mining techniques to address a variety of questions, such as the following:

- What snack foods do customers purchase most when purchasing Pepsi® products?
- What age group from what geographic region downloads the most top 10 songs from iTunes?
- What hotel chain and rental car combinations are most popular among Delta Air Lines passengers flying into Salt Lake City?

Questions similar to those above help organizations prepare their marketing plans to capitalize on consumer spending patterns. The more you know about your customer demographics, the better you can focus your strategic plans to increase market share.

A ***PivotTable*** is a powerful, interactive data-mining feature that enables you to summarize and analyze data, especially helpful when working with large datasets. An advantage of using a PivotTable is that you can group data into one or more categories and perform a variety of calculations without altering the original dataset. The most important benefit of a PivotTable is that it is dynamic. You can easily and quickly *pivot*, or rearrange, data to analyze them from different viewpoints, such as expanding or collapsing details, organizing and grouping data differently, and switching row and column categories. Viewing the PivotTable from different perspectives helps you more easily identify trends and patterns among the variables in the data that might not be obvious from looking at the data from only one viewpoint.

In this section, you will learn how to create a PivotTable by organizing data into columns and rows to aggregate data.

## Creating a PivotTable

Before you create a PivotTable, ensure the data source is well structured. Applying the rules for good table design is a start: Use meaningful column labels, ensure data accuracy, and avoid blank rows and columns in the dataset. To consolidate and aggregate data, at least one column must have duplicate values, such as the same city, state, or department name for several records. You then use these columns of duplicate values to create categories for organizing and summarizing data. Another column must have numeric values that can be aggregated to produce quantitative summaries, such as averages or sums.

### Create a PivotTable from the Quick Analysis Gallery

You can create a PivotTable from the Quick Analysis gallery. A benefit of this method is that Excel displays recommended PivotTables based on the data. To create a PivotTable using Quick Analysis, do the following:

STEP 1»

1. Select the entire dataset, including the field names (column labels).
2. Click the Quick Analysis button in the bottom-right corner of the selected range.
3. Click TABLES in the Quick Analysis gallery.
4. Position the mouse pointer over the PivotTable thumbnails to see a preview of the different recommended PivotTables (see Figure 10.9).
5. Click the PivotTable thumbnail to create the desired PivotTable.

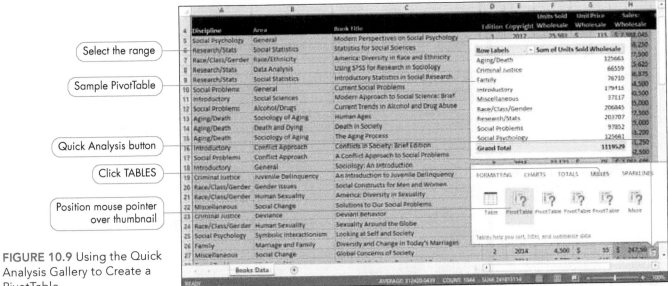

Select the range

Sample PivotTable

Quick Analysis button

Click TABLES

Position mouse pointer over thumbnail

**FIGURE 10.9** Using the Quick Analysis Gallery to Create a PivotTable

## TIP | PivotTable or Subtotals?

At first glance, PivotTables are similar to subtotals because they both produce subtotals, but PivotTables are more robust. PivotTables provide more flexibility than subtotals provide. If you need complex subtotals cross-referenced by two or more categories with filtering and other specifications, create a PivotTable.

## Create a PivotTable from the Ribbon

You can also create a PivotTable by using commands on the Ribbon. The Insert tab contains PivotTable and Recommended PivotTables commands. If you click PivotTable, Excel displays the Create PivotTable dialog box so that you can create a blank PivotTable from scratch. However, if you click Recommended PivotTables, Excel displays a dialog box so that you can select from a gallery of PivotTables. This option is similar to using the Quick Analysis gallery. To create a recommended PivotTable using the Ribbon, do the following:

1. Click inside the dataset (the range of cells or table).
2. Click the INSERT tab and click Recommended PivotTables in the Tables group to open the Recommended PivotTables dialog box (see Figure 10.10).
3. Click a thumbnail in the gallery on the left side of the dialog box to see a preview of the PivotTable on the right side.
4. Click OK to create the desired PivotTable.

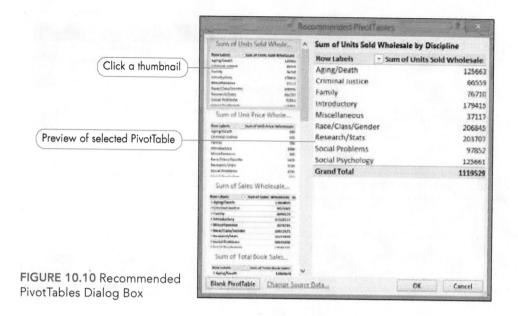

FIGURE 10.10 Recommended PivotTables Dialog Box

After you use the Recommended PivotTables dialog box or the Quick Analysis gallery, Excel creates a PivotTable on a new worksheet (see Figure 10.11). The ROWS area contains the category names of the summarized data. For example, each discipline, such as Family, is listed in only one row, regardless of how many times each category name appears in the original dataset.

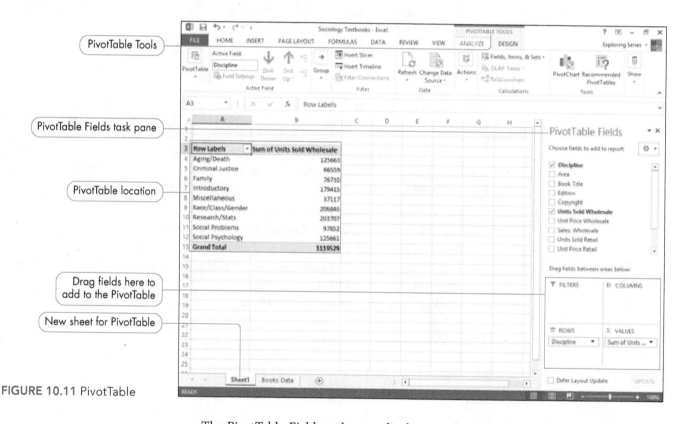

FIGURE 10.11 PivotTable

The PivotTable Fields task pane displays on the right side, and the PivotTable Tools Analyze and Design contextual tabs appear on the Ribbon. If you click outside the PivotTable, the contextual tabs and the task pane disappear. Click within the PivotTable to display these elements again.

The **PivotTable Fields task pane** contains two sections. The *Choose fields to add to report* section lists all the fields or column labels from the original data source. You can click either drag a field to an area in the bottom of the task pane or click the check box to add the field to the PivotTable. Use the *Drag fields between areas below* section to arrange fields in one of the four PivotTable areas. Table 10.3 describes the areas of a PivotTable.

| TABLE 10.3 | Areas of a PivotTable |
|---|---|
| **Area** | **Description** |
| **Filters Area** | Filters the data to display results based on particular conditions you set. |
| **Columns Area** | Subdivides data into one or more additional categories. |
| **Rows Area** | Organizes and groups data into categories on the left side. Each group name occupies a single row. |
| **Values Area** | Displays summary statistics, such as totals or averages. |

## Modifying a PivotTable

After you create a PivotTable, you might want to modify it to see the data from a different perspective. For example, you might want to add fields to the rows, values, and columns areas of the PivotTable. In addition, you might want to collapse the PivotTable to show fewer details or expand it to show more details.

### Add Rows

You can add fields to provide a more detailed analysis. For example, you might want to organize data by discipline by adding the Discipline field to the ROWS area in the PivotTable Fields task pane. To add a field as a row, do one of the following:

**STEP 2 »**
- Click the field's check box in the *Choose fields to add to report* section. Excel adds the field to a PivotTable area based on the type of data stored in the field. If the field contains text, Excel usually places that field in the ROWS area.
- Drag the field from the *Choose fields to add to report* section and drop it in the ROWS area.
- Right-click the field name in the *Choose fields to add to report* section and select *Add to Row Labels*.

### Add Values

A PivotTable has meaning when you include quantitative fields, such as quantities and monetary values, to aggregate the data. For example, you might want to display the total wholesale sales for each discipline and area. To add values, do one of the following:

- Click the field's check box in the *Choose fields to add to report* section. Excel makes it the value aggregate, such as *Sum of Sales*.

- Drag the field from the *Choose fields to add to report* section and drop it in the VALUES area.
- Right-click the field name in the *Choose fields to add to report* section and select *Add to Values*.

Excel sums the values for each group listed in the ROWS area. For example, the total number of units sold wholesale for the Family discipline is 76,710. If you drag a text field, such as Book Title, to the VALUES area, Excel counts the number of records for each group listed in the ROWS area. In this case, Excel counts seven books in the Family discipline.

## Add Columns

Although you can create subdivisions of data by adding more fields to the ROWS area, you might want to arrange the subdivision categories in columns. Doing so minimizes the redundancy of duplicating subdivision row labels and helps consolidate data. To subdivide data into columns, drag a field from the *Choose fields to add to report* section and drop it in the COLUMNS area. Excel updates the aggregated values by the combination of row and column categories.

Figure 10.12 shows a PivotTable that uses the Discipline field as rows, the *Sum of Units Sold Wholesale* field as values, and Copyright field as columns. Each discipline label and each copyright year label appears only once in the PivotTable. This added level of detail enables you to see the total sales for each discipline based on its copyright year. The PivotTable includes grand totals for each discipline and grand totals for each year.

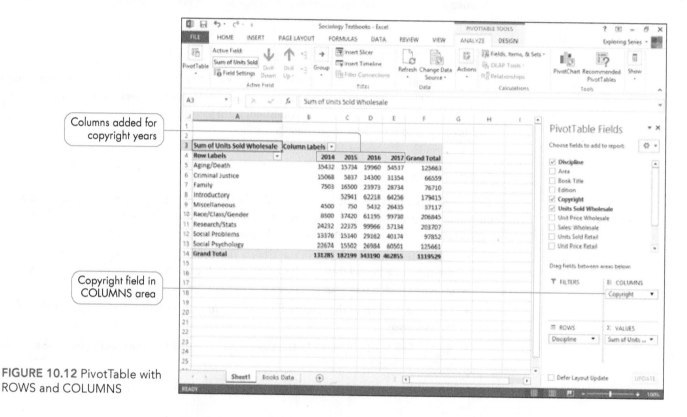

**FIGURE 10.12** PivotTable with ROWS and COLUMNS

## Collapse and Expand Items

If you include two fields as ROWS, the PivotTable displays more depth but may be overwhelming. You can hide or collapse the secondary field rows. For example, if the PivotTable contains both Discipline and Copyright row labels, you might want to collapse copyright years for some disciplines. The collapse and expand buttons display to the left of the row labels. If they do not, click Show and click the +/− buttons on the Analyze tab. Figure 10.13 shows the collapse and expand buttons.

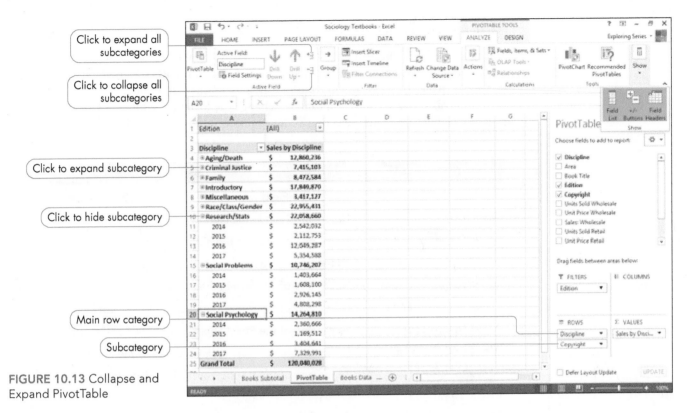

Click to expand all subcategories

Click to collapse all subcategories

Click to expand subcategory

Click to hide subcategory

Main row category

Subcategory

**FIGURE 10.13** Collapse and Expand PivotTable

To hide the subcategories for a particular category, click the collapse button (–) on the left side of the specific category you wish to collapse. Excel hides the subcategories for that particular category and shows only the aggregated totals for the category. Continue collapsing other categories as needed to focus on a particular category's details.

To expand the subcategories again, click the expand button (+) on the left side of the category labels.

---

### TIP   Collapse and Expand All

You can collapse all categories at one time by clicking Collapse Field in the Active Field group on the Analyze tab. To expand all categories at one time, click Expand Field. This approach is faster than collapsing or expanding each category individually.

---

## Remove Fields

You can remove fields to reduce the amount of data to analyze. To remove a field from the PivotTable, do one of the following:

**STEP 3**

- Click the field name in the *Drag fields between areas below* section and select Remove Field.
- Deselect the check box next to the field name in the *Choose fields to add to report* section.
- Drag a field name in the *Drag fields between areas below* section outside the PivotTable Fields task pane.

## Rearrange Fields

You can rearrange fields in a PivotTable to improve readability. For example, you might want more columns than rows, so you can switch the fields in the ROWS and COLUMNS areas in the task pane. To move a field from one area to another, drag the field in the *Drag fields between areas below* section. You can also change the location or hierarchy of the fields by clicking the field arrow and selecting a Move option. Table 10.4 explains the Move options.

| TABLE 10.4 Move Options | |
| --- | --- |
| Option | Moves the Field... |
| Move Up | Up one position in the hierarchy within the same area |
| Move Down | Down one position in the hierarchy within the same area |
| Move to Beginning | To the beginning of all fields in the same area |
| Move to End | To the end of all fields in the same area |
| Move to Report Filter | To the end of the Report Filter area of the PivotTable |
| Move to Row Labels | To the end of the Row Labels area of the PivotTable |
| Move to Column Labels | To the end of the Column Labels area of the PivotTable |
| Move to Values | To the end of the VALUES area of the PivotTable |

## Change the Values Field Settings

Although Excel uses the SUM function as the default summary statistic for numerical fields, you can select a different function. For example, you might want to calculate the average, lowest, or highest value within each group, or identify the lowest sales for each discipline/copyright year combination to see if the older books have decreased sales. In addition to changing the summary statistic, you might want to change the column label that appears above the summary statistics. By default, words indicate the summary statistic function applied, such as *Sum of Total Sales by Book* or *Average of Total Sales by Book*, depending on the summary statistic applied to the values. Finally, you might need to format the aggregated values. To modify any of these value settings, do the following:

**STEP 4 >>**

1. Click a value in the appropriate field in the PivotTable and click Field Settings in the Active Field group on the ANALYZE tab. Alternatively, click the field's arrow in the VALUES area of the task pane and select Value Field Settings. The Value Field Settings dialog box opens (see Figure 10.14).

2. Type the name you want to appear as the column label in the Custom Name box. For example, you might want the heading to appear as *Total Sales* instead of *Sum of Total Book Sales*.

3. Select the summary statistical function you want to use to summarize the values in the *Summarize value field by* list.

4. Click Number Format to open an abbreviated version of the Format Cells dialog box. Select a number type, such as Accounting, in the Category list; select other settings, such as number of decimal places in the *Decimal places* spin arrow; and then click OK.

5. Click OK in the Value Field Settings dialog box.

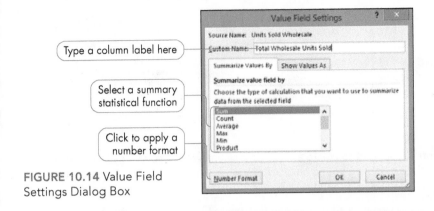

 Type a column label here

Select a summary statistical function

Click to apply a number format

**FIGURE 10.14** Value Field Settings Dialog Box

> **TIP** | **Multiple Summary Statistics**
>
> You can display more than one function for a field. For example, you might want to show *both* the total book sales and the average book sales. To display multiple summary statistics, drag another copy of the same field to the VALUES area and set each value setting separately.

## Refresh a PivotTable

Although PivotTables are powerful, they do not update automatically if you make any changes to the underlying data in the data source. For example, if you change a sales value or delete a row in the data source, the PivotTable does not reflect the changed data. Unfortunately, this causes PivotTable summary statistics to be outdated with inaccurate results. If you change the data source, you must update the PivotTable by doing the following:

**STEP 5 »**
1. Click in the PivotTable.
2. Click the ANALYZE tab.
3. Click Refresh in the Data group to refresh the current PivotTable only, or click the Refresh arrow and select Refresh All to refresh all PivotTables in the workbook.

If you want to ensure your PivotTable is up to date when you open the workbook, click the Analyze tab, click the PivotTable arrow on the left side of the Ribbon, select Options to open the PivotTable Options dialog box, click the Data tab, select *Refresh data when opening the file*, and then click OK.

*Quick* Concepts

1. What are the advantages of using a PivotTable instead of a subtotal? *p. 336*
2. What is the main benefit of creating a PivotTable using the Quick Analysis gallery or from the Recommended PivotTables dialog box over creating a blank PivotTable? *pp. 336–337*
3. List the four areas of a PivotTable. *p. 339*

# Hands-On Exercises

## 2 PivotTable Basics

After exhausting the possibilities of outlines and subtotals, you want to create a PivotTable to analyze the sociology book sales. You realize you can see the data from different perspectives, enabling you to have a stronger understanding of the sales by various categories.

**Skills covered:** Create a PivotTable • Add Rows, Values, and Columns • Remove and Rearrange Fields • Change the Values Field Settings • Refresh a PivotTable

### STEP 1 ≫ CREATE A PIVOTTABLE

Because you want to keep the subtotals you created in the Books Subtotal worksheet, you will create a PivotTable from the Books Data worksheet. Refer to Figures 10.10 and 10.15 as you complete Step 1.

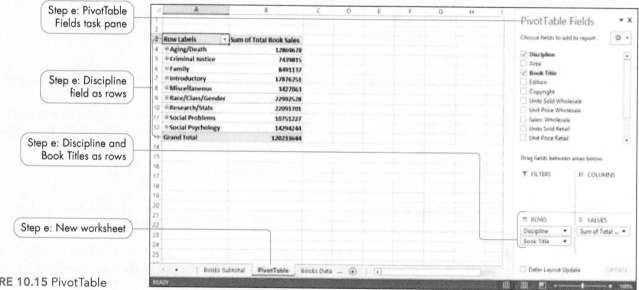

FIGURE 10.15 PivotTable

a. Open *e10h1Sociology_LastFirst* if you closed it at the end of Hands-On Exercise 1 and save it as **e10h2Sociology_LastFirst**, changing *h1* to *h2*.

b. Click the **Books Data worksheet tab**.

   Excel does not let you create a PivotTable using subtotaled data. To preserve the subtotals you created in Hands-On Exercise 1, you will use the dataset in the Books Data worksheet.

c. Click in **cell A5**, click the **INSERT tab**, and then click **Recommended PivotTables** in the Tables group.

   The Recommended PivotTables dialog box opens (see Figure 10.10).

d. Scroll the thumbnails of recommended PivotTables and click the **Sum of Total Book Sales by Discipline thumbnail**. (NOTE: Hover the mouse pointer over the thumbnails to see the full names.)

   You selected this PivotTable to show the overall total book sales for each discipline. The dialog box shows a preview of the selected PivotTable.

**e.** Click **OK** and click within the PivotTable, if necessary. Rename Sheet1 as **PivotTable**. Save the workbook.

Excel inserts a new Sheet1 worksheet, which you renamed as PivotTable, with the PivotTable on the left side and the PivotTable Fields task pane on the right side (see Figure 10.15).

## STEP 2 ADD ROWS, VALUES, AND COLUMNS

You want to compare sales combinations by discipline, copyright year, and edition. The discipline field is already in the PivotTable, but you need to add the copyright year and edition fields. Refer to Figure 10.16 as you complete Step 2.

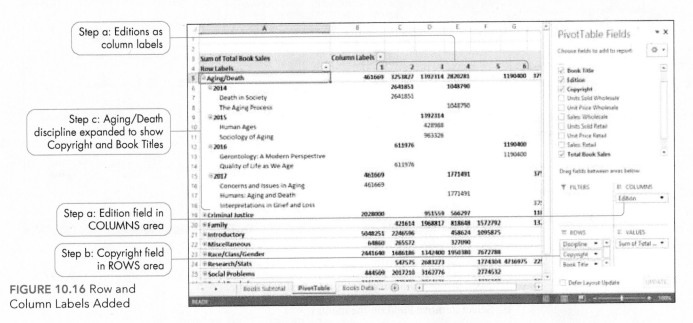

**FIGURE 10.16** Row and Column Labels Added

**a.** Drag the **Edition field** to the COLUMNS area in the PivotTable Fields task pane.

Excel displays the total book sales by a combination of discipline and edition. This enables you to compare sales of current editions within each discipline. Blanks appear in the PivotTable when a discipline does not have a specific edition. For example, the Family discipline does not have any first-edition books currently being published.

**b.** Drag the **Copyright field** to be between the Discipline and Book Title fields in the ROWS area.

The Copyright and Book Titles are not showing because they are collapsed within the Discipline rows.

**c.** Click the **Aging/Death expand (+) button**. Save the workbook.

You expanded the Aging/Death discipline to show the copyright years and titles.

### TIP Field ScreenTip

It may be confusing to see *Sum of Total...* in the VALUES box. Position the pointer over a field name in the area to see a ScreenTip with the full name, such as *Sum of Total Book Sales*.

## STEP 3 ≫ REMOVE AND REARRANGE FIELDS

Although it is informative to compare sales by edition, you think that the PivotTable contains too much detail, so you will remove the Edition field. In addition, the ROWS area contains the Book Titles field, but those data are collapsed; therefore, you will remove it as well. After you remove the fields, you will rearrange other fields to simplify the PivotTable. Refer to Figure 10.17 as you complete Step 3.

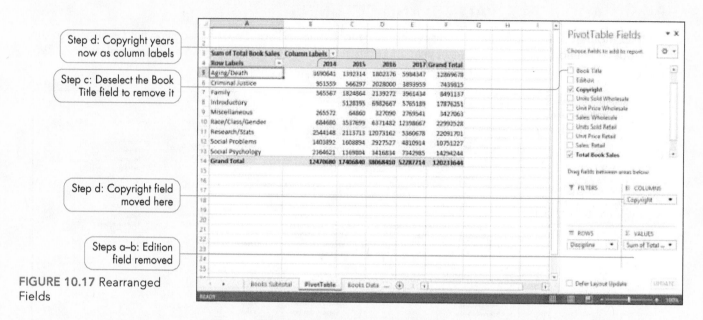

**FIGURE 10.17** Rearranged Fields

a. Click the **Edition arrow** in the Column Labels area.

Excel displays a menu of options to apply to this field.

b. Select **Remove Field** on the menu.

You removed the Edition field from the PivotTable. Instead of several sales columns, Excel consolidates the sales into one sales column. Although you find it helpful to have sales breakdowns by copyright year, you think the PivotTable will be easier to read if you move the Copyright field to the COLUMNS area.

c. Deselect the **Book Title check box** in the *Choose fields to add to report* section of the task pane.

You removed the Book Title field from the PivotTable.

d. Drag the **Copyright field** from the ROWS area to the COLUMNS area. Save the workbook.

This arrangement consolidates the data better. Instead of repeating the copyright years for each discipline, the copyright years are listed only once each at the top of the sales columns.

# STEP 4 ›› CHANGE THE VALUES FIELD SETTINGS

After selecting the PivotTable fields, you want to improve the appearance of the sociology textbook PivotTable. You will format the values for Accounting Number Format and replace the generic Row Labels description with a label that indicates the sociology disciplines. Refer to Figure 10.18 as you complete Step 4.

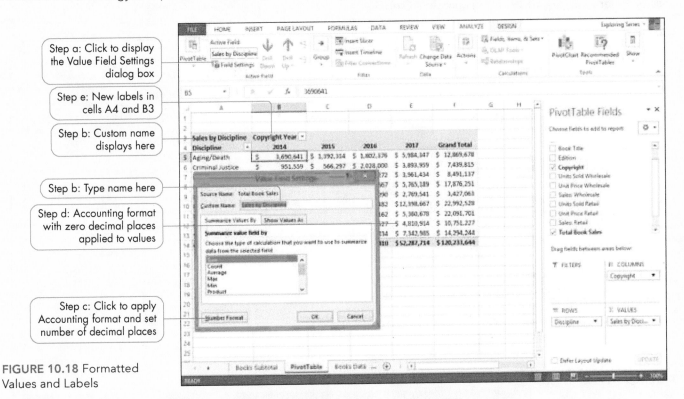

Step a: Click to display the Value Field Settings dialog box

Step e: New labels in cells A4 and B3

Step b: Custom name displays here

Step b: Type name here

Step d: Accounting format with zero decimal places applied to values

Step c: Click to apply Accounting format and set number of decimal places

**FIGURE 10.18** Formatted Values and Labels

a. Click **cell B5** and click **Field Settings** in the Active Field group on the ANALYZE tab.

The Value Field Settings dialog box opens so that you can format the field.

b. Type **Sales by Discipline** in the **Custom Name box**.

Leave Sum as the selected calculation type in the *Summarize value field by* section.

c. Click **Number Format**.

Excel opens a Format Cells dialog box with only one tab: the Number tab.

d. Click **Accounting** in the Category list, change the **Decimal places value** to **0**, click **OK** in the Format Cells dialog box, and then click **OK** in the Value Field Settings dialog box.

You formatted the values with Accounting Number Format with no decimal places, and the heading *Sales by Discipline* appears in cell A3.

e. Type **Discipline** in **cell A4** and type **Copyright Year** in **cell B3**.

You replaced the generic *Row Labels* heading with *Discipline* to describe the contents of the first column, and you replaced the *Column Labels* heading with *Copyright Year*. Although you can create custom names for values, you cannot create custom names for row and column labels. However, you can edit the labels directly in the cells.

f. Select the **range B4:F4** and center the labels horizontally. Save the workbook.

# STEP 5 >> REFRESH A PIVOTTABLE

After consulting with the Accounting Department, you realize that the retail prices are incorrect. The unit retail prices are based on a percentage of the wholesale price. The retail unit price is 30% more than the wholesale unit price, but it should be 25%. You will edit the input cell in the original worksheet and refresh the PivotTable to see the corrected results. Refer to Figure 10.19 as you complete Step 5.

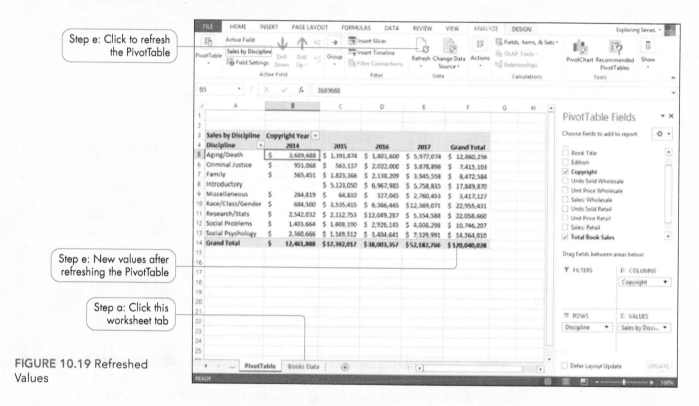

**FIGURE 10.19** Refreshed Values

a. Click the **Books Data worksheet tab**.

You need to locate and change the retail price percentage.

b. Click **cell J1**, the cell that contains the current retail price percentage.

c. Type **125%** and press **Enter**. Save the workbook to update the formula results on the Books Data worksheet.

> **TROUBLESHOOTING**: If the formula results in the Unit Price Retail, Sales: Retail, and Total Book Sales columns do not change after you edit the data in step c, the workbook may be set for manual calculation. To ensure that formulas update automatically, click the File tab, click Options, click Formulas, click Automatic as the Workbook Calculation setting, and then click OK.

d. Click the **PivotTable worksheet tab**.

Notice that the PivotTable aggregate values did not change. The grand total is $120,233,644. You must refresh the PivotTable.

e. Click the **ANALYZE tab** and click **Refresh** in the Data group.

Excel updates the PivotTable values based on the change you made in the Books Data worksheet.

f. Save the workbook. Keep the workbook open if you plan to continue with Hands-On Exercise 3. If not, close the workbook and exit Excel.

# PivotTable Options

As you have experienced, PivotTables consolidate and aggregate large amounts of data to facilitate data analysis. You can customize the PivotTable for more in-depth analysis. In the previous section, you used the Analyze tab to display the Value Field Settings dialog box and refresh the PivotTable. However, the Analyze tab contains more ways for you to customize your PivotTable. For example, you can filter groups, display or hide particular groups temporarily, and add subtotals.

In this section, you will learn how to filter data in a PivotTable. In addition, you will create a calculated field and display subtotals.

## Filtering and Slicing a PivotTable

By default, PivotTables display aggregated data for each category. However, you may want to set a filter to exclude particular categories or values. You can specify a particular field to use to filter the PivotTable. In addition, you can include slicers to easily set filters to designate which specific data to include in the PivotTable.

### Add Filters

Although PivotTables consolidate data from the original data source into groups, the PivotTable might contain more details than you want. You can apply filters to show only a subset of the PivotTable. Drag a field to the FILTERS area in the task pane when you want to engage a filter based on a particular field. For example, you might want to filter the PivotTable to show only aggregates for first- and second-edition books. When you drag a field to the FILTERS area, Excel displays the field name in cell A1 with a filter arrow in cell B1. To set the filter, click the filter arrow and do one of the following and then click OK:

**STEP 1** ≫

- Select the value in the list to filter the data by that value only.

- Click the *Select Multiple Items* check box if you want to select more than one value to filter the PivotTable. Then click the check boxes by each value you want to set (see Figure 10.20).

- Type a value in the Search box if the list is too long and you want to find a value quickly.

Only a subset of the data that meet those conditions appears in the PivotTable; Excel hides the unselected items.

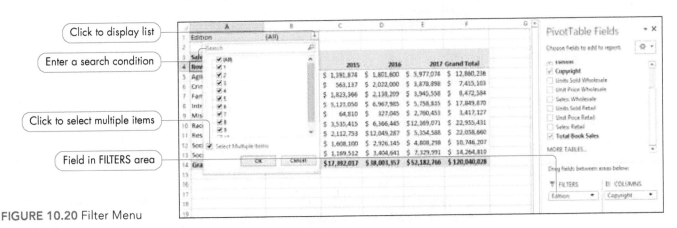

**FIGURE 10.20** Filter Menu

Cell B1 displays (All) when no filter is enabled, the value if one filter is enabled, or (Multiple Items) if more than one item is selected. To remove the filter entirely, remove it from the FILTER area. To remove the filter temporarily, click the filter arrow in cell B1, select (All), and then click OK.

You can apply additional filters based on the row and column label groupings. For example, you can apply date filters to display summary statistics for data occurring within a particular time frame or apply filters for values within a designated range. To apply group filters, click the Row Labels or Column Labels arrow in the PivotTable and specify the settings (see Figure 10.21). Excel calculates the summary statistics based on the filtered data rather than the complete dataset.

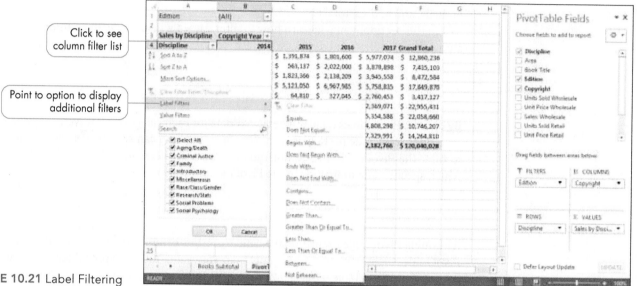

Click to see column filter list

Point to option to display additional filters

**FIGURE 10.21** Label Filtering

## Insert Slicers

You can insert a *slicer*, a small window containing one button for each unique item in a field so that you can filter the PivotTable quickly. Slicers are especially helpful to filter data when a PivotTable is based on multiple tables. The visual representation is easier to manipulate than adding more fields to the FILTERS area and then setting each field's filter through drop-down lists. To insert a slicer, do the following:

**STEP 2** ▶▶

1. Click the ANALYZE tab.
2. Click Insert Slicer in the Filter group to display the Insert Slicers dialog box (see Figure 10.22).
3. Click one or more field check boxes to display one or more slicers and click OK.

**FIGURE 10.22** Insert Slicers Dialog Box

Excel inserts slicers into the worksheet. You can manipulate a slicer by doing the following:

- **Move the Slicer.** Drag a slicer to move it onscreen.
- **Filter Data.** Click the slicer button to filter by the value represented by the button. Press Ctrl to select several slicers to apply additional filters. Excel highlights the item to make it clear how you filtered the PivotTable. For example, in Figure 10.23, the Discipline field is filtered by Family, Introductory, and Social Problems. Although

no filter has been enabled for the Edition field, the 6th and 9th edition buttons are unavailable because the three disciplines selected do not have books that are in their 6th or 9th editions.

- **Remove a Filter.** Click Remove Filter in the top-right corner of the slicer window.

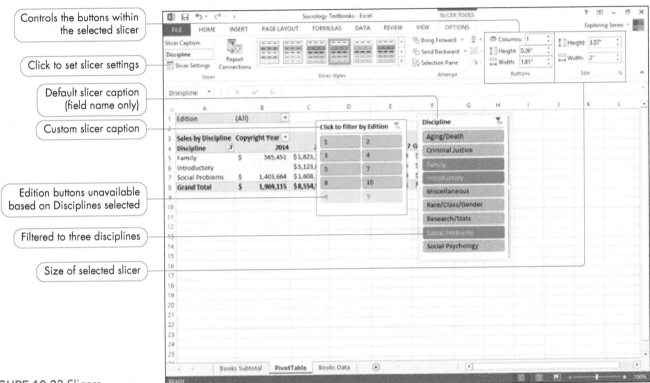

**FIGURE 10.23** Slicers

## Customize Slicers

When you select a slicer, the Slicer Tools Options tab displays so that you can customize a slicer. The default slicer caption displays the field name only. The *slicer caption* is text that displays in the header at the top of the slicer window. However, you can customize the slicer by changing its caption. In Figure 10.23, the left slicer's caption displays an instruction to the user, whereas the right slicer's caption displays the default field name. Table 10.5 lists and describes the commands on the Slicer Tools Options tab.

**TABLE 10.5  Slicer Tools Commands**

| Group | Commands |
|---|---|
| Slicer | Enables you to change the slicer caption, display the Slicer Settings dialog box for further customization, and manage the PivotTable connected to the slicer. In Figure 10.23, the Edition slicer has been sorted in ascending order. The light blue items 6 and 9 do not apply to the selected disciplines. |
| Slicer Styles | Applies a style to the slicer by specifying the color of the filtered item in the slicer. For example, given the workbook theme, the default active filters appear in blue and unavailable items appear in light blue. In Figure 10.23, Slicer Style Dark 2 has been applied to the Discipline style. |
| Arrange | Specifies the slicer's placement in relation to other groups, such as placing a slicer on top of other slicers. |
| Buttons | Defines how many columns are displayed in the selected slicer and the height and width of each button inside the slicer. For example, the Edition slicer contains two columns, and the Discipline slicer contains one column in Figure 10.23. |
| Size | Sets the height and width of the slicer window. For example, the Discipline slicer's height is 3.07" in Figure 10.23. |

# Creating a Calculated Field

You can create a *calculated field*, which is a user-defined field that does not exist in the original dataset. It derives its values based on performing calculations on other original dataset values. For example, you can create a calculated field that converts totals to percentages for easier relative comparison among categories, or you might want to create a calculated field that determines what the number of units a 10% increase in units sold for the upcoming year would be. To create a calculated field, do the following:

STEP 3 ❯❯

1. Select a cell within the PivotTable.
2. Click the PIVOTTABLE TOOLS ANALYZE tab.
3. Click Fields, Items, & Sets in the Calculations group and select Calculated Field to display the Insert Calculated Field dialog box (see Figure 10.24).

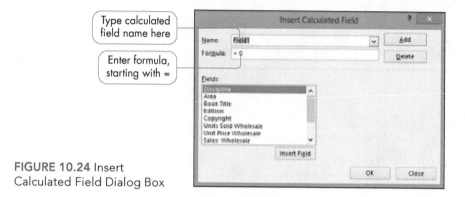

**FIGURE 10.24** Insert Calculated Field Dialog Box

Type a descriptive label for the calculated field in the Name box. Build a formula starting with the equal sign (=). Instead of using cell references, insert the field names and other operands. For example ='Total Book Sales'*.1 calculates a 10% royalty amount on the total book sales. Click OK to insert the calculated field in the PivotTable. Format the numerical values in the calculated field column as needed.

## Show Values as a Specific Calculation Result

In addition to creating calculated fields, you can apply built-in custom calculations that display relationships between values in rows and columns in the PivotTable. For example, you can show each value as a percentage of the grand total or each value's percentage of the row total. To display values in relation to others, do the following:

STEP 4 ❯❯

1. Click the field in the VALUES area of the task pane and select Value Field Settings (or click within the field in the PivotTable and click Field Settings in the Active Field group on the ANALYZE tab).
2. Click the Show Values As tab within the Value Field Settings dialog box.
3. Click the *Show values as* arrow and select the desired calculation type. Table 10.6 lists and describes some of the calculation options.
4. Click Number Format to set number formats, click OK to close the Format Cells dialog box, and then click OK to close the Value Field Settings dialog box.

**TABLE 10.6  Calculation Options**

| Option | Description |
|---|---|
| % of Grand Total | Displays each value as a percentage of the grand total. |
| % of Column Total | Displays each value as a percentage of the respective column total. The values in each column total 100%. |
| % of Row Total | Displays each value as a percentage of the respective row total. The values in each row total 100%. |
| % of Parent Row Total | Displays values as: (value for the item) / (value for the parent item on rows). |
| Running Total | Displays values as running totals. |
| Rank Smallest to Largest | Displays the rank of values in a specific field where 1 represents the smallest value. |
| Rank Largest to Smallest | Displays the rank of values in a specific field where 1 represents the largest value. |

*Quick* Concepts

1. What is the purpose of applying a filter to a PivotTable? How do you apply a main filter and additional filters? *p. 349*

2. What is a slicer? What do the three different colors indicate in a slicer? *p. 350*

3. When would you create a calculated field in a PivotTable? *p. 352*

# Hands-On Exercises

Watch the Video
for this Hands-
On Exercise!

MyITLab®
HOE3 Training

# 3 PivotTable Options

The PivotTable you created has been beneficial for you to review sales data by discipline for each copyright year. In addition, you have used the PivotTable to compare grand total sales among disciplines and grand totals by copyright year. Now you want to extend your analysis. You will calculate author royalties from the sales and impose filters to focus your attention on each analysis.

**Skills covered:** Set Filters • Insert and Customize a Slicer • Create a Calculated Field • Show Values as Calculations

## STEP 1 ≫ SET FILTERS

The level of success of the first two editions especially determines the likelihood of approving subsequent revisions and editions. To display aggregated sales for these editions, you need to set a filter to remove the other editions from being included in the calculated sales data. After you review the first- and second-edition data, you will enable additional filters to review books published in the past two years. Refer to Figure 10.25 as you complete Step 1.

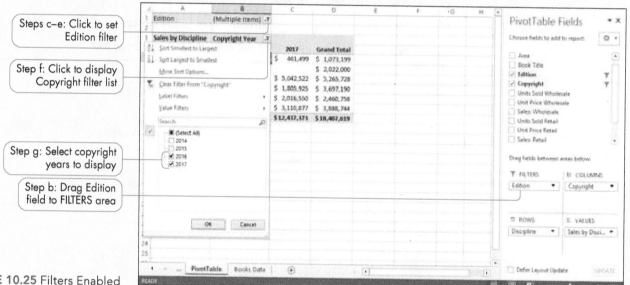

**FIGURE 10.25** Filters Enabled

a. Open *e10h2Sociology_LastFirst* if you closed it at the end of Hands-On Exercise 2 and save it as **e10h3Sociology_LastFirst**, changing *h2* to *h3*.

> **TROUBLESHOOTING:** Click in the PivotTable to display the PivotTable Field task pane if necessary.

b. Make sure the PivotTable worksheet tab is active and drag the **Edition field** from the *Choose fields to add to report* section to the FILTERS area.

You can now filter the PivotTable based on the Edition field. Cell A1 displays the field name, and cell B1 displays (All) and the filter arrow.

c. Click the **Edition filter arrow** in **cell B1** and click the **Select Multiple Items check box**.

The list displays a check box for each item.

d. Click the **(All) check box** to deselect it.

**e.** Click the **1** and **2 check boxes** and click **OK**.

The summary statistics reflect sales data for only first- and second-edition publications. The filter arrow changes to a funnel icon in cell B1.

**f.** Click the **Copyright Year filter arrow** in **cell B3** and click the **(Select All) check box** to deselect it.

**g.** Click the **2016** and **2017 check boxes** and click **OK**.

Excel filters out data for years that do not meet the condition you set. The filter arrow changes to a funnel icon in cell B3.

**h.** Save the workbook.

## STEP 2 »  INSERT AND CUSTOMIZE A SLICER

You might distribute the workbook to colleagues who are not as skilled in Excel as you are. To help them set their own filters, you insert slicers. Refer to Figure 10.26 as you complete Step 2.

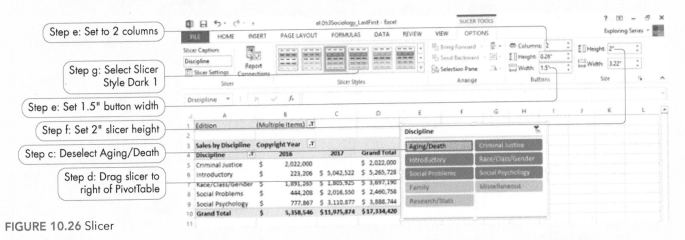

**FIGURE 10.26** Slicer

**a.** Click **Insert Slicer** in the Filter group on the ANALYZE tab.

The Insert Slicers dialog box opens, listing each field name.

**b.** Click **Discipline** and click **OK**.

Excel inserts the Discipline slicer in the worksheet. Six slicer buttons are blue, indicating that those disciplines are selected. The grayed-out buttons at the bottom of the slicer indicate those disciplines are not applicable based on other engaged filters you set (first and second editions and 2016 and 2017 copyright years).

**c.** Press and hold **Ctrl** as you click **Aging/Death** in the Discipline slicer.

This deselects the Aging/Death discipline.

> **TROUBLESHOOTING:** Because several disciplines are selected, if you click Aging/Death instead of pressing Ctrl as you click it, you set Aging/Death as the only discipline. The others are filtered out. If this happens, immediately click Undo and repeat step c.

**d.** Drag the slicer to the right side of the PivotTable.

You moved the slicer so that it does not cover up data in the PivotTable.

**e.** Change the **Columns value** to **2** in the Buttons group on the SLICER TOOLS OPTIONS tab. Change the button **Width** to **1.5"** in the Buttons group.

The slicer now displays buttons in two columns. You changed the width of the buttons to 1.5" to display the full discipline names within the buttons.

**f.** Change the slicer **Height** to **2** in the Size group.

The slicer window is now only 2" tall.

**g.** Click the **More button** in the Slicer Styles group and click **Slicer Style Dark 1**. Save the workbook.

Based on the selected workbook theme, Slicer Style Dark 1 applies a dark blue fill color for selected disciplines, dark gray and black font for available but not currently selected disciplines, and light gray fill with medium gray font for nonapplicable disciplines.

## STEP 3 ⟫ CREATE A CALCULATED FIELD

You want to calculate the amount of the sales returned to the authors as royalties. Although the 10% royalty rate is stored in cell J2 in the Books Data worksheet, the value must be used in the calculated field because range names and cell references outside the PivotTable cannot be used. Refer to Figure 10.27 as you complete Step 3.

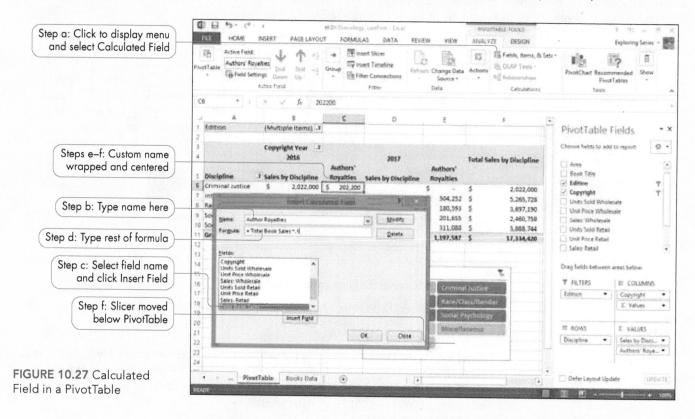

**FIGURE 10.27** Calculated Field in a PivotTable

**a.** Click within the PivotTable, click the **ANALYZE tab**, click **Fields, Items, & Sets** in the Calculations group, and then select **Calculated Field**.

The Insert Calculated Field dialog box opens.

**b.** Type **Author Royalties** in the **Name box**.

**c.** Scroll down the Fields list, click **Total Book Sales**, and then click **Insert Field**.

Excel starts to build the formula, which is currently ='Total Book Sales'.

**d.** Type **\*.1** at the end of the **Formula box** and click **OK**.

Excel adds Sum of Author Royalties calculated field columns, one for each copyright year category. It calculates the authors' royalties as 10% of the total sales for each copyright year.

**e.** Right-click the **Sum of Author Royalties heading** in **cell C5**, select **Value Field Settings**, type **Authors' Royalties** in the **Custom Name box**, and then click **OK**.

**f.** Move the slicer below the PivotTable. Select **cells C5 and E5**, wrap text for field names, set **30** row height, **12** column widths, and center column labels.

**g.** Save the workbook.

# STEP 4 ≫ SHOW VALUES AS CALCULATIONS

You want to see what copyright year generated the largest sales for each discipline, which discipline contributes the largest percentage of the total sociology sales, and which introductory book has the largest sales contribution within that discipline. Refer to Figure 10.28 as you complete Step 4.

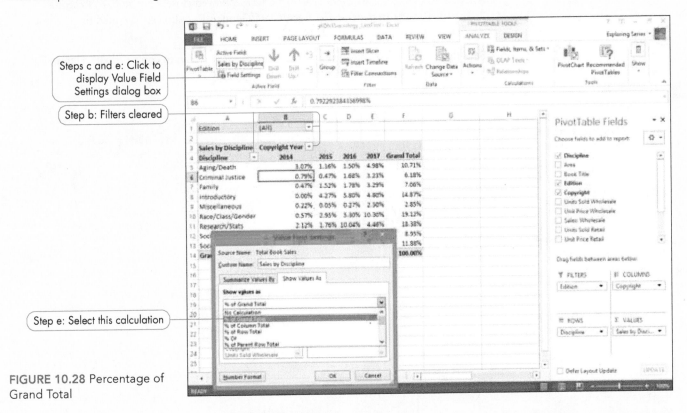

**FIGURE 10.28** Percentage of Grand Total

a. Right-click the **PivotTable worksheet tab**, select **Move or Copy**, click **Books Data** in the *Before sheet* list, click the **Create a copy check box**, and then click **OK**.

You copied the PivotTable worksheet to maintain the previous tasks you completed as evidence. You will work with the PivotTable (2) worksheet, which is the active worksheet.

b. Do the following to remove filters, slicer, and Authors' Royalties field:

- Click the **Edition filter** in **cell B1**, click the **(All) check box**, and then click **OK** to clear the Edition filter.
- Click the **Discipline filter** in **cell A5** and select **Clear Filter From "Discipline"**.
- Click the **Copyright Year filter** in **cell B3** and select **Clear Filter From "Copyright"**.
- Select the slicer and press **Delete**.
- Click the **Authors' Royalties** in the VALUES area of the task pane and select **Remove Field**.

c. Click within any value in the PivotTable, click the **ANALYZE tab**, and then click **Field Settings** in the Active Field group.

The Value Field Settings dialog box opens.

d. Click the **Show Values As tab**, click the **Show values as arrow**, select **% of Row Total**, and then click **OK**.

Excel displays each copyright year's values as percentages for that discipline. All disciplines except Introductory and Research/Stats had the highest percentage of sales for the books with a 2017 copyright. These two disciplines had their highest percentage of sales for books with a 2016 copyright.

e. Click the **Field Settings** in the Active Field group, click the **Show Values As tab** within the dialog box, select **% of Grand Total**, and then click **OK**.

See Figure 10.28. Each discipline's yearly value displays as a percentage of the total sales. Which discipline and for what copyright year produces the highest percentage of total sales? Answer: 2017 Race/Class/Gender with 10.30%, followed closely by the 2016 Research/Stats with 10.04%. In general, the Race/Class/Gender discipline contributed the highest percentage of the total sales with 19.12%.

f. Save the workbook and keep the workbook open if you plan to continue with Hands-On Exercise 4. If not, close the workbook and exit Excel.

# PivotTable Design and PivotCharts

After you create and modify the structure of a PivotTable, you can focus on the overall appearance and format of the PivotTable. The PivotTable Tools Design tab enables you to control the position of grouped calculations and the PivotTable style. In addition to finalizing the PivotTable's appearance, you might want to create a PivotChart to depict the consolidated data in a visual form.

In this section, you will apply a different style to and change the layout of a PivotTable. In addition, you will create and format a PivotChart.

## Formatting a PivotTable

Excel applies basic formatting to PivotTables. For example, it formats primary row labels in bold to distinguish those categories from the subcategories. In addition, the subtotals are bold to offset these values from the subcategory values. The PivotTable Tools Design tab contains commands for enhancing the format of a PivotTable (see Figure 10.29).

FIGURE 10.29 PivotTable Tools Design Tab

**STEP 1 ≫** A PivotTable style controls bold formatting, font colors, shading colors, and border lines. To change the style, click the PivotTable Tools Design tab and click the More button in the PivotTable Styles group to display the PivotTable Styles gallery (see Figure 10.30). Select the most appropriate style that accentuates the data in your PivotTable. As you move the pointer over the gallery, Excel shows how that style will affect the PivotTable. Click a style to apply it to the PivotTable.

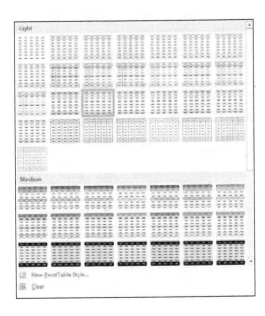

FIGURE 10.30 PivotTable Styles

After you apply a style, you can select which areas of the PivotTable are affected by the style. Select check boxes in the PivotTable Style Options group to apply formats to row headers, column headers, banded rows, and banded columns.

By default, the VALUES area consolidates data by showing subtotals for each category. You can customize the location of subtotals by clicking Subtotals in the Layout group on the

Design tab. For example, when the PivotTable is large, displaying the subtotals at the top of the group draws attention to the totals and enables you to scroll to view all of the supporting data if necessary. Table 10.7 describes the Subtotals options.

| TABLE 10.7 PivotTable Subtotals Options | |
|---|---|
| **Option** | **Description** |
| Do Not Show Subtotals | Removes subtotals for each category but retains the category names and displays aggregated values for the subcategories. |
| Show All Subtotals at Bottom of Group | Displays category subtotals below the last subcategory value within each category. Subtotal labels and values appear in bold. |
| Show All Subtotals at Top of Group | Displays category subtotals at the top of the list on the same row as the category labels. This approach takes up fewer rows than Show All Subtotals at Bottom of Group. |
| Include Filtered Items in Totals | Includes values for filtered items in the total rows and columns. (Active only when a filter has been applied.) |

# Using PowerPivot Functionality

*PowerPivot* is a built-in add-in program in Excel 2013 that enables you to import millions of rows of data from multiple data sources, create a relationship between two or more related tables within one workbook (similar to creating relationships among tables in Access), and maintain connections. For example, one table contains sales representatives' names and IDs. A related table contains the sales dates and sales amounts but only the sales reps' IDs to avoid mistyping a person's name. You must create a relationship based on a common field (such as ID) between the tables. A *relationship* is an association between two related tables where both tables contain a related field of data, such as IDs.

After you create a relationship between tables, you can use PowerPivot to create a PivotTable from both tables. After you create the relationship, you can use the common field to display the sales reps' names instead of their IDs. To create a relationship, do the following:

1. Click the DATA tab and click Relationships in the Data Tools group to open the Manage Relationships dialog box.
2. Click New in the dialog box to open the Create Relationship dialog box (see Figure 10.31).
3. Click the Table arrow and select the name of the primary table. The primary table in this example is SALES.
4. Click the Column (Foreign) arrow and select the name of the column that contains a relationship to the related or lookup table. For example, the column that relates to the other table is REPS.
5. Click the Related Table arrow and select the name of the related or lookup table. For example, the related table is REPS.
6. Click the Related Column (Primary) arrow and select the name of the column that is related to the primary table. For example, the ID column relates to the Rep column in the SALES table. Click OK.

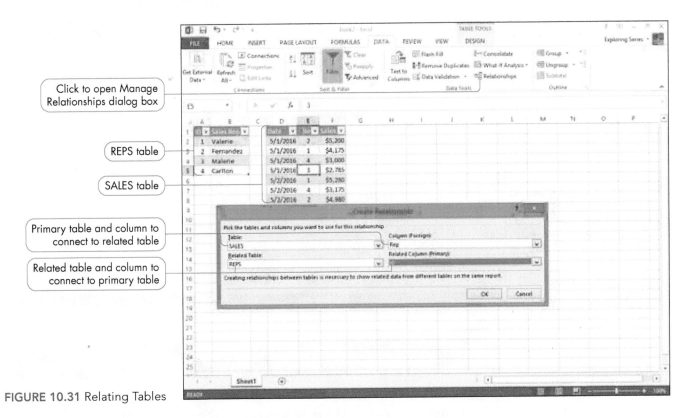

**Click to open Manage Relationships dialog box**

**REPS table**

**SALES table**

**Primary table and column to connect to related table**

**Related table and column to connect to primary table**

**FIGURE 10.31** Relating Tables

After you create a relationship between the tables, you can use PowerPivot to create a PivotTable based on the relationship. Do the following to create a PivotTable using two related tables:

1. Click within the primary table.
2. Click the INSERT tab and click PivotTable in the Tables group to open the Create PivotTable dialog box (see Figure 10.32).
3. Make sure the primary table name displays in the Table/Range box.
4. Click the *Add this data to the Data Model* check box and click OK.

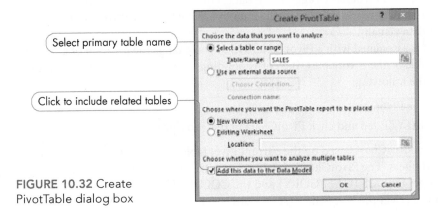

**Select primary table name**

**Click to include related tables**

**FIGURE 10.32** Create PivotTable dialog box

In the PivotTable Fields task pane, click ALL to display the names of all related tables. Then click the table names to display their field names. From there, you can arrange the fields in the different area boxes at the bottom of the task pane (see Figure 10.33).

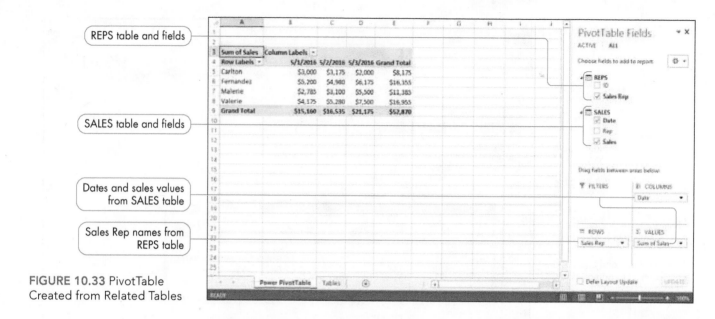

REPS table and fields

SALES table and fields

Dates and sales values
from SALES table

Sales Rep names from
REPS table

**FIGURE 10.33** PivotTable
Created from Related Tables

>  **TIP** | **More Information on Power PivotTables**
>
> Look up the topic *What's new in PowerPivot in Excel 2013* to learn more about the
> PowerPivot functionality and how to create PivotTables from related tables. The Help
> menu also informs you which versions of Microsoft Office 2013 contain this feature and
> how you can enable it.

# Creating a PivotChart

Charts display data visually. This visual representation may help you and your audience
understand the data better than merely presenting the data in a spreadsheet. Although
PivotTables help reduce the amount of data to analyze, PivotTables can be overwhelming.
Another way to display a PivotTable's aggregated data is through a PivotChart. A **PivotChart**
is an interactive graphical representation of the data in a PivotTable. A PivotChart presents
the consolidated data visually.

A PivotChart is associated with a PivotTable. When you change the position of a field in
either the PivotTable or the PivotChart, the corresponding object changes as well. To create
a PivotChart, do the following:

**STEP 2》**

1. Click inside the PivotTable.
2. Click the ANALYZE tab and click PivotChart in the Tools group.

Excel creates a PivotChart based on the current PivotTable settings—row labels, column
labels, values, and filters. The PivotChart contains elements that enable you to set filters. The
ROWS area changes to AXIS (CATEGORY) and the COLUMNS area changes to LEGEND
(SERIES) when you select the PivotChart (see Figure 10.34).

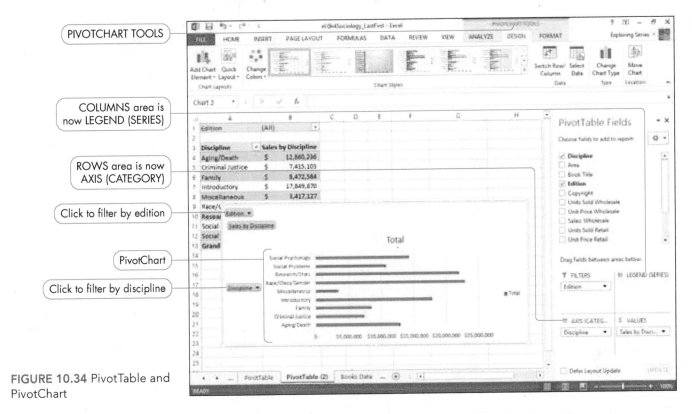

Labels pointing to the figure:

- PIVOTCHART TOOLS
- COLUMNS area is now LEGEND (SERIES)
- ROWS area is now AXIS (CATEGORY)
- Click to filter by edition
- PivotChart
- Click to filter by discipline

**FIGURE 10.34** PivotTable and PivotChart

Although Excel creates the PivotChart based on the current PivotTable settings, you can change the settings using the PivotTable Field List. Click the FILTERS arrow and select values to filter the chart. Click the AXIS (CATEGORY) arrows to sort or filter the categories and subcategories in rows. Click the LEGEND (SERIES) to filter the chart representation based on the values. Changes you make to the PivotChart also affect the corresponding PivotTable. For example, if you apply a filter to the PivotChart, Excel also filters the PivotTable.

The Chart Tools Analyze tab contains the same options that you used to customize a PivotTable. In addition, the Actions group contains the Move Chart option so that you can move a PivotChart to a different worksheet.

The Chart Tools Design tab contains options to add a chart element, apply a layout, change colors, and apply a chart style. In addition, you can switch the data between the category axis and the legend, select the data used to create the chart, change the chart type, and move the chart to a different worksheet.

You can further customize PivotChart elements the same way you can customize regular charts—display data labels, change the fill color for a data series, display axis titles, and so forth. Use Help to learn more about customizing PivotCharts.

*Quick* Concepts

1. What types of specific elements can you select to be controlled by PivotTable styles? **p. 359**

2. What must be done to create a PivotTable from more than one table? **p. 360**

3. What replaces the ROWS and COLUMNS in the task pane when you create a PivotChart? **p. 362**

## 4 PivotTable Design and PivotCharts

You want to format the PivotTable to make it easier for you to analyze the sales data. In addition, you want to create a PivotChart to depict sales data.

**Skills covered:** Apply a PivotTable Style • Create a PivotChart

### STEP 1 >> APPLY A PIVOTTABLE STYLE

To enhance the readability of the sociology textbook PivotTable, you will apply a style. Refer to Figure 10.35 as you complete Step 1.

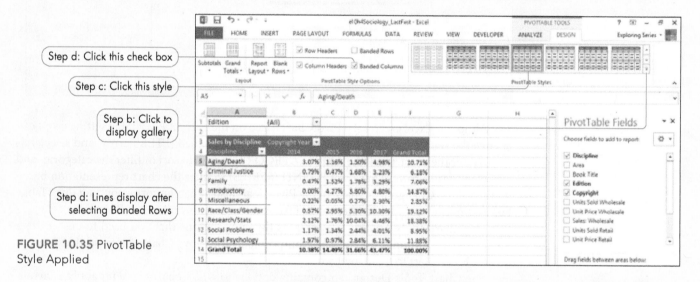

Step d: Click this check box

Step c: Click this style

Step b: Click to display gallery

Step d: Lines display after selecting Banded Rows

**FIGURE 10.35** PivotTable Style Applied

a. Open *e10h3Sociology_LastFirst* if you closed it at the end of Hands-On Exercise 3 and save it as **e10h4Sociology_LastFirst**, changing *h3* to *h4*.

b. Make sure the PivotTable (2) sheet is active. Click a cell within the PivotTable, click the **DESIGN tab**, and then click the **More button** in the PivotTable Styles group.

The PivotTable Style gallery displays styles that you can apply.

c. Click **Pivot Style Medium 3** to apply a dark red style to the PivotTable.

d. Click the **Banded Columns check box** in the PivotTable Style Options group to add dark red vertical lines between the columns. Save the workbook.

# STEP 2 ›› CREATE A PIVOTCHART

You want to create a PivotChart to depict the sales data by discipline. Refer to Figure 10.36 as you complete Step 2.

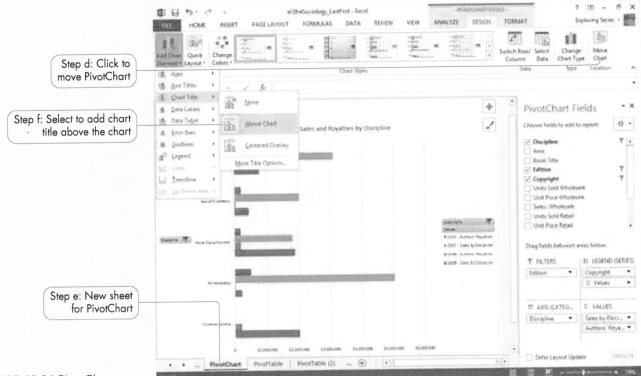

**FIGURE 10.36** PivotChart

a. Click the **PivotTable sheet tab** and click inside the PivotTable.

b. Click the **ANALYZE tab** and click **PivotChart** in the Tools group.

   The Insert Chart dialog box opens.

c. Click **Bar** and click **OK**.

   Excel creates a clustered bar PivotChart based on the PivotTable. Any changes you make to the PivotChart will also affect the PivotTable.

d. Click the **PIVOTCHART TOOLS DESIGN tab** and click **Move Chart** in the Location group.

   The Move Sheet dialog box opens.

e. Click **New sheet**, type **PivotChart**, and then click **OK**.

   The PivotChart is now on its own sheet.

f. Click the **DESIGN tab**, click **Add Chart Element**, point to *Chart Title*, and then select **Above Chart**.

   A Chart Title placeholder displays above the plot area in the PivotChart.

g. Type **Sales and Royalties by Discipline** and press **Enter**.

h. Save and close the workbook, and submit based on your instructor's directions.

# Action and Specialized Queries

## Moving Beyond the Select Query

Yuri Arcurs/Shutterstock

## OBJECTIVES    AFTER YOU READ THIS CHAPTER, YOU WILL BE ABLE TO:

1. Determine when to use an action query p. 368

2. Update data with an update query p. 370

3. Add records to a table with an append query p. 373

4. Create a table with a make table query p. 376

5. Delete records with a delete query p. 377

## CASE STUDY | Replacement China, Inc.

Replacement China, Inc., is an international firm that sells china, crystal, and flatware replacement pieces. You are the database administrator for Replacement China, Inc., and need to perform several database management operations. The most urgent is the need to increase retail prices for a key manufacturer, Spode China, by 5 percent. You will use an update query to make this price increase; you will create other action queries to make additional changes to the firm's database.

Before you run the action queries, you decide to make a backup copy of the database. If a problem exists with any of the queries, you will be able to easily recover from the error by reverting to the backup copy. In addition to backing up the database as a precaution, you need to develop a method of verifying that each action query works properly. One method of verifying an action query is to check the values before running the update query and again after running it, ensuring that the values are updated properly.

You will also create another special type of query known as the crosstab query; a crosstab query will summarize data in the Replacement China, Inc., database and help the managers evaluate the sales and other company statistics. Finally, you will create two queries that will reveal tables with missing data and tables with duplicate data.

# Action Queries

When you create a query, by default you are creating a select query. You begin your query design by selecting the necessary tables and then selecting the required fields to add to the query design grid. Select queries provide a subset of the data that answers most questions that users ask about the data in their databases. A select query is also flexible; you can update the underlying table data if you see an error or discover a blank field value. Another advantage of a select query is that you can create a query for one condition—for example, banquet sales in Boston hotels—and then copy the query, rename the copy, and change the criteria to extract data for a second city, for example, Miami.

Access provides four additional query types—update, append, make table, and delete—that you can use to add, edit, or delete data. The four queries are collectively referred to as action queries. An *action query* adds, edits, or deletes data in a database. You use these queries to update records that meet certain criteria, to append records to a table, to make a new table, and to delete specific records from a table. Because action queries change data, Access gives a warning when you attempt to run one. Access warns you that you are about to change data in the specified number of records and gives you a chance to cancel the changes.

## TIP  Database Administrator Career

A database administrator (DBA) helps manage databases, including performing back-ups, security checks, and upgrades to keep data both safe and accessible. According to the U.S. Department of Labor (www.bls.gov/ooh/computer-and-information-technology/database-administrators.htm), you need a bachelor's degree in Management Information Technology, Information Systems, or Computer Science to work in this field. This Web site also contains salary information.

In this section, you will learn about action queries and how they are used to maintain databases. Specifically, you will create the following types of action queries: update, append, make table, and delete.

## Determining When to Use an Action Query

Four main action queries can be used to maintain a database:

- **Update query.** An update query is used to update or change data automatically based on criteria that you specify. Rather than modifying data manually or using the find and replace tool, the update query is fast and accurate.

- **Append query.** An append query is used for adding records to an existing table. Records can be selected from various sources, such as external databases and spreadsheets. Rather than entering data manually or performing multiple copy-and-paste operations to a table, the append query is an automated process.

- **Make Table query.** A make table query automatically creates a new table from data that already exist in a database. You can create the new table in the current or another database. For example, a make table query can use criteria to make a table that archives older records that need to be stored outside of the current table. The process is automated and saves the trouble of tedious copy-and-paste operations. A make table query overwrites existing data in a table of the same name.

- **Delete query.** A delete query removes records from a table based on criteria that you specify. For example, after a make table query is run to create records in another table, you may want to remove those same records from the current table. The delete query saves the chore of having to locate and delete records manually.

The Replacement China, Inc., database, like most Access databases, requires some type of regular maintenance—usually performed by the DBA or another person assigned to these tasks. For example, customer orders that were entered last month but not filled might now be outdated. Over time, those outdated orders must be dealt with so they are not just taking up space in the database. One way to handle this type of outdated data is to move it from the primary order table to an inactive order table. You can accomplish this task using a make table query, an append query, and a delete query. First, design a make table query to create an inactive orders table based on existing data, create an append query to add future outdated orders to the inactive orders table, and then create a delete query to remove the outdated orders from the primary order table.

Another condition that exists in the Replacement China, Inc., database (and many Access databases) is null (i.e., blank) values in numeric data fields. In a list of products, each with a cost and a retail price, it is not uncommon for one of the fields to contain a null value. Access does not always calculate properly when a null is in the list of values. It is usually better to enter the value zero rather than have a null value. When null values exist, you can use an update query to replace null values with a zero. First, find all the records with null values using a select query, and then create an update query that will replace the null values with zeros. This is a good alternative to a manual or some other filter-and-replace operation. Once the update query has been created, it can be used on a regular basis to remedy this condition.

## Recognize the Benefits of an Action Query

One situation that requires an action query is when an end user is required to enter the same information into many records. For example, at Replacement China, Inc., if all of the customers who had Julia as their sales representative are now going to be handled by Susan, then Julia will need to be replaced by Susan for each of her customers. An employee could complete this task manually, or you could create an action query and replace "Julia" with "Susan" automatically. To handle this situation, create a select query that lists all the customers who have Julia as their sales representative. Next, change the select query to an update query and enter Susan as the new sales representative. Run the update query, and the task is finished! Once an update query has been created, it can be used repeatedly or modified to handle different situations.

A student database in a college is another situation where an Access designer needs to use action queries. When students enroll in a school or program, they are classified as current students and are entered into the Students table. After graduation, the school likely moves them to a Graduates table. An append query is the easiest way to move records from one table to another. Create a select query to select all the records from the Students table in which the graduation date is not blank (i.e., the student *has* a graduation date). Change the select query to an append query, specify the Graduates table as the *append to* table, and then run the query. The students are now in the Graduates table. Use a delete query to remove the students from the Students table (to avoid storing duplicate data).

## Back Up a Database When Testing an Action Query

STEP 1 >> Action queries locate and alter data that meet specific criteria. You cannot undo updates or deletions performed with an action query. Therefore, you should exercise caution when executing an action query. Before running an action query, it is best to back up the entire database. This provides you with some insurance in case you need to recover from a mistake. After the backup is made, you usually want to create a simple select query first to test your criteria and determine which data will be modified, appended, or deleted before switching to an action query. Once you run an action query, you are committing yourself to an irreversible change.

# Updating Data with an Update Query

An *update query* changes the data values in one or more fields for all records that meet specific criteria. For example, the phone company announces that all of your customers in a specific area code will now have a different area code. You construct an update query to identify records of all customers who live in the specific area code and then change their existing area code to the new area code. Another example might be in a database storing information about student athletes and their academic eligibility. At the end of each semester, you would create an update query to identify all academically eligible athletes based on their grade point average (GPA). All athletes with a GPA of 2.5 or higher would be updated to eligible.

## Create a Select Query Before Running an Update Query

Prior to updating data in a table, you may first want to locate the records that need to be modified. For example, you discover that one or more orders have a missing order date—key information required to process the order. To find other orders with a missing order date, you would first create a select query.

To create a select query, do the following:

1. Click Query Design in the Queries group on the CREATE tab.
2. Add the order data table to the query design and add all fields to the query design grid.
3. Add Is Null to the criterion of the order date field, as shown in Figure 11.1.
4. Run the query to see how many orders have a missing order date, as shown in Figure 11.2.

You could then ask a customer service employee to research the orders with missing dates, perhaps by talking with user 8580, the employee who entered the orders.

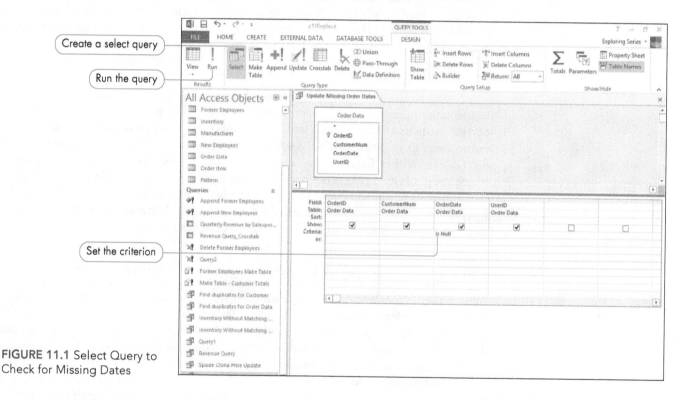

**FIGURE 11.1** Select Query to Check for Missing Dates

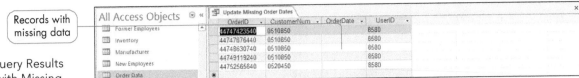

FIGURE 11.2 Query Results
Show Records with Missing
Dates

Records with
missing data

## Convert a Select Query to an Update Query

**STEP 2 »**  Your goal is to update records with a missing order date. Once the records with a missing order date are found by a select query, you decide to convert it to an update query and insert the current date into any record with a blank order date so that the orders can be processed.

To create the update query, do the following:

1. View the select query in Design view (as shown in Figure 11.1).
2. Click Update in the Query Type group.
3. Enter the new value into the Update To row. In the missing order date example, type the Date() function into the Update To row of the OrderDate field (as shown in Figure 11.3).
4. Click Run in the Results group. (If you want to verify which records the update query will affect before running the query, test the query as described in the next section.)

The current date is inserted into the OrderDate field for all records with a missing order date.

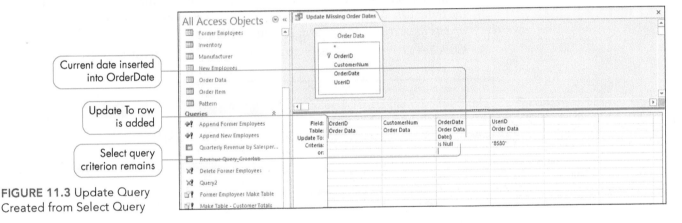

Current date inserted
into OrderDate

Update To row
is added

Select query
criterion remains

FIGURE 11.3 Update Query
Created from Select Query

## Test an Update Query

**STEP 3 »**  You can test an update query (before clicking Run) and verify that the correct records will be updated by switching to Datasheet view first. Once an update query is run, you cannot undo the action, so it is important to view the eligible records beforehand.

To test an update query before running it, do the following:

From Design view, click View in the Results group and click Datasheet view.

Datasheet view will look different than usual—most of the columns that were showing in the Datasheet view of the select query are no longer showing in the Datasheet view of the update query (see Figure 11.4). Only the column and records that conform to the Update To criteria are showing. You can use this information to evaluate the number of records that will be updated when you run the update query. Look at the number of records shown in the navigation bar at the bottom of the Datasheet view. If the number of records is what you expect, then it is safe to run the update query.

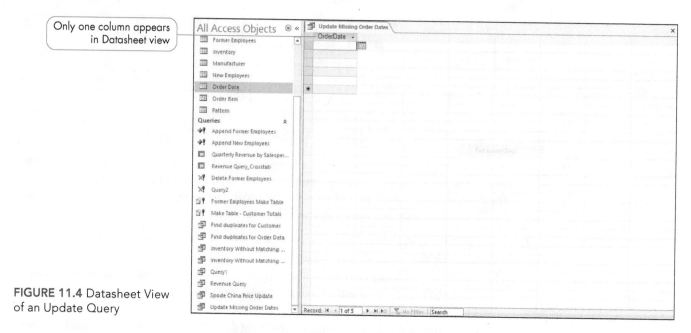

**FIGURE 11.4** Datasheet View of an Update Query

To run the update query, do the following:

1. Return to the query Design view.
2. Verify that Update is selected in the Query Type group.
3. Click Run in the Results group. The five records will have the current date inserted into the order date field, after you click Yes to the Access message *Are you sure you want to update these records?* (as shown in Figure 11.5).
4. Click Yes to the warning message and the update query executes.

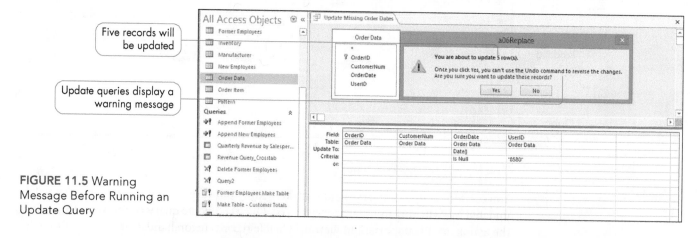

**FIGURE 11.5** Warning Message Before Running an Update Query

 **TIP** **Add a New Field Before Running an Update Query**

Backing up the database prior to running an update query is the best precaution. Additionally, there may be times when adding a new field to a table may be a practical option. For example, if you are reducing the values of retail prices by 15 percent, you lose the original prices after changing them with an update query. To avoid this, add a new field to the table named Retail Original (for example). Then create an update query that updates the Retail Original field with the current retail price. Next, run the update query to decrease the current retail prices by 15 percent. Now you have both the original retail price (Retail Original) and the new retail price (Retail New).

## Verify an Update Query

Running an action query from Design view does not display a view of the results; Access simply returns you to the query design window. No records (with the new data) are displayed. One way to test the results would be to create a query to locate the updated records. Click Select in the Query Type group and modify the query's criteria to select the updated data. In the sample database, we inserted the current date into the missing order date fields. You would change the order date criterion from Is Null to today's date and run the query to view the corrected records.

Another method is to try to locate the original records prior to their being updated and discovering that those records no longer exist in their original state. In the example, you could select orders for User (employee) 8580 where the order dates are null. With Is Null as the criterion in the order date field, enter 8580 in the User ID criteria row and run the query. The query results show that there are no longer records for this user with missing (null) order dates (as shown in Figure 11.6).

**FIGURE 11.6** Verify the Data After an Update Query

---

### TIP Do Not Rerun Action Queries

After you run an action query, it might appear that nothing has happened except that the warning box disappears. You might be tempted to click Run again—but you should not; you may find that data is changed again unnecessarily. For example, if you created an update query to lower the sale price of all products by 15 percent, entering *[Sale Price]* * .85 into the Update To row for the sale price field would work correctly. However, running the query a second time would lower the price an additional 15 percent from the current price. In this case, the total reduction would be a 27.75 percent discount (lower than the intended 15 percent).

---

## Adding Records to a Table with an Append Query

**STEP 4 >>** Another type of action query is the append query. An *append query* copies records from one or more tables (the source) and adds them to an existing table (the destination). The appended records appear in the destination table in primary key order, or they are added to the bottom of the table if no primary key exists. If any appended record violates the primary key rule or another rule created for the destination table, the record is rejected. For example, you might use an append query to copy employee records in the Replacement China, Inc., database. Suppose the company hires new employees each week. The company may place new hires into a Candidates table until the background checks are complete. Once the checks are completed, the candidates can be appended to the Employees table and then deleted from the Candidates table. Moving records from one table to another can be accomplished with the combination of an append query and a delete query. Append queries are frequently used in conjunction with delete queries. If you use an append query to copy a record from one table to another, the original record still exists. The same data is now stored in two different places—a practice that must be avoided in a database. After the criteria for an append query are established, you can reuse the same criteria to create a delete query and delete the records from the source table. This is a common practice when working with append queries.

Often, organizations store the active records (today's or this week's activities) in one table and then append them to a more permanent table after they are completed. The tables involved with an append query—the source and destination—usually contain the same field names. In most cases, the data types of the source fields must match the data types of the destination fields. The rules for appending are as follows:

- Data types of the fields in both tables must match in most cases; however, some exceptions to this rule exist.

- All the normal rules for adding a new record to the destination table apply. For example, the records are not added if a value is missing in the source table when the field is required in the destination table.

- If a field from the source table does not exist in the destination table, Access leaves a blank in the Append To row, and you will need to manually specify the destination field name (or just delete the unneeded source field from the query design grid). If the destination table has non required fields that are not in the source table, the record appends, and the missing field values are blank.

- The destination table should not contain an AutoNumber field. An AutoNumber in the source table should append to a Number field in the destination table.

## Create a Select Query Before Running an Append Query

Similar to an update query, the first step in creating an append query is to create a select query. You can use one or multiple tables for the data source. Next, select the fields you want to append from the table(s) to the query design grid. Enter the criteria to filter only the records you want to append. For example, if Replacement China, Inc., wanted to move its former employees from the Employees table to the Former Employees table, it could create a select query, and then add criteria to find employees where the termination date is not null. The results of this query are shown in Datasheet view in Figure 11.7.

**FIGURE 11.7** Verify Records Before Running the Append Query

## Set Append To Fields in an Append Query

After you verify that the correct records are selected, switch to Design view, and then change the select query to an append query.

To convert the select query to an append query, do the following:

1. In Design view, click Append in the Query Type group.
2. Select the destination table using the table name arrow and click OK.

Figure 11.8 shows the Append dialog box that displays, in which you specify the destination table.

When you change to an append query, Access removes the Show row in the query design grid and adds the Append To row in its place. If the fields in the source and destination tables are the same, Access automatically inserts the correct field names into the Append To row, as shown in Figure 11.9.

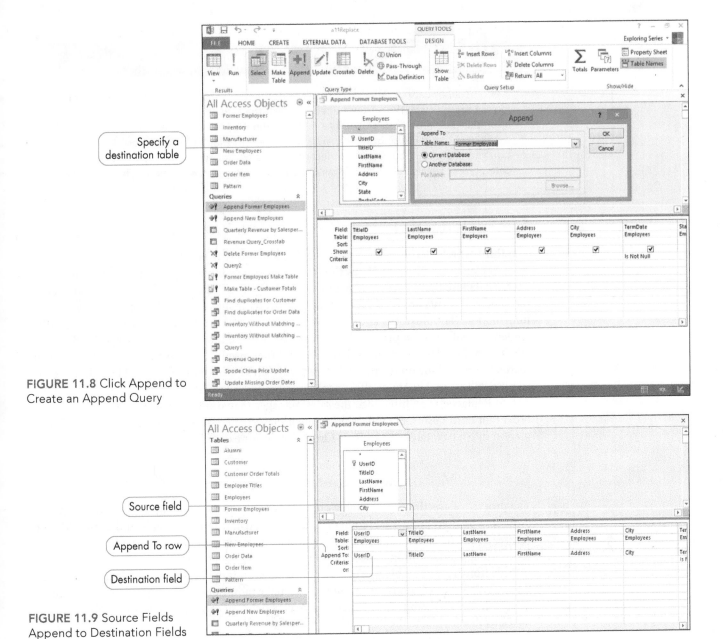

FIGURE 11.8 Click Append to Create an Append Query

Specify a destination table

Source field

Append To row

Destination field

FIGURE 11.9 Source Fields Append to Destination Fields

## Run an Append Query

If you need to verify the records to be appended, you can click View in the Results group to double-check in Datasheet view. After verifying the records, switch back to Design view.

To run an append query, do the following:

1. In Design view, click Run in the Results group. You will receive a warning message telling you that you are about to append the number of records selected, as shown in Figure 11.10.

2. Click Yes to continue. As with all the action queries, you cannot undo the action after it is run.

3. Save and close the append query (if required).

4. Open the destination table and verify that the appended records are in the table.

Four rows will be appended

Append query warning message

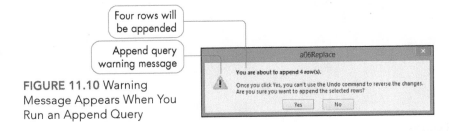

FIGURE 11.10 Warning Message Appears When You Run an Append Query

If Access cannot append the records to the destination table, a message appears explaining the reasons why the append query failed. If the primary key value of a record you are attempting to append already exists in the destination table, you will not be able to add the record that is causing the key violation. When this failure occurs, close the message box and examine the source and destination tables. Locate the records that have duplicate primary key values and determine the best way to handle necessary changes.

# Creating a Table with a Make Table Query

The third type of action query is the make table query. A *make table query* selects records from one or more tables and uses them to create a new table. Suppose that your school has a large database that stores information about students. The database has information about the classes students are registered for each term, their majors, and their emergency contact information. The Business and Technology Department needs to know the names of the students enrolled in its programs. You can use a make table query to extract the Business and Technology Department student data and then use it to create a new table. Subsequent searches can be done on the new table, reducing the response time required by searching the larger database that contains all student records.

At Replacement China, Inc., the sales manager may want to know the total year-to-date orders for each customer. You could create a make table query that would insert this information into a new table—Customer Order Totals, for example.

## Create a Make Table Query

**STEP 5** The process of creating a make table query is very similar to creating an append query. The difference is that a make table query creates the structure of the table and then adds the records to the table. An append query requires the destination table to exist first; otherwise, it cannot append additional records. You can use the make table query to copy some or all records from a source table to a destination table even if the destination table does not exist. If the destination table exists and you run the make table query, Access prompts you before it deletes the original table. If you click Yes, Access deletes the source table and replaces it with data specified by the make table query.

To create a make table query, do the following:

1. Create a select query; specify the tables and field names that you want to add to the new table to the query design window.
2. Specify the criteria that will result in selecting the correct records for your new table.
3. In Design view, click Make Table in the Query Type group.
4. Specify the table name that you want to create in the Table Name box.
5. Click OK.

Figure 11.11 displays the setup for a make table query that will copy aggregate order data to a new table.

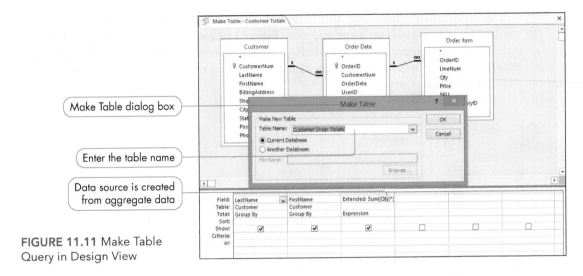

**FIGURE 11.11** Make Table Query in Design View

Labels pointing to the figure:
- Make Table dialog box
- Enter the table name
- Data source is created from aggregate data

## Test and Run a Make Table Query

As with the other action queries, you should preview the datasheet prior to running the query to verify that the records are those that you intend to insert into a new table.

To test and run a make table query, do the following:

1. Click View in the Results group to view the records in Datasheet view.
2. After you verify that the records are correct, click View again to return to Design view.
3. Click Run in the Results group and Access displays a warning telling you that you are about to append records to a new table.
4. Click Yes and the new table is created.
5. Open the new table and verify the records are correct.
6. Save and close the query (if required).

If you run the same make table query at a later date, the first table is replaced with a new, up-to-date table.

# Deleting Records with a Delete Query

**STEP 6 》** The final type of action query is the delete query. A ***delete query*** selects records from a table, and then removes them from the table. Sometimes it is necessary to identify and delete data in a database. However, it should always be done with caution. For example, if you copy the Replacement China, Inc., database inactive customers from the Customers table to the Inactive Customers table using an append query, you will want to delete those records from the Customers table. Take precautions prior to running a delete query. If you create a backup copy of the database prior to running a delete query, you can always recover from an error.

## Create a Delete Query

The delete query begins the same way as all of the other action queries, with a select query.

To create a delete query, do the following:

1. Create a select query; specify the tables and field names that you want to remove from the table in the query design window.
2. Specify the criteria in the fields that will result in deleting the correct records from your table.
3. In Design view, click Delete in the Query Type group.

At Replacement China, Inc., there may be times when they need to remove orders that were incorrectly entered on a specific date. Figure 11.12 shows the criterion to delete the orders that were placed on 6/10/2016. If you fail to specify a criterion, Access deletes all the records in the Orders table. Access displays a warning message and enables you to avoid running the delete query.

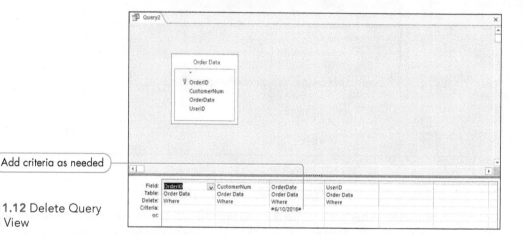

**Add criteria as needed**

**FIGURE 11.12** Delete Query in Design View

## Test and Run a Delete Query

As with the other action queries, always view the records to be deleted in Datasheet view prior to running the delete query. After you verify the number of records in the datasheet, run the query.

To run the delete query, do the following:

1. Switch to Design view, if you were testing the query in Datasheet view.
2. Click Run in the Results group to run the query and delete the records.
3. Click Yes when the warning message appears. Verify the results of the delete query by opening the table to confirm that the records were deleted.
4. Save and close the query (if required).

### TIP  Action Query Icons

Access denotes the action queries differently from select queries by displaying a specific icon for each action query type in the Navigation Pane (see Figure 11.13). This may prevent users from accidentally running an action query and getting unexpected results. For example, if an update query is created to increase prices by 10 percent, running the query a second time would increase those prices again. Exercise caution when running action queries.

**Action query icons**

**FIGURE 11.13** Action Query Icons

You will experiment with creating and running action queries in Hands-On Exercise 1 using the data from Replacement China, Inc. You will run an update query to identify all of the products in inventory from a specified manufacturer and increase their prices by

5 percent. You will use an append query to add new employees to the Employees table. Next, you will make a table containing the employees who are no longer with the firm. You will use a delete query to remove the employees from the Employees table who no longer work for Replacement China, Inc.

*Quick* Concepts

1. What is a benefit of creating an append query? *p. 368*

2. What is a potential disadvantage of running an update query? *p. 372*

3. What is a good strategy for handling mistakes that can occur while running action queries? *p. 372*

# Hands-On Exercises

## 1 Action Queries

Several maintenance tasks are required at Replacement China, Inc. Before work begins, you decide to back up the database to make it easy to recover from a mistake. Each task requires an action query. After you create and run each query, you verify the changes by checking the records in the modified table.

**Skills covered:** Back Up a Database When Testing an Action Query • Create an Update Query • Test an Update Query • Create an Append Query • Create a Make Table Query • Create a Delete Query

---

### STEP 1 ≫ BACK UP A DATABASE WHEN TESTING AN ACTION QUERY

Create a backup copy of the Replacement China, Inc., database before you create any action queries. If you make a mistake along the way, revert to the original file and start again. Refer to Figure 11.14 as you complete Step 1.

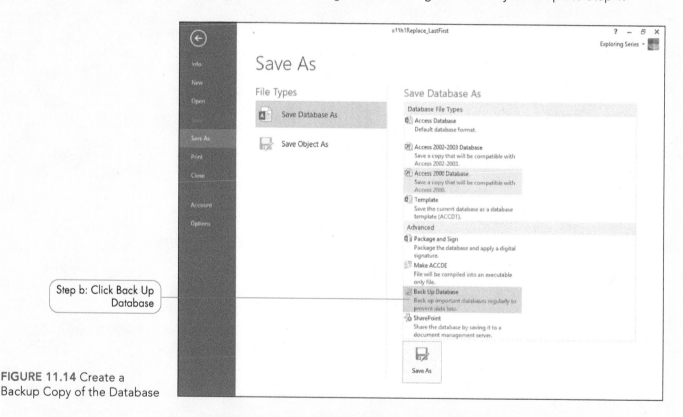

Step b: Click Back Up Database

**FIGURE 11.14** Create a Backup Copy of the Database

a.  Open *a11h1Replace*. Click **Save As** on the FILE tab, click **Save As**, and then type **a11h1Replace_LastFirst**. Click **Save**.

> **TROUBLESHOOTING:** Throughout the remainder of this chapter and textbook, click Enable Content whenever you are working with student files.

> **TROUBLESHOOTING:** If you make any major mistakes in this exercise, you can close the file, repeat step a above, and then start over.

**b.** Click **Save As** on the FILE tab, and double-click **Back Up Database**.

Before you execute an action query, it is recommended that you make a backup copy of the entire database first. If a problem occurs, you can use the backup copy to recover.

**c.** Click **Save** to accept the default file name for the backup copy of the *a11h1Replace_LastFirst_date* database.

A backup copy of the database now exists in your default folder.

**d.** Verify the backup file exists in your default folder.

## STEP 2 >> CREATE AN UPDATE QUERY

One of your manufacturers, Spode China, has increased its prices for the upcoming year. You decide to increase your retail prices as well. You create an update query to increase the retail price by 5 percent but only for items that are supplied by Spode China. Refer to Figure 11.15 as you complete Step 2.

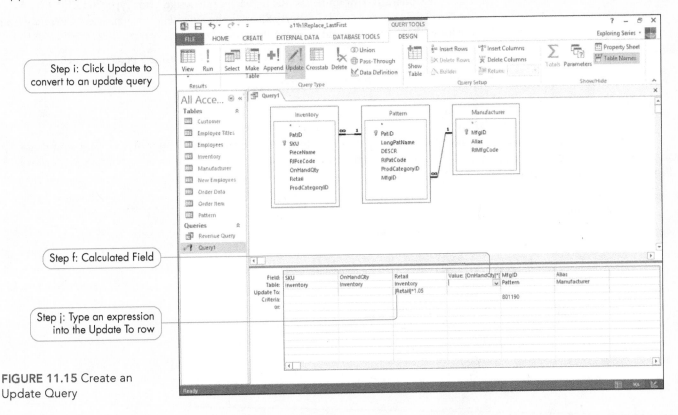

**FIGURE 11.15** Create an Update Query

**a.** Click **Query Design** in the Queries group on the CREATE tab.

The Show Table dialog box opens.

**b.** Double-click the **Inventory**, **Pattern**, and **Manufacturer tables** to add these tables to the query design space. Close the Show Table dialog box.

**c.** Add the SKU, OnHandQty, and Retail fields from the Inventory table, MfgID field from the Pattern table, and Alias field from the Manufacturer table to the design grid. Type **801190** in the **Criteria row** of the MfgID column.

You added the criteria to select only Spode China pieces to update the prices. The MfgID for Spode China is 801190.

**d.** Switch to Datasheet view and verify the correct records are selected.

The results include 1,129 Spode China records.

**e.** Switch to Design view. Click the **MfgID column** and click **Insert Columns** in the Query Setup group.

A new blank column appears between Retail and MfgID.

f. Type **Value: [OnHandQty]\*[Retail]** in the first row of the new blank column. Click **Property Sheet** in the Show/Hide group. Select **Currency** from the list in the Format box and close the Property Sheet.

You created a calculated field so that you can check the total value of the inventory before and after the update.

g. Switch to Datasheet view. Click **Totals** in the Records group. Advance to the last record.

h. Click in the **Total row** of the Value column, click the arrow, and then select **Sum**.

The total of the Value column is $911,415.88. The value after the update should be $956,986.67 (911,415.88 × 1.05).

i. Click **View** to return to Design view. Click **Update** in the Query Type group.

You changed the query type from a select to an update query. The Sort and Show rows are replaced by the Update To row in the grid.

j. Click the **Update To row** under the Retail field in the design grid. Type **[Retail] \* 1.05**. With the Retail field selected, click **Property Sheet** in the Show/Hide group. Select **Currency** from the list in the Format box and close the Property Sheet.

The expression will replace the current retail value with a value 5 percent higher.

k. Compare your screen to Figure 11.15.

## STEP 3 ≫ TEST AN UPDATE QUERY

You created an update query to increase the retail price of Spode China products by 5 percent, but you want to verify the values before you run the query. Once you update the prices, you will not be able to undo the changes. Refer to Figure 11.16 as you complete Step 3.

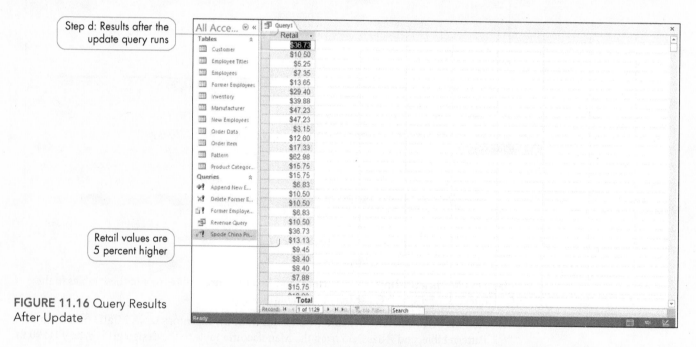

**FIGURE 11.16** Query Results After Update

a. Switch to Datasheet view and examine the records before running the query.

You should see a list of retail prices ($34.98, $10.00, $5.00, $7.00, etc.) but no other columns. Access only displays the columns that have a value in the Update To row. These are the current prices that will be updated.

b. Click **View** to return to Design view.

c. Click **Run** in the Results group to execute the query. Click **Yes** in response to the *You are about to update 1129 row(s)* warning.

Although it may seem as though nothing happened, your prices have changed.

**d.** View the results in Datasheet view.

The first four retail prices are now $36.73, $10.50, $5.25, and $7.35, as shown in Figure 11.16. These prices are 5 percent higher than the original retail prices you saw in step a above.

**e.** Return to Design view. Click **Select** in the Query Type group.

**f.** Switch to Datasheet view.

The prices in the Retail column reflect the updated prices, and the bottom of the Retail column is now $956,986.67, which verifies that the update query worked correctly.

**g.** Return to Design view.

**h.** Click **Update** in the Query Type group to change back to an update query. Save the query as **Spode China Price Update**. Close the query.

The query icon in the Navigation Pane indicates the query is an update query.

## STEP 4 ≫ CREATE AN APPEND QUERY

Replacement China, Inc., hired several new employees who were placed into the New Employees table for a 30-day probation period. The probation period is over, and now you need to add them to the Employees table. Refer to Figure 11.17 as you complete Step 4.

Step i: Append query will add four records

**FIGURE 11.17** New Employees to Be Appended to the Employees Table

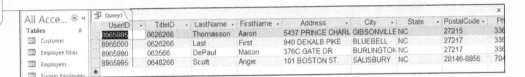

> **TROUBLESHOOTING:** You could make a backup copy of the database to revert back to in the event of an error. You backed up the database at the beginning of this exercise, but you may want another backup in case the append query causes a problem. If you complete this step on the same day as you completed the last step, Access adds _(1) to the end of the backup file name to distinguish it from the earlier file name.

**a.** Open the New Employees table in Datasheet view. Add yourself as a new record. Type **8966000** in the **UserID field**; **0626266** in the **TitleID field**; your last name, first name, address, city, state, postal code, and phone number in the respective name fields; and **9/11/2016** in the **HireDate field**.

**b.** Close the New Employees table.

**c.** Open the Employees table and note the total records in the navigation bar at the bottom of the window.

The navigation bar shows 115 current employees.

**d.** Close the Employees table.

**e.** Click **Query Design** in the Queries group on the CREATE tab. Double-click the **New Employees table**. Close the Show Table dialog box.

You have begun to create a select query.

**f.** Click **Append** in the Query Type group.

You need to change the query design to an append query to add the newly hired employees to the Employees table. The Append dialog box opens, prompting you to supply the destination table name.

**g.** Click the **Table Name arrow** and select **Employees**. Verify the Current Database option is selected and click **OK**.

The Append To row appears on the design grid, ready for you to add fields. You need all of the fields in the New Employees table added to the Employees table.

h. Double-click the title bar of the New Employees table in the top portion of the Design view window. All of the fields are selected. Drag the selected fields to the first field box in the design grid.

i. Click **View** in the Results group and preview the data you are about to append.

You should see 4 rows and 10 fields, as shown in Figure 11.17.

j. Click **View** in the Views group to return to Design view.

k. Click **Run** in the Results group to run the query. Click **Yes** in response to the *You are about to append 4 row(s)* warning.

l. Open the Employees table. Sort the table in descending order (Newest to Oldest) by the HireDate field and make sure the four newest records were added.

The Employees table should now contain a total of 119 employees. Your own name should be one of the top four records.

m. Click the **Query1 tab** and click **Save** on the Quick Access Toolbar. Save the query as **Append New Employees**. Close the open objects. Save the design of the New Employees table.

The query icon in the Navigation Pane indicates the query is an append query.

## STEP 5 ›› CREATE A MAKE TABLE QUERY

Replacement China, Inc., needs to create a Former Employees table for all employees who are no longer with the company. The records of these former employees are currently stored in the Employees table. You need to move them to a Former Employees table. Refer to Figure 11.18 as you complete Step 5.

Step j: Nine records added to the Former Employees table

**FIGURE 11.18** Use Make Table to Create a New Table

| FirstName | Address | City | State | PostalCode | Phone | HireDate | TermDate | TermReaso |
|---|---|---|---|---|---|---|---|---|
| Trevor | 10729 TRAPF | RALEIGH | NC | 27615-5313 | 9198463129 | 6/1/2004 | 1/2/2009 | Ret |
| Angie | 108 LOCHBEI | RALEIGH | NC | 27615-2815 | 3362991750 | 1/31/2009 | 2/3/2010 | Vol |
| Tim | 1012 TRADEF | SAN FRANCIS | CA | 94116-3039 | 9195671893 | 1/31/2009 | 3/4/2010 | Term |
| Jeanette | 1018 WENTW | SALISBURY | NC | 28146-8856 | 9198512318 | 4/18/2001 | 4/5/2007 | Vol |
| Carol | 104 LITTLE R | ROCKY MOU | NC | 27801-3052 | 9198512318 | 7/21/2009 | 5/6/2012 | Ret |
| Joni | 1010 MEADO' | SCOTIA | NY | 12302 | 9198469158 | 1/20/1995 | 8/7/2009 | Vol |
| John | 1102 KINDLE' | RALEIGH | NC | 27609-2800 | 9197839369 | 12/25/2011 | 2/2/2012 | Term |
| Judy | 100 CIRCLEV | STEAMBOAT | CO | 80488-1895 | 9103926711 | 12/12/1999 | 8/9/2005 | Ret |
| Bev | 1102 BRITTLE | RALEIGH | NC | 27609-3625 | 9198472095 | 12/12/1999 | 9/10/2008 | Vol |

a. Click **Query Design** in the Queries group on the CREATE tab.

b. Double-click the **Employees table** to add it to the query. Close the Show Table dialog box.

Some of the employees listed in the Employees table no longer work for Replacement China, Inc. You need to retain this information but do not want these records included in the Employees table; the records will be stored in the archived Former Employees table.

c. Double-click the title bar of the Employees table in the top portion of the Design view window to select all the fields. Drag the selected fields to the first field box in the design grid.

d. Type **Is Not Null** in the **Criteria row** of the TermDate field.

This criterion will select only those employees with a value in the termination date field.

e. Display the results in Datasheet view.

You should find that nine employees are no longer with the company. These are the employees you want to move to a new table using a make table query.

f. Click **View** to switch back to Design view.

g. Click **Make Table** in the Query Type group.

The Make Table dialog box opens and asks that you name and provide storage location information for the new table. You want to archive this data, but the new table can reside in the same database.

**h.** Type **Former Employees** in the **Table Name box**. Make sure the Current Database option is selected. Click **OK**.

**i.** Click **Run** in the Results group to run the query. Click **Yes** in response to the *You are about to paste 9 row(s) into a new table* warning.

**j.** Examine the Navigation Pane to make sure that the new Former Employees table exists. Open the Former Employees table to verify the nine former employees are present, as shown in Figure 11.18. Close the table.

> **TROUBLESHOOTING:** If your table did not come out properly, delete the query and the newly created table. You can try this query again by beginning from Step 5b. Be sure to check that the correct criterion is entered to locate employees with termination dates.

**k.** Save the query as **Former Employees Make Table**.

The query icon in the Navigation Pane indicates the query is a make table query.

**l.** Close the query.

## STEP 6 ≫ CREATE A DELETE QUERY

You moved the former employees from the Employees table to the Former Employees table in the Replacement China, Inc., database. Now you need to delete the former employees from the Employees table. It is not a good practice to have the same data stored in two different tables. Refer to Figure 11.19 as you complete Step 6.

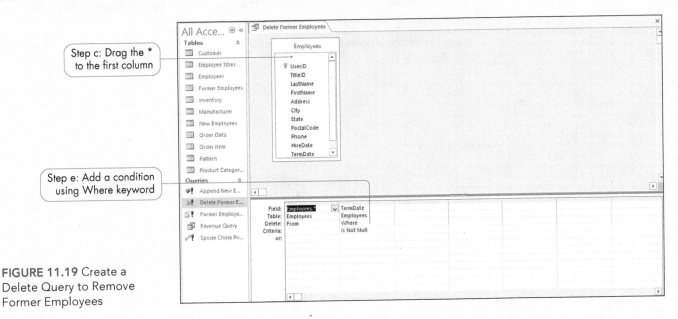

**FIGURE 11.19** Create a Delete Query to Remove Former Employees

**a.** Click **Query Design** in the Queries group on the CREATE tab.

**b.** Double-click the **Employees table** in the Show Table dialog box to add it to the query. Close the Show Table dialog box.

**c.** Drag the * from the Employees table to the first column of the query design grid.

The * field only takes up one column in the design grid. The * field represents all the fields in the Employees table. This is a shortcut for adding all of the fields to the design grid in one step rather than one by one.

**d.** Drag the **TermDate field** from the Employees table to the second column of the query design grid.

You need to add the TermDate a second time to use it to set the criteria for the select query.

**e.** Type **Is Not Null** in the **Criteria row** for the TermDate field. Click **View** to switch to Datasheet view.

You created a select query to make sure you have correctly identified the nine records for deletion prior to changing it to a delete query. Nine records are shown in Datasheet view.

**f.** Switch to Design view. Click **Delete** in the Query Type group.

The Delete row now contains From in the Employees.* column and Where in the TermDate column. This delete query will delete all records in the Employees table that have a termination date.

**g.** Click **Run** in the Results group. Click **Yes** in response to the *You are about to delete 9 row(s) from the specified table* warning.

You deleted the nine former employees from the Employees table.

**h.** Save the query as **Delete Former Employees**. Close the query.

**i.** Open the Employees table and verify that the total employees has been reduced from 119 to 110. Close the table.

**j.** Click **Compact & Repair Database** on the FILE tab.

**k.** Click **Save As** on the FILE tab, and double-click **Back Up Database**. Name the backup **a11h1Replace_LastFirst_date_(1)**.

You just created a backup of the database you used to complete Hands-On Exercise 1. The *a11h1Replace_LastFirst* database remains open. If you complete this step on the same day as you worked the last step, Access adds_*(1)* to the end of the backup file name to distinguish it from the earlier file name.

**l.** Keep the database open if you plan to continue with Hands-On Exercise 2. If not, close the database and exit Access.

# MIS Cases

## Piedmont Trailer Manufacturing Company

**Spreadsheet Case**                    **Difficulty Rating:** ★

## SKILLS CHECK    YOU SHOULD REVIEW THE FOLLOWING AREAS:

### SPREADSHEET SKILLS

- Cell Formatting
- Cell Reference
- Chart
- Consolidating Worksheets
- Formula

- IRR Function
- Protecting Cells
- Range Name
- SUM Function
- Worksheet Formatting

## Case Background

Piedmont Trailer Manufacturing Company, a nationally recognized trailer manufacturer, produces a wide range of quality standard and custom-built trailers, ranging from gooseneck to bumper pull trailers. Although the Piedmont Trailer Manufacturing Company uses state-of-the-art information systems for most of its business processes, its custom order-tracking process is primarily manual-based and requires major renovations. In an effort to improve the custom order-tracking process, a systems analysis and design project is currently underway. As part of the systems development team, one of your responsibilities is to prepare an economic feasibility analysis for an upcoming presentation to management.

Ms. Geraldine Pablo, the project manager, asks you to construct an Economic Feasibility workbook. The purpose of this workbook is to summarize and analyze the benefits and costs associated with the proposed custom order-tracking project. The preparation of an Economic Feasibility workbook requires you to design five worksheets, use several formulas and functions, use basic cell and worksheet formatting, and consolidate data from multiple worksheets into a summary worksheet.

## Case Scenario

Quality trailers and excellent customer service are the two primary reasons why the Piedmont Trailer Manufacturing Company is the nation's largest manufacturer of standard and custom-built trailers. Although the majority of the company's income is derived from the sale of standard trailers, the number of custom orders is on the rise. When a custom order is placed, the request is captured on several paper forms and then routed to the production department. Often it takes three months before a custom order is released to production. This is due in part to the careful attention given to the customer by helping him select the right finishes, fixtures, trailer size, and other amenities. Management has decided that the custom ordering process is inefficient, time-consuming, and costly. In an effort to improve the custom order-tracking process, your project team is assigned the task of developing a custom order-tracking system.

During the planning phase, your project team identified several tangible benefits and costs. The new custom order-tracking system will save the company money by decreasing storage, staff, and order rework expenses. Additionally, the proposed system should increase sales, improve order processing speed, provide better data management, and streamline activities. Table 12.1 summarizes these benefits and their respective savings.

The proposed custom order-tracking system will incur both one-time and recurring costs. From one of your business courses, you recall that one-time costs often occur during the start up and development of a project, and recurring costs occur throughout the useful life of the new system. The one-time costs for this project currently include development personnel, training, project-related technology purchases, site-preparation, and miscellaneous costs. Table 12.2 lists the one-time costs and their estimated dollar values. Recurring

### TABLE 12.1 Yearly Recurring Benefits

| Benefit | Approximate Dollar Value |
| --- | --- |
| Storage Savings | $30,000 |
| Staff Reduction (2 people) | $45,000 |
| Reduced Order Rework | $14,000 |
| Increased Sales | $100,000 |
| Faster Order Processing | $40,000 |
| Better Data Management | $125,000 |
| Streamline Activities | $80,000 |

### TABLE 12.2 One-Time Costs

| One-Time Cost | Approximate Dollar Value |
| --- | --- |
| Development Personnel | $142,000 |
| Training | $45,000 |
| Project-Related Technology Purchases | $65,000 |
| Site Preparation | $105,250 |
| Miscellaneous | |
| Conference-Related | $7,500 |
| Supplies | $2,704 |
| Duplication | $3,249 |

## TABLE 12.3   Yearly Recurring Costs

| Cost | Approximate Dollar Value |
|------|--------------------------|
| Software Maintenance | $55,000 |
| Hardware | $30,000 |
| Supplies | $35,000 |
| IT Positions (3 people) | $160,000 |
| Site Rental | $38,000 |

costs include software maintenance, hardware, supplies, new information technology positions, and site rental costs. Table 12.3 summarizes these recurring costs.

# Design Specifications

Since the project is in the early stages of development, you want your workbook to be as flexible as possible, so that additional costs and benefits, when identified, are easily added to the Economic Feasibility workbook. You decide that the Economic Feasibility workbook should contain at least five worksheets: Documentation, One-Time Cost, Recurring Cost, Tangible Benefit, and Economic Feasibility Summary. The Documentation worksheet provides information about the creator, each individual worksheet, and the date created. (Your professor will provide additional guidelines for the Documentation worksheet.)

You decide to construct the One-Time Cost, Recurring Cost, and Tangible Benefit worksheets first, because these worksheets have a simple design. These worksheets each contain two columns, with the first column identifying the items in the category, and the second column containing the dollar values associated with the items. Each worksheet totals the dollar values; these totals are then used in the Economic Feasibility Summary worksheet.

As Figure 12.1 shows, the Economic Feasibility Summary worksheet has a more complex design. Since the Economic Feasibility Summary worksheet is a summary worksheet, it consolidates data from the One-Time Cost, Recurring Cost, and Tangible Benefit worksheets, requiring you to reference specific cells on these worksheets.

As part of the Economic Feasibility Summary worksheet design, you must discount the recurring benefits and costs to their present values. Although several ways exist to determine the present value of the benefits, you decide to multiply the recurring benefit (or cost) by a present value factor. Since each year requires a different present value factor, the worksheet must compute the present value factor for each year. You decide to use the formula provided below to determine each year's present value factor. (In the following formula, "i" refers to the discount rate, and "n" refers to the year. The worksheet shown in Figure 12.1 assumes that the project's useful life is five years.) To determine the present value of a benefit or cost for a particular year, you multiply the recurring value of the benefit or cost for that year by the present value factor for that year. The net present value of all benefits (or costs) is a summation of the benefits (or costs) up to and including the current year. The overall net present value is the difference between the net present value of all benefits and the net present value of all costs. The cash flow section provides a summary of the cash flows on a yearly basis, as well as a summation of the overall cash flows.

$$PVF = 1/(1+i)^n$$

Although Ms. Pablo is the primary user of the Economic Feasibility workbook, other project team members will have access to this workbook. Therefore, you decide that all cells, other

## Piedmont Trailer Manufacturing Company
## Custom Order-Tracking Project
### (Current Date)

| Discount Rate | .14 | | | | | | |
|---|---|---|---|---|---|---|---|
| Year | 0 | 1 | 2 | 3 | 4 | 5 | Totals |
| **Benefits** | | | | | | | |
| Recurring Value of Benefits | $0.00 | $434,000.00 | $434,000.00 | $434,000.00 | $434,000.00 | $434,000.00 | |
| Present Value Factor | 1.000000 | .877193 | .769468 | .674972 | .592080 | .519369 | |
| Present Value of Benefits | $0.00 | $380,701.75 | $333,948.91 | $292,937.64 | $256,962.84 | $225,406.00 | |
| Net Present Value of All Benefits | $0.00 | $380,701.75 | $714,650.66 | $1,007,588.30 | $1,264,551.14 | $1,489,957.14 | $1,489,957.14 |
| | | | | | | | |
| **Costs** | | | | | | | |
| One-Time Costs | ($370,703.00) | | | | | | |
| Recurring Costs | | ($318,000.00) | ($318,000.00) | ($318,000.00) | ($318,000.00) | ($318,000.00) | |
| Present Value Factor | | .877193 | .769468 | .674972 | .592080 | .519369 | |
| Present Value of Recurring Costs | | ($278,947.37) | ($244,690.67) | ($214,640.94) | ($188,281.53) | ($165,159.24) | |
| Net Present Value of All Costs | ($370,703.00) | ($649,650.37) | ($894,341.04) | ($1,108,981.98) | ($1,297,263.51) | ($1,462,422.75) | ($1,462,422.75) |
| | | | | | | | |
| Overall Net Present Value | | | | | | | $27,534.39 |
| **Cash Flow Analysis** | | | | | | | |
| Yearly NPV Cash Flow | ($370,703.00) | $101,754.39 | $89,258.23 | $78,296.70 | $68,681.31 | $60,246.77 | |
| Overall NPV Cash Flow | ($370,703.00) | ($268,948.61) | ($179,690.38) | ($101,393.68) | ($32,712.37) | $27,534.39 | |

FIGURE 12.1 Economic Feasibility Summary Worksheet*

*Adapted from Modern Systems Analysis and Design, fifth edition, Jeffrey A. Hoffer, Joey F. George, and Joseph S. Valacich

than input cells, should be protected. (You may wish to use your system's online help feature to review worksheet protection.)

# Information Specifications

Ms. Pablo wants to generate optimistic, realistic, and pessimistic views of the data, so she requests the ability to quickly change the discount rate. To satisfy this requirement, you include a cell on your Economic Feasibility Summary worksheet to hold the discount rate. Figure 12.1 shows that the discount rate is placed at the top of the worksheet. The discount rate is used in several formulas, so referencing this cell in a formula facilitates the economic feasibility analysis.

The Economic Feasibility Summary worksheet summarizes the costs and benefits, shows the present values of the costs and benefits, calculates the overall net present value, and shows the yearly and overall cash flows for the project. Although not shown in Figure 12.1, Ms. Pablo requests that the project's breakeven point and internal rate of return be determined. During her presentation to management, Ms. Pablo will use the breakeven point to help justify the project's viability and show how quickly management will recover its investment in the project. Since the internal rate of return provides an indication of the project's profitability, Ms. Pablo will use the internal rate of return to help justify management's investment in the project.

Ms. Pablo needs answers to the following questions. Using your newly designed Economic Feasibility workbook, provide Ms. Pablo with answers to her questions.

1. How will discount rates of 8, 10, 12, 14, and 16 percent affect the project's feasibility?
2. Reset the discount rate to 14 percent. Prepare a breakeven chart that compares the net present value of all benefits to the net present value of all costs.
3. If management stipulates that the internal rate of return must be equal to or greater than the discount rate, is this project still justifiable?
4. Assuming the discount rate is 14 percent, how will eliminating an additional staff position of $32,500 affect the economic feasibility assessment?
5. Assume that the staff position mentioned in Step 3 is eliminated, the site preparation cost increases to $120,000, and the discount rate is 14 percent. What impact will these changes have on the project's feasibility?
6. Assume that management has enough money to fund two development projects. After you determine this project's internal rate of return, compare its internal rate of return to the internal rate of returns for the proposed development projects listed in the following table. Based on the projects' internal rate of returns, do you think management will fund the custom order-tracking system?

| Proposed Project | IRR |
| --- | --- |
| Delivery System | 15.7 percent |
| Human Resources System | 27.8 percent |
| Inventory Tracking System | 18.9 percent |
| Forecasting System | 23.7 percent |

# Implementation Concerns

To design the Economic Feasibility workbook described in the case scenario, you will create a workbook consisting of five worksheets. You should create separate worksheets for the documentation, one-time costs, recurring costs, recurring benefits, and economic feasibility summary. Since the Economic Feasibility Summary worksheet consolidates data from three of the worksheets, you should create this worksheet last.

Although you are free to work with the design of your worksheets, each worksheet should have a consistent, professional appearance. You should also use proper formatting for the cells. For instance, dollar values should display with a dollar sign and be formatted to two decimal places.

## Test Your Design

After creating the Economic Feasibility workbook described in the case scenario, you should test the design of your worksheets. Perform the following operations.

1. What recommendations would you make if the useful life of the project is three years instead of five years? Six years? (Use the original case values and assume a discount rate of 14 percent.)
2. Identify at least three additional benefits that might be derived from this project. Estimate their value and include the values in your analysis. What impact do these new benefits have on your economic feasibility?
3. Identify at least one additional one-time cost and at least three additional recurring costs. Estimate their values and include these values in your analysis. What impact do these new costs have on your economic feasibility? Is the project still justifiable? Why or why not?

## Case Deliverables

In order to satisfactorily complete this case, you should build the workbook as described in the case scenario and then prepare both written and oral presentations. Unless otherwise specified, submit the following deliverables to your professor.

1. A written report discussing any assumptions you have made about the case and the key elements of the case. Additionally, what features did you add to make the worksheets more functional? User friendly? (Please note that these assumptions cannot violate any of the requirements specified above and must be approved by your professor.)
2. A printout of each worksheet.
3. A printout of each worksheet's formulas.
4. An electronic, working copy of your workbook that meets the criteria mentioned in the case scenario and specifications sections.
5. Results for each question posed above. (A memo to your instructor discussing these results should also be provided.)
6. As mentioned above, you should prepare an oral presentation. (Your instructor will establish the time allocated for your presentation.) You should use a presentation package and discuss the key features of your worksheets. Also, discuss how the workbook is beneficial for Ms. Pablo. What additional information should be included in the workbook to make it more useful?

# Francisco's Lawn Care

Difficulty Rating: ★

YOU SHOULD REVIEW THE FOLLOWING AREAS:

## SPREADSHEET SKILLS

- Cell Formatting
- Cell Reference
- Chart
- COUNTA Function
- COUNTIF Function
- Formula

- PMT Function
- Sort
- SUM Function
- SUMIF Function
- VLOOKUP Function
- Worksheet Formatting

# Case Background

Fernando Francisco owns and operates a small, growing lawn care business called Francisco's Lawn Care. Record keeping for the business has reached a point where Mr. Francisco needs a better system for tracking his customers, service dates, customer payments, and revenue. After considering several options for improving his record keeping system, Mr. Fernando decided that a Microsoft Excel workbook will be beneficial for him. The Lawn Care workbook contains several worksheets, including Customer, Payment, and Amortization worksheets. The preparation of this workbook requires you to create and format multiple worksheets, create several formulas, use several functions, and prepare charts.

# Case Scenario

As Mr. Francisco's client base continues to grow, he does not want to rely on his memory for price quotes, service dates, payments, and business revenue. Instead he will use Microsoft Excel to track this information. As you are familiar with Microsoft Excel, you agree to develop Mr. Francisco's Lawn Care workbook.

Currently, Mr. Francisco keeps basic information about his lawn care customers in a spiral notebook. In the notebook, he records the customer's first and last names, standard fee, additional weekly charges, total weekly charges, service day, lawn size, and start date. When a customer requests an estimate, Mr. Francisco provides an initial price quote based on the standard fees shown in Figure 12.2. The standard fee is the minimum price charged for a certain lawn size. Before giving a final quote, Mr. Francisco visits the customer's site and may adjust the initial quote based on his site visit. Any additional weekly charges are determined after Mr. Francisco visits the customer's site. Additional charges include such things as extra weed eating, yard fertilization, or cleaning a flower bed. For each customer, the total weekly charges include the standard fee plus additional weekly charges.

| Francisco's Lawn Care Standard Pricing Guide | |
|---|---|
| **Lawn Size** | **Standard Price** |
| Small | $25.00 |
| Medium | $35.00 |
| Large | $50.00 |
| Commercial | $75.00 |

**FIGURE 12.2:** Pricing Guide

After Mr. Francisco's site visit, the customer is given a final quote for the total weekly charges. If the customer agrees to the final quote, a weekly lawn maintenance schedule is arranged. Mr. Francisco wants a quote sheet developed, summing the weekly charges. After he returns to his office, he will prepare the quote sheet and mail it to the customer.

In one of your conversations with Mr. Francisco, he mentions that he needs to purchase new lawn care equipment, and he will purchase the lawn care equipment on credit. Before purchasing the lawn care equipment, he will evaluate different payment scenarios. As part of the workbook's design, he asks you to build an amortization schedule for him.

## Design Specifications

The Lawn Care workbook will store the customer, service, and payment information that is currently kept in the spiral notebook. In the Lawn Care workbook, a worksheet should be created and named Customers. The Customers worksheet will store customer information. The Customers worksheet should have columns for customer first and last names, standard fee, additional weekly charges, total weekly charges, service day, lawn size, start date, and comments. Mr. Francisco will use the Comments column to record relevant comments about the customer's service, such as why additional charges were applied. When viewing the Customers worksheet, Mr. Francisco wants to see a total count of his customers, anticipated total revenue by day, anticipated total weekly revenue, and anticipated total monthly revenue. As the standard fee is based on lawn size, Mr. Francisco recommends that you recreate the standard pricing guide in the Customers worksheet, and then use the VLOOKUP function to retrieve the standard lawn size price. (If you are unfamiliar with the VLOOKUP function, consider using your system's online help feature to learn more about it.) The customer entries should be sorted alphabetically by last name.

Mr. Francisco asks you to create a Payment worksheet for him. The Payment worksheet enables Mr. Francisco to track customer payments. The Payment worksheet should include the payment date, customer's first and last name, total weekly charges, one-time fees, this week's total charges, amount paid, remaining balance, and comments columns.

Periodically, a customer will ask Mr. Francisco if he can remove a tree limb or trim a hedge. As this one-time fee is not reflected in the established total weekly charges, Mr. Francisco wants a one-time fee column included in the Payment worksheet. Sometimes a customer does not pay the correct amount, so Mr. Francisco wants a column to track the remaining balance. The Comments column enables Mr. Francisco to enter any comments about the transaction for later reference. For the total weekly charges column, Mr. Francisco recommends that you look up this value from the Customer worksheet.

Mr. Francisco asks you to prepare a quote sheet for him. After the initial site visit, Mr. Francisco will use the quote sheet to prepare a summary of the quoted charges. The quote sheet should show the standard fee, any additional weekly charges and the total weekly charges. Mr. Francisco wants the business name, current date and start date provided on the quote sheet.

Mr. Francisco will purchase new lawn care equipment on credit. To help him manage his payments, he asks you to create an amortization schedule. For each month, the schedule shows how much of the payment applies to interest, how much of the payment applies to the principle, and the remaining loan balance. Mr. Francisco will periodically make additional monthly payments of differing amounts, so he wants this capability built into the schedule.

## Information Specifications

In addition to the information requirements specified above, Mr. Francisco requests answers to the following questions.

1. Mr. Francisco wants a list of his customers based on service day. Provide Mr. Francisco with this list.
2. Mr. Francisco wants to compare the business's anticipated revenue by week day. Prepare a chart that compares the anticipated revenue by week day. (You select the chart.)
3. Mr. Francisco wants to compare the business's weekly revenue by lawn size. Prepare a chart that compares weekly revenue by lawn size. (You select the chart.)
4. A local hardware store is advertising zero percent interest on all purchases, as long as the balance is paid within one year of the purchase date. If Mr. Francisco takes advantage of this offer, what will his monthly payments be? (Assume he spends $12,000 on new equipment and makes monthly payments.)
5. If the interest rate is 5 percent and the loan period is for two years, what are Mr. Francisco's monthly payments?

## Implementation Concerns

Although you are free to work with the design of your workbook, it should have a consistent, professional appearance. You should apply appropriate formatting to the cells and worksheets. For instance, all cells containing dollar values should use a currency format and be formatted to two decimal places. Your worksheets should have appropriate headers, as well as appropriate column and row headings.

To prepare the Lawn Care workbook according to the specifications provided above, you will design several worksheets, construct formulas, may use the IF, COUNTIF, COUNTA, SUM, SUMIF, and VLOOKUP functions, and create charts. If you are not familiar with any of these skills, use your system's online help feature to learn more about the skill.)

## Test Your Design

After creating your workbook, you should test your design. Perform the following steps.

1. If the lawn care business operates seven months out of the year, what is the projected revenue for the year? (Assume no new clients are added.)
2. Mr. Francisco has five new clients. Add the following new clients to your Lawn Care workbook. (Make any additional assumptions that you feel are necessary.)

| Last Name | First Name | Additional Weekly Charges | Scheduled Day | Lawn Size | Start Date |
|---|---|---|---|---|---|
| Your Last Name | Your First Name | $10.00 | Tuesday | Small | 5/6/2008 |
| Malcom | Loretta | $15.00 | Tuesday | Large | 5/6/2008 |
| Orosco | Amilso | | Tuesday | Commercial | 5/6/2008 |
| Popoola | Rajesh | | Wednesday | Medium | 5/7/2008 |
| Rishel | Ravi | $25.00 | Wednesday | Medium | 5/7/2008 |

3. Mr. Francisco may raise his prices for next year. Using his current customer data for analysis, what impact will these prices have on next year's revenue?

| New Lawn Care Prices | |
|---|---|
| Commercial | $90.00 |
| Large | $60.00 |
| Medium | $45.00 |
| Small | $35.00 |

## Case Deliverables

In order to satisfactorily complete this case, you should build the worksheet as described in the case scenario and then prepare both written and oral presentations. Unless otherwise specified, submit the following deliverables to your professor.

1. A written report discussing any assumptions you have made about the case and the key elements of the case. Additionally, what features did you add to make the worksheet(s) more functional? User friendly? (Please note that these assumptions cannot violate any of the requirements specified above and must be approved by your professor.)

2. A printout of each worksheet and chart.

3. A printout of each worksheet's formulas.

4. An electronic, working copy of your workbook that meets the criteria mentioned in the case scenario and specifications sections.

5. Results for each question posed above. (A memo to your instructor discussing these results should also be provided.)

6. As mentioned above, you should prepare an oral presentation. (Your instructor will establish the time allocated for your presentation.) You should use a presentation package and discuss the key features of your workbook. Also, discuss how the workbook is beneficial for Mr. Francisco. What additional information should be included in the workbook to make it more useful?

# Maxi's Grocery Mart

SKILLS CHECK   YOU SHOULD REVIEW THE FOLLOWING AREAS:

## SPREADSHEET SKILLS

- Absolute Cell Reference
- Cell Formatting
- Chart
- Formula
- IF Function

- Page Break
- Protecting Cells
- Relative Cell Reference
- SUM Function
- Worksheet Formatting

# Case Background

Since its opening almost 50 years ago, Maxi's Grocery Mart has continued to grow and evolve with the times. The family-owned business has survived many ups and downs and is currently experiencing a modest growth in business. Leroy Feronti, the current owner, wants to expand his family's business by renovating the grocery mart building. While Mr. Feronti has some personal funds available, he will need to procure a loan from the local bank. Before approaching the local bank, he would like to prepare and review several pro forma financial statements. If Mr. Feronti decides to go forward with the renovation, he will use the pro forma financial statements as part of his loan application. Mr. Feronti wants the pro forma income statement prepared first, and he asks you to prepare it for him. Preparation of the pro forma income statement requires you to design a worksheet with input and information sections, properly format the worksheet, construct simple formulas, perform what-if analysis, and generate a chart.

# Case Scenario

Maxi's Grocery Mart is a family-owned business that has been in operation since the 1950s. Although Leroy Feronti is very active with his business, he does employ a store manager, assistant manager, and 17 full-time employees. The store manager and assistant manager are paid a salary, and the employees are paid an hourly wage. Each employee works 40 hours a week, 50 weeks a year.

Having recently assumed ownership of the business from his parents, Mr. Feronti feels that one of the keys to the business's continued success is the renovation of the grocery mart building. Renovating the existing building will cost approximately $450,000. Mr. Feronti must borrow $300,000 from the local bank and will use income generated from the grocery mart to repay the loan. Mr. Feronti asks you to prepare a set of pro forma financial statements for him. He will use these statements to analyze his business. If he decides to pursue the renovation project, he will use the pro forma statements as part of his loan application.

| | | | | |
|---|---|---|---|---|
| **Maxi's Food Mart** | | | | |
| **Pro Forma Income Statement** | | | | |
| | **2008** | **2009** | **2010** | **2011** |
| **Sales** | | | | |
| Deli | Assume 5 percent of total sales each year. | | | |
| Dairy | Assume 19 percent of total sales each year. | | | |
| Canned Goods | Assume 10 percent of total sales each year. | | | |
| Frozen Foods | Assume 22 percent of total sales each year. | | | |
| Meats | Assume 21 percent of total sales each year. | | | |
| Produce | Assume 12.5 percent of total sales each year. | | | |
| Dry Goods | Assume 9 percent of total sales each year. | | | |
| Video Sales | Assume 1.5 percent of total sales each year. | | | |
| Total Sales | Assume $3,750,000.00 in total sales for 2008. | | | |
| **Cost of Goods Sold** | | | | |
| Deli | Assume 50 percent of deli sales each year. | | | |
| Dairy | Assume 50 percent of dairy sales each year. | | | |
| Canned Goods | Assume 75 percent of canned good sales each year. | | | |
| Frozen Foods | Assume 65 percent of frozen food sales each year. | | | |
| Meats | Assume 50 percent of meat sales each year. | | | |
| Produce | Assume 65 percent of produce sales each year. | | | |
| Dry Goods | Assume 66 percent of dry good sales each year. | | | |
| Video Sales | Assume 30 percent of video sales each year. | | | |
| **Total Cost of Goods Sold** | | | | |
| **Gross Profit** | | | | |
| | | | | |
| **Operating Expenses** | | | | |
| Sales and Marketing | Assume 5.5 percent of total sales each year. | | | |
| General and Administrative | Assume 8.75 percent of total sales each year. | | | |
| Depreciation | Assume $20,000 per year. | | | |
| Wages | Includes the employees' wages, store manager's salary, and assistant manager's salary. | | | |
| Common Costs | Mr. Feronti's salary. | | | |
| **Total Operating Expenses** | | | | |
| | | | | |
| Income Before Taxes | | | | |
| Income Taxes | | | | |
| **Net Income** | | | | |

FIGURE 12.3: Maxi's Food Mart Income Statement Outline

| Maxi's Food Mart | |
| :-- | :-- |
| **Assumptions and Additional Information** | |
| **Growth and Tax Rates** | **Salary** |
| 2009 Growth: 6.25 percent | Mr. Feronti: 12 percent of gross profit |
| 2010 Growth: 7.75 percent | Store Manager: $57,000 |
| 2011 Growth: 8.25 percent | Assistant Manager: $42,000 |
| Tax Rate: 35 percent | Employee Hourly Wage: $13.00 |

**FIGURE 12.4:** Assumptions and Additional Information

Mr. Feronti asks you to use the income statement outline shown in Figure 12.3 and use the grocery mart's 2008 sales as the base period. You will use the 2008 sales to estimate Mr. Feronti's sales, cost of goods sold, expenses, taxes, and net income for the next three years. When preparing the pro forma income statement, several assumptions and additional information are necessary. Figure 12.4 provides these assumptions and additional information.

## Design Specifications

As Mr. Feronti will use the pro forma income statement as part of his loan application, he requests that it have a consistent, professional, and well-organized appearance. Mr. Feronti specifically requests that you include an appropriate header and apply proper formatting to the cells and worksheet.

Using Figures 12.3 and 12.4 as guides, you decide that the worksheet requires both input and information sections. Figure 12.3 provides an outline and guidelines for constructing the information section and Figure 12.4 provides the necessary data for the input section. By creating separate sections, it is easy for Mr. Feronti to not only view the input data to his income statement, but also, if necessary, change the parameters, thus facilitating his decision-making activities.

The information section contains the pro forma income statement, and this section provides Mr. Feronti with information about his projected sales, cost of goods sold, operating expenses, and net income for years 2009 - 2011. The information section uses the grocery mart's 2008 sales as the basis for these projections. You make sure that, where appropriate, the information section formulas reference the cell values contained in the input section.

As you study Figure 12.3, you realize that Mr. Feronti wants his store item sales, cost of goods sold, and operating expenses expressed as a percentage of total sales. To facilitate Mr. Feronti's analysis, you place the total sales value in the input section, along with the other assumptions. By doing this, your formulas in the information section can reference the actual total sales figure. As you study Figure 12.4, you notice that Mr. Feronti's salary is 12 percent of gross profit. Since Mr. Feronti only draws his salary if the grocery mart makes a profit, you must build this logic into the income statement. You do so by using the IF function. To keep the information section's formulas from accidentally being updated, you protect the cells in the information section.

Mr. Feronti wants the input and information sections printed on separate pages. For each section's printout, he wants the results printed on a single page. The printouts should utilize a portrait orientation and be centered horizontally and vertically.

## Information Specifications

Mr. Feronti needs information to support his decision making about the upcoming renovation to Maxi's Grocery Mart. Using the newly constructed pro forma income statement, provide Mr. Feronti with the information that he needs. (Before answering each of the following questions, reset your worksheet to its original values.)

1. What impact will sales growths of 9 percent in 2009, 9.5 percent in 2010, and 10 percent in 2011 have on the grocery mart's net income?

2. What impact will sales growths of 4 percent in 2009, 5 percent in 2010, and 5.5 in 2011 have on Mr. Feronti's net income?

3. Mr. Feronti wants a chart that compares the store items based on their 2008 sales. He asks you to select an appropriate chart type and then prepare the chart.

4. If Mr. Feronti decreases his salary to 8 percent and increases the employees' hourly wages to $15, what impact will this have on the grocery mart's net income?

5. Assume Mr. Feronti has 19 employees instead of 17. What impact will two additional employees have on the business's net income?

## Implementation Concerns

The preparation of this case requires you to apply basic spreadsheet construction concepts. Since Mr. Feronti will change the input values during his decision-making activities, you should have a separate input section for the input values. Keep in mind that the formulas in the information section will reference the input cells. You should use absolute and relative cell references, as opposed to constant values.

## Test Your Design

After creating the pro forma income statement worksheet, you should test your design. Perform the following steps.

1. Assume sales in 2008 were $2.5 million, instead of $3.75 million. Now, assume sales in 2008 were $7 million. What impact, if any, do these changes have? Are there any significant changes in the sales, expenses, or net income? (Other than the changes specified in this question, use the original case values.)

2. Make the following changes to the percent of sales for the following items. The deli accounts for 4 percent of sales; dairy items account for 18 percent of sales; canned goods account for 18 percent; frozen food items account for 20 percent; and meats account for 17 percent.

3. Make the following salary changes. Mr. Feronti takes home 16 percent of the gross profit, the store manager makes $60,000, and the assistant manager makes $48,000. How will these changes impact the grocery mart's net income?

4. Reset your sales percentages and salaries back to their original values and then make the following changes. Assume a discount chain is opening a grocery store in a neighboring town. Mr. Feronti thinks this may cause his sales to decrease. He thinks his growth may decrease in 2009 by 12 percent, 2010 by 10 percent and 2011 by 5 percent. Would you still recommend renovating the grocery mart? Why or why not?

### Case Deliverables

In order to satisfactorily complete this case, you should build the worksheet as described in the case scenario and then prepare both written and oral presentations. Unless otherwise specified, submit the following deliverables to your professor.

1. A written report discussing any assumptions you have made about the case and the key elements of the case. Additionally, what features did you add to make the worksheet more functional? User friendly? (Please note that these assumptions cannot violate any of the requirements specified above and must be approved by your professor.)

2. A printout of each worksheet and chart.

3. A printout of the worksheet's formulas.

4. An electronic, working copy of your worksheet that meets the criteria mentioned in the case scenario and specifications sections.

5. Results for each question posed above. (A memo to your instructor discussing these results should also be provided.)

6. As mentioned above, you should prepare an oral presentation. (Your instructor will establish the time allocated for your presentation.) You should use a presentation package and discuss the key features of your worksheet. Also, discuss how the worksheet is beneficial for Mr. Feronti. What additional information should be included in the worksheet to make it more useful?

# Klein Technology Seminars

**Spreadsheet Case**                    **Difficulty Rating:** ★ ★

# Case Background

Klein Technology Seminars provides information technology seminars to local corporations and continuously strives to provide its corporate clients with quality, timely instruction. As part of its quality-first strategy, seminar students are asked to complete customer satisfaction surveys. These satisfaction surveys are then reviewed by Dr. Klein, the company's founder. Based on the survey results, Dr. Klein makes adjustments to the company's courses.

To facilitate his analysis of the customer satisfaction surveys, Dr. Klein asks you to develop a Survey Results workbook. The preparation of this workbook requires you to design worksheets, use formulas, use several functions, use basic cell and worksheet formatting techniques, and prepare PivotTable and PivotChart reports.

# Case Scenario

Dr. Earl Klein is the founder and president of Klein Technology Seminars. As a former university vice president, Dr. Klein came into contact with many corporate executives. Frequently, the corporate executives would remark about the necessity of keeping their employees up-to-date in their field. Dr. Klein took this message to heart, and when he retired a few years ago, he formed Klein Technology Seminars.

Since its beginning, Klein Technology Seminars has seen a steady growth in its business and has a reputation for providing quality instruction to its clients. The company's reputation is due in part to its 10 full-time, highly qualified instructors. The instructors teach a variety of courses, ranging from productivity to certification courses. The courses are one-week courses, last from 8 a.m. to 5 p.m. each day, and are limited to 24 students. The company offers its courses on its campus, at the client's site, and at other off-site locations.

Once seminar attendees finish a course, they complete satisfaction surveys. The surveys help Dr. Klein judge the quality of the courses, as well as the instructors. Figure 12.5 shows a copy of the survey.

Until now, Dr. Klein has just read through the surveys and has not had time to analyze the survey data. Dr. Klein realizes the surveys contain a wealth of information, and he wants to

**Klein Technology Seminars**
**Satisfaction Survey**

1. **Have you previously attended a technology seminar offered by Klein Technology Seminars?**

   a. No
   b. Yes

2. **Have you attended a technology seminar offered by another company?**

   a. No
   b. Yes

3. **Overall, I am satisfied with the course.**

   Strongly Agree  Agree  Neutral  Disagree  Strongly Disagree

4. **I will take another course with Klein Technology Seminars.**

   Strongly Agree  Agree  Neutral  Disagree  Strongly Disagree

5. **The information presented will be useful on my job.**

   Strongly Agree  Agree  Neutral  Disagree  Strongly Disagree

6. **The instructor was knowledgeable about the subject matter.**

   Strongly Agree  Agree  Neutral  Disagree  Strongly Disagree

7. **The seminar's content is timely.**

   Strongly Agree  Agree  Neutral  Disagree  Strongly Disagree

8. **The instructor met the stated course objectives.**

   Strongly Agree  Agree  Neutral  Disagree  Strongly Disagree

FIGURE 12.5: Customer Satisfaction Survey

analyze the data with a spreadsheet application. Dr. Klein assigns you the task of developing a Survey Results workbook that will enable him to enter and track the results of the satisfaction surveys.

Once the surveys are collected, Dr. Klein or his secretary will code each survey respondent's answers. For each question, the possible responses are given a unique number. For instance, if a respondent answers "no" for Question 1, then Dr. Klein will record "1" in the worksheet cell. If the respondent answers "yes" for Question 1, then Dr. Klein will record "2" in the worksheet cell. Figure 12.6 shows how the questionnaire responses are coded.

## Design Specifications

Dr. Klein hands you a copy of an incomplete workbook called Klein Survey. The Klein Survey workbook currently contains sample survey data in the Response worksheet. Dr. Klein asks you to use the data from the Response worksheet when designing the Survey Results

| If Response Is: | Code |
|---|---|
| No | 1 |
| Yes | 2 |
| Strongly Agree | 5 |
| Agree | 4 |
| Neutral | 3 |
| Disagree | 2 |
| Strongly Disagree | 1 |

**FIGURE 12.6:** Customer Satisfaction Survey Codes

workbook. Figures 12.7 and 12.8 show how the survey data are currently organized in the Response worksheet. Columns A through E provide general information about the course. As the general information is readily available, it is not necessary to collect this information from the survey respondent. Instead, Dr. Klein will enter the general course information as he enters the respondent's answers into the worksheet. Figure 12.9 explains the codes for Columns A through E.

|   | A | B | C | D | E |
|---|---|---|---|---|---|
| 1 | Course No. | Location | Instructor ID | Class Size | Seminar Start Date |
| 2 | RTS1 | 2 | 2 | 10 | 10/6/2008 |
| 3 | RTS1 | 2 | 2 | 10 | 10/6/2008 |
| 4 | RTS1 | 2 | 2 | 10 | 10/6/2008 |
| 5 | RTS1 | 2 | 2 | 10 | 10/6/2008 |
| 6 | RTS3 | 3 | 5 | 12 | 10/6/2008 |
| 7 | RTS3 | 3 | 5 | 12 | 10/6/2008 |
| 8 | RTS3 | 3 | 5 | 12 | 10/6/2008 |

**FIGURE 12.7:** Survey Results Sample Data Columns A–E

Columns F - M display data that have been captured on the survey forms. The data displayed in these columns have been coded, meaning the survey responses have been coded using the codes displayed in Figure 12.6. For instance, if a student circled "no" as her answer for Question 1 on the survey form, then a "1" is displayed in Column F. Likewise, if a student circled "yes" as her answer for Question 1, then a "2" is displayed in Column F. (The codes help facilitate the analysis of the data.)

|   | F | G | H | I | J | K | L | M |
|---|---|---|---|---|---|---|---|---|
| 1 | Question 1 | Question 2 | Question 3 | Question 4 | Question 5 | Question 6 | Question 7 | Question 8 |
| 2 | 1 | 2 | 4 | 3 | 4 | 4 | 4 | 4 |
| 3 | 2 | 2 | 5 | 4 | 4 | 5 | 4 | 5 |
| 4 | 1 | 2 | 1 | 2 | 5 | 1 | 2 | 5 |
| 5 | 2 | 1 | 1 | 2 | 4 | 4 | 4 | 4 |
| 6 | 2 | 2 | 4 | 4 | 2 | 5 | 4 | 5 |
| 7 | 2 | 1 | 4 | 2 | 1 | 5 | 5 | 2 |
| 8 | 2 | 1 | 5 | 5 | 5 | 4 | 5 | 2 |

**FIGURE 12.8:** Survey Results Sample Data Columns F–M

The Response worksheet contains survey responses for a two-week period. Dr. Klein wants you to add a Summary worksheet to the Klein Survey workbook and then save the workbook as Survey Results. The purpose of the Summary worksheet is to summarize the survey response data contained in the Response worksheet. For each worksheet, you should include a worksheet title. Dr. Klein wants the title to reflect the contents of the worksheet, as well as the date range for the data the worksheet covers. Dr. Klein wants descriptive names for the column headings.

| Column | Codes | Explanation |
|---|---|---|
| A | Uses the actual course number. | Contains the course number. |
| B | 1 = Client's Site<br><br>2 = Klein Technology Seminars<br><br>3 = Another Location | Indicates where the course was offered. The course can be offered at the client's site, at Klein Technology Seminars or at another location. |
| C | Uses the instructor's identification number. | Contains the instructor's identification number. |
| D | Uses the number of students enrolled in the class. | Indicates the number of students enrolled in the class. (Not all students submit a survey.) |
| E | Uses the start date of the seminar. | Indicates the starting date of the seminar. |

**FIGURE 12.9:** General Course Information Codes

When the survey forms are returned, Dr. Klein or his assistant will code and then enter the individual survey results into the Response worksheet. When entering survey data into the Response worksheet, Dr. Klein wants the results for each survey assigned a respondent number. This request requires the insertion of a new column. This column should be the leftmost column in the worksheet, and should include a unique number for each row that contains survey results. So, if you have 20 surveys, the surveys would be numbered 1 through 20, respectively.

As previously mentioned, the purpose of the Summary worksheet is to summarize the data contained in the Response worksheet. For each question, the Summary worksheet should provide a count for each possible response. The count should reflect the number of times a particular response for the question was given. For instance, the Summary worksheet should show how many "1" entries, "2" entries, and "3" entries appear in the Location column for the Response worksheet. For Questions 3 - 8, Dr. Klein wants to see their averages, modes, and medians displayed in the Summary worksheet. The Summary worksheet should also provide the average, mode, and median class size.

Where possible, Dr. Klein wants the Summary worksheet information displayed in a graphic format. Specifically, he asks you to prepare several charts, including a column chart comparing the user satisfaction ratings for each course, a column chart comparing the satisfaction ratings by instructor, and a bar chart showing the number of respondents who strongly agreed that the courses were useful.

## Information Specifications

Dr. Klein will analyze the survey data at varying levels of detail. As mentioned above, Dr. Klein wants the survey results entered into a Response worksheet, and in the Summary worksheet he wants to see summarized results. Dr. Klein also wants to view data based on multiple conditions (such as satisfaction ratings for instructors by course). You suggest to Dr. Klein that the PivotTable and PivotChart reports are excellent tools for this type of analysis. Dr. Klein will use these tools to view the overall satisfaction ratings for each of his instructors by course, as well as the objectives met ratings for each course by instructor.

In addition to the information requests specified above, Dr. Klein wants answers for the following questions.

1. For each course, what is its average class size?
2. What percentage of respondents has attended a seminar before? Use a pie chart to summarize the results.

3. How many respondents who have taken a seminar course with another company agreed or strongly agreed that they would take another course with Klein Technology Seminars?

4. How many students strongly agreed that their instructor was knowledgeable about the subject matter? Display this information on a separate page for each course.

5. How did the students rate their instructor on the instructor's ability to meet course objectives? For each instructor, provide a count for each response. If possible, Dr. Klein wants this information summarized in a chart. (You select the chart.)

6. Which instructor had the highest percent of strongly agreed responses for Question 6?

## Implementation Concerns

Although you are free to work with the design of your workbook, the worksheets should have a consistent, professional appearance. Also, you should use appropriate formatting for the cells and worksheets.

This case requires you to insert columns into worksheets, consolidate information into a summary worksheet, use formulas, use several functions, and use the PivotTable and PivotChart report tools. Although it depends on how you design the Summary worksheet, the COUNTIF function can be used in a formula to determine the response counts.

## Test Your Design

After creating the Survey Results workbook, you should test your design. Perform the following steps.

1. Copy the survey results from the TYD Data worksheet located in the Klein Survey workbook and then paste these results immediately below the row containing the last October 13, 2008 entry.

2. Figures 12.10, 12.11, and 12.12 provide the results for three surveys. Enter the results for each survey into the Response worksheet. (You will need to code the response data.) For the survey results shown in Figure 12.10, the course was offered during the week of October 13th; the course number is RTS4; the location is 3; the Instructor ID is 2, and the course was conducted with 15 students. For the survey results shown in Figure 12.11, the course was offered during the week of October 20th; the course number is RTS4; the location is 2; the Instructor ID is 3, and the course was conducted with 23 students. For the survey results shown in Figure 12.12, the course was offered during the week of October 27th; the course number is RTS2; the location is 1; the Instructor ID is 4, and the course was conducted with 10 students.

3. Provide counts of the satisfaction ratings by class size for each instructor. Summarize this information in a PivotTable.

4. Which instructor had the highest percent of strongly disagree responses for Question 8?

5. Of those students who attended a seminar provided by another company, how did they rate Klein Technology Seminars? How do these results compare to students who have not attended a seminar offered by another company? Use a PivotTable to summarize this information. Also, prepare a chart that summarizes this information. (You select the chart.)

6. By class, how many students strongly agreed that the class provided useful information for their jobs? Summarize your results in a bar chart.

# Klein Technology Seminars
## Satisfaction Survey

1. **Have you previously attended a technology seminar offered by Klein Technology Seminars?**

   a. No ⬭(circled)
   b. Yes

2. **Have you attended a technology seminar offered by another company?**

   a. No
   b. Yes ⬭(circled)

3. **Overall, I am satisfied with the course.**

   Strongly Agree  (Agree)  Neutral  Disagree  Strongly Disagree

4. **I will take another course with Klein Technology Seminars.**

   Strongly Agree  (Agree)  Neutral  Disagree  Strongly Disagree

5. **The information presented will be useful on my job.**

   (Strongly Agree)  Agree  Neutral  Disagree  Strongly Disagree

6. **The instructor was knowledgeable about the subject matter.**

   Strongly Agree  (Agree)  Neutral  Disagree  Strongly Disagree

7. **The seminar's content is timely.**

   (Strongly Agree)  Agree  Neutral  Disagree  Strongly Disagree

8. **The instructor met the stated course objectives.**

   (Strongly Agree)  Agree  Neutral  Disagree  Strongly Disagree

FIGURE 12.10: Survey Results

# Klein Technology Seminars
## Satisfaction Survey

1.  **Have you previously attended a technology seminar offered by Klein Technology Seminars?**

    a. No

    ⟨b. Yes⟩

2.  **Have you attended a technology seminar offered by another company?**

    a. No

    ⟨b. Yes⟩

3.  **Overall, I am satisfied with the course.**

    Strongly Agree    Agree    Neutral    Disagree    ⟨Strongly Disagree⟩

4.  **I will take another course with Klein Technology Seminars.**

    Strongly Agree    Agree    Neutral    Disagree    ⟨Strongly Disagree⟩

5.  **The information presented will be useful on my job.**

    Strongly Agree    Agree    Neutral    ⟨Disagree⟩    Strongly Disagree

6.  **The instructor was knowledgeable about the subject matter.**

    Strongly Agree    Agree    Neutral    ⟨Disagree⟩    Strongly Disagree

7.  **The seminar's content is timely.**

    Strongly Agree    Agree    Neutral    ⟨Disagree⟩    Strongly Disagree

8.  **The instructor met the stated course objectives.**

    Strongly Agree    Agree    Neutral    Disagree    ⟨Strongly Disagree⟩

**FIGURE 12.11:** Second Survey Results

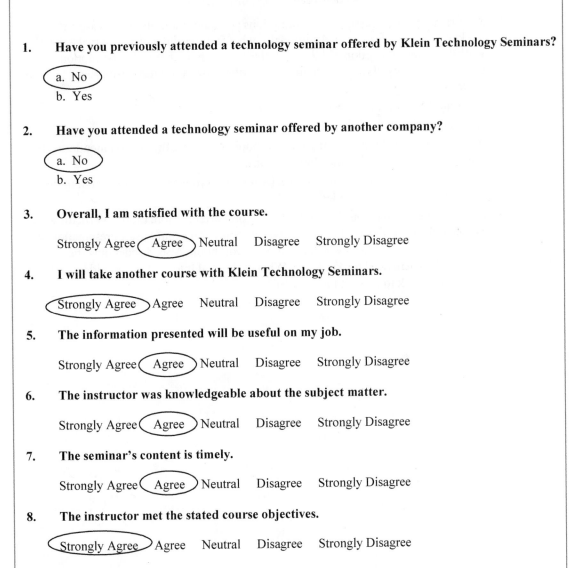

**Klein Technology Seminars**
**Satisfaction Survey**

1. **Have you previously attended a technology seminar offered by Klein Technology Seminars?**

   (a. No)
   b. Yes

2. **Have you attended a technology seminar offered by another company?**

   (a. No)
   b. Yes

3. **Overall, I am satisfied with the course.**

   Strongly Agree (Agree) Neutral  Disagree  Strongly Disagree

4. **I will take another course with Klein Technology Seminars.**

   (Strongly Agree) Agree  Neutral  Disagree  Strongly Disagree

5. **The information presented will be useful on my job.**

   Strongly Agree (Agree) Neutral  Disagree  Strongly Disagree

6. **The instructor was knowledgeable about the subject matter.**

   Strongly Agree (Agree) Neutral  Disagree  Strongly Disagree

7. **The seminar's content is timely.**

   Strongly Agree (Agree) Neutral  Disagree  Strongly Disagree

8. **The instructor met the stated course objectives.**

   (Strongly Agree) Agree  Neutral  Disagree  Strongly Disagree

**FIGURE 12.12:** Third Survey Results

## Case Deliverables

In order to satisfactorily complete this case, you should build the workbook as described in the case scenario and then prepare both written and oral presentations. Unless otherwise specified, submit the following deliverables to your professor.

1. A written report discussing any assumptions you have made about the case and the key elements of the case. Additionally, what features did you add to make the worksheets more functional? User friendly? (Please note that these assumptions cannot violate any of the requirements specified above and must be approved by your professor.)

2. A printout of each worksheet.

3. A printout of each worksheet's formulas.

4. An electronic, working copy of your workbook that meets the criteria mentioned in the case scenario and specifications sections.

5. Results for each question posed above. (A memo to your instructor discussing these results should also be provided.)

6. As mentioned above, you should prepare an oral presentation. (Your instructor will establish the time allocated for your presentation.) You should use a presentation package and discuss the key features of your workbook. Also, discuss how the workbook is beneficial for Dr. Klein. What additional information should be included in the workbook to make it more useful?

# Lake West University

## SKILLS CHECK YOU SHOULD REVIEW THE FOLLOWING AREAS:

### SPREADSHEET SKILLS

- Chart
- Conditional Formatting
- COUNTA Function
- COUNTIF Function
- COUNTIFS Function
- Filter (Optional)

- IF Function
- Nesting Functions
- PivotChart
- PivotTable
- Template
- Worksheet Formatting

# Case Background

Lake West University places a major emphasis on helping its students learn. To accomplish this mission, departments are strongly encouraged to assess their programs, majors, and courses. To better assess their courses, the Lake West University's Economics faculty include standard questions on final exams given in core Economics courses. Once exams are graded, Dr. Hash Haddock, the Economics Department chairperson, reviews student responses to the standard exam questions to determine how well course objectives are met.

Dr. Haddock asks you to finish designing a Lake West Assessment workbook for him. The workbook should provide a convenient way to analyze student responses for the ECON 2103 final exam's standard questions. This workbook will eventually serve as a template for other economics courses. When designing the workbook, the COUNTA, COUNTIF, COUNTIFS, and IF functions will prove useful. Conditional formatting should be used to highlight all questions with responses below a set minimum. To facilitate his analysis, Dr. Haddock will use the Filter command, PivotTable, PivotChart, and charting tools.

# Case Scenario

Lake West University is a four-year university located in the Midwestern United States. As part of a campus-wide initiative, Lake West University's Economics Department recently updated its assessment plan. As part of its updated assessment plan, the Economics Department includes a standard set of questions on all ECON 2103 final exams. ECON 2103 is an introductory economics course, and all business majors take this course as part of their degree plan. As the ECON 2103 course does not have prerequisite courses, freshmen, sophomores, juniors, and seniors enroll in the course. Each semester several ECON 2103 sections are offered.

Dr. Haddock needs a system that enables him to analyze results for the standard questions across all ECON 2103 sections, as well as the individual sections of the course. Dr. Haddock envisions using this system to compare responses between various semesters as well. He wants a standard template developed, so he can use the same format for other Economics Department course offerings. As you are Dr. Haddock's assistant, you are tasked with developing a Microsoft Excel workbook to track student responses for the ECON 2103 final exam standard questions.

# Design Specifications

At the end of the semester, all ECON 2103 section instructors give Dr. Haddock their student responses for the final exams. No standardized reporting format has been implemented, so Dr. Haddock wants a standard workbook developed so all instructors will use the same reporting format. He feels that a standard workbook format enables him to easily consolidate section data into the Lake View Assessment workbook, allowing him to analyze results across all sections.

Dr. Haddock hands you a copy of an incomplete workbook called Lake West Assessment. Although Dr. Haddock has begun incorporating each section's student responses into the workbook, he has not had time to format the workbook or complete its design. Figure 12.13 shows how data are currently organized for one of the sections.

| Section 1: Instructor Jones | | | Q1 | Q2 | Q3 | Q4 | Q5 | Q6 | Q7 | Q8 | Q9 | Q10 |
|---|---|---|---|---|---|---|---|---|---|---|---|---|---|
| Student | Major | Classification | Q1 | Q2 | Q3 | Q4 | Q5 | Q6 | Q7 | Q8 | Q9 | Q10 |
| 1 | ACCT | Freshman | b | b | d | b | b | d | c | b | e | a |
| 2 | MIS | Senior | a | c | d | b | a | d | c | c | d | a |
| 3 | ACCT | Sophomore | a | c | d | b | a | b | c | c | e | a |
| 4 | ECON | Junior | a | c | e | b | a | b | c | c | e | a |
| 5 | MRKT | Sophomore | a | c | c | e | a | b | c | c | e | a |
| Correct Answer | | | a | c | d | b | a | b | c | c | e | a |

FIGURE 12.13: Sample Worksheet

As you study the workbook, you notice that the workbook contains several worksheets. Although Dr. Haddock initially created a separate worksheet for each section, he mentions that he would now like all student responses included on a single worksheet called Response. In the Response worksheet, Dr. Haddock wants counts of the correct and incorrect responses for each question. He also wants to see correct and incorrect counts by major and by classification.

As you study the student response data, you notice that student names are not included. Dr. Haddock indicates that he wants a number assigned to each student and does not want to include student names. He does want the student's major, classification, and response to each of the 10 standard questions included.

Dr. Haddock asks you to create a summary worksheet. For each section, the summary worksheet should show the correct response counts, incorrect response counts, and correct response percentages for each question by section. He also would like to see a correct response percentage for each question for all sections.

Dr. Haddock considers a correct response rate of 70 percent as acceptable. Response percentages lower than 70 percent are unacceptable and are marked for further analysis. Correct response percentages lower than 70 percent should display with a light red fill and dark red text. Dr. Haddock wants to see a count for correct responses, a count for incorrect responses, and the percentage of correct responses for each major. He also would like the same information organized by classification.

To facilitate his analysis, Dr. Haddock asks you to prepare Correct Response, Major Comparison, and Classification charts. You are free to select the chart format. The Correct Response chart compares each major's correct response percentages for each question. Dr. Haddock wants to know the majors of the students enrolled in the ECON 2103 sections. He will use the Major Comparison chart to view a breakdown by major. He asks that the Major Comparison chart provide both a count and a percentage for each major. Dr. Haddock wants to know how many seniors, juniors, sophomores, and freshmen took the ECON 2103 course. The Classification chart provides counts and percentages for the freshmen, sophomores, juniors, and seniors taking ECON 2103.

As Dr. Haddock is the department chairperson, he manages several economics classes. He wants to use this workbook for other classes, and requests that you create a template based on your newly created workbook.

# Information Specifications

In addition to the information requests specified above, Dr. Haddock requests answers for the following questions.

1. Overall, which major's students answered the most questions correctly?
2. Which major's students answered the least number of questions correctly?
3. Which student(s) answered the most questions correctly?
4. Which section's students answered the most questions correctly?
5. Overall, which classification answered the most questions correctly?
6. How do freshmen economics majors compare to freshmen MIS majors?
7. For final exam Question 10, prepare a chart that compares the correct responses given by the different classifications across all sections. (You select the chart.)

# Implementation Concerns

Although you are free to work with the design of your workbook, the worksheets should have a consistent, professional appearance. When designing the worksheets, you should apply basic cell and worksheet formatting principles.

Depending on how you choose to design the workbook, this case may require you to create new worksheets, modify existing worksheets, and consolidate information into a summary worksheet. To prepare this workbook according to Dr. Haddock's specifications, you will create formulas, use several functions, and use the PivotTable and PivotChart report tools. Your worksheet's design may require you to use the COUNTIFS function to determine response counts. The COUNTIFS function allows you to use multiple criteria to evaluate multiple cell ranges and count when the multiple criteria are met. You should use your system's online help feature to learn more about the COUNTIFS function.

When designing the workbook, cells containing a correct response percentage less than 70 percent use a light red fill with dark text. The conditional formatting command can accomplish this task. If you are unfamiliar with conditional formatting, use your system's online help feature to learn more about conditional formatting.

Flexibility is one of the key aspects of this case. Dr. Haddock will use this workbook as a template for other classes. When designing the workbook, you should design a workbook that is easily adaptable as Dr. Haddock's information needs change. For instance, the Test Your Design section asks you to modify the workbook's design to match the standard questions to their objective.

# Test Your Design

After creating the Lake View Assessment workbook, you should test your design. Perform the following steps.

1. Professor Jones submitted responses for two addition students from Section 1. Please enter the following information into the appropriate worksheet(s).

| Section 1: Instructor Jones | | | | | | | | | | | | | |
|---|---|---|---|---|---|---|---|---|---|---|---|---|---|
| Student | Student Major | Classification | Q1 | Q2 | Q3 | Q4 | Q5 | Q6 | Q7 | Q8 | Q9 | Q10 |
| Assign Next Available Number | MIS | Junior | c | e | d | e | e | d | c | d | e | c |
| Assign Next Available Number | FIN | Sophomore | c | d | d | b | b | d | c | d | c | c |

2. Based on the following table, identify the sections achieving course objectives.

| Objectives and Matching Questions | |
|---|---|
| Objective 1 | Questions 1, 4, and 10 |
| Objective 2 | Questions 2, 5, and 7 |
| Objective 3 | Questions 3 and 8 |
| Objective 4 | Questions 6 and 9 |

3. Based on the acceptable percentage rate, which section did not meet at least 4 of its objectives?

4. Based on the acceptable percentage rate, did any section meet all of its objectives?

## Case Deliverables

In order to satisfactorily complete this case, you should build the workbook as described in the case scenario and then prepare both written and oral presentations. Unless otherwise specified, submit the following deliverables to your professor.

1. A written report discussing any assumptions you have made about the case and the key elements of the case. Additionally, what features did you add to make the worksheets more functional? User friendly? (Please note that these assumptions cannot violate any of the requirements specified above and must be approved by your professor.)
2. A printout of each worksheet. (This includes your charts and PivotTables.)
3. A printout of each worksheet's formulas.
4. An electronic, working copy of your workbook that meets the criteria mentioned in the case scenario and specifications sections.
5. Results for each question posed above. (A memo to your instructor discussing these results should also be provided.)
6. As mentioned above, you should prepare an oral presentation. (Your instructor will establish the time allocated for your presentation.) You should use a presentation package and discuss the key features of your workbook. Also, discuss how the workbook is beneficial for Dr. Haddock. What additional information should be included in the workbook to make it more useful?

# Edmund Grant Pharmaceutical Company

**Spreadsheet Case**

**Difficulty Rating: ★ ★ ★ ★ ★**

**YOU SHOULD REVIEW THE FOLLOWING AREAS:**

## SPREADSHEET SKILLS

- Advanced Filter
- Button
- Conditional Formatting
- DAVERAGE Function
- DMAX Function
- DMIN Function
- DSUM Function
- Excel Table

- Filter
- IF Function
- Macro
- Nesting Functions
- PivotChart
- PivotTable
- Template
- VLOOKUP Function

# Case Background

Keiko Lapeer is a district sales manager for the Edmund Grant Pharmaceutical Company. Ms. Lapeer has many responsibilities, including traveling, visiting with current and potential customers, supervising a growing sales staff, preparing numerous reports, and tracking her sales region's expenses. Each week, members of Ms. Lapeer's sales staff submit weekly expense claim forms. Currently, she scans through the expense forms, checks for anything out of the ordinary, and then authorizes reimbursement checks. Ms. Lapeer needs to become more organized about tracking her sales staff's expenses, and asks you to design an Expense worksheet for her. Specifically, she requests you to organize the expense data into an Excel table. To design the worksheet according to Ms. Lapeer's specifications, you are required to use database functions, other Microsoft Excel functions, and nest functions. You will then use the Filter, Advanced Filter, PivotTable, and PivotChart tools to analyze the data.

# Case Scenario

The Edmund Grant Pharmaceutical Company (EGPC) is a multinational company, well known in the United States for its anti-infective, wound care, and pain management products. The Edmund Grant Pharmaceutical Company's sales force is responsible for promoting EGPC products to doctors, pharmacists, and opticians around the globe. Keiko Lapeer is one of EGPC's many district sales managers and is responsible for supervising four sales areas.

As a district sales manager, Ms. Lapeer stays very busy. She often travels, attends several meetings a month, visits with customers, supervises a 23-member sales force, and performs managerial duties. As a manager, Ms. Lapeer's paperwork is often overwhelming, and she is looking for avenues of improvement. One area for improvement is the expense tracking of her sales force. She can easily spend an entire day just processing budget and expense reports.

By using a spreadsheet application to analyze her sales force's expenses, she feels that she will save time and make better decisions.

Sales representatives are reimbursed for business meals and calls, gas, hotel, airfare, and other miscellaneous expenses. Each week, sales representatives complete expense claim forms and submit these forms to Ms. Lapeer. Figure 12.14 provides an example of the expense claim form. Ms. Lapeer summarizes the expense data contained on these forms and prepares several weekly reports. Report preparation is a tedious, time-consuming task, often requiring her to wade through the expense claim forms numerous times.

## Edmund Grant Pharmaceutical Company
## Expense Claim Form

Employee Name:_____          For Week Ending: _____

Division Number: _____

### Expense

Meals:_____

Phone: _____

Gas: _____

Hotel: _____

Airfare: _____

Miscellaneous: _____

_____

_____

_____

Total Expenses Claimed:_____

### Mileage

Beginning Mileage: _____

Ending Mileage: _____

Comments: _____

_____

_____

_____

_____

Notice:  All expense claims must be accompanied by receipts.

**FIGURE 12.14:** Expense Claim Form

When a sales representative is hired, he is issued a company car. The sales representative may use his car for both business and personal travel, and he is given a weekly mileage limit. Each week, the sales representative reports the number of miles that he has driven that week. For any miles over the mileage limit, the employee is charged an overage fee. The allowable mileage and charge rate vary by sales position within the company. Table 12.4 summarizes the allowable mileage and charge rates. Ms. Lapeer wants the new Expense worksheet to determine the mileage overage amount and applicable charges for each sales representative.

## TABLE 12.4  Allowable Mileage and Rates

| Edmund Grant Pharmaceutical Company Allowable Mileage and Rates | | |
|---|---|---|
| **Position** | **Allowable Miles** | **Rate** |
| MN | 700 | 0.20 |
| SU | 600 | 0.22 |
| S2 | 550 | 0.25 |
| S1 | 500 | 0.32 |

When a car has 60,000 miles, the sales representative can request a new car. Ms. Lapeer wonders if there is some way that she can quickly determine when a car is reaching its end-of-service date. You recommend using conditional formatting to highlight ending mileage readings that are greater than 55,000 miles. If a sales representative has a car that is approaching its end-of-service date, Ms. Lapeer can remind the sales representative that it is time to request a new car.

Ms. Lapeer has used a spreadsheet application before and would like to organize the weekly expense data into a worksheet. She asks you to create an Expense worksheet for her. She specifically requests that you prepare an Excel table, establish a criteria range to support Advanced Filtering, include several database functions, insert four new columns, prepare pivot tables, and prepare several charts. Ms. Lapeer also requests that the new worksheet be saved as a template, so she can reuse it each week.

# Design Specifications

As you examine the Expense worksheet, you realize that the worksheet columns need formatting. After formatting the columns, you decide that a mileage lookup table and four additional columns are necessary. Before inserting the four columns, you build the mileage lookup table. As you want to keep the mileage lookup table separate from the expense data, you place the table in its own worksheet. After creating the mileage lookup table, you insert the actual mileage, overage, overage charge, and total expense columns into the Expense worksheet. The actual mileage column calculates the actual miles that each employee drove during the week. Actual mileage is the difference between the week's ending mileage and the week's beginning mileage. You want the overage column to reference the mileage lookup table and then determine how many miles over the limit, if any, the employee has driven. (Performing this operation requires nesting IF and VLOOKUP functions. At this point, you may wish to use your system's online help feature to review how to nest functions.) The overage charge column uses the VLOOKUP function as well. This column multiplies the overage by the rate specified in the mileage table. The total expenses column is a summation of the expenses for that week.

Ms. Lapeer will use the Advanced Filter capability. Using the Advanced Filter requires the inclusion of a criteria range. For Ms. Lapeer's purposes, you decide the best place for the criteria range is above the Excel table. (At this point, you may wish to use your system's online help feature to review the Advanced Filter topic.) As Ms. Lapeer uses the criteria range, she needs to clear the range of the current conditions and enter new conditions in the criteria range. You decide to create a macro that will clear the criteria range and position the pointer in the upper left-hand cell of the criteria range. Once you have created the macro, you then assign it to a button named "Clear Criteria."

As you study the contents of the Expense worksheet, you realize that the contents are in a format suitable for creating an Excel table. You recall from one of your business courses that an Excel table is a collection of data, similar in concept to a database table. The data in this Excel table can be filtered, sorted, and manipulated in a variety of ways, thus facilitating Ms. Lapeer's decision-making activities. In fact, several database functions are available for usage with an Excel table, and you decide to use these functions in the Expense worksheet. Ms. Lapeer wants average, minimum, maximum, and total values for the meal, actual mileage, phone, gas, hotel, miscellaneous, airfare, overage, overage charge, and total expense columns in the table. Since Ms. Lapeer will manipulate the data in the Excel table, you use the DAVERAGE, DMIN, DMAX, and DSUM functions. (At this point, you may wish to use your system's online help feature to review list creation and usage.)

After you design the worksheet, Ms. Lapeer wants a template created. Then each week, she can use the template to create a worksheet for that week.

# Information Specifications

Ms. Lapeer asks if it is possible to view the expense data at varying levels of detail and from different perspectives. She specifically requests a summary of all expenses categorized by division, the total expenses displayed by sales position and the total expenses for the meals, phone and gas expense categories by division and position. As the PivotTable tool can quickly change the way data are displayed and the level of summarization, you recommend that Ms. Lapeer use a pivot table.

As mentioned previously, Ms. Lapeer wants to know when a salesperson's car is approaching 60,000 miles. For any vehicle that has more than 55,000 miles, the spreadsheet application should highlight the ending mileage for that vehicle.

In addition to the information requirements specified above, Ms. Lapeer requests that you perform the following operations.

1. Identify which managers claimed airfare expenses totaling more than $1,700 and which supervisors claimed airfare expenses totaling more than $750.
2. Identify which sales representative(s) did not submit an expense claim form.
3. Identify hotel and airfare expenses by position.
4. Identify which managers traveled via airplane during the week.
5. Identify sales positions by division.
6. Identify which division had the lowest expenses for the week.
7. Identify which S1 sales representative(s) submitted hotel and airfare expenses this past week.
8. Identify which individuals went over their mileage limits.

# Implementation Concerns

Although you are free to work with the design of your worksheet, it should have a consistent, professional appearance. You should also use proper formatting for the cells. For instance, dollar values should display with a dollar sign and be formatted to two decimal places.

This case scenario requires you to use an Excel table. Extracting the data requires you to prepare charts; use the DAVERAGE, DSUM, DMIN, DMAX, IF, and VLOOKUP functions; nest functions; establish a criteria range; prepare PivotTables and charts; and use the Filter and Advanced Filter tools. (You may wish to use your system's online help feature to review each of these areas.)

The determination of the overage amount for each salesperson requires the spreadsheet application to look up the mileage allowance, determine if the mileage is greater than the allowance, and then compute the actual overage amount, if any. Performance of this task requires nesting the VLOOKUP function inside the IF function. (At this point, you may wish to use your system's online help feature to review nesting functions.) Keep in mind that Ms. Lapeer wants the mileage overage amount to display in one column.

You should carefully consider the placement of the criteria range and the mileage table. It is generally recommended that the criteria range be placed above or below the Excel table. Placement of the criteria range in either of these locations facilitates the viewing of the criteria and filter results. Although your mileage lookup table may be placed in the Expense worksheet, consider placing the lookup table in its own worksheet. Using a separate worksheet for the mileage lookup table facilitates table maintenance and accessibility.

# Test Your Design

After creating the Expense worksheet described in the case scenario, you should test your worksheet design. Perform the following operations.

1. Add the following three new employees to your Excel table.

| Employee 1 | Employee 2 | Employee 3 |
|---|---|---|
| Last Name: Ruokangas<br>First Name: Leota | Last Name: Saghafi<br>First Name: Abduellah | Last Name: Omari<br>First Name: Kyleena |
| Division: 1<br>Position: MN | Division: 3<br>Position: S1 | Division: 4<br>Position: S2 |
| Meals: $376.89<br>Phone: $79.86<br>Hotel: $478.78<br>Miscellaneous: $2,987.42<br>Airfare: $894.87 | Meals: $102.78<br>Phone: $10.07<br>Hotel $0.00<br>Miscellaneous: $0.00<br>Airfare: $0.00 | Meals: $257.88<br>Phone: $58.77<br>Hotel: $509.78<br>Miscellaneous: $877.89<br>Airfare: $250.75 |
| Beginning Mileage: 101<br>Ending Mileage: 372 | Beginning Mileage: 904<br>Ending Mileage: 1,150 | Beginning Mileage: 67<br>Ending Mileage: 803 |

2. Make the following changes to your mileage table.

**Allowable Mileage Table**

| Position | Allowable Miles | Rate |
|---|---|---|
| MN | 700 | 0.25 |
| SU | 600 | 0.28 |
| S2 | 550 | 0.30 |
| S1 | 500 | 0.32 |

3. Within each division, Ms. Lapeer wants to examine the expenses incurred by each employee. She would like to view the divisions one "page" at a time.

4. Prepare a column chart that compares the gas, hotel, airfare, and meal expenses for each division.

5. For each division, Ms. Lapeer wants to see the person's last name and the number of miles she/he drove last week. She would like to see a grand total for each division. Prepare a pivot table and also prepare a chart for Division 1. (Choose an appropriate chart.)

## Case Deliverables

In order to satisfactorily complete this case, you should build the workbook as described in the case scenario and then prepare both written and oral presentations. Unless otherwise specified, submit the following deliverables to your professor.

1. A written report discussing any assumptions you have made about the case and the key elements of the case. Additionally, what features did you add to make the worksheets more functional? User friendly? (Please note that these assumptions cannot violate any of the requirements specified above and must be approved by your professor.)

2. A printout of each worksheet. (This includes your charts and pivot tables.)

3. A printout of each worksheet's formulas.

4. An electronic, working copy of your workbook that meets the criteria mentioned in the case scenario and specifications sections.

5. Results for each question posed above. (A memo to your instructor discussing these results should also be provided.)

6. As mentioned above, you should prepare an oral presentation. (Your instructor will establish the time allocated for your presentation.) You should use a presentation package and discuss the key features of your workbook. Also, discuss how the workbook is beneficial for Ms. Lapeer. What additional information should be included in the workbook to make it more useful?

# Index

↓ (move down one cell), 4
↑ (move up one cell), 4
← (move left one cell), 4
→ (move right one cell), 4
##### (pound signs), 26
, (comma)
   number format, 45
   reference operator, 13
: (reference operator), 13
& (ampersand), 13, 283
% (percent), 13
[ ] (brackets), 73
( ) (parentheses), 13
^ (exponentiation), 13
* (multiplication), 13
/ (division), 13
+ (addition), 13
- (subtraction), 13
= (equal sign)
   formula and, 12
   logical operator, 86
> (greater than), 13, 86
>= (greater than or equal to), 86
< (less than), 13, 86
<= (less than or equal to), 86
<> (not equal to), 86
1.5 option, line spacing
3-D charts, 111
3-D formulas, 245–247
3-D reference, 245
100% stacked column charts, 110
.xlsb, 309
.xlsm, 309
.xlsx, 300, 309
.xltm, 309
.xltx, 300

## A

ABS function, 76
absolute cell references, 62–63
Access database table, importing, 271–272
Accounting number format, 45, 233, 271, 290
active cell, 3, 4
adding
   filters, to PivotTables, 349–350
   rows, to PivotTables, 339
   second level of subtotals, 330
   subtotals, 328
adding chart elements, 123–126
add-ins. See also PowerPivot; Solver
   PowerPivot, 360
   Trust Center option, 314
Add Watch dialog box, 257
addition (+), 13
aggregation, table, 201–203. See also
   table(s)

alert, error, 259–260
alignment
   horizontal cell alignment, 43
   vertical cell alignment, 43
   worksheets and, 42–43
ampersand (&), 13, 283
Analysis Services, import data, 272
AND function, 160–162
AND truth table, 160–161
Append dialog box, 374
append queries
   defined, 368, 373
   running, 375
   select queries before, 374
area charts, 115
areas, of PivotTable, 339
arguments. See also functions
   AVERAGEIF function, 145
   COUNTIF function, 146
   defined, 70
   Function Arguments dialog box, 147, 159, 164
   IF function, 85–86, 158
   INDEX function, 163
   logical_test, 158, 161
   Lookup_array, 162, 163
   Lookup_value, 162, 163
   Match_type, 163
   nest functions as, 76
   PERCENTRANK.EXC function, 148–149
   PERCENTRANK.INC function, 148–149
   QUARTILE function, 149
   range_lookup, 90
   RANK.AVG function, 148
   RANK.EQ function, 148
   SUBTOTAL function, 329
   SUMIF function, 145
   SUMIFS function, 146
   value_if_false, 86, 158, 159, 160
   value_if_true, 86, 158, 160
arithmetic operations, date functions and, 79
arrange and open windows, worksheets, 236
array argument, 149, 150, 163
arrows
   commands and, 24
   filter arrows, 179, 180, 193
   move down one cell (↓), 4
   move left one cell (←), 4
   move right one cell (→), 4
   move up one cell (↑), 4
   SUM arrow, 74
   tracer, 255
Assign Macro dialog box, 313
audit formulas. See formula auditing
Auto Fill, 14–15

AutoComplete
   cell data, 6
   Formula AutoComplete, 70, 72, 98, 201
AutoFit, 27
AVERAGE function, 74, 203
AVERAGEIF function, 144, 145–146
AVERAGEIFS function, 144, 146–147
axes
   category axis, 104, 108, 109, 112
   defined, 123
   formatting, 127–128
   horizontal axis, 106, 111, 125, 137
   titles, 123, 125
   value axis, 104, 108, 109, 110
   vertical axis, 106, 111, 115, 125, 138
   X-axis, 104, 108
   Y-axis, 104, 108
AXIS (CATEGORY), 362, 363

## B

background(s), 292–293
   in worksheets, 51
backups, database
   action queries and, 369
   DBAs and, 368
   update queries and, 372
bar charts, 106, 111
blank fields, 368
blue arrows, 255
bold argument names, 71
border(s)
   cells, 44
   defined, 44
brackets [ ], 73
breakpoint, 88
browsing *Help and Support*
bubble charts, 115
buttons
   macro, 312–313
   outline, 330

## C

calculated fields
   calculation options, 353
   creating, 352–353
   defined, 352
CamelCase notation, 245
Cancel icon, 3
career information, DBAs, 368
case
   CamelCase notation, 245
   text, 283–284
category axis, 104, 108, 109, 112, 362, 363
category labels, 104

caution
    action queries, 369, 378
    backups, 372
    delete queries, 377
cell(s). *See also* column(s); formula(s);
    functions; range(s); row(s); table(s);
    worksheet(s)
    active, 3, 4
    address, 4
    Auto Fill, 14–15
    AutoComplete feature, 6
    borders, 44
    clear contents, 7
    color scales, conditional formatting, 209,
       211–212
    conditional formatting, 208–214
    data bars, conditional formatting, 209,
       211–212
    dates in, 7
    defined, 4
    deleting, 26
    deleting contents, 7
    dependent, 255–256
    editing contents, 7
    Flash Fill feature, 285
    Format Cells dialog box, 42, 44, 45, 213,
       301, 342, 349, 352
    formulas displayed in, 15–16
    Highlight Cell Rules, 209–210
    horizontal alignment, 43
    icon sets, conditional formatting, 209,
       211–212
    indenting contents, 43–44
    inserting, 25–26
    line break in, 7
    locked, 300–301
    merge options, 42–43
    number formats, 44–45
    pound signs (######), 26
    precedent, 255–256
    rotate data, 43
    semi-selection, 14
    sparklines in, 137–138
    times in, 7
    Top/Bottom Rules, 209, 210–211
    unlock, 300–301
    unmerge, 43
    vertical alignment, 43
    Watch Windows, 257–258
    wrap text feature, 43
cell references. *See also* values
    absolute, 62–63
    circular, 64–65
    in formulas, 12–13, 62–65
    lookup value, 89, 90
    mixed, 64
    relative, 62
    toggle between relative, absolute, mixed
       cell references (F4), 64
    values *versus*, 12–13
cell styles, 293–295
central tendency, 74
chart(s). *See also* axes; worksheet(s)
    100% stacked column, 110

area charts, 115
    bar, 106, 111
    bubble, 115
    change type, 113
    clustered column, 108–109
    colors for, 135–136
    column, 106, 107–110
    combo, 115
    creating, 106–107
    data labels, 123, 125–126, 128–129
    data series, 104, 109, 112, 127
    data sources, 104–105, 136–137
    data table, 123
    defined, 104
    design, 135–138
    doughnut, 115
    elements, 104, 123–130
    error bars, 123
    exploded pie, 112
    gridlines, 123
    legends, 104, 108, 109, 112, 123, 126
    line, 106, 111–112
    moving, 115–116
    pie, 106, 112, 129
    plot area, 104, 108, 127
    printing, 117
    Quick Layout, 126
    radar, 115
    scatter (X Y), 113
    sizing, 116
    sparklines, 137–138
    stacked column, 109–110
    stock, 113–114
    surface charts, 115
    3-D, 111
    trendlines, 123
    types, 105–115
    update, 105
    X Y (scatter), 113
chart area, 104, 108, 127
chart elements, 104, 123–130
chart filters, 136
Chart Filters button, 135, 136
chart gallery, 106, 107
chart sheets, 115, 117, 123
chart styles, 135–136
Chart Styles Gallery, 135
chart titles, 123, 125
Chart Tools Format tab, 129–130
check for errors, 256–257
circles, invalid text, 260
circular cell references, 64–65
clear cell contents, 7
clear conditional formatting, 212
clear filters, Excel tables, 195
Clipboard, Office
    Clipboard tasks, worksheets, 34–38
clustered column charts, 108–109
Collapse Field, 341
collapse items, PivotTables, 340–341
collapse outlined group, 336
collapse subtotals, 330
colon (:), reference operator, 13
color(s)

for charts, 135–136
    fill color, worksheets, 44
    worksheet tabs, 23
color scales, conditional formatting, 209,
    211–212
column(s). *See also* table(s); worksheet(s)
    deleting, 26
    Flash Fill feature, 285
    freezing, 171
    headings, 3, 4
    hide, 28
    inserting, 25–26
    managing, 25–28
    in PivotTables, 340
    print column headings, 55
    Switch Row/Column, 137
    table style options, 184
    Text to Columns feature, 282
    transposing, 38
    unhide, 28
    width, 26–27
column charts, 106, 107–110
column index number, 89
column sparkline, 137–138
column widths
    worksheets, 26–27
Column_num, 163
COLUMNS area, 339, 340, 342, 362, 363
combo charts, 115
comma (, )
    number format, 45
    reference operator, 13
comma separated values (CSV), 269
command(s). *See also specific commands*
    arrows and, 24
comments, 319–320
comparison operators, 13
completing sequences, Auto Fill, 15
CONCATENATE function, 283, 284
concatenation, 13
conditional formatting, 208–214
    defined, 208
    grouped worksheets, 234, 235
    New Formatting Rule dialog box,
       213–214
    Quick Analysis Tool, 208–209
conditional math functions, 144–147. *See
    also statistical functions*
connections, 274–275
constants
    in formulas, 13
control(s). *See also specific controls*
    in worksheets, 312–313
conversions
    Excel tables to ranges, 181
convert
    select query to append query, 374–375
    select query to update query, 371
converting text, to columns, 282
Copy as Picture, 36
copy data, from Web page, 273
copying
    Auto Fill feature, 14–15
    Excel data, to other programs, 38

formulas, 14–15
  ranges, 35–36
  worksheets, 24–25
COUNT function, 75, 203
COUNTA function, 75, 203
COUNTBLANK function, 75
COUNTIF function, 144, 145–146
COUNTIFS function, 144, 146–147
criteria
  data validation, 258–259
criteria argument, 145, 146
criteria1 argument, 146
criteria2 argument, 146
criteria_range1 argument, 146
Ctrl+End, 4
Ctrl+G, 4, 170
Ctrl+Home, 4
Currency
  number format, 45
custom filter, Excel tables, 194
custom functions, 321–322
Custom Office Templates folder, 303
custom sort, Excel tables, 191
Custom style, number format, 45
customization
  cell styles, 294–295
  slicers, 351
  themes, 292
customize sparklines, 138

**D**

data. See also importing; XML
  copying, from Web page, 273
  download, from Web page, 273
  embed, 268
  external, 268–275
  Get External Data group, 271, 272, 274
  Import Data dialog box, 271–272, 273
  importing, from external sources, 268–273
  validation, 258–260
data, external, 268–275
data bars, conditional formatting, 209, 211–212
Data Connection Wizard, import data, 272
data entry, grouped worksheets, 233
data labels, 123, 125–126, 128–129
data mining, 336. See also PivotTable(s)
data point, 104, 112
data range properties, 275
data series, 104, 109, 112, 127
data sources
  charts, 104–105, 136–137
  external, 268–273
  Select Data Source dialog box, 271
  source file, 247
data table, 123. See also chart(s)
data validation, 258–260
database(s). See also field(s); table(s)
  table, importing, 271–272
database administrators (DBAs)
  career information, 368
  database maintenance, 369

database backups
  action queries and, 369
  DBAs and, 368
  update queries and, 372
database security. See also protecting
  macro, 313–314
  Trust Center, 313–314
datasets, large, 170–174. See also
    PivotTable(s); subtotal(s),
    worksheet(s)
  PivotTables, 336–343
  Subtotal feature, 328–330
dates
  in cells, 7
  date functions, 70, 77–79
  Date number format, 45
  header and footer option, 54
  missing, 370–371
date filters, Excel tables, 194
DATE function, 78
DAY function, 78
DBAs (database administrators)
  career information, 368
  database maintenance, 369
decimal places, increase/decrease, 46, 76
decrease decimal places, 46, 76
delete queries
  creating, 377–378
  defined, 368, 377
  test and run, 378–379
deleting. See also removing
  background images, 293
  cell contents, worksheet, 7
  cells, 26
  macros, 312
  range names, 97
  rows/columns, in worksheets, 26
  worksheets, 24
delimiters, 268–269
dependent cells, 255–256
design
  charts, 135–138
  Excel tables, 179–184
  Header & Footer Tools Design
    contextual tab, 53–54
  Sparkline Tools Design tab, 138
  Table Tools Design tab, 180, 181
  worksheets, 5
destination file, 247
dialog boxes
  Append, 374
  Format Cells, 42, 44, 45, 213
  Go To, 4, 98, 170
  Insert Function, 3, 71, 72
  Make Table, 377
  Move or Copy, 24–25
  Name Manager, 96, 97
  New Formatting Rule, 213–214
  Page Setup, 51–52
  Paste Special, 37
Dialog Box Launcher
  Page Setup, 51–52
display connections, 274
displaying cell formulas, 15–16

#DIV/0! error, 254, 257, 299
division (/), 13
double-click
  fill handle, 15
doughnut charts, 115
download data, from Web page, 273
drag worksheet tab, 24

**E**

EDATE function, 78
Edit Links, 248, 249
editing
  cell contents, 7
  hyperlinks, 239
  range names, 97
Edmund Grant Pharmaceutical Company
  case background, 415
  case deliverables, 419–420
  case scenario, 415–417
  design specifications, 417
  implementation concerns, 418
  information specifications, 418
  testing of design, 419
educators' salary table, statistical functions, 144
embed data, 268
Enter icon, 3
EOMONTH function, 78
equal sign (=)
  formula and, 12
  logical operator, 86
error(s)
  check for, 256–257
  #DIV/0!, 254, 257, 299
  formula, 254–257
  formula auditing and, 255–257
  IFERROR function, 257, 299
  ISERROR function, 257
  logic, 254–257
  #N/A, 254, 257
  #NAME?, 254, 257
  #NULL!, 254
  #NUM!, 150, 254, 257
  #REF!, 254, 257
  repair, 256
  run time, 320–321
  #VALUE!, 161, 254, 257
error alert, 259–260
error bars, 123
ERROR.TYPE function, 257
Evaluate Formula dialog box, 256–257
Excel 2013. See also chart(s); table(s);
    worksheet(s)
  window elements, 2–5
Excel Binary Workbook, 309
Excel Macro-Enabled Template, 309
Excel Macro-Enabled Workbook, 309
expand items, PivotTables, 340–341
expand outlined group, 336
expand subtotals, 330
exploded pie charts, 112
exploded slice, pie chart, 112
exponentiation (^), 13

eXtensible Markup Language (XML)
  data import, 272
external data, 268–275
External Data Range Properties dialog box, 275
external data sources, import data, 268–273
external reference, 247–248

## F

F4 (toggle between relative, absolute, mixed cell references), 64
F5 (Go To dialog box), 4, 170
field(s). *See also* data validation
  adding, update queries, 372
  blank, 368
  Excel tables, 181, 190–191
field(s), PivotTable
  rearrange, 342
  remove, 341
file name, header and footer option, 54
file path, header and footer option, 54
files
  defined, 268
  import, 268–271
fill across worksheets, 234–235
fill color, worksheets, 44
fill handle, 14–15
filter arrows, 179, 180, 193
filtering
  conditional formatting and, 212
  defined, 192
  Excel table data, 192–195
filters, PivotTables, 349–350
FILTERS area, 339, 349, 350, 363
financial functions, 70, 85–91
Find & Select, 170
fixed-width text files, 269–270
Flash Fill, 285
flowchart, nested IF function, 158–159
folder(s)
  Custom Office Templates folder, 303
  templates, 300
footers. *See* headers and footers
Format Cells dialog box, 42, 44, 45, 213, 301, 342, 349, 352
formats, number, 44–45
formatting. *See also* conditional formatting
  Accounting Number Format, 233, 271, 290
  axes, 127–128
  chart elements, 126–130
  conditional, cells, 208–214
  data in worksheet, 5
  data labels, 128–129
  grouped worksheets, 233–234
  PivotTables, 359–360
  worksheets, 42–46
formula(s), 62–65. *See also* functions; error(s)
  Auto Fill, 14–15
  calculated fields, 352
  cell references in, 12–13, 62–65
  constants in, 13

copying, 14–15
creating, 12–14
defined, 7
displaying, in cells, 15–16
equal sign (=) and, 12
errors, 254–257
Evaluate Formula dialog box, 256–257
with external references, 247–248
functions *versus*, 73
order of precedence, 13–14
parentheses in, 13
range names in, 98
structured references in, 201–202
text in, 87
3-D, 245–247
values in, 89
Watch Windows, 257–258
formula auditing, 255–257
Formula AutoComplete, 70, 72, 98, 201
Formula Bar, 3, 12
Fraction, number format, 45
Francisco's Lawn Care
  case background, 393
  case deliverables, 396
  case scenario, 393–394
  design specifications, 394–395
  implementation concerns, 395
  information specifications, 395
  testing of design, 395–396
Freeze Panes, 170, 171, 179, 237
freezing rows and columns, 171
FREQUENCY function, 76
Function Arguments dialog box, 147, 159, 164
functions, 70–79. *See also* arguments; formula(s); IF function; nested functions; statistical functions
  ABS, 76
  AND, 160–162
  AVERAGE, 74, 203
  AVERAGEIF, 144, 145–146
  AVERAGEIFS, 144, 146–147
  categories, 70
  CONCATENATE, 283, 284
  COUNT, 75, 203
  COUNTA, 75, 203
  COUNTBLANK, 75
  COUNTIF, 144, 145–146
  COUNTIFS, 144, 146–147
  custom, 321–322
  DATE, 78
  date, 70, 77–79
  DAY, 78
  EDATE, 78
  EOMONTH, 78
  ERROR.TYPE, 257
  financial, 70, 85–91
  formulas *versus*, 73
  FREQUENCY, 76
  HLOOKUP, 90, 158, 162, 254
  IF, 85–87, 208
  IFERROR, 257, 299
  INDEX, 163
  information, 257

Insert Function dialog box, 3, 71, 72
inserting, 70–74
INT, 76
ISERROR, 257
LEFT, 284
logical, 70, 85–91, 158–162
lookup, 70, 88–90
LOWER, 284
MATCH, 162–163, 164
Math & Trig, 70, 72–76
MAX, 75, 203
MEDIAN, 74
MID, 284
MIN, 75, 203
MODE.SNGL, 76
MONTH, 78
#NAME?, 72
nest, 76, 87, 90
NOT, 162
NOW, 77
OR, 161–162
PERCENTILE.EXC, 150–151
PERCENTILE.INC, 150–151
PERCENTRANK.EXC, 148–149, 150
PMT, 91, 246
PRODUCT, 203
PROPER, 283
QUARTILE, 149–150
QUARTILE.EXC, 149–150
RANK.AVG, 76, 147–148
RANK.EQ, 76, 147–148
reference, 70
RIGHT, 284
ROUND, 76
ScreenTip, 71
statistical, 70, 72–76, 144–151
STDEV, 203
STDEVP, 203
SUBTOTAL, 202–203, 329
SUM, 72–74, 203
SUMIF, 144, 145–146
SUMIFS, 144, 146–147
syntax, 73
text, 283–284
text manipulation with, 283–285
time, 70, 77–79
TODAY, 77
Trig & Math, 70, 72–76
TRIM, 284
UPPER, 284
VAR, 203
VARP, 203
VLOOKUP, 88–90, 158, 162, 246, 254
WEEKDAY, 78
YEAR, 78
YEARFRAC, 78

## G

General, number format, 44, 45
Go To dialog box, 4, 98, 170
greater than (>), 13, 86
greater than or equal to (>=), 86
green triangle, logic errors, 255

gridlines
    charts, 123
    printing, 55
grouped worksheets, 232–235
grouping data, 331

## H

handles
    fill handles, 14–15
    sizing handles, 116
headers and footers
    Header & Footer Tools Design
        contextual tab, 53–54
    worksheets, 53–54
heading(s), rows and columns, 3, 4
height, row, 27. *See also* cell(s)
hide columns and rows, 28
hide worksheets, 235
hierarchical structure, outlines, 330–331
high and low values, 75
Highlight Cell Rules, conditional
        formatting, 209–210
High-Low-Close stock chart, 113, 114
HLOOKUP function, 90, 158, 162, 254
horizontal axis, 106, 111, 125, 137
horizontal cell alignment, 43
hyperlinks
    ScreenTips, 238
    using, 237–239

## I

icon(s). *See also specific icons*
    action query, 378
icon sets, conditional formatting, 209,
    211–212
IF functions, 85–87, 208. *See also*
    conditional formatting
    arguments, 158
    logical_test, 158, 161
    nested, within IF, 158–160
    purpose of, 158
    Value_if_false, 158, 159, 160
    Value_if_true, 158, 160
IFERROR function, 257, 299
Import Data dialog box, 271–272, 273
importing
    data, from external sources, 268–273
    database table or query, 271–272
    defined, 268
    text files, 268–271
increase decimal places, 46, 76
indents
    cell contents, 43–44
    values, 44
INDEX function, 163
information functions, 257
input area, absolute cell references and, 63
input messages, 259
input range, statistical functions, 145
Insert Function dialog box, 3, 71, 72,
    164, 283
Insert Function icon, 3

inserting
    cells, 25–26
    columns/rows, in worksheets, 25–26
    data labels, 128–129
    functions, 70–74
    hyperlinks, in Web pages, 237–239
    range names, in worksheet, 98
    rows/columns, in worksheets, 25–26
    slicers, in PivotTables, 350–351
    3-D formulas, 245–247
    worksheets, in workbooks, 24
INT function, 76
invalid text, circles, 260
ISERROR function, 257

## K

k argument, 150, 151
keystroke commands
    navigation in worksheets, 4
keywords, 319
Klein Technology Seminars
    case background, 402
    case deliverables, 410
    case scenario, 402–403
    design specifications, 403–405
    implementation concerns, 406
    information specifications, 405–406
    testing of design, 406–409

## L

Lake West University
    case background, 411
    case deliverables, 414
    case scenario, 411–412
    design specifications, 412–413
    implementation concerns, 413
    information specifications, 413
    testing of design, 413–414
landscape orientation, 51
large datasets, 170–174
large worksheets, 170–174
ledger, paper-based, 2. *See also*
    worksheet(s)
LEFT function, 284
LEGEND (SERIES), 362, 363
legends, charts, 104, 108, 109, 112, 123, 126
less than (<), 13, 86
less than or equal to (<=), 86
line break, in cells, 7
line charts, 106, 111–112
line sparkline, 137–138
link(s)
    ScreenTips, 238
    using, 237–239
linked workbooks, 247–249
linking, 247
locked cells, 300–301
logical functions, 70, 85–91, 158–162
logical operators, 86
logical test, 86
logical_test, IF function, 158, 161
logic errors, 254–257. *See also* error(s)

Lookup_array, 162, 163
lookup functions, 70, 88–90
    HLOOKUP, 158, 162, 254
    MATCH, 162–163
    NEST, 163
    purpose of, 158
    VLOOKUP, 158, 162, 246, 254
Lookup_value, 162, 163
lookup table, 88–89
lookup value, cell reference, 89, 90
low and high values, 75
LOWER function, 284

## M

macro(s)
    creating, 309–312
    custom functions, 321–322
    defined, 309
    Excel Macro-Enabled Workbook, 309
    security, 313–314
    sub procedures, 319–321
    Visual Basic Editor, 319, 321
macro buttons, 312–313
Macro dialog box, 312
Macro Recorder, 309–310
Make Table dialog box, 377
make table queries
    creating, 376–377
    defined, 368, 376
    running, 377
    testing, 377
manage connections, 274–275
manipulating text, 282–285
manipulation, table, 190–195. *See also*
    table(s)
manual page break, 172
margins
    worksheet data, 51, 52
MATCH function, 162–163, 164
Match_type, 163
math functions, 144–147. *See also* statistical
    functions
Math & Trig functions, 70, 72–76, 147
mathematical order of precedence,
    13–14
mathematics and formulas, 62–65. *See also*
    functions
    Auto Fill, 14–15
    cell references in, 12–13, 62–65
    constants in, 13
    copying, 14–15
    creating, 12–14
    defined, 7
    displaying, in cells, 15–16
    equal sign (=) and, 12
    functions *versus*, 73
    order of precedence, 13–14
    parentheses in, 13
    range names in, 98
    structured references in, 201–202
    text in, 87
    values in, 89
MAX function, 75, 203

Maxi's Grocery Mart
  case background, 397
  case deliverables, 400–401
  case scenario, 397–399
  design specifications, 399
  implementation concerns, 400
  information specifications, 399–400
  testing of design, 400
MEDIAN function, 74
Merge & Center command, 42, 43
merge options, cells, 42–43
Merge Styles dialog box, 295
message(s)
  error alert, 259–260
  input, 259
Microsoft Query, 272
MIN function, 75, 203, 284
minus sign, on Start screen
missing dates, update query, 370–371
mixed cell references, 64
MODE.SNGL function, 76
modifying. *See also* editing
  cell styles, 295
  data sources, charts, 136–137
  hyperlinks, 239
  PivotTables, 339–343
modules, 319
MONTH function, 78
move down one cell (↓), 4
move left one cell (←), 4
*Move or Copy* dialog box, 24–25
move right one cell (→), 4
move up one cell (↑), 4
moving
  charts, 115–116
  ranges, 35
  worksheets, 24–25
multiple column widths and row
    heights, 27
multiple summary statistics, 343
multiple worksheets, 232–239. *See also*
    worksheet(s)
  printing, 55
multiplication (*), 13

**N**

#N/A, 254, 257
#NAME?, 72, 254, 257
Name Box, 3, 35
Name Manager dialog box, 96, 97
naming
  worksheets, 23
navigating
  in worksheets, 4–5
nest functions
  as arguments, 76
  in IF functions, 90
  in VLOOKUP function, 90
nested functions
  logical, 158–162
  nested AND, 160–161
  nested IF, 158
  nested IF, within IF, 158–160

nested MATCH, 163
nested NOT, 162
nested OR, 161
nested text, 284
New Formatting Rule dialog box, 213–214
New sheet icon, 3
New Web Query dialog box, 273
newline character, 268
nonadjacent range, 34
Normal view
  worksheets, 4
not equal to (<>), 86
NOT function, 162
Notepad, 268, 269
NOW function, 77
nper, PMT function, 91
#NULL!, 254
#NUM!, 150, 254, 257
number argument, 148
number filters, Excel tables, 193
number formats, 44–45
number of pages, header and footer
    option, 54
Number style, number format, 45

**O**

Objects, 320
OData Data Feed, 272
100% stacked column charts, 110
open and arrange windows, worksheets,
    236
Open dialog box, 268, 269
Open-High-Low-Close stock chart,
    113, 114
order argument, 148
order of precedence, 13–14
OR function, 161–162
orientation, page
  landscape, 51
  Page Setup option, 51
  portrait, 51
outline buttons, 330
outlines
  creating, 331
  defined, 330

**P**

Page Break Preview, worksheets, 4
page breaks
  large datasets, 172–173
  Page Setup option, 51
Page Layout view, worksheets, 4
page layouts, grouped worksheets, 233–234
page number, header and footer option, 54
page orientation
  landscape, 51
  Page Setup option, 51
  portrait, 51
Page Setup dialog box, 51–52
Page Setup Dialog Box Launcher, 51–52
Page Setup options, worksheets, 51–55, 174
paper-based ledger, 2. *See also* worksheet(s)

parentheses ( ), 13
password(s). *See also* security
  worksheet protection, 301–302
Paste Options, 36–37
Paste Special, 36–38
Paste Special dialog box, 37
pasting ranges, 35–36
percent (%), 13
PERCENTILE.EXC function, 150–151
PERCENTILE.INC function, 150–151
PERCENTRANK.EXC function, 148–149,
    150
PERCENTRANK.INC, 148–149, 150
Percent Style, number format, 45
Personal Macro Workbook, 311
picture(s). *See also* chart(s);
  charts as, 104
  Copy as Picture feature, 36
  worksheet header and footer option, 54
pie charts, 106, 112
pie chart data labels, 129
Piedmont Trailer Manufacturing Company
  case background, 387
  case deliverables, 392
  case scenario, 387–389
  design specifications, 389–391
  implementation concerns, 391–392
  information specifications, 391
  testing of design, 392
pivot, 336
PivotCharts, 362–363. *See also*
    PivotTable(s)
PivotTable(s)
  areas of, 339
  collapse items, 340–341
  columns added, 340
  COLUMNS area, 339, 340, 342, 362, 363
  creating, 336–339
  data-mining feature, 336
  defined, 336
  expand items, 340–341
  FILTERS area, 339, 349, 350, 363
  filters in, 349–350
  formatting, 359–360
  modifying, 339–343
  multiple worksheets and, 232
  PivotCharts compared to, 362–363
  PowerPivot program, 360–362
  rearrange fields, 342
  Recommended PivotTables dialog box,
    336–338
  refresh, 343
  related tables and, 360–362
  remove fields, 341
  rows added, 339
  ROWS area, 339, 340, 342, 362, 363
  slicers, 350–351
  styles, 359–360
  subtotals compared to, 337
  Subtotals options, 360
  update, 343
  value field settings, 342–343
  values added, 339–340
  VALUES area, 339, 340, 342, 343, 352, 359

PivotTable Fields task pane, 338–339, 341, 361
PivotTable Tools, 338
PivotTable Tools Analyze tab, 352
PivotTable Tools Design tab, 359–360
plot area, 104, 108, 127
PMT function, 91, 246
pointing, semi-selection, 14
portrait orientation, 51
positioning
    axis titles, 125
    data labels, 125–126
    legend, 126
pound signs (######), 26
PowerPivot, 360–362
precedence, order of, 13–14
precedent cells, 255–256
previewing
    worksheets, 55
print area
    large datasets, 173
    Page Setup option, 51
print order, worksheets, 174
Print Titles, Page Setup option, 51, 174
printing
    charts, 117
    column/row headings, 55
    gridlines, 55
    grouped worksheets, 233
    landscape orientation, 51
    large datasets, 171–174
    multiple worksheets, 55
    part of worksheet, 173
    portrait orientation, 51
    row/column headings, 55
procedures, 319
PRODUCT function, 203
Project Explorer, 319
PROPER function, 283
protecting
    cells, 300–301
    workbooks, 302–303
    worksheets, 301–302, 320–321
pv, PMT function, 91

Q

quart argument, 149
quartile, 149
QUARTILE function, 149–150
quartile grouping, 150
QUARTILE.EXC function, 149–150
queries. See also append queries; delete queries; make table queries; select queries; update queries
    action, 368–379
    importing, 271–272
    Web, 272–273
query design grid, 368, 370, 374
Quick Analysis gallery, PivotTable creation, 336–337
Quick Analysis tools
    button, 34, 35, 74
    conditional formatting on cells, 208–209

defined, 76
    Excel charts, 105–106
    Excel table creation, 180
Quick Layout, charts, 126

R

radar charts, 115
range(s). See also cell(s)
    copying, 35–36
    defined, 34
    Excel tables to ranges (conversion), 181
    moving, 35
    nonadjacent, 34
    pasting, 35–36
    selecting, 34–35
range argument, 145, 146
range names, 96–98
range_lookup argument, 90
RANK.AVG function, 76, 147–148
RANK.EQ function, 76, 147–148
rate, PMT function, 91
recoloring
    for charts, 135–136
    fill color, worksheets, 44
    worksheet tabs, 23
Recommended PivotTables dialog box, 336–338
record macros, 310–311
records. See also table(s)
    Excel tables, 179, 182
red arrows, 255, 256
#REF!, 254, 257
ref argument, 148
reference form, INDEX function, 163
references. See also cell references
    external, 247–248
    relative, 311
    structured, in formulas, 201–202
    3-D, 245
reference functions, 70. See also lookup functions
reference operators, 13
refresh connections, 274
refresh PivotTables, 343
related tables, PivotTables, 360–362
relationship(s)
    defined, 360
    PowerPivot program, 360–362
relative cell references, 62
relative references, 311
relative standing, statistical functions, 147–151
removing. See also deleting
    cell styles, 295
    chart elements, 124
    duplicate rows, Excel tables, 182–183
    fields, from PivotTables, 341
    groups, 331
    hyperlinks, 238
    subtotals, 330
    tracer arrows, 256
renaming. See naming
repair errors, 256

Replace current subtotals check box, 330
rerun action queries, 373
resizing
    Chart Tools Format tab, 130
    charts, 116
    Page Setup option, 51
reverse phone number lookup, 162
Ribbon, PivotTable creation, 337–339
RIGHT function, 284
rotate cell data, 43
ROUND function, 76
row(s). See also table(s); worksheet(s)
    deleting, 26
    duplicate, Excel tables, 182–183
    freezing, 171
    headings, 3, 4
    height, 27
    hide, 28
    inserting, 25–26
    managing, 25–28
    PivotTables, 339
    print row headings, 55
    Switch Row/Column, 137
    table style options, 184
    Total row, 202–203
    transposing, 38
    unhide, 28
Row_num, 163
ROWS area, 339, 340, 342, 362, 363
rules, conditional formatting, 208–218. See also cell(s)
run time errors, 320–321
running
    append queries, 375
    delete queries, 378–379
    macros, 312
    make table queries, 377

S

salary table, statistical functions, 144
scatter (X Y) chart, 113
Scenario Manager, multiple worksheets and, 232
Scientific style, number format, 45
ScreenTips, 238
    function ScreenTip, 71
scrolling, synchronous, 237
security. See also protecting
    macro, 313–314
    Trust Center, 313–314
security warnings
    macros, 313
    Protected View option, 314
    Security Warning Message Bar, 248, 249, 273
    Trusted Documents option, 314
Select All icon, 3
Select Data Source dialog box, 271
select queries
    advantages, 368
    before append queries, 374
    before update queries, 370–371
Select Table dialog box, 271

selecting
ranges, 34–35
selecting templates, 290–291
semi-selection, 14
SERIES (LEGEND), 362, 363
set connection properties, 275
Set Hyperlink ScreenTip dialog box, 238
shape(s)
Chart Tools Format tab, 130
SharePoint, 179
Sheet Options, 54. *See also* worksheet(s)
sheet tabs (worksheet tabs)
colors, 23
defined, 3
dragging, 24
navigation buttons, 3
sizing
Chart Tools Format tab, 130
charts, 116
Page Setup option, 51
sizing handles, 116
Slicer Tools Options tab, commands, 351
slicers, PivotTables, 350–351
Solver, multiple worksheets and, 232
sorting
conditional formatting and, 212
defined, 190
Excel table data, 190–191
source file, 247
spaces
reference operator, 13
sparklines, 137–138
Sparkline Tools Design tab, 138
Special style, number format, 45
split bars, 236
spreadsheets, 2. *See also* worksheet(s)
spreadsheet skills, case examples
Edmund Grant Pharmaceutical
Company, 415–420
Francisco's Lawn Care, 393–396
Klein Technology Seminars, 402–410
Lake West University, 411–414
Maxi's Grocery Mart, 397–401
Piedmont Trailer Manufacturing
Company, 387–392
SQL Server, import data, 272
stacked column charts, 109–110
statistical functions, 70, 72–76
conditional math and, 144–147
relative standing and, 147–151
statistics, described, 144
status bar
worksheet, 4
STDEV function, 203
STDEVP function, 203
stock charts, 113–114
structural changes, grouped worksheets,
233
structured references, in formulas, 201–202
style(s)
cell, 293–295
chart, 135–136
Excel table styles, 183–184
PivotTable, 359–360

sub procedures, 319–321
SUBSTITUTE function, 284
subtotal(s)
add second level of, 330
adding, 328
collapse, 330
defined, 329
expand, 330
PivotTables compared to, 337
removing, 330
*Replace current subtotals* check
box, 330
Subtotal feature, 328–330
SUBTOTAL function, 202–203, 329
Subtotals dialog box, 328, 330
Subtotals options, PivotTables, 360
subtraction (-), 13
SUM arrow, 74
SUM function, 72–74, 203, 351
SUMIF function, 144, 145–146
SUMIFS function, 144, 146–147
summary statistics
multiple, 343
value field settings, 342–343
sum_range argument, 145, 146
surface charts, 115
Switch Row/Column, 137
synchronous scrolling, 237
syntax
check for, 256–257
#DIV/0!, 254, 257, 299
formula, 254–257
formula auditing and, 255–257
functions, 73
IFERROR function, 257, 299
ISERROR function, 257
logic, 254–257
#N/A, 254, 257
#NAME?, 254, 257
#NULL!, 254
#NUM!, 150, 254, 257
#REF!, 254, 257
repair, 256
run time, 320–321
#VALUE!, 161, 254, 257

**T**

tab-delimited text file, 268–269
table, lookup, 88–89
table(s), database. *See also* data validation;
queries
make table queries, 368, 376–377
Quick Analysis gallery, 336, 337
table(s), Excel, 179–184
creating, 179–181
defined, 179
designing, 179–184
duplicate rows, 182–183
fields, 181, 190–191
filtering data, 192–195
manipulating data, 190–195
Quick Analysis, 180
records, 179, 182

sorting data, 190–191
structured references in formulas,
201–202
styles, 183–184
table aggregation, 201–203
tables to ranges (conversion), 181
total row, 202–203
table array, 89
Table Styles group, 183
Table Tools Design tab, 180, 181
templates
creating, 299–300
Custom Office Templates folder, 303
defined, 290
Excel Macro-Enabled Template, 309
selecting, 290–291
templates folder, 300
testing
delete queries, 378–379
make table queries, 377
update queries, 371–372
text
circles around, 260
in formulas, 87
manipulation, 282–285
worksheet, 6
wrap text feature, cells, 43
text files
defined, 268
import, 268–271
text filters, Excel tables, 192
text functions, 283–284
Text Import Wizard, 269–270, 282
Text style, number format, 45
Text to Columns feature, 282
text wrapping
wrap text feature, cells, 43
theme(s), defined, 291–293
themed cell styles, 294
3-D charts, 111
3-D formulas, 245–247
3-D reference, 245
times
in cells, 7
header and footer option, 54
time functions, 70, 77–79
Time number format, 45
TODAY function, 77
toggle between relative, absolute, mixed cell
references (F4), 64
Top/Bottom Rules, conditional formatting,
209, 210–211
Total row, 202–203
tracer arrows, 255–256
transposing columns and rows, 38
trap errors, IFERROR function, 257, 299
trendlines, 123
Trig & Math functions, 70, 72–76
TRIM function, 284
Trust Center
macro security, 313–314
truth tables
AND, 160–161
OR function, 161

## U

unavailable tasks, grouped worksheets, 234
Unfreeze Panes, 171
ungroup worksheets, 232–234
ungrouping data, 331
unhide columns and rows, 28
unhide worksheets, 235
unlock cells, 300–301
unmerge cells, 43
unprotect workbooks, 303
update queries
    add field, 372
    defined, 368, 370
    select queries before, 370–371
    testing, 371–372
    verify, 373
updates
    charts, 105
    linked workbooks, 248–249
    PivotTables, 343
UPPER function, 284

## V

validation of data, 258–260
validation criteria, 258–259
#VALUE! error, 161, 254, 257
value(s). *See also* cell references
    cell references *versus*, 12–13
    defined, 7
    in formulas, 89
    indenting, 44
    in PivotTables, 339–340
    as specific calculation result, 352–353
value, lookup, 89, 90
value arguments, 257
value axis, 104, 108, 109, 110
value field settings, PivotTables, 342–343
value_if_error argument, 257
Value_if_false, 86, 158, 159, 160
Value_if_true, 86, 158, 160
VALUES area, 339, 340, 342, 343, 352, 359
VAR function, 203
variables. object as, 320
VARP function, 203
VBA (Visual Basic for Applications), 319–322
    defined, 309, 319
    protected worksheets and, 320–321
    relative references and, 311
verifying, update query, 373
vertical axis, 106, 111, 115, 125, 138
vertical cell alignment, 43
view controls, worksheets, 4
views. *See specific views*
visibility
    backgrounds, 293
    worksheets, 235
Visual Basic Editor, 319, 321
Visual Basics for Applications (VBA), 319–322
    defined, 309, 319

protected worksheets and, 320–321
relative references and, 311
VLOOKUP function, 88–90, 158, 162, 246, 254
Volume-High-Low-Close stock chart, 113, 114
Volume-Open-High-Low-Close stock chart, 113, 114

## W

warning message
    append query, 375
    delete query, 378
    update query, 372
Watch Windows, 257–258
Web page, copy data from, 273
Web queries, 272–273
WEEKDAY function, 78
width, column, 26–27. *See also* cell(s)
window(s). *See also* dialog boxes
    Excel window elements, 2–5
windows, worksheets
    open and arrange, 236
    settings, 237
    split, 236–237
Windows Azure Marketplace, import data, 272
Win/Loss sparkline, 137–138
WordArt
    Chart Tools Format tab, 130
workbook(s). *See also* worksheet(s)
    completing, 6
    connections, 274–275
    defined, 2
    deleting worksheets, 24
    linked, 247–249
    management, 22–28
    protecting, 302–303
    unprotect, 303
    worksheets and, 232
    worksheets inserted in, 24
Workbook Connections dialog box, 274
worksheet(s). *See also* cell(s); chart(s);
        column(s); formula(s); functions;
        rows; table(s); workbook(s)
    alignment options, 42–44
    backgrounds in, 51
    chart sheets, 115, 117, 123
    Clipboard tasks, 34–38
    controls in, 312–313
    copying, 24–25
    data, in other programs, 38
    defined, 2
    deleting, 24
    design, 5
    elements, 2–5
    enter and format data, 5–6
    fill across, 234–235
    fill color, 44
    Find & Select feature, 170
    footers and headers, 53–54
    formatting, 42–46
    Go To dialog box, 4, 98, 170

group and ungroup, 232–234
headers and footers, 53–54
hide, 235
hyperlinks in, 237–239
inserted in workbooks, 24
introduction, 2–7
large, 170–174
large datasets, 170–174
management, 22–28
margins, 51, 52
move down one cell (↓), 4
move left one cell (←), 4
move right one cell (→), 4
move up one cell (↑), 4
moving, 24–25
multiple, 232–239
multiple, printing, 55
name, header and footer option, 54
naming, 23
navigating in, 4–5
Page Setup options, 51–55, 174
paper-based ledger *versus*, 2
part of, printing, 173
previewing, 55
print order, 174
printing, 55
protecting, 301–302, 320–321
range names in, 98
Sheet Options, 54
split windows, 236–237
as spreadsheets, 2
status bar, 4
text, 6
3-D formulas, 245–247
unhide, 235
view controls, 4
visibility, 235
windows, 236–237
workbooks and, 232
worksheet tabs (sheet tabs)
    colors, 23
    defined, 3
    dragging, 24
    navigation buttons, 3
wrapping
    wrap text feature, cells, 43

## X

x argument, 149
X-axis, 104, 108
XML (eXtensible Markup Language)
    data import, 272
X Y (scatter) chart, 113

## Y

Y-axis, 104, 108
YEAR function, 78
YEARFRAC function, 78

## Z

Zoom control, 4